D0707667

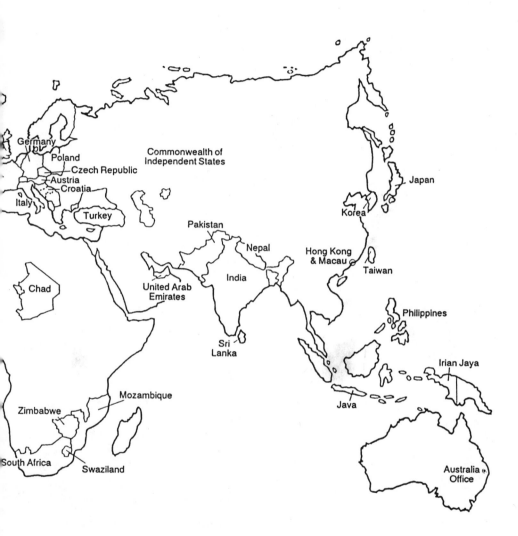

266.06
T253
M887g

GOD MADE IT GROW

Historical Sketches
of
TEAM's Church Planting Work

by
Vernon Mortenson

William Carey Library
Pasadena, California

77103

© 1994 by The Evangelical Alliance Mission

All rights reserved. No part of this publication may be reproduced, stored in a retrieval system, or transmitted in any form by any means—electronic, mechanical, photocopy, recording, or any other—except for brief quotations embodied in critical articles or printed reviews, without prior permission of the publisher.

Scripture taken from the HOLY BIBLE, NEW INTERNATIONAL VERSION. Copyright © 1973, 1978, 1984 by International Bible Society. Used by permission of Zondervan Publishing House.

Published by
William Carey Library
P.O. Box 40129, Pasadena, California 91114

in cooperation with
The Evangelical Alliance Mission
P.O. Box 969, Wheaton, IL 60189-0969

ISBN: 0-87808-257-3

Cover art: Dwight Walles

Printed in the United States of America

77103

CONTENTS

Slow Growth? Radio Work Considered, Growing Listener Response, At Last—A Bible School, Bible Translation. AFGHANISTAN: A Way Into Afghanistan, Proposal for International Mission, Related to Pakistan Field, Surmounting Obstacles to Witness, The Spiritual Battle Rages On.

Chapter 37 - Desert Oasis 586

Board Approves Near East Field, Kennedys to Iraq, Lebanon and Palestine, The Lord Directs to Trucial Oman, The First Permanent Entry, Preparing the First Hospital, The Purpose is Witness, Sensitivity and Restriction, Oil Flow Beckons Immigrants, Beginning of Group Ministries, Lebanon Not Forgotten, Church Development Begins, Growth of the Filipino Work, Theological Education by Extension, Church Fellowship Becomes a Reality, Soul-winning Continues, Oasis Hospital Still a Key, New Hospital Building Approved, Is it Worth the Cost? An Unanticipated Harvest.

G.3 THE CONTINENT OF AFRICA

Chapter 38 - Changes in South Africa 616

Life Around the Cities, Separate but Not Equal, Soweto Township, Orange Free State, Post-War Influx, Malla Moe and the King, The Lord's Gracious Response, A Field Headquarters, Need for a Hospital, Training of Nurses, Air Service, Reaching the Coloured Community, Indian Community Reached, Evangelical Bible Churches Formed, Autonomy for the African Church.

Chapter 39 - Struggle and Progress 632

Uncertainty and Questions, Slowly Attaining Self-support, Learning Lessons, A New Bible School and a Question, An EBC School in Capetown, Widening Literature Outreach, Retail Stores Purchased, WLP Transferred, Zulu Concordance. SWAZILAND: TEAM's Social Influence, A Price for Principle, What About Race Relations? Goals by Church and Mission, New Open Doors. MOZAMBIQUE: Another Attempt to Enter, Four Ready and Willing.

Chapter 40 - Zimbabwe—Toward Maturity 649

Post-war Reinforcements, A Separate Field, Evangelism in the Townships, Schools and Bush Clinics Required, Maranatha Teacher Training School, Urgent Need for a Doctor, Hospital Dedicated, Nurses' Training, Beginning Churches, Church Fellowship Organized, Training Christian Workers, War Closing In, Missionary Aviation, Guerilla War Intensifies, Ministry to the Keeps, A Most Difficult Decision, A Greatly Welcomed Armistice, Walking a Fine Line, Church Planting During the War, Church Relationships Over the Years, A Small Spark

Ignites a Flame, Efforts to Reach Understanding, Continued Hope, Tension Not the Whole Story, Broadcast Evangelism and TEE, Smaller Force but Gospel Work Goes On.

Beginnings of the Work, Growth in the First Twenty Years, Formal Request for Merger, The Work in 1969, Broad Benefits of Self-Support, Field-wide Church Organization Formed, Saturation Evangelism, Lake Chad Evangelism, Essential Help for Medical Work, Independence and a President, Initiation Practices Revived, Persecution of Pastors, Withstanding the Pressures, A Courageous Voice, A Timely Intervention, What To Do About Those Defeated, An Act of True Humility and Courage, Scripture Translation, Printing and Publishing, Church Requests Agricultural Help, Famine, Civil War and its Effects, Growth Continues, Tribes Yet Unreached.

G.4 EUROPE FOUND TO BE A MISSION FIELD

A New Field to the Southeast, Nineteen Recruits, Eight Early Losses, Methods of Work, Field Strategy, Growth in Beja, Ministries in Lisbon, A Bold and Effective Move, Lessons, Upswing in Work.

First Steps in Ministry, Emphasis on Youth, Disappointment and Resolve, Beginnings in Vitry, Prayers Answered in Orly, Planning a Strategy, A National Association, French Co-laborers, The Fruit of Careful Sowing, A Permanent TEAM Camp, Conference Grounds at Houlgate, Developing Momentum, Joint Evangelistic Campaigns, A Web Movement in Orly, Self-supporting Leaders, Training Programs Launched, Changing Church-Mission Relationships, Preparing for Even Greater Growth, Disagreement Over Praz de Lys, A Time of Slow Growth, A New Permanent Camp Site, Theological Education by Extension, Churches Growing and Multiplying, Ministries Supporting Church Growth, Why Has the Church in France Grown?

John and Betty Aerni Join TEAM, Visa Problems Bring Gholdstons, Surmounting the Obstacles, Reinforcements and a Bible School, Restrictions Easing, Church Planting Begins, Correspondence Courses, Two Decades of Slow Progress, Why the Slow Growth? Theological Education by Extension, Joining a Church Association, TEAM in Sevilla, Growing Pains, New Outreach Through Literature, Progress in the Churches, Developing a Camping Ministry, Reaping a Harvest.

PREFACE

ABOUT THIS BOOK—GOD MADE IT GROW

"I planted the seed, Apollos watered it, but God made it grow. "
—I Corinthians 3:6, NIV

One metaphor the Apostle Paul uses to describe the growth of the Church of Jesus Christ is growing grain. Nothing better describes the history of the church planted by the national Christians and missionaries of TEAM than this Scripture: "God made it grow." This book seeks to tell this story.

There is living seed to sow. It is good seed—the gospel of the atoning death and resurrection of Jesus Christ and His offer of salvation to all who receive Him. In it is revealed the "mystery that through the gospel the Gentiles are heirs together with Israel, members together of one body, and sharers together in the promise in Christ Jesus" (Ephesians 3:6, NIV).

On a wheat farm much work goes into soil preparation and sowing. When the grain ripens, there is urgency to garner the harvest lest much of it be lost. In countries where harvesting is done with hand sickles or other primitive equipment, many laborers are needed. Modern grain-growing countries harvest with combines—huge machines which, in one operation, cut, thresh, and recover the grain for delivery to the market.

It is interesting to observe the process and to study the economics. Yet while the people, the process, and the economics are important, of greatest importance is the grain itself. This is the objective of the whole undertaking. It is what counts. It is the staff of life. It is the hope for feeding the world. Interestingly, there is much attention to the process; comparatively little to the grain itself.

The same danger exists in telling the story of TEAM in this book. The people and process seem to be given most prominence. They are important—even indispensable—but the heart of missions is the church which is being planted. This is the "it" that God made grow. The mission is necessary, even as the farmer is necessary for planting and reaping. We have the example of the New Testament, which reveals the growth and development of the church by relating the stories of the apostles and describing the expanding movement. But most vital is the seed itself which God makes grow into the church.

In telling the story of the laborers in TEAM, we must not miss the real story, the church. True, it is the movement of missionaries and their aspirations, encouragements, and disappointments that first capture our attention. But it is the church being planted that has eternal significance. "To Him be glory in the church and in Christ Jesus throughout all generations, for ever and ever" (Ephesians 3:21, NIV).

Laced throughout the history—the facts and figures, the plans and performance—is the thread of the church, which we trust you will discern and follow to an understanding of the glory that is God's greatest handiwork; "the church, which is His body, the fullness of Him who fills everything in every way" (Ephesians 1:22,23, NIV).

* * * * *

Some explanation is needed concerning the names and initials used for the mission. Except in the very early years when there were several different names in use, the mission was The Scandinavian Alliance Mission of North America for somewhat more than the first half of it existence; thus the initials S.A.M. I have used these initials until the change was made in May 1949 to The Evangelical Alliance Mission. The initials without periods have been used since that time and the mission is generally known as TEAM. So S.A.M. and TEAM are one and the same.

Place names are given as they appear in the mission's files except where confusion would result. Chinese names present the greatest difficulty. Chinese writing is in ideograms—which we know as characters. The accurate rendering of these characters in our Roman alphabet is difficult, particularly when the pronunciation differs according to the region. I have followed the Wade system of Romanization except in a few cases where the postal spelling differs. Since TEAM left its work on the mainland of China, the Peoples Republic has revised and simplified many of the characters and has set arbitrary phonetic representations which differ somewhat from the past. Thus, the city where TEAM had its field headquarters is now designated as Xi'an, Shaanxi, rather than Sian, Shensi. The pronunciation is the same either way. We have chosen to stay with the old because our readers who followed the China mainland work will feel more at home that way.

A writer of history should be completely objective, standing apart from any personal involvement. This is difficult in this instance because I have been involved for over fifty years. Frances and I had what must be acknowledged as the great privilege of living and serving in China as the foundation experience of our share in missionary work. Then being involved in administration for many years, I had opportunity to see the work of missionaries and many national leaders at first hand and to enter into the joys and sorrows of the spiritual battle to take over territory for the Lord which for a hundred or more generations had been held by the enemy of souls—and uncontested. That there have been failures and defeats in the mission work must be admitted. So it was in New Testament times and so it is today. But the "bottom line" is that there have been victories—outstanding victories—as is clearly and amply testified by the existence of the church of our Lord Jesus Christ among formerly benighted people in thirty different world areas. "To Him be glory in the church and in Christ Jesus through-out all generations, for ever and ever! Amen."

Those listed in the "Acknowledgments" join me in praying that you will gain new understanding of the past investment in world missions and what is still needed if the goal of planting the church of Jesus Christ around the world is to be fully realized.

Vernon Mortenson

ACKNOWLEDGMENTS
AND THANKS

Successfully telling the story of an active work of 100 years is beyond one person's capability even though one person is listed as author. The real authors are the "accomplishers" by the enabling of the Spirit of God—men and women, missionary and national, whose service we relate and to whom we give heartfelt thanks. We praise the Lord of the harvest for calling them out, giving them a clear concept of the work to be accomplished, and empowering them to serve. Their memorial is the men, women, boys, and girls won to Christ and now in more than 2,500 churches around the world.

One Chinese pastor in particular should be mentioned here because, for his own safety, his story could not be told while he was still living. Pastor Huang Hsingmin of China passed away last April (1992) at the age of 84. For nearly forty-five years he had been under house arrest and other restrictions which cut off most of his public preaching. On the few occasions when permitted, he preached with clarity and power. Some of us had the privilege of visiting with him in China in recent years and exchanging letters from time to time. I, personally, acknowledge the inspiration of his example and fellowship across the many miles and many years. How happy he must be in the presence of the Lord whom he worshipped and served so faithfully under great difficulties.

Then there are many who helped this book project with research, review, consultation, and correction. Serving as editorial consultant and reviewer for the entire book has been Mrs. Beth Bennett Tetzel, a skilled editor who brought to this work a background as a TEAM MK (South Africa), degrees in communications and journalism, and a period of service in the TEAM Publications Department. Because of my illness and several hospitalizations, she has taken the lead in research, writing, and editing of the final chapters while I have been limited to reviewing her work.

Dr. Richard Winchell, general director of TEAM, has read every chapter and has given valuable information and suggestions. Other

TEAM staff members have assisted with research and review. I would name in particular Jack MacDonald, Ron Brett, Lynn Everswick, Norman Niemeyer, Gary Bowman, David Davis, Ed Lewis, Sylvia Fuller, Dorothy Vust, Janet Moody, Elizabeth Ostenson, Myra Dye, and Jack Kilgore. Three helpful friends who are no longer on the active staff are Janet Hyland, Bonnie Pratt, and August Ramsland.

Missionaries who came to my assistance by reading the initial draft relating to their fields of service are Verner Strom (Japan); Stuart Gunzel (Mongolia); John Rathbun (Korea); Morris Beck (Taiwan); J. W. Bergstrom, now deceased (China); Victor Veary, Ben Strohschein, and Nelson Bezanson (Chad); Einer Berthelsen (Western India); Charles Warren (North India); David Greene and Wesley Carlson (South Africa); James Carmean (Venezuela); Tom Jackson (Zimbabwe); Norman Kapp (France); Anne Vought (Spain); Barry Hancock (Peru); and Edvard Torjesen (Franson ministry).

Whatever the input has been from others—whom I thank wholeheartedly—I take full responsibility for the contents as the author and in the final chapters the reviewer.

Vernon Mortenson
December 1992

INTRODUCTION

When the author of this TEAM history answered my 1946 letter of inquiry, he replied with such Christian grace that I wondered if he had not noticed that I was only of high school age. He was then general director David H. Johnson's assistant. Several years passed before we met. Since then our friendship has steadily grown. At first I was the young applicant for missionary service awed by the stature, both physical and administrative, of this man. His spiritual stature, so evident from that first letter, seemed to grow with the years.

In time my wife and I were young candidates in orientation classes experiencing his effective teaching. After that we were in Africa watching from a distance as his careful, godly administration developed a growing support team in the home office. His visits to our mission field during those years were especially effective. We all knew that we had among us one who had walked where we were walking—learning a language, coping with culture, preaching, praying, and working with churches. This was no "ivory tower" executive—he was one of us. His years in China provided innumerable case studies for missionaries whether in Africa, Europe, or South America.

Soon he was chosen—to no one's surprise—to succeed Dr. Johnson as general director. It was during this time that he asked me to join the home staff. At least one significant reason I accepted his invitation was my deep admiration for this man. The thought of working near him, learning from him, and sharing in what he was doing was an honor I knew I did not deserve but could not decline.

The work grew under his leadership. His emphasis on the importance of founding reproducing churches echoed the heartbeat of founder Fredrik Franson and called us all to task to analyze our activities, evaluating them as to their contribution to the primary goal.

That penchant for evaluation is evident in this work. The author does not just relate our history; he asks hard questions about it. He does not hesitate to give credit to those who were used effectively, though he always points to the divine power that made it all happen. Hence the title: *GOD MADE IT GROW*. He also points out when we got away from our primary goal and calls us back to it. These are lessons we must constantly relearn.

I am sure you will enjoy this book as much as I enjoyed reading the manuscript. I shall never forget the excitement I felt as I read about the evangelistic fervor in northwest China; about the gospel hall in Xian seating over a thousand and packed full, not just every month or every week but every night!

But not all of the reading brings such exhilaration. You will learn how Franson started a field in East Africa, but gave it up as one missionary after another succumbed to disease. Victory did not come in every situation, and when it did this was often at a high price. There are tales of the martyrs, of those who were repatriated with illnesses, and those who buried their children, spouses, or fellow workers on foreign soil. Such is the stuff of missionary work. Dr. Mortenson shares it all with compassion. No wonder— he and Mrs. Mortenson left the body of a beloved baby son in China.

Walk with the author, then, through this account of a hundred years of faith and fruit-bearing, beset on occasion by fears and frustrations. Watch the saga unfold and, as you near the end of the story, may God give you, with us, a fresh vision of what can happen in the years ahead.

TEAM has been sending out near-record numbers of new missionaries in recent years. At the present writing there are over two hundred in the "pipeline" and applications are being received each week.

We may indeed be one hundred years old, but more than half of our active staff has joined us in the last ten years. This has been necessary as post-World War II veterans have been retiring, but it is also necessary as we face ever-increasing opportunities on our thirty fields.

This remarkable record of growth is prophetic of what can

happen in the days ahead. The first ten years of our mission's second century are the last ten years of the second millennium. God made TEAM and its resultant churches grow for one hundred years. We believe He will make them grow even more in the next hundred. Foundations laid and directions set by men like our author point the way. It is for us, now, to follow.

Enjoy the experiences of these pages and I know you will want to join with us as we begin TEAM's next chapter. Your prayers for mission supporters, new missionaries, and faithful leadership will assure more growth in the mission—and consequently in the churches—in the days ahead.

Richard Winchell,
General Director

CALL AND RESPONSE

The year was 1890. It was with a great sense of urgency that evangelist Fredrik Franson called for missionaries to reach lost multitudes in China with the gospel. World population was one and a half billion; it had doubled in just over a century. There was a new and growing concern among Christians that the multiplying numbers be reached for Christ. When William Carey had responded to God's call to India a century earlier, thus initiating the era of modern missions, there were many who maintained that God would have a way of saving the heathen without missionaries getting all stirred up about it.

But now in 1890 the Christians of the West were awakening to the need. The personal example and writings of J. Hudson Taylor had made a deep impression. Even more influential was his call, in December 1889, for 1,000 missionaries to go to China's inland provinces and evangelize its 250 million people.

It was not only the growing population that urged Fredrik Franson forward, but more particularly his anticipation of the early return of Christ. He longed for and daily expected Christ's return and this motivated him to win as many to the Savior as possible. Furthermore, he sought to inspire and train others to be equally involved. His short-term training sessions for lay evangelists had begun in Norway in 1884 and a growing number of young people had been helped to become more effective witnesses to their faith.

Franson was in Germany engaged in intensive evangelistic activity when he heard of Taylor's call for 1,000 missionaries for China. He immediately took this up as a prayer burden and was soon convinced that he should seek to raise up 100 of that number.

He informed Hudson Taylor accordingly. With conviction came action, and his first strategy was to adapt his Bible course ministry as a tool for recruiting and training. Werner Schnepper of Germany records:

> Franson's zeal for Christ and for His work, and for the Chinese, burned at that time with the brightest flame.... He began at once with the Bible Courses for the training of men and women to go out as missionaries.[1]

Franson's belief that America should become a base for his foreign mission thrust was first revealed in a report in the Swedish-American newspaper *Chicago Bladet* of August 26, 1890.

> His purpose is...to seek to get believers into action for the Lord...so that a large throng would go out from America to the heathen countries, particularly China and Japan.[2]

Arriving in New York from Europe Sunday, September 7, 1890, Franson immediately began working to accomplish his goal. He actually held four different meetings on the day he arrived.

On September 16, he announced that his first Bible course would begin at the Pilgrim Church in Brooklyn, New York, on October 14. Fifty young people attended, of whom sixteen were appointed to be included in the first China party to sail.

This necessary initial event marked the founding of the world-wide evangelization and church planting organization now known as The Evangelical Alliance Mission (TEAM). First called the China Alliance Mission and then simply the Alliance Mission, it became The Scandinavian Alliance Mission of North America (S.A.M.), the name it carried until 1949. In time, October 14, 1890, came to be recognized as the founding date of the mission.[3]

The sixteen recruits from the Brooklyn course were joined by nineteen others who attended Franson's courses in Chicago, Omaha, and Minneapolis. The first party of thirty-five, eighteen women and seventeen men, left San Francisco on January 22, 1891, arriving in Shanghai, China, on February 17. On February 5, a second party, fifteen in number, sailed, and arrived March 8.

In the same year, on November 3, a group of fifteen missionaries sailed for Japan, arriving in Yokohama on the twenty-third. Word of Japan's spiritual need and openness had come in letters from the China-bound missionaries who stopped briefly en route. The next year—1892—saw additional workers go forth, twelve more to China, twelve to Northeast India and twelve to South Africa. Between 1893 and 1895 additional missionaries were sent to these countries and to East Africa and Mongolia.

The requirements for service were simple but basic. Candidates should:

1. possess true life in the Lord;
2. have good references as to their Christian life;
3. have had experience in ministry for the Lord;
4. give good reasons for their call as missionaries;
5. have a congregation or individuals responsible for their support;
6. during the first three years be willing to work as traveling evangelists without settling down at their own stations; and,
7. for this reason continue unmarried during these three years.[4]

Franson was himself an evangelist both in his personal contacts and in his public meetings. He was eager to have missionaries who were gifted as evangelists and willing to undertake itinerant evangelism. He was also a churchman, having founded churches in the American Midwest and Europe. In fact, his exposition of the New Testament church structure and organization had formed the pattern for many of the revival churches among Scandinavian settlers in the American Midwest.

Tracing a Legacy

We shall follow the work of many of these first 100 missionaries and seek to determine the extent to which they and their successors were faithful to the mandate given in Scripture and emphasized by Franson. They have been followed in the work by several thousand men and women, of whom more than a thousand remain in active service as The Evangelical Alliance Mission (TEAM), their mission channel, approaches its centennial.[5]

Have the leaders overseas and at home clearly set forth Scriptural objectives and have the missionaries been seriously committed to them? To what degree has the work of these pioneer missionaries and their successors been fruitful?

Who Was Franson?

But first of all, who was Fredrik Franson, a man so greatly used by the Lord to catch a vision, communicate it to others, and see a good beginning to the harvest? He has been described by some as the spiritual giant that church historians overlooked. It is not that his ministry went unnoticed at the time it was taking place. In fact, there is a wealth of material in archives in North America, Europe, and even South Africa. But most of it is in Swedish, Norwegian, Danish, German, Finnish, French, Dutch, Flemish, Armeno-Turkish, or Afrikaans. Considering the extent of Franson's ministry in North America, very little is in English. It is not surprising that the story is not widely known.

Fredrik Franson was born in Nora, Sweden, June 17, 1852. His father died when he was five. His mother and stepfather moved the family to the United States in 1869, settling in eastern Nebraska. His conversion to Christ came about three years later at age twenty. For a year and a half he said little about his faith but did make a careful study of the Bible. After he was challenged to yield himself fully to Christ, there came a dedication from which he never wavered. Before long he discerned that God had gifted him as an evangelist and teacher of the Word.

His Work in Broad Outline

There followed several years of intensive evangelistic meetings in the Midwest; then ten months of service in Utah seeking to win Scandinavians who had been drawn into Mormonism. He was also associated for a time with the D. L. Moody evangelistic campaigns and did much writing and counseling on the biblical teaching regarding the local church. The Moody Church of Chicago commissioned him as an evangelist "wherever his labors call him."

For the next nine years, beginning in 1881, Franson ministered in Europe, mostly in the Scandinavian countries and Germany. He returned to the United States in 1890, and from that time onward much of his ministry was directed toward foreign missions.

Franson made two extensive world tours (1894-1895, 1902-

1908), in which he worked with and counseled the missionaries sent out from Europe and North America. He also ministered in many countries other than where these missionaries were serving. Spiritual awakenings followed in many of these places, outstandingly so in Korea and Armenian Turkey. Nearing the end of his second tour he visited Venezuela, where the newest field of the mission had been opened in April 1906.

The last weeks of his ministry were spent on the various islands of the Caribbean area and in Mexico. From Mexico he crossed the Rio Grande River at Laredo, Texas, to return to his homeland. He arranged for a few weeks of quiet prayer, study, and planning and chose to spend it serving as an interim pastor in a small church in the mountains of Colorado. It was there in Idaho Springs that his death occurred August 2, 1908. He was just fifty-six.

Franson scholar Edvard P. Torjesen lists fourteen mission organizations and church fellowships either founded by or greatly influenced by Fredrik Franson which still exist today.[5]

The Biblical Mandate

The objectives of missionary work set forth in Scripture are clear. It is not our purpose here to give a full exposition of the many passages which emphasize that the gospel of the Lord Jesus Christ is to be preached to all peoples so that many will, indeed, become His disciples. The familiar words of the commission the resurrected Christ gave to His disciples are sufficient to make the point:

> All authority has been given to Me in heaven and on earth. Go therefore and make disciples of all nations, baptizing them in the name of the Father and the Son and the Holy Spirit, teaching them to observe all that I commanded you; and lo, I am with you always, even to the end of the age (Matthew 28:18-20, NASB).

> Go into all the world and preach the gospel to all creation (Mark 16:15, NASB).

> And He said to them, Thus it is written, that the Christ should suffer and rise again from the dead the third day; and that repentance for forgiveness of sins should be proclaimed in His name to all nations—beginning from Jerusalem (Luke 24:46,47, NASB).

As the Father has sent Me, I also send you (John 20:21, NASB).

But you shall receive power when the Holy Spirit has come upon you; and you shall be My witnesses both in Jerusalem, and in all Judea and Samaria, and even to the remotest part of the earth (Acts 1:8, NASB).[7]

The mandate to proclaim the good news is clear: to all the world, to all creatures, and to the end of the age. Even as it was necessary for Christ to suffer, die, and rise again to accomplish man's redemption, so is it necessary that the gospel be proclaimed in His name to all nations if it is to be effective in the lives of individuals.

Christ's reference to the church in His statement, "I will build My church" (Matt. 16:18) introduced the truth which the Apostle Paul refers to as the mystery he was directed to reveal by inspiration in Ephesians 3:6. This was that in the eternal purposes of God, the Gentiles are to be "fellow-heirs and fellow-members of the body and fellow-partakers of the promise in Christ Jesus through the gospel."

The ministry of Paul illustrates God's purpose and pattern. His very first missionary journey with Barnabas, recorded in Acts 13 and 14, gives valuable lessons in missionary objectives and strategy. In quick review we see that Paul and Barnabas, having been sent out from the church in Antioch of Syria, preached evangelistic messages in Cyprus, Antioch of Pisidia, Iconium, and Lystra. Many believed and turned to the Lord, both Jews and Gentiles. But in each place the missionaries were opposed and had to leave under extreme pressure, apparently before their work was really finished. The ultimate act of opposition was at Lystra when the mob stoned Paul and left him for dead.

A look at the map of Asia Minor will reveal that the missionaries' journey from Antioch of Pisidia to the place of stoning was on the way back toward their starting place, Antioch of Syria. The remaining distance was a fraction of what they had already traveled. After Paul's stoning they went on to Derbe, which was the last major center en route back to their base. There they preached and made many disciples (14:21), perhaps an indication that they were there for a longer period of time and were not driven out as they had been from three other cities. But they apparently were not satisfied with what had been accomplished in these cities because we find that they reversed course and returned to Lystra, Iconium, and Antioch, where they had encountered such violent persecution.

Why did they return? The key may be in what they did in those places and what the Word says about their ministry the second time around. In Lystra, Iconium, and Antioch they now strengthened the souls of the disciples, encouraged them to continue in the faith, appointed elders for them in every church, and commended them to the Lord. Then—and only then—we read that "they sailed to Antioch, from which they had been commended to the grace of God for the work which they accomplished" (14:26) (KJV: "fulfilled").

The Apostolic Objective

Is this story telling us that their objective, yes, their work instructions from the Holy Spirit, would not have been fulfilled if they had not gone back to disciple the converts and appoint spiritual leaders?

The epistles define more fully what the gospel is, what it is to disciple, and what is necessary to plant and nurture a local church. Paul defines "the gospel which I preached to you" as being "that Christ died for our sins according to the Scriptures, and that He was buried, and that He was raised on the third day according to the Scriptures" (I Cor. 15:1-4). In Romans 1:17 he states that "in it [the gospel] the righteousness of God is revealed." This, then, is the central core of the evangelistic message committed to the missionaries.

Those who by faith receive the gospel message are by the Holy Spirit made members of the Body of Christ, a living, vital organism of which the Lord Jesus Christ is the Head. The objective of missions is more than the proclamation of the evangelistic message. It includes discipling the converts and teaching them clearly their relationship to the Body of Christ and the visible representation of that body, the local church. Paul, in particular, gave much teaching regarding the spiritual maturing of believers. He outlined carefully the requirements and responsibilities of church leadership by elders and deacons.

In almost every place where Paul went he left behind a live, functioning local church with spiritually qualified leaders where believers ministered to each other and reached out to the unsaved around them. This, then, is the clear New Testament pattern of missionary activity.

The apostle did not take a simplistic view of missionary activity—just go in, proclaim the message, encourage the people to associate together in a visible church, and then move quickly on to another place so that he could point to a large number of places having been evangelized. His message to the Ephesian elders, as recorded in Acts 20, lets us know what he believed to be essential and what he, himself, had done before he could say that he had fully discharged his responsibility. He was able to claim this in the statement, "Therefore I testify to you this day, that I am innocent of the blood of all men" (v. 26).

In brief, Paul reminded the Ephesian elders that he had lived among them so that they could know "how I was with you the whole time, serving the Lord with humility." They also knew his tears and trials because of the plots of the Jews. In spite of opposition, he did not hold back in declaring to them anything that was profitable, and this he did publicly and from house to house. Whether it was to Jews or Greeks, his message was of repentance toward God and faith in the Lord Jesus Christ. That further bonds and afflictions awaited him did not deter him. After all, he did not put such great value on his own safety or even on his own life. He was intent on fulfilling the ministry committed to him.

He further declared that he sought to teach them the whole purpose of God. He also solemnly warned them to be prepared against enemies who would attack the church from both within and without. Then, on a very positive note, he committed them "to God and to the word of His grace, which can build you up and give you an inheritance among all those who are sanctified" (v. 32). In an epilogue he reminded them about his instructions regarding giving, a lesson the young churches all needed to learn.

The Apostolic Pattern

In summary, what Paul had done to completely discharge his responsibility was to live the Christ-life among them, communicate the gospel message publicly and privately, teach the whole counsel of God, appoint leaders, warn, instruct in giving, and then entrust them to the Spirit of God to develop His life in them. The apostle's future relationship was primarily one of continued prayer and communication.

This apostolic example gives a measuring stick by which missionary work can be fairly evaluated. Ideally, it should have all the elements of the Pauline pattern. Sometimes this is not possible, as even Paul found in regard to Cyprus, a place to which he did not return. It may be that he was satisfied that Barnabas was to go there to complete the work they both had begun.

One may object that this message to the Ephesian elders said nothing about social concern. True, Paul's priority was clearly on the preaching of salvation in Jesus Christ and the planting of the church. But even so, he counseled these elders that they must "help the weak." He taught and practiced what he had written to the Galatian believers: "Let us do good to all men, and especially to those who are of the household of faith" (6:10).

Christ's example in giving a higher priority to the paralytic's need for forgiveness than the healing of his body and also the later teaching of the Apostles provide the charter for special ministries of alleviating suffering and helping the needy. Such ministries are of themselves not the gospel but are the fruit of redeemed lives possessed of godly altruism. Concern for the soul is to be paramount.

2

THE FIRST YEARS

Critics and doubters of the time would have been surprised indeed if "Franson's missionaries" persevered long enough to be able to celebrate even a first anniversary. It certainly was not expected that this "imprudent venture" would have a stable existence and a fruitful future. Sending out sixty-five workers in one year would have been a considerable undertaking for even a well-established mission of moderate size. The only organization that existed to carry out Franson's vision when he first started appealing for missionaries was in his heart and mind. His first published principles for a mission society were in an article in *Chicago Bladet,* November 25, 1890, which was also the beginning date of the Bible course for volunteers held in Chicago. In faith he had already called for workers to commit themselves for China when no mission to assist them yet existed.

The Plan

One of Franson's biographers, Josephine Princell, quotes his outline for the mission he conceived—at first to be called the China Alliance Mission:[1]

1. It is international—not only Swedes, Norwegians and Danes are included, but both Finland and Germany are represented in one division....
2. It is interdenominational—all who confess the truth in Christ may be involved in this work.
3. It appoints both men and women but only the unmarried. They may neither become engaged nor marry within three years.
4. It is primarily a mission of itinerating missionaries.
5. Each congregation, society or Sunday school may choose its own missionary to support. The following advantages will be apparent: (a) more workers can be sent out; (b) greater interest will be directed to the support of the missionary in that reports

will come direct to the supporting group from its own missionary; (c) it will be easier for the central committee which will be organized after the completion of this course in Chicago and which will be as representative as possible; the committee will have less responsibility and less work; (d) it will be better for the congregation in that, after the passage of three years, it can decide with its missionary about any changes in affiliation or methods of work (from itineration to a settled ministry).

This plan of finance does not seem strange in the present day when personalized support of missionary ministry, even in denominations, is often the preferred method. Yet in that day it was indeed different and seemed to some to be lacking in stability. To others, it seemed inconsistent with faith to have promises of support. The recent emphasis on a close relationship between missionary and supporting group is not new. Franson was one of its pioneers a century ago. "Every mission undertaking should be a matter of faith," Franson wrote in an open letter in April 1891, "and so should the China Alliance Mission be. In faith we have prayed for workers and their travel money and in faith these missionaries have left American soil.... In our evangelists' courses we have sought to learn something of the truth that the quickest way to reach the hearts of people—even when it comes to the pocketbook—*is by way of God, himself.* "[2]

Initial Principles

It would be well to examine Franson's outline. First, the mission was to be international. By 1890 Franson had ministered widely in America and Europe, using the English, Swedish, German, and French languages. He found it easy to work closely with various nationalities and wanted to draw on the strengths of dedicated Christians whatever their national background. Franson assumed that this mission would have an associate relationship with the China Inland Mission, as did the German China Alliance Mission which he had founded in Germany. His correspondence with J. Hudson Taylor seems to have sufficed not only for the German missionaries but also for the groups he was planning to send from

America.

In his early ministry, Franson had observed and been troubled by denominational divisions and tensions. He worked well across lines and was prepared to serve wherever called, so wherever he found true believers he easily assimilated them into a team for evangelism. He felt keenly that Christians of various fellowships should concentrate and cooperate on the major task confronting the church, the winning of the lost, particularly the heathen.

Franson's third point, that of calling only for single workers, was related quite closely to Hudson Taylor's timetable for getting the gospel to "every creature" in China. Taylor wanted men and women to go from door to door and lead people to Christ. His schedule called for each worker to make fifty evangelistic visits a day for a thousand days! There would be no time for the ordinary pursuits of life and so only workers without family ties could be used.

A second reason for a schedule of three years was that Franson wholeheartedly believed in the soon return of Christ and wanted to win the Chinese before that day came. Furthermore, he believed that these evangelists could be used to hasten the day of Christ's return as the Body of Christ would be completed.

The fourth point, that the mission would be primarily a group of itinerating evangelists, was related to the urgency of the task, but Franson was realistic enough to know that a more settled work would be necessary and therefore he provided that a change in method could take place after the initial three years.

In retrospect, Franson's emphasis on itinerant evangelism rather than on church planting and discipling of believers seems out of character. His previous thirteen years of evangelism had been accompanied by careful training of believers. More than many evangelists, he instructed believers in the New Testament pattern and function of the local church. His basic principle on the strategy of missions was revealed in a position he stated in 1892, less than eighteen months after he had sent at least two groups of missionaries to China.

> Our common goal must in every case be the salvation of souls and their continuing both in grace and in the work until the Lord returns. The essential task thus will not be to set up stations, but to get living congregations into being, whose continuing joy it will be to send out new missionaries from their own midst, until all of China shall have heard the good news of redemption.[3]

The final point, the missionaries' direct relationship with a supporting group, was vital. Franson believed that a church, young people's society, or Sunday school could easily take on the support of one missionary—giving to the needs of his ministry, supporting him in prayer, maintaining communication with him, and receiving regular reports of his work. This different approach put far more responsibility on both the missionary and the supporting group and should, he felt, result in more participation by supporters. At the same time it would ease the work of the mission society.

A Committee is Formed

The committee members for the China Alliance Mission were named by the end of the Chicago course. They were Pastor C. W. Holm, chairman; L. Michaelsen, vice chairman; Pastor August Pohl, treasurer; Professor Fridolf Risberg, secretary; Pastor C. T. Dyrness, vice secretary.[4]

A committee of ladies was also appointed: Mrs. Josephine Princell, Mrs. Tea Pohl, and a Mrs. Linden. In her biography of Franson, Mrs. Princell relates without comment that "the Ladies Committee was soon dissolved because one of its members moved from Chicago and the brothers considered that they could, without the help of the ladies, care for the important matters which pertained to the committee."[5]

Franson was right in anticipating that the arrangement he proposed would make the work of the committee quite light. The minutes of two of its early meetings testify to that fact.

> Minutes of the Meeting of April 2, 1891.
> Present: Holm, Michaelsen, Risberg, Mrs. Princell.
> Inasmuch as nothing of importance was up for consideration, the meeting was dismissed without any decisions (Fridolf Risberg).

> Minutes of Meeting, January 22, 1892. The committee came

together for prayer and thanksgiving. Present were Holm, Michaelsen, Dyrness, Pohl, and Risberg, together with Mrs. Pohl and brother Franson. No decisions of importance were made (C. T. Dyrness).[6]

One important decision had been made earlier, however. Mrs. Princell quotes a letter of Franson's:

The committee of the China Alliance Mission has decided to observe annually the Sunday nearest January 22 with services of thanksgiving and preaching on missions.[7]

This was the first anniversary of the sailing of the initial China party. After other mission fields were entered, that date became less significant than the forming of the mission in North America. October 14, 1890, the beginning of the first training course, was therefore considered to be the founding date.

Other Fields and a Change in Name

The widening of the mission's work into countries other than China necessitated a change in the name. It could no longer be identified alone with the first-entered country. Because those who were sending out the missionaries were in the Swedish and Norwegian-Danish churches, it seemed a logical choice would be The Scandinavian Alliance Mission (S.A.M.). To identify its organizational base, the words "of North America" were added at the time of incorporation.

Japan

Japan came into focus as a mission field when missionaries en route to China stopped there, were impressed by both the need and the opportunity, and wrote to Franson stating that they "had received an inner burden to pray God to send missionaries there also." Franson had ministered to Japanese on a visit to San Francisco and had conferred with a missionary who had spent many years in Japan. In his typical way, Franson had tried to glean from him as much information as possible about the Japanese and the best way to reach them.

The prayers of concerned people and the facts about the country led Franson to make an appeal for Japan. The result was a group of fifteen who offered themselves out of the training courses in Seattle, Denver, Phelps Center (Nebraska), and Des Moines, with some from the earlier course at Lindsborg, Kansas. Their preparations were quickly completed and they sailed for Yokohama on November 3, 1891, arriving there on the twenty-third.[8]

India

India, the next country entered, was not the primary target. Franson's objective was actually Tibet. He shared the outlook of the rulers of China that the country included not only the Chinese but the bordering Manchus, Mongols, and Tibetans.

During the summer of 1891 Franson met his close friend, Pastor John F. Frederickson, who twelve years earlier had worked with him in Minnesota and among the Mormons in Utah. They spent time together in prayer seeking the Lord's will about Frederickson's going to China. Franson valued his friend's gift of leadership and his experience in the work.

At the mission committee meeting early in 1892, it was decided to send missionaries to the Tibetans on China's southwest border and Frederickson was appointed the leader of the first group. The approach to Tibet from the south by way of India was thought to be the easier way. A group of twelve left Vancouver, B.C., on March 9, 1892. Two of these, more interested in getting directly to the Chinese, left the party in Shanghai. The remaining ten arrived in Calcutta April 30.

While the Tibet group was preparing, a third China party of twelve embarked for Shanghai.

South Africa

The mission committee meeting of January 22, 1892, also decided to send a party to Africa. Franson had earlier ministered among blacks in the United States, and had even mentioned in his China appeal of November 1890 that perhaps he should try to interest black American Christians in a mission to Africa; so when he received feelers about sending missionaries to that continent he was willing to accept this challenge also. He at first considered Angola as a field, but as further information came to hand decided on a work among the populous Zulu tribe in South Africa.

The first Africa group was a party of eight, most of whom had more than average training and experience. Their leader was Andrew Haugerud. One with the least training was Malla Moe, who nevertheless had great zeal for the gospel and was to work more fruitfully than most for over sixty years. The Africa party sailed from New York on April 2, 1892, and disembarked in Durban in mid-May. Their goal was Transvaal but they went first to Ekutandaneni, Natal, to study Zulu.

While the Africa and Tibet parties were en route, Franson reported the death of one of the Japan missionaries, Mary Engstrom; the return from China for health reasons of another; and that "the Alliance Mission [note the dropping of China as part of the name] now had 59 missionaries in China proper, 14 in Japan, 10 on the way to Tibet and 8 on the way to Africa—altogether 91."[9]

East Africa

The fifth field to be entered was East Africa. Franson had met missionary Eric Hedenstrom in Sweden and learned from him about his years of service among the Galla people of Kenya. The great need was for missionaries. Franson advised him to go to the United States and, with introductory letters and other publicity from Franson, Hedenstrom was able in a short time to recruit a party of eleven to accompany him. That party of twelve (to be increased to thirteen when Mrs. Hedenstrom joined it in London) sailed from the East Coast on July 10, 1893. It arrived in Mombasa, East Africa, on August 26, 1893. On November 6 the missionaries boarded ship for Kulesa on the River Tana. Their ship was grounded at the mouth of the Tana but there was no loss of life or injury to any.

After arrival at Kulesa, all were busily engaged in studying the Galla language and building missionary homes and a church. The area proved to be extremely unhealthful. One after the other became ill with malaria and one of the young ladies, Augusta Nelson, passed away February 17, 1894, less than six months after arrival.

In the following months there was much flooding and the missionaries fell victim to repeated fevers. All became greatly discouraged, with the result that four decided to return to America and four left for India to enter missionary work there. One missionary, Ole Alme, went two days' journey farther inland and opened a mission station at Makere. His work was showing promise when he, too, died. The work at Makere was turned over to a German mission.

There were only three left on the field, Mr. and Mrs. Hedenstrom and Frank Palmquist. Through their diligent efforts in the face of repeated illnesses (malaria, bilharzia, etc.), a congregation of sixty-five converts was raised up at Kulesa from among Galla tribespeople, freed slaves, and several former Muslims.

Just as these missionaries were much encouraged because the work was progressing well, Mrs. Hedenstrom passed away on September 22, 1901. Palmquist had, meanwhile, opened a mission work in Lamu where the climate was more tolerable. After a brief furlough Hedenstrom joined Palmquist at Lamu, but their time together was not long as Hedenstrom passed away April 8, 1904.

Palmquist was then alone and in poor health. He continued on until June 1908, when he turned the work over to German missionaries and returned to Chicago. He had been on that tropical mission field—with only one brief furlough—for almost fifteen years.[10]

Mongolia

When Franson visited missionaries of the Swedish Holiness Union in North China in 1895 he was very near that section of the country known as Inner Mongolia. The Mongolians are a nomadic people without towns or cities. Living mostly in tents, they move from place to place pasturing their animals. The only settled communities were the temples where Lama priests congregated and went through their Buddhist ceremonies.

In reporting on his visit, Franson wrote about a meeting for prayer on the Mongolian desert, where he joined three missionaries of the Swedish Holiness Mission in earnest intercession for Mongolia. When David Stenberg, a seminary student who had earlier attended one of Franson's Bible courses in Sweden, read this report he determined to apply to The Scandinavian Alliance Mission for Mongolia.

Stenberg arrived in Mongolia before the end of 1895, making it the mission's sixth field. He was later joined by a fellow seminarian, Carl Suber, who went out in 1896. Four more were added to the field in 1897.[11]

A Review of the First Five Years

Thus in five years' time six countries had been entered by Franson's American-based mission. At least eleven of the workers from North America had died in their early years (in some cases, early months) of service. Others had to be repatriated for health reasons and a few had transferred to other mission work. There remained about one hundred on the fields. This new work, started without a fully established mission organization, had an outstanding record of growth and stability and only a very small percentage of loss along the way.

To what can that stability be attributed? Certainly the help and guidance of the China Inland Mission was a great factor in the early years of the China field. The missionaries, themselves, were very resourceful and soon adopted their own form of organization—that of holding of an Annual Field Conference and electing a Field Committee—which has, through the years, proved to be an excellent form of field government.

The prayers of the founder and the supporters were also decisive. Probably the greatest factor was the sense of the Lord's call that each missionary possessed. It was true that Franson had been the instrument to move them out to the fields, but they were going at the Lord's command and recognized their dependence on Him.

LAYING FOUNDATIONS

It is not surprising that Franson was eager to visit the missionaries in China, Japan, and India, as he was the one God had used to send them out. But there was another compelling reason. Franson had continually stressed the dire spiritual need of people languishing in pagan darkness and was fully convinced that they were lost. He also knew that many would receive Christ if they but heard the good news of salvation through faith in Him. Franson therefore planned a trip that took him through Southeastern Europe and the Near East en route to India, with many opportunities for preaching along the way. Departing from Cairo, Egypt, on March 9, 1894, he arrived in Bombay on the seventeenth.

Tibet from the India Side

By early April he had reached Ghoom, Northeast India, where the S.A.M. workers had made a good start in three locations, preaching and teaching the gospel to Tibetans. He was not content to only observe their activities but soon proved himself a diligent and effective coworker. He preached at every opportunity— through interpreters—and, as he and his companions traveled through the rugged Himalayan Mountains "he talked with every heathen he met on the trail about Christ."[1]

Many wondered how this frail-looking man could endure the hardships of such travel. Missionary A. E. André wrote of him at the time:

> Franson was tireless as a walker. The two of us have traveled several hundred miles in the Himalayan Mountains. No matter the circumstances, he got along with and even seemed to enjoy what was provided. He really did not give much thought to what he ate.... He was, however, much frightened of precipices. It often happened when we were on the very narrow paths with a sheer mountain cliff on one side and a dizzying chasm on the

other that he cried out to God for strength and crept forward on all fours with his eyes almost closed. On the other hand, he had a great deal of courage when it came to something of an adventuresome nature. He was very anxious that we should enter closed Tibet without delay.[2]

In May, Franson and two of the men started out on a long and rugged tour of the border areas as far west as Mussourie. Altogether, Franson spent three or four months with the S.A.M. missionaries who were working along the frontier. His visit left a permanent impact on the work. Of exceptional value was the book he wrote on how Buddhism had erred, *The Religion of Tibet and the True Religion: for English Speaking Tibetans,* and a series of eight tracts to be translated into Tibetan. Another was the winning to Christ of a young man, David McDonald, the son of a British father and a Tibetan mother. In later years McDonald was greatly used to translate Scripture into Tibetan.[3]

First Visit to Japan

In September 1894 Franson boarded ship in Calcutta for Hong Kong. After a short stop there and in Macao and Canton he went on to Japan. There he worked alongside the fourteen missionaries for several months and was most pleased with the progress they were making in winning Japanese and gathering them into churches. He reported:

> They are working at no less than twelve stations and have nearly thirty outstations with a total of seven hundred children in their Sunday schools. They are supporting fourteen national fellow workers, some of whom are good preachers.... The number of baptized believers is over sixty and the most of these are converts won through the work of our brothers and sisters. In addition to these, there are, of course, those who have joined the work of other missions, as well as those who now are being prepared for baptism.[4]

The small group had taken up work in three areas—Tokyo, Kobe, and Takayama. After Franson had conducted a two-week training course for evangelists in Tokyo, he, along with a Japanese evangelist and two missionaries, made a survey trip in Hida province seeking other places for ministry. Torjesen reports that the small party of four divided into two groups, the two missionaries going together and Franson and the evangelist together. Franson and his Japanese friend covered about 150 miles, walking twenty to thirty miles a day and holding meetings along the way.

Franson was very pleased with the literacy of the Japanese and their interest in reading gospel portions and tracts. He was becoming more than ever convinced of the message to be preached to those in heathen darkness and wrote about his convictions in a letter to a Swedish paper.

> I have found during all my visits in these pagan societies how it is most important to keep to the main issue, and to seek to make this as clear as possible.... In what way can you best make the pagan acknowledge his sin? Preach Christ, the crucified One. In what way can they best come to understand God's love? Preach Christ, the crucified One. Oh, how we must admire the Master's wisdom in sending out those who either did not know anything except this one thing, or else, who like Paul refused to know anything but Jesus Christ and Him crucified!

> It works, this old doctrine about the entrance of sin into our human society and about forgiveness of sin, freely and for nothing. It works, to let people know there is a God of love, who has opened communication with fallen men through the Mediator—through His only Son. It works, to show that God in all ages past has sought to come near to man...through messages written down by holy men—and that nineteen hundred years ago God sent His one Son.... I will not criticize others, but my, oh my, what one gets to hear in many of Japan's churches from highly learned missionaries, both foreign and national! Yes, dissertations about philosophy, science, civilization, and at the highest level about Christianity as a teaching! But this is not all that the people need in order to get to heaven. They need to hear about a personal, living, present Savior—not only Christianity, but Christ![5]

To the Middle Kingdom

In early 1894 when Franson left Scandinavia to begin his first worldwide tour, events of great importance to the future of the mission were transpiring in China. The missionaries were scattered over four provinces in the work of the China Inland Mission—

Chekiang and Kiangsi in the south and Shansi and Shensi in the north.

As we have seen, the agreement between Franson and Taylor stipulated a three-year period when the missionaries would work with and under the direction of the China Inland Mission. Their main responsibility was itinerating with the gospel message. Taylor's fervent hope was that 1,000 new missionaries could complete the evangelization of China in three years. The missionaries had agreed to this plan and its related requirement that they remain unmarried during that period. Correspondence and reports from the year 1894 reveal that the workers had the completion of the three-year period much in mind; but even so, they remained faithful to the agreement.

These missionaries, all culturally linked by their Scandinavian backgrounds and language; their allegiance to their new homeland, the United States; and Franson's recruitment and training were now separated in four widespread areas. This weighed rather heavily on many of them. Furthermore, they were associates of the China Inland Mission, not full members. Could they not work closer to each other? There was one other factor, briefly alluded to in the historical record, that naturally was on the minds of not a few—marriage.

When I visited one of the pioneer workers, Mrs. Kristina Nelson, in her retirement years and mentioned that I had heard that she and her husband, John, were the first couple married after the three-year period had been completed, she in effect asked, "When eighteen young women and seventeen young men with natures the same as young people today travel together across the ocean for over three weeks, don't you expect attachments to develop?" She could have added that they had been together several weeks in the homeland while preparing, and were also linked by many common interests, above all by their dedication to the Lord for service in China.

Torjesen reports that this question of marriage was one of the points to be discussed at the 1894 conference of twenty S.A.M.

missionaries working in the south. There are intimations that the single missionaries may have been cautioned against any thoughts of early marriage.

> The conference deliberated, among other things, on the question of whether or not a new field should be opened. The conference came to the agreement that they should seek to be transferred by the China Inland Mission to the northern part of China. Moreover, the conference discussed the question of to what extent, if any, it might be harmful to the missionaries to enter into matrimony, since they soon will have been three years on the field. The majority saw it as beneficial to the mission, when those who so wished would enter into matrimony.[6]

In May 1893 the missionaries in Shensi province had been able to secure premises and thus a base for evangelism in three cities: Sian, Lunghsien, and Hsingping. Sian had been the capital of China for over 700 years and was clearly the most important city in China's northwest. Because of this the missionaries were convinced that it should be their center of operations and that they also should seek to enter many of the county seats on the heavily populated Sian plain.

The developments which followed are related in the twenty-fifth anniversary story of the China field.

> Encouraged by the progress [in establishing bases on the Sian plain] and foreseeing the advantage of taking up a field of work together—the mission already having over fifty missionaries in China—a conference was called to be held in February 1894 in Kuwu, Shansi, for consultation on the best plan for proceeding. The Sian Plain had been found to be a "land with wide boundaries." At the time of the missionaries' arrival in China in 1891, Hudson Taylor had pointed out this area on the map as their future field. It seemed to those gathered that the time had come to take up this field and that it should be as a joint work of these missionaries. Concentrating their work in this manner in one field instead of being spread widely North and South, as previously, could bring unity to the work. At the same time the missionaries could support each other in spiritual and practical ways. They needed to be together to meet all the demands that growth of the work would make on them.[7]

Seeking a Field of Their Own

The Kuwu conference of twenty-one missionaries began February 3, 1894, and continued for eight days. The decision was confirmed to take up a field in Shensi and neighboring parts of Kansu and to invite the other S.A.M. workers to join them. P. E. Henriksen seems to have been the leader of the conference. He reported further:

> In addition, we were to elect our own committee on the field, which was to stand by us in both counsel and deed. The committee was to regulate and lead the work as a whole. We were to have annual conferences at which the more important aspects of the work would be deliberated. If the China Inland Mission was willing to consent to this, then we wished to cooperate with them as before. If not, we would work as an independent mission. Since we wished to get the work on the new field started as soon as possible, the brothers began at once to seek to get some more stations opened, preparing thereby for the sisters also to come into the work.[8]

The group elected Henriksen as field chairman, a position he held until his death from typhus in May 1898. This is the first record of the setting up of the field administrative structure that has served so well throughout the years.

> It was with complete unity of heart that this little group, meeting in conference in Kuwu, laid prayerful plans for the new work. They foresaw that money would be needed if new stations were to be opened and in faith committed this matter to their Heavenly Father. They also decided that they themselves should contribute to the need. Their resources were very limited, but they had a love for the Lord and His work and the result was that they gathered $50.00. With this small fund they proceeded to open new stations on the field.[9]

The missionaries did not forget their relationship to their sponsoring group.

> The mission committee in Chicago was advised by letter about the decisions of the conference, as was also the directorship of the China Inland Mission in Shanghai. But before the letters had time to reach their destinations—the postal service being so slow—the missionaries had already begun to set their plans in motion.

This matter was admittedly handled in a rather independent way and their procedure was misunderstood by the China Inland Mission. This led to the decision of Mr. Hudson Taylor to undertake the long trip from Shanghai to Sian to inquire into their action and to seek to prevent any serious results, which according to the thought of the China Inland Mission could arise from what was done.

After Hudson Taylor had more closely studied their decision and had seen how it had been brought about, he not only agreed, but supported it by apportioning the southeastern region of the province of Kansu as a widened field of labor....

It can be said that from this time the work of the Scandinavian Alliance Mission began. Previous to this they had only shared in the work of others. The conference with Mr. Taylor was held in Sian, June 18-21, 1894.[10]

The historian's assessment was correct as far as the beginning of the work in the mission's name in China was concerned, but it overlooked the good start the mission was already making in Japan, India, and Africa.

Franson Confers with Hudson Taylor

On December 31, 1894, Franson arrived in Shanghai to begin more than six months of consultation, encouragement, instruction, and evangelism in China. He first conferred with Hudson Taylor, apparently his first face-to-face meeting with the one whose great burden for China was such an important factor in igniting the flame of missionary zeal and action in Franson. Taylor, on his part, had come to have great respect for the evangelist and missionary enthusiast who in a relatively short time had been instrumental in adding so many dedicated missionaries to the force in China.

With the transfer of the S.A.M. missionaries to the north already agreed, there was apparently little discussion of that subject. However, Franson wanted to visit the workers in the south. Taylor accordingly arranged an escort so that he could travel to Chekiang and Kiangsi where they were cooperating with the China Inland Mission as per the earlier agreement.

Before going to the northwest provinces of Shensi and Kansu

Franson spent several months in north China with missionaries he had sent out under other Swedish boards and the International Missionary Alliance (now the Christian and Missionary Alliance).

With the Missionaries in Shensi

The conference of the missionaries in Sian began May 29, 1895, with Franson having arrived just the evening before. He reported later that he was impressed by the systematic plans for evangelism that the workers had implemented, including home visits, street preaching, chapel meetings, Sunday schools, and teaching of lay workers. He assisted in securing a tent for the evangelistic meetings and arranged to buy a printing press for their literature needs. He was gratified by one statistic in particular. Of the sixty-nine workers sent out, fifty-eight were still active in the work, forty-two of them in the new field of Shensi and Kansu. Four had died in China; five or six had returned home because of illness. Apparently one or two had transferred to other activity.[11]

As he had done along the Tibetan Frontier, Franson also worked alongside the missionaries in China. One of the early China missionaries, C. J. Anderson, told me that he had seen little fruit from his work in the first years. But when Franson visited his station in 1895, Anderson interpreted for him and many responded to the gospel. What impressed Anderson was that the Chinese heard the same voice speaking Chinese as before, but now they responded. The same limitations of language were present, but that did not prevent their understanding and coming under conviction of their need of the Savior. To Anderson it was a great lesson in the absolute necessity of the message being given in full dependence on the Spirit of God and with much prayer.

After a second stop in Japan, this time of three weeks, Franson left for North America, arriving September 4, 1895. With his ministry in Europe and Asia he been away for more than three years.

Beginnings in South Africa

This first world tour did not include South and East Africa, to which earlier parties had been sent (see chapter 2). The South Africa group went to Ekutandaneni in Zululand and began studying the Zulu language. Andrew Haugerud, the leader, accompanied by a Danish missionary, Sofus Nielsen, set out to find a place to work farther inland in Matabeleland, part of the present country of Zimbabwe.

Disappointment, Success, Grave Loss

The Matabeles were ruled by a pagan king, and when the men reached that area and presented their request to settle among the people, he replied in very definite terms that permission would not be given and they could return the way they had come.

As they traveled they conferred with missionaries along the way, seeking information about the needs of the people. Thus Swaziland, a protectorate of Great Britain, came to their attention, and they were directed to a place named Bulunga. Here Haugerud obtained permission from the authorities for the missionaries to take up their ministry. He wrote to tell the others the good news and urged them to join him. Unknown to Haugerud, however, Bulunga was notoriously unhealthful. The next word his coworkers had was upon the return of Nielsen, who brought the sad news that Haugerud had died of malaria. He had been in Africa less than eight months.

This loss was a heavy blow to the others. One of the men decided to serve with another mission and that left only five women and one man. This man, Paul Gullander, had married one of the women, Augusta Hultberg. The group continued language study and awaited the birth of the Gullanders' baby. The "baby" turned out to be twin boys. Mrs. Gullander did not survive and one of the boys lived only six weeks. Mr. Gullander felt he had only one course to follow—return home and care for the surviving twin. The loss of the leader, Andrew Haugerud; Paul Gullander, a seminarian; and his wife, a nurse, left the group greatly reduced. Even so, the remaining four women decided to go ahead to the field which Haugerud had chosen. But the Lord provided help from an unexpected source.

There was a young man at Ekutandaneni by the name of William Dawson. His fellow missionaries agreed to let him accompany the four ladies so he could provide help along the way and in the building of living quarters. He later married one of the four, Emma Homme. The early history does not indicate whether interest in Emma was one of the motivating factors in his offer to help. Whatever the situation, it was surely the Lord's provision. Dawson was not only a help in the move and settling in, but, after joining the mission, was appointed by Franson as field leader. He became a tremendous asset in the training of African evangelists and the development of churches in Swaziland.

The Swazis did not manifest any need for the missionaries and their message. They were far more interested in getting salt and matches than in becoming "the salt of the earth" and "the light of the world." One great hindrance was their fear of the king's threats of death if they became Christians. The beginnings of the work seemed unpromising. [12]

The Mission Tour Evaluated

Mrs. Josephine Princell summarizes Franson's first world mission tour:

> On this world trip Franson spent six months in India, three in Japan, and seven in China. He visited many mission stations, saw all the missionaries whom he had sent out to these countries, helped and encouraged them with words and deeds, preached the gospel for the heathen by interpretation and met with universal acceptance and kindness.
>
> Only God has the count of how many heathen who listened to missionary Franson's Spirit-anointed and zealous evangelistic messages turned from the darkness of heathenism to the gospel of life and freedom. But the number was not small as the missionaries have borne witness in their letters. Franson, himself, tells of one conversion in the following words:
>
> "In one of my meetings in China, as I was kneeling and praying

with one heathen about his soul's salvation, his tears happened to fall on my hand. When he noticed this, he looked up as if to apologize. I said nothing, but I thought, 'My dear man, if you really knew how happy I am to see the tears of the heathen you would never think of apologizing for them. I would not be as happy if pearls and jewels rained on me, as I am now when I feel your tears on my hand.'"

Franson would have liked very much to have stayed for a longer time on the mission fields; but various urgent concerns related to the Alliance Mission's work made it necessary for him to return to America. He must be present for the fifth annual meeting of the mission, and so his steps must be directed that way. [13]

THE HEART CONCERNS
OF LEADERSHIP

In retrospect, it is amazing that Franson, now the administrator of a fair-sized mission with about a hundred missionaries in five different countries, could keep current on its progress. Mails were slow and forwarding points, as he traveled, were few and far between. The S.A.M. committee undoubtedly felt the need of his presence and help, particularly as he had been the key instrument the Lord had used to recruit workers and develop the prayer and financial support which were essential to this undertaking. The severe financial panic of 1893 was followed by a period of deep economic depression which seriously affected missionary giving. It was too much to expect churches to send out new missionaries when it was not easy for them to keep the commitments already made.

A General Director Selected

The need of an official leader for the mission was becoming evident. The work in the countries Franson visited seemed to be progressing satisfactorily under stable leadership, but a homeland committee whose members were hard pressed with their own individual responsibilities could hardly meet the mission's home base needs to build a relationship with the supporting constituency and recruit new workers.

Franson, as founder, had filled the role of director but now suggested that a formal appointment be made of one he thought gifted for the task. At the annual meeting in Chicago, January 1896, he nominated a Swedish pastor and former coworker in Europe, C. W. Gillen, for the position. Upon careful reflection Gillen, though at first receptive to the idea, decided that he should not accept. The conference then elected Franson general director "for life," a position he did not seek and which he accepted with reluctance. For this very active evangelist, churchman, and founder of mission societies, this was the first and only formal appointment to position on record.[1]

Not Immune to Criticism

This was a rather difficult period for the young mission. Franson's long absence on his world missionary tour meant that his only contact with supporters was through articles in various periodicals. Upon his return he found that criticisms of the mission were circulating, questioning a financial support system that made the missionaries dependent on the faithfulness and financial health of individual donors in the various churches. Critics also wondered about the effectiveness of the missionaries because they saw no published statistics of progress in the work. (Missionaries did report to their supporting churches, however.)

Franson's reaction to criticism was to bring his concerns to the Lord, spending much time in prayer for the supporters and the missionaries. He was willing to let needs be known but he also understood that because of the economic depression, many who earnestly desired to be faithful were unemployed or had experienced financial loss and were themselves suffering. In spite of the circumstances, his faith did not waver. It was the Lord who had called the workers and sent them overseas. He would not fail them.

A friend of his, who in writing to the periodical *Ansgarii Post* identified himself only as "J.E.B.", commented on Franson's confidence in the Lord's being fully able and willing to hear and answer prayer.

> Were his prayers heard? Yes, the experience confirms this. Is it not remarkable that during this time when missionaries backed by large denominations at times have suffered physical need Franson's missionaries have never seriously lacked? The treasuries of other groups—even large denominations—have often been empty, and more than empty, but Franson's missionaries have in proper time received what they have needed. The prayer of faith prevails![2]

When the criticism was directed at him personally, Franson seems not to have responded or sought to justify his course of action.

Arriving on the West Coast in September 1895, he was encouraged by the warm reception he received. Doors for his evangelistic and Bible teaching ministry were open on every hand, so it was four months before he reached the Midwest. Only after the fifth anniversary conference did he begin to write in explanation of the work of the missionaries and to answer questions about their effectiveness. He had now seen them at work and had opportunity to compare their work with that of others. He was personally convinced that they were proving to be diligent and useful workers.

Itinerant Evangelists, Yes—and More

Concerning the effectiveness of the missionaries, Franson wrote in May 1896 under the heading of "Information Concerning the Alliance Mission":

> The Alliance Mission establishes stations and its aim is to raise up Christian congregations. Some of our workers serve as ground-breakers in new areas, but even these do more than home visitation and distribution of tracts. They preach the gospel—at times to large crowds. Other missionaries assist and instruct the newly established churches and direct the work of the mission stations. It has been of great interest to me to notice that many of the missionaries who while here at home were most gifted in evangelism, on the field have developed excellent gifts of leadership, teaching, and pastoring.[3]

Franson's response to Hudson Taylor's call for itinerant evangelists had been immediate and wholehearted. He, too, was an evangelist and knew that the message of life must be widely proclaimed. But he was also a church planter, as proved by his broad and effective ministry in North America, Sweden, Norway, and Germany, so it is not surprising to detect his concern for a continuing ministry to converts.

We have seen how he anticipated that after the first three years of itinerant evangelism some of the missionaries might be called to a ministry in depth. Now in 1896 he clearly states that the missionaries work from established bases and endeavor to establish churches. Franson's growing understanding of the missionary task led him to an early conclusion that the fruits of evangelism must be preserved in New Testament congregations of believers, and that these believers must be trained to effectively witness for Christ. It was this pattern he had developed in his homeland ministry, both in the Midwest and in Europe.

A Constitution and Incorporation

Franson's time in North America gave him and the mission committee time to work out some organizational matters that were essential to the continued stability of the mission. The committee requested that he frame a constitution so steps could be taken to formally incorporate the work. This he did, and though there have been amendments through the years, much of the basic outline remains. The mission's solid evangelical stance, its evangelistic outreach, its relationship with its supporters, and the basic spiritual and practical requirements for missionaries remain unchanged. The Scandinavian Alliance Mission of North America was incorporated in the state of Illinois on November 12, 1897, and its Mission Committee changed to a Board of Directors with seven members. (In 1949, the name was changed to The Evangelical Alliance Mission and became commonly known by its initials T.E.A.M.—TEAM.)

In a pattern quite different from many other mission organizations without denominational affiliation, the corporate membership was drawn from the supporting churches. The annual meetings in the early years were of the mission treasurers of these supporting churches. In time other groups, such as youth organizations and women's missionary societies, were included.

Today, these churches and groups along with individual donors of a certain level of interest, board members, missionaries, and permanent home staff make up the membership which elects members to the board and makes other corporate decisions. There is an eligibility requirement that they be "in accord with the objectives, purposes, and Statement of Faith of this mission."[4]

In Torjesen's evaluation of Franson's early years with the mission he notes:

> In his major undertaking, he had developed a mission concept that sought to combine two specific New Testament models: (1) the involvement of the local church in missionary expansion; and (2) the mobilization of a specialized interchurch missionary team on the model of Paul's apostolic teams. To develop such a mission concept for interdenominational application was Franson's most significant contribution to foreign missions during this period.[5]

His detractors at the time did not give him credit for a carefully thought-through plan of operation. To them it seemed all was hasty and without adequate foundation. One key to the success of the undertaking—and the years have proved the validity of Franson's approach—was his thorough knowledge of the Word of God. He understood that Scripture set forth principles for mission and church and naturally adopted these principles for his work. Another key was his criteria for selecting missionaries. They must be sure of their call and have been active in witness.

Although the board members may have hoped that Franson would remain in North America for a protracted period so he could more actively participate in the administration of the mission, such was not to be. Franson was back in Europe by June 1897. He ministered in Norway, Sweden, Finland, Germany, and southern Europe. In 1900 he helped organize a Swedish division of the mission to be responsible for nine new missionaries he was sending out from Sweden. Though these missionaries for the most part joined the existing work of the S.A.M., the division founded in Sweden became a separate organization, the Swedish Alliance Mission, which has developed extensive missionary work in a number of countries. Cooperation with that mission has continued and there is a consciousness of common beginnings and common interests.

In reviewing the early history, one gains the impression that Franson tended to think of the missionaries from the various home countries (with the exception of those in the International Missionary Alliance) as all part of the same mission. He did, however, arrange for separate home committees. Franson, himself, was the unifying factor; and it was only natural, as each national committee matured and Franson's participation was reduced, that distinct mission organizations should emerge in each country—the German China Alliance being the first.

"If one...suffers, all...suffer."

Events on several fields caused much concern during this period. The Boer War in South Africa between the Dutch and the English colonists, 1899 to 1902, seriously affected the S.A.M. missionary work. The station at Bulunga had to be evacuated and eventually given up. All the missionaries had to leave their work areas except Malla Moe, who somehow managed to get permission to stay, first when the Boers were in control and later under the British. She wanted to be close to the African Christians.[6]

China and the Boxers

In China, 1900 was a time of terrible persecution and bloodshed when the Boxers, demon-worshipping fanatics spurred on by the urging of the Imperial Throne, sought to exterminate foreigners, especially missionaries, and deal similarly with their Christian converts. The Boxers, or "Righteous Fists," were so named by the Chinese because of their boxing motions and incantations intended to make themselves invulnerable to the swords and bullets of opponents. They had followed the deposed governor of Shantung province into Shansi where their anti-foreign hatred infected much of the general population.

> The bands were organized into three classes: (1) those who were to go to Peking "to fight for the Empire"; (2) those who were to stay in their own villages "to fight for their homes"; and (3) those who were "to fight for the gods" by attacking missionaries and Chinese Christians. In the middle of May 1900 these bands began to attack the homes of Chinese Christians. They carried flags bearing the inscription: "By Imperial command, exterminate the Church".... The movement was openly supported and

encouraged by the Empress Dowager and by the powerful conservative forces in her government....[7]

Franson was particularly concerned about these threatening developments. Over a hundred of his missionaries were in China at the time. These included forty-eight on the S.A.M. China field, thirty-two with the International Missionary Alliance, fifteen or sixteen with the German China Alliance, ten with the Swedish Holiness Mission, six on the S.A.M. Mongolia field, three with the Swedish Mongol Mission, three with the China Inland Mission, and two with the Norwegian Covenant Mission.

Of the missionaries Franson had sent out to work under the International Missionary Alliance and several Swedish missions, forty-two adults and sixteen children died at the hands of the Boxers.[8]

The Shensi missionaries were spared from martyrdom through the concern and disobedience of the provincial governor, Tuan Fang. The empress had ordered the death of foreigners but:

> Tuan Fang wrote to all the district magistrates in the province that they should protect all the foreigners in their regions and not kill them.[9]

Even so, the missionaries were ordered by their consulates to leave for the coast without delay. One new missionary, Mrs. Ruth Ahlstrand, who was in the refugee group, wrote, as reported by Mrs. Princell in the twenty-fifth anniversary story:

> The missionaries later recognized it as being the leading of the Lord that they waited to travel [until the governor provided an escort] because an ambush had been laid for them on the way when the word had gone out that they were traveling. The missionaries left the field at the end of July in two groups, one from Sian and one from Kansu. The Lord protected them in a wonderful way from known and unknown dangers which lay in wait during the long journey. The intense heat seemed unbearable at times, because this was an unusually hot summer.
>
> Mr. and Mrs. Ulrik Soderstrom, who were in the party from Kansu, had to sorrowfully lay to rest their little two-year-old daughter, Laura. The hardships of the journey were too much for this tender plant and so the Lord transplanted her into a better garden. In spite of the anguish, the bereaved parents could still

say, "He makes no mistakes." The refugee travelers could not even arrange a proper burial—a simple wooden box was not available —but under cover of darkness the father and two other missionaries, without even a tool for digging, scooped out a little grave on the bank of the river and hid the little body of the beloved child. Early the next day they had to hurry on. No one knows the little one's resting place but the Lord and that is enough.

The Kansu party traveled for eight weeks, often on foot, before they came to the coast. They truly experienced that the name of the Lord is "Almighty" and "Wonderful," for there were others, only four or five days distant from the coast, who were murdered along the way.[10]

Mongolia Martyrs

For the Mongolia field the story was much more tragic. Two of the earliest missionaries, David Stenberg and Carl Suber, had tried to reach the Mongols by widespread itineration throughout both Inner and Outer Mongolia. They decided, however, that it would be advisable to attract Mongols to a settled area where they could hear the gospel repeatedly and converts could be discipled. They actually began to develop two such areas, but did not abandon itineration. Torjesen summarizes the activity and circumstances:

> In the spring of 1899, N. J. Friedstrom and Suber started out on a long itineration into Outer Mongolia, which was to occupy them until the summer of 1900. Meanwhile Stenberg would be supervising the building and development of the colony in the desert at Wuyuan. By the summer of 1900 this colony had begun to function. A Chinese evangelist had been put in charge.

> Three lady missionaries, Hanna Lund and Hilda and Clara Anderson, also had moved out to the area. These four in the desert of Inner Mongolia had at that time heard that there was some trouble in connection with Boxer bands in Shansi. They had no idea, however, of the seriousness of the situation until they found themselves at the beginning of August 1900 in immediate danger. They were unfortunately betrayed by a corrupt lower rank Mongol chieftain who was acting in collusion with Chinese bandits. As a result they lost whatever they possessed and they fled. Hiding out in the desert for twenty days and nights, they were given food by friendly Mongols. Ultimately they returned to their own half-finished buildings and continued

in hiding there. But the night of September 1, they were caught by surprise and had to make a hasty flight. They were never seen again. They were put to death out in the desert where their bodies were then hidden.

Not knowing anything of these tragic events, Friedstrom and Suber came into the area on September 10 with their camel caravan from Uliasutai, Outer Mongolia. Friendly Mongols told them to stop and be most careful, but they would give them no further information. The two retreated to a safer place, and there they sent out feelers in different directions. When they still could find out nothing, Suber decided to go personally and check. He never returned. He was killed in a most brutal fashion.

After ten days, Friedstrom pulled back still farther until he was able to make contact with a Mongol friend. This man came to see him with utmost caution one night, and he then went secretly to a trusted high Mongol prince for advice. Friedstrom's life was in gravest danger at this time. The prince instructed the Mongolian friend to personally escort Friedstrom to Outer Mongolia as fast as he could, which he did. Friedstrom thus became the only survivor of the S.A.M.'s early Mongolian ministry.[11]

Franson was in Norway, Sweden, and Finland while these shocking events were occurring. In September 1900, some of the Swedish International Missionary Alliance survivors from China, who had escaped over the Gobi desert and reached the Trans-Siberian Railway, came as far as Helsinki, Finland, where Franson was ministering. It was indeed an emotional meeting. Particularly gratifying to Franson was the positive attitude these survivors held toward the Chinese people. They had not turned against the ones they were called to serve.

Franson saw most of these missionaries again after they had returned to north China. The hardships of their frightening experiences had not discouraged them or turned them aside from the path of the Lord's calling. The Shensi missionaries and Friedstrom were back in their respective places of service when Franson visited. Their spirit was reminiscent of the Apostle Paul's, who affirmed, "But none of these things move me, neither count I my life dear unto myself, so that I might finish my course with joy, and the ministry, which I have received of the Lord Jesus, to testify the gospel of the grace of God."

Whether they thought of it or not, their actions were much like those of Paul and Barnabas as recorded in Acts 14. They, too, returned to the places of persecution and suffering because they had not, up to that time, fulfilled their commission or reached their goal. True, they had preached the gospel and distributed literature. They had even seen men and women turn to Christ. But they had little opportunity to make disciples or to plant the church of the Lord Jesus Christ. It was for them to go back with the expectation of seeing His church established in those heretofore hostile hearts.

SIX YEARS OF WORLDWIDE MINISTRY

On his first world mission tour, Franson had not been able to visit South Africa, but the missionaries there were now much on his mind because of the Boer War. Thinking that the war would not last much longer, he set out from the Scandinavian countries in early 1901, stopping for evangelistic services in Belgium, Spain, and Portugal. But with the war continuing, he changed course and went through Algiers, Tunisia, Italy, Greece, Macedonia, Bulgaria, Romania, Russia, and on to Finland. There he arrived early in July 1901, having held meetings along the way. It is of interest to note that he had preached the gospel in every country of Europe in the course of two decades.[1]

Not being able to visit South Africa at this time, he returned to the United States. In Chicago he had opportunity to consult with the board of directors. Though no one realized it at the time, this was his last visit to the city he had chosen for the headquarters of the mission.

> For many reasons, Franson felt especially bound to Chicago for it was here that he first received genuine recognition as an evangelist of unusual caliber and a Bible teacher of more than ordinary insight and deep understanding of prophetic truth.[2]

To the Lands Down Under—and Around

On August 14, 1902, Franson began his second world tour, a trip that would keep him away from North America for six years. Other books recount the story of his remarkable ministry during this time, some of which related directly to the fields where S.A.M. missionaries served and some to other areas and groups. His time was spent mostly in evangelistic meetings, deeper life services, and prophetic conferences. The very clear evidence that the hand of the

Lord was on him provided all the open doors he needed.

As Franson was the first and undoubtedly the most effective missionary of the S.A.M., some brief mention must be made of the results of his work in areas other than the established fields of the mission. This chapter will describe some of these periods of ministry.[3]

When he left North America, Franson's immediate destination was New Zealand and Australia. Following three busy months "down under," he went on to Hong Kong, arriving there on December 24, 1902. For the next three months he traveled throughout southern China, holding meetings in cooperation with various missions. The usual fruit in souls converted and churches revived was seen. One pertinent development was a clear statement on an important aspect of mission strategy, the training of national workers. Franson wrote from Wenchow, Chekiang, March 7, 1903, to a periodical in Sweden:

> One matter occupies our thoughts unceasingly, and that is, What is the best way by which to foster national workers. Pray for us, dear brothers and sisters, that we may be able to implement the plans we do have, if they are from God; and also that large groups of national fellow workers may gradually stand side by side with the foreign workers.... The foreign missionaries will have their task then more and more in the training of the nationals.[4]

This emphasis on training workers should not be surprising, because it had been a strong point in Franson's earlier ministry as he trained hundreds of lay workers in his short-term Bible courses. Note there is no suggestion that itineration by foreign missionaries would be sufficient, in itself, to finish the job of evangelizing the Chinese.

To Japan Again

Franson arrived in Japan on March 26, 1903. He preached and taught for almost six months throughout the largest island, Honshu, and then for a short period in Hokkaido. He was gratified by the increased opportunities to preach the gospel to interested and receptive people and referred to this in a letter to a Swedish paper:

The mighty work of God's Spirit, particularly in these last eight years, has caused quite a turn around. The truth presses itself home on these people. They are learning more and more to discern the difference between being converted to the new teaching, and being converted to a person—Christ.[5]

Beginnings of Revival in Korea

Korea, the next country visited, was not then a field of the S.A.M. His time there, late September to early November 1903, was filled with services mostly for missionaries and Korean Christians, whom he found hungry for spiritual refreshing. His preaching of the Word was used by the Spirit of God to strengthen the beginning revival which moved onward and outward after he departed for China. It has been acknowledged as a significant factor in the continuing revival which had such an outstanding impact in the years 1903 to 1910.[6]

"The Blood of the Martyrs...."

From early November 1903 to January 1904, Franson worked with many missionaries in North China before he came to the S.A.M. Mongolia field. Here the lone survivor of the Boxer Uprising, N. J. Friedstrom, welcomed him warmly. Friedstrom was now married and he and his bride were working diligently to overcome the losses the work had suffered. One major goal was to reactivate the agricultural project begun before 1900. They wanted to encourage the otherwise nomadic Mongols to settle in one place for their livelihood and thus have a greater opportunity to hear the gospel in a sustained way. The leased land had been occupied by Chinese and was being denied to mission use. Franson assisted in the negotiations with the local authorities.

Following his time in Mongolia Franson spent four months preaching and teaching at the stations of various missions in Shansi and eastern Shensi before he arrived at the S.A.M. field headquarters in Sian in early April. The China field "had fifty missionaries on the field at the time, working in twenty stations, sixteen in Shensi Province and four in neighboring Kansu. Franson ministered on the field for over four months. He held meetings, ranging from a few days to up to a week, at most of the stations. Also an eight-day Bible Course for evangelists, elders, and Bible women had been planned. The 1904 annual field conference was scheduled for Pingliang, Kansu, toward the end of June."[7]

The missionaries who had been forced to leave because of the Boxer violence were now back at work. In many places the Chinese people had suffered greatly because of the upset conditions. Now when they saw the missionaries who had been the target of much of the violence return with relief supplies, they could not help but be impressed by their forgiving attitude. It had taken years to make even small beginnings in winning Chinese to Christ and bringing them together in small churches. At last there was a modest increase in interest and response. Franson described these encouraging developments as he wrote to a paper in Norway:

> Since the Boxer period, the work has been developing in a beautiful way. During the last conference year seventy persons were baptized after they first had been thoroughly examined concerning the condition of their souls. Many more now stand ready to take the same step. Our missionaries are generally full of courage and initiative. During the conference in Pingliang at the end of June they adopted several resolutions concerning the expanding of the work...[deciding that] missionaries at each station [would] conduct practical Bible courses for national evangelists...[and deciding to establish] a theological seminary and normal college for the training of both preachers and teachers.[8]

Franson, himself, allocated $1,000 from the bequest of a former fellow worker in Europe for the seminary project, which got under way quite soon. By 1907 the school had opened in Sian. Through the years, scores of Christian workers received training and went on to work in the churches.

To India

En route to India, Franson ministered in southeast China, the Malay Peninsula, and Burma. By early 1905 he was with the missionaries in northeast India.

The Alliance Mission situation in India had changed considerably since Franson's 1894 visit. The Finnish Alliance Mission, which Franson helped to organize in 1898, now had eight missionaries in India. The Swedish division of S.A.M., which Franson helped bring into being in 1899-1900, had six missionaries there. The S.A.M. from North America had nine. Moreover, in September 1900, John F. Frederickson, the original field leader, had suddenly died in Ahmadabad, Western India, where he had gone to distribute famine relief and set up a refuge for some two hundred destitute children. His loss was felt throughout the far-flung S.A.M. work.

When Franson arrived in 1905, the twenty-three Alliance missionaries in India were working out from seven main stations: Ghoom in Northeast India, Ringim and Lachung in Sikkim, Cooch Behar in Bengal (near the Bhutan border), Shigar in Baltistan (in Northeastern Kashmir), and Mandulwar and Nandurbar in Khandesh, West India. Despite this wide geographic distribution, the missionaries still were meeting in only one field conference.[9]

Responsive Bhils

A new movement developing in a more remote area was to have a marked effect on the India work. In Khandesh (part of the present state of Maharashtra), Swedish missionary A. P. Franklin began work among aboriginal Bhil tribespeople. These people, of whom there were about 400,000, were not in the Hindu religious system but were animistic and much more open to the gospel. Missionary O. A. Dahlgren from America, who was working in Baltistan, far to the north, paid a visit to Franklin and thus was introduced to the possibilities among the Bhils.

Up to this point the closed land of Tibet had been the focal point of interest. Spread out from that center were many Tibetan people outside the borders of mountainous, forbidding Tibet. Denied entry into the closed land, the missionaries could still work among the Tibetan people with the expectation that, as these nomadic people went in and out of their country, those who knew the Lord could become witnesses for Him. The S.A.M. missionaries, having started in the eastern area near Bhutan, entered Sikkim and, far to the west, Baltistan in northeast Kashmir.

With entry into the Bhil work, the extremities of the field now formed a triangle of 1,500 miles on each side. The northern section where the Tibetans were to be found was all mountainous—the highest mountains in the world at that, the Himalayas. Travel was a major undertaking and mail communication difficult. It was no easy matter for the field committee to coordinate the work of the twenty-three missionaries and give necessary guidance and help. Added to this was the administrative problem of dealing with home boards in three different countries—Sweden, Finland, and the United States.

On his arrival, Franson quickly evaluated the situation but waited to make adjustments until he first consulted and worked with the missionaries for several months. He wanted, in particular, to see the promising new work among the Bhils and be assured of their receptivity. His decision concerning the further placement of workers was announced in a letter from Ghoom, dated April 3, 1905, to a periodical in Sweden:

> We have no intention of lying around and waiting for Tibet and Bhutan to open, while other doors are wide open. We don't intend to place more missionaries up in the mountains than will have good opportunity to work there. Although Tibet might open up, it will not, despite the poetic glow that rests upon this closed land, be able to cause the missionaries to the Bhils to regret their choice, since the Bhils are far more responsive than the Tibetans and the Mongols, two peoples that are deeply entangled in the web of Buddhism.[10]

Franson was eager to take full advantage of the opportunity given by the openness of the Bhils. Mr. and Mrs. O. A. Dahlgren, who had been working with Mr. Fred Gustafson in Baltistan, were now back in Ghoom. Dahlgren related: "In a letter to me Franson wrote, 'In Ghoom kings sit waiting for a kingdom, but among the Bhils there is a kingdom waiting for kings.'" He and his wife readily responded to Franson's request that they transfer to West Khandesh.[11]

Having recently been in Burma where he had seen what had happened among the responsive Karens, Franson realized that opportunities could easily slip away. There, in areas where missionaries were available to enter, great numbers came to Christ; but where there were no missionaries, the animistic Karens turned to Buddhism. He feared that the Bhil people without the gospel could be similarly lured into Hinduism. To the question whether missionaries should be sent only to the responsive, his answer was to send to resistant people those who felt a strong call in that direction and at the same time not miss the opportunity of bringing the gospel to those who were ripe for the harvest. Conviction led to action and Franson penned an appeal for eight new missionaries to work among the Bhils.

With the Dahlgrens transferring to the Bhil ministry in 1905, western India became the principal focus of the American S.A.M.—in cooperation with the branch in Sweden. Finnish missionaries were taking an increasing interest in the Ghoom area and in 1906 it became the full responsibility of the Finnish Alliance Mission. In the meantime, the S.A.M. missionaries in Bengal and Bhutan continued their work among the Tibetans.

An Administrative Advance

Franson's method of administering the mission work grew more out of observation and experience than by following any traditional pattern. As general director, he did not hesitate to actively direct when he was personally present, but in his absence—and even while he was on the field—he placed great responsibility on the field committee and the annual conference of missionaries. He was learning that confusion could arise when different home centers established policies for their missionaries without taking adequate steps to coordinate with the other sending countries. His solution was simple and direct. He divided the responsibility. Each of the sending missions was to have full authority over its own personnel and work—the Finnish Alliance Mission in northeast India and the Scandinavian Alliance Mission and the Swedish Alliance Mission in the west. (Division of responsibility in the west between the American and Swedish missions would take place in 1907.)[12]

As the Baltistan field was to continue under S.A.M. responsibility, Franson went directly there from the Bhil work. He conferred with the three remaining missionaries and joined them in planning future expansion, including the opening of another station.

Franson's farewell word as he left India was one of victory: "Just since my arrival we have had the privilege of baptizing about one hundred sixty people on our mission stations in India. All glory to God!"[13]

Detoured by Political Disturbances

Franson had intended to travel from Baltistan in Kashmir up toward Siberia into the Trans-Caspian provinces and thus to Asiatic Turkey, but political disturbances in Russia closed its borders to travelers. He wrote about the enforced change in his plans:

> When I came to Lek in Ladakh [in northeastern Kashmir] I was informed by the British Commissioner that Russia had forbidden foreigners to travel through the Trans-Caspian Provinces.... I have, therefore, had to choose another way to get to the many Americans serving in eastern and central Turkey—by way of Baghdad and through a part of Persia.[14]

More than three years had passed since Franson left America and he was just half way around the world. One of his principal objectives was to visit the missionaries in South Africa, but before reaching there in April 1906 he would have what must be regarded as the most outstandingly fruitful period of his consistently fruitful career of harvesting souls for the Lord. We shall follow him into Armenia.

Overflowing Blessing in Armenia

From Baltistan Franson journeyed to Karachi in present-day Pakistan and took ship to Basra (Al Basrah in Iraq). There followed several weeks of extremely hard traveling in Iran in order to preach to a settlement of Nestorian Christians. From there he crossed into Turkey.

The trip went well and he arrived in the city of Van, Armenia, where the doors of the largest Gregorian church were opened for him. More than five thousand Armenians listened with marked attention to his preaching.[15]

Most of the Armenians were Gregorian Catholics. These people had suffered greatly at the hands of the Turkish Moslems and many had lost loved ones in the massacres of Christians. In Diyarbakir and a nearby village, Franson heard much about the recent persecution of the Christians. He wrote that many in this place had suffered greatly in the bloodbath and unrest of 1895, when 228 of the village's 600 inhabitants were massacred by the Turks. The family where he ate his noon meal had seven of its members murdered and one girl kidnapped. They did not know her fate. They estimated that 100,000 Armenians and Syrians had been killed during the terrible years when Turks and Kurds attacked the Christians.[16]

Missionaries of the American Board were doing much work in Eastern Turkey and eagerly welcomed Franson's help. Dr. Atkinson, of that board, wrote to the local missionaries introducing this Swedish-American evangelist. His letter is of special interest because of what it tells about Franson personally. He described Franson as small in stature, about five feet six inches tall, having blue eyes and a happy expression and with a countenance reminding one of Charles Dickens.

> He is of a deeply religious nature and is constantly praying, sometimes aloud, when he is home and feels himself free. His preaching is simple, illustrated with many pertinent stories. Everything is aimed at inviting people to come to Christ. He points to Christ as the only source of salvation and power and gives Him all the glory.[17]

An example of Franson's fruitful work in Armenia was given in Dr. Torjesen's research of the meetings in Marash, one of ten centers where Franson preached:

> In the evening of the very day of Franson's arrival, the building was packed to its utmost capacity. The word of life fell on his audience with burning power. Revival broke out which continued six weeks or longer. The attendance grew so great that the people packed every available space within the church and clung

to the doors and windows to hear the Word of God. The building was crowded hours before the appointed time. Even before Franson's words were interpreted, souls were convicted by their impact. The sermons were short and simple and generously filled with pungent parables, quickening illustrations, and anecdotes which made the truth live. He spoke to his listeners of the need of repentance, the joy of obedience to the will of God, the brevity of human life, and the certainty of judgment to come. Behind the words was the personality of one who was passionately convinced of a divine mission to his hearers.[18]

Over a period of eighty years following the Armenian revivals, the TEAM headquarters has received occasional inquiries from evangelical Armenians in the United States asking for information about Franson's work. These letters usually had some indication of a parent or grandparent who had been won to Christ through his ministry.

On to South Africa

Going by way of Lebanon, Egypt, and East Africa, Franson arrived at Durban, South Africa, on April 25, 1906. As usual, he was pressed into service immediately, and worked with a number of missions in various parts of Natal province over the next two months. The work of the S.A.M. missionaries was in northern Natal and the Protectorate of Swaziland. There he attended the annual missionary conference and ministered in the churches established by the missionaries. These missionaries had mostly relocated as a result of the Boer War but could rejoice that the new planting was beginning to bear fruit.

Franson was able to report that there were four head stations, forty out-stations, twenty-eight partly supported African evangelists, and fifty self-supporting African evangelists and workers. There were a total of 456 communicants and an equal number of adherents. Eleven foreign missionaries served among them. He was delighted to see and hear the groups of converted Africans singing with their rich, melodious voices as they walked from various places to the church conference at Bethel. At each place he ministered he saw many coming to the Savior. "We had the joy

73

of baptizing not less than fifty-six people—those who had some time back acknowledged that they wanted to belong to the Lord," Franson reported.[19]

With Andrew Murray

A friend in Turkey had written to Dr. Andrew Murray, renowned Dutch Reformed minister, about the spiritual results of Franson's work there. As a result the churches under Dr. Murray's influence in South Africa were open to Franson. He preached in fifty of them, held Bible studies for lay evangelists, and greatly encouraged missionary interest among the Boer people.

When, after sixteen months, Franson was to leave for South America, Murray sent along a letter of introduction. He wrote: "Through God's blessing, his preaching has borne fruit in the salvation of many souls and in the thrust it has given believers to renew their dedication to more fully involve themselves in the service of Christ." Franson left Capetown, South Africa, early in September 1907 for Buenos Aires, Argentina.[20]

Eight and a Half Months in Latin America

After working in Argentina, Brazil, and Chile for five months, Franson boarded ship at Valparaiso for Panama with stops in port cities along the western coast of the continent, among them Lima, Peru, where a little more than half a century later the mission he founded would have missionaries at work. He crossed the equator February 27 and not long after arrived in Panama, where he found an open door for ministry among English-speaking Jamaicans working on the canal project. From Panama he took ship to Maracaibo, Venezuela, the site of the newest field of the mission.

Bach and Christiansen Pioneer New Field

We do not know whether Thomas Johan Bach and John Christiansen had met Franson before he left the United States almost six years earlier, but they could not have escaped knowledge of his extensive and fruitful work. When Franson started on his last world mission tour in August 1902, Bach had just begun his Bible preparation as a student of professor Fridolf Risberg at the Swedish Seminary in Chicago. John Christiansen was in the Danish-Norwegian division of the same school. Bach's story of his call is related in the mission's twenty-fifth anniversary book. In the spring of 1901 he was working in a machine shop in Racine, Wisconsin. While resting during the noon hour he caught sight of a bit of newsprint on which he saw the question, "Will you not go to South America with the gospel of Christ?" He laid the paper aside but God brought the words back to his mind again and again and within a week Bach was praying, "Send me to South America." When he shared his vision with Risberg, he was encouraged to keep pressing toward that continent, even if at the time the Scandinavian Alliance Mission had no plans for work there.

Three years later, with his seminary work completed, Bach made plans for a survey trip to the southern continent. He left New Orleans on January 1, 1905, for Venezuela, where he spent two months. He found no evidence of missionary activity or of any evangelical witness in western Venezuela. Before returning to the United States he spent two months in Brazil.

With his burden greatly increased for western Venezuela and finding no mission working in that area, Bach contemplated forming a new organization. First, however, he asked if the Scandinavian Alliance Mission would be interested in opening a new field. The S.A.M. board agreed to begin work in Venezuela and Mr. and Mrs. Bach were accepted as the first appointees. Four months later, Mr. and Mrs. John Christiansen were also appointed.

Arriving in Maracaibo April 17, 1906, the two couples found it to be a small city of about fifty thousand people of largely Spanish-Indian blood with some African mixture. The Roman Catholic church dominated the life of the people. Protestant missionaries were not welcome. Bach wrote: "Difficulties and persecutions were great in the beginning, but God was with us."[21]

Franson Reaches Venezuela

Franson found the Bachs and Christiansens busy in the work

and commented:

> Though they have not been here a full two years they seem to have a good hold of the language and served as my interpreters at the meetings. In addition to the religious literature they give out, they publish a paper with the beautiful name of *La Estrella de La Mañana* (The Star of the Morning). The paper's appearance brought on a fierce attack in the local papers by the Catholic priests of the city. It is no wonder that the priests were annoyed because a newspaper exercises great influence, especially among these people. The storm quieted when some of the missionaries' friends came to their defense.[22]

The missionaries had laid plans to reach out to the towns along the shores of the large Lake Maracaibo and tributary rivers and so had constructed a small boat. Franson joined in the dedication of this boat to its evangelistic purposes.

To the Islands of the Caribbean

From Venezuela, Franson took ship to Curaçao in the Netherlands Antilles, where he ministered to the local people and the Dutch. In less than twenty-five years S.A.M. would have missionaries stationed in the islands, beginning what would become an extensive church work. From there Franson went to Puerto Rico, Haiti, Jamaica, Cuba, and then on to Mexico.

To Mexico and Back to the U.S.A.

The month of May 1908 was spent in Mexico with meetings in Mexico City and surrounding areas. On June 5 he crossed the Rio Grande and was back in the United States after six years away. "Our dear friends in Texas were glad to have me back among them and I was equally glad to be with them," Franson wrote. After several weeks of rest in the mountains of Colorado I expect to travel through the beloved States again. Plans are developing in my heart and mind for a campaign with the particular goal: Children and Youth for Christ!"[23]

Though rest was Franson's immediate goal, he did not refuse invitations to minister and so each Sunday was filled. To have opportunity for more extended quiet he accepted an invitation to supply the pulpit of the small Mission Church in Idaho Springs, Colorado. Here during the month of July he preached seven times with apparently as much strength and power as before. Sunday morning, August 2, 1908, word came to the church leader, Mr. A. Brostrom, that he was not well. By the time Mr. Brostrom could get over to the house where Franson was staying, this humble yet outstanding servant of the Lord was peacefully breathing his last. Brostrom noted: "Franson came to Idaho Springs to rest. But could this restless man ever really rest? Not literally. He actually came here for quiet to lay plans about the expansion of the mission work both in so-called Christian lands and throughout the heathen world."[24]

The Founder's Heritage

Looking back over the history of almost a century, it is interesting to evaluate Franson's impact on the lives of the missionaries he personally touched, on the ministry they performed, and on the mission society he founded. The founder of an organization generally leaves a distinct imprint on it. The missionaries of the first generation have long since left the harvest fields; there is not one missionary now alive who has personal memory of Franson's ministry. But not a few of the present older missionaries were coworkers of the pioneers and have a keen sense of the heritage he left.

A reading of the early history reveals a great deal of love and appreciation by the missionaries, and even a measure of awe at the very evident hand of the Lord on him. The early histories include many references to him as "beloved friend," "zealous and diligent worker," "self-sacrificing servant," etc. It is clear that he was a greatly respected leader.

One reason for the respect was the fruit of his work. Whenever he came to a mission station his first concern was to have opportunity to lead men and women to Christ by personal contact and through public meetings. There was fruit from his preaching even in hard, resistant areas. Many whom he touched for the Lord went on to lives of fruitful service, such as David McDonald of Tibet and Nathan Ma of China. Others he taught in his short-term Bible courses went out as effective evangelists to reap the ripening harvest around them.

In Franson's basic principles for foreign missionary work we see an application of the Pauline example of multicultural teams sent out from a variety of backgrounds—Hebrew, Hellenistic, Greek. The missionary force of the S.A.M. was drawn from several different national backgrounds and church relationships and was united in one purpose: to win men and women for Christ in cultures where His name was not being proclaimed.

To the missionary body as a whole he left the pattern of effective evangelism, follow-through discipling, and the establishing of churches in the New Testament model—all based on full confidence in the Word of God, the atoning work of Christ, and the expectation of His soon appearing. Though succeeding generations of missionaries were farther and farther removed in time from the direct impact of Franson's ministry, the heritage was passed down from one generation to the next and those same characteristics are present almost a century later.

If one thing has changed it may be the sense of urgency that characterized the founder. For him the need was *now*. Souls were dying *now*. Christ could return before they would have an opportunity to hear the message of life and be saved. Yet nine decades later the coming of the Lord is even closer. The unreached multitudes have multiplied in number. The urgency is as great as in Franson's day.

THE SEARCH FOR A LEADER

Fredrik Franson's example continued to influence the work of the S.A.M. even after his death, but the inspiration of his personal leadership was greatly missed. For almost eighteen years his ministry had been a major factor sustaining interest in the mission. Most of the missionaries had come in direct response to his appeals and were indoctrinated into his scriptural concepts concerning soul-winning, discipling of believers, and founding of churches— all in the light of the Lord's longed-for soon return.

The supporting churches, too, had benefitted from Franson's ministry. They had gained a clear understanding of the plight of the heathen and the possibility that many would respond to the saving message in Christ. Even during Franson's long absences from the homeland on his missionary journeys, his stream of inspiring reports and letters, published in many of the Scandinavian papers, kept interest high.

It is true that missionaries corresponded with their supporters and, and when on furlough, contacted prospective missionaries in the churches they visited. It is also true that a number of gifted men, particularly Pastors A. J. Thorander and G. A. Young, were actively serving the mission's interests by visiting churches and presenting the missionary message. In addition, there was a board of directors whose members carried out the responsibilities of home administration. But with all this, the S.A.M. was now perceived as being a mission without leadership. As we shall see later, this perception surfaced sporadically in the denominations whose churches furnished missionaries and support.

Long Search for a Director

Though correspondence files are scanty for the period, the minutes of the monthly meetings of the board of directors tell the story quite well. The S.A.M. needed a leader, whatever he might be called—general director, general secretary, superintendent, chairman, or president. The search for one is recorded again and again in the minutes.

March 7, 1911—Resolved to call Rev. C. T. Dyrness to be general director. G. A. Young and F. Risberg to confer with him.

April 11, 1911—C. T. Dyrness did not accept the call.

December 9, 1911—Resolved to call Rev. Gustaf F. Johnson of Rockford to be mission chairman.

February 14, 1912—Gustaf F. Johnson could not accept the call.

September 3, 1912—Pastor N. W. Nelson of Jersey City, New Jersey, called as mission president.

September 11, 1912—Nelson greatly appreciated the confidence but declined.

February 4, 1913—Pastor Ludwig Johnson of Oslo, Norway, was called to be general secretary.

May 6, 1913—Ludwig Johnson declined call.

May 6, 1913—Gustaf F. Johnson was again asked to become general secretary.

June 6, 1913—Dyrness and Carlson talked with Gustaf F. Johnson and felt he might accept the call.

August 16, 1913—The same committee is to continue consultations with Gustaf F. Johnson about being general secretary.

August 1, 1916—Rev. J. H. Hedstrom of Roseland, Chicago, was invited to become a member of the board.

April 8, 1919—J. H. Hedstrom resigned as a member and chairman of the board to take a pastorate in Tacoma, Washington.

October 4, 1920—J. H. Hedstrom was called as general director and representative. [He declined, possibly because of his short time in the Tacoma pastorate.]

November 15, 1920—Decided to call Gustaf F. Johnson of Minneapolis as general director or general secretary of the Alliance Mission. Brother Dyrness was given the responsibility of personally visiting Johnson to present the call.

June 9, 1921—[Annual meeting report] A telegram from J. H.

Hedstrom was received accepting the renewed call to become general director, effective in September.

August 1, 1921—Brother Hedstrom was given a standing welcome to his position as general director and in quiet prayer before God was commissioned for his important work. The Tacoma church requested permission for Hedstrom to serve the congregation two months in each quarter beginning the first of August 1921.[1]

So, for a while, at least, a leader had been found.

Hedstrom's Brief Service and Death

John Henry Hedstrom was born in Sweden on January 28, 1874, and came to the United States at the age of nineteen. It was an S.A.M. representative, the Rev. G. A. Young, who influenced him in his early years and invited him along on a preaching tour. Young later encouraged him to enter the ministry. While serving a church in McPherson, Kansas, Hedstrom studied at Bethany College, Lindsborg. Closer contact with the mission came as he served the independent Swedish Mission Church in Roseland, Chicago.

Hedstrom was a strong spiritual leader and an able administrator. His time as general director was tragically cut short as he lost his life in a train-car accident September 14, 1923. The extensive reporting in Christian periodicals of the time reveals the esteem in which he was held and an awareness of the great loss to the family and the mission.

Having given part of his time to his church in Tacoma, Hedstrom had just made a start on what all expected to be a fruitful time of mission leadership. In writing to missionary T. J. Bach in Venezuela, February 20, 1923, he expressed his feeling about the work and his early involvement:

I rejoice greatly in hearing of progress on your field. God has in a special way blessed you as I can understand from letters I have received. Our God is wonderful and great in His grace! We stand at times, as it were, in a corner and look on what He accomplishes. *As you can well understand I have not yet gotten into the work to the extent that I feel at home. There is such an enormous amount and so many threads to keep in the grasp* [Italics supplied].[2]

Questions about the Future

Major problems faced the S.A.M. The search for a general director had to be renewed. The work of administering a mission with 125 missionaries had to go forward. Support for the many new missionaries who wanted to be sent out was very slow in coming. One pressing need mentioned from time to time was for a headquarters and a home for furloughing missionaries. The basic question about the mission's future also came onto the board agenda from time to time and certainly came to mind again at this time of crisis.

Several steps were taken without delay. At an emergency meeting the day after Hedstrom's funeral five decisions were recorded. (1) To extend a vote of thanks to Miss Siri Malmstrom for her willingness to care for the office and assist the board in this trying time. (2) To request board member Professor Algoth Ohlson to work out a plan whereby he could take care of matters in an executive way until proper help could be had. (3) To seek a source of financial help for the bereaved family. (4) To ascertain whether the Rev. Gustaf F. Johnson would, in fact, consider a call to become general director. (5) To call the Rev. G. A. Young back into service as traveling representative.[3]

Professor Risberg had shared his office at the Chicago Theological Seminary with the mission and, as treasurer, had cared for necessary office details, which were kept to the bare minimum. When Risberg's health began to fail, Miss Malmstrom was asked to become office secretary and bookkeeper. She began her work the day after Christmas in 1920 and continued in the office for fifty years until shortly before her death December 16, 1970. She had worked with four successive general directors. Whether there was an emergency such as in 1923 or just the routine of office detail, her service was done as to the Lord and was marked by skill, faithfulness, and cheerfulness. Several generations of missionaries knew her well and thanked the Lord for her.

The assignment to Algoth Ohlson to come up with a plan to handle the executive functions was given to one who was a busy pastor and later a college president. The office did have occasional help from several missionaries on furlough, but the need in this area gave more urgency to finding a general director.

The third decision, about finding a source of financial help for the Hedstrom family, resulted in a sum being received which provided assistance for a time but not enough to relieve the family of financial pressures and concerns. The S.A.M., in keeping with the situation in many missions of that period, had no provision for such emergencies. Because the contributors expected their contributions to go in full to the work of the missionary of their particular interest, there was no margin or surplus to provide for such other needs. Even though financial support was a pressing need, there was another need equally as great, that of spiritual and emotional support and practical counsel. The mission, at that time, had no plan in operation and no adequate home staff to provide help for its missionaries who had been invalided home or bereaved. The Hedstrom family faced the hardships common to missionaries of the day. In later years more adequate provisions have been made for similar situations. Mrs. Hedstrom survived her husband by more than thirty-seven years, passing away December 2, 1960. Often in attendance at annual mission conferences, she was a continued inspiration to those who knew her well.

The invitation to Gustaf F. Johnson to become general director was now the fourth time the men of the board of directors had officially turned to him for the help they felt he could give. In October 1923 he was in Chicago and spent some time conferring with the board, but then in December word came that he could not accept the call.

At the same December meeting, and undoubtedly as an indication of the feeling of urgency on the part of the members, the board discussed the situation at length and then voted to ask the Rev. G. E. Pihl of New Britain, Connecticut, to take the leadership post. A night letter telegram was immediately dispatched. On the last day of the year, a surprising time for a board meeting, the men met with Pihl to discuss the position and learn of any possible interest on his part. Again the matter was high on the agenda at the February meeting, but the information revealed only a possible interest. When the men gathered for the April meeting the word from Pihl was that he had heard doubts about the future of the mission and wondered how certain discussions about its future might affect him, should he accept the leadership.

The minutes of the meetings refer often to prayer but do not detail the burden the men felt in properly administering the work. It is safe to say that there was much waiting on the Lord to show a clear way to go.

The men felt led to turn once again to the long-term chairman, Pastor C. T. Dyrness, and ask him to take the position of general director. With his growing local church ministry so close to his heart, Dyrness again declined, but countered with an offer to help as he could on a part-time basis until a permanent solution was found. So, for the next three and a half years, C. T. Dyrness was acting general director. This was made possible in part by his church offering to provide secretarial help if he would continue his work with the mission. The secretary provided was his own daughter, Camilla. Miss Dyrness later served on the mission office staff for almost thirty years.

Throughout the history of the S.A.M. up to that time, no one had served as full-time director, not even Franson. He was fully occupied but his work included a majority of time spent in direct missionary ministry overseas. In the 1920s the need was urgent for a leader to give himself wholly to the guidance, representation, and administration of this growing work.

The Men Who Were Approached

All of those approached about accepting a call to lead the mission were holding successful pastorates. They were men held in confidence and esteem by the supporting Scandinavian constituency. Some of them had very close association with the mission. Let us review the names.

The Rev. C. T. Dyrness was pastor of the Salem Evangelical

Free Church of Chicago with a thriving ministry among Norwegian immigrants. In a short biographical sketch written about Dyrness in 1934, Dr. O. C. Grauer, secretary of the S.A.M. board, wrote, "The same year he began his ministry in Salem—1890—he became involved with Fredrik Franson, who had just started a missionary organization and with him became one of the co-founders of The Scandinavian Alliance Mission."[4] Dyrness became a member of the original committee organized in February 1891 after the sailing of the first party of missionaries. He and the Rev. Fridolf Risberg were truly the mainstays of the home organization and both are referred to in early information as "founders" with Franson of the mission. Dyrness, with some brief breaks in continuity, served as either secretary or chairman for almost forty-two years.

Gustaf F. Johnson went to Japan in 1891 as a missionary with the first party, but returned home after only two and a half years due to poor health, reported to be tuberculosis. For a time he joined Franson in evangelistic services in North America. He pastored large churches in Rockford, Illinois, and Minneapolis, Minnesota, and was also particularly gifted as an evangelist.

Pastors N. W. Nelson and Ludwig Johnson ministered to Norwegian congregations. Johnson served as pastor of the Bethlehem Church in Oslo, Norway, a church which resulted from Franson's evangelistic work in the city in the 1880s.

The Rev. G. E. Pihl was pastor of the Swedish Bethany Church of New Britain, Connecticut, which had a strong interest in the work of the Gustaf Ahlstrands in northwest China. He was the only one of those under consideration to have expressed a desire to visit the mission fields. This he did later, in 1926 and 1927, when he spent time in Japan, Mongolia, China, and India.

Why No Success?

Why did five different men decline the invitation to direct the S.A.M.? Two reasons appear in the letters: first, the demands of their present ministries, and second, the potential effect on their families of the much traveling required to represent the mission. Some reading between the lines is necessary to find a third reason. This may have been the perceived instability of an organization with no visible headquarters, no adequate staff, and what seemed to be very uncertain financing. This general perception was held by leaders of the denominations which were most closely related to the mission through the support contributed by the individual churches. It had led to a number of attempts from outside the mission over a dozen years to alter the S.A.M.'s basic organization and even to divide it among several denominational groups. These well-meaning attempts would have fragmented the work overseas and were rightly discerned to be a threat to the mission's continued existence.

SHOULD THE MISSION BE DISMEMBERED?

To understand the makeup of the S.A.M. in the early years and the somewhat proprietary feeling that certain church groups had toward it, we must go back to its beginnings and even farther back to Franson's evangelistic work and church polity discussions.

The Major Supporting Constituency

Franson had become widely known in the Scandinavian churches and, with some exceptions, warmly welcomed and greatly appreciated. His missionary appointees had come in large numbers from these churches. The Swedish Mission Covenant (now known as the Evangelical Covenant Church) had begun small mission works in Alaska and China. The Swedish Free Church (now united with the Norwegian-Danish Free and known as the Evangelical Free Church of America) had a beginning mission in south China. With the S.A.M.'s rapid growth in missionaries and support, it was inevitable that some would feel that at least part of this growth was at the expense of the struggling new denominational missionary work. The Swedish churches in the northeastern part of the United States were separately organized as the Eastern Missionary Association (EMA) and some of them had church loans which put them under obligation to the Congregational denomination. They had no missionary work of their own. The Norwegian-Danish Free Churches, for their part, looked to the S.A.M. to provide a channel for their missionary outreach.

The basic mission organization as drafted in the first constitution by Franson has persisted through the years. The S.A.M. was to have a relationship to the churches, societies, and individuals participating in its support. These contributors were entitled to vote at the annual meetings to elect members of the board of directors. The missionaries were responsible to report to their supporters and their ministries, were, in some undefined way, to be "controlled" by the contributors. At the same time, the board of directors was to "have general oversight and care of the mission" and "to give advice to the missionaries while on the field and at home; also to the conferences held by the missionaries on each foreign field."[1]

The organizational charter made no provision for denominational representation or proportionate control.

The EMA Makes an Approach

There is no record in the minutes during Franson's lifetime of any request for a modification of the basic structure of the S.A.M. But on November 10, 1908, only three months after his death, a minute is recorded: "A committee of the Eastern Missionary Association requests to meet the S.A.M. committee to discuss a possible change in the supervision of their missionaries who belong to the S.A.M. It was agreed to meet them here in Chicago."[2]

That meeting took place the following February 2. Pastor C. G. Ellstrom, representing the EMA, introduced the subject they were delegated to present.

> It is essentially a question if the separate associations can be given more control over the Alliance Mission, for example in the election of the board, or if the mission could come entirely under the control of these groups. There was much discussion about what would be the best for the mission's future, without coming to any definite conclusion. It was decided to suggest that the EMA review our constitution and propose to us any amendments which they consider necessary. It was also decided to arrange a meeting where constitutional amendments can be studied. The missionaries on the various fields must be consulted so they can express their desires concerning any changing of the constitution.[3]

The Free Church Plan

Before any further action was recorded on this suggestion, a somewhat similar move came from another direction:

The December 1911 meeting of the board was informed of the

plan of the Swedish Free Church to write all its missionaries and their supporters recommending that they leave the Alliance Mission and transfer to the Free Church. To hinder the accomplishment of this purpose it was decided to send a letter to the committee which was acting on this plan and ask it to delay until the Alliance Mission committee had called together a meeting of the Eastern Missionary Association, Norwegian Free Church, and Swedish Free Church and from this meeting send notice to individual local treasurers to confer regarding the administration of the Alliance Mission work.[4]

This action in late 1911 apparently blunted any official move by the Swedish Free Church to take direct responsibility for the missionaries it supported. There were isolated actions involving several missionary couples in China which may have been initiated by the missionaries involved or by the supporting churches.

Proposal to Shift Control

Two and a half years passed before the files reveal any further discussion with the EMA. Then on July 1, 1914, the Rev. C. V. Bowman of Boston wrote to Risberg stating that the Eastern Missionary Association had for some time increasingly felt that it should direct the foreign mission work carried on by missionaries its churches supported, and that its recent annual meeting had set up a committee of three pastors to study the matter and bring a proposal to the next annual meeting. To obtain the desired facts, Bowman set forth thirteen questions asking about the various missionaries supported—which EMA churches contributed and in what amounts, whether their support of the missionaries was full or partial, etc.[5]

Risberg's reply of July 13, after the board had studied the questions, was full, helpful, and courteous. Many of the missionaries involved received only part of their support from EMA churches, with the balance being made up from other sources. He suggested that the individual supporting churches probably would not give consent to a transfer of missionaries away from the S.A.M. Furthermore, the mission's constitution would not permit such a transfer without the supporting churches' approval. At the same

time the constitution would not forbid the transfer of any missionary and his support to another mission society.

Risberg's letter seemed to offer the Mongolia field to the EMA
as the only one where both the missionary staff and the support
came wholly from EMA churches. As for the fields—China, Japan,
India, South Africa, and South America—where most missionaries
were supported from elsewhere and only a limited number had full
or partial support from EMA churches, he said that the effect of
the plan, if carried out, would be to seriously fragment the S.A.M.
In such a case, the EMA mission work would also be fragmented
as their missionaries would be scattered in five countries among
those of the S.A.M., but under different organizational control.[6]

Though Risberg's response should have politely closed the door
to further discussion, the EMA committee continued its pursuit of
the matter in a letter from the Rev. C. E. Peterson dated April 20,
1915. The approach in this letter was summarized in one paragraph: "The question to which I request an answer is this: How
would it work out in the mission if our congregations relinquished
their control over their missionaries to the Eastern Missionary
Association and the Association then became represented in the
Alliance Mission?"[7]

Peterson further suggested the possibility that funds could be
channeled by the churches to the EMA treasury which in turn
would send them either to the S.A.M. office or direct to the field,
whichever would be best.

Up to this point, the correspondence leaves the impression that
the S.A.M. board felt the need of some administrative help or
financial backing and was somewhat open to the inquiries about
its future. Its response to the latest letter, however, was more clear
and decisive:

> First of all, we want to repeat what we have previously said, that
> we have nothing else in mind than the mission's best interests,
> and faithfulness to its constitution. With the constitution we
> have, we can think of no other way in which the Eastern Mis-
> sionary Association can be represented than by voting for the
> members of the board and by that means promoting its purpose.

Because so many missionaries have support from different sources the matter is even more difficult to change. In many instances supporters give to the mission because they know the missionary and if we should try to make some exchange a large number of them would say, "We will do as we please in this matter."[8]

An Effort to Change the Constitution

The move to gain greater control of the S.A.M. did not end there. The EMA annual meeting held in October 1915 set up a committee to communicate with the Swedish Free Church, the Norwegian-Danish Free Church, and the S.A.M. board to work out a change in the S.A.M. The three denominational committees met in Chicago on August 15, 1916, to plan their approach. The next day they met with all the members of the mission board. The report which came out of these meetings stated that the fourteen participants voted "unanimously" to recommend changes in the constitution which would alter the nature of the mission, putting it to a large degree under denominational control.[9]

The report of "unanimity" was premature because on September 18, 1916, the S.A.M. board officially wrote to the committee presenting "changes to the changes" along with carefully thought-through substitute wording which served to maintain the basic organizational concept. Special concern was expressed that the unrelated churches and individual contributors should not lose their right to share in the election of members of the board.[10]

Two and a half years passed before the subject of mission control and administration appeared in the minutes again. A committee was appointed to study the question of the mission's future and representatives of the three groups which had previously met on the subject were invited to participate. The result of that joint effort was that certain amendments were adopted at the annual meeting held February 2, 1920. These amendments were apparently the same or little altered from the board's proposal of September 1916, which meant that the mission structure remained intact.

Maintaining the organizational status quo did not mean that

existing problems were solved. The mission still had no general director. Fridolf Risberg, who was the key figure in administration, was failing in health. Interestingly enough, the mission was steadily growing in size even though some of the early pioneers were retiring. The missionary total reached 124. Fifteen new workers were sent out in the most difficult year. Annual income passed the $100,000 mark for the first time. China reported 1,200 baptisms in a two-year period. Then in 1921 the long search for a general director ended successfully when the Lord led the Rev. J. H. Hedstrom to accept the post. All too soon the hopes for smoother administrative sailing were dashed when Hedstrom was suddenly taken from them and they were back to the same problems.

Added to these problems was the post-war economic distress of the early 1920s which led the board to pass a resolution on February 22, 1924: "Further Appointment of Applicants: The financial outlook, the difficulty of getting funds for new missionaries and adequate support for those on the fields at present was discussed. It was voted that we discontinue making further appointments until the financial situation is better."[11]

The Final "Rescue" Attempt

The Rev. G. A. Young, who was representing the mission in church contacts, was also fully aware of the prevailing crisis and at this same February board meeting proposed that a joint conference be held with representatives of the Covenant and Free Churches. The board voted to request such an emergency meeting. This meeting was held in Chicago on March 15, 1924, and was attended by individuals in the leadership of four Scandinavian denominations along with a number from the mission board. The leader in the movement apparently was Pastor Gustaf F. Johnson, the one who had been invited on four different occasions to become general director and who had declined the position. The minutes tell the story in less words than would a rewrite:

> Present were—Covenant: E. G. Hjerpe [president], Gustaf F. Johnson, Algoth Ohlson, Otto Hogfeldt; Swedish Free: E. A. Halleen [president], Gustaf Edwards, August H. Modig, Frank

W. Anderson; Norwegian Free: C. T. Dyrness. [Edwards, Anderson, and Dyrness were at the same time members of the S.A.M. board.]

Pastor Gustaf F. Johnson, who had taken the initiative in bringing about this meeting, opened the consultation with a statement of its purpose. He pointed out, among other things, the importance and necessity of the Scandinavian free denominations (Covenant, Norwegian Free, Swedish Free, and the Eastern Missionary Association) positioning themselves in a more full and united collaboration with the Scandinavian Alliance Mission. The speaker pointed out that there could be two possible ways to better assure the future of the Alliance Mission; the one through dividing the work and the fields among the four denominations named; the other, which was considered more ideal, was that these organizations take over the Alliance Mission as their joint foreign mission. In the discussion that followed it became clear that many obstacles and difficulties would be encountered whichever of these two plans was followed.

Inasmuch as this meeting could not officially deal with or take measures with reference to the position of the separate denominations regarding the Alliance Mission, it was decided to select two from each denomination with the request that they lay this matter before the annual meetings of the denominations. The following were chosen: C. T. Dyrness and N. W. Nelson for the Norwegian Free, E. A. Halleen and Aug. H. Modig for the Swedish Free, E. G. Hjerpe and Gustaf F. Johnson for the Mission Covenant, and E. G. Pihl and Gustav Anderson for the Eastern Missionary Association.

It was further decided to recommend to the respective denominational annual meetings through these appointees that two representatives be named for each of these organizations to form a joint working committee to present a workable plan on which all can unite. It was also considered appropriate that the board of the Alliance Mission should be represented on this committee with four members, one for each denomination.

It also became clear that the most progress that could be expected for the present in regard to a united effort in furthering and safeguarding the Alliance Mission would be that the denominations at their annual meetings would set up a permanent board for the mission and that the denominations take upon themselves the responsibility for the mission and all its concerns.

The secretary was requested to send a report of the meeting's deliberations to the boards of the respective denominations.[12]

The March 15 meeting was not an official gathering and it is to be noted that no provision was made for the S.A.M. board to be officially informed of the preparations made for its funeral! It is further noted that the minutes made no claim of unanimity. Of the three S.A.M. board members present, at least one, and probably all three, went away from that meeting with contrary thoughts. They probably were thinking, "Yes, we have had difficulty in finding a leader, and for the time being money is in short supply. Some of our board members are carrying far too heavy a work load during this difficult period. But is this to be the dismembering of a worldwide work built on the vision, zeal, and wisdom of Fredrik Franson? With reports from overseas relating victories in souls saved and churches developing, must we now tell our 125 missionaries that henceforth they will serve under different auspices, with some of them having to transfer to different countries and learn new languages?"

A Resolute Stand

One board member, in particular, believed strongly that the mission had been raised up by the Lord and must continue. Years later, in 1960, T. J. Bach wrote concerning C. T. Dyrness: "Because of Pastor Dyrness' wise counsel and firm conviction the mission was spared from being divided into four."[13]

The turning point for the S.A.M. came at the April board meeting, when the board took a firm stand against the mission's dismemberment in a resolution which would be presented later that day to the annual meeting of the mission. On Monday afternoon, April 28, 1924, Professor O. C. Grauer, secretary of the board, read a proposed resolution, which was then adopted:

> Whereas, an informal conference was held in Chicago, March 15, 1924, to consider ways and means by which the Scandinavian free churches might in the future come into closer cooperation in foreign missionary work, and whereas, this conference decided to present the matter to the annual meetings of the Swedish

Covenant, the Swedish Free Church, the Eastern Missionary Association and the Norwegian-Danish Free Churches by representatives named at this meeting;

BE IT THEREFORE RESOLVED, that concerning any proposed change in the agencies directing the foreign missionary work of the Scandinavian churches, organizations and people, no other change can be considered by the Scandinavian Alliance Mission than this, namely, that the S.A.M. be continued and enlarged as the one union corporation to direct and carry on unitedly all the foreign missionary work of the Scandinavian free churches.

The annual meeting of the S.A.M. held in Chicago April 28, 1924, expresses the hope that whatever action may be taken by the church associations above mentioned may result in the enlargement and strengthening of the work of the S.A.M.[14]

Ironically, the plan to have the S.A.M. swallowed up by a combination of denominations was turned, in this proposal, to a swallowing up of the missionary ministries of the other groups. Well, in the sovereignty of God, neither proposal materialized. While deeply grateful to these evangelical denominations for their significant provision of personnel and support for the expanding ministry on six fields, it was seen that the S.A.M. could serve most usefully as a mission not denominationally related. Its subsequent history has given ample proof of the Lord's sovereign direction to those board members and voting constituents who felt strongly that it would be pleasing to the Lord that the mission continue to exist and serve.

Undoubtedly an indication of the real strength of the mission was the minute recorded in the session immediately preceding:

The secretary read interesting reports from the fields in China, Mongolia, South America, and Africa. Those from India and Japan had not arrived in time for the meeting. After the reading of the reports, the conference knelt in prayer and thanksgiving to the Lord of the harvest for His many blessings on our fields this past year.[15]

When one of the China missionaries, Julius W. Bergstrom, heard T. J. Bach refer to the move to divide the mission, his remark was, "There may have been a crisis and uncertainty at home, but out on the field the work was strong and going forward with fruitfulness and blessing."

In the vocabulary of the 1980s a familiar term is a "hostile takeover." The events described in this chapter cannot be characterized in that way. It undoubtedly seemed to earnest Christians familiar with the circumstances and even to some of the board members that the mission was in dire need of help. In contemporary mission history certain missions have sought to help their situation by suitable mergers. Such arrangements have generally strengthened the ministry and advanced the gospel cause. But for the mission founded as a result of Fredrik Franson's vision, faith, and prayers, the Lord's will was that it continue on into the future.

Still Seeking a Leader

Even with renewed determination to maintain the mission as a going concern, there remained the unresolved problem of finding the Lord's choice for general director. The previous chapter detailed the continued unsuccessful efforts. But during this time of waiting, the Lord was preparing the one who would be called to the office.

In Venezuela, the work of T. J. Bach was coming of age. It had started with personal witness, the production of simple tracts, and the publication of an evangelistic magazine. The ministry expanded in the face of opposition from the priests. At first, the social outcasts were those most willing to listen. In time a small group of converts was assembled and a congregation organized. Finally in 1926 a church structure was being erected, its foundation made up in part of stones which had been thrown at the *protestantes*. Mrs. Bach had remained in the homeland for a number of years due to her health and the needs of their five children, and now, with the church building dedicated, Bach considered resignation from the field or at least a leave of absence.

When the board received Bach's letter, the men quickly decided against a resignation and instead voted a leave of absence. They further decided "to confer with him about the possibility of undertaking a campaign to raise $100,000 to provide a headquarters for the mission in Chicago and a permanent fund to help missionaries on furlough."[16]

For the next two years Bach worked closely with the board, planning his ministry and reporting not only on the financial results but, more importantly, on the spiritual fruit in the lives of those ministered to. Like Franson, Bach believed the most important work he could do was to win souls and nurture the Christians as he went from place to place. He was confident that the Lord would lay on the hearts of the people to contribute to the needs of the work.

As the board members were praying earnestly one day, it became obvious to one of them that the man the Lord was preparing to lead the mission was right there working with them, so he spoke up, "Has anyone ever thought of Brother T. J. Bach?" One who was present reported that it came like an electric shock and all were initially silent.[17]

Action soon followed and on that day, April 23, 1928, the board unanimously voted to extend a call to Bach to become general director.[18]

After some consultation about details, Bach responded by letter on May 1.

> After prayerful consideration, and believing that it is God's will, I accept the call. I accept the conditions and the responsibility attached to it. It is my earnest prayer and desire to carry on my duties in cooperation with you and according to the rules and regulations laid down for the work and the workers of the Scandinavian Alliance Mission, which were so nobly presented in the wishes and lives of the founders of our mission. In all circumstances I shall endeavor to honor and glorify our dear Lord and Master.[19]

That the Lord used the men of the board to hold the mission together through two decades of pressure and disappointments was freely acknowledged by Bach and he entered into a beautiful working relationship with them. Together they saw the work grow and the S.A.M. gain broad acceptance in the homeland.

THE WORD OF GOD IS NOT BOUND

It was no exaggeration for missionary Julius Bergstrom to say of the China field that "the work was strong and going forward" even as the home base was experiencing uncertainty. It was nevertheless a surprising statement, for there is often a relationship between the strength of the home base and the health of the field work. This is undoubtedly more true in these days of rapid communications than when an exchange of correspondence took several months and administrative visits were rare.

Under those conditions, strong local leadership was most determinative. Some of the missionaries had gifts of leadership and in each place of work there seemed to be a clear concept that the objective was evangelism that would result in strong churches.

Early Shallow Interest

Another reason it was surprising that the work was going forward strongly was the formidable obstacles faced by the messengers of the gospel, both missionaries and Chinese coworkers. Our last glimpse of China was in connection with Franson's 1905 visit, when the work was getting under way in a promising manner after the disruption of the Boxer Uprising.

In the years following these troubles, there paradoxically came a period of favor and interest which was not necessarily a true seeking for spiritual truth. Because the Roman Catholic missionaries often helped their converts with their lawsuits, the Protestant missionaries found people coming to them with offers to join the Christian church in return for help with their legal difficulties. Others came asking a price to follow "the Jesus doctrine."

Even though the missionaries tried to be very careful before baptizing professing believers, they began to realize that there were many in the churches who were either unsaved or at least living on a very low plane of faith and experience. As the author of the twenty-fifth anniversary China story wrote, "We were almost tempted to believe that the Chinese were a people of a different nature who could not receive the same deep spiritual impressions as Westerners."[1]

Longing for Revival

Faced with this distressing situation, many of the missionaries began to pray for a true revival. They heard of revival blessings in Wales, Korea, and Manchuria and wanted God to do the same in China. Their heart cry became one of near desperation. About Christmas time 1908 in Hsingping, where Mr. and Mrs. Solomon Bergstrom had a ministry that was growing rapidly in numerical response, there began to be "mercy drops falling" that gave the missionaries courage to pray for genuine "showers of blessing."

In the spring of 1909 the missionaries invited the Rev. A. Lutely and Chinese evangelist Wang Changlao from the neighboring province of Shansi to come for revival meetings. About four hundred people gathered in a tent set up in the courtyard. "The meetings went on for four days during which the Holy Spirit did a thoroughgoing work in the hearts of many. Most of those present came under deep conviction of sin.... The heathen became aware of what was happening and said that the Christians' God had come among them." Lutely and Wang moved on to the city of Sian and several other places where "the realization of God's nearness was overpowering; both old and young being gripped by it."[2]

The results of the revival were felt in many of the churches. A higher level of spiritual interest and understanding was very apparent, and a change was also seen in practical ways in a greater willingness to serve and contribute.

Preparation for Loss

Two years later, in the fall of 1911, Lutely and Wang returned to hold meetings in Sian from October 7 to 15. On the twelfth the missionary children were present and were greatly moved by the

Word of God. These were wonderful, unforgettable days and many later felt that God had "lit a lamp in advance of their going through the dark tunnel which many of them shortly were to experience," because the meetings took place on the eve of the breakout of the revolution in this area. The last day of the meetings was October 15 and on the following Sunday, the twenty-second, the storm broke loose in Sian, where the S.A.M. was the hardest hit by its furor.[3]

Just after midnight in the early morning of October 23, a lawless mob attacked the school for missionary children which had been opened south of the city. Mr. and Mrs. Richard Beckman and Mr. William Vatne were the adults present and with them seven children. While the attackers were setting fire to the large entry gate, the missionaries tried to scale the seven-foot wall but only Mr. Vatne and young Selma Beckman succeeded before the attempted escape was discovered.

The others took temporary refuge in a small outbuilding adjacent to the wall and there Beckman made a futile attempt to dig through the hard-packed clay. When the mob gained entry to the grounds, the rioters set fire to the large dormitory classroom building. When, at last, they found the hiding place of the little group, Mrs. Beckman, leading the others, tried to rush through the crowd but most were felled by the blows of clubs and other weapons. Only Mr. Beckman, carrying four-year-old Thyra, was able to escape into the darkness. Once outside, he fled with members of the mob in pursuit.

When Beckman came to a large pit partially filled with water, he was able to slip down and hide in the shelter of the bank. There he held Thyra above the water, all the while praying that his little one would not give away their location by any cry or question. After several hours, when he sensed that one side of the pit was being poorly guarded, Beckman was able to climb up and slip away. Within an hour he was at the door of a missionary residence several miles away sharing the awful news of the attack and finding that the missionaries there were also in great danger. When a closer investigation could be made, there was no trace of Vatne and Selma, but Mrs. Beckman, her daughter Ruth, Oscar and Hulda Bergstrom, George Ahlstrand, and Hilda Nelson had given their lives as the price of the gospel being preached to the Chinese. The bodies of Vatne and Selma were found two days later.[4]

Forced Evacuation

This was a terrible blow, not only to the parents but also to the entire mission. Those most closely affected returned to the homeland for a while, but then the call of the Lord became so strong that they soon found their way back to China to minister in love to those who had so cruelly treated them. They came back to a ministry made more fruitful by their having contributed precious seed to China's soil and to the great harvest that has been reaped in the years following.

In a look forward, we note that the Bergstroms spent the rest of their days building up the large work already started in Hsingping. Their son, Julius, in time married Thyra Beckman and these two had a ministry of forty-five years among Chinese in northwest China, Taiwan, Japan, and Korea. Mr. and Mrs. Ahlstrand, having given up their one remaining child, continued in the work, developing a strong church ministry in Kienhsien until their retirement in 1944. The Philip Nelsons served until retirement and three of the next generation went on to serve the Lord among the Chinese until they in turn retired. Such is the love of Christ which shields against bitterness and changes it into loving concern.

Widespread Turmoil

The attack on the missionary children's school was by no means an isolated affair. There was revolutionary activity in the city of Sian, in the province of Shensi, and throughout the Chinese Empire. The Ching Dynasty, which was a rule by Manchurians, had been in power since 1644. It had become increasingly arrogant and insensitive both in domestic and foreign relationships. There is no doubt that Christian teaching had raised the expectations of thinking Chinese generally, and especially of the students.

One who had revolutionary plans and was able to attract a following was Dr. Sun Yatsen. Though others were involved and Sun's leadership was not accepted by many, he is generally considered the Father of the Revolution. The revolution broke out on October 10 and within ten or twelve days had engulfed much of the country. Fighting between the revolutionaries and the Imperial troops persisted for some time and it was this fighting that created such a hazard for the people and for foreigners in particular.

Because of these troubles, missionaries due for furlough were urged to go home. Soon the consulates ordered their citizens to leave the troubled areas. The result was that most of the missionaries had to withdraw. When they could return they did so, but not to a peaceful situation. There followed sixteen or eighteen years of civil war, banditry, and war lord rule and misrule. The China field annual report for 1919 summed up the situation graphically:

> In the midst of heavy fighting, terrible siege experiences, attacks by various forces—truly "in perils of robbers, ... in perils in the city, in perils in the wilderness"—the Lord has protected His witnesses and also caused the extreme need to bring people into contact with His word. It is true that some of the believers here and there have lost their lives in these troubled times but by God's grace it has been more endurable for the Christians than for the people in general. At the same time it must be acknowledged that these war activities, widespread lawlessness, opium planting, high cost of necessities and other circumstances associated with these troubles have been hindrances. Even so, the work has gone forward and new victories have been won in the name of the Lord. Proof of this is the fact that over 1,200 have been baptized in the last two calendar years, which is about as many as the entire number that were members in the churches four years earlier at the twenty-fifth anniversary of the field.[5]

Reaping in Troublous Times

The station reports at the time tell of more receptivity by the people, progress by the Chinese in evangelism, growth in the churches, and an advance in bearing responsibility. By 1925 it was possible to report a total baptized membership in the churches of

4,414 in forty-seven churches, with 221 national workers active.

Telling about opposition in Lantien County, the Rev. William Englund went on to report:

> However, nothing could hinder the people from coming to the meetings. This opposition seemed rather to have increased the interest. From countryside and villages men and women came and filled the church every day and at times there was not room for all who wanted to be in the meetings. The Spirit of God gripped the hearts of the people, and sinners sought the Lord. About fifty came forward to be prayed for.... Twenty-five were baptized at one service.[6]

The following year, 1926, was a particularly trying time. The provincial capital, Sian, was besieged for eight months and Mr. and Mrs. C. J. Jensen, who remained in the city to help many of the suffering people, had a most difficult time. It was estimated that 30,000 died in the city from war, disease, and starvation. That year and 1927 saw a major effort by communist elements to take control of China. In Sian, the huge ornate bell tower at the center of the city was painted red and the Marxists thought they had won the day. Many of the students were subverted and were in the forefront of anti-foreign activity. The consulates of various nations ordered their people to the coast for better protection. The S.A.M. missionaries from the provinces of Shensi and Kansu were among the evacuees. Only one remained behind, a single man, Roy Brehm. In the homelands there were pronouncements from pulpits and in periodicals that China had indeed forfeited its opportunity to accept the gospel.

Islands of Peace and Progress

The Japan missionaries, in the meantime, faced a problem of another kind—the perception that Japan was rapidly being Westernized. In the minds of many, modern education, Western-type clothing, adequate medical facilities, and material progress made missionary work unnecessary. Such thinking apparently penetrated the Christian church in the homeland with the result that Japan was not given much consideration as a mission field.

In the first three years of the mission's work in Japan, beginning in 1891, it had sent out nineteen workers. When Franson visited in 1894, fourteen were on the field. At the twenty-fifth anniversary there were just seven missionaries. From the time when the Rev. and Mrs. C. E. Carlson arrived in Japan in 1913 until 1936—a stretch of twenty-three years—no new S.A.M. missionaries came to this truly heathen field.

Those who were on the field, however—the Joel Andersons, the F. O. Bergstroms, Albertina Peterson, and the C. E. Carlsons—and their Japanese coworkers built solidly and well so that when the twenty-fifth anniversary story was written four districts were named as having S.A.M. ministries: Chiba, Tokyo, Izu, and Hida. Cities and towns referred to were Tokyo, Chiba, Mohara, Honjo, Ito, Takayama, Furukawa, Funatsu, Kamakura, and the islands of Oshima, Nijima, and Miyakejima. A picture from the period shows eleven pastors and evangelists. The directory printed in the first issue of *The Missionary Broadcaster* in 1925, however, shows only two places as having resident missionaries, Tokyo and Chiba.

Northeast India Field Transferred

By 1925 the India missionaries were still working in two distinct areas, the original field in the northeast and western India, where most of the missionaries were posted. Though the bulk of the work in the northeast was now the responsibility of Finnish missionaries sent out by Franson, several North American workers continued to try to reach Tibetans and even worked into Bhutan. The last to carry on that ministry were Mr. and Mrs. Claude Dover, who, upon leaving Baksa Duar in 1928, recommended that the work be turned over to a Swedish mission. (Mrs. Dover was the widow of the first field leader, the Rev. John F. Frederickson.) The board was guided in part by that recommendation and in January 1929 the minutes record an action transferring Baksa Duar to the Finnish board.

The great investment made by missionaries among scattered people in a rugged mountain area paid dividends in souls. TEAM missionaries working farther west along the Tibetan Frontier forty years later were made aware of the impact of that earlier ministry in the printed material still in use and the continued effective witness of Franson's Tibetan-British convert, David McDonald. Jumping forward to 1985, the Finnish Free Church reported that there were then thirty-five functioning churches even though no missionaries had been assigned there for over thirty years. When the church is planted, it is a living organism that continues to grow and bear fruit.

Reaching the Bhils

As we have seen in an earlier chapter, Franson was eager that the receptive Bhil aboriginal tribespeople of western India be evangelized and so urged the O. A. Dahlgrens to undertake this ministry in cooperation with missionaries of the Swedish Alliance Mission. When each mission became responsible for a separate area of work, the S.A.M. developed stations in Navapur, Pimpalner, and Chinchpada in West Khandesh and Amalner, Parola, and Yaval in East Khandesh. These places are located in the present state of Maharashtra. The Dahlgrens were later joined by Mr. and Mrs. Thorvald Johansen and Miss Esther Ritzman. The next to come were Mr. and Mrs. O. E. Meberg and Mr. and Mrs. Joseph Otteson.

India was at this time under the rule of Great Britain, which gave the missionaries some advantage in securing land for mission stations. Though the work was primarily among the Bhil people, the missionaries were affected by the predominant Hinduism with its caste system. Not being members of a caste, they would have been at a great disadvantage in purchasing property without the help of the British government. As non-caste people they were as limited as outcastes in their right to live in the city. Later observers wondered why the missionaries chose to live outside the towns, farther removed from the people. The answer is that they were not permitted to live in the towns at that time.

As the Bhils were poverty-stricken when the missionaries first started their work, early efforts were directed toward helping them gain a livelihood. While this was a demonstration of love and concern, it did have its severe drawbacks in creating the impression that the missionaries were in a way buying converts. Along with the early help went a great deal of preaching and teaching to make sure adherents understood the gospel and were rightly related to the Lord. The Bhils were animists and even after conversion much teaching was necessary before some who clung to false beliefs and fears were delivered.

The early missionaries soon saw the importance of opening village schools to bring the children under the teaching of the Word of God. The government encouraged that endeavor and even seemed to make it a requirement that the missions function in this way. These schools and the intensive village evangelism carried on in the cool season began to bear fruit for eternity.

RESISTANCE AND RESPONSE

From the time of the Boer War through World War I, the S.A.M. work in southern Africa centered very much around the activities of two couples and one single lady—Mr. and Mrs. Severin Bang in Zululand and Mr. and Mrs. William Dawson and Miss Malla Moe in Swaziland. Other missionaries also served and some of them died in service because of tropical diseases. Others had to return home because of health problems. During this period the number of missionaries varied from seven to ten.

Dawson, Linguist and Teacher

William Dawson came to Africa from England in 1888 and worked as a builder while studying the Zulu language. In 1891 he joined the East Africa Mission of Norway and was at work in Ekutandaneni when the original party of eight S.A.M. missionaries came there to study Zulu. After the death of their leader, Andrew Haugerud, and the loss of the two other men, Dawson was asked by Franson to become the leader of the group.

Dawson was very proficient in Zulu and made a number of valuable translations of English Christian literature. In addition to his work among the Swazis, Dawson initiated work among the Eurafrican or Coloured population, thus laying the foundation for a later thriving ministry which grew into the Evangelical Bible Church. He was also concerned that Africans be trained and later, when a Bible school was developed, taught at the school.

Bang, Church Developer

Severin Bang has been described by one of the more recent missionaries, Dr. Ralph Christensen, as a missionary "not too many people knew about, and yet in terms of the indigenous church and getting the church on its feet, Bang stands in the forefront of our early missionary team."[1]

Malla Moe, Pathfinder and Evangelist

Malla Moe was destined to become the most widely known of the missionaries, not only in southern Africa but also in the homelands where the story of the evangelization of Africa is told. Several quick glimpses will have to suffice here.[2]

> When the Boer War came on and the Government advised all the missionaries to leave, Miss Moe stayed at her post, and rendered great service in various ways. This was greatly appreciated by the British, especially by General Allenby, who sung her praises. The urge was constantly upon her to itinerate in the various parts of Swaziland and Zululand and going even into the Transvaal. In the early days it was on donkey back or by wagon and oxen or on foot. In later years her friends provided her with her famous gospel wagon, a sort of home on wheels, with her donkeys and helpers, going everywhere spreading the gospel. The light of her devoted life and clear and gracious testimony has shined in the many dark places bringing salvation to many hundreds of black people.[3]

Ralph Christensen's comment about her was, "There are two sides, because all these heroes of the faith are very human. I think what is lasting for our field from Malla Moe was that she was a pioneer who opened up the field and contacted the leaders in such a way that other missionaries could come in. She also recognized the fact that she didn't have all the gifts.... Her gift was to move the gospel wagon all over Swaziland, even into the King's kraal, and reach people."[4]

In his own unpublished story of the work in Swaziland, William Dawson tells of the spiritual wisdom displayed by Malla Moe in dealing with the practical training of new converts in the Christian walk.

> When Miss Moe first came to Enyatini she found a Wesleyan convert, named Stefanu, and his wife who were associated with the work in the beginning. Trouble now came up in this little company of believers. Up to this time nothing had been said against the drinking of native beer—*utshwala*—but it was found that this was going to prove a great hindrance to the work. In fact, it threatened to upset it. Stefanu's wife brewed beer and

invited the Christians to come and drink with them. Several times these drinking parties ended in quarreling and fighting. Both Miss Moe and Evangelist John Gamede saw that this could not go on.

In talking with Gamede, Miss Moe advised that all the believers should go out one day and pray to God about this matter and get it settled. This they did, going out early in the morning, fasting and praying until about two o'clock. Those who could read had their Testaments with them. When they came back they held a meeting in the little room and there talked the matter over. The almost unanimous opinion, and their conviction, as they expressed it, was that it was God's will that they should give up *utshwala* altogether and have nothing to do with it as it was an evil thing that caused quarreling, fighting and other sins among them, and certainly was not of God, but of Satan.[5]

Bible School Proposed

Malla Moe was concerned that the converts receive adequate teaching, and the key to this was to have evangelists and pastors trained in the Word of God. On her third and last furlough in 1920, she met two promising couples, Mr. and Mrs. M. D. Christensen and Mr. and Mrs. Arthur Jensen, and recruited them to develop a Bible school. They arrived in Swaziland early in 1921 and were taken in hand by Dawson to insure that they would obtain a good knowledge of the Zulu language.

The Franson Memorial Bible School, as it was then called, was developed on what had been a farm at a place called Mhlosheni. It opened to four students on February 12, 1924, and was the source of trained evangelists for about twenty years until a higher level inter-mission school opened. The ministry of the school did not stop, however, but continued to serve the evangelical witness in the country.

The baptized membership in the churches in Swaziland and Zululand totaled about two thousand at the twenty-fifth anniversary of the mission, and probably doubled in the next ten years. Pastors and evangelists served small congregations in rural areas and tilled their own land for their support. As the local economy was not on a cash basis, self-support through cash contributions was rare. The African believers had the example of effective personal witness and soul-winning in Malla Moe and other missionaries, and their following of this example was a strong factor in their growth.

Barren Mongolia

Taking the fields in the order of their entry, Mongolia is next in line. It was a field greatly different from the others. The nomadic lifestyle of the Mongol herdsmen who traveled over the broad grasslands had convinced the early missionaries that they must somehow motivate the Mongols to come to a more settled way of life where they could receive a witness over a longer period of time. Those who were open to the message could then be taught in the Word.

A large tract of land, about nine square miles, was leased at a place called Patsebolong. An irrigation channel ten miles long brought in water from the Yellow River. The hope that the Mongols would be attracted to this land did not materialize. In the trouble of 1900 and during the revolution of 1911, the Chinese took advantage of the missionaries' absence to occupy available areas for themselves. In time, Patsebolong became a Chinese settlement with only a very few Mongols and they were ones who were intermarried with Chinese.

Chinese Work Undertaken

A Chinese congregation was planted and flourished. Chinese Christians sought to witness to Mongols, but the historic tensions between these two related but different peoples made that witness very difficult, if not entirely fruitless. That the early missionaries persevered was not due to responsiveness by the people, but to a deep sense of God's call to reach the Mongol people. Mr. and Mrs N. J. Friedstrom invested about twenty years of their lives in this work and passed away on the field. Mr. and Mrs. A. B. Magnuson gave fifteen years to seeking out the Mongols. Mr. and Mrs. P. L. Danielson served almost eight years, working part of the time with the Chinese in Shensi. A single man from Sweden, Folke Boberg, was with the mission for seven years, 1922 to 1929. He developed a largely Chinese church at Wangiefu, later turned over to the Swedish Alliance Mission to which Boberg transferred.

Work among the Mongols had many similarities to Muslim work, in that the investment of prayer, effort, money, strength, and even lives seemed all out of proportion to the harvest reaped. Seed was planted. Some germinated. There has been a harvest even though it seems small. The Lord's teaching about the rescue of even one lost lamb helps to put this field in perspective.

A Forgotten Continent No Longer

For more than half a century the mission was active in no more than six countries. Venezuela was the newest in the time period we are now considering. Franson visited the newly arrived missionaries, the T. J. Bachs and the John Christiansens, in 1908 and found them making a good beginning in the work, though not without difficulties and opposition. Maracaibo, the second largest population center in Venezuela, had never had any previous evangelical witness.

Stepped-up Opposition

When the missionaries began distributing Christian literature and holding public meetings, the opposition of the priests intensified. John Christiansen gives some illustrations in his book *Under the Southern Cross*. As the Catholic women were the ones who most regularly went to the confessional, the priests pressured them to confess any interest they might have shown in the Protestant preaching. The women, in turn, were expected to influence their men away from what the priests charged to be heretical teaching.

The missionaries and their teaching also got quite a lot of attention in sermons. Though the preaching in the Catholic churches was generally in Latin, which the people did not understand, the priests would use Spanish to denounce the missionaries.

Another means of attack was the press. Newspapers were usually willing to print anything the priest demanded. In the Maracaibo paper *El Avisador* of May 19, 1911, the readers found this bit of news: "There is not one of the founders of the Protestant religion that deserves the name of virtuous or even the qualification of honorable." In another issue of the same paper was a description of Protestantism: "It is the most horrible and most corrupt of all religious sects. It is the curse of the bad children of the church of Christ. It is error working to prostitute man. It is the dark workings of evil and crime and it is the shameful den of dishonor and misery."[6]

The newspaper attacks became specific in naming the missionaries. *El Tesoro del Hogar* of January 25, 1912, reported: "It is not the first time that we have made to stand out in these columns what the Protestant ministers, T. J. Bach and John Christiansen, are doing. We have tried to call the attention of the government to the necessity of putting a stop to this wave of corruption that tends to break down the foundation of Christian morals."[7]

In one attack on the evangelical magazine *La Estrella de la Mañana,* the priest wrote in his church paper, "We have already on another occasion said that it is not permitted for any Catholic to read or subscribe to the loathsome paper, *'La Estrella de la Mañana.'* The pernicious plant of the false reformers will never take root in Venezuela."[8]

Christiansen's comment was, "Publications like these do give us free advertising but it is natural that they also hold back for a time the progress of missionary work." If those priests could have visited Maracaibo seventy-five years later and found over three hundred live, evangelical churches, how horrified they would have been; or, just maybe, the truth would have penetrated to cause them to bow before the Risen Savior and receive His all-sufficient salvation.

A Second Mission Station Opened
Because Mrs. Christiansen could not maintain her health in the heat of Maracaibo, the decision was made that the Christiansens

should open up work at a higher elevation. In January 1913 they moved to Rubio in the state of Táchira, close to the border of Colombia. From here Christiansen could itinerate to the various towns in the Andes Mountains, on the *llanos*—plains—south of the mountains and into the easternmost state of Colombia. They were joined in 1920 by Mr. and Mrs. Olav Eikland.

In the meantime, the ministry in Maracaibo was slowly taking root. A key to the spread of the gospel was the printed page. Bach kept himself busy producing *La Estrella de la Mañana*, tracts, and even books. Opposition continued, sometimes in less overt ways. Bach told about a boycott on the sale of supplies for the print shop. The suppliers had been warned that if they sold ink and paper to the Protestants they would lose the Catholic business. On one occasion, when the supply of ink did not arrive by boat and an edition of the magazine was due, he climbed up on the roof and scraped soot out of the chimney. Following a formula from an encyclopedia, he made his own ink for the press and the deadline was met.

Writing to the C. T. Dyrness family in Norwegian on January 7, 1914, Bach told a little about the work done in the year just ended. (It is interesting to find letters in the files written by Bach in Danish, Norwegian, Swedish, Spanish, and English—reminiscent of Franson's language ability.) Bach reported, "Even if in the year 1913 we haven't seen so much by way of visible results, yet it has been the best year in the Protestant-Evangelical mission history of Venezuela. Thousands of tracts, books and Bibles have been distributed. During the last six months about 7,000 Bibles have been sold or given away and according to God's promise we shall some day see a glorious harvest."

Other coworkers joined Bach. Among the earliest were C. P. Sutherland, who had a special gift for reaching young men, and Levi Hagberg, who with his wife developed the Christian day school *Colegio Libertador*. Among the early workers were George Holmberg and his wife, Karin, and just a little later John F. Swanson, who with his wife, Grace, worked in Venezuela for twenty years before being called to the home office to assist the general director.

Planting Maracaibo El Salvador Church

In Bach's report for 1924 the membership of El Salvador Church was given as 107. During that year twenty-four new converts were baptized, with fourteen more to be baptized shortly. In the congregations with which he worked on the *llanos* there were forty-two more baptisms. The average attendance in the Sunday school was 105.

One effective means of evangelism initiated by Bach was what he called the One by One Evangelistic League. He wrote in a short recounting of the early work that he was concerned about a more widespread distribution of the tracts being printed in his print shop. One night as he was praying, the Holy Spirit prompted him to "ask for men and women whose hearts God has touched to offer themselves for the distribution of tracts." At first only four people offered their services. In time the group grew to more than fifty who, the first Sunday of each month, took a bundle of thirty tracts to be given directly to individuals, one each day of the month. Fifty years later the Evangelistic League was still active and its work bearing fruit.

El Salvador Church in Maracaibo completed its church building in 1926, just before Bach was to return home to serve the wider interests of the mission. The field was not left without strong missionary leadership, however. John Christiansen in Rubio was a man of outstanding vision for the development of the church work. In the Maracaibo area, George Holmberg was found to have considerable gifts. J. F. Swanson commented about him:

> After Bach left the field the spiritual burden of the work fell on Holmberg. He was an honest student of the Word and developed as a powerful preacher who wielded a mighty sword. Holmberg was also a man of outstanding courage. He went into areas where a robust man might hesitate to go, and when threatened with mutilation or death by machete if he'd return, went in anyway. The Spirit of God moved mightily and many were gloriously saved.[9]

A Basic Principle

The question might well be asked how it was that the work overseas made such clear progress when there was not strong direction from the home base. The answer to that question reveals a principle that has been basic in the ministry of the mission since its earliest years. In a way, it reflects a principle laid down by J. Hudson Taylor when he founded the China Inland Mission. Decisions for the work on the field should be made on the field, not thousands of miles away. There are necessary decisions to be made at home, but missionaries with vision and spiritual wisdom who know local conditions are best entrusted with decisions related to the placement of workers, methods of work, and relationships with the developing churches.

Another important point is that to these early missionaries, the church was central. Coming from a background where ministry flowed naturally out of their relationship to a local church, they did not expect the church's responsibilities to be carried out by unrelated para-church organizations. Missionaries who had been closely related to their own churches were quite well equipped to reproduce churches on the mission field. The first thirty-five years of the mission's history give strong evidence of this fact.

T.J. BACH'S LEADERSHIP

Thomas Johan Bach was installed as the third general director of the Scandinavian Alliance Mission in a public service of the annual meeting on April 28, 1928. Immediately after the service he hurried to the hospital where his beloved wife and co-laborer of many years in Venezuela was near death's door. A week later, May 5, Anna Bach passed into the presence of her Savior and Lord. The one whose prayers, encouragement, and sacrificial labor had supported Bach in the pioneering of the Venezuela missionary work was not permitted to enter into what would be a most fruitful ministry in the leadership of the mission. The five Bach children had reached ages where they could assume much responsibility and with the special help of the oldest, Elizabeth, Bach did remarkably well as both father and mother, while carrying heavy responsibilities in the mission work.

Bach often spoke of the lessons learned in his years on the mission field—lessons of dependence on the Lord for the supply of the needs of the work, lessons of spiritual warfare in which the weapons of faith, prayer, and the Word of God had to be employed with utmost dedication and diligence. There were also lessons of working together in harmony with missionaries and national Christians. These lessons, well learned, stood him in good stead as he assumed the direction of a going work which at this juncture had great need for a full-time leader.

Bach's Early Priorities

While Bach's responsibilities included the work of the mission around the world, his immediate concern was for the needs of the home base. For the preceding eighteen months Bach had visited churches, presenting the Franson-Risberg Memorial. After the death of Fridolf Risberg in 1921, the board members had felt that his tremendous contribution as treasurer and part-time administrator over a period of thirty years merited a suitable memorial and therefore proposed gathering a fund of $100,000 for the purpose. Accommodation for missionaries on furlough and those detained for health reasons was a pressing problem, and the board hoped that a suitable building could be provided to serve them.

When, as we have seen (chapter 7), Bach felt that he should not return to Maracaibo, the board asked him to head the Risberg Memorial project. He agreed only if the memorial could be broadened to included Franson and if he could, with this responsibility, have a spiritual ministry. In the months since the project was started, Bach had made considerable progress in enlisting the interest of the friends of the mission. By the board meeting of January 10, 1928, Mr. Carl A. Gundersen, a young Christian building contractor who had been made a member of the Franson-Risberg Memorial committee, was able to report that a Chicago site had been located at the southwest corner of Mozart and McLean. Gundersen also presented a sketch of an architect's plan for a building of three floors and basement. There would be space for offices, board room, assembly hall, guest rooms, and twenty-one small and medium apartments. Most of the apartments could be rented out to help finance the building—until these apartments were needed by furloughing missionaries.[1]

The choice of a location was not difficult because it was right across the street from the Salem Evangelical Free Church. This was the large church work in Norwegian and English built up by the Rev. C. T. Dyrness. The energetic young builder, Carl Gundersen, was also a member. The close proximity to the Salem Evangelical Free Church proved to be a happy and mutually advantageous arrangement. The church had a lively interest in S.A.M.'s missionary work and, in turn, missionaries in residence provided help in the church ministries.

The Challenge of the Great Depression

The decade of the 1930s brought challenges quite different from those of the 1910s and 1920s. True, these earlier decades had brought World War I and financial inflation, but these did not harm the work of the S.A.M. The year 1929 seemed to hold promise of growing prosperity for the American-educated sons and daughters of the Scandinavian immigrants who were the original supporters of the mission. The language question did trouble the Scandinavian churches for a while but by 1929 was largely solved as English was coming to the fore in the church ministries. Thoughts of business expansion and prosperity filled the minds of Americans— Christians included.

Then on October 29, 1929, the stock market crashed, ending the hope of continued prosperity and ushering in the Great Depression which was to last for most of the ensuing decade. With business stagnating, unemployment increasing, farm cash income drying up, banks failing, and people generally distressed, the outlook for a faith mission did not seem encouraging. Long-established denominational mission boards were retrenching. Could a denominationally unrelated mission survive?

The S.A.M. was not spared the effects of the economic situation. Some of the money—happily, not much—for the new headquarters building was lost in a bank failure. It was a real answer to prayer that financing did become available to complete the building so it could be dedicated and begin to serve its purpose early in 1930. Contributions to the mission, which totaled $125,278 in 1929 and $148,594 in 1930, were down to $90,043 in 1932. By 1933, income had fallen 40 percent from the 1930 high to a low of $85,778.

Without a cushion or margin in their support allowances it was not expected that the missionaries could trim their living expenses. The Lord had other ways of making provision. The value of the dollar actually went up. That meant it was worth more in commodities and this meant generally lower prices. In some countries foreign exchange rates improved and this meant more local currency for each of the fewer dollars. The Lord used these circumstances to supply his servants in part. It was not necessary to call the missionaries home.

Nationalistic Movements and War

The 1930s also saw the growth of movements that led to devastating wars. Communist parties took advantage of depressed economies in many countries to increase their power. Fascism in Italy and Naziism in Germany first attracted, then subverted the Italians and Germans and then moved aggressively across their borders to subjugate neighboring nations. Extreme nationalism in Japan led to resurgent Shintoism as the strongest expression of the national spirit, with militarism and aggression being the natural result. Japan's attack on China, July 7, 1937, was really the opening battle of the war that within a few years engulfed most of the world.

It was not to be expected that the missionary cause would be untouched by these events and movements. Missionaries in Mongolia were the first to be affected; then those in China had to contend with war conditions for eight years before there was a period of temporary peace. Missionaries to Japan withdrew before that country felt the brunt of the war, but the Japanese pastors and Christian people had to face much suspicion, opposition, persecution, and war devastation.

In the face of the financial stringency at home and turbulent conditions abroad, general director Bach, the board of directors, and missionaries very evidently were guided by the principle set forth by Solomon in Ecclesiastes 11:4: "He who watches the wind will not sow, and he who looks at the clouds will not reap."

The history of that period is replete with accounts of supporters and prayer helpers wholeheartedly demonstrating their confidence in the primacy of the task they were backing; of seasoned missionaries pressing on in spite of travel difficulties and dangers, persisting in their ministry in spite of inflation, famine, and war. Recruits were eager to reach the work areas and often found roundabout ways to proceed when war cut off the normal routes of travel. When many young men and women were diverted into military service before having had an opportunity to apply as missionaries, they considered the experience as excellent training for the Lord's work and upon being finally released pressed eagerly forward to make up, as it were, for lost time. For not a few, indeed, the military experience and a first-hand view of the need was used by the Lord as their call to serve.

Tours of Encouragement

To discharge his responsibilities properly, a general director of a mission must know the work on its cutting edge—among the people on the mission fields. This is necessary so that he can counsel the missionaries and field organizations, properly represent the workers to the board and supporting constituency, and be equipped by first-hand observation to enlist recruits for the mission fields.

In addition, the general director's presence overseas gives opportunities for the missionaries to arrange special evangelistic services and other meetings with the nationals. Consultations of church and mission leaders often take place during such visits.

Of no less importance is the ministry to the missionaries themselves. Being isolated from the Bible teaching and worship services which are a normal experience for Christian workers in the homeland and, of necessity, mostly giving out evangelistic messages and the "milk of the Word," missionaries hunger for times of deeper study. The presence of an administrative officer, board member, or Bible teacher provides a welcome opportunity for the exposition of biblical truth that is so necessary for the missionaries' spiritual health.

T. J. Bach made four extensive mission field visits during his eighteen years as general director: in 1931 to Venezuela and Colombia; in 1933 to South Africa and India; in 1935 to Japan, Mongolia, and China; and a return to Latin America in 1937 for a tour of Venezuela, Colombia, and the Netherlands Antilles. The necessity of traveling by boat lengthened the trips, but that is only part of the reason one trip extended to eight months and another to seven. Everywhere he went, Bach was pressed into preaching and teaching the Word of God to missionaries and nationals. Malla Moe wrote concerning Bach's visit to Swaziland:

> God used him to be a voice from heaven for us. But the most wonderful thing was that we could see Jesus in him. We prayed God should make our dear director, when he came, a cloud full of rain to us. We were so dry; our thirsty hearts needed to be filled.[2]

He also was very well received by national Christians and years later his visits were remembered and mentioned with appreciation.

Bach as Administrator

Bach's administrative style was interestingly different and yet very effective. His training and experience, combined with his understanding of and genuine love for people, made him a truly effective leader. His early training as an engineer contributed to a logical approach to any problem; he saw that certain actions would necessarily result in a predictable outcome. His work in Venezuela included a print shop for Christian literature, but he also found it an advantage both financially and in making contacts for Christ to accept printing orders from the public, mostly business firms. This gave him a basic understanding of finances and particularly of the necessity of careful stewardship and accountability. A key New Testament instruction which he rarely quoted but which exemplified his lifestyle and administration was I Corinthians 14:40, "Let all things be done decently and in order."

He was most meticulous in his correspondence and he constantly counseled the missionaries to take care to answer letters and have a ministry in how they wrote. He stressed the importance of words which could bless or, on the other hand, offend, and which when once written could not be withdrawn. He often quoted Pontius Pilate's words, "What I have written, I have written."

His letters were models of friendliness, personal interest, and spiritual counsel. They invariably commenced with a nugget of Scripture truth and some pertinent application. The influence of his Scandinavian upbringing and later Spanish study and ministry were at times evident. His salutation often was, "Esteemed brother Anderson," etc., reflecting the Spanish usage. Terminology was occasionally suggestive of Danish. Spelling was accurate, giving evidence of his typesetting and editing experience.

Rarely did Bach write in detail or at length. In writing, as in speaking, he depended on suggestions or questions which came out of his meditation or experience to convey his counsel or instructions. A verse of Scripture might be quoted and the reader left to think through its application to his situation. When, once, in my pre-candidacy days, I asked Bach for definite directions on how to proceed, Bach's answer was limited to these words from Acts 26:16: "I have appeared unto thee.... I will appear unto thee." Though this did not satisfy my desire for detailed guidance, it became an unforgettable principle, teaching that the one called of the Lord into His service can depend on the necessary guidance unfolding before him as he moves forward in obedience to the Lord.

In contrast to the letters written to field leaders by his successors, which usually dealt with questions in detail, Bach wrote very few letters on strategy or development of the work. He did write general letters of spiritual encouragement on a quarterly basis when the support remittances were sent out. A factor in the administration of field work in those years was the slowness of boat mail—a slowness frequently compounded by political situations or war. If, as was true for the work in China for many years, a letter could take three months for delivery and another three months for the return of a prompt reply, it was difficult to keep in close communication. The administrative philosophy of placing confidence in the local decisions made by field conference and field committee was the key to the continued strengthening of the work.

Another characteristic of Bach's leadership was his confidence that many situations could be solved without direct action. He was not quick to involve himself or the board of directors in matters where time and local concern would bring a solution. It was not unusual for him to counsel others in the administration with the words from the experience of Moses at the burning bush: "God told Moses to take the serpent by the tail...and it became a rod in his hand."

Widening the Outreach

When Bach first began his work as general director the supporting churches were mostly of Scandinavian orientation. It was to these churches that he first received invitations. As time passed, interest began to widen and he became a welcomed speaker in many other churches and in the various Bible schools. Though the mission still bore the Scandinavian name, an increasing number of non-Scandinavian names began appearing in the mission directory, names like Barville, Gunzel, Maluske, Hillis, Saunders, DeVries, and Dunkeld. Their supporting churches readily welcomed Bach's visits and ministry. By 1940 the non-Scandinavians accounted for about 20 percent of the active missionary force. At the hundredth anniversary that figure is close to 95 percent.

As the general director of the Scandinavian Alliance Mission went into missionary conferences where well-known leaders of the more recognized mission societies were participating, he quickly won acceptance and approval as a man with a spiritual message who spoke against the background of a positive and fruitful field experience. The 1930s marked the coming out of the S.A.M. into the mainstream of evangelical foreign mission activity.

Bach had a clear understanding of and firm convictions about the mission's position regarding the fundamentals of the faith. He knew where he stood and what the position of the mission must be. There are indications that some earlier board members did not see the ecclesiastical situation as clearly and were not fully alert to the changes taking place in the Foreign Missions Conference, linked with the International Missionary Council. The board minutes and files do not reveal any active relationship, but there had been occasional attendance by a representative of the mission at inter-mission conferences, although with perceptive and critical comment.

Bach knew that the S.A.M. position did not coincide with that of many of the so-called mainline denominations, and he questioned why the mission should be on the mailing lists of the various inter-mission committees requesting mission statistics and budget participation. The question he reportedly asked again and again was, "Where do you have any request that the Scandinavian Alliance Mission be a part of your organization?" It remained for his successor, David H. Johnson, to take that serpent by the head and by determined action guarantee that the official situation agreed with the actual, as will be explained in a later chapter.

With the widening of the mission's constituency to include churches and individuals of non-Scandinavian roots, a proposal was floated in early 1936 that the name of the mission be changed. The board of directors decided to present an amendment on the agenda of the annual meeting to change the name to "The Alliance Mission of North America." It was pointed out that this change, after receiving preliminary approval, could only become effective if adopted at the annual meeting in 1937. The proposal was not adopted and was not again considered for a dozen years, though sentiment for a change continued strong in some quarters.[3]

"Whatever you do...."

Very much in the pattern of Fredrik Franson, Bach was able to attach spiritual significance to the ordinary business activity of the mission. He correctly discerned that every phase of the work must be under the control and direction of the Spirit of God. A case in point was the annual meeting. True, such a meeting was necessary to fulfill a legal requirement, but more than that, it was an opportunity to unite supporters, board members, and missionaries in a bond of spiritual fellowship for the furtherance of the overseas ministry. The conference meetings were expanded to cover most of a week. Missionaries at home were encouraged—almost required—to attend. For some who came weary and discouraged, the gathering became an opportunity for refreshing and renewal as the Word of God was shared and experiences compared.

Friends in attendance rejoiced as they listened to the reports of victories won and were even greatly moved by accounts of frustrations and disappointments as the enemy sought to hinder the progress of the gospel. As inspirational as the conferences were, those who understood knew that success could not be measured by the warmth of a missionary meeting in the homeland. The measure had to be taken out where the battle for souls was being fought. So, we turn, once again, for a look at the front-line activity where the soldiers of the cross were engaged.

OPPORTUNITY AND ADVERSITY IN CHINA

During the entire period of Dr. T. J. Bach's leadership, the largest S.A.M. field, China, endured two or more calamities at the same time—either war-lord domination, international war, banditry, famine, disease epidemics, inflation, or civil war and unrest. At the beginning of the period—1928—the China missionaries, with the exception of Roy H. Brehm, were all evacuated from Shensi and Kansu. At the end of Bach's tenure—1946—most were once again away from the field of service because of a military situation requiring evacuation.

Fertile Seedbed for Unrest

The roots of China's troubles were interwoven but quite easy to identify. The inward-looking policies of the Manchu Dynasty and its arrogance toward other peoples and cultures provided the soil in which the troubles germinated. The forcing open of China by

the Western nations, much against its will; the tragic Opium War with Great Britain; the internal disintegration—financially, physically, and morally—due to the cultivation and use of opium; the impact of Western education on a limited number of restless, would-be leaders; the Boxer Uprising of 1900 and the Revolution of 1911 (themselves results of the other pressures); Japanese expansion designs; and the introduction of Communism all contributed to a century of turmoil. This was in a nation which for almost four thousand years had a stable culture with a governmental structure that maintained its integrity while other great empires disintegrated.

The 1911 Revolution and the later rise of the Communist Party brought two great forces into the arena and their struggle had a lasting impact on the Chinese people. The Communist Party in China was founded by Michael Borodin in 1924. About the same time, Dr. Sun Yatsen, the father of the Revolution, opened the Whampoa Military Academy in Canton. Chiang Kaishek, who in a short time would head the Nationalist Party and government, was its first president. Chou Enlai, later to be one of the top Communist Party leaders, headed the Academy's political department. He was a founding member of the Communist Party. In Hunan province, Mao Tsetung had organized twenty-two trade unions and aspired to the leadership of the provincial Communist Party.

Civil War—Its Effect on the Northwest

Chiang Kaishek, in 1927, broke violently with the Communist Party and thus began the civil strife that was to last for more than twenty years, interrupted only for a time by the Sino-Japanese War. Turmoil resulted. This admittedly was of a different kind from the years of competing war-lord struggles. William Pape, in his book on William Englund's life work, describes its effect in the area where the S.A.M. worked:

The restless Northwest felt the repercussions of the violent political struggles of South and Central China. The anti-foreign spirit of the terrible Boxers had not died out with the passing of Manchu rule. Calling themselves "Hard Bellies," "Red Spears" or simply "Old Brothers," they spread terror through Shensi Province. After more than a quarter of a century of incessant war, banditry, bloodshed, and suffering, weary missionaries asked each other if peace would ever come.[1]

When the Nationalist government gained the supremacy in 1928, the missionaries forced out the previous year by the anarchy, turmoil, and fighting came back to their work stations. But all was not peaceful in the nation and particularly in north China, as Leslie T. Lyall points out:

> In 1931 the political and economic stress in China reached an appalling magnitude. It was a crisis unprecedented since the Revolution. Half-a-dozen wars raged in North China, while China had to look on helplessly as the Japanese carried out a lightning occupation of Manchuria, the three provinces so vital to China's existence for their oil reserves and industry. A Japanese attack on Shanghai followed in September. A catastrophic flooding of the River Yangtze affected fifty million people. A Muslim revolt and a famine in the northwest left millions dead. And, to crown it all, the Nationalist forces failed again to defeat the Red armies in Kiangsi and Hunan; in fact the Communists were overflowing into neighboring provinces. Wherever they went hundreds of civilians died, Christians among them, as victims of Red terror.[2]

The immediate problems in Shensi and Kansu in 1929 and the early 1930s were typhus, cholera, organized banditry, and famine. Disease, mostly typhus, robbed the missionary staff of five valuable workers and one missionary son in a period of less than two years. Included was Solomon Bergstrom, who not only developed a strong Chinese work in Hsingping but also set an example for other missionaries in building the Chinese church. One very effective second-generation missionary, Gustav Tornvall, suffered martyrdom July 23, 1932. The principal cities were fought over by contesting groups and it was not always easy to identify who were the "cops" and who were the "robbers." Defeated soldiers often turned to banditry.

While each of the missionaries deserves far more mention than can be given in these pages, Solomon Bergstrom is one who must have special attention. His fellow missionary, Gustaf Ahlstrand, wrote concerning him:

> Our dear brother was a man of prayer as few, and in that as well as many other things he was an example and inspiration to us all. That probably was the secret of his success in winning men for Christ and in building up a large and flourishing church.[3]

Assistant to the general director Roy H. Brehm, who served in China, was deeply impressed by what he observed of Mr. Bergstrom's work and wrote at some length concerning him:

> His ability as a leader was remarkably evident. It was intensely interesting and educational to watch him direct the work at the station and the sixteen outstations. From the outset of the work he was keenly conscious that he would eventually have to leave the work to the Chinese and, therefore, indigenous leadership was the great need of the church. He sought diligently by prayer and effort for men who gave promise of such capacity. Actually one hundred fifty visits were made to one Chinese scholar [Huang] before he yielded to the Lord and His service.[4]

As bad as was war and as terrifying as were bandit raids, they did not take the emotional and physical toll that famine did. Violence may last for hours or even days, but famine goes on and on with people wasting away and dying all around. When men and women, boys and girls were weakened by hunger they easily fell prey to diseases such as cholera. The ever-present wolves in the countryside, having eaten bodies of some who died, were emboldened to attack children and the elderly. Even the comparatively strong were not safe from attack. The missionaries grieved for the people they were serving who had little defense against these dangers. It has been correctly stated that a person who views suffering must do something about it. If nothing can be done, then he must, to a certain extent, harden his heart in the face of the hopelessness of it all.

Compelled by Compassion

One thing that could be done was famine relief. The missionaries petitioned the International Famine Relief Commission for funds and an engineer with a plan to improve the fabled old Silk Road which extended from Sian northwestward for several hundred miles across rugged mountains and into Kansu. Other roads were also targeted for development, the immediate need being for a better means to transport relief supplies. Money and engineering skill were not sufficient of themselves to get the job done. Laborers were required and preference was given to those who desperately needed income to buy grain for food. Bilingual supervisors were a must and here is where missionaries could fit in and at the same time find a receptive audience for the gospel message. Names attached to this effort include Oscar Beckon, Gustav Tornvall, Arthur Nelson, and Reuben Gustafson. Several hundred miles were upgraded to all-weather roads. The narrow, steep, twisting roads through the mountains were rebuilt into grades which cars and trucks could use. One particularly difficult mountain area was Liupanshan. Twenty-five years later a Communist periodical falsely took credit for this road-building as a demonstration of development that had been accomplished for the people by the Marxist regime.

Direct results in the number of churches, if any, started through this type of help would be hard to identify, but the missionaries involved rightly claimed that a reservoir of good will was established that paid dividends. In later years, with starvation no longer staring them in the face, the people remembered and listened with growing interest to the gospel message. This service could have been one factor in the growing responsiveness of the Chinese people.

Remembering Forty Years

In his story of the ministry of William Englund, a particularly gifted and fruitful missionary whose service extended over more than fifty years, William Pape refers to this period and notes the atmosphere of encouragement and victory at the fortieth anniversary field conference.

> Sufferings, dangers, and difficulties were eclipsed by a review of four decades of blessing. War, drought, famine, revolution, and disease had ebbed and flowed across the unhappy land, but the gates of hell had not prevailed. Thousands of people had

turned to Christ. Churches had been established. Even priests, saturated with the vague doctrines of Buddhism or lost in the mysteries of Taoism, had been delivered from the power of darkness and brought into the kingdom of God's dear Son. The fire of revival had not been extinguished and an increasing number of Chinese men and women were being trained to witness effectively for Christ. God's power and glory were being revealed and so they sang together, those missionaries in conference, rejoicing in what God had done and expecting yet greater things. It was for this they had prayed.[5]

Positive developments continued. Two evangelists of the Bethel Band of Shanghai came at New Year's time 1934 to work with the teachers and students of the Sian Bible Institute in a city-wide campaign. Other missionaries cooperated. By the time the campaign had ended, more than 300 men and women had accepted Christ.

A welcome milestone of this period was the formation of a church fellowship which gave opportunity for the leaders of the various churches to come together for fellowship, inspiration, and consultation. Pastor Kuo Mingyueh of Hsingping was the leader and gave "abundant evidence of increasing ability and rich spiritual gifts."[6]

Communists in the Back Yard

In 1934 Chiang Kaishek began what he called his "final extermination campaign" against the Communists. Facing intense military pressure, the leaders of the Communist Central Committee decided to move out of south central China, and so began what is now known as the Long March. Starting from Kiangsi with 85,000 soldiers and 15,000 party and government cadres, the Communists struggled and fought forward by a circuitous route of about 6,000 miles over a two-year period to the northwest, finally entering Shensi. They had lost large numbers through battles, disease, and exhaustion so only 7-8,000 men and women survived to reach Shensi. Along the way they had wreaked their fury on landlords and others in senseless destruction and killing. Several missionaries of the China Inland Mission were killed and others were kidnaped and held for months.

Eventually settling in Yenan, about 170 miles north of Sian, Shensi, the remaining Communists established their base with Mao Tsetung now firmly in control. We shall note in later chapters how they spread out from this base to eventually control all of China. For our purpose now, it is sufficient to point out that the local territory they occupied was adjacent to the field of operations of the S.A.M. missionaries. The Reds were carefully watched by the Nationalist armies and their presence did not directly affect the mission work except for one serious convulsion late in 1936.

Bach's One China Visit

General Director Bach was able to visit China during a tour that included Japan and Mongolia. Reuben Gustafson was one of the missionaries who accompanied Bach to visit the churches in Shensi and Kansu. His diary of that period is sparing on words but summarizes the visit very well.

> Bach visited China Field November 16, 1935, and left January 25, 1936. He captioned the experience, "Ruts, Robbers, and Reds." He should have added "Revival." In a 1928-29 Ford station wagon driven by Reuben with Fred Nelson as extra mechanic, Julius [Bergstrom] as interpreter, Bach spent 70 days in Kuyuan, Pingliang, Kingchow, Sifengchen, Changwu, Pinhsien, Kienhsien, Lichuan, Lantien, [Sian], and smaller places. In a number of places we were warned against bandits and in some narrowly escaped being cut off. In the north some of these were Communist bands. Driving averaged ten miles an hour. Many flats—five a day. Wiring ablaze. Mechanical break-downs. But much blessing and revival to missionaries. Recap 120 miles. All appointments kept.[7]

Other diary entries by Gustafson include brief descriptions such as: "A touching service with the workers." "There was not a dry eye." "A melting service indeed." "A blessed time at Tsingning; at least 12 accepted Christ and many were touched."

The "Sian Incident"

Generalissimo Chiang planned an attack on the new Communist base in Yenan but when he came to Sian he was taken captive by a rebel army group supposedly loyal to the National government but actually under the control of a local war-lord, the "young marshall" Chang Hsuehliang. The generalissimo's bodyguards were gunned down and he was forced to bargain for his life. Just what kind of an understanding was reached is not clear, but what resulted was that his captor, the young marshall, and the generalissimo were flown to the capital, Nanking, where the young marshall was kept under arrest for many years. There apparently was some agreement that Japan would be recognized as the greater threat and the pressure on the Communists would be eased. The local situation was not improved by this surprising development. Communist troops swarmed in to join the rebel units in Sian and it seemed that a full-scale battle would erupt. Many British and American missionaries and business people were in the city and this became a matter of grave concern to the consular authorities, who hurried to arrange for their evacuation.

When the missionaries were able to return after several months, they enjoyed almost a year and a half of peace and quiet. The completion of the Lunghai railroad from the seacoast to Sian opened a new era of communication and supply. But then on July 7, 1937, Japan attacked China and thus began the Sino-Japanese War which was to last more than eight years and which seriously threatened the nation, eventually involved the United States, and made missionary work much more difficult than it had been for many years.

Japan's Forces Push Inland

China's military force was no match for Japanese might. Railroads and navigable rivers made it easy for the Japanese army to overrun most of the eastern provinces, occupy the larger cities, neutralize sources of military equipment, disrupt its government base, and isolate the country from outside supply. The Japanese armies which pushed westward along the Lunghai railroad toward the western provinces were stopped because of a difficult decision and desperate action by Generalissimo Chiang. He ordered the blowing up of the Yellow River dikes.

To understand the situation, one must know something about the remarkable Yellow River. It drains a vast area characterized by deep deposits of loess soil. Silt from erosion has been carried down the river for many centuries, slowly filling up the river bed. The result has been serious flooding every rainy season and this, in turn, has led to the building of ever higher dikes to contain the river. In time the river flowing through the flat central provinces was higher than the surrounding countryside.

When the dikes were blown up, the river, which deservedly bore its appellation of "China's Sorrow," cut new channels across the countryside for more than 400 miles to the Yangtze River and the sea. The destruction and loss of life were horrendous, but the advance of the Japanese Army was stopped and there remained a Free China to continue its resistance. Japan quickly occupied the provinces north and east of the river and this brought the enemy to a position only eighty miles from Sian, with its air fields only fifteen to twenty minutes away from this strategic city.

Sian Bombing Begins

By early 1938 Sian began to feel the pounding of Japanese bombing raids from the not-too-distant air bases. Missionaries continued their work, taking refuge as necessary in small dugouts or foxholes. Because the William Englunds were due for furlough, and the Julius Bergstroms were already on furlough, it was decided to close the Sian Bible Institute for the time being. Its moderately large building was quite close to the airport and students were also somewhat nervous about the danger. Elsewhere in Shensi and Kansu the work continued, with little concern about the war.

War Complicates Travel Inland

The biggest problem faced by new and returning missionaries was getting to Shensi across the area where fighting often raged. The distance from Shanghai to Sian was roughly 1,000 miles and all the normal routes were cut off. Julius and Thyra Bergstrom were the first to try to go in through the difficult and dangerous route of Japanese-occupied area and the flood plain of the Yellow River. They escorted the senior Mrs. Bergstrom and a new worker, Mildred Nelson. Train travel was possible as far as Kaifeng, which was about halfway to Sian and only ten or twelve miles from the new course of the Yellow River. They then went by cart to the village of Chungmou at the river which the Japanese still showed on their maps as being under their control. (The Japanese did not want to admit they had lost control of that point.) With some difficulty the travelers obtained permits from local Chinese officials to cross the river into Free China. Their going was often within sound of artillery. The Lord protected and after several weeks of travel they reached Sian.

Making up the next party to return from furlough—in the fall of 1939—were the Oscar Beckons, the Reuben Gustafsons, the Arthur Nelsons, and Miss Ruth Nelson. When they arrived in Shanghai with two Model A Ford sedans it was thought unwise to attempt to cross the Japanese-occupied territory and war zone. They also wanted to bring in amplifying equipment for outdoor evangelism, necessary supplies, and Bibles. Their choice, by necessity, was to tranship to Haiphong in French Indochina (now Vietnam) and then set out to negotiate the long and rugged mountain roads of western China en route to Shensi in the northwest.

Frances and I, as new missionaries, arrived in Hong Kong in December 1939, uncertain whether we would have to go inland by way of French Indochina or by the Burma Road into mountainous Yunnan province in the southwest. Missionary Edwin Fisch informed us in January that he had been able to take the shorter inland route through the war zone to come to the coast for supplies and advised us that, for the time being, it was a reasonably safe route. Oscar Beckon then came out to the coast, as his wife had remained there to put their daughter in school. We then joined the Beckons for the inland trip which took almost a full month, counting travel time and delays along the way. Travel was by train, ricksha cart, on mule back, and on foot over the same route and with the same conditions the Bergstroms had experienced a year earlier.

In the fall of 1940, Mr. and Mrs. William Englund also crossed Japanese-occupied area but by a longer route. Several months later Edwin Fisch and his bride, Laura, along with three new missionaries, Hugo Johnson, Oliver Olson, and Elmer Peterson, tried to travel the inland route but were turned back. After several unsuccessful attempts they settled at the coast for language study. They made another attempt in late 1941 by way of a French-controlled port near the border of Indochina. The party cleared the adjoining Japanese-held area just hours before word was broadcast of the Japanese attack on Pearl Harbor. Hours later they might well have been detained and interned by the Japanese military. Three months of hard travel were ahead of them before they reached their mission field.

Two of the families, the Beckons and the Englunds, were immediately affected by the outbreak of war between Japan and the United States. Their daughters, Fronsie and Winifred, were interned, as were all of the students and staff of the Chefoo school for missionary children. Almost two years were to pass before they were repatriated—two difficult years in a crowded camp, through seasons of intense cold and oppressive heat, with only makeshift facilities and the plainest of food.

Outreach and Short-term Courses

While some of the missionaries were necessarily concerned with logistics—travel, supplies, obtaining Bibles, exchange of money, etc.—the main thrust of the work was going forward in the twenty-two counties of Shensi and Kansu where the S.A.M. served. Here was a vast area where the mission had primary responsibility among people estimated as being up to ten million in number. There were close to a hundred organized churches, most cared for by Chinese pastors and evangelists. Some groups, in the mountain counties, were rather small, but on the populous Sian plain the congregations were large and active. Several pressing needs were felt: for a way to more adequately make the multitudes of people aware of the message of salvation in Christ, for follow-up teaching of believers, and for renewed training of young men and women for service in the churches.

Reuben Gustafson had returned to China with an amplifying system and a small generator. During his first years in China he had experienced the difficulty of reaching crowds with unaided voice. When the first trial of the equipment was made in Lunghsien, he and fellow missionaries were delighted to see over 1,000 people gather and listen attentively to the message of life. Not only did those assembled hear, but I, as an observer on the city wall, looked down into several score family courtyards and saw other hundreds of listeners. A new way had been found to reach out with the gospel message.

To facilitate the outreach, Gustafson had a cart built to carry the equipment and provide sleeping accommodations for the family, somewhat along the pattern of Malla Moe's famous gospel wagon in Swaziland, Africa. He then offered to come to the churches for evangelistic campaigns in the open air. The churches usually provided an ox to move the cart and also found a supply of hard-to-get gasoline to operate the generator. Gustafson projected color slides of the life of Christ using a large cloth screen while a Chinese coworker told the story, mostly in the exact words of Scripture. A gospel message followed, usually by a Chinese pastor.

Those who responded, and there were many, were counseled and followed up by workers of the local church. The size of the audience varied with the size of the city or town. In Kienyang, a town of about 4,000, it seemed that at least 3,000 people were present to view the pictures on the silk screen strung from side to side across the main street. In Sian, with a population of 800,000 at the time, meeting after meeting filled Nanyuanmen, a large city square. Some estimated the crowd to be 30,000. Many who had never before heard the gospel learned of the possibility of finding forgiveness and peace in Christ. In their idol worship they certainly found no assurance or peace of heart.

When the Englunds returned to China, Mr. Englund was requested by the churches to teach short-term Bible courses and so spent many months in that ministry. Julius Bergstrom, freed from the business office by my availability to handle the financial work, embarked on a training ministry among the many church workers in the large Hsingping church circuit, and elsewhere as he had time.

Fiftieth Anniversary Meetings

The year 1941 marked the fiftieth anniversary of S.A.M. in China, commemorating the arrival of the first group of missionaries, thirty-five in number, several of whom were still active. To celebrate the anniversary, a team of Chinese pastors and missionaries visited all the church areas. Included were Hsieh Szuta, Tuan Hsiohai, Huang Hsingmin, Julius Bergstrom, William Englund, Reuben Gustafson, and Arthur Nelson. The churches did need encouragement. Not only was there a war going on with the attendant pressures of high taxes, conscription of soldiers, and rising inflation, but there were also pressures relating directly to the church work.

Certain persons, with a doctrinal emphasis including speaking in tongues, wild so-called prophecies, and turbulent worship practices, had invaded one church and were seeking to gain advantage in others. Both missionaries and Chinese leaders sought to give corrective Scriptural teaching to stabilize the believers. Their efforts were generally successful, so the churches were spared divisions and strife.

Another concern was for the churches' support of their pastors and the meeting of other expenses. Much of the work was already self-supporting, but some congregations continued to receive help from the mission. With inflation worsening and the rate of foreign exchange remaining low, there was little possibility of continued help. What the churches had been taught as a goal had to quickly become a reality.

War Pressures

In his account of William Englund's ministry, William Pape

138

describes the situation that affected both Chinese and missionaries in that period.

> In the decade beginning in 1940 the faith of God's people in China was tested to the limit by crisis after crisis, revolving around such basic issues as daily food, personal safety and family needs. Shensi, deeply scarred by years of bitter fighting, was lashed with the full fury of war.... Millions of Chinese, as if inoculated against despair, improvised, repaired, worked, struggled, laughed, fought and died. Churches, sharing in the common suffering, were alert to their golden opportunity and reaped a harvest in Christ's name. Rocketing prices robbed money of its value. Missionaries dependent on funds from America grappled with the problem of a more or less fixed income, a fixed rate of exchange, and an uncontrolled cost of living.[8]

Missionaries, although isolated in a vulnerable war zone, read reports of the bombing attacks in Europe and the devastation resulting from Nazi ground warfare and were inclined to feel they were in a relatively safe place. Weeks and even months passed with no visits from Japanese bombers; then when all tended to feel quite secure there would be a wave of attacks day after day. On several occasions the bombing coincided with the gathering of Christians for a church conference. Some mission houses and chapels were destroyed and others badly damaged. Missionaries were spared from injury. In these situations their confidence was often expressed in the words of Psalm 91:6, "He shall cover thee with his feathers, and under his wings shalt thou trust: his truth shall be thy shield and buckler."

Sharp Demand for Scarce Bibles

With the number of Christians increasing rapidly came a pressing need for Bibles and New Testaments. There was no known source of supply in Free China. Though the Shanghai International Settlement, where the Bible Society was located, was now occupied by Japanese troops, the Chinese postal system was still operating. In the winter of 1941-1942, during my time in the field headquarters, I learned that the Bible Society had mailed some packages of Bibles to Chungmou, the small village on the Japanese side of the Yellow River's new channel. I also recalled that when we went through there in 1940 I had seen a Chinese mailman making his rounds in no-man's-land near the village and so decided to try an order of about 4,000 Bibles to be sent to Chungmou. The Lord blessed the effort and the order of Bibles—in small bundles— was delivered to Chungmou.

I do not now recall how I arranged for someone to readdress and remail the bundles but I well recall that in a reasonable time these precious packages began reaching Sian until we had a fairly large supply of God's Word in Chinese print. Supplies were then shared with churches and missionaries with the caution to distribute them very sparingly. When a person came to buy a Bible he was asked whether he already had one. Those who had Bibles in usable condition were told to wait until supplies were plentiful.

Inflation and Famine

It was not only Bibles and other Christian literature that were in short supply. Many commonly used necessities were not available. With the Japanese controlling lines of communication, the Chinese and the foreigners among them were obliged to live only on local supplies. This also meant that imports from other parts of China were equally scarce. To meet its expenses the Chinese government printed more and more paper currency. Inflation was the inevitable result. As difficult as it was for the average Chinese farmer, merchant, or professional person, it was many times harder for the foreigner among them—be he embassy official or missionary— whose source of income was the American dollar or the British pound. The rate of exchange was kept low to help the Chinese government in its purchase of military supplies or services. By the way of comparison, a bushel of wheat cost $40, American currency, and a five-gallon can of kerosene, $200. It was a time of extreme pressure, but also a time of great spiritual satisfaction to see how the Lord graciously made provision—even in some instances through support from Chinese Christians.

As trying as were war and inflation, by far the most distressing were the effects of the great famine of 1942-43 in Honan province to the east. Drought ruined the harvests while military necessity prevented the movement of grain to the stricken population. People tried to subsist on roots, weeds, and the bark of trees. Travelers told of seeing trees stripped clean of their bark. With word that food was available in Shensi, people who could migrate did so, and it was commonly reported that two million Honan refugees crowded into Shensi. How accurate the figures were is hard to say, but it was very evident that starving people crowded into the city of Sian and its suburbs. A walk along the street in the early morning revealed corpses of those who had not survived the cold of the night.

Missionaries tried to help from their limited means and finally rescue came in part from United China Relief. The availability of inflated money could not bring in any new supplies of grain, but it did make possible some redistribution and many people were saved from starvation. Wherever possible, the missionaries, in cooperation with the churches, instituted work programs and used the opportunity to give out the gospel message. It is sometimes charged that missionaries give help only as a bribe to make people willing to listen. Such was far from the case. The critics should have visited Miss Anna Jensen, who was in her seventies and not strong, and observed her standing long hours, day after day, handing out supplies of grain, along with a greeting in Christ's name, to provide the minimum needs of the hundreds who came to her mission station.

A Rapidly Maturing Church

The war and economic pressures could not be forgotten, yet in the midst of these experiences a positive ministry was moving forward. The workers were taking advantage of opportunities around them. Churches welcomed the cooperation and assistance of missionaries. Some Chinese professionals wanted to learn English, and a limited amount of such teaching was done where it opened doors for witness.

The churches were eager that the Bible Institute be reopened, but not in Sian which was still being subjected to bombing raids. The buildings of the Women's Bible School in Hsingping were vacant so it was decided to open a co-educational school there— about 28 miles distant from the bombing hazard. Julius Bergstrom, who had taught at the Sian school, wisely counseled that the Institute should be the responsibility of a special board related to the churches, with mission cooperation, rather than a strictly mission project. The school did reopen October 15, 1944, with seventy-one students taught by three capable, experienced, and spiritually mature Chinese pastors, Sun K'ueiko, Ts'ui Weihsin, and Huang Hsingmin. The churches cooperated well in giving and in student support. The Bible Institute was able to continue for seven or eight years until the Communist regime forced its closure.

The Lord used the inflation and low exchange rate of the American dollar to accomplish what missionaries had only succeeded in part by their teaching. The churches were forced by the missionaries' near impoverishment to take full responsibility for the support of their own work. This, too, prepared them for the coming time of Communist restrictions and pressures.

The Church Association took a further step forward. It recognized its close spiritual relationship with the churches founded by the China Inland Mission and the Christian and Missionary Alliance in the northwest and entered into a fellowship which lasted until the new government ruled out all church organizations based on relationships with foreign missions.

Reluctant Evacuation

With America's entry into the war there came a slow build-up of U.S. air bases, many of them behind the forward lines of Japanese occupation. Fearing the possibility of bombing attacks on its home islands, Japan began a campaign to dislodge the Americans. The year 1944 saw a great deal of such fighting and the eventual expansion of Japanese-held territory. Many missionaries of various groups were affected and as they moved ahead of the threat of invasion, large numbers came through Sian.

Later, Shensi itself was seriously threatened and the American consular officials urged us to evacuate. For six months after the most serious threat developed, many of us continued our work in the exposed areas, but when, late in 1944, we were told that any emergency transportation the Air Force might provide would be at the cost of leaving some of their own military personnel behind, most of us decided to heed the counsel and evacuate to India. There was no easy way to do so as it involved many days of hard travel over mountain roads and then a flight over the "Hump" into India.

Two Kansu missionaries, Marie Wistrand in Chenyuan and Didrik Kilen in Sifengchen, felt their stations were so remote from danger that they chose to stay. Those who went had to leave responsibility with the church leaders and they did so with confidence, because these men had demonstrated both maturity in caring for the flock of God and practical ability in administering church affairs. Two single missionaries, Oliver Olson and Elmer Peterson, remained in China for the duration of the war, having offered their services as language officers to the American military.

Plans to Reenter

V-J Day in August 1945 brought an end to the long war that had engulfed China. Several months later the furloughed China missionaries gathered at mission headquarters in Chicago to begin plans for return. Because of continued uncertainty in China, largely due to the presence of many armed Communist units, and also because of some difficulty in obtaining passports and securing passage, it was decided that families should wait and rather that two of the men should go out first. So, in April 1946, Oscar Beckon and Reuben Gustafson sailed for Shanghai as the vanguard of a group of workers eager to enter the whitened harvest fields once again.

JAPAN ON A SLIPPERY PATH

When T. J. Bach addressed the students of the Moody Bible Institute in 1936 after his return from a visit to Japan, Mongolia, and China, he spoke prophetically of the future of the Far East mission fields. He first referred to Revelation 2:5 and the possibility of the removing of the candlestick of witness. Bach looked to the day when the candlestick would be moved to the church of China. It would take half a century before that prediction would begin to be fulfilled.[1]

Disturbing Prediction

The second prediction had much earlier fulfillment. Having learned at first hand how Japan was using its Shinto religion to whip up nationalistic fervor and a spirit of militarism, he commented on the failure of the United States to manifest equal fervor for the evangelization of the Japanese. He predicted that if the U.S. was unwilling to send its sons as missionaries, the day would soon come when it would have to send its sons as soldiers. He was five years ahead of time but otherwise right on target.

Missionary Numbers Decreased

Though the number of experienced S.A.M. missionaries in Japan over a period of thirty years was always small—sometimes two or three, or even just one—the progress in the work was encouraging. Of particular note was the work of venerable Pastor Doi of Atami, who had a unique ministry intercepting and leading to Christ many who were trying to commit suicide at the high seaside cliffs. Joel Anderson reported concerning him:

> Pastor Doi is the Moses within our group! He is loved and respected by all. He is now having a contraption made for warning suicide candidates. He is writing this time with a certain kind of chemical that will show even in the night. This signboard

will be placed at the most dangerous spot, in such a way as to be plainly seen. Of course, the Buddhists are not pleased and are trying to put obstacles in the way. The Buddhists had tried their "sutras" and the burning of incense at the spot only seemed to encourage the unfortunate ones in their dangerous undertaking. It is all right to them to stop people from committing suicide, but to have it done in Christ's name is not to their taste.[2]

A single lady missionary, Miss Albertina Peterson, who came to Japan with the first party in 1891, labored effectively for forty-two years. She returned home in late 1933 on only her fourth furlough and passed away in January of 1934. She had laid a good foundation for a growing work in Chiba and before that in Kamakura. A visitor to Japan had earlier written concerning her: "Sister Peterson was the first white person to gain entrance in the Imperial Palace, where she presented the crown prince with a copy of the Holy Bible." If the full story of her faithful work could be told she would indeed be numbered among the noteworthy pioneers.[3]

In the summer of 1933 Joel Anderson was able to report strong evangelistic activity by the Japanese churches with "hundreds having been given an opportunity to hear the gospel and quite a few having found the Saviour—or, rather having been found by Him."[4]

Storm Clouds on the Horizon

The same report by Anderson gives one of the early warnings about future difficulties for the country and for Christians in particular.

Japan is launching upon a new program of development of the national defence which will call for an expenditure that will greatly add to the already heavy burden of the people. A rekindling and fostering of the national spirit is also in the program. Ancestral worship, too, is to be more encouraged!... If a radical change in Shintoism, the national religion of Japan, is not brought about soon, I am afraid the Christians will yet have to go through days of severe persecution.... It would come tomorrow if the leading Christians took as definite a stand as the early Christians did toward Rome's idolatry.[5]

C. E. Carlson, who had served in Japan since 1913, also was not blind to the changing national and religious climate. He wrote from Tokyo in 1936:

> Priests take advantage of the present intense nationalism to work up confidence in the old religions, and on the surface they seem to enjoy some measure of success.[6]

While being alert to growing threats to the church, the missionaries were also conscious of the gracious work of the Spirit of God in many lives. Joel Anderson shared this word with his prayer partners:

> I had occasion to thank God for what he is doing in Ito through our young pastor, Brother Matsumoto, and his faithful lay workers. Many precious souls have been won to the Lord during the year.[7]

War with China

With the attack of Japan on China, July 7, 1937, the nation went onto a war footing and the earlier foreboding of trouble began to be realized, as Carlson mentioned in his reports.

> Since the war broke out the authorities exercise stricter watch over the Christian work, so that open-air meetings and other special activities have in some places been forbidden.... Idolatry is rather enjoying a revival these days; people flock to the temples to pray for victory.[8]

At the same time Carlson was encouraged by certain positive developments in the broader Christian work.

> We note nevertheless, with satisfaction, that modernism is losing ground. Some are coming back to the program of winning souls for Christ rather than social work.... We are also happy to note signs of hunger among God's people for the deeper things of God. A union convention held here last month for the deepening of the spiritual life bore testimony to this fact. The leaders had not expected more than four hundred to attend, but as many as fifteen hundred gathered. And they were not drawn by unusual preaching so it was generally conceded that it was the work of the Spirit.[9]

Christian workers were not exempted from military service and at one time Carlson reported that four of the ministers in the

146

mission-related Japanese Domei church had been drafted to fight in China. In their letters both Anderson and Carlson mentioned instances of Christian soldiers having lost their lives in battle.

Increased Government Harassment

Letters from missionaries began to allude increasingly to government pressures, such as Joel Anderson's comment, "We are living in an age when everything is demanded by Caesar.... We have something which we cannot sacrifice on Caesar's altar—our faith in the true and living God and the worship which belongs to Him."[10]

C. E. Carlson echoed the same concern: "We do not fear government oppression as much as the compromising attitude of the Christian movement. The Japan Christian Council has taken the lead in compromising on the Shrine Worship question."[11]

The argument that a visit to a national shrine was an act of patriotic duty reportedly swayed the majority of Protestant churches. It is also true that there were thousands of believers who did not "bow the knees to Baal." A spiritual battle was raging. The Japanese government steadily increased restrictions on Christian churches. In fact, it even wanted to control religious belief and expression. Whether this was generally possible or not, the government tried certain legal maneuvers.

> The Religious Organizations Bill became effective as of April 1, 1940; and although this granted recognition to the Christian religion, it also added severe restrictions. No organization with less than five thousand members could be maintained with government sanction. Thus eleven blocs were formed and received recognition from the Department of Education. Bloc Number Six was the one in which our Alliance Church was incorporated together with the Nazarenes, the Free Methodists and one or two others.[12]

At the end of 1939, according to the last formal Japan field report before World War II, there were 775 communicants in twelve organized churches in what had been established as the Nihon Domei Kirisuto Kyokai (Japan Alliance Christian Church). These Domei churches were served by sixteen Japanese pastors and evangelists. After April 1, 1940, these churches were all linked with the larger group—Bloc Number Six. This evangelical grouping could not be maintained for long, however, because in 1941 all eleven blocs were forced to join together as the United Church of Christ in Japan, a decision made by the government.

For those denominations of world-church persuasion this uniting may have seemed like a welcome assist to their goal of one world-wide super church and they were happy to stay with the United Church when peace finally came. However, this union posed problems of conscience for the evangelicals and the Nihon Domei Kirisuto Kyokai was one of a number that severed connections with the United Church, as will be explained in a later chapter.

Missionaries Withdrawn

No S.A.M. missionaries remained in Japan after late 1940. Because of the severe tensions between Japan and the United States, the U.S. consular officials had urged withdrawal of all Americans. Though hesitant about heeding that advice, the missionaries were moved to decision by the Domei church representatives who, in a split vote, decided that foreigners should no longer be members of the church association.

Though the situation looked bleak, both on the national scene and for the churches planted by the mission, the positive accomplishments of fifty years of ministry must be recognized—twelve active churches by so small a missionary and pastoral force. In spite of the evident embarrassment the churches faced at having been established by Americans who were soon to be counted by Japan as enemies, the churches observed in a victorious way the fiftieth anniversary of the coming of the first party of missionaries. As they did so they could have had no premonition of all the fiery trials they would face—as citizens of a warring nation and as followers of Jesus Christ—before they would once again welcome servants of Christ from overseas into their midst.

LIGHTING LAMPS IN WESTERN INDIA

When, in 1930, missionaries in western India looked at the small band of 300 baptized believers—the results of twenty-five years of work—and then considered how many millions of Hindus, Muslims, and Animists surrounded them, they may have felt much like Gideon when ordered to confront the Midianite hordes—questioning the possibility of victory yet believing. Like the heroes of faith of old, the missionaries' confidence was in God's promise and His power.

Twenty-five Year Recap

Observing the twenty-fifth anniversary of the opening of the Western India field in 1905, the annual conference in 1930 recapped some of the history. Thirty-one missionaries had served in East and West Khandesh since Fredrik Franson chose, under the Lord's guidance, to send missionaries there. Two had died, ten had left for other fields, six were delayed at home and thirteen were on the field in India. Thirty-five Indian coworkers were numbered in the force.

Through the combined witness of missionaries and Indians there were now a total of 300 baptized believers. An additional 98 were listed as adherents and 575 persons were under instruction. Sunday schools were teaching 476 pupils and 366 boys and girls were receiving Christian witness and

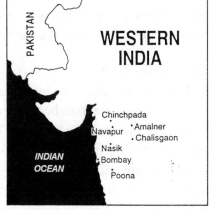

Bible teaching in day schools.

As "a journey of a thousand miles must start with a single step," so could the India missionaries look at the steps taken so far and in faith anticipate what another fifty or sixty years would bring.

Bach's Observations

T. J. Bach arrived on his first and only visit to India on October 21, 1933, after several months of ministry in South Africa. He had been in India only eight days when he received a cablegram with the sad news that Dr. C. T. Dyrness had passed away. Dyrness, associated with the work from the very beginning at the invitation of Franson, had been a tower of strength on the board and through the leadership he gave when the S.A.M. had no general director. Bach keenly felt the loss of a valued counselor.

It did not take Bach very long in India to become aware that all was not well in this huge country. In his first report he noted:

> Politically, economically, and religiously at first glance everything may seem rather quiet among the great masses of India. But when we get to know what is going on in New Delhi, where the legislative bodies meet, or at Poona where Mahatma Gandhi sits in prison, and works on his spinning wheel; or the continual strong undercurrent of strife between Mohammedans and Hindus in Bombay; we soon discover that India is very much disturbed.[1]

Bach noted the predominance of religion in the culture and also the degrading impact of much of it. "The people give the impression of being intelligent, with great possibilities for good if the yoke of idolatry and caste system could be removed."[2]

Currents of Unrest

The Untouchables or Outcastes, as the Scheduled Castes were known at that time, numbered then about eighty million and were becoming increasingly restless. Thus, there were several major currents stirring up the sea of humanity on the Indian subcontinent—communal strife because of the caste system, religious animosities, and broad resentment against Great Britain's colonial rule, particularly on the part of the more educated people.

A keen observer of the situation was Augusta Swanson, who reported to the mission's periodical that the 80 million Untouchables in India had become restless and were questioning any benefit to them of the Hindu religion. They protest, "We are worshippers of the Hindu gods, but are never allowed to behold them. [They were excluded from the temples.] After all, what good have these gods done us? Are they not the very ones who keep us in bondage?" Miss Swanson further noted that Dr. Amedkar, himself an Untouchable, and a recognized leader among them, received very shabby treatment after returning to India from Europe. His high level of education gave him no standing among the Hindus. He startled the nation by announcing his caste would leave the Hindu fold. The Untouchables responded by burning their holy books and tearing the holy beads from their necks. This new attitude made them respond more openly to the Christian message.[3]

Missionaries of some groups involved themselves in the political struggles, feeling this was the way to bring the kingdom of heaven to earth. The S.A.M. missionaries were convinced that their responsibility was to "take out a people for His name" (Acts 15:14b), and thus serve both God and the people. The largest share of their ministry was to the aboriginal Bhils but they did work among all segments of the people as they found openings for ministry. Reports refer to some of the highest caste, Brahmins, receiving Christ and becoming active witnesses. When they were in the body of Christ and in the local body of believers, caste and cultural differences melted away.

Growth in the Field and Force

The missionary count in India increased during Bach's tenure as general director. Chinchpada, Dharangaon, Sakri, Raver, and Yaval were added to the mission stations of Navapur, Pimpalner, Parola, and Amalner. Reinforcing the earlier staff of Mr. and Mrs. Joseph Otteson, Mr. and Mrs. O. E. Meberg, Miss Esther Ritzman, Mr. and Mrs. John Ribe, Mr. and Mrs. Paul Ringdahl, and Miss Marie Christensen were many new missionaries, including names that would be recognized in later years for their work in India and in other aspects of the mission activity: Richard and Martine Thomas, Lucille Guiley Kent, Esther Sorensen, Gladys Henriksen, Margot Kvaase, Wayne and Evelyn Saunders, Alexander and Beatrice Wilson, Don and Doris Hillis, Dr. Karl and Esther Klokke, and Walter Olsen.

With paramedical training, Richard Thomas set up a dispensary in Parola to which crowds of ailing people came six days a week and received the message of life as well as medication. When Dr. Klokke, the mission's first qualified physician, arrived on the field and had completed language study he began a hospital ministry at Chinchpada, the first regular hospital in the work of the S.A.M. This hospital, with easy access by Bhil villagers, was to become a key factor in the growth of the Christian churches in West Khandesh.

Joseph Otteson was concerned that there be a multiplication of trained witnesses. He wrote in 1938:

> This is the third year God has opened the way for me to carry on the most important work I could do in India, namely, to help a few more get into a living and vital contact with Christ, and to give instruction sufficient to enable young men to be effective, either as lay witnesses or mission workers. The numbers have increased each year to the present fifteen.[4]

There are three distinct groups of Bhils in West Khandesh, with the principal S.A.M. work being done among the Mauchi Bhils. These aboriginal tribal people live in grass huts, have no furniture and just a few brass utensils. They are not idol worshippers, but worship the god of the mountains, "Dongeri." Their religion is animism which is, in reality, demon worship. They have a vague idea of one God but suppose he is far away with absolutely no interest in the jungle people.

The Bhils' receptivity to the gospel was cause for much praise on the part of the missionaries, who were all too aware of the resistance of the Hindus to the Christian message. One reported anonymously in the mission magazine:

> I do want you to experience with me the joy that was ours as we

saw fifteen Bhils, babes in Christ, declare openly through baptism, before a group of Bhil Christians and others of their own village, their faith in Him alone as the Way, the Truth and the Life.[5]

Reporting to the annual field conference in November 1941, field chairman O. E. Meberg could point to 77 baptisms during the year and to a church membership of 1,315. A total of 1,554 Sunday school children were taught by 83 teachers. Village schools totaled 39 with 634 pupils. Sixty-one boys and fifty-seven girls were being instructed and given Christian guidance in separate boarding schools. Dr. Klokke handled 12,883 patients at the newly opened hospital. Missionaries and Indian fellow workers were reaching out to the villages in their districts. The larger towns, quite solidly Hindu, or in some instances, Muslim, were harder to penetrate. One missionary, viewing the hopelessness of Hinduism, sent a clipping from an Indian newspaper that revealed the sad plight of the Hindu devotee:

The Hindu's Weariness[6]

Weary are we of empty creeds,
Of deafening calls to fruitless deeds;
Weary of priests who cannot pray,
Of guides who show no man the way.

Weary of rites wise men condemn,
Of worship linked with lust and shame;
Weary of custom, blind, enthroned,
Of conscience trampled, God disowned.

Weary of men in sections cleft,
Hindu life of love bereft;
Woman debased, no more a queen,
Nor knowledge what she once hath seen.

Weary of babbling about birth,
And of mockery men call mirth;
Weary of life not understood,
A Babel, not a brotherhood.

Weary of *Kali Yuga** years.
Freighted with chaos, darkness, fears—
Life is an ill, the sea of births is wide,
And we are weary; who will be our guide?

*According to the Hindu belief, *Kali Yuga* is the fourth age of the world, the age of universal degeneracy, and the age at that particular time of writing.

War and Protest

World War II affected India but not as directly as it did China or Japan. Transportation to and from India was difficult because all shipping gave priority to national needs. India was a supply base and a staging area for troops fighting the Japanese on the Indo-Burma Front. It was part of the only route open to communicate with and supply China. Rationing of food, fuel, and cloth was enforced. Japan made some incursions into the eastern area and bombed Calcutta to a limited extent. The British-trained Indian Army was sent into action on several fronts.

Though the Congress Party in India with leaders such as Mahatma Gandhi, Jawaharlal Nehru, and Patel and the Muslim Brotherhood led by Mohammed Ali Jinnah had different goals, they were united in opposition to British rule. They tried to make the point that the Indian people should not have to fight to preserve freedom for others when they were still bound in the colonial system. Their opposition landed them in prison, where they remained until near the end of the war in 1945.[7]

Encouraging Prospects

New missionaries were able to reach India in 1943, 1944, and 1945. Included were Miss Henrietta Watson, Miss Jane McNally, Miss Catherine Iobst, Robert and Margaret Cooper, Robert and Jean Couture, Einer Berthelsen, Miss Zoe Anne Alford, and Miss Carol Hastings. Some of these names will come before us again, but their names are well known to our Lord and Savior, who sent them out and equipped them for His service.

Field chairman O. E. Meberg reported to the annual field conference in November 1945 that sixteen new missionaries were present and more were expected. The mission had also expanded into the Nasik District, adjoining Khandesh to the south, which increased the mission's responsibility by one million souls.

Meberg also referred to the rapid political changes taking place which could greatly affect missionary work. His emphasis in the face of the changing situation: "Our missionaries are in India to serve the people in the pattern of Him *'Who came not to be ministered unto but to minister, and to give His life a ransom for many'.*"

LIGHT FOR THE DARK CONTINENT

General director Bach's first morning in Swaziland set the tone for his heart-warming experience among the Africans. The evangelists at Franson Memorial Bible School were to leave early in the morning to walk to a Bible conference some fifteen miles away. At 5:30 A.M. they came to Bach's door and "sang softly and with unusual harmony one of their hymns in the Zulu language." He learned with real appreciation what so many others have noted, that the Zulus and Swazis have outstanding gifts for musical harmony. "If it is so pleasing to be awakened in a foreign land with a song of words which are not understood, what will it not be to be awakened by the heavenly voice and music!"[1]

Bach Visits South Africa

When Bach made this his first visit to the S.A.M. mission work in Swaziland and Zululand in southern Africa, forty years of its history had been completed. The fruit of the work had been gathered into 79 organized churches which had a membership of 4,953. Evangelism was emphasized strongly but that was not all. The importance of discipling new converts was recognized and they were taught to take a clear-cut stand for Christ by being baptized. Bach reported that 434 converts were baptized in 1932.[2]

Bach had immediate opportunity to view the work. Arriving in Swaziland on July 31, 1933, he and Arthur Jensen started off the next day on a trip of about three weeks, going

from mission station to mission station and visiting as many outlying preaching points as possible. The Africans were very much interested in the visit of this small-of-stature "Big Chief" from overseas and came readily to the meetings which were arranged. Many responded to the invitation to receive Christ. Christians listened to his kindly counsel and responded to his warmth.

Meeting Malla Moe

Though Bach was well informed about Malla Moe and her work, he had never met her. True to form, Malla was out on tour with the gospel wagon visiting African kraals—this time in low-lying malarial Tongaland—when Bach and Jensen wanted to get in touch with her. Bach described their search:

> When we started out to look for Malla Moe we knew she was in a certain district in the "bush" but were not sure of the location. At six in the evening it was dark and there was no road to follow. One of the Africans at a kraal promised to go with us to the next kraal to show us the best way through the bushes. When we came to the next kraal we asked two questions: "Have you seen Malla Moe's Gospel Wagon?" and "Who will go with us to the next kraal?" I do not believe there is a person in all Swaziland, Zululand, and Tongaland who is so well known as Malla Moe.... Well, we kept on until 12 o'clock, when in answer to much prayer, we found the Gospel Wagon near a kraal. There was no road over there. We were so happy and dear Sister Moe just wept for joy.[3]

The first trip surveying the mission work covered about 1,100 miles; then after one day back at the Jensens' home they were off again on another trip of the same length. Reporting on the tour, M. D. Christensen wrote: "Many, many souls found the Lord and the work all over received a new quickening touch of the Spirit of God."[4]

In Conference with Missionaries

Bach next met with the missionaries at the annual field conference. There were now forty-one missionaries in the Africa work, and the conference sessions were times of outstanding spiritual refreshing. Several decisions made at the conference were of prime importance for the local work, though many years would pass before they were fully implemented. As M. D. Christensen explained:

> The first question was about self-support, self-government, and self-propagation of the African Church. This does not mean that this will be accomplished in one day, but it does mean that we will work toward the achievement of this as soon as possible. After 40 years of mission work carried on chiefly with foreign money we think it is time for them to carry their own burdens. We do not wish that we may have less burdens but that we may be released to preach the gospel in the regions beyond.[5]

An Expanded Vision

Another decision related to expansion. Looking at the excellent response among the Swazis and Zulus, the missionaries were becoming increasingly aware of a large, inadequately reached territory just across the eastern border of Swaziland—Portuguese East Africa (also known as Mozambique). Several missions were active in the southern part of the country but the extreme northern district of Tete beyond the Zambezi River was largely unreached. Here was an area eleven times the size of Swaziland with only two missionary couples. The Portuguese government's reluctance to allow more missionaries to enter was a concern that called for much prayer. Though not clear how the S.A.M. would go about obtaining entry, the missionaries nevertheless took the first step, that of a decision. The conference voted unanimously to enter Portuguese East Africa. It would be only after many decades and several unsuccessful attempts that this door would open. But the call of a needy field would remain strong.[6]

Pastor John Gamede and Malla Moe

Malla Moe's evangelistic outreach continued to be a significant factor in the expansion of the work. She had unusual gifts for contacting people and opening new places for the gospel. John Gamede, the Swazi pastor who worked with Malla for many years, wrote in a letter to Arthur Jensen: "We are happy all the time with our mother, Malla Moe. Some time ago she planned for a big meeting at Chief Mhlosta's at Odakeni. Then grown-up people came to Christ. Now she says, 'Let's have a similar meeting at Ndungunye.' Yes, it is her life to push the gospel to help people get saved."[7]

Miss Moe was not the only one who earned the appreciation of the pastor. In the same letter he also wrote, "We had a meeting at Esinceni, a farewell for Miss Dagny Iversen and Miss Borghild Frogner. The people wept many tears because these missionaries have great love for the work of Jesus. I, too, sympathize with those who cried on account of the ladies leaving. They have been zealous in working for Jesus with great love. We are asking the Lord to bring them back to Swaziland speedily."[8]

Changing Roles

In the mid-1930s, missionary letters and magazine articles give evidence of development in thinking about the missionaries' role in Africa and the future of the African church. Surrounded, as the early missionaries were, by almost unrelieved paganism, the one thought was to share the liberating and cleansing gospel of salvation. The African evangelists were taught to do what the missionaries were doing—proclaim the message of salvation as simply as possible and win people to Christ. That, of course, was fundamental.

More Bible Teaching

But now more thought began to be given to helping believers mature, particularly those who were evangelists and workers in other capacities. Missionary Tom Olsen reported on a week of Bible studies with the African evangelists and said that such studies were arranged twice a year. At first he wondered if the evangelists would be able to persevere for a solid week of study, but then was delighted to see their eagerness to learn all that was being taught.[9]

Christian Christiansen noted in particular the increasing ability of the African evangelists to absorb spiritual teaching and articulate it in word pictures easily understandable by the common people. In one letter he reported:

> When we had our last quarterly meeting with the African workers, we decided to have some extra meetings at different places in order to help the Christians dig deeper into the Word of God. We are so happy to state that there is definitely a deeper hunger for more of the Word of God than before. The churches all over the field are longing to be taught in the Scriptures. We praise God for this. There was a time when one could hardly detect any longing whatever in this direction. But it is different now![10]

On one occasion when the missionary presented the ministry of the Holy Spirit, one of the workers spoke up, "Mfundisi [pastor] we would ask you to speak more on this subject—the Holy Spirit—because so many of the native sects preach all kinds of fairy tales in regard to the working of the Holy Spirit."

Committing Responsibility

Though there were now many churches with basic organization, missionaries realized that greater responsibility had to be committed to the African leaders.

> It is quite evident that the attitude of the present missionary should not be the same as our missionary pioneers had to take. This is simply because there has been growth and change. The missionary is wanted and is needed, but not for the same things he had to do when there were no churches and but few Christians. As the years pass, we turn over as much as possible of the administrative side of the churches to the people themselves. Definite steps were taken this year to get all the churches started on the road to self support.[11]

Self-support had to be viewed in a different context than in North America. The Africans did not have a cash economy. Whatever assets they had were largely in cattle, and land for tilling was available at the pleasure of the chief. The people had little money and actually did not need much. The evangelists had land to plow and some cattle, so were largely self-supporting. Efforts were made to teach the people to bring tithes of grain they raised. It was a lesson they learned in time, but all too slowly.

Pastor John Gamede served as general overseer and advisor to the other pastors and evangelists, all of whom gathered each quarter for fellowship, instruction, and to consider solutions to any problems they faced. The Quarterly Meeting thus became the principal church administrative instrument.

About 75 percent of church members were women, so it is not surprising that they took much of the responsibility for lay witness. In 1936 a committee was set up for Church Women's Evangelistic Bands.

Peaceful Work Climate

After the Boer War, 1899-1902, no political disturbances hindered the movement or work of the missionaries. They did face many health hazards, one of the principal ones being malaria. World War II, beginning in September 1939, brought one danger in particular. That was sea travel. The usual route from North America to South Africa was across the North Atlantic to Great Britain and then from Southampton to Cape Town or Durban. With the outbreak of hostilities between England and Germany came immediate danger from German submarines and surface raiders. The regular routes of travel were interrupted and missionaries were forced to book passage on less vulnerable vessels than British lines.

Hazardous Sea Travel

Irl and Florence McCallister and Lydia Rogalsky were new missionaries who were needed in South Africa and anxious to go. They finally obtained passage on an Egyptian freighter, the S.S. *Zam Zam*, which sailed from New York on March 19, 1941. Its route was by way of the U.S. east coast to Trinidad and from there to the eastern bulge of Brazil, from whence the ship started across the South Atlantic, sailing blackout.

At daybreak on April 19, the passengers were awakened by the explosion of a shell hitting the ship. They quickly dressed and prepared to abandon ship, while shells continued to find their mark. The lifeboats filled rapidly and the sailors anxiously pushed clear of the sinking vessel. Irl had started climbing down a rope. Seeing the lifeboat, with Florence in it, move away he let go to jump into the sea, thinking perhaps he could swim to it, when a wave washed the lifeboat back alongside and he unexpectedly landed in it.

It was not many minutes before the German raider came toward the lifeboat and called out an order to come alongside. Wounded passengers were helped by the German sailors. Others climbed rope ladders and in time all were taken on board. The raider, the M.S. *Tamesis,* rendezvoused with a supply vessel, the M.S. *Dresden,* and this ship became their home for almost five weeks until they were disembarked in German-occupied France on May 20.

The American passengers were taken across Spain to Lisbon, Portugal, from where they sailed, June 15, to return to New York, arriving June 24. As the S.S. *Zam Zam* had been presumed lost, it was front-page news when the passengers were disembarked.

So after more than three months of travel, the missionaries returned empty-handed to where they had started. True, they had enjoyed the rich experience of the Lord's marvelous protection. These hardships and losses did not deter the McCallisters and Miss Rogalsky from continuing to press toward South Africa and about two years later they were able to enter the Swaziland work.[12]

Celebrating Fifty Years

The fiftieth anniversary of the South Africa work was celebrated by African Christians and missionaries at a jubilee conference beginning July 15, 1943. Of special interest was the presence of several pioneers, Miss Malla Moe, Mr. and Mrs. William Dawson, and Mr. and Mrs. Severin Bang. It must have been with overflowing joy that they viewed the African church ministries flourishing all around them. Baptized believers in the churches numbered about 6,000. There were still enough pagans in the Swazi and Zulu kraals to remind them that the area was one of unrelieved darkness when they came a half century earlier.

The Christians found their way to the conference at Bethel Mission Station from settlements near and far to join the celebration. Christian Christiansen was deeply moved as he described the scene at the opening meeting:

> As the sun was setting, Thursday, we heard singing from various directions. At first it was faint, but as it became more audible, we realized that groups from the various outstations were coming in for the Jubilee. The singing groups had come onto the station grounds and each group stood over against the other singing different melodies and then after a while meeting for greetings. The women and the girls carried their sleeping mats and blankets on their heads. Many of them were tired after a long day's walk—tired but happy. Some had even spent two full days on the road, and a few, three days.

> The meeting on Sunday was termed the big meeting, lasting six hours. The station grounds were filled with people who had come to celebrate with us. Most of them had to sit on the ground.... Our hearts were warmed as we realized the tremendous change the gospel has brought in the lives of these people. There was a time when the countryside heard no gospel songs, no preaching, no invitation to accept Christ as Saviour. In those days there were the weird and subtle chanting of the witch doctor and his aides, the thumping of feet of the women dancers to scare away the evil spirits, the fear and dread of what some revengeful neighbor might do. Sundays, too, were like all other dreary days. Now— look at this sea of happy faces reflecting the peace and joy the heart possesses.[13]

One of the early missionaries, Miss Dagny Iversen, who in true pioneer spirit opened the work in Ekuseni, Tongaland, and saw the gospel win victories in the lives of the people, summed up the situation very well as it could be viewed in 1940:

> Africa! Who has not from early childhood looked at the map, at the great land south, and wondered? Wild forests, wild animals, snakes and dark-skinned people drew out our imagination. Africa has been called "The Dark Continent", the land of superstition, the blood-stained, tear-stained continent.

> Today it is the land of opportunity and great riches—gold, diamonds, ivory, copper, and radium invite the white nations. But the dark people of this wealthy land are still living in superstition and witchcraft and their ignorance is still at its height. But, praise God, if China has no sore which the gospel cannot heal, India no problem which the gospel cannot solve, then Africa has no dense darkness that the gospel cannot penetrate.[14]

MONGOLIA—
RELIGION AND DARKNESS

Burden and Concern

As a lone S.A.M. missionary in Inner Mongolia in late 1933, and with just one other missionary couple assigned to Mongolia but living in China, Stuart J. Gunzel thought deeply about the unmet need of the people around him. He also recalled the history of almost forty years of S.A.M. efforts to bring the gospel to these people. In this mood he wrote to the editor of *The Missionary Broadcaster*, Dr. O. C. Grauer, pouring out his heart:

> Some days ago when my mail came it brought the *Broadcaster*. I sat down and read with the greatest joy of the beautiful way that the Lord is blessing on the other fields. Praise God for the way He has been saving souls in the other parts of the world. But many times since reading that *Broadcaster* my joy has turned to sorrow as I think of these poor people here. There is not any revival in Mongolia. We are not able to give any report of people seeking their Lord and Master. Cannot the Lord save Mongols as well as others? I know that He can, and I trust Him for it. Last evening I walked the floor of my room with tears in my eyes as I thought of the blood of our dear fellow missionaries that has been poured out. It seems that so few people have heard their voice calling. At one time we had quite a few missionaries to the Mongols and now we have only three. Does the blood of our brothers have to call out these thirty-three years and then see the work go backward instead of forward.[1]

Though this brought sorrow to Gunzel, it did not deter him from full obedience to the Lord's call. He continued his letter to Dr. Grauer:

> When I dedicated my life to the field of Mongolia, I thought I had given my all, but last night as I thought of these things, by the grace of God, I said a far bigger "Yes" to Jesus than ever before. I just want to tell you, Brother Grauer, in a very humble way, that I trust the Holy Spirit will find in me a wholly dedicated

servant whom He can use to speak to these poor souls.[2]

More than half a century has passed since those sincere words were written. It would be Gunzel's privilege to spend less than one more decade in Mongolia. But the dedication revealed in his letter has characterized the service of his many succeeding decades outside of Mongolia. Few men have served as faithfully and well in keeping the needs of the Mongols before the Christian public and few are as well received and appreciated by the Mongols as he.

A Costly Undertaking

No field has exacted a greater toll in blood and health than Mongolia, when calculated in proportion to the size of the missionary staff. To the five martyrs of 1900—Hilda Anderson, Clara Anderson, Hanna Lund, David Stenberg, and Carl Suber—can be added the names of Mr. and Mrs. N. J. Friedstrom, Mr. and Mrs. A. B. Magnuson, Folke Boberg, and Anna Lundberg, who toiled hard and died early.

When T. J. Bach assumed leadership of the mission in 1928, only one missionary, Mr. Folke Boberg, was on the Mongolia field. He was seeking to establish a church at Wangiefu among Mongols and Chinese. His fiancée, Anna E. Lundberg, who trained at the Moody Bible Institute and a New York City hospital, was the first recruit commissioned for Mongolia by Bach. She arrived in Kalgan, China, on December 19, 1928, to begin language study. Nine months later she had passed into the presence of the Lord whom she loved and served. This was a terribly hard blow to Boberg, weakened by illness and the strain of trying circumstances. He decided to go home to Sweden and in 1930 left the mission. He did, however, return to Mongolia under a Swedish mission and by agreement continued the work at Wangiefu.

Lindholm Taken by Bandits

Another couple, Mr. and Mrs. A. Godfrey Lindholm, arrived in Mongolia in 1929. After a period of language study in Kalgan, Mr.

Lindholm decided to visit Patsebolong—the agricultural project where earlier missionaries had hoped Mongols would settle—and evaluate the situation. The colony had been confiscated by provincial officials and land parcels were being offered for sale. Lindholm left for Patsebolong on April 10, 1931, accompanied by his Mongol teacher, Mr. Daktoho. Four days later, within a day's journey of Patsebolong, both men were kidnapped by a bandit gang and held for ransom. They were robbed of all personal possessions of interest to the bandits, including personal clothing, and were given Chinese winter coats to wear.

Daktoho was particularly helpful and was certainly God's provision for the time; he had earlier been taken by bandits and knew what to expect. The ransom demand amounted to over $10,000 in U.S. money plus medicines and other valuables. Lindholm and Daktoho explained that this was an exorbitant demand beyond the possibility of paying. The demand was reduced to about one fourth and a time limit of five days was imposed or Lindholm would be shot. Daktoho was dispatched to try to gather the ransom.

The bandits kept moving around the area to avoid the authorities, which made it hard for Daktoho to locate them once he had the ransom in hand. In the meantime, Lindholm was sustained by Scripture promises such as, "My presence shall go with thee, and I will give thee rest," "Lo, I am with you always, even unto the end of the world," and many others. Contact was finally made, the ransom paid, and Lindholm released.[3]

Earlier histories do not reveal whether the ransom demand was communicated to the Chicago headquarters of the mission. If such a demand had come in later years, the kidnappers would have been informed that it is the mission's policy not to accede to such demands. While this policy may seem hard and unyielding, it is necessary to avoid making all missionaries targets for kidnappers in the hopes of extorting large sums of money.

Gunzel Chooses Mongol Lifestyle

Stuart Gunzel had arrived in Mongolia early in 1933. At the

invitation of the Mongol Prince, Sunnit Wang, Gunzel located in the royal settlement to help the prince's son with English and at the same time study Mongolian. This required him to live in a small Chinese-style room with a Mongol man. He ate native food and in most respects lived the life of a Mongol. In most—but not all, because the life of the Mongol was deeply influenced by his Buddhist religion, Lamaism.

Religious but Lost

The Lamaism of Mongolia is directly related to that of Tibet and the Dalai Lama at Lhasa is venerated as a living Buddha and god. The first son of each family becomes a lama. Where there are temples there are often great concentrations of lamas.

While Gunzel adapted very quickly to the Mongol way of life, the heathen darkness and superstition which surrounded him weighed heavily on him. Writing about his joy in being allowed to serve the Lord there, he commented on the life around him:

> I have had to live in the midst of heathenism. Just now as I write, the Mongol lamas are in a room not over one hundred feet from mine, beating their drums and saying the Tibetan prayers by memory. I hear the sounds of horns and drums all day and many times all night. I see these poor people crushed under the burden of sin with no one to help them. They are plenty religious for I do not think that there is another people in all the world more devoted to their religion than the Mongols. But their gods are nothing more than clay or metal—or a sinful man such as the Living Buddha who made his home right next to mine for over a month this summer.... I have seen people fall down and worship a lama and then could see on the face of the lama a large canker of syphilis.[4]

In the summer of 1934 Gunzel spent several months in the nearest station of the Swedish Mongol Mission (also founded by Fredrik Franson) where he had fellowship with Dr. Joel Eriksson while continuing his language study. He also reported that Mr. Lindholm and another missionary had come from Kalgan on an evangelistic tour of Mongolia, traveling by oxcart.

Move to Pailingmiao

Pailingmiao, Suiyuan, was important as the newly designated capital of Inner Mongolia and was a center of Buddhism. As such, it was home to many priests as well as government officials and workers. Mongols from all parts of the country converged there on pilgrimages. As far as Gunzel could determine, no missionary work had ever been done there and certainly no missionary had ever settled there. This place began to come into focus in Gunzel's vision and prayers.

First, a Visit to Patsebolong

In communication with Lindholm, the decision was made that Gunzel should locate at Pailingmiao. Hjalmar Ekblad of the Swedish Alliance Mission agreed to drive them first to Pailingmiao and from there to Patsebolong to study the situation in view of the confiscation by provincial authorities. Leaving Kweihua on November 20, 1934, they covered 115 miles in two days; then waited several days for gasoline and other supplies which Gunzel had sent earlier by camel. The remaining 210 miles to Patsebolong involved detours and delays, but they finally saw a large cluster of trees rising from the flat level plain. Coming to the buildings among the trees they found the Patsebolong gate guarded by several soldiers of the occupying force.

The earlier agricultural project of 6,000 acres had been reduced to thirty and that was occupied by a hundred soldiers. Their thoughts turned to the earlier vision of a place where Mongols would congregate and have extended contact with the gospel. They thought also of the investment in labor, life blood, and tears with seemingly so little fruit among the Mongols. Gunzel recorded their thoughts:

> While we rejoiced to see the place, endeared to so many hearts, we could not but lift up our hearts to God in prayer because of the present condition. The place where work had begun among the Mongols forty years ago had been converted into a place of almost all Chinese and very few Mongols. The work is now in the hands of Chinese Christians and they are carrying on in their own way. There are over a hundred names on the roll, yet only

about twenty are regular in attendance. Besides Sunday services they have a prayer service each night. It was our joy to speak at these services. Hands were raised by some, signifying a desire to follow Jesus.... We spent part of a day at Lungchenteng and met some of the people. It was encouraging to see the people carrying on their own work.[5]

Cold Welcome

In Pailingmiao, Gunzel settled into two small Mongol tents. The weather was so cold that a five-gallon tin of water inside the tent froze solid during the night. Not only was the weather cold, but his reception by the officials seemed equally cold. The missionary was told that the Prince would not allow him to preach the gospel there. The people, however, were more friendly and often came to the tent to visit and receive medical help. When Gunzel talked to them about God they laughed and told him he was crazy. Even so, he persevered and gave out many Scripture portions.

Three months later the missionary could report a better relationship with the officials, although some opposition continued. But contact with the people was possible.

> I am finding that it takes a lot of patience and love. Their religion is such a curse and sometimes it is rather hard to work with them because of their religious customs. They have certain days when they can do certain things. For instance, the 15th of the month is called *spirit's day* and a person is not allowed to prick his body with a pin or cut himself, for if he does the spirit might take its flight and cause great sickness. The sick cannot receive an injection on such days.... This is a time of opening the hearts of the people, for the story of Jesus is all new to them. While we do not limit the power of God to save souls we realize that this is the time for patience and love to be shown and the seeds of the gospel to be planted. Later we will have the gathering of the sheaves.[6]

Eager Waiting

As the summer months of 1935 approached, expectations heightened for this lone missionary, who for more than two years had lived among people of a vastly different culture with few opportunities for fellowship with other believers. How good it was that he knew the reality of "constant, conscious communion with Christ," as Franson would have described it. One expectation was that general director Bach would be arriving in Mongolia on October 18. Even better news was that Gunzel's fiancée, Margaret Leir, had been commissioned and was to travel on the same boat as Bach. Gunzel met them in Tientsin and for the next few weeks, together with a Swedish couple, they toured Mongolia and ministered to Chinese and Mongols.

A field conference with four missionaries and the general director was held at Patsebolong, where Mr. and Mrs. Godfrey Lindholm were now located. Several important decisions were made. One was that a Chinese-speaking missionary be sought for Patsebolong and that the Lindholms should locate in a Mongol area. Another was that Pailingmiao should be established as a mission station. A third: "Considering the circumstances, we recommend that brother Gunzel and sister Leir be joined in marriage in the near future." The circumstances in the mind of the general director were his conviction that Gunzel had been alone long enough and that his fiancée should not have to live alone in the Mongol culture just to satisfy a mission rule which required a wait of one year after arrival on the field.[7]

When Bach was escorted back to the coast it was a convenient time for him to officiate at the wedding on November 14, 1935, of these two young missionaries. From there the bridal pair went back to tent life in bleak Mongolia where, in obedience to the call of the Lord, they gave themselves in a ministry of love to the Lord and these resistant people.

Constant Pressure and Upset

In the years that followed, military developments interrupted the work of the missionaries many times. The Japanese army had occupied Manchuria to the east in 1931 and set up a puppet government for renamed Manchukuo. Japanese military units ranged westward beyond the borders of Manchukuo and into Inner Mongolia. Pailingmiao came under their control in 1936 and missionary work began to feel the tensions and restrictions imposed by the occupation forces. In November 1936, the Japanese military ordered the mission work to stop and missionaries to leave. Before the Gunzels could remove their possessions to a new location at Chao Ho, renewed fighting broke out between the Japanese and Chinese. When the Chinese gained the upper hand their soldiers looted the missionary property and everything was lost. The Chinese government and the American consul agreed that Americans should be evacuated from the fighting zone. Because the Lindholms were due for furlough they arranged for the work at Patsebolong to be cared for by a committee of seven Chinese Christians.

At the new location in Chao Ho, circumstances were much the same as at Pailingmiao. The Mongols were very suspicious of the missionaries' motives and the rumor was circulated that they had come as spies and would be taking away their land. After only six months at Chao Ho the Gunzels had to endure another military takeover as the Japanese forces came in and drove out the Chinese. Over a period of almost four years it was a continual struggle to maintain a foothold. The Japanese were in control most of the time and put severe restrictions on the missionaries.

Mr. and Mrs. Lindholm returned to Mongolia in 1940, allowing the Gunzels to leave for furlough. Reporting to the S.A.M. board of directors, Gunzel described some of the conditions they and other missionaries faced, including the Lindholms and workers of the Swedish Mongol Mission:

> All missionaries are regarded as spies and are under suspicion. Some missionaries have been thrown in jail for no reason and have had to go through weeks and months of grueling experiences, not being allowed a trial, nor visits by their relatives or government representatives. They eventually are released with broken health and forced to leave the country with the warning to keep their mouths shut. The Japanese have questioned all people in contact with us and have threatened our workers and even have gone so far as to beat up some masons who were working for us. We have been continuously questioned by Japanese who call purposely for that reason. We have been called

to police stations and questioned thoroughly. The state of affairs is an effective, indirect method against us as the people fear to work for us. For many months last year we were without help. Imagine having to carry water two blocks, besides caring for the multitude of other chores when we possess no modern conveniences. Under such conditions the missionary can do little more than live. On top of this we had to move our entire household three times during the past year. However, the Mongols, who at first were against us as missionaries, have in the last months defended us in the face of Japanese accusations.[8]

In the Pattern of the Pioneer

James Gilmour, honored as the Apostle to the Mongols, worked among them tirelessly for twelve years beginning in 1870 and saw very little fruit. That the Gunzels went through the same kind of experience and retained the deep sense of call to work among them is testimony to their love for the Lord and the Mongols.

During the years at Chao Ho [1937-1940] we worked largely without help. No Mongol gospel workers seemed available but we tried to carry on along four lines: colportage, direct personal work and chapel meetings, ministering to the sick, and definite time set aside for working through prayer.... Up to the time we left we could not point to one Mongol, who under our labors could be called a born again, baptized Christian. There was one Mongol who was driven from our district because he affirmed publicly that he was praying to Jesus.... About three months before we left, two men—one a former priest and the other a Mongolian-speaking Chinese—desired baptism. While both of them seemed to confess and pray we felt it the part of wisdom to put them on probation for some time.[9]

It would be more than six years—until early 1947—before missionaries could return to build upon the foundation so sacrificially laid down in Mongolia.

LIGHT PENETRATING LATIN AMERICA

Widening Lay Witness

The work in South America, which T. J. Bach had so great a part in developing, continued to expand. One key reason was the shouldering of responsibility by national believers, mostly laymen. The One by One Evangelistic League of the Evangelical Church in Maracaibo, Venezuela, grew in activity, strength, and fruitfulness. Similar widening of ministry was experienced in the Venezuela state of Táchira where Mr. and Mrs. John Christiansen and others worked and in the city of Cúcuta, Colombia.

A Sense of Oneness

The believers may have been scattered in many towns but they were bound together by an understanding of their oneness in Christ. The evangelical paper *La Estrella de la Mañana* also created a strong bond as it gave reports of the gospel work in the different areas and shared news about various believers. The sense of oneness began to crystalize at the time of the dedication of the Maracaibo church in 1926, just before T. J. Bach returned to the homeland. John Christiansen, when reporting about the conference of churches in 1930, reviewed the history of the united evangelical efforts:

> At the time of the dedication of the Maracaibo church a representation of missionaries and national workers drew up some recommendations, which were circulated in all the evangelical churches of the

Republic of Venezuela. These recommendations have had a very hearty reception and have greatly helped toward bringing about a spirit of unity and cooperation. Acting upon these recommendations the church in Maracaibo sent out an invitation to the churches in the western part of Venezuela and Cúcuta, Colombia, to send official representatives to a conference in Maracaibo in August 1927, and since then two more such conferences have been held. These are constantly growing in influence and confidence. This year the conference is to be held in San Cristóbal and we expect a better representation than ever before.[1]

Church Dedication and Mob Riot

Though the evangelical witness in Cúcuta began in July 1918 with visits by Christiansen, followed up later by Olav Eikland, it was only in January 1923 that Mr. and Mrs. Eikland moved in to carry on regular work. They met at first in a corridor chapel connected to their house and with encouraging response. By 1926 the believers were able to buy a well-situated lot and begin plans for a building. Christiansen prepared a beautiful design and the men of the congregation started construction—a task which took over two years. Like Nehemiah's workers of old at Jerusalem, the Cúcuta church builders had to suffer ridicule, threats, opposition, and persecution. But they persevered and by autumn 1928 were ready to dedicate their attractive new building. When their enemies saw the progress being made their threats increased and rumors surfaced that the building would be blown up.

The police had been alerted, so when the dedication began on a Sunday afternoon a large squad of police was posted at the door. When the meeting got under way the bells of the Catholic church were tolled as a signal and the crowd gathered by the priests in the central plaza started to fire rockets. Carrying other noisemakers, the agitated protesters marched up the avenue and filled the whole block in front of the *Templo Evangélico*.

The combined noise of the shouting, noisemakers, and stones raining on the church building threatened to drown out the dedicatory sermon by Pastor Domingo Irwin. But the louder the noise, the more strongly he preached, and the greater liberty he had. When the preaching concluded, the outside noise seemed to increase. The evangelicals inside kept on singing hymn after hymn. The mob had no intention of dispersing and the believers chose not to venture out into the hostile crowd. The police tried hard to restore quiet, and when they failed, the governor came to appeal for order. He, too, failed. But he had the authority to call out the military and he did just that. The soldiers managed to clear the street quite rapidly.

The local newspapers were united in heaping reproach on the fanatic actions of the priests. God actually used this persecution to bring the gospel to the attention of a much greater number of people than ever before.

Twenty-fifth Anniversary

As the year 1931 approached, the national church leaders and missionaries decided to observe the twenty-fifth anniversary of the work. Central to that observance would be evangelistic campaigns in as many places as possible. An urgent invitation asked Bach to spend an extended time in the various districts. To have the leader of the mission present for such an anniversary seemed appropriate, but more than that, Bach was honored as one of the pioneers of the work. Moreover, he could minister effectively in Spanish.

Bach accepted the invitation and left New York by boat in February. Several stops were made en route, one of the most significant being in the Netherlands Antilles. Mr. and Mrs. Elmer Paulson accompanied him to take up their post, assigned by the field conference, as the first missionaries to reside in Curaçao. Bach conducted evangelistic meetings in Curaçao and Aruba and was well received. From there he sailed to Barranquilla, Colombia, accompanied by Charles Johnson. By various means of transportation—four days on river boat, one day by cable railway, and three days on mule back—they traversed extremely rugged terrain to reach Cúcuta on the Venezuelan border. Bach was burdened anew by what he encountered and recorded his thoughts:[2]

> When we travelled past one place after another and saw the multitudes, I often seemed to hear the words of the Psalmist saying, "No man cared for my soul." Is it possible that so near

to us there should remain so vast a field without a messenger of the gospel?"[3]

Years of Growth

Writing to *The Missionary Broadcaster,* Christiansen reported information shared with the anniversary conference. After twenty-five years of work there were now ten organized congregations and many other groups of believers that had not yet been organized. "Some of the churches had already become self-supporting, self-governing, and self-propagating. Most of the churches have their own pastors or evangelists, whom God has called out from among their own people." He named a number of men who were active witnesses, including Buenaventura Angulo, Pedro Vicente Saavedra, Eduardo Meleán, Sacramento Cobos, and Francisco García. The conferences of the churches had helped strengthen the bond of fellowship among the groups of believers. The missionaries could not help but rejoice as they reflected on the gospel's impact in the face of determined opposition and persecution by the priests.[4]

A Bible Institute is Founded

This same anniversary year saw a forward step in the training of workers. Some young men had previously been sent to a seminary in Puerto Rico, but the Christians wanted training to be given closer to the churches from which the men came and to which they would return. The conference decided to open a Bible institute in Maracaibo. John F. Swanson was given the responsibility of directing the school and George Holmberg, S. B. Mosby, Juliann Jacobson, and others shared teaching duties. One of the first students was Asdrúbal Ríos, who thus began his long association with the mission and the evangelical churches in western Venezuela. The Maracaibo Bible Institute, which later was transferred to San Cristóbal with a change of name to Ebenezer Bible Institute, was the first evangelical Bible school in Venezuela. One early difficulty was securing satisfactory textbooks in Spanish.

Seizing the Opportunity

It is interesting to note that the annual conference was not just to give the believers opportunity to get together, but was planned as a means of reaching out to unbelievers. To the 1934 conference in Valera came pastors and delegates from twenty-two congregations—altogether a total of one hundred out-of-town visitors. The Valera members were determined to take advantage of the opportunity.

> For months the members and workers in Valera had been busy visiting and distributing literature, not only in Valera, but also in surrounding towns and villages. They would go out two and two and when they could not afford to pay the fare on a truck they would go on foot for miles to spread the gospel. In this way the surrounding towns and villages had been visited an average of nine times a month. The result of all this preparation was felt from the very beginning as sinners began to seek salvation.... The evening meetings were held in the open air outside the chapel as there was not room for half the people inside. Some evenings the space left vacant near the entrance was crowded with people standing and at times the crowd reached all the way across the street.... Sunday evening, August 12, was the last meeting of the conference and at the close of that service those who had come to Christ during the conference meetings were asked to come forward. It filled our hearts with joy and praise to see more than thirty people crowd around the platform.[5]

Of present interest is the note in the conference report that Asdrúbal Ríos was consecrated to the Lord's service and given ministerial license. The remarkably fruitful life of the Reverend Asdrúbal Ríos Traconis in its relationship to the evangelical cause in Venezuela and throughout the Hispanic world deserves to be related fully, but only a brief account can be included here.

Asdrúbal, born April 24, 1913, attended grades five through eight of *Colegio Libertador*, the S.A.M.-founded day school, and was in the first class to be graduated from the Bible Institute of Maracaibo. He served a number of pastorates between 1933 and 1939 and then taught at the Bible Institute for five years. He was named editor of *La Estrella de la Mañana* in 1939, adding the responsibilities of administrator in 1956. Though the work on the magazine should have been a full-time job, he also served as Pastor-Elder of El Salvador Church in Maracaibo for ten years. He was also radio pastor for twenty-four years of weekly broadcast ministry. Ríos served repeated terms as president of OVICE, the Organization of Evangelical Churches in Western Venezuela, and for twenty years was president of the United Convention. In a very real sense he was *Mr. Evangelical* of Venezuela. While the foregoing outlines some of his work, it does not come near revealing the outstanding impact his life has had and continues to have on the evangelical cause throughout Latin America.

Also of present interest is John Christiansen's role in assisting the churches of the Orinoco River Mission in setting up the Eastern Convention of Churches at this time (1934). This had a bearing on the later formation of the United Convention of Churches and established a relationship of mutual interest and purpose with the ORM that bore fruit in a significant way when that mission was merged into TEAM in 1980.

Mérida and Environs

Maracaibo was situated at sea level on Lake Maracaibo not far from the Caribbean Sea. Tropical lowlands lay to the south and west of the lake and beyond them loomed the Andes Mountains. To cross three different spines of the mountains, the road reached elevations of eight and ten thousand feet and in one place over thirteen thousand. Sizable towns were located in the mountains. One of the first to be occupied by missionaries was Mérida, the capital of Mérida state and the location of high dignitaries of the Roman Catholic Church. The Catholic clergy dominated the religious and social life of the people, who were very conservative and seemingly less responsive to the message of deliverance from sin and the shackles of dead religion.

While keeping up the faithful proclamation of the gospel in Mérida, missionary George Holmberg tried to visit outlying settlements where people were more open. Holmberg reported, in 1936, on one tour he made to many small places at the foot of the mountains and in the lowlands:

> After twelve days we were ready to go back to Mérida. We had
> held seventeen meetings in all. The number of baptized believers
> had been increased to twenty-five, while among the believers
> some twenty or twenty-five more are receiving instruction and
> are definitely looking forward to being baptized. Some twenty
> adults and a number of children responded to the invitation to
> seek the forgiveness of sins and follow Jesus, while others
> reconsecrated their lives to the Lord. Two fine young men are
> planning to go to the Maracaibo Bible Institute this fall to prepare
> for Christian service.[6]

Reaching the Scattered Plains People

South of the towering Andes Range, Venezuela leveled off in
the *llanos*—plains—which extended for hundreds of miles and
were intersected by several large rivers. During the rainy season
the rivers overflowed and many places were flooded. In the dry
season, dust took over. George Holmberg was the first of the
S.A.M. missionaries to venture into the far-away regions of the
fever-infested plains—in early 1919. He did so at great hazard to
his health, his life hanging in balance for some weeks after he
completed that first tour.

In 1935 Christiansen spent a month on the *llanos* traveling
"1,000 miles by car, 200 miles in a dugout canoe, 45 miles in a
saddle, and quite a number of miles on foot, going through jungles,
mud holes, over rough roads and by fording rivers. He conducted
32 evangelistic meetings, held 11 prayer meetings, 4 Sunday
schools, and one communion service."[7]

The paper *La Estrella de la Mañana* was frequently the forerun-
ner introducing the gospel to scattered ranchers. Missionaries
sought to build on the work of the messages in print and often were
warmly welcomed by men and women whose hearts had been thus
prepared for the gospel. By 1930 Gustav and Tillie Bostrom had
accepted responsibility for the *llanos* outreach and for much of the
time lived in Barinitas to be closer to the work. Bostrom's tours as
unofficial "Evangelical Bishop of the Plains" extended over many
months as he ministered to the scattered groups of believers and

introduced others to the Savior. The Bostroms persevered in this difficult work for many years.

So much of the reporting of the missionary ministry tells of the work of the men; and while these are accurate reports, there is the danger of overlooking the great part the missionary wives had in the ministry. As responsibility for care of small children decreased, the wives often took part in the itineration. Mrs. Gustav Bostrom wrote interestingly of a missionary tour of four months to the *llanos* by her husband and four nationals during which time she was present for two months. Travel and accommodations were quite primitive but these matters did not deter her or diminish the joy of firsthand involvement.

La Estrella Observes Thirty Years

General director Bach was again invited to the Netherlands Antilles, Venezuela, and Colombia in 1937 to help observe the thirtieth anniversary of the founding of *La Estrella de la Mañana*. As he planned the trip, his mind ranged over the history of the region and particularly its missionary history. The first evangelical missionary to Latin America was James Thomas, who went to Buenos Aires, Argentina, in 1818. Now Bach could report that there were throughout the whole of Latin America about 2,500 missionaries, 3,200 national workers, with over 4,000 evangelical churches and approximately two million evangelical Christians.[8]

No doubt Bach thought of the time thirty years earlier when the region in which the S.A.M. was now working suffered total spiritual darkness. Now he could report it had thirty-five missionaries working in forty stations and outstations. His article did not refer to the part he personally had played in bringing the gospel to a large number of these people and thus beginning a chain reaction which was now expanding in scope and force.

The field Bach toured this time was larger than on his earlier visit and there were more places to stop for services. His visit to the *llanos* involved very hard travel—in an open Model T Ford and on mule back. Many nights were spent in most primitive quarters. Bach had learned in earlier years how to get a reasonable night of sleep in a hammock. Officials of the mission often have the opportunity to share experiences common to the missionaries in regard to travel, food, lodging, heat, and insects, as well as the joy of giving out the life-changing gospel message to many who have never before heard it.

Of particular interest was the general director's participation in the dedication of the nearly completed Evangelical Church building in San Cristóbal where John and Anna Christiansen had worked productively for so many years. Then another highlight was the observance of the thirtieth anniversary of *La Estrella de la Mañana,* when he heard testimonies of a number who had their first introduction to the gospel through the "Star of the Morning." Bach also attended the annual field conference of the missionaries. Anna Christiansen wrote a conference report which included a comment on Bach's part in it.

> At the opening of each session brother Bach gave us a devotional message which was heart-searching and inspiring. He spoke on the need of faithfulness by the servants of the Lord in spite of persecution and indifference in those around them; of the importance of a life of intercession, and a broken and contrite heart which alone the Lord can use; of the yearning of God's heart for those who can "stand in the gap" and take on their hearts the burden for the salvation of the lost and the strengthening of the believers; the need of reviving fervent prayer in each one and on the field as a whole. How these messages stirred our hearts and awakened in each one the fervent desire to be wholly yielded and used as an intercessor and the Lord's messenger as never before.[9]

Lay Evangelism

A key to the progress of the gospel in Venezuela was the active participation of most of the believers in evangelization. A new missionary, Elva Vasby, described the activity:

> We have in our church in Valera an Evangelistic League composed of practically every member. Each month the League's directors meet to make out the itinerary for the month. From twelve to fifteen commissions, consisting of two to five members, go to some part of the immediate vicinity, a neighboring

village, or one farther away to give out the gospel, presenting tracts or Scripture portions. If there is a Christian home in the vicinity, an evangelistic service is conducted in the evening and to this the people are invited.[10]

Church Convention Hears of Growth

At the time of the fourteenth convention of the evangelical churches in western Venezuela and North Santander, Colombia, in August 1940, George Holmberg could report 400 in attendance and gave statistics about the development of the work. There were now 33 organized churches with 1,912 members in full communion and an average attendance of about 2,500. Since the convention a year earlier, 274 believers had been baptized. The Bible messages given by the national pastors and evangelists were on the whole of a higher order than ever before, not only in form and content, but also in spiritual power. Most of the groups reporting were in the S.A.M. work but several other evangelical works were also included.[11]

Radio Broadcasting Begins

The 1943 convention included several items of lasting interest. Asdrúbal Ríos, recently ordained, was elected president of the church association. Plans were advanced toward developing a United Convention of Evangelical Churches, which would bring together churches from western, eastern, and central Venezuela in conference and consultation meetings every five years. This convention was initiated in 1945. At the 1943 convention, also, the first radio broadcasts of the evangelical message were aired as a precursor to a regular radio ministry.

> Three times during the week the convention had the unusual privilege of giving half-hour programs over a local broadcasting station. This aroused great interest, and, as might be expected, intense opposition on the part of the Roman Catholic Church which threatened reprisals against the broadcasting station. As a result, the local Evangelical church in Maracaibo made the decision to continue broadcasting half-hour programs each Sunday over *Ondas del Lago*.[12]

Advances in Colombia

Writing in 1938, Bach reminisced that Cúcuta was first visited by missionaries thirty years earlier, and mentioned something of the burden and concern that resulted in the seed being sown in those early years:

> The fruits of those first visits were not encouraging. With much effort and prayer a few copies of the Bible were sold and a very small number of friends were found who subscribed to the evangelical paper, *La Estrella de la Mañana.* Those who dared possess the Bible and read the paper were generally persecuted. Every inch of the ground for the Lord's garden in Cúcuta, as well as everywhere else on the mission field, has been obtained at the cost of sacrifice, prayer, and suffering. Thanks be unto God for the faithful workers and His own watchful care over each little plant. Today there is a beautiful and suitable church building in Cúcuta. The membership of the church, including outstations, is 193. There is a Sunday school of 183 members. The church is completely self-supporting, and even gives a little help to other needy places. It calls its own national pastor. [13]

In the meantime, the work was expanding in Colombia. Restrictions on visas for entry into Venezuela resulted in many of the newer missionaries being assigned to Colombia. La Donjuana, not far from Cúcuta, was one of the early churches planted and its membership grew steadily. Asdrúbal Ríos served as pastor from 1935 to 1939.

Work was also opened in Ocaña, Convención, El Carmen, Pamplona, Salazar, and elsewhere. Response to the gospel was quite good and by 1943 the churches had decided to meet in an annual Assembly while still continuing their relationship with the Convention in Venezuela. The second meeting of the Assembly was held in La Donjuana in 1944 with a total of 150 delegates and visitors participating.

An impressive occurrence, which brought great joy to the assembled throng, was the presence of a group of fifteen from El Páramo de la Paz, all of whom accepted the Lord Jesus as personal Savior at the gathering. These fifteen went back to their mountain homes to live their new Christian lives before their neighbors, backed by the intercession of their brothers and sisters in Christ. In less than two years, José de la Cruz Bolívar, one of the new believers and a promising leader in the work, had suffered martyrdom.[14]

After Forty Years—Still Serving

The fortieth anniversary of the opening of the South America work—April 17, 1906—was observed in San Cristóbal where John and Anna Christiansen were still fruitfully serving. The field committee members and several visitors, including Dr. and Mrs. H. H. Savage of Pontiac, Michigan, joined them to observe the anniversary date. A decision was made that day to recommend to each mission station that the anniversary year be a time of renewed emphasis on evangelization. The honor the Christiansens received at the time was very modest, a reflection of the self-effacing way in which they worked.

The Christiansens' ministry throughout the forty years had been monumental, not just in developing churches in Rubio, San Cristóbal, and surrounding areas, but in helping churches throughout the field to mature. Bach commented, when he found Christiansen sitting in the back row at one of the big meetings, that it was typical of him to put the national Christian workers forward while he literally took the back seat, in honor preferring the other. Christiansen was clearly the mind behind the cooperation that developed among the churches in Venezuela. While teaching at the Ebenezer Bible Institute he was able to inculcate scriptural principles regarding the church into the minds of future leaders.

The work of the S.A.M. in 1946 extended to six states in Venezuela, four in Colombia, and two islands in the Netherlands Antilles. In Venezuela, alone, there were over fifty places where meetings were regularly held.[15]

Broad statistics are of value in tracing the progress of a work of God, but God's work really is done in individual hearts. For each true believer there has been a life-changing experience. The change brought about in the life of Carlos Vielma, of the state of Barinas, has been repeated in the lives of thousands who have been led out of darkness into the Savior's marvelous light.

When he was a young man, Carlos traveled the country towns working as an actor and clown. The bright young girl who helped him kept on living with him after they gave up this work. When they heard the gospel and received Christ into their hearts, they recognized that a change in their lifestyle was imperative and so were married. Their enthusiasm for the gospel and love for the Lord motivated them to preach the good news and do person-to-person soul-winning work. Carlos, with amusement, loved to relate how astonished the people of the towns were to see this former clown now preaching the gospel.[16]

NEW FIELDS ENTERED

The existence of still unreached people beckons continually to a missionary, "Come over and help us." That surely was the Apostle Paul's experience when needy Macedonia lay just beyond the water from Troas. For Paul the call came through a vision in the night. For the present-day missionary it is the urging of the Spirit of God using various means to bring the need to his or her attention. It is usually more than a subjective desire that results in a new field being entered. The simple knowledge that an adjacent territory has little or no permanent gospel witness often stirs up an earnest desire to move in with the Word of life. Confirmation of the unfilled need by personal observation or by testimony of others is important. So is the availability of missionaries on whose hearts the Lord has laid the burden of that particular "Macedonia."

The areas where missionary ministry was either begun or the initial decisions to enter were made during the period of T. J. Bach's leadership were Netherlands Antilles, Portugal, Southern Rhodesia (as a hoped-for way into Mozambique), Pakistan, and the Tibetan Frontier of North India. Let us follow the beginning work in several of these areas.

Netherlands Antilles

At the time the mission began work here, six islands under the rule of Holland made up what was called the Netherlands West Indies. Political changes have occurred in the intervening years, mainly to provide for more local rule and autonomy. Three islands—Aruba, Curaçao, and Bonaire—lie off the north coast of Venezuela, with the closest point being only about thirty-five miles away. Because Aruba and Curaçao were usual stopping points for ships sailing from North America to Venezuela, the early missionaries became somewhat familiar with them and actually made friends with certain local people.

These missionaries learned that the people of the islands were a blend, mostly European with some Carib Indian and African, and with a culture that drew from both Dutch and Latin American backgrounds. The islands making up the Antilles had been under the past rule and influence of several nations. Dutch was the official language, but that which was commonly spoken was Papiamento, a polyglot of at least six languages, with the strongest influence said to be Portuguese. Many of the Antilleans were also fluent in Spanish and English.

When the Dutch Protestant Church sent ministers from Holland for the Dutch settlers, only white Europeans were allowed to enter the churches. Roman Catholics, sensing an opportunity, opened their churches to all and the result, not surprisingly, is that 85% of the people are Roman Catholic. The established Dutch Protestant Church is now a minority group.

The missionaries assigned to the S.A.M. South America work who stopped in the Antilles on March 21, 1931, to consider the possibility of establishing a beachhead on the islands were Mr. and Mrs. G. A. Holmberg, Mr. and Mrs. C. G. Johnson, and new workers Mr. and Mrs. E. O. Paulson. T. J. Bach, just beginning a tour of his former field of service, had come on the same ship from New York. All except Bach faced the problem of visa difficulties for entry into Venezuela.

The board of directors had in January 1931 accepted the recommendation of missionaries George Holmberg and John Swanson that a work be started in the islands. Now it was up to the small group to view the situation and seek the Lord's guidance. Out of that meeting came the decision to launch the work as an extension of the Venezuela-Colombia mission. The Holmbergs would serve in Aruba until a visa for Venezuela became available; Mr. and Mrs. Elmer Paulson would be the first resident S.A.M. missionaries in Curaçao. This step initiated a ministry that has grown and expanded over the years.

Reporting in 1932 on their first year of work on Curaçao, the

Paulsons mentioned two Sunday schools with a total of sixty children. Regular evangelism in their own living quarters sparked growth in interest and response. The Paulsons undertook to learn the Papiamento language. They soon discovered that there was little written material to support their study or to share with the people. General education was in Dutch but the heart language was, of course, Papiamento. The Paulsons set about to supply some of the lack by translating tracts from English.

A Papiamento version of the New Testament existed, but it clearly needed revision. Where a language has an oral and not a written base, it lacks stability and can go through changes quite quickly. Without a literature it tends to develop different idioms and meanings in different localities. Several years later a revision of the Gospel of John was completed which the American Bible Society agreed to publish.

The Paulsons found no hymnal in the common language. They selected hymns which those familiar with Spanish and English were using and, with the help of local Christians, prepared Papiamento translations. These translations formed the heart of a hymnbook published somewhat later. By early 1935 Elmer Paulson was able to report the first group meeting of believers for communion. "It was a precious service and it seems that the blessings the Lord shed upon us at that service linger with us."[1]

When the Paulsons went on furlough in 1936, they were followed in the Curaçao ministry by Mr. and Mrs. George C. Barville, who transferred from Venezuela. Edith Barville had served in Venezuela from 1923. George was a British businessman who spent a number of years working for an oil company. When he married Edith he joined the mission and they continued on in the Spanish work. In Curaçao they could minister to many in either Spanish or English.

The Holmbergs were able to enter Venezuela again but left behind them in Aruba both good will and some lasting fruit. Richard and Lillian Ekstedt joined the Barvilles in Curaçao in 1940 and with some interruptions continued in that work until 1962. One of those interruptions was for Richard to serve as editor of *The Missionary Broadcaster* during a period of family medical needs.

Aruba

Paul and Charlotte Sheetz had hoped to serve in India, but when passport and travel restrictions during World War II closed that door they responded to the call to Curaçao, arriving in 1943. After language study and a period of work there they moved to the smaller island of Aruba. Their first contacts were among those who had been in the Dutch Protestant Church. When asked why they would do missionary work in a place where there was already a Protestant church, Paul had an answer which was later included in a letter printed in the mission magazine.

> Let me remind you that the existence of a church does not always constitute a gospel witness, and it is just as possible that those who call themselves Protestant are as ignorant of the way of salvation as Catholics or any other religious group. We must give the gospel to those who have never heard, whether they have been baptized Catholic, Protestant, or not at all. We cannot truly consider this island evangelized until a Holy Spirit empowered witness of the gospel has been established in the language of the people.[2]

After a year and half Paul and Charlotte Sheetz could look at the ministry the Lord had given them and rejoice in what He had done in Aruba. Their activities had included home visits, Bible classes, preaching and—most of all—use of the printed page. Beginning in November 1945 they published a monthly magazine in Papiamento. They also had written, translated, printed or mimeographed, and distributed thousands of tracts and sold many New Testaments and gospel portions. This literature was well received, and a group of fifteen or twenty had openly confessed the Lord and were standing by the missionaries in the work.

Portugal

Missionaries working in Swaziland and the Union of South Africa were much aware of a large territory on their borders which generally went by the name of Portuguese East Africa but was also known by an older name, Mozambique. They knew of work carried on there by missionaries of the Nazarene Church and the South Africa General Mission but were also aware of large areas with little or no gospel witness. When Bach visited Africa in 1933 that concern crystallized into a unanimous recommendation to the board of directors that missionaries be sought for Portuguese East Africa. It is interesting to note that the decision prayerfully made by a group of concerned missionaries actually led to the opening of *two* fields—Portugal and Southern Rhodesia.

It took several years after the board's approval before candidates offered themselves for this new field. Miss Mary Maluske and Mr. and Mrs. Magnus Foreid were among the first to be appointed to Portuguese East Africa. Mr. Rudolph Danielson, engaged to Miss Maluske, was next. Because Portugal required that those applying for entry into one of its colonies should first study the language in Portugal, these four proceeded to do that, Mary and the Foreids in 1936 and Rudy in 1937. After studying Portuguese Rudy and Mary, now married, went on to Swaziland to probe for an entry into the field of their appointment. The Foreids stayed in Portugal for more study and with the hope of seeing the door open to Mozambique.

As Magnus and Clara Foreid became more fluent in Portuguese, they gained greater knowledge of the history of this extensive colonial power. One of its early seafaring adventurers, Vasco da Gama, had found the way around the southern tip of Africa to reach India. In time, Portugal had colonies as scattered as Macao on the coast of China, Goa in India, Timor in the East Indies, Mozambique and Angola in Africa, and Brazil in South America. By 1936 Portugal was no longer an empire but a republic and its population was only about seven million. Wealthy property owners were in the minority but held economic power over the larger number of poorly educated and generally poor people. Roman Catholicism was the religion most professed, but for many it was just a form and without real significance in their lives. Foreid saw them as needy people and wondered if those in Mozambique he hoped to reach in the future could be more needy than these right at his door.

Even though continuing to pray about Africa, the Foreids' thoughts turned more and more to the unevangelized towns around them, such as Alges and Queluz. Here were spiritually needy people, some perhaps even hungering for the gospel message. The best thing to do was to launch out. This they did, as their letter of late September 1939 to *The Missionary Broadcaster* reveals:

> In the meantime God has opened for us a door of service here in poor, needy Portugal. Where he leads, we follow. At times our disappointments are God's appointments. Last August we started meetings in our home in Alges with a group of over twenty people. Our home was too small so we were fortunate in renting a hall with two rooms at one side which can be used for children's classes. We are calling the new work the "Evangelical Mission of Alges." We have bought sixty chairs and rented a piano. Our first meeting was September 21 and we had the honor of having Rev. Eduardo Moreira as the first speaker. We also opened a Sunday School with a fine group of children. There is no other evangelical work in Alges. We are also interested in starting a new work in a place called Sintra about fourteen miles from Alges.[3]

By late October the Foreids were able to report a wonderful meeting with about 120 people in attendance.

> The need in Portugal is great and the workers so few. There are whole cities without the gospel. How we wish there were other S.A.M. missionaries here![4]

During the year 1940 the Alges work progressed well. Twenty-seven believers took the step of confessing Christ in baptism before their families and friends. A letter from a missionary in Mozambique was especially heartening, reporting that two of the Alges Sunday school boys who were now in the colony with their parents were continuing their Christian walk.

As the Foreids worked in Portugal they were very conscious of the war raging in western Europe. France had fallen and Great Britain was being fiercely attacked by Hitler's bombers. The Foreids' native country of Norway had been invaded and occupied. By late 1942 they had been in Portugal six years and were advised by the American Consul that they should return to the United States to protect their standing as naturalized citizens. When they left Portugal they were sure they would not return until the war was over, but they purposed in their hearts to return—if the S.A.M. board of directors would look favorably on a recommendation they were preparing to put before the men.

When the board members met on November 17, 1942, they welcomed Magnus and Clara Foreid to the meeting and listened to their earnest plea that Portugal be considered the seventh field of the mission and that recruits be sent forth. The missionaries presented convincing information about the people and their need and shared written appeals from people who knew the situation firsthand. Later, the secretary recorded the following minute:

> After much consideration and prayer, the brethren felt led of God to make Portugal a permanent field of the S.A.M., to support the work now established and further develop the work as soon as possible after the present war is over and peace has come.[5]

In the spring of 1946, after spending several years in a pastorate in Pennsylvania and also trying to inform churches that Portugal was indeed a needy mission field, the Foreids returned to the land of their calling. They wrote back to the mission office that they found the work encouraging in both Alges and Queluz.

Thus, by God's sovereign leading, the seventh field of the mission was opened, the first since 1906 that had not been an expansion from an existing S.A.M. work.

Southern Rhodesia

Meanwhile, back in Swaziland, the evidently God-directed decision of the 1933 annual conference was about to produce another development. The burden for Portuguese East Africa remained heavy. With field conference permission, Rudy and Mary Danielson accepted an invitation to work for a year at Mavuradonha with the Zambezi Mission, which was operating in the northeastern section of Southern Rhodesia bordering Portuguese East Africa. The Africa field made an official decision to station missionaries in this area and sent the field chairman, Arthur Jensen, to plan the new advance together with those assigned.

Orval and Helen Dunkeld, newly commissioned, had arrived in Swaziland with a strong desire to serve in a pioneer advance. They were assigned to join the Danielsons in the new undertaking.

While the missionaries' aim was to work as close to the border of Portuguese East Africa as possible, it was necessary to find a suitable and yet needy, unreached area. Southern Rhodesia was a colony of the British Empire with a small population of colonists engaged in developing its fertile farming land and exploiting its mineral wealth. Two principal African groups made up the bulk of the African population, the N'debele in the south and the Shona in the north. Several missions were at work with both of these groups. From the information they supplied, there was one large area with no gospel witness and that was the extensive Zambezi Valley.

Much of Southern Rhodesia was high plateau which, at a point approaching the valley, descended sharply about 3,000 feet over what was called the Escarpment. Here lay the broad Zambezi Valley, some sixty miles across, with the Zambezi River flowing out toward Portuguese East Africa and the sea. The principal reason it was still unreached by missionaries was its unhealthful climate—tropical, malarial, and plagued by the tsetse fly carrier of sleeping sickness. Those who pointed out this area did so with mixed admiration and apprehension—admiration for the willingness of the new missionaries to select a district which all white people carefully avoided, and apprehension about their welfare.

In May 1942—the relatively cool season—Rudy and Orval headed down into the valley in an old Ford and a fully loaded one-ton Chevrolet truck to begin building a mission station close to the Msengedzi River. It was here they found people more in abundance. They were deeply impressed by the primitive living, unhealthful conditions, and the superstition of the Shona people, and more assured than ever that it was from among these people they should seek to call out followers for the Lord Jesus Christ. As they built the first small house of pole and mud they had opportunity to tell the Africans why they were there—to bring them the good news of a loving God in heaven who cares for them enough to forgive their sins and make them His children through faith in His crucified Son. They found that the early morning hours before the people went to their fields was the best time to gather them together for simple services.

As soon as the first thatched hut was completed, Mary Danielson and year-old Muriel joined them. When a second, somewhat more substantial, hut was completed, Helen Dunkeld and boys, Fred and Dick, joined them. With the coming of the rains life became much more difficult. Their garden—on which they placed much hope—was flooded out. Then as a reminder of the nature of the territory they were in, a leopard got into their goat pen and killed all the animals they were depending on for their milk supply.

More difficulties lay ahead. Malaria felled most of the little group. Rudy, who was quite run down, was hardest hit, and to save his life they all made the exhausting trip to Mavuradonha for cooler weather and a more healthful climate. With medical care and rest came revived strength and once again the little group returned to the valley.

Now they could begin getting out among the people and found their message well received by many. They continued the practice of holding early morning services and as interest grew they began services on Sunday.

As hot and humid weather returned, Rudy's strength began to wane. A hard trip into Portuguese East Africa was particularly taxing and his condition worsened. The only hope was to take him out to the nearest hospital at Bindura, 160 miles away. The trip over the barely passable roads was made at night. After five fever-ridden weeks—even with the best doctors and nurses could do—Rudy Danielson slipped away into the presence of the Lord, on Thanksgiving Day, November 25, 1943. So even in the mid-twentieth century this new field had to face the same cost in missionary life that was true in the earlier years of the mission's history in China, Japan, Swaziland, northeast India, and Mongolia. The bereaved wife and daughter returned to North America on an overdue furlough but not to turn away from a commission by the Lord to a lifetime of service.

Orval and Helen Dunkeld remained in the pioneer work until a furlough was possible after World War II ended. Before they left they were able to welcome new recruits—Miss Eunice Ott, in January 1945, and Norman and Thelma Everswick in 1946. A field had been found, the soil broken up to a certain extent, some seed sown, and the first fruits of a harvest brought in.

Northern India—Again

In late 1945 and early 1946, the board of directors decided to enter two new areas, the first in the Northwest Frontier Province of India in what later became Pakistan, and the second in north India along the Tibet-Nepal border. It is interesting to note the proximity of these new fields to the areas Franson had pointed out and where a number of the early missionaries had worked.

With the actual entry into these areas not taking place until Bach's successor was in office, the story will be picked up in later chapters. What was particularly a cause for thanksgiving was that young men and women were coming forward with very deep interest in the work of missions and with a dedication that gave assurance that the Lord was still at work calling out laborers for His harvest fields.

RUNNING THE RACE WELL

World-wide Doctrinal Drift

Evangelical strength in North America reached a low point in the 1920s and 1930s—at least in the general perception of its influence as compared to the rising tide of liberalism. Some of the mainline denominations were having serious internal struggles and it seemed that the battle was being won by those who questioned or denied outright the inspiration, reliability, and authority of the Bible. The teaching of the deity of Jesus Christ was being directly challenged, while belief in the uniqueness and exclusiveness of salvation through Jesus Christ was termed intolerant and outdated. Heathen religions were given credence as alternative ways to God. Arthur P. Johnston, commenting on the background of this particular period, speaks of the theological uncertainty:

> Stephen Neill observes that "the liberal was not by any means sure that Jesus Christ was the *last* Word of God to man." The result was that uncertainty began to replace the authoritative Bible and its evangelistic message. Troeltsch went even further—to suggest that among religions, Christianity should be considered the highest up to the present time.[1]

When T. J. Bach was laying the foundations of the evangelical witness in Western Venezuela, an area in total spiritual darkness in spite of—or because of—the Catholic Church, he was shocked to read that the great World Missionary Conference of 1910 in Edinburgh, Scotland, had refused to consider either Europe or Latin America as mission fields. In the view of most participants, the existence of the Roman Catholic Church on those continents and the universality of its acceptance there made evangelical mission activity not only unnecessary, but actually offensive. This opened Bach's eyes to the drift in Protestantism. While not a fighter against others, Bach was determined to record his views and what he sincerely believed should be the position of the mission.

A Biblical Position

A burning issue surfaced in late 1932 on which Bach focused his attention. This was the *Laymen's Foreign Missions Inquiry Report* published in a book of fourteen chapters and given wide publicity in both religious and secular press. The thirty-five laymen who made the inquiry were from seven Protestant denominations. Their report called for syncretism—a standing upon the common ground of all religion. It recommended a turning away from emphasis on the lostness of men to a happier conception of destiny. It wanted a shift of concern from other-worldly issues to problems of sin and suffering in the present life.

Bach's response:

> As Christians who believe in an open Bible and a living Christ, we do not turn to such a group concerning the Christian missionary program. No, we turn to the Word of God which is clear in stating WHO shall carry on the work of missions—HOW, WHERE, and WHEN it shall be done.... The Report is a betrayal of the missionaries, their supporters, and the Church of Christ. The Commission has betrayed the heathen who need the gospel. It has betrayed the Word of God and our Lord and Saviour. The Commission's investigation and report will prove that we are at a crossroad in missionary work within Protestant missions.[2]

No Room for Syncretism

As time went by there was further drift and decline in much of the older denominational mission work and at the same time a surge in growth in evangelical response. The subject was on Bach's mind as he prepared his annual report for 1936.

> Great efforts are being made today, not only in the non-Christian lands, but also here at home by men and women who once were true to the gospel, to compare Christ with Buddha, Confucius, Mohammed, and Zoroaster. We desire to have nothing to do with that kind of comparison. We not only accept the teaching of the New Testament and claims of Christ, but we will defend them and commend them. Christ shall be first or not at all. We find no second place given to Christ in the Bible and we do not want to give Him second place in our lives or in our missionary message.[3]

A Seasoned Board

While it is the responsibility of the annual meeting of the mission to elect members to the board of directors, the general practice is that the board itself fills vacancies that occur between annual meetings. The recommendation of the general director bears great weight. It is interesting to note the men invited to join the board during Bach's tenure. One of the earliest to become a member after Bach was installed was Carl A. Gundersen, earlier mentioned for his cooperation with Bach in the development of the Franson-Risberg Memorial Building. Gundersen's participation continued from 1929 until his death in 1964. For the last eleven years of his life he served as chairman of the board.

The man whose stationery firm sold supplies to the mission received his first strong missions impulse when he read a book on the life of Franson, given him by Bach. Noting the keen interest of Charles E. Bodeen, Bach invited him to consider board membership. His association, which began in 1930, continued until 1969. For twenty-five years he was treasurer and chairman of the finance committee.

A pastor-evangelist-attorney by the name of David H. Johnson was the next one to be invited onto the board in 1931. Did the men at that time have any thought of the vital role he would have in the later development and expansion of the mission? The pastor of the large Evangelical Free Church in Rockford, Illinois, the Rev. Elmer Johnson, was elected a member that same year.

After the death of C. T. Dyrness, pastor Morris Johnson of the Gospel Tabernacle of Racine, Wisconsin, was chosen to fill the vacancy. Dr. Gustav Edwards, professor of the Free Church Bible Institute, former Swedish Alliance missionary to China, and a board member since 1915, became chairman. The Rev. Otto Hogfeldt, editor of the *Mission Friend*, served as vice chairman. Upon the death, in 1939, of businessman John Olson, Dr. Enock C. Dyrness, registrar of Wheaton College, was appointed and served until 1979, for most of the time as secretary of the board and chairman of its candidate committee. Two more Christian leaders served as board members during that period, Dr. Harold Lundquist, dean of Moody Bible Institute, and Dr. Charles Porter, associate pastor of the Moody Memorial Church.

During those years the number of board members was limited to nine and it was required that they live in the greater Chicago area to be readily available for the monthly meetings. Because of the long periods of service, their three-year terms being renewed again and again, these men gained intimate knowledge of the mission family and the work.

Workers Together

Bach's ministry in the churches was very well received and this necessitated a great deal of travel from coast to coast. Train travel was slow and the need for economy dictated that as many responses to invitations as possible should be grouped together. The result was long absences from the office. To keep the work flowing smoothly, regular and reliable help was critical. Miss Siri Malmstrom, who had come to the office in December 1920, continued as secretary during the various changes and served well as the general director's secretary—beyond the terms of Bach and his successor and until shortly before her death December 16, 1970.

When the Franson-Risberg Memorial Building was completed there was a growing load of work, so the board invited furloughed China missionary Roy H. Brehm to help. In January 1931, the board appointed him assistant to the general director, a position he held until November 1938.

For about two years after Brehm's resignation, the position of assistant to the general director remained vacant, but Bach kept thinking of one with whom he had worked in Maracaibo and prayed about calling him to the work. John F. Swanson had responded to the need of the Maracaibo print shop in 1922. Having worked in the building trades at home in Tacoma, Washington, he was a practical and useful man. John had met and married Grace Jacobson in Venezuela. In his early years in Maracaibo, he went into the office equipment and supply business to provide support for his missionary activities and as a means of contacting business people with the gospel. Later he was asked to begin the Maracaibo Bible Institute and served as its administrator. His work with the periodical *La Estrella de la Mañana* gave him publication and editorial experience. Furlough Bible study provided further preparation.

Sensing that the call, in 1941, from the board of directors was in the will of the Lord, John and Grace Swanson joined the home staff where John ably and conscientiously served as assistant to the general director until Mr. Bach retired. He was then given a new assignment, a channel through which his considerable gifts would continue to be used in the work of the mission for the next sixteen years.

Golden Jubilee

The period when Bach was without an appointed assistant was made extra busy because the year 1940 was observed as the mission's Golden Jubilee—its fiftieth anniversary. A series of anniversary conferences was planned for churches across the country. The mission already had the help of the Rev. M. D. Christensen of the South Africa field in the conference ministry. His strong Bible teaching messages were greatly used to bring the work of missions before God's people. The counsel he gave to one young missionary was: "Speak to the conscience." That was what Christensen did in the power of the Holy Spirit.

Another missionary on furlough was also brought into the anniversary services—the Rev. William Englund of China. He not only had gifts of Bible exposition but could also draw on a fruitful revival meeting experience in China to present the mission field to the Lord's people. Missionary Earl Peterson, also of China, rendered valuable service on the conference circuit during part of the anniversary year.

During the jubilee year the statistical reports revealed the fruit of much of the work since its inception in 1891. There were 146 missionaries working in 52 central stations. An additional 27 were on furlough and 52 had been retired or were detained at home. There were 181 organized churches with 16,655 communicants. In the year 1939, 1,057 new believers were baptized. How many members had been in the churches and had gone on to their eternal reward was not reported.[4]

Grauer, an Early Link

After fifty years of S.A.M. history there was a thinning of the ranks of pioneers and thus fewer links with the founder. One long-standing link was Dr. O. C. Grauer, who had been invited to join the work in 1894 as auditor and then as board member. While Franson was still on his second world tour he wrote to Grauer expressing the hope that he could produce a paper or magazine to serve as a link between the missionaries and the churches and individuals who backed them in prayer and support. It took quite a number of years before this busy seminary professor felt he could give the time needed for such a task. When he did begin, he produced *The Missionary Broadcaster,* a quarterly magazine which had its first issue at the beginning of 1925. The present-day researcher of the mission's history finds its volumes a rich and interesting source of facts and inspiration through the missionary letters which were its main format.

In his annual report for 1944, Bach included the following paragraph about Grauer:

> Our beloved Dr. O. C. Grauer, who for fifty years rendered untold service to the Scandinavian Alliance Mission, departed to be with the Lord, August 26, 1944, from his home in Oak Park, Illinois. After Dr. Grauer's departure, brother J. F. Swanson was asked to assume the principal responsibility for editing *The Missionary Broadcaster* in addition to his many other duties in the office.[5]

Growth in Western Canada

Until the early 1940s there had been no appointment of a missionary with Canadian citizenship who was also resident in and supported from Canada. Four or five Canadians who were resident in the United States or whose supporters were in the U.S. were serving with the mission. With the onset of World War II, Canada, as a member of the British Empire, found it necessary to strictly control foreign exchange. Money could not be remitted to the United States and most other countries except by a licensing arrangement. Remittances to sterling block countries—those related to the British Empire—were permissible for Canadian organizations. The Scandinavian Alliance Mission did not qualify for such permission as it legally did not exist in Canada.

The Peoples Church in Toronto, of which Dr. Oswald J. Smith was pastor, offered to help. Peoples Church not only took on support of several Canadian missionaries but also offered to send the support direct to India and South Africa, which were in the sterling block. So for the time being the remittance problem was solved.

There was at the same time a growing interest in the foreign missionary cause by Canadians. One result was that general director Bach began to receive invitations to speak in Canada, particularly at certain Bible schools. Sensing an open door of interest and knowing his own limitations of time, Bach invited Stuart J. Gunzel, Mongolia missionary on furlough, to take meetings in western Canada. Gunzel laid the foundation for the mission's ministry in that region and later, after he and Mrs. Gunzel had spent a further term of service on behalf of the Mongols, accepted an appointment to serve as Western Canada Representative, a ministry that extended over thirty years.

The need for a home base in Canada soon became apparent. With the encouragement of Mr. S. Whittaker and the Rev. Henry Hildebrand, who were associated with the Briercrest Bible Institute in Briercrest, Saskatchewan, a home was located in that town and Arthur and Helen Dalke were asked to set up a Canadian center.

Mr. Bach and Mr. Gundersen visited Briercrest in late 1945 and came back with a recommendation that steps be taken "to effect an incorporation in Canada in order to enable us to hold property in that country."[6]

A Saskatchewan non-profit society was organized with the

assistance of attorney O. D. Hill, who was also asked to become a member of the board of trustees. The following year the center was moved to the rail junction city of Moose Jaw for greater convenience in travel. In the meantime, the Canadian response in candidates was on the increase, particularly from the western provinces.

Getting Ready for Retirement

The men of the board of directors, concerned about Bach's high blood pressure and uncertain heart condition, often urged him to secure more help and lighten his load—counsel which was not easy for him to follow with the growing interest in the mission. With the end of the war in August 1945 came a surge in activity. One measure of the growth was the need to double the office space, which was accomplished by taking over one of the residence apartments. But to find someone to share the workload was not easy. For the public ministry, one would be needed who had special gifts for such work.

To complicate the problem, M. D. Christensen, mission representative, had been asked to take an interim pastorate while board member David H. Johnson was serving in the military as chaplain. When Johnson was released to return to his church, Christensen was then drafted to return to South Africa to fill an urgent leadership need.

Several board members had remembered and were impressed by the public ministry gifts of first-term India missionary Don W. Hillis. For a year of his furlough he had been teaching at the Bible Institute of Los Angeles. Under the guidance of the Lord, Don and Doris Hillis were invited to move to Chicago and join the staff. Hillis was able to share the load of public ministry and was a welcome conference speaker.

Bach had informed the board and the annual meeting as early as May 1944 that he intended to retire from the position of general director in May 1946:

> If Christ tarries and I live, within two years I will have reached the age of sixty-five years. It is my desire then to be released from my present position in my relationship to the Scandinavian

Alliance Mission. I express this desire under the firm conviction that it will be for the best interests of the mission which I love so dearly and for the greatest glory of our Lord and Saviour. I am confident that you will be united with me in praying that among you may be found a man of God who will take the mantle and carry the torch higher and farther.[7]

Restructuring

When the board members realized that Bach really meant to retire they began to seek the Lord's will concerning a successor. In their February 1946 meeting they took formal action to approve Bach's retirement and voted him the title of general director emeritus. At the same meeting they asked Don Hillis to become acting general director for one year and appointed John F. Swanson associate general director and editor of *The Missionary Broadcaster*. However, at the next meeting Hillis presented a letter asking the board to reconsider its action; then the following month he and his wife requested recommissioning to India.

The heavy load of headquarters administration remained a problem as it was left primarily for Swanson to bear. As early as August 1945 when Frances and I arrived on furlough from China, Swanson had asked if I would not consider joining the office staff, but with plans in mind for return to China, we quickly declined that invitation. In March 1946, with the office load becoming far too heavy, Swanson received the board's approval to draft me for a three-month period, perhaps feeling that my earlier experience in the business world and several years of China field administrative work might have prepared me to be helpful. That three-month assignment was accepted, as were several extensions of the time while we continued to prepare to return to China.

Bach was still very concerned that a successor soon be found so the mission would not have a period without a leader. One day he approached board member David H. Johnson with the question: "What would brother Johnson say, if the board should ask him to become general director?"

"Why don't you ask him?" Johnson replied.[8]

This exchange showed the characteristics of the two men. One was indirect and yet effective as a leader. The other was direct and forthright and yet equally effective in his leadership.

David H. Johnson was ready for a new and wider open door in the Lord's service, so when the board extended a unanimous call at its March 3, 1946, meeting for him to become general director, he was immediately responsive to it. At the meeting of April 30 he formally accepted the call. With a background quite different from that of T. J. Bach, he nevertheless brought to the mission the gifts and dedication that were needed for the postwar period of widening opportunity to reach the world for Christ.

19

A VIEW FROM THE MOUNTAIN

Writing a historical sketch has some similarities to climbing a mountain. Pressing forward, we see how much of the steep grade lies ahead and wonder if we will find the right pathway to take us to the peak.

But then we stop to look back on the way we have come. We note the breath-taking view and discover that the terrain through which we have labored becomes more understandable. Climbing through a steep mountain valley on the way up we were fascinated by the immediate sights—to the left some awesome cliffs and a majestic tumbling waterfall, to the right some tree shade inviting us to sit and rest.

At times the experience was not that pleasant. Down in a deep valley we lost sight of the height to which we had climbed and even, looking back, could not see beyond the valley rim. But then farther on a promontory allowed us a more studied look back. The ridges and valleys began to form a pattern. We could now see clearly the plain below where our climb began. We also discovered, to our chagrin, that some of the pathway we chose caused us more effort than necessary because in our lack of experience we took what seemed the easiest way, only to find grave difficulties farther up. Looking back from the promontory, we were happy we had come as far as we had. Lessons were learned that would help us all along the way to the heights above.

Similarly, in this historical sketch we are at a level which suggests that a good look back over the ground covered might help us to a better understanding of the way ahead.

A Reassuring Review

The first fifty-six years of the history of the Scandinavian Alliance Mission can be divided into three roughly equal periods:

1. The time of Fredrik Franson's leadership—18 years.

2. The period without a general director (except for J. H. Hedstrom's brief administration)—20 years.

3. The administration of T. J. Bach—18 years.

The Missionary Force

During the first period there was initial, rapid growth of the missionary force followed by constant replacement which kept the missionary staff at a level of about one hundred. During the second period there were sufficient replacements and new growth to increase the number about twenty-five percent. The third period saw a doubling of the number to a total of 228.

Franson was used by the Lord to call out a large number of workers. Though very different in his call for workers, Bach was equally used to lay the missionary opportunities before prospective missionaries and so the numbers increased at a satisfactory pace.

What is surprising is that there was no net loss of personnel— and actually a small increase—during the second period when the mission had no visible or stable leadership. Two factors are hinted at as having been the means of keeping missions before prospects: the publishing of missionary letters by the Swedish and Norwegian periodicals, and the missionaries' diligence in writing and making personal contacts.

In the number of missionaries at work over the years, China had by far the most until the late 1930s, followed by Africa, Latin America, and India. Japan had few missionaries after the first decade and Mongolia fared the worst. Portugal barely had a start by the end of the Bach administration.

The Message Emphasized

Franson's message stressed Christ's imminent return, and thus the urgency for sinners to receive Christ and for the Lord's people to hasten out with the message of salvation. Also paramount was the need for believers to live in constant, conscious, communion with Christ. The Franson emphasis greatly influenced all who were sent out by him and continued to characterize the message of Bach and the missionaries in general. Bach also dwelt much on the relationships which should exist between Christians, both missionary and national, particularly those who were working together.

The Objective—Churches

Franson's strong teaching on the church in his pre-foreign missions ministry is not spelled out as strongly in his written communications during his years as mission director, but the evidence of his convictions is seen in what the missionaries did. They established churches in the New Testament pattern. Bach referred to the church often but not so much to its formation or polity as to its spiritual progress. Bach had devoted twenty years to planting the church in Maracaibo and environs; his work undoubtedly had a strong influence in Venezuela and elsewhere.

The Methods Employed

Itineration characterized the early years of the work in China. This method included personal conversations, the selling of Scripture portions, and public preaching when there was opportunity. This, after all, was the agreement with Hudson Taylor, who had a program to try to reach every person in China in three years. At first the China missionaries aimed to reach new towns, but once having gained entry and not being driven out, they combined home visits with preaching in market places and chapels. The shift was to a more settled approach that gave repeated opportunities to proclaim the message. An example was the opium refuges established where the addicts could be counseled, prayed with, preached to, and helped over a period of months. Schools for children were started. Even with a great deal of illiteracy, gospel literature was produced and distributed. Famine relief brought humanitarian aid and helped commend the gospel to suffering people.

In Africa, the main method was preaching to family groups in the kraals, although personal contact was also effective, as in the ministry of Malla Moe.

Northeast India saw a great deal of personal work, largely due to the scattered population. Surprising as it was because of widespread illiteracy, the written word was used effectively. Schools for children were another effective means. In western India among the Bhils, village itineration featured much public proclamation. Schools and particularly hostels for children were good means for winning them.

In Japan, it was the group proclamation, even when numbers were few, that seemed the most fruitful method of evangelism.

Mongolia offered little opportunity for public preaching but allowed many personal conversations about Christ. Medical help provided listeners, even among an extremely resistant people.

Venezuela and Colombia, with less personal resistance but more outright opposition, responded initially to the printed message through Scripture portions, books, magazines, and tracts. Sunday schools led to the formation of congregations and organized churches. Preaching in the church buildings drew many, even to just listen through the open windows.

Bible study groups, such as have become common in recent years, were not reported as a frequently used method of ministry in any of the countries. Using tents for evangelistic meetings was common mostly in China, where it was a fruitful method of making the multitudes of people aware of the gospel message, as was the later use of amplifiers.

Churches were formed most rapidly in China, Africa, Latin America, and Japan, but not all were formally organized with responsible elders and deacons in the New Testament pattern. That came later, as did the sense of oneness with other congregations. Association in a church fellowship must have been implied in Japan through the close relationship with the mission. A church association became a reality in Venezuela and Colombia before the work was twenty years old. In China it was almost forty years before taking formal shape. Until the church ministries were strong and conscious of one another, the work apparently centered around the missionary.

Self-support, self-government, and self-propagation progressed most rapidly in Latin America. In China full self-support was slower—until forced by the Lord's special intervention through economic conditions which eliminated the supply of foreign funds. By 1946, the churches in China and Latin America were bearing full responsibility for their own ministries, while still receiving cooperation and ministry help from the missionaries. The same was true in Japan, although the serious war situation temporarily impoverished the church.

The churches in Africa had progressed quite well in propagating the message, but more on the responsibility of the mission than on their own. The African pastors and evangelists supported themselves in part from their own land but monetary support for church ministries was difficult.

In the number of communicants, China was first, Africa second, followed in order by Latin America, Japan, and India, with Portugal showing a good start. The number in Mongolia was not reported. The total number of baptized members on all the fields exceeded 20,000 by 1946.

Bach—on the Church

Research did not reveal much that Bach had written about the establishment of churches on the mission field, but constant references seemed to take for granted that missionaries understood that planting churches and nurturing believers was the scriptural pattern for the follow-up of evangelism, which he constantly stressed. Bach's only discovered treatment of this vital subject was in his first annual report of March 31, 1929. Less than a year after he was installed as general director, he wrote:

> As missionaries and as a missionary organization we must be willing and able to face the continual growing and changing conditions on the fields of the mission. There is the work of leading the national to Christ, there is also the work of directing him in the service for Christ, and sooner or later there is the work in cooperation with the national Christian. We recognize that to every nation or people to whom the gospel is given there is also given the duty of self-supporting, the right of self-governing, and

the privilege of self-propagating churches.

Throughout the history of our mission it has principally been the work of our missionaries to establish churches, but today, on most of the fields at many of the stations, there must be a gradual transfer of oversight and leadership of the national church from the missionaries to the national Christian leaders. Have we the vision and the grace of God to do it in the right time and in the right spirit? Such steps involve very serious problems for the missionaries as well as for the national Christian Church. There must be Christian love and willingness on both sides to sacrifice, if it shall be accomplished.

Wherever our missionaries are thus able to transfer their leadership in the work to the national Christians, there they are able to answer God's call to go forth and take up new work for Christ in the "regions beyond." In order to enter into new fields, where millions live without Christ, there must be new manifestation of the spirit of love and sacrifice for Christ, not only on the part of national Christians and missionaries, but also of the supporters.

As followers of Christ we are again asked to face the question: Will we do aggressive evangelistic work in the more needy and unevangelized fields? If Christ is going to use us to have a share in the unfinished task of missions, we will be called on to manifest even more self-denial in service and more humility in spirit than ever before.[1]

There is a great deal of truth and wisdom in those short paragraphs.

The Training of Workers

While informal training took place at the various mission stations, the establishment of training institutions was delayed until there were Christians who wanted formal training and places in the churches where their service could be used effectively. China opened its seminary (on a Bible institute level) in 1907 with financial help from Fredrik Franson. Japan sent its trainees to existing evangelical schools, as did India. Africa began its Bible training ministry in 1921; Venezuela in 1931. Many of the leading national pastors had training at these early schools—an outstanding example is the Rev. Asdrúbal Ríos of Venezuela.

Part of the Cost

Research for a historical sketch such as this must cover a great deal of material, yet can draw on only a small percentage. But the subjective impression is that the first fifty-six years of history entailed a great deal of sacrifice. There were at least fifteen martyrs and scores who died before their time from disease and other rigors of the way, not to speak of the many children laid in the grave. The impression is that great victories were won for the Savior, and this brings to mind the word in Revelation 12:11 about victory: "They overcame him [the accuser of the brethren] by the blood of the Lamb, and by the word of their testimony; they did not love their lives so much as to shrink from death" (NIV).

20

NEW DIRECTOR,
NEW OPPORTUNITIES

It was with a sense of expectation that missionaries, candidates, board members, and supporters of the S.A.M. gathered in Brooklyn, New York, in early May 1946 for the first annual conference after the ending of World War II. Eight years of terrible warfare—including the earlier invasion of China—had devastated whole countries, uprooted millions of people, caused untold suffering and loss, and turned people from many of their normal pursuits of life.

Time to Press Forward

For those assembled, the years of warfare had affected the concern that was uppermost in their minds—missions. Now, though problems for many nations were still extremely serious, means of travel were limited, and passports and visas were difficult to obtain, it seemed to the mission family that it was time to press forward. The fields were indeed white unto harvest and reapers must be sent out to gather precious souls for the Savior. Added to the sense of expectation was the appointment of a successor to the much-loved and respected T. J. Bach.

General Director Installed

The formal installation of David H. Johnson as the fourth general director took place May 3, 1946, at the conference. There was greater than usual attendance of furloughed missionaries and candidates, all greatly interested in meeting their new leader. Johnson was not yet personally known to many, although most knew his name as a member of the mission's board of directors for sixteen years and knew also that he had recently returned to his Chicago pastorate after almost two years of overseas service as a chaplain in the military.

The new general director's wife, Edna, was not able to attend the installation due to poor health. In fact, Mrs. Johnson, who had often traveled with her husband as a soloist in his earlier years of evangelism, was able to only rarely accompany him in local ministry for TEAM and never on overseas trips. Those of us who knew her well cherished her friendship and recognized her ministry of intercession for the work of her husband and the mission.

Johnson's Background Ministry

Those who had been with the mission for a number of years recalled that Johnson had spent about ten years as a gifted evangelist in the eastern and central states among the churches of the Evangelical Covenant denomination, and knew that he now was pastor of the Lake View Mission Covenant Church of Chicago. Some knew more about his background as an attorney who had felt a strong call from the Lord to prepare himself for full-time Christian work and had completed both Moody Bible Institute and North Park Seminary. It was about 1926, at the age of 33, that he turned from a promising career in law (he had been a top student at the Kent College of Law in Chicago) and set out to win men and women and boys and girls for Christ.

As a chaplain on a U.S. Army hospital ship bringing wounded men home from southern Europe, Johnson's zeal for souls led him to diligently share the gospel message with every man on board ship through services over the public address system, personal conversations, and the printed page. To wounded men apprehensive of their future he held out the promise of both an earthly life made much better and a blessed eternity through a personal relationship with Christ.

Fields Reopening

At this 1946 conference the three fields from which S.A.M. missionaries had been evacuated due to the war came in for special attention. Mongolia was again beckoning for Stuart and Margaret Gunzel. They had the promise of being joined by Edvard and Jenny

Torjesen and Angeline Bernklau. The three missionaries in China—Marie Wistrand, Didrik Kilen, and Elmer Peterson—who were overdue for furlough, had recently been joined by Oscar Beckon and Reuben Gustafson. The missionaries who had been evacuated from that war-torn country and an encouraging number of appointees were eager to go forward. Japan, for which missionary concern had been seriously lacking for many years, was now a special center of interest. General Douglas MacArthur, supreme commander of the U.S. occupation forces, had issued a call to American churches for 1,500 missionaries. The conference was challenged to pray for twenty-five new workers for the S.A.M.

Learning and Leading

As Johnson became fully involved in the duties of his office he was concerned about getting to know the names of the 228 active missionaries. Moreover, he was eager to learn about their work. There were also many appointees waiting to enter service—some delayed because of the hostilities, lack of travel facilities, and passport and visa difficulties. To learn to know the missionaries' supporting groups was also one of his goals. As soon as possible he set out to visit churches—at first with T. J. Bach, his predecessor. With the announcements that had been made about his appointment, it was not long before invitations to speak kept him as busy as he could afford to be along with his desk duties as director.

J. F. Swanson was fully occupied with headquarters management, editing *The Missionary Broadcaster,* and other duties such as trying to book hard-to-obtain passage for all outgoing missionaries. Eager for all the help he could get, he asked the board to draft me for another three months. At the end of that period, late in 1946, the request was renewed for an additional six months.

At the first meeting of the board of directors after the new general director was installed, an important forward-looking decision was recorded concerning the Japan work. The boldest aspect, considering the virtual apathy that had existed before the war, was "to send forth as rapidly as possible twenty-five or more missionaries, as the Lord may lead, and funds be raised for passage, equipment and salary to the extent of approximately $2,500 each, per year."[1]

Administrative Field Visits

Many years had passed since most fields had been visited by home office or board personnel. (Bach did go to South America in 1946 for the fortieth anniversary of the beginning of work there.) Now in early 1947 requests came for Bach to visit southern Africa and Swanson to go to Venezuela for the fortieth anniversary of the founding of *La Estrella de la Mañana*. Johnson was eager to respond to the invitations to visit Japan, Mongolia, and China. Don Hillis and his family had already returned to India so his help was no longer available for the public ministry.

With this depletion of the men of the staff at the time of an increased load of work, there seemed nothing else for me to do than to accede to the request to continue on at the Chicago headquarters for a time, even though the China missionaries had petitioned the board to release us for return to the field. Without official appointment or position, I nevertheless had to substitute for the general director and the associate general director and respond to speaking invitations. Correspondence with prospective candidates and counseling of those accepted occupied a large portion of my time.

Johnson Trip to be Five Months

David Johnson planned his trip to the mission fields in the Far East to cover a period of five months beginning in July 1947. Almost a third of that time was required for boat travel. To get around in the countries visited was also time-consuming because of primitive transportation. Johnson was anxious that this first trip should provide a good opportunity to observe and study the situation on each field. He was aware that, different from Franson and Bach, he had not been personally involved in foreign missionary work. On several occasions when speaking to me about remaining on the home staff he mentioned the need for one with field experience to deal with missionaries and candidates.

Introduction to Far East

Johnson did indeed get an initiation into missionary life and service. Japan had been devastated and very little recovery was apparent even by early August 1947 when he docked at Yokohama. He saw poverty and deprivation at first hand. He met with the Japanese pastors and people who were beginning to pull their lives together after the havoc of war and was encouraged by their friendliness to their former enemies. Though harassed and battered, the church was alive. He also ministered to the unsaved and was impressed by their openness to the gospel message. He was convinced that Japan must have many missionaries to take advantage of that openness.

Mongolia presented quite a different picture—not the devastation of war, but the barrenness of desert and drought. Here he experienced the rigors of service on that difficult field. China missionary Fred Nelson, who escorted him all through his China visit, told of the breakdown of the old Ford as they, with Stuart Gunzel, drove across the barren plains. There was no other choice than to spend several days in a Mongol yurt, with their only food being unfamiliar barley cakes and rancid butter-flavored tea. What was no great difficulty for the missionaries seemed at first quite trying for the visitor. Gunzel overheard Nelson thanking the Lord that this had happened to the general director so he could have first-hand experience of rugged missionary life. That trip gave him many such opportunities, and he adjusted rapidly and well.

Northwest China provided Johnson's first opportunity to see and experience extensive missionary work at first hand. Travel arrangements were not much different than those experienced by the early missionaries and this gave him further appreciation of the cost, in part, of bringing into existence the widespread church ministries in Shensi and Kansu. But he was tremendously inspired by the response as he preached in most of the church centers. He found that the simple gospel, clearly presented, brought men and women to Christ. He hesitated to quote numbers but simply said that those responding could be counted in four figures.

Upon returning from his lengthy journey, Johnson was asked to speak at a dinner for all mission-related people in the greater Chicago area. Missionaries may have wondered if one who had not gone through the apprenticeship of missionary service would really be able to understand missionary life and work. As they listened to him they were more than convinced that here was a leader with keen powers of observation and quick understanding of what was involved in the front-line ministry. He clearly perceived the nature of the spiritual battle and knew that the weapons of faith, prayer, and the Word of God must be faithfully employed.

Reports of his visits began to reach the mission office and the board of directors from the three Far East fields. It was evident that the acceptance of the new leader was whole-hearted and complete. Like his predecessors, he had come to serve. Wherever there was an opportunity for an evangelistic service he took advantage of it and had the joy of seeing many turn to the Lord. His field apprenticeship might have seemed short but it was thorough and gave him a good foundation for informed leadership, representation, and appeal.

Returning to a Full Desk

Back at his desk in early January 1948, after five months of overseas travel, Johnson found some urgent matters requiring early attention. Foremost was his earnest desire to share with prospective missionaries and potential supporters what he had seen and heard on the mission fields. This would require much time away from the office. At the same time the pressure of work in the office was increasing as the mission grew in size and activity. Several matters had to be dealt with promptly—a question affecting the churches in Japan, the unclear situation of an apparent Foreign Missions Conference relationship, and the suggested change of mission name.

To complicate matters, Johnson found on his desk a letter from Frances and me asking the board to release us from home office duty so we could return to China. The general director and the board at first acceded to our request. Then a few months later, in March 1948, when it became evident that the work was rapidly increasing and China also seemed to be closing because of the Communist takeover, they reversed the decision and requested that I remain on the staff as assistant general director. As this now seemed to be the leading of the Lord, we accepted the decision; however, with mixed emotions. I was asked to take responsibility for office management, financial procedures, and—without official designation—was left with candidate correspondence and counseling.

Appeal to Students

Johnson was eager to get to the schools where prospective missionaries were being trained. In these schools were many young men who had served in the military overseas where their personal walk with the Lord had been strengthened and their eyes opened to the spiritual need of people without the gospel. Johnson's invitation was clear and direct: "There is a field to be harvested; reapers are needed; you can be a reaper in that harvest field."

He told of what he had seen in China, where the people, dependent for food on the grain they produced in the fields, cut and gathered grain enough to feed the most populous nation on earth using only ten-inch sickles. They succeeded because they turned out en masse to gather in the harvest.

Students responded to his appeal and applications for service came in at an accelerated pace. Young women whose schooling had been delayed because of war work were equally responsive. The mission began to grow rapidly. In his report of March 31, 1948, Johnson listed 51 candidates accepted during the year. The total active missionary force was 341.

Decisive Action—Japan

In his visit to Japan, Johnson had opportunity to acquaint himself with concerns of the mission-related (Domei) churches. The larger evangelical church group with which the Domei was associated had, by government action, been made part of the United Church (see chapter 12). Several pastors had clearly understood the potential doctrinal compromise involved in this relationship and had withdrawn from membership, along with their churches. Others saw only the immediate fellowship with those of like precious faith and saw no reason to withdraw. After several months of correspondence and consultation, Johnson took the matter to the board of directors for study and decision. The following action of the board was communicated to the churches, to the Japan field conference as a body, and to the individual missionaries:

> As to the Kyodan or United Church, it is the decision of the board of directors that our missionaries, [Domei] churches and national pastors in Japan should carry on their work separate and apart from the same. All new churches hereafter organized by or affiliated with the S.A.M. must not accept membership in or in any manner be associated with the Kyodan.... After January 1, 1949, no pastor or church belonging to the Scandinavian Alliance Mission is to have any membership or affiliation with the Kyodan or United Church.[2]

Several churches chose to remain in the United Church and therefore their affiliation with the S.A.M. was terminated. One was the largest church of the Domei, with a large Sunday school. This decision seemed costly, but Johnson and the board were convinced that obedience to the Lord would be honored by Him.

Decisive Action—Foreign Missions Conference

Johnson noted that regular requests were being received from the Foreign Missions Conference (FMC) for statistical information on the mission's work and assigning a financial support quota. Though these requests were ignored, their receipt indicated to Johnson that the mission was considered to be a member in spite of Bach's earlier protests. (In the world mission scene there were several organizations for consultation. The Foreign Missions Conference was a grouping of major denominational and certain independent missions in North America. It was a member of the International Missionary Council, organized in 1921, which linked the councils of various regions. The World Council of Churches, with which the IMC amalgamated in 1962, did not come into being until 1948.)

Though the mission did not participate in conciliar activities, Johnson was alert to the perception of compromise. He was concerned about the theological inclusiveness of the FMC, which allowed participation by missions not faithful to the Word of God. He wrote to the FMC executive secretary certifying that nothing could be found in the mission's records to indicate that the S.A.M. had applied for membership. The board requested that the mission's name be removed from the list of members. This official approach brought the desired action. The board minutes of September 2, 1948, recorded this response from the FMC.

> Whereas The Scandinavian Alliance Mission of North America has certified that the appearance of its name in the list of members of the Foreign Missions Conference for many years has occurred without any action of its Board of Directors authorizing it, and is apparently due to some misunderstanding; and whereas it is not the present desire of the Mission to be a member of the Foreign Missions Conference; therefore be it voted that the Committee of Reference and Counsel recommend to the next Annual Meeting of the Foreign Missions Conference that Article 1 of the Constitution be amended by omitting from the list of members the words: "The Scandinavian Alliance Mission of North America;" and that the Executive Secretary be instructed to convey to the Mission the regret of the Committee at this decision on the part of the Mission.[3]

The recommended action was taken and a situation which understandably confused some was clarified by Johnson's forthright approach. The only membership which the mission maintained was in the Interdenominational Foreign Mission Association (IFMA)—a grouping of conservative evangelical missions without denominational affiliation.

S.A.M. Becomes TEAM

From workers on the three Far East fields came questions about the continued use of the Scandinavian name of the mission. There was strong sentiment among them that the name should not have national connotations, both for the sake of the churches being planted and because of relations with host governments. It is easy to understand that Johnson counseled the missionaries to put their feelings into formal wording for the board of directors to consider. This presentation moved the long-delayed subject up to priority status and at the 1948 annual meeting it was voted to initiate the process by recommending to the 1949 meeting that the change be effected.[4]

So, on May 12, 1949, official action was taken by the membership to amend the charter on file with the State of Illinois to change the name to *The Evangelical Alliance Mission*. There was a clear purpose in having "The" as part of the name. As Johnson pointed out, the initials would then spell TEAM, which would fit nicely with the Scripture motto used by the mission, "Workers together with Him" (II Corinthians 6:1). To protect its use in the field of Christian mission organizations and to avoid confusion, the acronym TEAM was later copyrighted. The new name quickly gained approval and acceptance.

A Manual Needed and Provided

When Frances and I were candidates in 1939, we had observed that prospective workers had many questions for which there were no ready answers, such as about the country of service, how to go about contacting churches and enlisting their interest, financial procedures, outfit needs, passports, visas, steamship bookings, immunizations, timing of departure, contact with field leaders, etc. Now in 1948 we found that candidates, not surprisingly, had the same kinds of questions. It seemed impractical to be repeating similar information in scores of letters and at the same time fearing that some did not know the right questions to ask. Many obviously were not receiving the help needed. The logical solution was an informative handbook. The first edition of forty-eight pages was ready for distribution in October 1948. Furloughed missionaries soon realized they needed the same kind of information and the manual was expanded to satisfy their needs. What started as forty-eight pages later grew to a volume of several hundred.

Candidate School Initiated

Missionaries serving with a denominational board usually have had years of acquaintanceship through their churches, but for an independent mission the situation is quite different. The independents lack the family ties of a denomination. Yet it is important that those who will be working together in one organization and particularly on the same field have similar goals and a sense of history. They must become a virtual family with great capacity for mutual understanding and cooperation. I had observed that some faith missions brought their appointees together for several weeks of study and work and asked if our mission could do the same. The problem was that the TEAM offices were already overcrowded and overburdened. There was neither space, time, nor personnel for what would admittedly be a very good thing.

The solution to the beginning of a candidate school—as it came to be called—was the availability during the summer months of an aging dormitory building, the C. T. Dyrness Memorial, which the mission had set up close to Wheaton College to provide rooms for missionary daughters who otherwise might not be admitted to the college for lack of dormitory space. This building could accommodate twenty-four people and there was a large parlor which could serve as a classroom. Meals could be bought at the college dining room or, for those who chose to do so, simple meals could be prepared on a burner in the basement.

With 120 candidates desiring to attend, it was necessary to divide them into groups by field and schedule them for two-week sessions for ten weeks of the summer, beginning June 13, 1949. Getting the needed personnel took a little longer, so with an initial staff of one teacher—the one whose idea it was—augmented from time to time by a staff member or a furloughed missionary, the classes of 1949 received orientation to TEAM and to the work ahead. The general director was enthusiastic about the project and welcomed opportunities to share his insights with the candidates. From that somewhat humble but not small or insignificant beginning, the annual candidate school, now held for three weeks on a college campus, has become a valuable tool for verifying the call, clarifying the objectives, creating family unity, and bonding for spiritual fellowship, plus the practical matter of instructing in headquarters procedures, methods of work, and cross-cultural adaptation.

Additional Field Visits

In his first five years as general director, David Johnson visited all the fields where TEAM was then serving and several additional areas which later became TEAM fields. His were not quick superficial visits but opportunities for observing, studying, counseling, and ministering. The trip to the Far East had lasted five months, as we have seen. The next, to Pakistan, Tibetan Frontier, western India, Hong Kong, China, and Japan, was no shorter, extending from October 1948 to March 1949. Considering that for the first time he now traveled by air, the time spent with the missionaries and national workers was greater. Pakistan and the Tibetan Frontier were new areas of work where missionaries had questions similar to pioneer fields—language arrangements for new workers, missionary housing, methods of work, agreements with other missions, financial provision and administration, etc. All of these matters were the responsibility of the field leaders but the counsel of the general director was not only helpful but most needful.

The following year found Johnson responding to invitations from Africa and Portugal. Both South Africa and Rhodesia had great increases in the number of missionaries, as well as many opportunities for new work which he noted and later brought before interested friends in the homeland.

Europe Comes into Focus

Johnson had previously observed some of Europe's need when serving as military chaplain. He wrote:

> Italy is another land in need of many Christian workers. I stopped there for only a day in September [1950] but during the recent World War II, I visited the land many times as Chaplain in the United States Army and gave time and effort to a study of its spiritual needs. The spiritual situation then was very dark and it continues to be dark, although we rejoice that some missionaries have gone there with the gospel since the close of that war. Italy has Catholicism but not Christ. It has an abundance of religion, but knows practically nothing of regeneration.[5]

The anguish and pleas voiced by Johnson for Italy, Spain, and France were honored by the Lord and were surely factors in the later opening of TEAM work in these countries. Concerning Spain, he wrote:

> Most of Spain's people will face eternity unsaved. They will die in their sins. Pray much for this people in spiritual darkness.[6]

It seems that the need of France touched Johnson even more deeply:

> I saw enough to realize that the need for gospel workers in that land is appalling. God is left out. He is unknown to the multitudes. The spiritual condition is one of dense darkness. The heathen in many distant lands face a brighter opportunity of being reached with the gospel than do the people of France. If this is to be part of the task of The Evangelical Alliance Mission, may the Lord direct us. We want to be obedient to his will.[7]

To Latin America

One more area remained to receive an initial visit from the general director—Latin America. Johnson found it possible to schedule a visit there in the summer of 1951, spending time in Colombia, Venezuela, and the Netherlands Antilles. Though the missionaries and national Christians were still facing much opposition and not a little persecution, there were evidences of encouraging response to the message of liberation from sin and a vain dependence on a false hope.

Still a Troubled World

Though the first five years of David Johnson's service as leader of the mission saw a great deal of growth and activity, this was not a time of peace in all the areas where TEAM missionaries served.

In the Far East, Russian influence increased as a result of its invasion of Manchuria in the last week of World War II. Its occupation of this strong military and industrial base contributed much to the defeat of Nationalist China by the Chinese Communists under Mao Tsetung from 1946 to 1949. It also brought North Korea under Communist control which, in turn, led to the attack on South Korea in June 1950.

Elsewhere in Asia, India gained independence from Great Britain in 1947, but the Moslem-Hindu division resulted in a separate country of Pakistan and severe persisting tensions. The Indonesians agitated for and obtained independence from the Netherlands in 1949.

The struggles for a Jewish homeland in Palestine resulted in the partition of the Holy Land in 1948 and the emerging of Israel as a nation. It also marked the beginning of a state of hostility with surrounding Arab countries.

The Soviet Union increased its hold on Eastern Europe, incorporating the Baltic States into its homeland. "D.P." became easily understood as denoting displaced persons, of whom there were millions in Europe as a result of the war and later oppression. After Russia blockaded Berlin, the Western nations became keenly aware of its growing threat to peace and organized the North Atlantic Treaty Organization (NATO).

Latin America was not directly affected by the Communist expansion in Europe and the Far East but suffered from serious political and religious tensions. Colombia, in particular, was torn by fighting between the Liberal and Conservative political factions. Evangelical Christians became the target of Conservative (Catholic) oppression and persecution during *Los Anos de Violencia* (the years of violence)—1948 to 1958.

No Holding Back

One day a supporter came into the TEAM office to see Johnson, thinking to caution him with the question: "In light of the hostilities in Korea, what are you doing about the safety of your people in Japan?"

"We are sending out more missionaries," was Johnson's response.

A DECADE OF RAPID EXPANSION

The sixtieth anniversary of TEAM was observed in May 1950 at the Salem Evangelical Free Church in Chicago. This church had faithfully supported the work ever since the day Franson had spoken to the young pastor, C. T. Dyrness, about assuming responsibility for a missionary.

A Growth Report

David H. Johnson's annual report of March 31, 1950, announced 122 candidates appointed, 74 new missionaries sent to the fields, and contributions of $787,429 received and used in the work. There were now 402 active missionaries compared with 228 four years earlier when Johnson took office.

These figures are a significant measure of the Lord's response in providing laborers. Of even greater significance are the believers gathered in congregations. For the first time since reporting was begun, shortly after the founding of the mission, no China statistics could be included in the annual report. Communist forces had occupied and were controlling China, and normal communications with the Chinese church leaders were cut off. Church membership of 18,746 in all TEAM's work reported in 1945 was now in 1950 listed as 8,422, a disappearance from TEAM's records—but not from God's—of more than fifty percent of the believers due to the unavoidable omission of the China figures. The adjusted membership of 8,422 in 167 congregations then became the new basis for comparison as the work continued to grow.

Closing and Opening Doors

While it was necessary to report the closing of the Mongolia work and the evacuation of most of the China missionaries, the general director could also report that Japan now had eighty TEAM missionaries, some of whom had recently had to leave China. New recruits were entering other fields and taking up work in several expansion areas—the Nasik district in western India, the Tibetan Frontier field in north India, and the new nation of Pakistan. Southern Rhodesia was recognized as a separate field. Indonesia, with a population of 70 million, was being studied as a possible future area of service. The South Africa field was initiating evangelism and church work near the large cities of Durban and Johannesburg where Africans from the "bush" were beginning to crowd into the surrounding townships. The South America fields were reaching out within their borders. This clearly was a time of "lengthening the cords and strengthening the stakes."

Some Unexpected Difficulties

Though this period was very satisfying because of new fields opening and new opportunities presented, it was not without difficulties. One such difficulty came from an unexpected source—certain fellow Christians in the homeland. Among the American Christians of fundamental and conservative doctrinal convictions there had arisen two separate cooperative movements—the National Association of Evangelicals (NAE) and the American Council of Christian Churches (ACCC). Though these two associations should have had much in common, there were certain policy and doctrinal positions that kept them apart. Because TEAM was neither a church nor a denomination, it was not a member of either group. It chose to have its membership only in the Interdenominational Foreign Mission Association.

The leaders of the ACCC were particularly zealous in pointing out and publicizing direct or indirect relationships, if any, which members of the NAE or IFMA had with the liberal National Council of Christian Churches (NCCC) or related bodies. If, for example, a local church of unquestioned evangelical position joined the NAE while still a member of an NCCC-related denomination, such membership would, in the view of the ACCC, compromise the NAE and any other member of the NAE.

An Unforeseen Criticism

To the surprise of TEAM, in 1950, it found its name in one of the ACCC-related publications as being a compromising mission. The writer of the article said that he had called an office in New York and was told that TEAM was a member of the Foreign Missions Conference and that its India field organization was a member of the National Council of Churches of India. In South Africa the field office had sent in reimbursement for some study reports and therefore was listed as a contributing member of the South African Council of Churches.

It was easy to answer the unfounded charge about membership in the Foreign Missions Conference. The clarifying action taken by the board two years earlier had settled that matter. The supposed South African Council relationship was also disposed of easily. The India connection came as a surprise and required some investigation. The TEAM field conference was a member of the Berar-Khandesh Christian Conference (BKCC). The BKCC, in turn, was a member of the Bombay Representative Council of Churches. When the National Council of India was organized—apart from any participation by TEAM—it was noted that the missions and churches in the Bombay Presidency were already organized so the Bombay Presidency Council was recognized as a part of the NCC without any action on the part of the missions in the area. The zeal for a world-church had motivated the promoters of union and they seemed surprised that there were some missions and churches which did not welcome such links.

A Correcting Action

Johnson counseled TEAM India field leaders to urge the other missions to have the Berar-Khandesh Christian Conference withdraw from the Bombay Representative Council. When that failed, he directed the field organization to leave the BKCC. Some missionaries objected, feeling that the mission was giving in to pressures that related mostly to the American ecclesiastical scene. Johnson was able to make a good case on the basis of scriptural principles and convictions and the field agreed that it would be the best course to follow. Some years later other missions in the BKCC saw the wisdom of the action and followed TEAM's lead.

A Necessary but Unhappy Termination

In December 1948, TEAM had requested the resignation of a young missionary in Japan on evidence of grave difficulties in personal relationships within the mission and with members of several other evangelical missions. There was no disagreement with him concerning separation from the Kyodan. The mission had earlier taken a stand on that question. While his zeal in advocating purity of the church had the full sympathy of the mission, the board noted that his approach was one which created dissension and injured the work.

After a period in the service of another mission which, in turn, dismissed him for similar reasons, this young missionary began a campaign of self-justification by intense and unwarranted criticism of TEAM and its Japanese pastors. His charges were fed to a number of men in the homeland who spread them widely.

Diligent Inquiry

Johnson kept in close touch with the Japan field leaders, wanting to make no response until he was sure that the criticisms against the pastors had no basis in fact. When he did answer, it was only to those who wrote directly to the mission. He made no counter-charges. Some critics, knowing that Johnson was an attorney, wanted to accuse him of twisting words to make the situation look good. But that was far from the case. He was untiring in seeking out the facts and thoroughly conscientious in responding truthfully. As I worked with him and read the most important correspondence, I felt that he could save himself a great deal of labor by writing a form letter that would cover the questions in a blanket approach. He chose not to do so because he wanted to deal with each question on the basis of fact for which there was clear evidence.

"Tried...as Silver is Tried"

The Lord honored Johnson's faithfulness. In early 1953 a group of men, mostly affiliated with the American Council of Christian Churches, asked to meet with Johnson and other leaders of TEAM in what seemed to be an attempt to justify the position of this young missionary. In a meeting of more than three hours there was opportunity to examine charge after charge. The result was that a joint committee issued a statement that none of the young missionary's charges had been proved. On the contrary, TEAM offered much evidence of the faithfulness of its pastors and missionaries. Not mentioned in the prepared statement was the young missionary's admission under questioning that he had sent out false information and had been guilty of falsehood in a number of situations.

That meeting solved the problem for the most part but did not silence this determined critic, who continued to spread the same kind of unfounded charges, but now with few who would believe them. This was an ordeal for the general director, but his confidence was in the Lord, believing he had allowed it so that all concerned in TEAM would be extremely careful that there be no compromise in the ministry.

Wider Recognition

Even as Bach's ministry was used by the Lord to bring the mission to wider attention, Johnson's ministry widened it much more. One factor was the great increase in missionaries. When a church sends out and backs a missionary in prayer and support, the mission agency also becomes known. While being known is not the sole objective of mission representation, it is necessary that the channel for the missionary outreach be sufficiently known to create confidence. This certainly became true for TEAM during Johnson's leadership.

An interesting innovation in this period was the holding of the annual meeting and Bible conference at the Winona Lake, Indiana, Christian Assembly grounds in 1953, 1954, and 1955. Most of the missionary and Bible messages were broadcast over the Moody Bible Institute station WMBI. Attendance was high, particularly over the Independence Day holiday weekend. Because of scheduling difficulties and also because some felt there was loss in not holding the conference in a supporting church, 1956 saw a return to the earlier practice.

Johnson's Administrative Style

In an earlier chapter we commented on T. J. Bach's administrative style. Johnson's was different. Bach gave much spiritual counsel—often in an indirect way. Johnson also gave spiritual counsel but was quite direct. Johnson corresponded much more with the field leaders on specifics in the field conference or field council minutes. Whereas earlier correspondence had been mostly with the secretary of the field council, Johnson chose to write to the field chairman. This gradually brought about a change in field administration, as field conferences began to choose chairmen who would not only chair the council meetings but would more actively administer the work and keep in touch with the home office.

Though Johnson had been a pastor for many years, he had been active in evangelism even longer. His concern—and rightly so—was that people be won to the Lord. While he wrote occasionally about establishing and nurturing churches and clearly believed in the importance of the church ministries, he was not particularly interested in disproportionate time spent in talking about strategy. He simply wanted missionaries to get to work. Being very resourceful himself, he felt that others should be equally resourceful, with little need of coaching. A typical message to the mission family—repeated in different words on many occasions—was the following:

> God has given us mission fields in various parts of the world. They are, in many instances, our sole responsibility. If we are faithful and diligent, increased numbers will be reached. If we are not, many who should have heard will not hear. God help us to be true! God help us to be incessant in prayer and labor! We cannot afford to be lax or careless. To be indifferent to our task is to fail God, and if we fail Him, we also fail those who made

it possible for us to go to the field. We are trustees of the gospel and as such we want to be faithful in the discharge of our duties. To be kept spiritual is our primary need. Without the Holy Spirit's anointing our work is in vain. By His provision we are enabled to go forward. We must reach the lost for Christ. If we do not, many will never get to know the Saviour. We have a tremendous responsibility. There is no escape from it. May the Lord help us all to abound in every good work and be faithful unto the end. We must all give an account of our stewardship. May yours and mine be commendable on that great day when we meet Him face to face.[1]

As long as missionaries were free to continue their work he urged them to be diligent, but he also foresaw a time when the day of opportunity might be past. Observing the strong nationalistic trends in that period, Johnson felt that foreign missions must be prepared for closing doors, and so he wrote:

Little by little the day appears to be approaching when missionary work will have to be done altogether by the national himself. In each land where foreign mission societies have missionaries there is a growing consciousness of the fact that on short notice we must be prepared to turn over much, if not all, of the mission work to the Christian national. We have, therefore, in our day a strong emphasis on making the national church indigenous. The sooner the Christians in the lands where we minister can take full and complete charge of the evangelization of their own people, the brighter is the future of the church in such lands.[2]

Not referred to as a possibility was the indigenous church as an effective tool for church planting even while the missionaries were still free to work with them, though that is one of the principal reasons for establishing and nurturing strong national churches.

Narrow Administrative Spread

Though the home staff grew with the growth of the mission, Johnson seemed to prefer to deal mainly with two people, his secretary and his assistant general director. What he wanted done in the office was usually communicated to one or the other, Siri Malmstrom or me, and we were to take it from there. When Johnson was out of the office—and that was often and for many weeks at a time—he left few instructions. He assumed that Miss

Malmstrom would acknowledge the letters that would have to await his return, respond for my signature on stewardship matters, and hand the other correspondence to me for my attention. The field leaders sometimes wondered what the proper procedure was. Should they write to the general director or to his assistant? Either way usually made no difference.

Divide Responsibilities? Not Yet

At one time I suggested that it would be more clear if Johnson would divide the field responsibility so that I would handle the correspondence with about half the fields and he would reserve the others to himself. No, he felt the general director should be in touch with all areas of the work. Even if I were the one who answered a letter he expected the field leader to accept the letter as if it were from him. There was some risk involved but it was great training for the assistant. The other side of the coin was that Johnson observed how I, with a missionary point of view, dealt with mission field questions. It was a great working relationship.

Expansion and Outreach

In the 1950s several new fields were opened, some by extension within countries already being served, others completely new to TEAM. The study of Indonesia as a possible field did open a way in an unexpected manner to Netherlands New Guinea, a territory adjacent to Indonesia which remained under Dutch control for almost fourteen years after Indonesia became independent in 1949. This territory became a TEAM field in January 1951. Taiwan was entered in 1951 with experienced China missionaries in the lead. France and Spain became TEAM fields in 1952.

Uruguay was entered in 1953 with the hope of setting up a radio station, but when this was found to be impossible missionaries withdrew in 1957. The Near East was drawn strongly to TEAM's attention in 1953 and 1954 and entered by missionaries in 1955. South Korea was first viewed as a possible field and entered in 1953 when the armistice was signed halting the fighting between

North and South Korea. At first under the Japan field council, it became separate in 1954.

The Netherlands Antilles, which had since 1931 been part of what was then called the South America field, became a separate field in 1955. Missionaries assigned to Turkey were first directed to work with the Near East field council but in 1960, when the Near East work was concentrated in the United Arab Emirates, the Turkey work was designated as the Southeastern Europe field. Though missionaries were engaged in radio work in Sri Lanka as early as 1955, that country was not considered a TEAM field until 1960.

Office Space Expansion Necessary

With the steady, rapid increase in missionaries it was necessary to expand the home staff that served their interests. By the time Johnson came into office, space had expanded from the three small rooms plus a board room in the Franson-Risberg Memorial Building into which Bach had moved the operation in 1930. To provide working space for the twelve staff members, the adjacent five-room apartment had been taken over. By 1950 there were twenty-six staff members to meet the needs of the doubled missionary force. Three more small apartments were requisitioned and the board of directors' meeting moved to the assembly hall downstairs. By the time there were thirty-five on the staff it was apparent that something needed to be done.

It was decided to build an annex to the west of the Franson-Risberg Memorial building and this was done in late 1955. Though I had to plan the layout of the building, the pressure of my work would not allow adequate time to confer with the contractor in the building process.

But the Lord made special provision just when needed. Rolf and Phyllis Egeland had been denied residence in Portugal after serving there two and a half years and were home awaiting reassignment. We put Egeland to work in the office, not recalling at the time his previous experience as a builder in the Navy Seabees and while in college. I requested his help in liaison with the contractor and when I learned of his past experience, turned over full responsibility to him. Through his careful scheduling the office building was completed by early February 1956—in just five months time. As I was to visit our Far East fields for fourteen weeks in 1956, I asked Egeland, who also had valuable past service as a camp manager, to take over my duties as office manager for that period and later gave it to him as a regular assignment.

Johnson Tours Fields Around the World

If Dr. Johnson was invited to visit a field on the other side of the world such as India or Pakistan, he figured he should stop at fields on the way and then return via the other side of the world to touch additional areas. This he did on the 1948-49 trip when the mission had relatively few fields. By 1953, with added areas to visit, he chose to travel in the same way. This trip to ten fields also lasted five months.

Again in 1957, his field visits were on a round-the-world ticket. Some savings in the circular fare appealed to him, too, as he was always very careful in the spending of mission money. With so many new areas of work being entered in that decade, Johnson was eager to see the work at first hand, both for purposes of administration and for presenting the ministry in the homeland.

Acting on Scriptural Convictions

In the decade of the '50s there was increasing emphasis in the Christian world on what some called cooperative evangelism. Churches and missions had often cooperated in a limited way in the past, but these recent movements were similar to the great Moody and Billy Sunday campaigns. There was a difference now, however. Some who wanted to join in the cooperative campaigns did not hold to sound doctrine. As TEAM had no churches in North America, its responsibility was solely for the churches on its mission fields. The mission was particularly anxious that converts in field evangelistic meetings be channeled into Bible-believing churches. It did not want liberal church leaders to be considered safe guides for mission field converts.

After receiving requests from several field councils for guidance on this sensitive but extremely important issue, Johnson proposed to the board of directors that it set forth a policy that would be binding on all who served in TEAM. After careful discussion of the historical position of the mission, the board assigned Johnson the responsibility of writing a suitable resolution, which was to deal with issues and principles, not personalities. He asked me to review the wording with him. The board approved the wording and, on May 13, 1958, adopted the following resolution:

> In view of the doctrinal position and the spiritual standards of The Evangelical Alliance Mission, its Board of Directors unanimously reaffirms its position that the spiritual ministry of The Evangelical Alliance Mission shall continue to be carried on at all times in a scriptural manner, with aims and procedures consistent therewith. Therefore, all of its home representatives, its missionaries and field conferences shall, in all joint undertakings, participate only in such evangelistic efforts or other spiritual ministries as are sponsored entirely by individuals and/or groups holding to the fundamental doctrines of the Christian faith concerning the Word of God and the Person and work of our Lord Jesus Christ and of the Holy Spirit, as revealed in the Holy Scriptures.[3]

That statement has proved to be a spiritually wise and valuable guideline for cooperation in spiritual ministries and for establishing limits to such cooperation. The occasional objection that it sets an impossible standard and forfeits opportunities for ministry has been more than outweighed by the testimonies of its practical benefits. Most important, there is the conviction that this position is in accordance with God's will for TEAM.

Home Base Growth

The number of fields had increased to fifteen and missionaries to 800 by March 31, 1959. Ladies of dedication and skill were handling the routine office matters, but with this growth, the directors began to recognize the need for more men on the headquarters staff. J. F. Swanson was dividing his time between the deputation (extension) department and *The Missionary Broadcaster*. Rolf Egeland continued to serve as administrative assistant and office manager. Julius Bergstrom, China missionary who had served from 1953 to 1955 as candidate secretary, was called to Korea to take responsibility for the Chinese department of the new radio station, HLKX. Once again, I had to assume leadership of the candidate department while continuing to oversee the accounting department and serve as deputy to Johnson in all aspects of his work. The board had approved installation of IBM tabulating equipment for receipting, record keeping, accounting, and mailing procedures. While this extensive change would, in time, expedite the work, it did add a great deal of pressure for Egeland and me in the conversion process.

Request for Help

As clearly as I could, I described the need for help to Johnson, who was understandably reluctant to increase home office overhead. At the same time he could understand that there must be limits to the workload some were carrying. The first to receive help was the deputation department—for church contacts—in the person of furloughed Japan missionary John Schone. When he returned to Japan, the board appointed former Japan missionary George D. Martin to the position. Martin's experience included evangelism, the pastorate, leadership on the Japan field, Bible school teaching, and a period as a TEAM representative.

To ease my load, Johnson invited Delbert A. Kuehl, recent chairman of the Japan field, to become candidate secretary. Kuehl had a background of service as pastor, chaplain in the military, Bible college teacher, and church planter. Miss Doris Frazer, former India missionary, was designated his assistant.

Carl A. Gundersen, chairman of the board since 1951, was conscious of the need for help and in 1959 approached former India missionary Don W. Hillis about rejoining the mission and considering a staff appointment. Gundersen had in mind that Johnson was nearing retirement age and the mission would need a man with a strong public ministry to replace that aspect of his work. Hillis, who had developed the Light of Life Correspondence ministry, had left TEAM in 1954 to promote the courses through the World Gospel Crusade but was at this time working with Overseas Crusades. The board welcomed Mr. Gundersen's recommendation and, after consultation with Overseas Crusades, invited Hillis to become home secretary with responsibilities in conference work and writing.

Annual Report, March 31, 1961

In his report to the annual meeting in May 1961, Johnson included mention of the death of a number of pioneer missionaries. William Hagquist, a member of the original China party, passed away June 25, 1960, at the age of eighty-eight. He was the first of the party of thirty-five to step ashore on Chinese soil, and his service extended over thirty-seven years. Mrs. John G. (Kristina) Nelson passed away on February 14, 1961, just three days short of the seventieth anniversary of her arrival in China. She was the last survivor of that group of pioneer missionaries. It is of interest to note that she and John Nelson were the first to marry after the three-year time limit set by Franson. The Nelsons had the first child in the mission, daughter Ruth, who later became a missionary to China. She and her brother, Arthur, were the first of many TEAM children to become second-generation missionaries. A third member of the family, Esther (Mrs. Reuben Gustafson), also gave a lifetime of service to win Chinese for Christ.

In the statistics reported, Johnson pointed out that the membership in 322 TEAM-related mission field churches was now 13,206, compared to 8,422 in 167 churches ten years earlier. Baptisms were 1,216 as compared to 629. Forty-two new missionaries were sent to thirteen of TEAM's sixteen mission fields. The number of active missionaries was 819, an increase of 358 over a decade earlier. He did not refer to the increase of 591 missionaries since 1946. Contributions from the Lord's people to carry on this extensive work had reached a level of $3,000,000 annually.

Retirement Looming

It would seem that, by 1961, the headquarters was well staffed, but both Dr. Johnson and Mr. Swanson had reached normal retirement age and were also having some health problems. In addition, because Mrs. Johnson did not enjoy good health, Johnson was finding it more difficult to be away for long periods. On June 27, 1961, Johnson requested the executive committee of the board to set a date for the transfer of his responsibilities to a successor. He suggested the mission anniversary date of October 14, 1961, just before his sixty-eighth birthday. After prayerful consideration, it was decided to pass a recommendation to the next board meeting, July 10, at which meeting it was voted:

> That Dr. David H. Johnson's request to give up the title of general director on October 14, 1961, be agreed to with the understanding that he will be given a suitable title to indicate the high level of work in which he will be engaged. The title of General Director Emeritus was suggested but for the specific work he is to do a suggestion was made that a more suitable title be given, such as Stewardship Counselor.[4]

Replacement Appointed

The approval of Johnson's retirement from leadership necessitated a follow-up decision. It was one which the general director and executive committee of the board had under study for some time:

> Motion carried to adopt the following recommendation of the Executive Committee: That the Board of Directors appoint Vernon Mortenson to be General Director, effective October 14, 1961. Mr. Mortenson commented on Joshua 5:13-15 in expressing his purpose that the Lord would fully control the activities of the mission.[5]

Choosing Vernon Mortenson as successor to Dr. Johnson was not a matter taken for granted by the executive committee. It was known in a limited circle that names of several well-qualified men had been suggested and—it is assumed—were given consideration. Johnson had a wide public ministry which seemed essential for any new appointee as well. While I was often out in meetings for TEAM, that aspect of my work could not be compared with Johnson's. Johnson also communicated with the supporting constituency by letter and through the pages of the mission magazine. The editor had often requested articles from me so that area was not seriously lacking.

Under the working arrangements at TEAM headquarters, Johnson had left much of the executive responsibility to me. With TEAM's rapid growth and expansion, my familiarity with and involvement in all aspects of the work were probably considered strong positive factors outweighing, in the minds of the executive committee members, other deficiencies.

To become general director of a mission such as TEAM was a position of responsibility I neither sought nor shunned. Knowing of the possibility, I truly desired the Lord's will for the mission and for me. I was encouraged by the knowledge that those responsible for the decision equally desired to know and follow the Lord's will. Even so, it seemed an awesome responsibility for me to be the successor to spiritual giants and gifted leaders such as Franson, Hedstrom, Bach, and Johnson.

The prayer of Moses in Exodus 33:13 became my personal petition: "Now therefore, I pray thee, if I have found grace in thy sight, shew me now thy way, that I may know thee, that I may find grace in thy sight: and consider that this nation [mission] is thy people." Assurance came from the Lord's answer to Moses: "My presence shall go with thee."

AN EASY TRANSITION

Recognition

A combined recognition and installation service was held October 12, 1961, to honor Dr. David H. Johnson for his fifteen years of leadership as general director, and to mark the beginning of my time in office. The setting was the Lake View Mission Covenant Church of Chicago, where both our families were members. Many missionaries, staff members, friends from local churches, and family members were present. At the age of over eighty, Dr. T. J. Bach, resident in California, made a special effort to be at the service. Speakers representing the board of directors, missionaries, pastors, and other organizations spoke with gratitude of the impact of Johnson's ministry.

Installation

TEAM board member Dr. Harold W. Erickson, pastor of the First Evangelical Free Church of Rockford, Illinois, gave the charge to the new general director, who in response spoke on *TEAM's Basic Goals.* A condensed outline follows:

> Several friends have asked me what changes are planned for TEAM as a new administration takes office. Some seem to feel that missionary activity must undergo drastic changes if it is to meet new challenges. This is the time to put the answer clearly on record.... Because the mission's authority is not derived from man and its responsibility is not primarily to man, the changing of its administration or the changing of world conditions does not change its objective or character.

> - There is an unchanging divine commission—*go.*
> - There is an unchanging world need—*lostness.*
> - There is an unchanging message—*Christ.*
> - There is an unchanging objective—*the church.*
> - There is an unchanging dependence upon the faithfulness of God— *"I am with you."*

- There is an unchanging agency— *"so send I you."*
- There is an unchanging fellowship— *"workers together."*

There are changes we seek even as did Bach and Johnson.
- More conformity to Christ.
- More dependence on the Spirit of God.
- Greater burden for the lost.
- Greater sense of urgency.
- More devotion and yieldedness to our Lord.[1]

Plans for the Future

In noting future plans by the new administration it is necessary to look back to the executive committee meeting of June 27, 1961, to get the thread. In preparation for that meeting, chairman Gundersen had asked me to be ready to discuss two topics—(1) home administrative structure and (2) more effective field direction. Though I knew these subjects would be on the agenda, I did not realize that Johnson's retirement and the appointment of a successor would also be discussed. Once I learned this, it was easy to adjust my presentation to the new situation and I proceeded to outline a division of responsibilities, incorporating a number of suggestions that had been made in earlier board sessions.

The structure presented and later confirmed for the administrative staff included: David H. Johnson, stewardship director; Rolf C. Egeland, administrative secretary; Delbert A. Kuehl, candidate secretary; Don W. Hillis, publications secretary; and George D. Martin, deputation secretary. I would retain responsibility for liaison with the fifteen fields, though I had in mind assigning future foreign secretary duties to one or more others.

The secretary's record of the second item was:

> Some time was spent in the discussion of procedures to be followed in strengthening the direction of the work on the fields. Mr. Mortenson pointed out the possibilities which have been opened up to the administration for more effective field direction through the provision of the new Constitution and Principles and Guiding Rules.[2]

These understandings established a firm basis for TEAM administration.

The Need for Guiding Rules Update

The mention in the minutes of the *new* Constitution and Principles and Guiding Rules referred to the extensive revision adopted at the 1960 annual meeting. The Constitution is a basic document which only occasionally needs to be amended, but the Principles and Guiding Rules must be adjusted as times change. No revision, other than in minor items, had been made for almost thirty years. The addition of many new missionaries to the older fields, the opening of new areas of work, and the growth of special ministries—such as hospitals, Bible institutes, orphanages, publication projects, and radio work—brought new conditions. Improved communications within the various countries and with the home office also changed the administrative requirements.

In 1953, when I visited the Venezuela-Colombia work, I began to realize that the Principles and Guiding Rules did not adequately provide the guidance that their title suggested. Working with the field council, we were able to outline in a clear way the relationships and lines of authority to exist among the missionaries, the field conference, and the field council.

The following year in South Africa and Southern Rhodesia, the missionaries welcomed similar clarification. Here it was also essential to clearly define and explain financial procedures and to delineate responsibilities within project ministries.

At the Japan field conference in 1956, I had further opportunity to explain the principles implied in the Constitution and Principles and Guiding Rules. My explanation had to be in the nature of an exegesis, as there were few direct statements on some of the subjects causing concern.

The reinforcement of a mission field with new workers was welcomed by the older missionaries, who were very much aware of the unfinished task before them. Yet along with the welcomed increase in missionaries came inevitable adjustments.

Older workers had, for the most part, learned to adapt to the host culture but in so doing seemed to the new arrivals to be quite different than expected in thought patterns and customs. Most new workers adjusted well but sometimes tensions arose even among dedicated missionaries.

Some speakers who visited the fields saw these tensions as evidence of a spiritual lack, requiring confession and rededication. While it is true that spiritual renewal is necessary, I considered the problem to be partly due to lack of clear administrative guidelines. I noted in the Pauline epistles that Paul first set forth spiritual principles and then followed up with practical teaching and exhortation. The epistle to the Ephesian church is a good example.

The Process of Revision

Having seen the need of clearer guidelines, I suggested to the board that a revision of the Principles and Guiding Rules would be helpful. The job was assigned to me. It took more than a year to carefully analyze the existing document and gather additional material for a draft revision. This draft was then sent to all missionaries, board members, and staff, soliciting their recommendations and suggested wording.

Being a firm believer that TEAM is not just an organization controlled by a board and staff, but an organism in which the missionaries are vital members, I wanted the finished document to truly be a joint undertaking in which all had participated. The responses were most helpful. Then followed the problem of evaluating and deciding on these suggestions. The solution was found in a seemingly unrelated decision the board had made earlier—in January 1958:

> Advisory Committee: Mr. Mortenson proposed a plan of having each field designate one person with the background of a term of satisfactory service, and particularly past membership on the field committee as chairman or secretary, to serve while on furlough as a member of a continuing advisory committee. Such committee would meet for a period of several days twice each year with members of the board of directors, to discuss mission objectives, methods of work, effectiveness of the ministry, and establishing of priorities of emphasis, discussion of language study, adjustment, candidate qualifications, etc. Approved.[3]

Now with responses in hand from several hundred TEAM

members, the advisory committee, with at least twelve mission field leaders participating, spent several days discussing the substance and wording of the proposed revision. The missionaries' views bore significant weight. This was highly desirable as they were qualified to give counsel; too, their work would be directly affected by the result. The revision—as reworked—was again sent to the entire mission family, reviewed once again by the advisory committee and the board, and adopted at the annual meeting in 1960.

This document—with some later amendments—has proved to be a necessary and helpful guide to administering the work overseas and at home. Designed to be a unifying factor in the widespread work of TEAM, it has served well. T. J. Bach once said that the mission's principles and guiding rules can be properly interpreted only if those involved are spiritual. There is truth to that observation. It is also true that careful administration removes obstacles to spiritual blessing.

The Value of the Advisory Committee

The advisory committee, which served so well in the revision of the basic documents, was actually an anomaly. It existed apart from any authorization in the Constitution and Principles and Guiding Rules. It had no legislative power or administrative function. Its sole purpose was to study the objectives, policies, methods, and work of the mission and make recommendations to the board of directors. If the men of the board found that the recommendations had merit—and they consistently found this to be so—then the board could and did give authority to the recommendations. Field organizations could do the same on recommendations affecting the field work.

A Matter for Concern

On a tour of eleven TEAM fields in 1960, I became aware of a trend that adversely affected our ministry. It was the result of a good thing that had gotten out of balance—specialization. On one field, for example, out of a total of thirty-five missionaries, only four couples and one single worker were involved in the basic church planting ministries. Others were in administration, Bible school teaching, correspondence courses, linguistic work, medical work, preparing audio-visual materials, radio work, and teaching missionary children. All of these ministries were not only useful but many were vital. What then was the problem?

The problem had two aspects. The first was that very often these specialties—even those whose purpose was evangelism—were thought of as ends in themselves and not adequately related to the basic mission objective of evangelism leading to planting and nurturing churches. The second was that not enough candidates were available for the "old-fashioned" work of church planting.

TEAM was not alone in facing this problem. In the post World War II period there was much emphasis on specialization in missionary work—often without definition of what specialization was needed. A common statement went something like this: "The day of the general missionary is past." The results of this attitude could be detected in TEAM's work by the early 1960s—a leveling off and even a decline on some fields of the central church planting ministry.

I began to share my observations in our newsletter *TEAM Topics,* which was sent to all missionaries quarterly. In one article I shared the concern expressed by the chairman of one of the larger fields:

> The statistics over the past five years reveal an alarming trend away from a church planting ministry. This presents a real danger and calls for our immediate prayer and attention. In 1960 we had 73 station missionaries on 28 different stations. This year we have 46 station missionaries on 20 stations. This is a loss of 27 station missionaries in less than five years. This loss is reflected in the number baptized. Five years ago missionaries baptized 255 and last year 104. Total baptisms—TEAM and national church—five years ago were 403; this year 290.[4]

Elsewhere in his report the chairman referred to the number who had entered project ministries. Extremely important in themselves, the projects were failing to reap the results which should be theirs because church planting was being neglected.

What to Do About It

This situation motivated me to make an "in-depth ministry" the subject of major emphasis. This was not an effort to deny the value of the special ministries but to instill a purpose that such work should be judged by its contribution to church development.

One point I tried to make, by way of illustration, related to Bible correspondence courses. It was possible to advertise widely and attract many students from scattered areas, with follow-up being difficult or impossible. The preferred alternative was to use the correspondence courses as a tool, distributing the invitations in a more restricted area where it would be possible to follow up, either by inviting the students to a study center to prepare their answers or to have occasional rallies of the students. Following that, there should be some opportunity to disciple the converts and bring them together into an embryo church, if an evangelical church did not already exist in the area. Other correspondence courses could be used as discipling tools. It was possible to give illustrations of success from TEAM and non-TEAM work.

Advisory Committee Study

The advisory committee chose church planting and development as a major topic for study over a period of several years. Its recommendations resulted in a renewed emphasis on a ministry which would gather the fruit of evangelism into New Testament-type congregations.

School Concern Enlisted

The advisory committee asked the candidate secretary, Delbert Kuehl, to share the mission's concerns with schools where missionaries are trained, which he did in the following statement from the committee:

> Due to the predominant emphasis today on technical skills, a
> large number of missionary volunteers have in mind some

technical ministry on the mission field. This has resulted in a serious dearth of evangelistic and Bible-teaching missionaries. The urgent need is for men with a burning passion to reach the lost, who will identify themselves with the people, who will preach from house to house, on the street, in the market place, to the few and to the many, in order to win them to Christ, making disciples and establishing, through the faithful teaching of the Word, vital functioning churches thoroughly equipped to carry on a spiritual ministry. For all such, missions can offer the most challenging opportunities for service today.[5]

Encouraging responses were received from the leaders of a number of schools.

A Hopeful Trend

A change in the direction of a trend does not take place overnight, nor in a year. But attention to the key factors can bring discernible progress to the desired goal. The minutes of field councils and annual field conferences began to mention increased concentration on church planting, and in time TEAM began to give far more serious effort to this central ministry.

It took longer to see a change in the general homeland attitude. But a change did come, at least enough to fan the flame of interest in this central purpose of missions. Applications increased perceptibly from men and women who understood the New Testament teaching and example of having the fruits of evangelism preserved in local churches. Candidate classes, under the direction of Delbert Kuehl, strengthened the emphasis. Annual conference sessions were planned to involve the furloughed missionaries in discussions.

In time it was gratifying to hear missionaries clearly describe TEAM as a mission with its goal as the church and its purpose to have its varied special ministries contribute strongly to that goal.

A Variety of Activities

While the principal work of the mission is done on the foreign fields, there is related activity at home which has a bearing on the work overseas. A quick perusal of reports and business items considered by the board in 1962 and 1963 reveals some areas of particular interest.

- January 1962—The general director suggested as a prayer burden that our national churches move out in foreign missions.
- January 1962—Field committee name changed to field council.
- January 1962—Richard Winchell, South Africa, reported Light of Life Bible Correspondence courses enrolled sixty thousand.
- January 1962—George Martin reported missionary participation in 1,442 homeland meetings in 1961.
- April 1962—Mortenson reported discussions about transfer of responsibility for Ebenezer Bible Institute, Venezuela, to the national church.
- May 1962—Recommendation to annual meeting that the constitution be amended to increase board membership to twelve.
- January 1963—General director reported accepting the presidency of the Interdenominational Foreign Mission Association (IFMA).
- March 1963—Mortenson outlined goals set for the seventy-fifth anniversary in 1965, including strong evangelistic programs on all fields.
- March 1963—General director reported on Europe trip where he emphasized TEAM's policy of church planting and noted steady progress in that direction. Investigated Austria as a new field.
- April 1963—Board favors Austria as a new field.
- May 1963—Tom Watson reported conversation with two men of the Caribbean Broadcasting Company about possible TEAM interest in Trinidad.
- June 1963—Trinidad approved as a new field, subject to an agreement with the Caribbean Broadcasting Company.
- December 1963—Agreement finalized to absorb the Caribbean Broadcasting Company.

Sharing the Foreign Administration
One matter the board of directors called to my attention in early

1963 was the delay in assigning responsibility for assistance in the foreign work, as I had earlier suggested would be done. The recorded minute of April 2, 1963, put it quite plainly:

> The general director is to recommend to the board, on or before the next annual meeting, a procedure whereby certain of the staff assistants be designated to take charge of correspondence, general supervision, and the making of recommendations with reference to the work of the mission in certain designated fields. This is in no way to lessen his being the final authority in decisions that are made, but to relieve him of the necessity of receiving and answering the large volume of mail pertaining to field matters.[6]

There were several obvious reasons for the board's concern. All the work previously handled by Johnson, except stewardship matters, was now coming to my desk. To add to the problem, I was getting requests from a number of field councils that I visit their fields to help with certain matters. The result was that in the eighteen months I had been in office, I had been overseas twelve weeks and was getting ready to go on another trip of three and a half weeks.

The board had a helpful recommendation related to the public ministry at home: that Don W. Hillis be named associate director for conference ministries and publications. This was work which Hillis was already doing, but the designation emphasized its importance at a time when my attention was directed more to executive responsibilities.

The question of who was to have final authority in my absence needed to be addressed. The board took action on that matter also, recommending that Delbert Kuehl become executive assistant director while continuing as candidate secretary. Kuehl would assist me in the foreign work generally, and particularly in certain specific field areas I was to designate, and he would also officially represent me in my absence.

In September I informed the board that I had assigned Kuehl the Latin America fields of Venezuela-Colombia, Netherlands Antilles, and Peru. Two years later George Martin was given responsibility for the Far East fields of Japan, Korea, and Taiwan and in 1967 his area was widened to include all the Asia fields.

Homecall of T. J. Bach

Dr. Bach had kept a full schedule through much of the seventeen years since his official retirement. At the request of field councils he had ministered in Africa, Europe, Latin America, and the Far East with much of his former vigor and continued spiritual blessing. He had served as chairman of the board of directors from 1948 to 1951, continued to accept invitations to speak at churches, and kept up wide personal correspondence. He tried to attend the TEAM conference each year.

Bach had several episodes of life-threatening health problems but the Lord restored him to activity each time. In his later years he made his home in Yucaipa, California, where on June 12, 1963, he passed unexpectedly and quietly into the presence of the Lord at the age of eighty-two. The memorial service was held at the Salem Evangelical Free Church of Chicago and burial was in the Mt. Olivet Cemetery, Chicago, not far from the grave of Fredrik Franson.

In the quarter century following Bach's death there were many who well remembered the spiritual impact of his life on theirs. He was truly a Spirit-filled apostle of love. His part in opening up western Venezuela to the gospel and laying the foundations for a widening church planting ministry must surely have received the Lord's "well done."

Gundersen Finishes Race

Mr. Carl Gundersen, in his position as chairman of the board of directors, made a number of trips to visit the work of the missionaries. These included a tour of the Africa and Europe fields in 1952, Latin America in 1949, 1955, and 1958, and a round-the-world trip to eleven fields with David Johnson in 1957. He and Mrs. Gundersen had a special interest in the hospital ministry in Rhodesia, radio work in Aruba and Peru, and the church building needs in Japan, to mention a few.

Mr. Gundersen's service on the board extended to thirty-five years. In the latter part of that time he attended and chaired the board meetings in spite of failing health, the last one being in April 1964. Only a few weeks later, on May 3, the Lord called him home. Fellow board members recall with appreciation Mr. Gundersen's love for the Word of God which led to his memorizing long passages of Scripture. One inspiring memory was when he quoted the entire epistle to the Ephesians in a way that brought out its powerful message. David H. Johnson was elected to succeed him as chairman.

Approaching Seventy-five Years

As the time for observing the diamond anniversary of TEAM approached, the administrative men on the staff began to outline plans for appropriate activity at home and on the mission fields. Just at that time I had the opportunity for renewed contact with Mr. and Mrs. Nolan F. Balman, who had served on TEAM's South Africa field. Balman had been principal of the Evangelical Teacher Training College, founder-principal of the Durban Bible College, and acting field chairman. He was now teaching at the Lancaster School of the Bible. Thinking of the need for someone to coordinate the planned anniversary activities I broached the possibility to him. Balman accepted the board's assignment and in cooperation with the administrative staff began to coordinate the activities. The publication department under Hillis had special articles in *The Missionary Broadcaster* to highlight the occasion. A book of pictures plus text, *Light is Sprung Up*, was readied for introduction at the conference held in Wheaton, Illinois.[7]

One rewarding aspect of the anniversary observance was the decision to involve the missionaries. They were urged to pray for at least seventy-five applicants during the anniversary year and particularly for those needed on their own fields. Kuehl was able to report that the goal was met with the receipt of 78 applications in 1965.

Goals for the Seventy-fifth Anniversary

The fields were also asked to prayerfully and carefully establish realistic goals in their work for 1965—goals that could be measured that year and extended into the future. The overall purpose set before them was *Intensified Evangelism and Church Planting*. These goals were also to be prayer topics that would be remembered faithfully and shared with other intercessors.

Only a selection can be given of the one hundred goals established by the fields but they are enough to reveal the purpose and longing of those who invested their lives in winning the lost.

Western India:

- Year-long concerted effort to win 300 souls to Christ.
- Seven new congregations in 1965.
- Train lay Christians in personal witnessing.
- Increase efforts to train nationals in spiritual leadership.
- Add two new Light of Life correspondence courses.

Pakistan:

- Tent evangelism ministry in six new areas in 1965.
- Carefully planned evangelistic visits in numerous villages.
- New efforts to reach secluded Muslim women with the gospel.
- Enroll 300 new students in Bible correspondence courses.

Irian Jaya:

- Extensive evangelistic visits in all areas.
- Home evangelistic visits in Manokwari with local Christians.
- Complete rough draft of Gospel of Mark for Manikion people.
- Establish three new Asmat churches.
- Make contacts and preach Christ in ten Awju villages.

Japan:

- Designate cities for advance and pray for 30 new workers
- Concentrated evangelism in key TEAM areas.
- Each national church to evangelize adjacent areas.
- Cooperate with Japanese churches in setting up a mission board.

- Establish new Bible camp in Nagoya area.

Many reports over the next two years revealed forward movement directly related to these goals. Not all goals were reached, it is true, but substantial progress was made. Some fields followed through by making goal-setting a yearly exercise, with gratifying results.

Seventy-fifth Anniversary Conference

The general director regularly gives a keynote address at each annual conference. At the 1965 conference my topic was *Build Upon This Foundation.* A few excerpts from that message will be of help as we try to put TEAM's history in perspective.

> It would have seemed bold in 1940, TEAM's fiftieth anniversary, to predict a doubling in size in the next 25 years. With China and Japan closed because of war, Europe overrun by the Nazis, and America soon to be involved, a spirit of defeat would have been understandable. But, on the contrary, Dr. T. J. Bach and other mission leaders called for more volunteers and encouraged advance. The 1940 annual report revealed the following statistics: 6 fields, 160 missionaries, 168 organized churches, and 16,892 communicants. There was one bookstore, one Christian magazine, one print shop, two Bible institutes, no radio station or programs, no hospitals, no teacher training schools, no linguistic work, no correspondence courses and no Bible camps.

> It would have seemed visionary then to predict tremendous growth in the postwar period; but now we can report 19 fields of service, 840 missionaries, 3 radio stations, 6 hospitals, 35 bookstores, 10 Bible colleges and institutes, and correspondence courses reaching hundreds of thousands. In 1940 there were 111 organized churches in addition to those on the China field, which had half of the national believers. This year's report [1965] shows 336 organized churches and 399 groups of believers in process of establishment.[8]

In a leap of imagination I tried to look ahead twenty-five years:

> What will the situation be if we are permitted to hold a centennial conference in 1990? Will there be continued expansion so we can look forward to having 1,500 missionaries, 2,500 churches, 250,000 members and 2,500 pastors and evangelists?[9]

Then I asked some additional questions: What kind of a mission will TEAM be? What are the threats? What kind of building material? What is the plan?

> Will we diligently press forward until our scriptural objectives are realized? In 1990, will these churches be true to the Word of God, uncompromising in their stand for the faith, unspotted by the world, and active in witness because of the truly spiritual and scriptural nature of our present work of building?[10]

Many—nationals and missionaries—have planted, others have watered. Only God can make it grow.

EXPANDING OUTREACH

At the time—1965—that the seventy-fifth anniversary conference was being held at the Evangelical Free Church in Wheaton, Illinois, plans for TEAM's new headquarters buildings just over three miles to the north were well under way. By early 1964 it had become clear that TEAM would soon need a larger headquarters facility. The mission continued to grow and there was no room for expansion on the Chicago property.

Some other Christian organizations had moved to Wheaton, twenty-five miles west, but TEAM resisted that move. Business contacts were more convenient in Chicago, foreign consular offices were near at hand, and missionaries coming by train or air could be easily met and assisted. There were also many church contacts in the metropolitan area.

As Rolf Egeland and I searched for a solution, we thought we might locate some vacant land to the northwest within the city limits, convenient to transportation. After several months we found a vacant plot of less than one acre about eight miles distant. It would be enough to provide for an office building and some apartments, although parking space would be marginal. On serious inquiry we learned that the price was $264,000. This sum, plus the construction costs, was far more than the mission could handle, with all the usual needs faced in the work. Nevertheless, we committed the matter to the Lord, knowing that our need was real.

When we took the question to the board of directors, one member of the board, Robert C. Van Kampen, spoke up and offered to contribute a plot of 4.9 acres just north of the border of Wheaton, in the village of Carol Stream. Thus the Lord had answered prayer in a remarkable way. It did not take the board long to agree that the move should be made and with little delay. We found later that the missionaries were most enthusiastic about the decision.

The three buildings which were started in August 1965—an office building, missionary furlough home, and staff apartments—were completed in time to move in on July 22, 1966. Rolf Egeland carried the main responsibility for this project. To represent TEAM in dealing with the builders, he enlisted the help of Lloyd Anderson, a skilled missionary builder who had served with the Unevangelized Fields Mission in Haiti. The move from Chicago to Wheaton was made smoothly, the office having to be closed only one day.

Other Headquarters Concerns

The years 1965-66 had other activities of interest at the home base. One was our concern and intercession for the Harold Lovestrand family in Indonesia. Harold had been arrested in September 1965 in Manokwari, Irian Jaya, on suspicion of aiding tribespeople who were rebelling against the Indonesian government. He and the family were taken by boat to Jakarta where Harold was kept in solitary confinement without any formal charge being filed against him. The two older children were in high school in the Philippines. Muriel and the younger children were at liberty to live in a guest facility in Jakarta.

At TEAM headquarters we prayed diligently for Harold's release and maintained frequent contact with the U.S. State Department and the parents of both Harold and Muriel. The State Department officers were eager to keep the negotiations on a low key and out of the news so as not to arouse the captors to manufacture false charges to justify their action.

I needed to be in Korea in October 1965, so I flew on to Indonesia to give assurance to Muriel and the families of our concern and to confer with the U.S. Ambassador. This visit to Jakarta would also allow me to speak at some length with the chairman of our Irian Jaya field, Calvin Roesler, who came out from his jungle station of Ayam for the purpose. I did not ask to see Harold or talk with the Indonesian authorities, feeling that this matter was best left to the U.S. consular officials, who were doing their best to obtain Harold's release. Months of waiting and praying followed until we received a cablegram in late March 1966 that Harold had been released and the family was en route home.

No charges were ever filed and there is some mystery as to why Harold was arrested. There was a rumor that radio transmissions from some source gave information to the rebels. The local authorities knew that Harold had been a radio operator in the military and that he used a Missavia two-way radio for missionary communication, as did many others. It should not have taken long for the police to satisfy themselves of his innocence.

Needless to say, it was with great joy and praise to God that those gathered at the TEAM conference in May 1966 welcomed the Lovestrands home from their extended ordeal. The Lord used the circumstance to bind the whole TEAM family together in concern and intercession.

A Base in Australia

TEAM's home base was in the United States. There was no particular desire to establish centers in other countries, and yet there was a willingness to do so, if necessary. That need arose in Canada in 1946 and in Australia in 1964. Several Australians had applied to TEAM: a couple for the Near East, a missionary in India married to a Canadian lady, several workers helping at the Oasis Hospital, and a couple in Japan. When this latter couple, Hugh and Frances Osborne, were on furlough in Australia they told us their interests would be better served if TEAM were recognized in that country.

As I was in Europe, the Near East, and India in late 1964, I continued on to Australia to confer with Mr. Osborne and others. As a result, a charter was drawn up for an Australian TEAM Council, with the Rev. A. R. Ritchie as the first chairman. An organization meeting was held in Camberwell, Victoria, April 1, 1965. One of the council members was the Rev. E. Arthur Collins, who became chairman after the resignation of Mr. Ritchie in 1968. By 1988 Mr. Collins had served as chairman for twenty years. With his background as field director of the Aborigines Inland Mission he has provided gifted leadership and continuity in representing TEAM and maintaining relationships with missionaries sent out from Australia.

The annual meeting of the Australia council in April 1966 informed the board that a full-time missionary representative was needed to expand TEAM's interests. Mr. and Mrs. Carl Davis were completing one phase of their work in Pakistan so the board invited them to represent TEAM in Australia, a ministry which they began in 1967 and continued until 1974. They established a headquarters center in Homebush, a suburb of Sydney. Their seven-year leadership brought TEAM recognition and an increase of missionaries commissioned and supported from Australia. Davis was succeeded by the Rev. Brian Thitchener and he, in turn, by David Brook, an Australian TEAM missionary to Japan whose wife is Canadian. In late 1988 there were ten active Australian missionaries on seven fields.

A New Try to Enter Nepal

For many decades, there has been much prayer for the closed areas and resistant peoples along the northern frontier of the Indian subcontinent. Early missionaries sent out by Franson penetrated and served in some of these border areas with reasonably good results. TEAM missionaries did not enter again until 1946 in northern Pakistan, earlier known as the Northwest Frontier Province, and in Bhot bordering Tibet and Nepal.

Missionaries of the Tibetan Frontier field often looked across the river to Nepal and prayed about entry with the gospel. Short trips were made on occasion and in September 1955 the Nepal government gave permission for TEAM to send in agricultural workers. However, Nepal asked the mission to sign an agreement that its missionaries would not preach the Christian gospel or seek converts. It was one thing to be aware of laws against such activity and another to actually promise not to preach. That opportunity was let pass, trusting that another would come when the terms were relaxed.

Ten years later the board was informed of the possibility of taking over an existing medical work in western Nepal which a Dr. Katharine Young had opened but must now leave for age and health reasons. Dr. and Mrs. Maynard Seaman were eager to enter. Seaman and missionary Albert Bowdish made a survey trip and submitted a full report to the board. At its meeting of June 14, 1968, the board gave its approval. The patient waiting of thirteen years was rewarded with a difficult work assignment to those who must travel by foot over rugged terrain and live under extremely primitive conditions. That was the reward the Seamans and Mr. and Mrs. Peter Hanks welcomed.

Afghanistan Opens—Slightly

Afghanistan was closed to missionaries. Some "tentmakers" had been able to have a quiet ministry there over a number of years. One of them was Dr. Christy Wilson, who held a teaching post. Dr. Wilson saw the possibility of forming a group which could negotiate with the Afghan government to place skilled personnel in teaching positions and medical work. He contacted a number of missions working in countries bordering Afghanistan and arranged an initial meeting in Pakistan. William Pietsch, chairman of TEAM's Pakistan field, sent a report and urged that I attend the organizational meeting in Kabul in February 1966.

Representatives of seven missions spent several days seeking a basis for cooperation. All present were fully evangelical in their personal faith but two were from missions whose relationships were broader than TEAM's. This broader spectrum created a problem for TEAM with its position of restricting cooperation in spiritual ministries to those sponsored by groups holding to fundamental doctrines. With two of the missions also being more broad in doctrinal interpretation, there was no way that TEAM could join the effort. But here was a group of individuals, evangelical in doctrine, sincerely desirous of finding a way to establish a gospel witness in Afghanistan. TEAM Pakistan missionaries, though not present in that meeting, had the same earnest desire to reach their nearest neighbors.

When it seemed that TEAM and two other missions would not participate, the others were ready to listen to a possible solution. I proposed that the International Afghan Mission (later called International Assistance Mission) be a mission of individual members and not of mission organizations. Board membership would be restricted to individuals who could without reservation subscribe to a biblical statement of faith.

The next necessity was to see that the statement of faith included a strong statement on the full inspiration of the Scriptures. The different definitions given by Americans and Europeans to theological terms presented a problem, but in time it was possible to reach an understanding. One other point needed to be made. We did not want this new mission ever to come under the influence of the World Council of Churches. A proposal was accepted that it was never to join any outside organization without the unanimous consent of the board. So the International Afghan Mission (IAM) became a reality in that country seemingly so fast-closed to the message of life in Jesus Christ.

Inter-Mission Conferences

The 1960s gave rise to a number of conferences and cooperative undertakings—World Vision Crusades, Billy Graham Crusades, Evangelism in Depth, New Life for All, the Wheaton Congress on the Church's Worldwide Mission, the Berlin Congress on Evangelism, to name a few. Field leaders and some national church representatives wanted to be involved in evangelism and also welcomed opportunities to participate in study conferences. If TEAM joined in the activity there would be criticism from some circles in the homeland; if it did not participate there would be criticism from others. It was clear that the mission's position could not be determined by popular opinion. How thankful we were for

Dr. Johnson's spiritual foresight in formulating the resolution of May 13, 1958, providing firm guidelines. Every opportunity for participation was measured by this position. TEAM personnel joined in some activities and refrained from joining in others.

The Congress on the Church's Worldwide Mission held in Wheaton in April 1966 was sponsored jointly by the Interdenominational Foreign Mission Association (IFMA) and the Evangelical Foreign Missions Association (EFMA). Dr. Louis L. King of the Christian and Missionary Alliance and I served as joint chairmen. More than a thousand mission personnel participated and worked out a carefully thought through and discussed *Wheaton Declaration* which presented guidelines on current mission questions.[1]

A Radio Secretary

Several staff changes were made in this period. Tom Watson, Jr., the founder of TEAM's HLKX radio station in Korea, was invited by the board chairman, Carl Gundersen, to become radio secretary on the staff. Gundersen hoped for greater coordination and better results in the representation of TEAM's three radio stations and five program recording centers. This was a new concept in the administration of the field ministries. The preferred and time-tested pattern in TEAM was that the annual field conference, through its field council, controlled the ministries—setting ministry policies, assigning personnel, and monitoring the finances. The radio secretary arrangement created administrative uncertainties which I had to deal with on field visits. Even more difficult was the bleak financial picture, caused by insufficient budget controls and a weakening of direct contact with the supporters of the radio ministries. It was necessary for me to return the radio administration to the proper field councils and responsibility for supporter contacts to the directors of the ministries. This slowed the downward financial trend, but full recovery took several years.

Watson was asked to become editor of the mission's magazine,

The Missionary Broadcaster. He proposed a change of name to *Horizons* and some modification of format. These proposals were approved by the board. Watson, a gifted writer, did an excellent job as editor. He also produced a number of mission films. In this he had the cooperation of Kenneth Semenchuk, who later became responsible for the film department.

Controller

A businessman friend of TEAM and treasurer of a TEAM east coast committee which functioned for a time, J. Carlton Seeland, was invited to join the accounting department and some months later was made controller. He had many years of experience in handling the accounting of a steamship business and brought a high degree of skill to the work. In the seventy-five years of TEAM's history he was the first to serve as controller, a long overdue provision. He continued with TEAM for more than twelve years until retirement.

Canadian Corporate Changes

A reorganization of TEAM's Canadian corporate structure became necessary in 1967. Stuart and Margaret Gunzel, who were in charge of the mission's center in Moose Jaw, Saskatchewan, had been invited to spend six months in Taiwan to minister to Mongols who had settled there. During their absence, Wilfred and Dorothy Strom of the Rhodesia field were asked to serve.

In March, Strom informed the board that there had been a change in the Canadian National Revenue Service regulations concerning non-profit organizations. It would be necessary for our Saskatchewan corporation to revise its charter and apply for new registration. As a step in qualifying, the board in Canada was required to give evidence of its corporate autonomy.

The legal formalities were easily cared for; then to insure that the U.S. and Canadian corporations would maintain unity of purpose, a formal agreement was drawn up defining their relationship. In essence this agreement provided that the work of the two corporations of TEAM would be carried on in harmony with the statement of faith and the principles and procedures outlined in the *Principles and Practices of TEAM*. It recognized one general director as the chief administrative officer and coordinator of the missionary work. Financial administration was also to be coordinated. Though existing as separate corporations in North America, missionaries were to work together as TEAM in the overseas fields. The Canadian corporation applied for and was granted federal incorporation as TEAM of Canada, Inc., in 1969.

Assistant to the General Director

One day in 1967, Joseph Horness, then the vice chairman of the board, had some questions for me.

"When Johnson was general director did he not have you to work alongside him, to share in the work, and to care for it when he was away? Shouldn't you have such an assistant?"

I responded by saying that I had able and dedicated coworkers sharing in the administrative responsibilities. He was not satisfied but asked, "If something should happen to you, who would be prepared to take over?"

I named one of my associates as being qualified.

"That is all very good," Horness replied, "but he has his own work and is not acquainted with the scope of your responsibilities the way you were with Johnson's."

About a month later, I came to Mr. Horness with a question of my own: "You know Dick Winchell on the South Africa field who heads up the extensive Word of Life Publication ministry. I have long been impressed by him and believe it is time to call him into the home office to work with me."

"Yes, I know him and respect him. I saw him at work on the field," Horness responded.

He then mentioned the name of another missionary with considerable gifts and asked if I had considered him. I had, but said that I questioned whether he would easily fit into the position of assistant to the general director, which was the need of the moment.

Richard Winchell Appointed

The matter of calling an assistant was brought to the executive committee of the board on December 15, 1967, and I was authorized to write to Winchell. I wrote first to the chairman of the South Africa field and from him received assurance that it would be all right to approach Winchell. He added that Winchell was filling an important post and having an excellent ministry but might be ready for a new challenge. I then wrote direct to Winchell. What I offered was work of a general nature without too many specifics. I did assure him that he would be supported in prayer as he considered what might be the Lord's leading. On January 26 I reported to the board that Winchell had replied favorably.

While in South Africa in March 1968, I spent some time with Winchell reviewing the type of work he could expect. Knowing of his gifts for effective public ministry I assured him that there would be a fair proportion of that kind of work, but not to the extent that it kept him away from the office a great deal.

My next stop was to be our Rhodesia field so I invited Winchell to join me for a week or so. When the scheduled Bible teacher had to cancel at the last minute, the Rhodesia field chairman, Roy Eichner, asked Winchell to take the twice-daily messages. This gave a good opportunity for the missionaries to get to know him. It also allowed me to hear him as a Bible teacher and I was pleased. While together, we agreed that Winchell should start his work at the Wheaton headquarters the first week of September 1968.

Joseph Horness Becomes Chairman

At the meeting of the board in June 1968, Johnson mentioned his approaching seventy-fifth birthday in October and requested that he not be reelected chairman of the board. The vice chairman, Joseph Horness, was named to succeed him. Horness had been a board member for twenty years. He was an active Christian layman and president of a company in Muskegon, Michigan, which manufactured office and laboratory furniture. Horness had visited TEAM mission fields in Africa and Europe and was a perceptive observer of the work. He had a gift for asking a question in a few words that focused on the heart of the subject under discussion.

Death of David H. Johnson

Johnson was preparing to reduce his activity in TEAM and proposed to give up the position of stewardship director at the time of his seventy-fifth birthday, October 23. He offered to come in weekly to help with legal questions. Johnson wanted to keep involved and active. On September 26, 1968, he came to the office in mid-forenoon, sat down at his desk, and immediately passed into the presence of his Master. The Lord knew his reluctance to retire. He was survived by his wife, Edna, and children, Doris and Donald. Burial was at the Wheaton Cemetery.

David H. Johnson's ministry, under the Lord's blessing, made a great impact on TEAM's missionary work. The scope was doubled and the number of workers more than tripled during his fifteen years of leadership. Fields increased from seven to fifteen and the count of active missionaries from 228 to 818. The harvest that followed was made possible by this expansion in the fields being reaped and the harvest crew at work. Johnson was described more than once in the words first applied to Barnabas in Acts 11:24, "For he was a good man, and full of the Holy Ghost and of faith, and many people were added to the Lord."

SUMNA Merger

When I was president of the IFMA, 1962-1965, I presented a paper describing the advantages of having some smaller missions of like purpose merge in order to enhance effectiveness. TEAM had some experience with mergers, as with the Tibetan Frontier Mission, Door of Hope Mission, and the Caribbean Broadcasting Company. My paper was not intended as a hint that TEAM was seeking further mergers. But the suggestion of merger remained in the memory of John Russell, U.S. secretary of the Sudan United Mission, North American Branch (SUMNA), when that mission had decided to separate from the international organization of the

SUM. He apparently shared his interest with the SUM North American Council in Toronto and in May 1968 representatives of the SUMNA met with TEAM administrative men to gather pertinent information.

SUMNA had a large, flourishing work on the continent of Africa, in the Republic of Chad. The council in Toronto decided to send council member Alex Stein and Canadian secretary Gerald Morehouse to Chad for the field conference in late December 1968 and urged me to be present also. I invited Arthur Johnston, chairman of TEAM's France field, to accompany me as interpreter and to help communicate TEAM principles and procedures to the missionaries and Chadian pastors. French is one of Chad's official languages, and there were also some European missionaries working with SUMNA whose language was French. After one long session when we answered numerous questions about TEAM and what the mission would do if it assumed responsibility for the Chad work, the missionaries went into a closed business session to decide on a recommendation to the home council. Johnston and I were in a separate part of the building. About forty-five minutes later we heard the missionaries singing the doxology. I remarked to Johnston, "They are either rejoicing that the Lord has led to a decision to join TEAM or else they are rejoicing that they escaped that prospect." We were called in and informed that the vote had been unanimous in favor of merger.

Additional studies were needed for a proper understanding of all that was involved. After both boards voted approval, the formal merger took place at the Wheaton headquarters April 25, 1969. The SUMNA headquarters in Toronto became TEAM of Canada's Eastern Canada Center under the responsibility of Gerald and Jean Morehouse and assisted by Gladys Lee, former Chad missionary.

Eightieth Anniversary

TEAM's eightieth anniversary, 1970-71, was marked by the publication of *The Sovereign Hand* by Paul H. Sheetz, concerning whom I wrote in the introduction to the book:

The author…has watched with understanding and discernment the unfolding of missionary work for more than a quarter of a century, having served in the Netherlands Antilles and Venezuela, at TEAM headquarters in the Publication Department, and in literature work in Latin America.[2]

My comment on the history presented in the book to that point was briefly stated in the introduction:

In TEAM's 80-year history we have seen a number of fields close. We know, too, that some workers have turned back from their field of battle. We also acknowledge that there are vast areas which have not been adequately evangelized. But, with thanksgiving to God, we acknowledge great victories where earlier, unrelieved darkness is now dotted with lighthouses of earnest, witnessing Christians.[3]

Administrative Philosophy

In earlier chapters I referred to the administrative styles of Bach and Johnson. To be consistent, I should do the same for my time as general director, but that is not easy. It is not possible to look objectively at one's own attitudes and work habits. What I consider strong points may not be viewed as such by my associates. Nevertheless, I will make some comments.

We were different in our written communication with the missionaries. Both Dr. Bach and Dr. Johnson wrote many articles for publication in *The Missionary Broadcaster*. Bach's were mostly mission-related devotional Bible studies. Johnson's were, in large part, exhortations to vision and diligence, coupled with relating the results as seen in the work on the fields. What they wrote was both helpful and necessary. Neither wrote much in the way of guidance for the missionaries or as explanations of the work to the supporters. My opportunities to do so were greater because there was not only *The Missionary Broadcaster* but also two papers that were sent to the missionary family, *TEAM Topics* and *Monthly TEAM Memo*. The general director had the privilege of writing the lead article in the papers to the missionaries. Going through copies I find a strong emphasis on the objectives of the mission—evangelism and discipling leading to planting and developing churches.

Missionaries were asked to evaluate their ministries as they related to the central work of church planting.

Field conferences and inter-field consultations gave further opportunity to speak on these ministry topics. A good opportunity came when I was assigned a paper on a pertinent subject. Several of these papers have had quite wide circulation within the mission family, such as *Guidelines for Church Planting* and *Directed Evangelism*. Some articles, originally published in *The Missionary Broadcaster,* were grouped together in the book *This is TEAM.*[4]

Even as the administrative styles of Bach and Johnson were influenced by the backgrounds of these men, the same was undoubtedly true of mine. Work of almost seven years in the business world plus the biblical teaching about the members of the Body of Christ provided the mold which gave shape to my thinking on administration.

My banking experience was divided into two segments, about six and a half years in a medium-sized bank and three months in a giant institution. Our work in the smaller bank allowed room for some individual judgment and initiative. We were free to recommend changes within the broader guidelines and such recommendations were given consideration. If we made a good case for their adoption we could go ahead.

In the large bank everything was structured. Procedures were not changed unless the department on forms and methods initiated the change. The latter method had some advantages, but it also stifled initiative and was quite boring. I never felt I was an integral part of the operation, whereas I felt so much a part of the smaller bank that I maintained friendly ties with its officers through the years and had no hesitation in recommending it to others.

Applying this background to the administration of the mission, I wanted very much to have my associates feel they were essential participants in the action and that their views on the work would be taken into consideration. Applying the lessons from Scripture, I viewed the fellow workers as members of the Body of Christ, indwelt and guided by the Spirit of God. The work of every member had significance. Others will have to judge whether my concept was translated into positive action that fellow staff members could see and appreciate.

International Coordination

The members of the official administrative staff met regularly—usually twice a month—for coordination and prayer. They also participated in an annual three-day study retreat for a more in-depth consideration of the administrative side of the work. This was different than the advisory committee of missionaries and staff which addressed broad field policies. In 1971, Carl Davis, Australia home secretary, was to attend so representatives from Canada—Stuart Gunzel, Sam Archer, and Gerald Morehouse—were also urged to be present.

One agenda item was the relationship among TEAM's home offices in Canada, the United States, and Australia. I felt this would be a good opportunity to consider thoroughly the subject of internationalization, which refers primarily to having home bases in a number of sending countries. My paper for that session was titled *The Organizational Nature of TEAM*. I compared TEAM with several other international missions. If there was one home base and a number of fields, the home base provided the unity. If there were several home bases but only one field, the field authority was the unifying factor. Multiple base/multiple field missions faced administrative problems unless there was one focus of unity. The question: how does TEAM insure that it will operate as one mission and not three? The unifying factor pointed out in the paper was what is now called the *Principles and Practice of TEAM* composed of Constitution, Bylaws, and Guiding Principles.[5]

Provision is made for adherence to one statement of faith, the seniority of one home board in the conduct of the foreign missionary work, the leadership of one general director, a unified financial system, and coordinated procedures. Though several corporations are involved, TEAM functions as one mission.

Staff Changes

A number of changes in the home staff were made in the years 1971 to 1973. Miss Goldye Gustafson, a former China missionary who had served as my secretary since 1951, was loaned to the Rhodesia field for one year while the secretary of that field, Miss Shirley Bradford, promised to serve for one year in the general director's office. It is of interest that these assignments both ended in marriage, Goldye Gustafson to Mr. Cecyl Till in Rhodesia and Shirley Bradford to Dr. John Bennett, TEAM medical director.

Nolan F. Balman, who had served as coordinator of the seventy-fifth anniversary observances, became deputation (extension) secretary for church relations. When he accepted an assignment in Pennsylvania, Lyle H. Petersen, Japan missionary, succeeded to that post. Tom Watson, Jr. resigned from TEAM and his position as editor of *Horizons*. Don Hillis resumed that work, followed in 1973 by Harry Genet. George Martin, area secretary for the Asia fields, became Pacific Northwest representative and coordinator of Target 7, a program mobilizing evangelism and discipling on the fields. Carl Davis, having completed his term in Australia, was appointed Asia foreign secretary. In April 1972, the board appointed Richard Winchell associate general director, effective May 16, "with executive responsibility for areas of the work to be determined by the general director."[6]

The board had changed Winchell's title with the understanding that this was a step toward his eventual appointment to succeed me as general director. His expanded executive assignment was to provide experience for the larger responsibilities. This appointment took into consideration that Delbert Kuehl, executive assistant director, who served as deputy in my absence, had requested that he not be in line to succeed me.

In March 1974 the board approved other staff changes. Jack F. MacDonald, who with his wife, Miriam, had served on the Venezuela field since 1955, including several terms as field chairman, was invited to join the home staff. During his latest furlough MacDonald had taught Spanish and mission subjects at the Moody

Bible Institute. He was appointed area foreign secretary for the Europe fields and to represent special projects. Rolf Egeland's title was changed to assistant director, administration. Dick H. Francisco was named stewardship secretary.

An Early Change Proposed

For some time I had been concerned about projects that should have my attention but which a combination of foreign trips, heavy correspondence, and necessary consultations kept me from accomplishing. One of these projects was updating the retirement plan for TEAM personnel. Missionaries served with modest allowances, and supporters felt that the mission should have a better retirement support system for them than it did. Major revision was necessary. The urgency increased when the U.S. Congress passed a comprehensive pension law that set strict standards.

This new law increased my feeling that I should devote time to these special administrative projects, but that would be possible only if my responsibilities as general director were transferred to someone else. That person had been in training and I believed he was fully prepared to take the helm. Furthermore, his being recognized as general director would enhance his already effective public ministry. Naturally, this became a matter to lay before the Lord for His guidance as to the timing.

At the administrative staff study retreat early in September 1974, I mentioned to Dick Winchell that I was just over two years away from TEAM's mandatory retirement age and felt I should transfer leadership to him well before that date. I assured him I was confident he was ready for the assignment.

Though this subject did not surprise Winchell, the proposed earlier date did. I felt so strongly that this plan was the Lord's leading that I sent a formal letter to board chairman Joseph Horness for attention at the meeting of September 20. The board not only agreed to my plan but went a step farther by naming Dr. Horness honorary board chairman and me as his successor. They directed that the changes be effective January 1, 1975.

The precedent was that the appointment of a general director be recognized in a formal way so announcements went out to the missionary family, the supporting constituency, and to leaders of other Christian organizations that Winchell's installation would take place December 29 at the Wheaton Evangelical Free Church.

A Time of Testing

In November Winchell visited the Venezuela field and while there became aware of a physical problem. Upon return he checked with his doctor, and several weeks of examinations followed. On the evening of December 6, the office staff met for its annual Christmas dinner. At the conclusion, Winchell asked me if Frances and I could stop at his house to talk with him and Marjorie about the urologist's report. Eager to know the results of the tests, we readily agreed.

Winchell had a cassette recording of the doctor's explanation and what we heard was extremely serious. A malignant tumor had been found which if not removed would surely be fatal. In cases where surgery could be performed the survival rate was only five percent. The outlook seemed grim indeed. But when the picture looked darkest the Lord reminded me of the assurance I had as I prayerfully planned to present Winchell's name as my successor. The board had acted with similar dependence on the Lord's leading when making the appointment and setting the date. Now, as we knelt before the Lord in the Winchells' living room, the Spirit of God renewed that assurance. The Scripture that brought confirmation was Philippians 1:6—"Being confident of this very thing, that he who hath begun a good work in you will perform it until the day of Jesus Christ."

I had no doubt about the outcome but I had to immediately confer with members of the board to report the new developments. Dr. Andrew Karsgaard, medical director, concurred with the board's decision to postpone the installation with no definite date being set. The notification to the mission family and constituency asked for prayer for the Winchells. The response was most heartening and increased the assurance that God would not only spare His servant but would turn this experience to his good through enlisting so much prayer support.

An interesting sidelight was Winchell's reaction to my announcement that I would be sending another letter to the supporting constituency telling about the delay of the installation service and asking for prayer support for the Winchells as they faced this crisis. Winchell's response: "With so much suffering and need around the world, do you have to call attention to me?"

I assured him that the letter was necessary, but the thought he planted led me to mention in my general letter some of the famine situations our missionaries were facing, particularly in sub-Saharan Africa and India. To our great delight, several tens of thousands of dollars came in as contributions to the mission's Christian Concern Fund. In the almost fifteen years since then contributions of several hundred thousand dollars have been received, making it possible to render timely relief to suffering Christians and help to outsiders for whom Christian charity became a strong positive testimony.

Forward with Confidence

The first stage of Winchell's surgery on December 14 took seven and a half hours. The outlook was guardedly promising, but the next stage, January 17, would reveal more. The executive committee of the board was in session at TEAM headquarters when a call came from the hospital. Winchell was on the line to report to me (rather groggily) that the surgeon had given him the good news that the just-completed second surgery revealed no spread of the malignancy. The surgeon expected full recovery. This good news triggered immediate praise. As a mark of its confidence, the board set March 1, 1975, as the effective date for the change of leadership and March 21 for the public installation. God had answered prayer in a way which made a difference in how this TEAM history would be written.

RICHARD WINCHELL
NAMED GENERAL DIRECTOR

Installation as Sixth General Director

The large group gathered at the Evangelical Free Church in Wheaton, Illinois, March 21, 1975, had come to share in the installation of Richard M. Winchell as the sixth general director of TEAM. Having heard about Winchell's major surgeries in December and January, many were eager to know if he would be strong enough to take on an assignment that had many physical demands, such as long foreign trips into some difficult traveling areas. They had reason to be reassured because the Lord had restored him to apparent full vigor. The whole Winchell family was present for the service—wife, Marjorie; son Peter and his wife, Joan; daughter Martha; and sons Leigh and Barry.

At the same service, Dr. Joseph Horness, chairman of the board since 1968, was honored for his twenty-seven years as a board member and as the new honorary chairman of the board. Kind and generous words were also spoken about my time as general director and it was announced that I had been named chairman of the board.

Principles Outlined

Subsequent to his appointment, Winchell summarized in one sentence his convictions concerning the work of the mission: "Committed to what is changeless in world evangelization and to strategic change [in order] to meet the challenges of a new day." He then spelled out some details:

> Standing in the evangelical fundamental tradition, TEAM is faithful to God's inerrant Word. Its philosophy of evangelism grows from the Word's revelation of man's lostness and need of the gospel. Its motivation to spread the gospel abroad comes

from Christ's death and victory over the grave. Remembering His promised return lends urgency to its task.

We shall continue to follow biblical principles of church planting and growth. We shall continue to manifest concern for man's needs but not merely to make life more comfortable for those "bound in the prison house of sin." The goal, while demonstrating true compassion, is release from "prison." Thus the ministries of medicine, education, literacy, and relief begun by my predecessors will continue to emphasize the paramount spiritual goals.

This is God's work. He will supply grace, guidance, gifted co-workers, and spiritual and material resources adequate to the need. We trust God for every financial requirement. When needs arise, we shall not hesitate to inform God's praying people, but our petitions will be to Him. While taking "no thought for the morrow," we shall render careful stewardship of God's supply for today—with sincere thanksgiving. Looking ahead, we expect to grow—not to become the biggest, but because in God's order growth is healthy.

We are aware the enemy will contest each advance in this spiritual warfare. TEAM's history is rich in answers to prayer. To the founder, Fredrik Franson, prayer was like breathing—absolutely essential. Recent leaders have placed great emphasis upon it. It is awesome to step into such a tradition. I do so reverently but confidently. My confidence is not in self, but in Him who has shown himself so abundantly present in those I follow.[1]

Naming the Administrative Staff

Winchell gave early thought to the appointment of his associates and brought his recommendations to the October 1974 board meeting for confirmation:

- Delbert A. Kuehl, executive assistant director, candidate secretary, and foreign secretary for Latin America;
- Don W. Hillis, associate director, conference ministries;
- Carl W. Davis, assistant general director, foreign secretary for Asia;
- Rolf C. Egeland, assistant director, administration;
- Jack F. MacDonald, foreign secretary for Europe and Middle East;
- J. Carlton Seeland, controller;

- Dick H. Francisco, stewardship secretary;
- Lyle H. Petersen, extension department supervisor;
- Dr. Andrew Karsgaard, medical director;
- Vernon Mortenson, consulting director.

Size and Extent of TEAM in 1975

TEAM had twenty-three fields with 998 missionaries on March 1, 1975, when Winchell assumed office. It had grown steadily in the thirteen-and-a-half-year period of my time in office from fifteen fields and 818 missionaries in October 1961. The total had reached the 1,000 mark of active missionaries several different times but then receded because of normal attrition. Staff size in proportion to the size of the missionary family remained quite constant through the years.

Introduction to Constituency

Early in Winchell's service as general director we thought it wise to give him a wide introduction to supporting churches and friends and so arranged a tour of the western, central, Canadian, and eastern centers of interest. It was a good opportunity for Frances and me to present him and his wife, Marjorie. We found that friends of the mission knew about the physical crisis at the time of Winchell's scheduled installation and had been backing him and the family in prayer. They could now see that the Lord had answered prayer. Winchell's messages revealed to them that he had an excellent grasp of Scripture, a clear understanding of mission principles, and a thorough knowledge of TEAM.

Known Widely by Missionaries

The transition to Winchell's administration went smoothly both in the home office and in the relationship with the fields. I was indeed gratified that the board of directors had enough confidence in the quality of the missionary family to look within the organization for the personnel needed to fill leadership positions. Winchell knew the missionaries and their work. He had visited five or six fields in the interests of literature en route home from Africa in 1962, and en route from the field in 1968 he had visited and conferred with missionary and church leaders in the Middle East and Europe. Since joining the staff he had been in the Far East, Latin America, and Europe, often serving as Bible teacher at a field conference.

Korean Conference Experience

One notable conference ministry had been in Korea in 1973. I had been invited to visit that field to assist in deliberations concerning a possible close working relationship with the Korean Laymen's Evangelical Fellowship. After I had agreed to come, the Fellowship asked that I bring with me a Bible teacher who could spend four to five hours a day for five days giving Bible studies. This was an assignment I could with confidence give to my associate, Dick Winchell.

When we arrived in Korea we found about two thousand Korean believers assembled, wanting long periods of teaching and preaching. No thirty-minute sermons for them. Every message must be two to two-and-a-half hours long, including interpretation. Dick taught the epistle of Ephesians and by the last day was part way through the fifth chapter. After two-and-a-half hours Dick closed his Bible and asked interpreter Chang to dismiss the meeting with prayer. Chang immediately objected that Dick had not finished the study.

"But we have gone the full time," Dick responded.

"Go on anyway," the interpreter urged.

"I will, if it is all right with the people."

So the question was put to the people and their hearty response was enthusiastically positive. Dick resumed preaching and went on another hour, for a total of three-and-a-half hours. That they sat quietly for so long eagerly drinking in the teaching was amazing, but it was all the more amazing when we considered that this was their first meeting of the day and they had not yet had a meal. This gave evidence of two things. The first was of their own hunger for the solid meat of the Word. The second was that they were now being fed that solid meat and the Spirit of God was making it full of meaning to them.

Winchell was also asked—on only ten minutes' notice—to give a message on baptism just preceding a service when 450 were baptized, and this message was an hour long.

Winchell's God-given gift of expository preaching was soon recognized by the missionary family and his presence at a field conference was indeed welcome for his Bible ministry as well as for the official counsel he gave.

Peruvian Merger

One unfinished item for consideration was the request of the Peruvian Gospel Fellowship to have its missionary staff of three active and two retired missionaries merged into TEAM. The active missionaries were working with the Evangelical Seminary in Lima though the Fellowship was not directly responsible for that ministry. Winchell and Kuehl worked out the details and arranged that the merger would be finalized in May in Kitchener, Ontario, where TEAM was to hold its 1975 annual conference.

TEAM Conference in Canada

Holding the annual conference in Canada was a first for TEAM, as the conference had never before been held outside the United States. TEAM is incorporated in the State of Illinois, which requires an annual meeting of the members but does not limit location. With a growing Canadian missionary family and supporting constituency it was felt that annual meetings of the Illinois and Canadian corporations should be held together on occasion. The 1975 gathering was at the invitation of the Benton Street Baptist Church in Kitchener, Ontario, of which the Rev. W. Arnold McNeill was pastor. It was not foreseen at the time that McNeill would become chairman of the board of directors twelve years later.

First CPA Appointed

Another first that year was the appointment of a certified public accountant (CPA) to the staff of the accounting department at TEAM headquarters. By 1975 the amount needed to support the ministry of a thousand missionaries and the extensive work being carried on in twenty-three fields was about nine million dollars a year. At that time, the U. S. Congress was considering legislation that would greatly affect non-profit organizations. In 1974 it had adopted legislation to regulate pension plans and this affected TEAM. Though the mission finances were properly accounted for and safeguarded, it did not have a professionally trained financial officer to deal with the complexities being forced on non-profit organizations.

Rolf Egeland recognized the need and in consultation with Winchell and Seeland, the controller, invited Donald Mortenson to join the staff. Don was a CPA working with a Seattle accounting firm. Just at that time in 1975 TEAM was making a change in its computer installation. (The mission had installed tabulating equipment for receipting, accounting, and record-keeping as early as 1960.) Don used the opportunity to conform TEAM accounting to currently accepted procedures for non-profit organizations. He also prepared a technical manual to guide IFMA missions in non-profit accounting. An additional CPA, Jim Fuoss, was brought on the staff in 1978 and in 1984 was made controller. Another CPA, Miss Audrey Uber, was employed as well and in 1990 was named manager of the accounting department.

Upgrading Accounting Practices

A compelling reason for having several professional accountants working with TEAM was the more strict requirements of auditors who were mindful of government regulations. These requirements related not only to safeguarding funds, but also to conforming to widely accepted standards of recording and reporting. Because a significant part of mission accounting is carried on overseas at the point of missionary service, the auditors have increasingly required that the records there be reviewed by professional accountants and subjected to periodic audits. Such thorough procedures would be possible only with professional accountants who could make occasional trips to the fields. Jim Fuoss and Audrey Uber have made a number of such trips.

Computerization

A related advancement in accounting and record keeping was the introduction of accounting by computer on many of the fields. The availability of personal computers made this development possible, but equipment alone does not suffice. A competent and resourceful computer consultant was also necessary. The Lord provided such a man in the person of William Jack and, later, Daniel Dick, who not only supervised computer installations at headquarters and in Canada but also on many TEAM fields. This development offered opportunity for spiritual service by some who had training and experience in this late twentieth century tool. (Missionaries doing Scripture translation found the computer to be a time-saver, cutting the time involvement by 50 percent.)

Recruitment Emphasized

Winchell recognized that a steady flow of recruits was necessary to replace the many missionaries approaching retirement as well as for the expansion of the work. The candidate department, under the direction of Delbert Kuehl, was doing excellent work in contacting prospective missionaries and helping them through the process of applying. Once a candidate had been accepted, however, there was no office or person with the principal responsibility of expediting his progress in reaching the field. Robert Couture, former missionary to western India, who had worked with the extension department since 1970, had his assignment redefined to include special responsibility to counsel and encourage appointees and help them arrange meetings in churches. Couture was later succeeded by Donald Hoyt, former missionary to Rhodesia.

In 1975, Winchell appointed June Salstrom, former missionary to South Africa, to the candidate department to work along with Doris Frazer assisting Kuehl and, later Michael Pocock, Kuehl's successor. Pocock and Miss Salstrom revamped the structure and curriculum of the three-week candidate classes.

A Missionary Magazine for Students

Winchell approved and encouraged the development of the magazine *WHEREVER* by Harry Genet, who conceived and edited it. This magazine was distributed widely on a request basis to students in Bible institutes, colleges, and seminaries. It was recognized as an effective means of furthering mission awareness among young people.

In setting goals for the future of TEAM, Winchell calculated that the fields would need a minimum of 1,300 active missionaries. This goal was set in 1987 when the total was 1,060; the target date for reaching the goal was the centennial year, 1990. Winchell recognized that the scriptural formula for requisitioning workers for the fields was that given by Christ in Matthew 9:36, 37: "The harvest is plentiful but the workers are few, ask the Lord of the harvest, therefore, to send out workers into his harvest field" (NIV).

The Target 1300 Prayer Program

As the staff discussed the need they came up with the name *TARGET 1300* which Winchell enthusiastically promoted. Missionaries were asked to pray for specific personnel needs of the fields, and periodic prayer services were scheduled at the mission centers. Ron Brett was asked to maintain graphs showing the number applying to TEAM, approved as appointees, and entering active service. The number of new missionaries entering service each year reveals the measure of answered prayer. The general director's annual reports give the following numbers:

1983—61
1984—60
1985—52
1986—80
1987—88

1988—83
1989—71

Coordinated Advance

"Reaping a Harvest and Reaching Goals" was the theme of the 1973 Advisory Committee which recommended that TEAM launch an enlarged reaping effort on all fields and an outreach into new areas. George Martin, Pacific-Northwest representative and former Asia area secretary, was appointed coordinator.

Martin proposed the "Target Seven" program for the period of October 14, 1974, through January 1977 with seven phases: (1) Prayer, (2) Spiritual Renewal, (3) Training, (4) Special Efforts, (5) Evangelism, (6) Follow Up, (7) Church Fellowships Organized.

In his first letter to field leaders, Martin set forth basic principles, among them the approach to the national church leaders:

> Any program of spiritual renewal and evangelism should involve not only our missionaries but also our national brethren and churches. We do not want to impose a mission program on them but rather share our burden and concern, hoping they will feel the same and enter such an emphasis with us.[2]

Martin recognized that some fields had careful plans for coordinated advance and did not want these set aside for Target Seven. Where possible they could be adapted to the program. An outstanding example was the Venezuela field's seventieth anniversary *AVANCES* plan. Each field was asked to appoint a coordinator who could give adequate time to this ministry.

Encouraging reports on Phase I came from the field coordinators. Probably the most outstanding was from Ocaña, Colombia:

> Daily prayer meetings have been held in six sections of town, from 2 to 3 P.M., with good attendance and some souls saved. The church has a program for opening six to eight branch Sunday schools in the next two years. Two have been opened already with about 100 in each. That's about 200 people who previously did not attend Sunday school at all. A third will open soon. Attendance at all services has also increased significantly.[3]

The western India field coordinator, Earl Conrad, reported that the village churches in the Chinchpada and Navapur districts entered fully into all phases of Target Seven and saw results in proportion. One report had the following items of progress:

> God saved a number of people in a recent campaign in Navagaon, Chinchpada area. Seven of them have been baptized. This constitutes a new group of believers.

> The youth group from the Chinchpada church preaches every Monday night in selected villages which have no resident Christians. In Tinmovli three youth now believe.

> Fifty-six believers from seven villages in the Chinchpada area have been baptized during 1976. A few of them belonged to a special religious sect from which no one had become a Christian before.

> Berean Bible School at Pimpalner is bursting its seams with the highest-ever attendance—a total of 41 students.[4]

Though Target Seven had fixed dates for reporting direct results it was conceived as a continuing plan because all elements were to be a regular part of missionary-national church activity. This pilot program proved the value of a coordinated effort.

TEAM REACH

REACH—Resources for Evangelism And Church Helps—was a department to maintain the impetus of Target Seven. Martin served as coordinator of this program also and worked hard to provide helps for field missionaries in furthering evangelism and church ministries.

In a letter to Martin, Winchell commented on the value of the REACH program:

> I am particularly impressed with the materials you have been selecting and sharing with our fields.... There is a certain satisfaction in knowing that important materials on church planting are being brought to the attention of our missionaries on a regular basis.[5]

One important part of the REACH program was the ministry of international cross-cultural teams for evangelism. What the ministry of these teams did—beyond informing the homeland constituencies about missionary work—was to arouse missionary interest in the churches on the mission fields. When team members saw people of other cultures and the fruits of the gospel among them, and experienced the joy of seeing response to the gospel, they were awakened to their responsibility to have a part in the harvest.

Teams were formed in India, Indonesia, Netherlands Antilles, Spain, Taiwan, Trinidad, and Venezuela. Indian pastor Emmanuel Endigeri from Agra ministered effectively among Indian communities in Trinidad and John Naidoo of South Africa did the same in India. One of the most active groups was the Grace Family Septet, made up of Jonathan and Margaret Cheng, their four daughters, and a son. They held evangelistic services—mostly in Chinese churches—in North America, South America, Europe, and the Far East with much blessing and fruit.

Pension Law Mandates Changes

The passage of a U.S. federal pension law in September 1974 pointed up the urgency of putting TEAM's retirement plan on a better footing. Winchell recognized that one of my goals when I transferred the general director's office to him was to free myself for work on projects such as this. Our plan, initiated in 1941, had several problems. It was inadequate at its inception and thirty-five years later inflation had made its schedule of benefits almost meaningless in spite of some interim adjustments. Even so it promised more to retirees than the plan would be able to pay. I once asked Dr. Johnson about that difficulty: "When this plan was set up did you think the fees would cover the benefits, modest as they were?"

"No, we didn't," was his reply. "We expect the Lord to return so there will be many who won't have to draw retirement."

That was my conviction also, but the federal government did not see it that way and required that pensions be funded. To catch up on funding according to the actuarial requirements would have been impossible except that the government allowed the make-up funding to extend over a period of years. That helped care for service already recorded. The next step was to bring the benefits up to a realistic level. Had we been forced to pay these added pension costs from the mission's general fund, it would have used up much of what was needed for administration and to help various field ministries. Instead, the Lord's provision came through the support system TEAM had been led to adopt. This system is not a general fund supporting all missionaries and ministries, but a partnership with missionaries trusting the Lord for the support to cover all aspects of their service and ministry. The combined faith of a thousand missionaries was rewarded by the Lord's provision through those who were partners in their ministries.

Better Care for Retirees

The changes in the pension plan made it possible to put the support of retirees on a better basis. All American and Canadian retirees were eligible for social security pensions, but given the low level of missionary salary allowances, these pensions were far from adequate. Another problem was that salary allowances differ depending on the cost of living in various countries. The solution was to give opportunity to the supporters of a retiring missionary to continue a portion of that support. Thus, the social security pension, the TEAM pension, and the support subsidy together would provide retirement support which was quite in line with the standards set by the mission.

The same law had a bearing on TEAM's plan for helping missionaries meet medical expenses. As early as 1955, TEAM had decided that a self-insurance plan for medical expenses would be far less expensive than commercially available insurance. Comparisons indicated that the costs were 70 to 75 percent of those of commercial plans. The law required that the plan be registered with the Internal Revenue Service. In this way, a member's reimbursed expenses—some running to tens of thousands of dollars and a few to more than a hundred thousand—would not have to be reported on the income tax return. TEAM missionaries have often thanked the Lord for this provision, and supporters have voiced appreciation for the orderly way such expenses are cared for, in contrast to special appeals for help when illness or surgery is faced.

These financial arrangements for the welfare of the Lord's missionary servants were among the special projects that I could care for when I turned my office over to Winchell.

Fashioning a Stronger Staff

By now the mission administration had reached a size that required a fairly large administrative staff. As a result, there were appointments and changes which were significant to those concerned and to the work of the mission, but which cannot all be recorded. Those of longer-term or special interest are mentioned. Michael Pocock, Venezuela missionary, was invited to become candidate secretary in 1977. Don Hillis retired in 1978 but continued to assist in conference ministries on a voluntary basis. *Horizons* and *WHEREVER* editor Harry Genet went to another local Christian publisher in 1979 and his place was filled by Douglas Wicks. Carlton Seeland's title was changed to assistant director for finance in 1978, and Don Mortenson was named controller. Seeland retired in 1979.

When Don left to join the staff of a Christian college in 1980, Ron Brett, assistant to the general director, was given the responsibility of managing the accounting department. Jim Fuoss, CPA, guided the accounting functions and was named controller in 1984.

The staff—and the whole mission family—sustained a great loss on October 31, 1979, when Carl W. Davis, assistant general director, and foreign secretary for Asia since 1973, passed away. Davis and his wife, Agnes, had begun their service in Pakistan in 1947 and in 1967 were asked to head up TEAM's Australia office and representation.

With the retirement of Delbert Kuehl in 1981, Winchell invited Elton Dresselhaus to become foreign secretary for the Latin America fields. Dresselhaus and his wife, Joyce, had served in Venezuela for sixteen years in student work and Bible teaching. Elton had also been chairman of the field. But the Lord had other plans for Elton, because He called him home on March 4, 1983. Thus, two experienced, capable, and dedicated coworkers were promoted from earthly service in what seemed to be the prime of life.

Senior Staff Team

Winchell gave much thought and prayer to the development of his senior staff team. Every position on the team was important. For most, missionary experience was not only desirable but essential. To call a field leader home from a vital responsibility overseas was a serious matter. The field had need of such missionaries and the missionaries wanted to be on the field of their call. Yet the general director could not recommend to the board for appointment any who had lost their vision and burden for the field or any whom fellow missionaries did not want to retain. So it boiled down to inviting some who wanted to stay on the field and whose fellow workers did not want to release them. However, this was the way to build a staff whose hearts were in the work and who also had the full confidence and respect of the missionary family.

Even before the deaths of Davis and Dresselhaus, Winchell had discussed with colleagues the need to have four foreign secretaries, with one of them being back-up for the others who were often away from the office in meetings or on foreign trips. For the fourth foreign secretary Winchell turned to a man who had served in Trinidad for eighteen years, part of the time as field chairman— Norman Niemeyer. Norman and Sue, in early 1979, were uncertain if their Trinidad residence permits would be renewed. The government was trying to limit such permits to the time that it felt would be necessary to train a local replacement, not realizing that a missionary wanted to do just that and then move on to another new area to repeat the process instead of leaving. Winchell reached the Niemeyers with the invitation to join the staff just as they were praying much about the next step should they have to leave Trinidad. Niemeyer was appointed administrative assistant to the foreign secretaries in March 1979. Later, after the death of Carl Davis, he was named foreign secretary for western Asia and southern Africa.

Foreign Secretary Positions Strengthened

There was still the need for a fourth man to assist the foreign secretaries. Considering the names of several promising men, the others agreed with Winchell that Lynn Everswick should be the next one to be recommended for a foreign secretary role. Everswick, a second generation missionary, and his wife, Judy, had been church planters in Zimbabwe (Rhodesia) since 1969. On a trip to the field in 1982, Winchell spoke to Everswick about the possibility and later invited him to join the staff to work with MacDonald, Dresselhaus, and Niemeyer, the appointment to become effective in early 1984. With the death of Dresselhaus, the need for help had become urgent and Everswick agreed to come six months earlier to take up the work in August 1983. Even with Everswick's appointment the goal of having four area secretaries had not been reached.

General Director Still Responsible

In organizing the mission, the board of directors had made one man, the general director, responsible to administer the work. By the time the Constitution was revised in 1960, growth of the work had made a better-defined administrative structure necessary, so provision was made for other administrative officers to be responsible to the board through the general director. Their authority and duties were to be determined by the general director, subject to board approval.

That directive could be implemented in one of a number of ways. Winchell's plan was a good one. He named three assistant directors to be responsible for three areas of administration:

- Jack F. MacDonald, foreign areas, candidate department. He was the senior foreign secretary. The medical director and office of pastoral care also reported to him. Later MacDonald was named associate director with executive authority in the absence of the general director.
- Rolf C. Egeland, administration. The operational departments of headquarters were his responsibility, including both person-

nel and general operations. This included donor relations in general. The growing number of retirees also came under his care as did the missionary sons and daughters in their college years in the homeland.

- Ronald A. Brett, finance. All aspects of financial administration and public relations had his attention and oversight. When it was realized—in 1989—that the general director needed someone to pick up some of his work, particularly in his absence, Brett was named assistant general director.

While all departments and staff members recognized that their main purpose was to further the work of the missionaries, it was understood that the foreign secretaries had major responsibility for the missionaries assigned to their areas.

This administrative structure was designed to enable each officer to give optimum attention to his primary assignment and the people committed to him and yet make him fully accountable to the general director. As required by the constitution and as expected by the board, the general director was to be adequately informed and fully responsible for the entire ministry. This arrangement served as well as—and undoubtedly better than—any in place in earlier administrations.

Through the years the general director was always faced with the pull between being out in public ministry to the supporting constituency and being at his desk to deal with executive correspondence, consultation, and planning. Franson was out in ministry with his missionaries and left what administrative matters there were to board members. Bach was out a great deal and kept administration very simple—probably too simple. Johnson was out much of the time and left most of the administrative responsibility to his assistant general director. I was at my desk more, except for some rather extensive foreign trips, and I depended on others—Don Hillis, George Martin, Nolan Balman, and representatives—to carry the main responsibility of public ministry.

Winchell carried those two broad areas of work in better balance, dividing his week more equally between public meetings and desk duties. It was undoubtedly true that his office associates wanted him on deck more as they felt the need of his counsel and direction. On the other hand, supporting churches which wanted his public ministry often had to accept Friday through Sunday rather than a longer stay. Some even had to wait until the next year and some on occasion had to accept a substitute. They did it with good grace for the most part.

A Meaningful Fifth Anniversary

At a meeting of the board, March 21, 1980, I referred to the fifth anniversary of Winchell's installation as general director and also pointed out that the surgeon had earlier stated that the passage of five symptom-free years provided clear evidence that there was no recurrence of malignancy. By 1990, fifteen years had passed with the tripled assurance that the board's appointment was indeed the right one. God had indeed honored the faith of many intercessors.

FAITHFUL TO THE LEGACY

Winchell's Administration

Each TEAM director in turn has addressed basic questions concerning recruitment, deployment, provision of resources, principles of ministry, prayer backing, spiritual unity, and practical effectiveness, and has diligently sought to strengthen the ministry. But while their purpose in each area has remained the same, each man's approach or emphasis has been different, yet necessary and effective for the time.

Looking at Richard Winchell's fifteen years of leadership from 1975 to 1990 it is apparent that he has not only been faithful to the legacy received from his predecessors but has diligently sought to strengthen and enhance the work. In no major area has there been retrogression. In most areas there has been measurable progress; in some, outstandingly so.

Philosophy of Leadership

To properly understand Winchell's administration it is essential to note his philosophy of leadership. In short, he places confidence in and entrusts responsibility to the men and women working with him. In his first letter to the missionary family after being appointed general director, Winchell referred to the administrative team in place and added:

> May I here pay tribute to that team? It takes typists, administrators, accountants, computer experts, secretaries, and many others to make the team complete, but it is the spirit of oneness on the team which makes working together such a pleasure. In particular I value the privilege of working so closely with the administrative officers of this team. It is the prospect of continuing with this group of men that makes it possible to acquiesce to the board's request. This shall continue to be a team. I shall rely heavily on the counsel of each of these servants of the Lord, and I shall encourage the continued exercise of their varying gifts.[1]

Confidence and Delegation

One of his first actions was to share responsibility for the foreign work more completely with the area foreign secretaries and have them meet as a committee for coordination and mutual counsel. Whereas I had, in effect, served as area foreign secretary for about one-third of the fields—and was often overloaded with correspondence—Winchell freed himself from much of this detail to invest himself more fully in development of the ministry. Even so, he kept well informed about all aspects of the work and involved himself deeply in major items.

Doing Something About Church Planting

While others before him strongly emphasized church planting, Winchell did more than talk and write about it. In keeping with the recommendation of the field chairmen's consultation in 1981, he determined to provide specific training in evangelism and church planting and selected Dr. Michael Pocock, candidate secretary, to develop such a program. A ten-day training course for furloughed missionaries and appointees began in 1983 and has been held each summer except 1988. Pocock brought in missionaries fresh from successful church planting experience to share lessons they had learned. Those who attended testified to the great value of the training, not only in the inspiration it gave, but also in the practical instructions which were communicated. Attendance ranged from a low of 35 to a high of 68.

Other Training Programs

Winchell thought of the Evangelism and Church Planting School, as it was later called, as one element of a program of continuing in-house education for missionaries. This program, initiated under the direction of Pocock, was developed under the leadership of Lee Hotchkiss, who was brought onto the staff in 1984. Hotchkiss was not in the administrative line but served rather to provide pastoral care and counselling for missionaries. His training in clinical counselling, coupled with experience in the pastorate and as a missionary in Latin America, prepared him well to work with the area foreign secretaries and the medical director, Dr. John Bennett, in meeting the pastoral care and continuing education needs of missionaries. David Brown, who with his wife, Donna, had served in Japan for ten years, was appointed candidate secretary when Pocock left in 1987 to join the faculty of Dallas Theological Seminary. In 1990 Brown's title was changed to director of personnel. In this position he worked closely with Hotchkiss in the training program.

Servant Leadership

One very beneficial program which Hotchkiss proposed in 1987, with Winchell's encouragement and the participation of the area secretaries, was a series of Servant Leadership Workshops. Five-day seminars were held in three central overseas areas—Sri Lanka, Germany, and Venezuela—in the fall of 1988 and spring of 1989, each with about fifty participants. The program was initially conceived as being a means of preserving to the mission the services of some who were having difficulty adjusting to the demands of living and working in another culture. Further consideration led to the conclusion that a ministry aiming to prevent problems would be better than waiting for difficulties to develop and then seeking to apply a remedy. Hotchkiss explained the concept:

> Growing out of the observation that a missionary's personal problems are often related to and at times complicated by the management of the individual on the field, a suggestion was made that we consider a program of organizational development and training. It was felt this training should include general leadership development as well as specific management skills appropriate to the unique needs of the missions community.... Our objective is to contribute to the development of those whom the Lord has gifted in leadership and management so they will be better equipped to exercise those gifts in a manner that brings glory to God.[2]

A Broader Training Program

As these elements of a training program began to materialize,

Winchell developed the idea further, linking some long-existing activities into a comprehensive plan which he called the "Franson Project" in recognition that the founder's earliest tool in building the mission was through training classes. In 1988, Winchell listed existing and projected components of the Franson Project as follows:

1. Candidate School [in existence since 1949].
2. Church Planting School [begun in 1983].
3. Servant Leadership Seminars [initiated in 1988].
4. Advisory Committee or Field Chairmen's Consultations [begun in 1958].
5. Computer classes [initiated in 1986].
6. Administrative Staff Retreat [in existence since 1959].
7. Annual Conference Workshops [from about 1976].
8. Occasional conferences for special types of service [medical personnel, field treasurers, etc.].[3]

A year later, Winchell presented a more detailed study to the board which spelled out the rationale for the training program and added new recommendations:

> One of our purposes is to encourage and stimulate growth in our missionaries' lives in spiritual and emotional health, in evangelistic and cross-cultural communication skills, and in discipling and church planting ability.... We also want to encourage our missionaries to keep current in this rapidly growing and constantly changing world.[4]

"Explore" Seminars

One recommendation made at the time was actualized with the holding—in the fall of 1989—of a three-day "Explore" seminar designed for those who wanted to explore the possibility of missionary service. "From the young person's point of view it was an opportunity to investigate his own fitness for missionary service. From TEAM's point of view it provided the opportunity to get to know the potential candidate, administer some testing, and conduct personal interviews prior to candidate school."[5]

Training Facilities at Wheaton

Provision of the Franson Center at headquarters to house these added activities was made by shifting several departments and utilizing space more efficiently. The modifications were coupled with certain necessary changes to accommodate the increased foreign secretary staff. It was gratifying that the Wheaton headquarters building—already nearing twenty-five years in use— could be adapted to meet the needs of administering an enlarged program of service for the missionary family, which itself had expanded 27 percent in number since it was built. It is true that the Robert C. Van Kampen missionary residence building, completed in 1979, provided much-appreciated meeting space to take pressure off of the office building.

Consultations: Chairmen and Treasurers

Special consultations with field chairmen and field treasurers held at the annual Advisory Committee meetings of field leaders won enthusiastic approval from the missionary body. In 1981, 1983, 1986, and 1989, field chairmen met with board members and headquarters staff under the leadership of Jack MacDonald, and in 1985 and 1990 the field treasurers met under the leadership of Ron Brett. One lasting benefit of these consultations was the preparation of manuals for the offices of field chairman and field treasurer. These were prepared in draft form by MacDonald and Brett and reviewed and revised as necessary by those in attendance.

Future Franson Center Plans

In his report to the annual meeting of TEAM in 1989, Winchell reviewed the developments in training and then suggested possibilities for the future:

> Others being planned include Reentry-Debriefing Sessions for missionaries and perhaps also for missionary children. These are not programs to replace formal training or continuing education available through existing institutions. We will continue to encourage missionaries to avail themselves of these while providing specialized programs of our own.[6]

More Mergers Implemented

In addition to Peruvian Fellowship's joining TEAM in 1975,

there were several other significant mergers. One, with the Orinoco River Mission in 1980, extended TEAM's work across the full width of Venezuela from west to east. Another, a short-lived arrangement with Mission of Baja in 1982, led indirectly to the opening of a TEAM field in Mexico, which was entered with a missionary staff in 1988. A third, with the Japan Evangelical Mission in 1983, enlarged the church planting work in Japan and brought TEAM into Brazil to work with Japanese and Brazilians. As in earlier mergers, these were not sought by TEAM but were welcomed as they preserved the investment by missionaries of the predecessor missions and provided—with the exception of Mexico—a good foundation for further church planting. The mergers will be dealt with more fully in the chapters covering the fields involved.

A Higher Canadian Profile

Though TEAM has an international supporting constituency and outreach, it is viewed as an American mission having one principal board and one chief executive, the general director. This is true even though it is incorporated separately in the United States and Canada and registered in Australia. Some in Canada felt that a higher Canadian profile would enhance TEAM's appeal to prospective missionaries and potential local supporters.

Winchell, who doubles as general director of TEAM of Canada, understood the Canadian point of view and encouraged various steps to strengthen the Canadian role in the total ministry of the mission. The first was to assure a minimum of two Canadian members on the U.S. board of directors. This was only a formal recognition of what was already true in practice. Of sixteen members in 1990, the board actually had four Canadians, including the chairman, W. Arnold McNeill.

His next step was to approve increasing the meetings of the Canadian board of trustees to two a year and having additional phone conferences as necessary. To satisfy the need for a Canadian candidate secretary, the trustees appointed Nelson Bezanson, a member of the candidate staff at Wheaton headquarters and former missionary to Chad. Nelson and his wife, Uda, had both received their missionary training in eastern Canada and were well oriented to Canadian evangelical interests.

Strom Appointed Canadian Director

There remained the need for a Canadian director who could be more closely related to the Canadian staff and constituency. In 1987, Winchell recommended to the trustees the appointment of Verner Strom, an Albertan who had served as chairman of the Japan field for much of the previous twenty-seven years. Though the Stroms had been in Japan most of the time since 1950, they were quite well known in Canadian evangelical circles. It was advantageous to have a director who was well acquainted with TEAM's principles and practices and had demonstrated gifts of spiritual and practical leadership. Strom began his new assignment on January 1, 1988.

Canadian Headquarters Relocated

Over several years, chairman Leonard Erickson led a discussion within the board of trustees about relocating the Canadian headquarters, which had been in Saskatchewan since 1946. Since 1969 there had also been an eastern Canada office in Toronto administered by Gerald Morehouse, former Chad missionary. There was some question as to whether the relocated headquarters should be in the east or the west. The populous province of Ontario had a concentration of evangelicals with strong mission interests but the western provinces from Manitoba to British Columbia had provided TEAM with the larger percentage of missionaries and their support.

After Strom took office he dealt with this question in an expeditious manner. The trustees were furnished information which led them to choose Calgary, Alberta, as the headquarters site for TEAM of Canada. A smaller facility in the Toronto suburb of Etobicoke was rented to serve the mission needs in eastern Canada.

The move from Regina to Calgary was made in September 1988. Sam Archer continued to have responsibility for general business activities as administrative secretary.

In January 1990, TEAM's personnel count showed 106 Canadian career missionaries, five associates, eight serving in the office or as representatives, and six staff wives with missionary service. An interesting figure was the forty retired Canadian workers who had given a lifetime of service.

Entering New Fields Justified

One of the goals proposed by Winchell in 1980 was to enter three new fields by 1990. Having this goal become reality was no easy matter. Beginning work in another country required answers to a number of questions: Was that country or people-group within the country so lacking in witness that entry of a mission was justified? If other missions were at work in the country, did they favor TEAM's entry? Were there national churches which would welcome TEAM's help? Could these national churches not carry on the work by themselves to evangelize the country? What restrictions might the government impose on the entry of North American missionaries or on the preaching of the gospel? Would there be need and opportunity for a church planting ministry along the lines TEAM was committed to? What would be the support needs for a missionary family? Where would missionaries get the necessary language instruction? Were there schools for missionary children or would the mission need to establish a school? Is there agreement by the administrative officers and board of directors that the country in question should be entered and that the timing is right? Does the proposed entry seem, indeed, to be the Lord's will? It was not a prerequisite that all conditions be favorable for entry, but there needed to be sufficient information for the guidance of the missionaries who entered the field.

Mentors for the Pioneers

Some of the early fields were entered by new missionaries with no cross-cultural experience and with little knowledge of what was involved in planting a church in a resistant culture, but in recent decades TEAM has tried to provide experienced missionary help and guidance for any new work. For example, when the Austria work began in 1965, the France field council was asked to advise and monitor the work for the first few years.

Italy Surveyed and Entered

As the general director and area secretaries were led to consider certain areas for entry in the 1980s, they set a firm policy of surveying the target area and then assigning missionaries of experience to lead the way. A case in point was Italy. In October 1980 Jack MacDonald, Michael Pocock, and Wallace Geiger, chairman of the France field, undertook a survey. They visited and interviewed missionaries and national pastors and came away convinced of the unevangelized condition of many areas of Italy. Murray and Florence Carter, fresh from church planting experience in India but lacking a visa to return, offered themselves for the new work in Italy and went there in 1981.

Philippines, Mozambique, and Hong Kong

The next two areas entered—Mexico and Brazil—came as a result of merger arrangements in 1982 and 1983. Nepal was designated a separate field in 1982. In 1986 Winchell and Norman Niemeyer, area secretary for the Far East fields, surveyed Luzon, the largest island of the Philippines. They were looking for an alternate field where appointees to Irian Jaya who had been refused visas could minister in tribes which needed linguists for Bible translation. The first TEAM missionaries entered in October 1986. About the same time the board voted to reaffirm the mission's long-standing interest in Mozambique. Actual entry came in late 1989. One other field—Hong Kong—was surveyed by Niemeyer and MacDonald in 1988 and entered that same year.

Linguists and Translators

Though TEAM does not specialize in linguistic reduction, many missionaries had such training and did this essential work with the purpose of providing the Scriptures and Christian literature. The late 1980s saw completion or significant progress in a number of translation projects. In Chad, the Nanjere Bible was finished, the Ngambai Bible was completely translated and checked and was scheduled for 1990 publication. Several other Chadian languages had a significant start in receiving the Word of God. In Taiwan, the Amis Old Testament was nearing completion to give the people a whole Bible. Much Bible translation was being done in Irian Jaya, where the Asmat and Sougb tribes received the New Testament and the Hatam New Testament neared completion. A Turkish modern-language New Testament was completed and published, as was a Mauchi Bhil New Testament in India. Earl Conrad finished work on a concordance of the Marathi New Testament and so provided Christians a most useful aid in Bible study.

Maintaining Harmony and Coordination

It is gratifying—and somewhat surprising to those outside the mission—to note the harmony of purpose and viewpoint among TEAM missionaries. How is this harmony and coordination possible when missionaries come from several different homelands, are drawn from various church backgrounds, have been trained at different schools, and serve in thirty different countries? First and foremost must be general agreement on Scripture and faithfulness to it. Serious differences in doctrine are rarely encountered. Having a clear statement of faith and additional clarifying statements on such subjects as relationships, cooperation, objectives in the work, and the ministry of the Holy Spirit promotes understanding of the guiding principles of the mission.

In addition, there are two family publications—*TEAM Topics,* issued quarterly, and *Monthly TEAM Memo* (MTM)—which draw the family together. *TEAM Topics* is a channel of information on mission procedures and contains articles or notices from various staff members or departments. The MTM differs in that it is a letter from the general director. Acting on an expressed need for a family letter, I began the MTM in September 1968, and Winchell has continued it in the same format. In addition to TEAM family news there is a spiritual message from the general director.

Winchell has used the MTM as a messenger to communicate relevant scriptural truth on timely subjects. His Bible teaching at conferences of missionaries relates the Word of God to personal life and service. The MTM follows the same pattern and is well received by the missionary family. Our younger daughter, who receives the MTM by virtue of being an MK (missionary kid), is one who values it highly and applies its lessons to her responsibilities as a Christian worker, homemaker, and mother. This is a good test of its acceptance, readability, and usefulness.

Another way for the missionaries to be made aware of their unity of purpose is to learn of resolute stands on vital principles as demonstrated by the general director and board members. In a day when even Christian organizations seem to be swayed by compromising trends, it is reassuring that the leaders are not only informed, but also alert and ready to stand by their scriptural convictions. An occasion which demonstrated this was in regard to Lausanne II, a widely hailed gathering in Manila of missionary leaders in 1989. The TEAM board of directors, following Winchell's counsel and lead, refused to participate because the sponsors disregarded vital principles of Christian cooperation.

Board Members, 1975 and 1990

When Winchell was installed as general director in 1975 the board of directors had twelve members:
- Joseph Horness, honorary chairman, businessman;
- Vernon Mortenson, chairman, mission executive;
- Iver Erickson, vice-chairman, businessman;
- Enock C. Dyrness, secretary, educator;
- Tory Lindland, vice-secretary, pastor;
- Robert C. Van Kampen, treasurer, businessman;
- Harold P. Halleen, assistant treasurer, businessman;
- S. Maxwell Coder, educator;

- P. Kenneth Gieser, ophthalmologist;
- Kenneth S. Kantzer, educator;
- Alex B. Stein, pastor; and
- Roy B. Zuck, educator.

By 1990 the membership had increased to sixteen:
- W. Arnold McNeill, chairman, pastor;
- Terry Hulbert, vice-chairman, educator;
- Howard Westlund, secretary, pastor;
- Roy B. Zuck, vice-secretary, educator;
- James Erickson, treasurer, businessman;
- Paul W. Anderson, assistant treasurer, pastor;
- Kenneth S. Kantzer, educator;
- Andrew T. Karsgaard, ophthalmologist;
- Tory Lindland, pastor;
- Jonathan Mosby, businessman;
- Delbert Kuehl, mission executive (ret.);
- Leonard Erickson, businessman;
- Keith Sinclair, businessman;
- Warren Wiersbe, Bible teacher;
- James Couture, businessman; and
- Vernon Mortenson, mission executive (ret.).

It is interesting to note that four of the members listed in 1990 had served as foreign missionaries, two were sons of missionaries, three were seminary professors, five were pastors, five were businessmen, and one was a doctor. The fact that this adds up to twenty positions simply indicates the dual roles some have filled.

Nomination of board members is done with great care as their responsibilities affect the spiritual welfare, financial integrity, and organizational strength of the mission. Board members generally serve for repeated three-year terms—adequate time to become fully acquainted with the stance, emphasis, philosophy, and principles of the mission, and acquainted with the scope of its worldwide work. All have been signally used by the Lord in their own individual callings.

Their counsel, encouragement, and support of the mission administration and missionaries have contributed immeasurably to the stability and progress of the mission work. When a member retires from active participation every effort is made to replace him with a young person of promise so that there will be a good age spread.

While various members of the administrative staff are mentioned in connection with their work, little has been said to identify many who make the work possible. They fill roles essential to the smooth operation of the mission. Administrative efficiency is necessary but there is another ingredient absolutely essential in a missionary ministry and that is the spiritual. All staff members are selected on the basis of their practical training, proficiency, and spiritual maturity and sensitivity. All are participants in the work for Christ. All join in a daily time of intercession for the work of the mission around the world. These morning prayer meetings often include a report by a returned missionary who shares topics for prayer. Many staff members also participate in the Monday night prayer meetings.

Administrative Staff

Administrative officers working with the general director in 1990 were:

- Jack F. MacDonald, associate director;
- Ronald A. Brett, assistant general director;
- Rolf C. Egeland, assistant director, administration;
- Norman B. Niemeyer, foreign secretary, East Asia;
- Lynn Everswick, foreign secretary, Southern Africa, West Asia;
- Gary Bowman, foreign secretary, Latin America;
- David Davis, foreign secretary, Europe and Chad;
- Dick H. Francisco, stewardship secretary;
- David L. Brown, personnel director;
- John E. Bennett, M.D., medical director;
- Vernon Mortenson, consulting director;
- Verner Strom, Canadian director;
- V. Sam Archer, Canadian administrative secretary;

- Gerald H. Morehouse, Canadian extension secretary;
- Nelson I. Bezanson, Canadian candidate secretary; and
- David Brook, Australian regional director.

Special Assignment Missionaries

In the mid-1970s the administration recognized that there were some missionaries who could not remain on their fields because of unavoidable matters such as poor health, closed doors, or family needs, but who nevertheless were eager to remain in active service with TEAM and could make a worthwhile contribution to its ministry. Some would need to be away from their regular work only temporarily; others would be embarking on long-term assignments. With a large Spanish-speaking population in the United States there were opportunities for a useful ministry. The Missionary Gospel Fellowship (MGF) ministered to Mexican migrant workers in California, Florida, and Michigan. TEAM agreed to provide several missionaries with their own support to work under the direction of MGF. Among those who served under this arrangement were Bruce and Betty Cole and Bruce and Nina Wakelin. Later, William and Karen Pietsch of the Pakistan field were asked to join the MGF staff so that Pietsch could serve for several years as director of the work founded by his father, Paul J. Pietsch, Sr.

Those still on active service with TEAM who were temporarily serving with another organization were listed as being under special assignment. These included William and Dorothy Pape (Japan) serving at the Brake Bible Institute in Germany; Gordon and Elaine Van Rooy (North India) and Armond and Lolly Fritz (Trinidad), with LIT; Duane and Muriel Elmer (South Africa) and Patricia Mortenson (Zimbabwe), with Missionary Internship; Dalmain and Audrey Congdon (South Africa) with IFMA.

Representation in Europe

Pape's contacts with German students at the Brake Bible Institute led him to recommend that TEAM appoint someone to recruit European missionaries.

The result was that in 1980 Winchell appointed Edvard and Jenny Torjesen as Europe representatives to live in Germany and travel in northern European countries. The Torjesens were U.S. citizens of Norwegian ancestry who could minister effectively in the Scandinavian languages. Their knowledge of German also was sufficient for their ministry. Torjesen had earlier done extensive research on Fredrik Franson's work in Europe and in this way had become well known to church groups, mission societies, and schools. He was often asked to lecture in the schools about missions and evangelical church history. He worked out arrangements with the Dutch Missionary Fellowship and the German Missionary Fellowship whereby a number of missionaries supported by those groups were sent to TEAM fields.

Upon the retirement of the Torjesens in 1989, Winchell appointed Herbert and Lorelei Apel (Austria) to succeed them. The Apels' fluency in German and knowledge of Europe prepared them well for this assignment.

TEAM Celebrates One Hundred Years

The centennial conference, the very nature of which made it unusual and special, opened the observance of TEAM's one hundredth anniversary at the Wheaton Evangelical Free Church, Wheaton, Illinois, May 8 to 13, 1990. As early as October 1982 the administrative staff began preliminary preparations for the centennial, the exact date of which would be October 14, 1990. At the outset, it was decided that its first public observance would be at the 1990 annual conference. This was actually preceded by a world-wide day of prayer participated in by the TEAM family in North America and thirty mission fields.

The next major event was the centennial banquet, October 13, 1990, at the Rosemont Holiday Inn near O'Hare Airport, Chicago, with 1,650 in attendance. The next day, October 14—the actual anniversary—TEAM participated in the services of the Moody Church, Chicago. It was this church which had commissioned Fredrik Franson in 1878 for the Lord's work wherever He should lead. The final celebration to remember the completed span of a hundred years and to launch a new century of dedication and service was announced as the 101st annual conference on the campus of Bryan College in Dayton, Tennessee, July 13 to 19, 1991.

A centennial song book, *Songs to Live By,* compiled by Jack MacDonald, was introduced at the 1990 conference. In addition to well-known hymns, it presented some new pieces authored and composed by TEAM personnel.

The centennial committee also commissioned me to write a hundredth anniversary history of the mission to cover the entire century of its work, not just the period since the eightieth anniversary book *The Sovereign Hand* by Paul Sheetz was published in 1971.

Winchell appointed Jack MacDonald, associate director, as coordinator of the centennial year activities, and after the fall of 1989—when David Davis joined the foreign secretary staff—to give his full time to this work.

General Director's Centennial Report

In his report to the annual meeting, Winchell took note that TEAM was completing its first century and entering the second while at the same time beginning the last decade of this present century. He reiterated the objective of the mission in a new, more direct wording as developed by the administrative staff:

> The purpose of TEAM is to help churches send missionaries to plant reproducing churches in other nations.[8]

Winchell then called for dedication to this central biblical purpose:

> All our endeavors must work toward this. We must weigh every potential ministry in light of its possible contribution to this purpose.[9]

Growth Since Seventy-fifth Anniversary

Winchell also took a look back at the seventy-fifth anniversary in 1965 and, referring to my keynote message and annual report, noted the growth the Lord had given in the intervening twenty-five years:

> Our total missionary force has grown from 840 to 1107 [in spite of many retirements]. There were 38 missionaries on the retired list then and there are 272 now, not to mention the many who have died. The number of fields has grown from 19 to 30, and the number of churches from 755 to approximately 2,500. In the year reported on at that conference there were 1,851 baptisms; last year there were 7,541. There were 6 hospitals (now we have 8 and 3 more planned), 40 clinics (now we have 151), 180,708 outpatients (this year 403,285) and 13,403 inpatients (current year 14,041). We had ten Bible colleges and institutes then, 33 now—355 students in our schools then, 1,751 now.[10]

A New Century, New Opportunities

The attention at the centennial conference was not only on the past, but very much on the present and future. The 1989 collapse of communist governments in Poland, East Germany, Hungary, Czechoslovakia, and Romania opened new and exciting possibilities of ministry. Preliminary reports were given of the April 1990 survey completed by Jack MacDonald and David Davis of the home staff and Europe missionaries Richard Baarendse, Kurt Schneider, Mike Cochrane, Elena Bogdan, and Ed Lewis. The survey team found a situation different from some other pioneer fields. That difference was in the existence of a live but embattled church in many places, whose need was not that foreign missionaries take over responsibility from the church but rather be "fellow helpers to the truth."

Conferring with evangelical church leaders, the team learned of needs for Christian education and youth work, leadership training and development, assistance in evangelism and church planting, and teaching English as a means of developing contacts for evangelism.

Being already positioned in central Europe, and working with Austrians and Yugoslavs, TEAM missionaries sensed a strong responsibility to enter the open door in the east. MacDonald and Davis accordingly requested "the board's permission to begin aggressive recruitment for East Germany, Czechoslovakia, and Romania as parts of our widened Eastern Europe field."[11]

Eastern Europe Field Approved

The board members, meeting May 8, 1990, agreed unanimously to move forward in this way. So at the threshold of TEAM's second century, there was a new field before the mission and promise of new missionaries to respond to the call. Winchell pointed to this development as evidence that a century-old mission could rightly be described as a young mission with a pioneering spirit.

EXPECTATION AND DISAPPOINTMENT IN CHINA AND MONGOLIA

Return to China

Oscar Beckon and Reuben Gustafson—who formed the vanguard of the return to China after Japan surrendered—arrived in Shanghai on April 28, 1946. They bought a truck and gathered supplies they would need inland. Christian literature was in short supply due to lack of paper but they did find 200 song books. The Pocket Testament League had ordered three tons of Scripture portions, which the men were able to transport. For the thousand-mile trip inland to Sian, Shensi, the truck was put on a railway flatcar for much of the way. There were a number of interruptions as guerrilla bands, intent on creating problems for the government, had broken up the tracks.

Beckon and Gustafson learned that Elmer Peterson had returned to Sian upon his release from military duties after hostilities ceased. They found that Peterson had been active in contacting churches—particularly those without pastors—seeking to encourage the lay leaders. He had attended the joint conference of the churches founded by the China Inland Mission, the Christian and Missionary Alliance, and the S.A.M. in the northwest provinces of Kansu, Ningsia, and Tsinghai. There he noted with approval the strong sense of responsibility exhibited by the Chinese leaders.

Churches Revisited

In their first four months, Beckon and Gustafson visited city after city through the length of the field to hold evangelistic services. Pastor Tuan Hsiohai, chairman of the church association, traveled with them desiring to take advantage of the open doors for evangelism. Their new amplifying equipment was put to good use, multiplying the number who could hear the message. Beckon reported:

> The number of men and women who have confessed Christ by accepting Him publicly is now much over five hundred. As Pastor Tuan said after a meeting when forty came and knelt before their newly found Savior, "This is the work of the Spirit, for otherwise you could not get these men and women—even with torture—to kneel and confess."[1]

Meanwhile, back at mission headquarters in Chicago, a large number of new and returning workers were preparing to sail for China. The only ships available were troop transports which had been fitted with large dormitory rooms. An item in a San Francisco newspaper reported that the Marine Lynx, with 970 passengers— 670 of them missionaries—had sailed and was to dock in Shanghai on January 2, 1947. On board were seven returning and four new S.A.M. workers. Another group left in mid-February. By October 1947, when general director David H. Johnson visited China, the number of missionaries had increased to forty-one.

General Director's Ministry

Johnson toured the large field—three hundred miles from end to end—accompanied by Pastor Tuan, Reuben and Esther Gustafson, Fred Nelson, and a Bible Institute student. He spoke an average of three times daily, with Nelson as interpreter. They covered twenty church areas in thirty-two days of constant travel, preaching, and consultation. Johnson was overwhelmed by the response to the gospel message. "The eagerness with which the people listened to the message of life gave evidence that the door for evangelism is wide open."[2]

Then followed five days of conference with the missionary family. This was Johnson's first such mission field conference as general director. The report referred to some of the positive planning in that gathering:

> In the many matters of importance considered at the business sessions, the understanding counsel of the general director was much appreciated. Plans for extension of the work were formu-

lated. Though there are now four preaching chapels in Sian where a thousand or more hear the message every evening, it was decided to launch out in a venture of faith in establishing a meeting hall large enough to accommodate three thousand people and thus take advantage of the eagerness of the people to hear the Word of God. It is expected that this hall will be filled night after night as the gospel is proclaimed.[3]

Paradoxically, the same report had the following ominous yet determined words: "Uncertainty is written over the days ahead, but with the fields ready for harvesting, present difficulties must not be permitted to interfere."[4]

Threatening Clouds

Uncertainty and *present difficulties* referred to the growing strength of the communist forces contesting with the nationalist armies for control of China. Julius Bergstrom wrote on March 29, 1948, describing the opportunities at the Chinese New Year season and also the threatening clouds:

> We were deeply impressed with the manifest hunger of the people who filled the gospel halls evening by evening. In many respects they were far more quiet than some of the audiences in our country churches here. Hundreds indicated their willingness to believe in the Lord.

> In view of the almost inevitable invasion of this area, and the consequent disruption of organized conditions, it seems best for all new missionaries and those who can leave to go to Szechwan and settle down in Chungking and Chengtu, there to study, work, and wait for developments. A few of us will try to stay as long as possible, and fly out e'er it is too late. This has been the policy in other cities which have been seriously threatened.... How loathe we are even to think of moving!"[5]

This reluctance even to contemplate withdrawal is understandable. The harvest fields were ripe. Missionaries were using several amplifying outfits to reach multitudes in the city of Sian. This was indeed the time of harvest.

Yet the situation continued to deteriorate, so over a period of eight to twelve months most of the missionaries, heeding orders from the consular officials, left for other parts of China. Several groups went to the western province of Szechwan. One group flew to Canton in southern China. Some of the Kansu missionaries moved northwest to the capital, Lanchow. One truckload of missionaries and equipment for public meetings went to Kweichow in the far southwest. Everywhere they went they seized opportunities for preaching the Word—truly a re-enactment of the experience of first-century Christians.

Evangelism Intensifies

In early 1949 general director Johnson, en route from a visit to India and Pakistan, stopped in China to confer with as many of the missionaries as possible in the major cities of Canton, Chungking, Chengtu, and Shanghai. He wrote in the mission magazine:

> Our home constituency will rejoice with us in the marvelous manner in which the Lord is using the missionaries in these days of dispersion. They are not idle. For example, at Chungking, a city of almost a million inhabitants, our missionaries are engaged in a tremendous outdoor evangelistic effort. On Chinese New Year, January 29 [1949], they used two cars, each equipped with a public address system. More than 25 meetings were held throughout the day in the crowded business sections. In the evening a large rally was held in the public park. Thirty thousand tracts were distributed; hundreds of gospel portions were sold! Upward of 50,000 people heard the gospel in this one day's effort in Chungking. At Chengtu our missionaries are also busily engaged with many Bible classes. Many, through these classes, have found the Saviour.... Preaching has also been carried on from boats, by means of amplifiers. Unnumbered thousands have thus heard the Word. This was especially true during the Dragon Feast Festival.[6]

The combination of danger and open doors of opportunity was not a new situation for the missionaries with longer years of service. They had worked under similar conditions during the period of war lord misrule and more recently in the war with Japan.

What made the decision of whether to go or stay so difficult in 1949? First, the unparalleled responsiveness of the threatened Chinese and, second, the knowledge that missionary work as previously carried on would be greatly handicapped or halted altogether when the communists took over. Once that happened, Chinese Christians who associated with foreigners would be considered anti-revolutionary. Field council leaders, a number of whom had repeatedly faced danger, were convinced that the churches would be better served by withdrawal of the foreign workers. They observed that missionaries of other missions were leaving.

On the other hand, they also knew that the general director of the China Inland Mission had ordered C.I.M. personnel to remain at their posts. It was understood that any missionary choosing to leave would forfeit his membership in the mission and be responsible to pay his own passage home.

Withdraw or Stay?

As the TEAM board members viewed this situation from the other side of the world, they cherished the hope that the missionaries could continue their work under communist control. On May 23, 1949, they approved sending a cable: "Board prefers no withdrawals from China unless absolutely necessary, transfers to other fields questionable."

On that same day Johnson followed up with a four-page explanatory letter. One sentence left the problem unresolved: "In expressing itself that it preferred there be no withdrawals from China unless absolutely necessary, the Board is fully aware that there may be emergency situations which would warrant a withdrawal from that field."

The question was how to define "absolutely necessary" and what would constitute "emergency situations." The known treatment of Chinese Christians and missionaries by the communists presented a confusing pattern. Some had been imprisoned, tortured, and murdered; Americans were particularly at risk. On the other hand, some missionaries testified that the "liberating armies" had treated them with consideration and allowed them to continue their work.

Dr. Johnson was not at the August 17, 1949, meeting of the

board as he was visiting churches in the western United States. It was, therefore, my responsibility to summarize the China question and present it to the board for decision. I did this in a brief of nine points:

1. Missionaries believe the board has ordered them to stay—this in spite of Johnson's letter which indicated that the field committee could authorize exceptions.
2. The leaders of the field—men of dedication and long experience—believe it is wisest to evacuate.
3. Most other American missions are leaving.
4. Missionaries have already left their own stations so cannot be of assistance to their Chinese friends.
5. The China Inland Mission stands alone in ordering its missionaries to remain.
6. The China Inland Mission will take no responsibility for our missionaries in its territory.
7. The U.S. State Department has given confidential notice of its intention to close its consulates in advance of the communist takeover.
8. It has not been found possible to transmit money to Communist China.
9. The New Testament gives examples of both courses of action—remaining to confront danger or moving out ahead.[7]

A Decision Reached

The board discussion was open and frank with a variety of views expressed. In the end, there was unanimous approval of "the decision of the field committee for withdrawal when the committee is in position to function; to leave it to the individual missionary where committee action is not possible, and that the board make it clear there will be no censure."[8]

Of the forty-one TEAM missionaries in China, two lady missionaries, Jeanette DeVries and Gladys Thompson, remained on the Shensi field. Mr. and Mrs. Fred Nelson and Mr. and Mrs. John Streater stayed in Szechwan, to which province they had previously moved, and in Shanghai Mr. and Mrs. Edwin Fisch continued their work with the China Sunday School Union. Angeline Bernklau of the Mongolia field stayed on in the northwestern province of Ningsia. After less than two years under communist rule these nine missionaries, finding that effective work was no longer possible, decided to move out. Officials of the China Inland Mission reached the same conclusion and withdrew their missionaries, also in 1951.

Sian and all of the Shensi and Kansu fields had come under communist control in 1949. From that time on, communication with church leaders was greatly diminished and before many months passed was completely severed.

Missionaries DeVries and Thompson maintained local contact and sent news of interest from time to time. Gladys reported from Lunghsien that the communist authorities had prohibited the church from holding any Christmas (1949) services—to the great disappointment of the Christians. Jeanette wrote that one of the Sian churches held a vacation Bible school (1950) in which 217 children were enrolled. The Sian Bible Institute opened its 1950 fall term on August 20. Students were taking vocational courses in addition to Bible so that they could be classified as laborers and thus "productive members of society."

Pastor Tuan Run Over

Pastor Tuan Hsiohai, chairman of the church association, enjoyed the confidence of the missionaries as they believed he would have both spiritual and practical wisdom in dealing with the new situation. But then in late 1949, Miss DeVries cabled the sad news that Tuan had been killed on a Sian street by a communist military truck. This was a great loss. He was mourned by church members and missionaries alike. When word reached me in the home office my reaction was as if a beloved brother had been taken from me.

A period of almost thirty years was to pass before any authentic word would be received about the condition of the churches. We who had served with the Chinese believers were sure the Lord was preserving a testimony for His name in spite of a series of pressure actions by the authorities. These actions cannot be reviewed in detail here. It is sufficient to say they were designed first to control, then to weaken, and finally to destroy the churches.

After sixty years of missionary work, the TEAM China field had more than 100 churches in twenty-two counties of Shensi and Kansu with more than 15,000 baptized believers. Countless others who had been won out of heathen darkness had already gone to their eternal reward with the Savior.

The American public viewed the loss of China to the communists as a failure of U.S. diplomacy and power. This attitude spilled over to Christian circles as well. It was not uncommon to read articles in Christian periodicals decrying missionary work as a failure for not having prevented the people from turning to godless communism. With no sure or authentic news there was little that the defenders of missions could offer to prove that the endeavor had not ended in failure.

Mao's Cultural Catastrophe

The Cultural Revolution instigated by Mao Tsetung in 1966 unleashed the radical and destructive Red Guard youth to persecute, destroy, and kill. By the time the revolution peaked the whole Christian movement seemed to have been wiped out, with little evidence that even a limited underground church survived.

Not Closed to Radio

There was ample reason for discouragement. Yet missionaries of vision and faith saw radio as a means of encouraging the Christian remnant who might have access to radios. Some unbelievers might even listen to the saving message. The stations of the Far East Broadcasting Company (FEBC) began broadcasts to China. At about the same time the first TEAM missionaries in Taiwan began a recording ministry preparing programs in Mandarin and Taiwanese for release over local stations. FEBC needed programs for broadcasts to China and so TEAM Radio Taiwan became a regular supplier.

In December 1956 when TEAM Radio HLKX was opened in Korea, Julius Bergstrom was drafted to head the Chinese department. The beaming of Mandarin evangelistic and Bible teaching programs became a continuing ministry in which Bergstrom was engaged for seventeen years—part of the time working in the homeland and part in Taiwan.

A Memorable Reunion

In 1979, after twenty-eight years of silence, it became possible to communicate with isolated individuals in China. This opened the way in April 1980 for four of us—Julius and Thyra Bergstrom and Frances and me—to join a tour group which included Sian in its itinerary. We had forty unforgettable hours in Sian during which we spent seven hours with nineteen Christian friends and former coworkers. We also made a quick unsanctioned side trip to Hsingping, twenty-eight miles to the west, in order to learn what remained of the extensive church work built up by the Bergstroms of two generations. There was little of material to see. The large church building had been destroyed, but we learned enough to know that out in the country districts the Lord had preserved an active witness for Himself. (We were amused to see a discarded five-foot plaster bust of Mao Tsetung left to face the wall of a partly demolished building. Was this prophetic? It was, indeed. I observed that by 1981 many of Mao's pictures, statues, and quotations had been removed from public places.)

The time together with Chinese Christians was informative, interesting, emotion-filled, and heart-stirring. We learned that some of the work had continued for seven or eight years, but all of the churches and chapels, except in several isolated country places, were eventually closed. A number of the church leaders had suffered martyrdom. We heard that Dr. P'ei of Pingliang and Pastor Hu Wentung, successor to Pastor Tuan as chairman of the church association, had died in prison. We could infer, from what was alluded to, that most Christian workers had suffered a great deal. Christians were now meeting in crowded house churches, still unsure of their right to gather. Our friends told us that the total in these meetings in Sian was about 4,000, exceeding the total number of church members at the time of the communist takeover. (This total included Christians formerly identified with several missions. No denominational or mission distinctions were now permitted.) These servants of the Lord exhibited a victorious spirit. "Christ is alive! The church is alive!" They also confessed they needed much prayer for future uncertain days. As we conferred and prayed together it was with a sense of thanksgiving, joy, and triumph. The gates of hell had not prevailed against the church of the Lord Jesus Christ!

Now, View the Harvest

The remarkable growth in the number of believers reported in recent years can be attributed to various factors. Surely the most notable is the personal witness of Christians who had heard the gospel in the days before the communists choked off the missionary ministry.

On a visit to Sian in 1981, general director Richard Winchell, his brother William, coordinator of TEAM radio outreach to China, and I attended a Wednesday morning worship service in the one reopened Sian church. There was an attendance that week-day morning of about 500! This was only one of six or seven services during the week which were similarly well attended. We also spent three evenings with evangelist CCK and learned much that convinced us that the Church of Jesus Christ in China is alive and growing—through the sovereign work of the Lord and the diligent witness of His own. The figures shared with us by CCK at that time have made it easy to accept the estimated total of 50-75 million believers in China as a whole.

The Overseas Missionary Fellowship (formerly China Inland Mission) publishes a small monthly paper which gives news about the churches and provides subjects for prayer. The January 1989 issue contains a lead article on the church in Shensi. (The new spelling is Shaanxi; no change in pronunciation.) Of the 30 million population there are said to be 100,000 Christians. The church is growing rapidly. In 1983 the Religious Affairs Bureau reported that in Sian there were 1,857 converts of whom 1,814 were in the house churches. There were reopened churches in at least half of Shaanxi's 89 counties and 8 cities. The pioneers who introduced the gospel in the face of much resistance and at the risk of health and even life certainly would rejoice to see such a harvest.[9]

Mongolia Closed—But Not Completely

The increased concern for unreached peoples following World War II extended even to sparsely populated Mongolia. Stuart and Margaret Gunzel were fully aware of the difficult task ahead as they returned to Patsebolong in 1947. Three new missionaries, Angeline Bernklau and Edvard and Jenny Torjesen, also answered the call. There was even promise of more new workers. Thirteen candidates had applied to serve on that difficult field.

A Brief Reentry

The Gunzels and Miss Bernklau were the only ones able to reach Patsebolong, where early missionaries had made so great an investment of love, labor, and life. The occupation of Patsebolong by Chinese settlers had caused the Mongols to move farther back onto the grasslands. Yet Gunzel found some fruit of the earlier witness and rejoiced that the price paid by the early missionaries had not been in vain.

It was not long after this that general director David Johnson visited Mongolia. His impressions of the spiritual darkness and physical and material backwardness were shared in the mission's magazine, on film, and through messages in churches and schools. They surely were a large factor in awakening the interest of potential missionaries.

A Hurried Withdrawal

The Torjesens reached Tientsin on the coast of China in late 1948 and Gunzel left Patsebolong to meet them. Just after he left, the military defense against communist attacks collapsed so quickly that Mrs. Gunzel and two children, Joy and James, had to evacuate their home. They joined a party leaving Mongolia by truck for Ningsia province, several hundred miles farther inland. (Two older children, Carol and David, were in school in Kuling, China. Miss Bernklau was out on a long gospel tour with missionaries of another mission and only later found her way to Ningsia.)

The military situation prevented Gunzel and the Torjesens from proceeding to Patsebolong so they found space on a chartered plane to take them directly to Lanchow, Kansu, not far from where Mrs. Gunzel and children had gone. Though their reunion was not at the expected place or time, the missionaries rejoiced in the Lord's protection and guidance. Their next step was to assess the circumstances through which they had been led and determine His will for their continued ministry to the Mongols.

Finding Mongols Elsewhere

This evacuation seemed to end TEAM's fifty-three year missionary ministry in Inner Mongolia but the Lord was not through working. With the communist occupation, missionaries could no longer hope to serve in Patsebolong, Pailingmiao, and Chao Ho. But this did not nullify their calling nor end their determined efforts to seek other means to reach Mongols. Having learned that there were Mongols in China's Tsinghai Province, Gunzel, Torjesen, and a representative of the China Bible House undertook a survey trip. They traveled among a mixed population—Chinese, Muslims, and Mongols. Gunzel's proficiency in Mongolian gave an open door to minister along the way and in scattered villages.

On another tour—with Leonard Street of the China Inland Mission and Arne Nordmark of the Swedish Free Mission—Gunzel traveled several hundred miles farther west into Tsinghai to a Mongol settlement at Tulan. This seemed like a promising area in which to begin a new work. The Mongol dialect was similar and the welcome extended by the people contrasted sharply with the indifference of the people on the older Mongol field. If the nationalist armies could turn back the communists so that peace would be restored, Tsinghai could become a new base for reaching Mongols. This was the hope.

New Testament Revision

In the meantime, Gunzel had responsibilities, accepted earlier, to assist in the revision of the Mongolian New Testament. The revision committee included missionary Gerda Ollen of the Swedish Mongol Mission and three qualified Mongol linguists, Mattai, Genden, and Erinchindorji. These Mongols, who had first-hand experience with the communists, would not accept the assignment unless they were away from the unsettled conditions in China. As they were indispensable members of the revision team, the missionaries decided to make Hong Kong their base.

It was no easy matter, in 1949, to find housing where several Mongol and missionary families could live and work together in crowded Hong Kong. The solution was to rent five small vacation houses high on the mountain ridge of Laantau Island, about fifteen miles by water from the city center. The isolation was welcome for the exacting work of translation and revision. Here, after more than two years of work, Gunzel and his coworkers completed the revision and also prepared an English-Mongol dictionary to replace the outdated and inadequate ones available.

Scriptures Through the Curtain

By the time the Mongol New Testament was published, the communist regime had consolidated its control over China, including Inner Mongolia. The missionaries, however, found ways to send copies inland to known believers. Where there were numbers of Mongols outside the China mainland, such as Taiwan, the New Testament could be sold as the foremost means of introducing Mongols to Christ.

When the first printing of New Testaments was exhausted, some deeply interested friends—including Priscilla, widow of Mattai, and Doris Ekblad, Evangelical Free Church missionary—arranged in 1988 for a reprint of 1,000 copies. They have continued to send copies in to Mongols, so the Word of God is still a potent factor in bringing light to these people.

Universities around the world with Mongolian studies purchased copies of the dictionary and the New Testament, recognizing them as valuable resource materials. Faith in God's wonderful providence tells us they will continue to be of benefit to the missionary cause.

Mongols in Taiwan

The Torjesens and Angeline Bernklau responded to an invitation to come to Taiwan to work among Mongol refugees from the Red onslaught on China. They found some who were in government positions as representatives of their people. Torjesen wrote glowingly of encouraging contacts:

> In recent weeks, three Mongols here have confessed Christ, and others are talking freely about the stand of their countrymen. One of them is Hugjintei, representative to the National Assembly of China; another is the 17-year-old son of Jagchid, secretary-general of the Mongolian National Assembly; the third, the 17-year-old daughter of Uljibayin, Prince Teh's personal representative to the national government. O, how we long to help these people for they undoubtedly are the ones to have a say in the future of Mongolia—should it be freed from the Communists.[10]

When the Gunzels visited Taiwan after completing their work in Hong Kong, Mongols came eagerly to the meetings held in the Mongolian language. Although a number of these Mongols were believers, others came because of their curiosity about an American couple who had lived and worked in their Mongolia homeland. The Gunzels rejoiced for these additional opportunities to unveil the gospel light to men and women in the heathen darkness of Lamaistic Buddhism.

Lasting Fruit

On visits to Taiwan over thirty-three years, I became personally acquainted with Mrs. Fu, the widow of Erinchindorji who had worked with Gunzel on the New Testament revision. I also came to know her son, Philip, a fine Christian layman, and her daughter, Hannah, the wife of Joseph Chiang, pastor of a TEAM-related Chinese church in Taipei. Each time I have fellowshipped with them, I have rejoiced that some Mongols have come to Christ—a few plucked out of the dense darkness of Lamaism. There will indeed be Mongol voices in the praise chorus around the throne of the Lamb!

JAPAN—A RENEWED OPPORTUNITY

Widespread Destruction

Pearl Harbor, Midway, Coral Sea, Guadalcanal, Tarawa, Leyte, Iwo Jima, Okinawa—these battle names are grim reminders of blood poured out in deadly conflict between resolute foes. By 1945, when the Japanese surrendered to General MacArthur, their homeland was in a desperate condition. Japan's factories, transportation facilities, businesses, schools, and communications were virtually demolished by the American bombing. What remained of infrastructure in the cities had been commandeered for the essential needs of the military occupation, with civilian needs taking a low priority. Because of the widespread destruction of Tokyo and other principal cities many of the people were without housing, and little material for rebuilding was available.

Food, medical supplies, and other civilian necessities were scarce. So when MacArthur issued his famous call for missionaries to come in large numbers, Japan was not an inviting place to work.

TEAM Approved for Re-entry

The American authorities had full control of entry permits and at first recognized only those missions which had been registered with the Japanese government before the war. The Evangelical Alliance Mission (under its previous Scandinavian Alliance name) not only had this recognition but had actually been the second mission to be incorporated and registered (1892) after the opening of Japan to the West. TEAM, therefore, was in an extremely favorable position to request entry for its missionaries.

It was advisable to send only men at first. The only prewar missionary available to go was C. E. Carlson. He reached Yokohama on October 15, 1946, and as the first representative of the mission was provided accommodations by the military in the Dai Ichi Hotel. As soon as possible he communicated with Pastor Matsuda Masaichi, of the Nakano, Tokyo, church, and arranged for the two to meet at the hotel. Carlson related afterwards that he was somewhat apprehensive. He wondered how Matsuda would feel toward him, an American, after suffering so much loss from the American bombing of Tokyo and especially when he recalled that the prewar Domei Church leaders had requested the missionaries to leave.

All Barriers Abolished

Matsuda, himself, had apprehensions. He later admitted that he was fearful about meeting Carlson, whose country had been attacked by Japan and which now was the conqueror. One small gesture in the spirit of the Master on Carlson's part cleared the air and set the tone for their fellowship. On the way to Mr. Carlson's room, they came to an elevator. Mr. Carlson stepped back and motioned Pastor Matsuda to enter first. Matsuda later revealed that at that moment he determined that he and the churches would work together with TEAM. Those first minutes together proved that their fellowship in Christ had not been ruptured or even weakened by six years of separation and four years of terrible war.

After Carlson had been in Tokyo for two months he summed up his impressions in a letter to his supporters:

My heart sank at the sight of Yokohama and Tokyo, these cities which were formerly so prosperous. Their fate is like that of Capernaum. I had read about the destruction before coming, but now it impressed me more painfully as I could see the homes and stores burned down for miles and miles; the trains, street cars, and buses with broken doors and windows, and the paint peeled off; and the people in rags standing in long lines for their turn to ride or hang on an already overcrowded car. When we see the pitiful condition of the people, and think of their boys who went to war, many of them never to return, then we can realize in some small measure what a heavy judgment has fallen on this nation. Their fanatical pride which made them think of themselves as a superior race with a divine ruler who was destined to rule the world; the belief that since they had never been defeated they never could be defeated; the confidence that their Shinto gods could give them victory over any foe—all such foolish ideas have been shattered. Their social and religious systems have suffered a serious blow.[1]

Battered but Alive

Carlson's primary interest was in the condition and welfare of the Christians. He searched them out as soon as possible. Pastor Matsuda had written a letter several months earlier which gave Carlson some information:

> During the war the Nakano Church was demolished, and on May 25 of last year [1945] the gospel hall, the Hongo church, and the Honan church were burned during air raids. A month later the Chiba church was also burned. Very fortunately, however, we were all safe. My family had been removed to Takayama, Hida, a month prior to the calamity and I alone remained at Uyenohara, taking care of your house. Most of the members of the Nakano church had left the city before the fire of May 25th and those who remained became victims of the fire, though none was killed. Immediately after the fire I built a little hut at Uyenohara and began Sunday services. At the beginning there were only a few in attendance, but gradually the congregation increased.[2]

Matsuda was not disheartened but steadfast in faith and hope. He continued in his letter to Carlson:

> The Christian Church in Japan has faced a grave trial since the end of the war. They have been fighting a good fight for Christ's sake. There are many serious problems such as housing, food, and finances. Nevertheless, they are never disappointed but rather have become more humble and are seeking earnestly after spiritual comfort and encouragement. At present we have a rare opportunity to preach and work for the gospel.[3]

The church was battered but very much alive.

Growing Homeland Interest

The mission's call for twenty-five workers for Japan was receiving a good response. By the annual mission conference in Turlock, California, in May 1948, general director Johnson could report that sixteen missionaries had already reached Japan and twenty-seven candidates in attendance were looking forward to service there. By the end of 1948 there were forty candidates listed for the field. Many of the young men had fought against Japan and some had served briefly in the occupation. The flow of new missionaries continued through 1949, 1950, 1951, and beyond.

One Hundred Mark Passed

When Verner and Dorothy Strom disembarked at Yokohama, January 5, 1951, they were numbers 100 and 101 of TEAM missionaries to reach Japan in the post-war period. This steady growth was in marked contrast to the scarcity of workers throughout the three decades before the war.

Solving Practical Problems

The influx of so many new missionaries was indeed gratifying but it also presented some problems. The lack of accommodations was a major problem because 50 percent of Japanese housing had been destroyed. In Tokyo the destruction of housing was 75 percent. TEAM set a policy of acquiring housing units and having each missionary be responsible for raising funds to make partial provision. Some missions adopted a policy of renting rather than buying; later when the price of land skyrocketed, they faced prohibitive costs. TEAM was able to buy several older—and often quite dilapidated—properties which would seem small according to Western standards but were larger than many Japanese homes. These later would be divided and a part sold to finance other needed housing. The Lord used these circumstances to make provision and thus the missionary force could grow.

Another sign of the Lord's leading was the provision of a field headquarters. In the home office we became conscious, shortly after the count of new missionaries began to rise, that newly arrived missionaries tended to feel they were on their own rather than being part of a family. Dr. Johnson and I began urging the field council to plan such a center. To provide greater incentive, Johnson presented the need to a certain church with the result that over

$10,000 was given for the center. When Johnson stopped in Japan in March 1949 he assisted in the purchase of a large frame residence that had escaped the bombing. With the addition of a small office building, several apartments, and some motel-like rooms, this property met the need for about twenty years. Its successor building served adequately for an additional twenty years. Having a center where missionaries from outlying districts could come for their business needs and for periodic prayer meetings, as well as for social contact with others, did much to bind the large force together as a family.

China Workers Come to Japan

Since the TEAM field in China had come under the control of the communist government, and with the thought that the China missionaries would be looking for a new field of service, the Japan field council extended a welcome to them to come to Japan. Here there were unlimited opportunities for open air evangelism for those with similar experience. Others could assist with Bible teaching and administration. Over a period of about a year twenty missionaries transferred to Japan. They had high hopes that the communist government would soon be brought down so they could return to China, and therefore chose to maintain their own field organization rather than come under the jurisdiction of the Japan field conference. It became apparent in time that this was not a good administrative arrangement; so, at the urging of the board of directors, the two separate groups joined as one at the field conference held in October 1950. An interesting development was the election of a China missionary, Oliver Olson, to be chairman of the united Japan field.

Several of the former China missionaries with valuable experience in open air evangelism and work in large street chapels set an example of vision and aggressive outreach that had a healthy influence on the Japan work. Oscar Beckon, Reuben Gustafson, and Arthur Nelson are particularly remembered for this ministry.

Remarkable Progress

A simplistic view of missionary work is that somehow the administrative chores essential to Christian work in the homeland are not necessary on the foreign field. But consider the situation the Japan field confronted. One hundred new missionaries arrived in Japan within three short years. All lacked a knowledge of the Japanese language and were unfamiliar with the culture and customs. They needed to have assistance in cultural adaptation, language study, logistics, work strategy, financial administration, education of children, and a score of other matters. This help normally comes from field council members chosen by their fellow missionaries because of their ability to make decisions and give appropriate assistance. In the first few years there were only two, and for a short while three, who knew the language and people—C. E. Carlson, G. W. Laug, and briefly, Timothy Pietsch. The tenure of Carlson and Laug in leadership was also quite brief. That the newer field leaders were not only able to give broad direction to the work, but also to make steady advance must be seen as it really was, a most significant undertaking. They set up a proper field administration, absorbed and interpreted mission principles and policies, gave guidance to newcomers, planned a strategy, and all the while kept up their own study of Japanese and a measure of direct evangelistic ministry. It could not have been accomplished without their full dedication and the direct help of the Lord.

How Important Is Language?

How important was language study for these new missionaries? Was it not more important to take advantage of the many open doors in evangelism? The people were open and friendly and seemed to respond well to the evangelistic messages. A crowd could easily be gathered in the open air. Public schools welcomed speakers. Was this not the strategic time to sow the seed and reap a harvest? Would not time taken for language study be at the expense of evangelism? In time, however, thoughtful missionaries began to realize that preaching and teaching through interpreters was far from satisfactory in presenting a clear and adequate message, except in the few situations where interpreters were unusually well qualified.

A 1951 article in the mission's magazine reviewed the work of many missions since 1947 and tried to put mass evangelism and careful follow-up into proper perspective:

> Church rolls and mission statistics have comparatively little to show for the hundreds of thousands who have responded to an invitation. In the first place there are far too few [missionaries] who are able to do follow-up work. There is the problem of knowing the language well and of understanding thoroughly the thought background of those who come to ask questions. Few of those who have gone to Japan since the war can qualify. New missionaries and foreign preachers on tour can draw the crowds to their mass meetings, but the intimate dealing with souls through an interpreter many times falls short in effectiveness.[4]

Another problem was that the Japanese had no background of biblical understanding and required spiritual counseling and teaching to ground them in the Christian faith. Missionaries needed a working knowledge of the language.

Understanding the Objective

One concern was that some missionaries without strong home church service lacked an adequate understanding of the church. The preparatory teaching in the pre-field candidate classes strongly emphasized church planting, which would be possible only if missionaries were proficient in Japanese. It took several years before the missionaries were united in their recognition that language attainment was an essential key to their church planting work. When they saw its importance they set up a good language program to make it possible.

Domei Re-established

The action taken to clarify the position and affiliation of the churches (see chapter 20) needed follow-up. This had occurred at a conference of the missionaries, pastors, and lay leaders of the S.A.M.-related churches held October 12 to 14, 1948, with forty in attendance. Coming so soon after the re-entry, this gave a much-needed opportunity for warm fellowship. The church fellowship was reorganized as the Nippon Domei Kirisuto Kyokai with Pastor Matsuda as chairman. It became generally known as the Domei—the word for Alliance. The Japanese chose to translate the name as Japan Evangelical Alliance Church, not an exact translation but one which emphasized its relationship to TEAM.

As a step toward getting new churches started, the program committee for the annual field conference in 1951 had assigned study papers on various aspects of church planting. These papers were carefully discussed and then bound together in a small volume to serve as helpful guidelines for the missionaries.

By the fall of 1952 there were several areas of growth and progress. The missionary force had grown to 157 and there were 72 children. To house this family and to provide for the beginning ministries there were 71 pieces of property in use of which 31 were mission-owned. The Word of Life had started a literature center and was also operating a printing press. The Alliance Bible Institute held classes on a new—though small—campus. There was a beginning of Bible Camp work at Matsubarako, and twenty of the 153 campers were reported to have made decisions for Christ.

Radio Ministry Commenced

The year 1952 marked the signing of the peace treaty between the United States and Japan. This restored to Japan much of the sovereignty which had been in the hands of the occupying forces. The control of radio was a case in point. Hopes for establishing a Christian station evaporated when the government decreed that no one religion would be granted that privilege. Not to be denied, a group of TEAM missionaries and several from the Far Eastern Gospel Crusade, all with radio experience, banded together to form the Pacific Orient Broadcasting Company (later changed to the Pacific Broadcasting Association). They hoped to buy time on national networks and local radio outlets. TEAM personnel were Arthur Seely, Bernard Holritz, Ralph Bell, and—later—Tom Watson. The first programs were placed on a Manila short-wave station of the Far East Broadcasting Company (FEBC). Later a plan was developed to place programs in local areas of Japan with churches or missionaries being responsible for the cost of air time and for handling follow-up. This proved to be an excellent method for conserving the fruit of radio evangelism in local churches.

Breaking With Custom

A troublesome question exercising the minds of the missionaries at this time in 1952 related to funeral customs. In a heathen funeral, a picture of the deceased was placed beside the urn containing the ashes. Those in attendance bowed to the picture in an act of worship to the spirit of the deceased. A Christian funeral had some similarities in that a picture was also placed beside the urn. Some Christians in attendance bowed in respect but did not at all consider the bow as worship. However, the uninstructed did not differentiate and may have construed the bow as worship of the spirit of the departed. Pastors and mature Christians were not confused, but there was a fear that new believers who were being warned not to compromise with idolatrous practices might consider a funeral as a time when Christians did recognize a departed spirit as deserving of worship.

The board of directors usually does not make decisions relating to details of church practices, but felt this was a matter which would affect the testimony of the mission work in Japan. It therefore took the matter under careful study and sent a recommendation to the field council to bring to the attention of the pastors and other church workers:

> We fear that there may be some who will interpret such bowing as an act of worship, following the practices of the non-Christian people, and thus prove a cause for stumbling among weaker Christians, as well as among unsaved. We believe that the teachings of the Word of God as set forth in First Corinthians, chapter eight, will prove helpful in bringing about a solution of this question. We must be careful, as stated in verse 9 of said chapter, that we "take heed lest by any means this liberty of yours become a stumbling block to them that are weak."[5]

The 1953 Revival

The mission field is a battleground. A superficial view is that the enemies of progress and blessing are such things as language difficulties, unsatisfactory living conditions, personal pressures, financial stringency, etc. When a true revival comes, the real reasons are seen through spiritual eyes—coolness of heart, dependence on self rather than on the Holy Spirit, interpersonal tensions, and personal spiritual needs. The revival that swept Japan missionaries and nationals in early 1953 was no shallow stirring but a deep moving of the Spirit.

Plans had been made some months in advance to hold a semi-annual business conference in February 1953, but as the time grew near, it was decided that rather than meet to discuss business concerns there should be a time of fasting and prayer for the financial needs of the missionaries and the work.

> About one hundred missionaries met in Tokyo, February 10 and 11, 1953, to seek the Lord for a special outpouring of blessing. One missionary had been asked to bring the message from the word of God. He read a Scripture passage but had not proceeded very far in his message before he was moved by the Spirit's convicting power. His own spirit was broken and he could proceed no farther. He felt his own personal need. There had been some misunderstanding between the missionary and two others in the conference. In the presence of all, he asked them to forgive him. Thus the Spirit of God began to work. The hearts of all were stirred. Others came under conviction. A time of confession followed. Many who had hardened hearts because of some unkind words which had been spoken, or because of jealousy, lack of brotherly love, or some other cause were immediately moved to straighten all differences with their fellow missionaries. God was softening hearts. Confession turned into praise, sorrow into joy, and silence into witnessing. Revival had come and revival fires began to burn and to spread.[6]

The revival expanded to TEAM missionaries not present, to other missions, and to many Japanese. One of the newer workers summarized the results in her life and as she observed them in others:

> (1) A new realization of the deceitfulness of sin. (2) A holy hatred of sin. (3) A new love for the Word. (4) A new love for the

brethren. (5) A greater brokenness for lost souls. (6) A greater faith to claim every promise in the Word. (7) A greater desire to live a holy life.[7]

The revival brought a heightened spiritual tone to the ministry with the realization of the truth of Zechariah 4:6 that victory comes "not by might nor by power, but by My Spirit, saith the Lord of hosts." As recently as 1988 one of the Japan missionaries stated that the revival has had a profound and lasting effect on the ministry. The Japanese people, although well educated and once again prosperous, are nevertheless steeped in idolatry. Missionaries to that country have generally been well prepared academically and theologically, but their training and experience were not found sufficient to lead men and women to an acknowledgment of their need and a willingness to follow the Savior. This was a task that would not yield to "might and power." Only the gentle wooing of the Spirit of God could cause souls to come to the One who alone could meet their need, satisfy their spiritual hunger, and convince them of the excellency of Christ. That a steady work of the Lord has gone forward in the planting of several hundred churches is attributable to the working of the Spirit of God through yielded channels at His disposal—missionary and national. This is what made the revival of 1953 a watershed event for the gospel in Japan.

The Churches in the Spotlight

New missionaries need time to get to know and understand the national church leaders. In addition to language barriers there are cultural differences and variations of church traditions and practices. These conditions were present in Japan and, additionally, there was one difficulty that was not generally present on other mission fields—the focus of the Christian world was on the Japanese churches. Questions were being asked of missions: Had the prewar church leaders been guilty of the fiction that bowing at Shinto shrines was only a show of respect and patriotism and not worship, as many of the liberal prewar churches had insisted? And were they properly penitent for their nation's background of Shinto idolatry and military aggression? Had there been cleansing from any past compromise? What about their present faithfulness? Even those pastors who had suffered for their testimony did not escape accusing questions.

Recent arrivals who lacked the language and the background of first-hand observation were particularly troubled by such questions. Some who had transferred from China made comparisons with the more mature Chinese churches and their observations were not always helpful. The problem was compounded by certain self-appointed judges outside the mission who made unfounded accusations.

Some of the newer workers felt that the safest way to proceed was to work only with those who had been won to the Lord in the post-war period, thus abandoning any thought of ministering to the Christians in already established churches or seeking their assistance in evangelizing Japan. For them it seemed the solution would be for the missionary body to declare itself separate from the Domei churches. This would also mean losing the advantage of having mature Japanese leadership in whatever new work would be undertaken.

The proposal under consideration at the annual field conference of 1954 was the required filing with the Japanese government of the constitution of the church and mission, linking the two in one organization. Older missionaries and newer workers with pastoral experience cautioned against hasty unscriptural reaction. Delbert Kuehl, field chairman, took the floor and read extensively from Paul's letters to the not-so-praiseworthy Corinthian church. When he had finished reading he asked the simple question, "Have our Japanese churches as much reason to be questioned or blamed as the church in Corinth which the apostle exhorted but from which he did not separate?"

Kuehl's presentation brought scriptural light on the subject with the result that the mission went ahead in fellowship with the Domei in a position for each to counsel and instruct the other. This had been a critical decision. The mature and wise action opened the way for an excellent and spiritually fruitful partnership.

AUXILIARY PROJECTS TO HELP THE CHURCH

The first post-war decade in Japan could be called a "decade of beginnings." The missionaries began many different projects. For a while TEAM in Japan was alluded to as the "project mission." This was not a particularly welcome name for a mission that had church planting as its main objective. It is true that the emphasis in that decade throughout many missions was on specialization. Many who had answered the call to Japan were qualified by interest or training to carry on types of work other than direct church ministries. Some sincerely believed that there were faster ways of completing the work of evangelization than the admittedly slow founding of churches and helping them grow.

In retrospect, the development of the work of the Domei Church and TEAM can be seen as the clear leading of the sovereign Lord. The Domei was an established church fellowship rooted in TEAM's pioneer work. The church needed various types of missionary assistance to be more effective. Pioneer evangelism did not come easily for most Japanese, possibly because of the more highly structured and formal code of courtesy and communication. Some Japanese Christian leaders frankly stated that missionaries were more acceptable as witnesses than the Japanese Christian who was viewed as a deserter from his own religion and culture. Missionaries could give effective assistance by getting churches started and then turn them over to full Japanese responsibility when organized

with mature believers.

Both the churches and the missionaries needed additional tools for their work. This need for tools prompted the earliest special projects—the Word of Life Press and the Alliance Bible Institute.

Word of Life Press Founded

When T. J. Bach visited Japan in 1950 he related that his own conversion in Denmark had come when a young man handed him a tract—which he at first angrily crumpled, then retrieved and read. Bach now asked the new missionaries what they were doing to reach the Japanese with gospel literature. Their reply was that they were doing nothing as yet.

Bach's question and the answer it elicited shot an arrow of conviction and holy resolve into the heart and mind of a young Canadian, Kenneth McVety. He had arrived in Japan in 1949 having worked in various Christian ministries in Saskatchewan. McVety had observed that the Japanese were avid readers. Even with shortages of most conveniences and many necessities in that period so soon after the war, the people were willing to spend money on books and other reading material. On the crowded commuter trains most riders were quietly reading a book or periodical.

While still engaged in language study and with as yet no plan for an extensive literature ministry, McVety wanted to help meet the very evident need for Christian literature. Twenty-five years later he recalled the very humble beginning of the Word of Life Press:

> When WLP's first stumbling production, Oswald J. Smith's *The Only Way,* was sent to the printers, there were few resources— only a part-time desk in an already crowded kitchen, a part-time missionary, a part-time interpreter, and 108,000 yen [$300] in beginning capital. But God had planted a seed of faith, and it began to grow.[1]

The work which began so inauspiciously in Olive McVety's kitchen soon had to find more space in rented quarters. By 1951 it had expanded into a section of an old, almost dilapidated, building which it used for the next fifteen years. Much of the early growth in publishing came as a result of homeland authors granting the right to translate articles or small books for publication and sale. At times the authors would donate the cost of the first printing, expecting that any new editions would be made from the proceeds of sales.

A monthly family magazine of Christian reading, *Gospel for the Millions,* was launched in 1951 and has had continuous circulation for more than 37 years with a peak of an estimated 100,000 readers per issue. A more recent magazine, *One Way*, is geared to the younger generation.

Nation-wide Impact

Word of Life has also distributed gospel booklets nation-wide for Every Home Crusade. Over a thirty-five-year period more than 135 million pieces of gospel literature were placed in the homes of the Japanese. The response? More than 380,000 individuals were enrolled in Bible correspondence courses and many were introduced to churches where the gospel is preached.

This publication ministry, initiated so modestly, has expanded to 1,500 titles published, with 1,200 still in print in 1988. Word of Life established a wholesale division to handle the distribution of WLP books along with those of other Christian publishers. Because of insufficient existing outlets, WLP opened its first Life Center bookstore in the busy Shibuya area of Tokyo in 1962. By 1988, Life Center bookstores had increased to eighteen, located from the northernmost island of Hokkaido to Okinawa in the south. Word of Life also launched a Christian weekly newspaper. It remembered the blind and produced Bibles and other material in Braille. The work expanded further with other ministries being developed. WLP also absorbed the Japan Sunday School Union.

Bible Translation

The New Japanese Bible was, without doubt, Word of Life's largest undertaking. It had the cooperation of forty-one evangelical

Bible scholars as translators and the participation of the Lockman Foundation, publishers of the New American Standard Bible. The New Testament edition came out in 1965 and the whole Bible in 1969. Five and a half million copies were published by 1988. With the cooperation of Living Bibles International, WLP became responsible for the translation and publication of the Japanese Living Bible.

With its constantly expanding outreach as Japan's most active Christian publisher, and providing other Christian services, Word of Life Press became Word of Life Press Ministries in 1988, and continued as an essential part of the Japan field work of TEAM.

Two Million Pages a Day

An interesting statistic is that Word of Life publishes two million pages of gospel material every business day—with printing done on commercial presses. The dollar amount is also a yardstick of activity with a budget in 1988 of U.S.$17,000,000. Of far greater importance is the number of individuals reached with Bibles and other Scripture material. Although the pages and dollars do not provide a precise measurement of that outreach, there is a significant relationship. God had His precious word committed to writing and pronounced His blessing on those who read it. The easy availability of that word in Japanese is certainly in line with His will.

In addition to Kenneth and Olive McVety, other missionaries participating in the Word of Life ministry have been Thelma Clark, Margaret Waldin, Kenneth and Gladys Henry, and Sam and Manda Archer.

Missionaries have given wise leadership, but a literature work in the difficult Japanese language must depend on the participation of able and dedicated Japanese. Many such national staff members have been involved and today carry forward the vision and work of the founder. McVety named six men who together had served over 180 years and described them as "outstanding, dedicated men of God:"

Rev. Kaoru Kohama, the very first staff member, and the first editor of *The Gospel for the Millions* magazine. Even in semi-retirement he continues doing translation work for WLP.

Mr. Kitao Iwasaki, for almost 30 years assistant to the director and the business manager.

Mr. Jiro Funaki, who headed the main editorial responsibilities in the publishing department for about 30 years.

Mr. Hideo Kubo, thirty years with WLP, serves on the managing board and as personnel director.

Mr. Masaru Saito, thirty years with WLP, headed the finance department and is a member of the managing board.

Mr. Hikaru Tanaka headed the Every Home Crusade department for 28 years.[2]

In a study I presented at the 1958 conference of Evangelical Literature Overseas, I shared some insights McVety had gained as he developed coworkers in the Word of Life Press:

The most difficult task has been to obtain in our workers the needed balance between natural ability or training and spiritual vision and maturity. The first step was to meet the Japanese workers often in prayer until God had given them some of the burden and vision we felt. When the spiritual was shared first we were often amazed at the wholeheartedness with which they took up extra burdens and responsibilities.[3]

Pastoral Training

The board of directors made a significant decision in May 1946 when discussing plans for re-entry to Japan. It was that "a Bible school be acquired at or near Tokyo with a faculty acceptable to evangelical Christian leaders."[4]

This decision recognized the need for trained leaders. With prewar governmental restrictions and pronounced liberalism in the training institutions of so many of the older denominations, pastoral training for the evangelical churches was now a high priority need. The Domei strongly endorsed the idea of a Bible institute. When David Johnson had an opportunity to present a project for consideration by the Park Street Church of Boston, he spoke for a Bible training school in Japan.

Bible Institute Founded

The Park Street Church provided an initial sum of $15,000 which made it possible to purchase a piece of property—quite limited in size—and erect a small building for the Alliance Bible Institute.

Early faculty included pastors Nobata and Sukigara and missionaries George Laug and George Martin. William Englund—recently transferred from Hong Kong—taught for about two years. His teaching combined three and even four languages. He wrote outlines on the blackboard in Chinese characters, which the Japanese understood. His lectures in English were interpreted into Japanese, and on occasion he wrote Greek sentences. His instruction abounded with interest and effectiveness.

A Christian College for Japan

When the plan for a Bible school was first considered, the Domei was still fairly small and it was felt that this might be too large an undertaking for the group. The board's earlier decision could be interpreted as favoring a school that would be acceptable to a wider group of evangelical leaders.

Dr. and Mrs. Fred Jarvis—both with earned doctorates—had gone to China in late 1946, hoping to launch a college ministry. The lack of high school education among most Chinese Christians, the political unrest, and the subsequent communist takeover made such an undertaking impossible. After leaving China, the Jarvises served briefly in Japan in evangelistic work before going on furlough in 1951. Jarvis was impressed by the evident need and potential in Japan for a Christian college to train future evangelists and pastors.

Hokes Appointed to College Ministry

While on furlough, Jarvis shared with Donald and Martha Hoke the vision of such a Christian college. Hoke was then serving as assistant to the president of Columbia Bible College of Columbia, South Carolina. Jarvis presented the need in Japan for a school that would be on a higher level than the Alliance Bible Institute and which might serve a wider circle of evangelical churches than the Domei. The Hokes applied to TEAM and their appointment to Japan carried the understanding that after language study they would be assigned to the Bible college ministry.

Committee Study of College Project

After the Hokes arrived in Japan in late 1952, Hoke was asked to join a committee with Jarvis and John Reid (who had a graduate degree in education administration) to work out detailed plans for a college. The field council instructed them to preserve to the Domei churches the benefits of the Alliance Bible Institute while at the same time planning a school that would interest a wider circle of evangelicals. This committee consulted regularly with the field council and at the annual field conference in 1954 presented a carefully worked out plan. The plan received unanimous approval by the missionaries and it was reported that the Japanese pastors were satisfied and pleased.[5]

In his first annual report as president of the Japan Christian College, Hoke referred to the inauguration of the college on April 12, 1955, with Pastor Matsuda, chairman of the Domei, bringing the opening message. The enrollment was reported as 101, of which 72 were new students. Of the new ones, fifty-five were in the third and fourth year Bible courses. Sixty-five students were from TEAM-related churches. The remaining thirty-six were from a variety of groups. "This is due to two reasons: (1) The size of TEAM and its vital interest in the school. (2) The as-yet undeveloped work of most of the other groups which are cooperating with us."[6]

Relationship to TEAM

Though Japan Christian College was formed to serve the training needs of other evangelical church groups as well, it was understood that TEAM had a special relationship—with its personnel responsible for the concept, detailed planning and financial underwriting and its having provided the Alliance Bible Institute property, originally used to train Domei pastors. Because of this relationship, TEAM/Domei was allowed a majority of seven of the thirteen members on the college board of directors. This board was responsible for safeguarding the doctrinal and spiritual integrity of the school, appointing the president, and holding the property. An administrative board with wider representation was responsible for day-to-day administration.

Don Hoke continued as president of the college until 1973 and saw the school through several major stages of development—a 1962–63 move to a larger campus at Kunitachi in outlying Tokyo and accreditation of three years of its four-year program. Accreditation made necessary a change of name to the Tokyo Christian College, which was viewed as having certain advantages, including greater appeal for prospective students. Hoke was succeeded as president of Tokyo Christian College by the Rev. Shinpei Higuchi and more recently Dr. Tadataka Maruyama.

Merger of Schools

Further development came with the merger process, extending over five years, which brought the Tokyo Christian College, Tokyo Christian Theological Seminary, and the Kyoritsu Christian Institute together as the Tokyo Christian Institute in March 1980.

Move to Chiba Prefecture

The combined school moved, in March 1989, to a new and more adequate campus in Chiba Prefecture, east of Tokyo, and was granted full accreditation as Tokyo Christian University in March 1990. The TEAM-related Domei churches were deeply involved, participating in the control, sharing in the administration, sending students, and receiving graduates into the service of the churches. A 1988 report showed an enrollment of 164 students of whom 60 were TEAM/Domei-related.

Bible Camp Work Begun

When the Lord has a special work for a missionary to do, he

346

often trains him or her in similar work in the homeland. That was true for the founders of the Matsubarako Bible Camp—John and Lucia Schone. They had served with a Bible camp ministry in Wisconsin. While still in language study in Karuizawa they decided that the central part of Honshu would be a good area in which to develop a camp for evangelism and Bible teaching. Somewhat to the north of Karuizawa they found a small lake, Matsubarako, in a picturesque setting, easily accessible by rail and highway.

Here, in 1952, the Schones began the first youth camp in a temporary quonset hut on rented land. Word went out to the Domei and other interested churches. The good response of both workers and campers surprised and gratified them. Later, an opportunity came to buy some lake-front property. When this was secured, the Japanese counselors and missionaries claimed the land for the Lord's use as they marched around the perimeter. As time passed, they were able to buy additional land and construct more substantial buildings.

Many young people and adults from the growing Domei churches profited spiritually from the time spent at Matsubarako. The counseling the workers received and which they in turn carried on provided excellent training for their participation as laymen in their own churches. Winterizing some of the buildings permitted many activities to extend into other seasons of the year.

Several years before the Schones were to retire they turned full responsibility for Matsubarako over to the Domei churches. The camp work at Kominato, Tateyama, and Yumori continued on a smaller scale under the direction of the local churches and missionaries.

Other Projects

TEAM AVED was the development and distribution of audio visual material—slides, films, and art work. A separate project for many years, it was later incorporated into the Word of Life Press. Ted and Phyllis Brannen had major responsibility for this work. Mrs. Brannen's artistic skills contributed greatly to the popularity of this material for use in the churches.

The Heaven House Orphanage served a good purpose for a time when Japan was struggling to recover from the disruption of war. Japanese families generally care for orphaned children, but following the war there was a breakdown with the result that many were neglected. Some of the most needy were children of the occupation forces. It was difficult to integrate children raised in an orphanage into Japanese society because of the stigma of having no family roots and being raised by foreigners. When the missionary ladies who had the original vision for that work left the field, the few children were placed elsewhere and the Heaven House work was discontinued.

English as a Wedge

The Helping Hand ministry was more of a concept than a project. The plan, first set forth by James Frens and carried forward by Ralph Cox, took advantage of the eagerness of Japanese to learn English. Short-term missionaries, willing to serve at least two years, were recruited to teach English in organized class settings. Along with instruction in English grammar and conversation there was teaching of the New Testament in English and Japanese. Thus, the teaching of English became a tool for evangelism which led to the formation of many congregations.

Indirectly Related Ministries

In addition to the projects which were the full responsibility of TEAM missionaries, there were a number of indirectly related ministries in which some served—a few of them originated and developed by TEAM personnel. While these projects were not officially administered by TEAM they contributed to the overall work and helped significantly in planting and developing churches. For this reason the field council assigned missionaries with certain special gifts and interests to these other activities such as radio, student ministries, and producing Sunday school material.

Reaching Out to Students

Japan places great emphasis on higher education. Competition for entry into universities is intense. Several major universities are located in Tokyo and it is estimated that 300,000 students are concentrated in a small area. After making a survey of the student population, John Schwab felt led to enter an Inter Varsity-type work in cooperation with British missionary Miss Irene Webster-Smith. To give tangible help, he raised funds for the Ochanomizu Student Christian Center in the heart of the university district. This work is administered by an interdenominational board of Japanese and missionaries, with participation by TEAM. Dr. Siegfried Buss directs a ministry of evangelism through language teaching. Many different Christian organizations base their ministries in the recently expanded Student Center building.

Radio, A Helper in Evangelism

Many TEAM missionaries participated in the radio ministry of Pacific Broadcasting Association although it had wider sponsorship and direction. These were: Arthur and Florence Seely, Bernard and Jeanette Holritz, Stephen and Alma Tygert, Joe and Frances Parker, Steve and Cynthia Snyder, and Tim and Aileen Selander. Dr. Akira Hatori, not a member but working in close cooperation with TEAM, has been the radio pastor for over thirty-five years. He also served as director for part of this time. Hatori's Bible messages have been broadcast widely over commercial radio stations to millions of listeners throughout Japan—and beyond Japan through Christian radio outlets such as World Radio Missionary Fellowship, Far East Broadcasting Company, and Trans World Radio.

Meeting Sunday School Needs

China missionaries Edwin and Laura Fisch had a great interest in Sunday school literature and in 1947 were loaned by TEAM to the China Sunday School Union in Shanghai. The communist regime took control of Shanghai in 1949, but the Fisches were able to continue working there until 1951 when increasing difficulties forced their evacuation to Japan.

Evangelical Sunday school material was a pressing need in the Japan churches, and Fisch set about doing there what he had been doing in China. When he organized the Japan Sunday School Union its funding was mostly through channels other than TEAM and thus it was separately administered. Fisch did a commendable job of developing the organization, but as is true of many men of ability, he did not prepare others—most notably the Japanese—to take responsibility. After his sudden death in 1975, and with Mrs. Fisch being in poor health, the Japan board of JSSU asked Word of Life Press to take over the work. This was a good move as Word of Life was well positioned to provide the writing, publication, distribution, and administrative direction that was needed.

Other special ministries which had a bearing on fulfilling the objectives of the mission were the language school, field headquarters, and the school for missionary children. Without them the missionaries would have been greatly handicapped in their work. Some of the most able and dedicated missionaries worked in these ministries. They usually sought opportunities to teach Bible classes or help with church activities and thus did double duty.

With these supporting projects in place, the Domei churches and the newer congregations being planted had a good supply of evangelistic and instructional literature, a trustworthy Bible translation, a Christian training institution, Bible camps, radio, and other programs. Now concentration could center more and more on church planting and expansion and on the believers' spiritual growth.

JAPANESE CHURCHES
GROWING

When I visited Japan in 1956 it was long enough after the rapid build-up of the missionary force to observe the progress—and some remaining problems. Looking back thirty-three years, what impresses me now is that many of these new missionaries had won souls, discipled them, and started planting churches. As one example among many, I particularly noted the work of the Allen Fadels and Delbert Kuehls in Aomori, where lay leaders were playing a strong role in the new church. When I contemplated the spiritual darkness that surrounded them, I rejoiced at every evidence of victory.

It wasn't every missionary who felt victorious. Some still struggled with the difficult Japanese language, caught between the necessarily strict requirements for study and their desire to be out working with the people. In the week I spent at the annual field conference, I found that language study was a major topic of discussion. This brought additional questions to the fore: "Does the field council have authority to monitor language progress, or is this reserved to the missionaries in field conference?" and "What do the Principles and Guiding Rules have to say about field council authority?"

Representing the home administration, I naturally became involved in the discussions. Though I could make a case for field council authority from the existing Principles and Guiding Rules, I realized that the guidelines needed to be clarified. This became possible when we revised the document several years later. It was good to see, though, how the missionaries in conference arrived at a decision in a mature way. What assurance it gave that the confidence placed in them in the conduct of field affairs was fully justified. These servants of the Lord enjoyed His leading in their decisions.

Slow and Exacting Work

More than half of the missionaries were involved in church ministries, mostly pioneer work. This was slow work requiring much faith, perseverance, and patience. For a few it seemed that the miracles in apostolic times not only could, but should be repeated if missionaries were in the right relationship to the Holy Spirit.

By Sight or By Faith?

This hunger for miracles led these few into contact with a visitor from North America who taught that the sign gifts of miracles, healing, and tongues were not limited to the first century but were for every Christian today. Several workers of another organization had already been influenced and were propagating these teachings.

Five missionaries of TEAM in the city of Toyama came strongly under this influence. They actually left the proclamation of the Word to wait for some miraculous gift. In the meantime, some from other missions had joined them and by 1957 a total of thirty-one were linked in what came to be called the "Toyama Group," among them eleven from TEAM. This represented only 6 percent of the TEAM force in Japan but it included missionaries of seemingly great promise in the work.

Resignations

General director Johnson met in Japan with those involved and undertook a great deal of correspondence with individuals, to little avail. He also conferred at length with the field council. The eleven workers involved voluntarily withdrew their membership over the next year. Though the percentage was small the loss was keenly felt both on the field and at home.

Those who resigned remained in Japan for a time seeking a superior spiritual experience. To many, their desire seemed to be to walk by sight rather than by faith. Little by little, they left the

Toyama group and returned to the homeland until only one couple—former TEAM missionaries—remained. Most of the others—at least as far as the mission has knowledge—had gone into secular activity and apparently were no longer fruitful in the gospel work.

Not All Loss

When I visited Japan in 1963, the field chairman informed me that the couple remaining in Toyama had given much thought and prayer to the events and now found themselves in agreement with TEAM's doctrinal emphasis rather than that of the Toyama group. I asked to talk with the couple, and we had a very satisfactory meeting indeed. They gave evidence of an attitude of dependence on the Spirit of God and a recognition that confidence in His Word rather than on signs and wonders was of paramount importance. They expressed a desire to return to TEAM at the proper time. I was confident they could indeed fit in with TEAM again and suggested an early application for reinstatement. Their reply was both enlightening and encouraging: "No, we had better delay. We are now carefully instructing the Toyama Christians in the Word to correct the unscriptural teaching they received." They later rejoined TEAM and their subsequent service was both solid and fruitful.

Blessing came unexpectedly from this unwelcome tension and loss. Missionaries, board members, and staff became more diligent to understand the ministry of the Holy Spirit and to proclaim a truly scriptural position. During the thirty-year period which has followed, no similar problem has resurfaced on the Japan field.

Protestant Centennial

It was in the preceding century, May 2, 1859, that the Rev. J. Liggins, first Protestant missionary to Japan, arrived in Nagasaki on the southern island of Kyushu. In the next twelve months, four ordained and two medical missionaries followed. The first convert was baptized five years later—in 1864. After thirteen years there were only ten converts.

Lacking any Christian literature in Japanese, these early missionaries did the best they could to introduce Japanese to the Word of God; they used the Chinese Bible. A characteristic of the Chinese written language made this possible. Though the Japanese had developed a phonetic alphabet, they had lacked a literature until, in an earlier century, they had adopted the Chinese system of writing and with it Chinese literature. They simply added the Chinese language to the Japanese, so a written character—which had no phonetic representation—now had at least two arbitrary pronunciations, the Japanese and the Chinese. It still had only the one meaning—that assigned to the written character. A very simple illustration is the word for mountain. In Chinese the pronunciation is *shan* and in Japanese *yama*. Thus for the city of Takayama (High Mountain), where there is a Domei church, the Chinese reading of the name is *Gaoshan*. Even the moderately educated Japanese use Chinese characters as part of their language so it was quite easy to introduce them to the message of the Chinese Bible. It conveyed the same meaning when read by the Japanese.

Protestant Centennial Observances

With Protestant pastors and missionaries of evangelical conviction now being the leading force for evangelism, they took the initiative in planning observances of the hundredth anniversary of the entry of the gospel into Japan. Rallies were planned for major cities—Tokyo, Yokohama, Nagoya, Osaka, Kyoto, Kobe, Sendai, Fukuoka, Hiroshima, and Okayama. The basis for cooperation was the Bible—"the fully inspired, infallible Word of God, the only rule of faith and practice."[1]

Domei pastors and missionaries were mindful of the opportunities made possible by the Protestant Centennial:

> Forty Japanese pastors and a large group of missionaries attending the two-day TEAM pastor-missionary prayer conference in October [1958] formed a joint committee for evangelism. They laid plans for evangelistic efforts during the centennial anniversary of missions in Japan [1959] and the seventieth anniversary

of TEAM in Japan [1961].... Pastor Matsuda of the Domei told the group: "We pastors alone cannot do the job and likewise you missionaries cannot do it alone. Let us join our hands and our hearts in united evangelism." The Word of Life Press and the Pacific Broadcasting Association gave assurance of full cooperation.[2]

Informing the General Public

The Protestant Centennial gave opportunity for wide publicity in the secular press about the Christian message and ministry. In the four leading English-language papers, which were widely read by Japanese, there were articles in April and May 1959 by TEAM missionaries Mrs. Dorothy Pape, Kenny Joseph, and Donald Hoke. One example is Hoke's article in the May 2, 1959, issue of *Asahi Evening News*, entitled "The Heart of Protestant Christianity." Hoke developed seven major Bible themes—the Godhead, Creation, Man, Sin, Salvation, the Church, and the Return of Jesus Christ.

> These seven points in brief sum up the Protestant Christian message to the world. It is a thrilling word of hope. It is a God-centered message. It is the purpose of the Christian gospel to bring men back into joyful fellowship with their Creator, to join them in the holy, happy fellowship of the Christian church, through which the Christian teachings of love, kindness, and unselfishness will be manifested to the world.[3]

Copies of Japanese-language newspapers giving similar coverage are not available, but it is assumed that the reading public gained some additional knowledge of the movement that was slowly advancing in their country and that some opened their minds and hearts to the gospel message.

After a Century—Still Too Few Witnesses

The slowness of the spread of the Christian message was brought out by Kenneth McVety in *The Japan Times* of April 20, 1959, in a listing of the ratio of the combined total of pastors and missionaries to the population. For Japan as a whole the ratio was one worker to 20,598. In Tokyo, where the concentration of missionaries is relatively high, the ratio was one to 7,670. In several prefectures where TEAM missionaries were serving the proportion of witnesses to the people was much lower—Niigata, one to 38,112, and one to 53,631 in Gifu.[4]

Leadership for a New Decade

As the decade of the '60s progressed it was evident that mature servants of the Lord were leading the TEAM work and this brought vision and stability. Verner Strom, who had served in church planting nine years, was elected chairman in 1960, a post to which he was reelected again and again.

The project ministries reached a level of Japanese participation where they were making major contributions and most required no increase of missionary assistance. From this time on, the field directed the missionary efforts more and more toward establishing churches. This work was by no means easy. In contrast to the ready response of the Japanese twelve to fifteen years earlier, a harvest could be reaped now only through faithful and persistent sowing and nurturing of the seed.

Resurgent Ethnic Religions

The resurgence of the ethnic religions and new expressions of these religions began to capture the attention of the people. One particularly active Buddhist sect that expanded rapidly was *Sokagakai*. It numbered its adherents in the millions. While these newly aggressive Shinto and Buddhist sects had little success in reclaiming those who had put faith Jesus Christ, they did offer a contemporary Japanese religious expression as an alternative to Christianity, which many considered a foreign import.

Willing to Count the Cost

That evangelism leading to church establishment required a great deal of patience and hard work did not deter those who had counted the cost and given themselves to the Lord for this ministry. The expansion from ten small congregations to almost two hundred in less than forty years, much of it by missionary pioneering, undoubtedly could be told in a hundred separate stories. Brief accounts will have to suffice. One is the story of the early days of planting the Yokosuka Church by Victor and Ann Springer and John and Mary Reid who, after spending several years in special ministries, felt strongly they should give themselves to church planting. Springer's account gives some insight into the required investment of time and dedicated effort:

> In 1963, Pastor Kenichi Fukazawa and I visited over 3,000 homes, inviting the people to church, and in many cases, giving personal witness. When people showed an interest in the gospel, we went back again and again. We visited one home forty times before that person finally came to church. By the beginning of 1964, there were twenty baptized believers plus other individuals who attended church regularly. The number might seem small to others, but only four years before we had yearned to see the attendance go over five.[5]

Growing National Responsibility

The annual reports of chairman Verner Strom during these years tabulate distribution of missionaries and indicate the number in church planting, projects, administration, or other work such as missionary children's education. Year after year the figures show from 53 to 57 percent of the missionaries giving their major time to directed evangelism with the church as its goal. Those in the projects averaged about 25 percent of the missionaries on the field. He reported that many of these individuals also held Bible study classes and helped the church ministries in other ways.

While the missionaries did much of the pioneer work that led to the founding of churches, they held before the believers their responsibility to witness so that others could be added to the number. The believers were also taught the importance of supporting their own work. At first the expense would be minimal. Later they would need to rent meeting places.

A Place to Meet

A welcome problem was outgrowing the meeting places. When that occurred the believers took seriously the need for a church building of their own. Missionaries prayed and worked to win whole families. That goal shaped the strategy in evangelism. If a start was made with a women's Bible study, then the converts were urged to pray faithfully for the salvation of the husbands. Activities were planned to bring men under the hearing of the gospel.

Praying for Leaders

When a number of families had become Christians the missionary prayed for spiritually qualified leaders and when such leaders emerged the congregation could be formally organized. It still might be a very small congregation, but with spiritual leadership it had the potential for growth in maturity and numbers. Some congregations continued with lay leaders while others believed that a trained full-time pastor could give the best leadership and aid in future growth.

Case Study—Shikoku

The mission's prewar ministry was mostly on the island of Honshu, which is somewhat smaller in area than the combined states of Illinois and Indiana. After the war, most of the missionaries were still assigned to Honshu, but a smaller group—David and Jacqueline Martin, Dan and Joan Dale, Ralph and Stella Cox, and later Neal and Clara Jean Browning—became concerned about the nearby large island of Shikoku (about the size of Massachusetts) and in 1955 began work in and near the major city of Takamatsu. By 1967 these missionaries, joined by Stan and Mary Barthold, had planted seven small churches. The Coxes have served in Takamatsu more than thirty years.

Concern for Growth

Cox reviewed the results to 1967 and was convinced that vision and faith called for more rapid expansion. After praying about it for some time he formed a plan to triple the number of congregations to twenty-one in ten years. His proposed strategy:

Cluster churches, house churches, lay-pastors, rotating pastors and missionaries. Missionaries pioneering, leading church planting teams, training potential new missionaries, rapidly laying foundations over vast areas, continuing supervision, discipling, etc.[6]

Cox reported that by 1977 the seven congregations had increased to twenty-two and the number of believers from 100 to 300—an average of fourteen per church. Consolidation rather than rapid expansion marked the years 1978 to 1982. The churches increased to twenty-four and total believers to 350.

A New Goal, One Hundred Churches

Noting that the ten-year goal had been met, Cox set forth an expanded plan in 1983—100 new churches in fifteen years. An interim report in July 1988 announced a total of 550 believers in forty-four churches—an average size of over twelve—and twenty-two pastors. Eighteen congregations had their own land and buildings. Cox believed that church planting was proceeding on schedule so that by 1997 there would be at least 124 fellowships of worshipping and witnessing Christians.

Obviously the territory covered had to expand beyond Takamatsu and nearby towns. It did so—to populous Hiroshima and Okayama prefectures across the water on Honshu. The vision was wider still. It included country towns of 20,000 to cities of one million on the major islands of Shikoku and Kyushu.

Although Ralph and Stella Cox led this outreach, they did not work alone. The Helping Hand program provided many short-term evangelists who used English teaching as a means to attract young business people, professionals, and students to classes where the New Testament was the most important—if not the most used—textbook.

An Excellent Recruiting Tool

One valuable result of the Helping Hand program was the vision it gave to many short-term workers to return to Japan as career church planters. Cox reported in 1988 that twenty-four had returned, of whom three couples were working with the Coxes in church planting.

While fellow missionaries commended the vision and rejoiced in the church growth seen, not all were convinced that this method could be widely adopted and followed successfully by others. This is where the flexibility of TEAM's work policy found justification. TEAM's objective is clear, but it makes allowance for different methods according to varying gifts.

Forty-four churches are actually forty-four lighthouses allowing the light to shine into the spiritual darkness so evident in these populous areas. These presently small churches have seen the example of reaching out and expecting growth. With solid Bible teaching the believers can grow in their walk with the Lord and service for Him. The vision of the Shikoku missionaries is that they will see growing churches in their field of work—not 124 small, struggling churches with only twelve to fifteen members, but large, active congregations which are continuing to reach out.

Case Study—Osaka

Osaka, with three million people, is Japan's second largest city and its metropolitan area has about fourteen million. It is not surprising that missionaries should consider this a priority area for evangelism and church planting. TEAM workers assigned there for longer or shorter periods have been Neal and Clara Jean Browning, David and Dorothy Brook, Stanley and Mary Barthold, and Mary Ellen Gudeman. To illustrate the growth of the church ministries in the Osaka area, we shall refer to the development of three churches—Hotarugaike, Kuzuha, and Kawanishi—as revealed in the annual reports of Stanley and Mary Barthold.

Hotarugaike—1966

After having served on Shikoku Island and in Ibaraki in their first terms, the Bartholds moved to Osaka in March 1966 and by May had started meetings in their home. The Christians at Hotarugaike consider this the beginning date of their church. Two years later, meeting in a farm co-op building, as many as sixty could gather. Mary Ellen Gudeman worked with the Bartholds in this ministry and they paid tribute to her effective help. Baptized believers still numbered only thirteen. Knowing that building with "gold, silver, and precious stones" takes time and perseverance, the missionaries were not at all discouraged. They took seriously the instruction of the Apostle Paul to be "pastors and teachers, to prepare God's people for works of service, so that the body of Christ may be built up" (Ephesians 4:11-12, NIV).

Edifying Believers

How this building up of believers was to be brought about is mentioned in the 1969 annual report:

> During 1969 we met with the Christians every Sunday afternoon from 1:00 to 5:00 o'clock. This time was broken up in the following way:
>
> 1:00 to 1:30—Discussion period for Christians.
>
> 2:00 to 3:00—Sunday school for children plus two English classes: one for students and one for adults.
>
> 3:00 to 4:00—Worship service in Japanese.
>
> 4:00 to 5:00—Fellowship time.[7]
>
> Another activity begun by the church in 1969 was "Service Sunday." Once a month the Christians gather together on Sunday morning and spend an hour or so going from house to house inviting people to the worship service. Many new contacts were made this way and it was a help to the Christians who took part.[8]

Barthold's report for 1973 listed a full schedule of body-building ministries:

- A bimonthly men's meeting has been introduced.
- A Thursday night men's prayer meeting also started this year.
- The Osaka men's supper is developing in a wonderful way and many in the Osaka business community are being reached with the gospel for the first time.
- University Bible classes are conducted on two campuses.
- The Sunday morning worship service maintains its position as the highlight of the week. The attendance has increased so that every Sunday the room is filled to capacity, and often beyond.
- Sunday School is always a busy time.
- God has clearly blessed in the women's meeting this year.
- A source of weekend power and preparation is the women's

prayer meeting every Friday morning.

- On the first and third weeks of each month home Bible studies go on in four homes. Mary teaches the lesson to the leaders (two for each group) and also leads one of the studies.[9]

A Pastor for Hotarugaike

In 1975 the church was able to extend the sanctuary to accommodate thirty more worshippers—to a seating total of ninety. It was ready to support a pastor and in 1976 called the Rev. Yoozoo Machikawa, a Domei pastor from Okinawa. The missionaries could now move on to another needy area to repeat the process. As long as there are great groups of people who have no adequate testimony among them the missionary's work is not finished.

Kuzuha—1977

Kuzuha is a growing city of high-rise apartments located midway between the large cities of Osaka and Kyoto. Stan and Mary Barthold chose this as their next place of service, intending to work within a high-rise apartment building. They selected as their living place a fifteenth floor apartment in a complex with 1,200 families—5,000 people—as their neighbors, ample scope indeed for missionary work.

Using the Barthold's living room as a meeting place the church held its first worship service September 18, 1977. The neighbors, having moved away from more conservative towns and villages, were themselves newcomers to apartment living. They welcomed contacts with the missionaries and some of them dropped in for visits. Attendance increased gradually and by mid-1980 the church bought another apartment which the Christians fixed up to seat forty people. There was also room for Sunday school classes.

Goals set for 1982 were ten baptisms (there were twelve), average attendance of fifty (by December it was fifty-four), twenty men in attendance (goal reached), an increase in home Bible studies (realized), and the calling of a Japanese pastor. The Rev. Nobukazu Takahashi was installed April 10, 1983, with all seven TEAM pastors from the greater Osaka area taking part. The

Bartholds were now free to move to another area of need and promise.

Kawanishi—1983

They moved back closer to their first Osaka parish. By 1983 one of the home Bible study classes of the Hotarugaike church was ready to become the nucleus of a new congregation, the Kawanishi Bible Church. Following much the same methods as in the earlier churches, the Kawanishi congregation grew steadily and by the end of March 1989 welcomed Pastor Akio Moriwaki as undershepherd.

Church growth in metropolitan Osaka can be measured somewhat by noting that a workers' retreat brought twelve area pastors together whereas there were none when the Bartholds came to Osaka in 1966. A full account would reveal all who had a part in this growth—national pastors, missionaries, and Japanese lay people. They all shared in planting and watering, but again it was God who made the work grow.

Case Study—Shakujii

Another interesting case study is the church at Shakujii, Tokyo. Letters by Verner and Dorothy Strom and Victor and Ann Springer, written over a period of fourteen years, relate a series of forward steps taken by busy people engaged in the administration of TEAM's largest field. When read together they reveal in part what is necessary to plant an active, growing, spiritually minded church.[10]

December 1973: Mrs. Tsuchiya has been over several times. I took her to a ladies' meeting where she heard a wonderful testimony. She was impressed and said again that she would like to hear more and would like to become a Christian sometime soon [D. Strom].

November 1977: Ann Springer and Dorothy Strom (with their husbands) live less than a mile apart here in Shakujii. But Vern Strom is TEAM's Japan field chairman, and I'm serving as treasurer. Though both families have had a burden for Shakujii souls, we haven't felt there was much we could do about it. After prayer and consultation together last week, we have decided to begin biweekly meetings for the Japanese in the Strom home [V. Springer].

November 1979: Our first three men in the Shakujii work have been saved—all this past Sunday—all are husbands of believing women. Isn't that thrilling [V. Springer].

March 1980: Here in Shakujii, the work has grown enough so that we feel it is time to switch from twice-monthly afternoon meetings to weekly morning meetings. Both Vern and I feel the need of a Japanese worker to join us, as we have heavy responsibilities at the office during the week. Mr. Tamai, a graduate of Dallas Seminary, has expressed a willingness to join us in April, so that is when the weekly meetings will begin [V. Springer].

December 1982: Attendance has jumped so that we're barely able to hold the people who now come on Sundays. Sometimes we fill every seat, with 60 in overall attendance. And 70 came to our recent evangelistic meetings. Pray for a larger meeting place [V. Springer].

October 1983: Tomoko Tsuchiya started weeping at the start of Vern Strom's message, made a clear decision at the end, and since then had a definite part in the salvation of her grandmother (who died shortly after that). We also are delighted to report that Tomoko's parents this summer pulled out the family Butsudan (symbol of Buddhism) that had been in storage and publicly burned it. Better than anything else this gives indication of a permanent break with the past [V. Springer].

March 1984: We have found a building! God's building for our Shakujii Gospel Church. No, it's not the place we featured in our newsletter a year ago, but rather a more modest building for a more modest price—$280,000 instead of $1,500,000. How we praise and thank the Lord for it! The vote was unanimous, "Let us buy it at once!" [The members immediately subscribed $50,000 toward the purchase. V. Strom.]

December 1984: We have been using our new church building since May and what a blessing it is...! The first Sunday of May, thirteen new believers were baptized. Our Sunday attendance has steadily increased since then to between 70 and 80 while the mid-week prayer meeting runs around 25 to 30. In September we started a new ladies' Bible class in the church and have been very pleased with the response [D. Strom].

October 1988: Our Shakujii Church family in Tokyo faithfully keeps us informed of blessings and prayer requests. Their vision of a bigger piece of property for a larger church building continues to grow and we still covet your prayers [D. Strom].

April 1989: It was my privilege to speak again Sunday morning and afternoon to our beloved Shakujii believers. How we thank God for the warmth and love of these dear believers and Pastor and Mrs. Tamai. The inspired leadership of Pastor Tamai has much to do with the fact that, though just begun in 1977, our church has climbed to #7 in attendance of the 138 churches with which it is affiliated and #5 in prayer meeting attendance [V. Springer].

The names of many other church planters and examples of their work should be given. With the author of Hebrews 11:32, I lament, "And what more shall I say? I do not have time [space] to tell about..." the many, many missionaries who learned the Japanese language, adjusted to oriental customs, witnessed faithfully, taught diligently, led souls to Christ, and planted churches among the Japanese. This is how churches have grown in Japan. From a small fellowship of churches—less than ten—with under 800 members, the churches which share their statistics have grown (by 1988) to 197 with a total of 7,800 communicants. Most of these churches are in the Domei.

Growing Maturity

Looking forward, in 1980, to the ninetieth anniversary of the entry of TEAM with the gospel, Strom commented in his annual report to the field conference:

In giving a general overview of the work in Japan, it appears to me that there is both an increased interest in the gospel on the part of individuals, and a rising tide in the quality of people that are responding. A number of our national churches have seen good growth in the past few years. One church has tripled its average Sunday morning attendance in a five-year period. Several have changed to double services in order to care for the increasing attendance. I have been encouraged over the past year to see the growing maturity on the part of our national pastors and church leaders.[11]

Strom's sense of encouragement about the growing maturity of national pastors and church leaders is an acknowledgement, in part, of the quality of godly leadership in the Domei. In Japan, as in other oriental societies, age and experience are valued and respected and contribute to effective leadership.

On the two occasions when it seemed that TEAM Japan might attempt to go forward on its own without mature Japanese leadership—after the separation from the Kyodan in 1948 and again when the question was the filing of a joint constitution in 1954—the sovereign leading of the Lord preserved that spiritually wise leadership to TEAM/Domei. Pastor Matsuda Masaichi was God's man for the Domei and TEAM at those critical junctures.

Ando Becomes Domei Chairman

When Matsuda's long fight with cancer made it necessary for him to retire from the chairmanship of the Domei in 1966, the Lord had another chosen vessel ready to take his place—Pastor Ando Nakaichi. Ando, born in 1900, received Christ at the age of nineteen and was baptized at age twenty. He was a student of the outstanding missionary of the Japan Evangelistic Band, Paget-Wilkes, and was graduated from that mission's Kobe Bible School four years after his baptism. Ando and his wife, Rutsuko, served as missionaries in Manchukuo (present-day Manchuria, China) and it was there that he came into conflict with the Japanese government's demand for shrine worship. Because he refused to compromise with the imperial cult system, the Japanese arrested and imprisoned him. He remained in prison for nine months until the end of the Pacific War in September 1945.

In the post-war era, Ando founded the Setagaya Chuo Church in Tokyo which he pastored until his death, November 6, 1987. The Chuo Church grew to be one of the larger churches in Japan and the Domei. Ando and Strom worked in full harmony in leading TEAM/Domei in its remarkable church growth.

Awakening Mission Interest

When Japanese Christians began seriously to think about missionary outreach, about 1965, an increasing number gave themselves to the Lord for this work. Several went out as independent missionaries. Without church or missionary society backing some became discouraged.

One young lady, Miss Toshiko Suzuki, went to Taiwan under a very small Japanese mission *Cho No Hate*. In the providence of the Lord, Pastor Ando had accepted the chairmanship of that mission. When Toshiko arrived in Taiwan she felt the helplessness of being a new missionary in a foreign country. TEAM had a sizeable missionary family there. With Ando's relationship to TEAM in Japan, it seemed only natural for Toshiko to turn to TEAM missionaries for counsel and fellowship.

The chairman of TEAM in Taiwan, Hugo Johnson, was happy to assist. In time, he suggested that he would be on safer ground in giving guarantees to the Taiwan government if there were some formal understanding between Toshiko's mission and TEAM. This led to a four-way agreement among the Japanese mission and TEAM offices in Japan, Taiwan, and the U.S. concerning the conditions under which TEAM Taiwan would accept responsibility to assist and guide Toshiko's ministry, while her mission would take full responsibility for support, medical coverage, furlough activities, etc.

This inter-mission arrangement served as a pattern for working arrangements between TEAM and the Domei in the sending of Mr. and Mrs. Katsuhiko Seino to Indonesia and Miss Lydia Goeku and Mr. and Mrs. Yoshihiro Terada to Taiwan. There they served in full participation with TEAM missionaries.

Interest in missionary outreach grew to the point that the Domei sent Seino and his wife, Hiroko, to attend TEAM's candidate classes, not only to prepare them for service in Indonesia, but to learn to give such training to candidates who would serve under the Domei. The Domei invited Michael Pocock, candidate secretary, to come to Japan in 1984 for special training sessions for prospective Japanese missionaries. Pocock reported that more than 200 gathered for this training. This included not only prospective missionaries but also pastors and members of church mission committees.

The leaders of the Domei were concerned for both their homeland and overseas. In 1981 they had set prayer and work goals to be reached by the 1991 centennial—increasing the number of churches to 200, doubling the church membership, and enlisting 500 young people to train as full-time Christian workers. The response to the training course in 1984 gave promise of progress toward that goal.[12]

JEM Merger

The leaders of the Japan Evangelical Mission (JEM) headquartered in Three Hills, Alberta, approached TEAM in 1981 about possible merger. This led to careful study as discussions continued in North America and Japan over a period of eighteen months. TEAM missionaries were quite well acquainted with JEM members in Japan. JEM had opened a field among Japanese settlers in Brazil in 1972 and the Brazil missionaries were also included in the negotiations.

The joint announcement made at the conclusion of the talks reveals something of the mutuality of purpose and unity of spirit of the two groups. The Rev. Brian R. Bates, chairman of JEM board of governors, made the official announcement on behalf of JEM:

> The challenge of the '80s has forced many missions to evaluate their performance, procedures of operation, and public accountability for their ministry. Japan Evangelical Mission has faced these areas of concern also. After much prayer and study of our viability, we have moved toward merger with The Evangelical Alliance Mission. Many factors make such a move beneficial at this time. Over the years a spirit of cooperation has developed between the two mission families, enabling them to work together in various ministries in Japan.... Another factor that has led to TEAM as our merger partner is the doctrinal position held by each mission. Both adhere to the same basic teachings of Scripture.[13]

As chairman of the board of directors of TEAM, I made the announcement to the TEAM missionaries and constituency:

> Certain spiritual and practical advantages should be present when one mission merges into another as the Japan Evangelical Mission is doing. The fact that JEM leaders and missionaries have requested the merger and TEAM has responded in full agreement proves that all believe the Lord's work will be furthered by the merger. What advantages do we all expect? Spiritual gain should come in the area of greater vision and widened prayer backing. JEM missionaries will now be related to 25 additional world areas. They will meet in conferences and consultations with TEAM fellow workers from around the world. TEAM will also learn from JEM's experience in Japan and Brazil and be enriched by it.[14]

JEM had a history of thirty-three years' work in Japan and ten years in Brazil. Its Japan work was mostly along the western coast of Honshu, where its missionaries had planted churches, founded the Kashiwazaki Bible Institute, and developed a Bible camp ministry. The churches were linked together in the *Nihon Dendo Fukuin Kyodan* (Japan Evangelical Gospel Association) which continued as a separate church fellowship having common aims with the Domei.

The long service of JEM leaders—Abram J. Block, Ben Itchikawa, Donald Bruck, and Alvin Doerksen—was recognized and greatly appreciated. But as is common in merger arrangements, not everyone in leadership could continue with the merged group. Alvin Doerksen, secretary-treasurer, was the exception. He cared for the winding up of JEM affairs in Canada and merged all that was necessary into the TEAM Canada administrative structure. After two years of special service in Brazil, he and his wife, Mary, joined the Canadian TEAM staff where he served for an additional two years before his early death in 1988.

Bill Friesen was the JEM Japan field chairman who handled much negotiation and correspondence with his TEAM counterparts, Vern Strom and John Reid. Bill and Lois Friesen continue in the work in Japan along with twenty other former JEM members. The merger was celebrated in Calgary, Alberta, in November 1982 and in Tokyo, Japan, in January 1983. In the six years following the merger, the missionaries of the two groups have truly served together as one and there has been unanimous agreement that the union has strengthened the ministry.

Is the Work Finished?

The evangelization of Japan is not complete—far from it. The figures most commonly quoted claim only a little more than 1 percent of the population as evangelical believers. Most of the larger urban centers have an active, permanent witness, but there remain towns as large as 20,000 that have no church.

As the TEAM and Domei approach the centennial in 1991, a new team is in leadership—J. Douglas Heck, church planter, chairman of the missionary body; Pastor Atsuyoshi Saito, chairman of the Domei churches; and missionary Katsuhiko Seino, mission secretary of the Domei.

With the planting already accomplished by TEAM missionaries, followed by the watering they and the Japanese have done, there should be steady growth. The messengers of the cross have been obedient to the commission to make disciples. With the door remaining open, there is still much work for missionaries to do.

They have faith to believe that if missionaries were no longer allowed entry, Japanese Christian workers would carry the work forward with the full blessing of the Lord of the harvest. After all, He is the only one who can make the planting grow.

TAIWAN, ISLAND OF BEAUTY

First Sighting by Portuguese

Named *Ilha Formosa* in 1590 by Portuguese sailors because of its outstanding beauty, the island of Taiwan was known as Formosa to the western world throughout most of its history. The aboriginal inhabitants were probably of Malay-Polynesian background, similar to those of Luzon in the Philippines. After a short period of Dutch rule (1620-62) the island came under the control of China from which it was separated by less than one hundred miles of sea. Chinese from the coastal province of Fujian came to the island in great numbers and their dialect of Chinese became the language of Taiwan—Taiwanese. The tribespeople were gradually crowded into the mountainous area along the east coast as the Chinese occupied the broad central and western plains.

Japan Takes over Taiwan

Japan had defeated China in 1895 and rewarded itself by taking possession of Taiwan, which it held until the end of World War II. As conqueror, Japan proceeded to remake Formosa to its own advantage as much as possible. Japanese became the required language in government and schools. Taiwan was made into an industrial base to support the war effort and became a principal staging area for the conquest of Southeast Asia.

China Repossesses the Island

After Japan's defeat in 1945, the Nationalist Chinese government sent troops to occupy the island. Expecting to be welcomed as liberators, the Chinese were taken aback by the attitude of many Taiwanese, who viewed them as conquerors, not brothers. The harshness with which the Nationalist government established its authority, the outlawing of the Japanese language in which the people had been educated, and the immediate imposition of the Chinese *Kuoyu* as the official language did much to disenchant the Taiwanese.

The withdrawal to Taiwan in 1949 of Chiang Kaishek's officials, his Nationalist army, and large numbers of refugees caused further shock to the Taiwanese. In all, two million people came to the already crowded island from the mainland to escape the communist advance. In addition to government officials there were businessmen and, of course, soldiers. The Taiwanese had no say in the government. The tensions created in those early years of Chinese rule took long to heal. It was only after several decades that Taiwanese were brought into meaningful positions in the government.

Early Missionary Work

A strong missionary work among the Taiwanese had been done by the English Presbyterian Church (beginning 1865) and the Canadian Presbyterian Church (1872) and this later was extended to the aboriginal tribes with great response.

China Missionaries Look to Taiwan

Mission societies closed out of China by the communist government had great interest in the mainland Chinese in Taiwan. TEAM missionaries working temporarily in Hong Kong after evacuation from China were attracted to this field where they could use the northern language. The first party of six—Fred and Blanche Nelson, Doris Brougham, Geraldine Petersen, Lola Phillips, and Nils Sunwall—arrived in February 1951, just sixty years after the first party of Franson's recruits disembarked in Shanghai in February 1891.

Some of the missionaries evacuated from the mainland had remained in Hong Kong for a time, about twenty had gone to Japan, some to the Philippines, and others returned to North America. Over the next two or three years most of these China workers found their way to Taiwan. Mongolia missionaries Edvard and Jenny Torjesen, Angeline Bernklau, and Edna Heinz also went to Taiwan to work among Mongols, and they were integrated into the larger missionary group.

Major Cities and Towns Entered

The missionaries learned that there were concentrations of mainland Chinese in cities and larger towns, so they spread out to places like Hualien on the east coast, Pingtung in the south, Taichung in the central area, Lotung, and the capital city of Taipei in the north. Smaller places like Changhwa, Chingshui, Fenglin, Kaliwan, and Yuanlin were not overlooked.

Speaking the language of the mainlanders the missionaries found a warm welcome among them. They discovered Christians among these displaced people, so when the missionaries began to hold services and Sunday schools they were not without help.

Summarizing the activity for the year 1958, field chairman Ed Torjesen reported that of forty-nine missionaries assigned to Taiwan, thirty-five were on the field at the end of the year, stationed in five counties and two municipalities. Regular services were held in thirty-three places, in thirteen of which the congregations had been organized with elders and deacons. A total of 674 persons had been baptized since TEAM started work and there were 506 active members at the end of 1958. This was encouraging progress for a new work.[1]

Difficult Indigenization

Missionaries discovered that many of the mainlanders had been reduced to near poverty. Soldiers were provided food and shelter, but because their cash income was meager their offerings did not cover the modest expenses of the small churches being planted. The groups needed places to meet and some missionaries found money to build or buy. When Chinese could serve as evangelists or pastors, their support was a problem because of the small offerings. The short-term solution was for missionaries to pay the salaries. Self-support was thus compromised.

With responsibility for the basic financial needs resting on the missionaries, most decisions concerning the work were made by them. Thus the church failed to make progress in self-government.

The ideal was to have churches be self-supporting, self-governing, and self-propagating. With two-thirds of this ideal not being realized, the third item—self-propagation—still remained a possibility. It is true that within the churches there was encouraging participation in such things as teaching Sunday school, but a greater sense of responsibility for self-support and self-government would likely have resulted in more outreach.

Why Was Mainland Example Not Followed?

It may seem strange that experienced missionaries who had worked hard to lead Chinese churches on the mainland to be truly indigenous were not fearful of the pitfalls of supporting with foreign money. It was true that some of those churches had attained self-support only when the economic crisis dried up the supply of mission money—truly the Lord's intervention—so it seemed that where no such economic crisis existed a path of lesser resistance was followed.

Compounding the Problem

The lack of a clear indigenous policy gave rise to later vexing problems regarding support of the church ministries. The first effort to correct the situation was to set up—about 1959—an Evangelistic Aid Budget which was intended to systematize financial assistance. When, after ten years, it was seen that this was not leading the churches to a position of self support, the annual field conference—with due notice—suspended all financial aid. Church-mission relationships naturally suffered.

Further complicating relationships, in the minds of many Chinese, was the development of other mission-administered ministries such as radio, camp work, a hospital, an improved headquarters, and large schools for missionary children. These obviously required mission support. The Chinese quite naturally assumed that the money previously used to help the churches was now going into these other projects.

Radio Ministry Begun

Opportunities for special ministries opened up to the missionaries soon after their arrival on the island. One of the first was radio. Doris Brougham and Geraldine Petersen—stationed in Hualien— learned that the local radio station was eager to get program material and readily accepted recorded gospel broadcasts. They assembled a radio team with Stanley Tang as speaker and his wife, Nancy, as narrator. When I first visited Taiwan in 1956, the staff had grown to over twenty and programs were aired in both Mandarin and Taiwanese from five cities. The Far East Broadcasting Company in Manila needed Chinese programs for broadcast to the mainland and TEAM radio became a regular supplier. Missionaries were excited about this expanded outreach and many contributed personally to keep the programs on the air.

Radio Ministry Expanded

A versatile musician, Leland Haggerty, and his wife, Dorothy, joined the radio work in 1957. The ministry was enlarged to include correspondence courses for follow up and a monthly magazine *Living Waters*. Hualien was not the best place to find radio talent so in 1958 the radio ministry was moved across the island to the large city of Taichung. Under the leadership of Haggerty and Miss Brougham the programming reached a high level of excellence. (Geraldine Petersen transferred to the North India field, having married Robert Remington.)

Could Radio Help Church Planting?

Though radio time was very reasonable in cost at the time, expenses for staff and equipment mounted. In an effort to balance the budget, we in the home office recommended that the Taiwan radio work seek the cooperation of missionaries involved in church work, following the successful pattern of the Japan field. There, churches (and also not a few missionaries) undertook the support of programs on local stations and followed up the contacts. We believed that radio could be an excellent tool to further the work of church planting. With hundreds taking correspondence courses and subscribing to the magazine, we viewed this ministry as a natural to enhance church growth. Furthermore, we believed we had a responsibility to gather the fruits of this radio ministry into local churches, which was clearly the New Testament pattern.

A Difficulty Surfaces

It was on the question of relating the radio work to the church ministries that difficulty arose. The directors of the radio work had a vision of wide radio outreach but seemed not to see the importance of the churches. In fact, they believed that a church connection would hamper their ministry. The missionaries who were trying to get churches solidly planted and growing did not agree. It was a question as to which approach would be most effective in the long run. One result of the differing viewpoints was that some missionaries stopped giving. An inherent radio ministry weakness was that the Chinese staff, though made up of Christian young people, included very few who were deeply involved in a local church and even fewer who were related to a TEAM church.

A Regrettable Schism

While the radio work was still under discussion in late 1959, Dr. Johnson received word that Haggerty wanted to separate it from TEAM. He brought this development to the board of directors, which carefully reviewed the extensive correspondence. The secretary recorded the decision:

> David Johnson reported the desire of Haggerty, Brougham, and certain Chinese to withdraw the radio ministry from TEAM to be attached to an unnamed organization. The board affirmed its stand that under no circumstances could the radio project be removed from TEAM control and sponsorship.[2]

This action by the board may have seemed rather unyielding,

but it was properly so because the mission had the responsibility of safeguarding the ministry. Doris Brougham came home in April 1960 and met at length with the directors and board. It seemed that a solution was in sight but then word came that the radio group had actually separated from TEAM. This separation included not only the Haggertys and Miss Brougham but also thirty Chinese staff members under their influence. Only three of the staff—Esther Chang, Jonathan Cheng, and John Tien—remained with TEAM.

The field council, of which Ed Torjesen was chairman at the time, assured the board that a radio ministry was necessary for accomplishing the objectives of the field. Johnson believed that donors to this ministry expected TEAM to safeguard its integrity, so he sent word to the chairman that the radio work should not be surrendered but rather should be rebuilt into an effective ministry once again.

Door of Hope Inquiry

In late 1958, field chairman Oliver Olson informed Dr. Johnson that several elderly missionaries of the Door of Hope Mission had approached him about the possibility of TEAM's taking over responsibility for the ministry to orphaned and partially orphaned girls in Taipei.

Long Record of Loving Service

Door of Hope had been founded in Shanghai in 1901 by Miss Cornelia Bonnell, who was greatly moved by the sight of young girls offered for sale. The work in Shanghai had to be left behind when the communists came into power, but the missionaries of the early 1950s—Gladys Dieterle, Edna Johnston, Winifred Watney, Inez Green, and Clara Nelson—then built up a similar work in Taiwan. Mrs. George Schuler served as secretary-treasurer in the homeland.

Merger Consummated

Dr. Johnson and I visited the Door of Hope headquarters in Orlando, Florida, and worked out an agreement that resulted in

TEAM's assuming responsibility beginning in early 1959. The assets and income were sufficient not only to continue the existing work but also to provide retirement help for the elderly missionaries.

About one hundred girls were being cared for, some of them full orphans, but many who had one or both living parents. These latter came from broken, impoverished, or neglectful homes. A concern expressed by Mrs. Schuler was that there was little contact with family members and inadequate follow-up of girls who had been withdrawn.

Clara Nelson, the only Door of Hope missionary available to continue the work in Taipei, assumed the main responsibility for running the orphanage. Nils and Lola Sunwall and other missionaries were assigned for shorter or longer periods.

After my visit to Taiwan in April 1963, my report to the board included comments on the Door of Hope ministry:

> The Door of Hope Children's Refuge continues to be operated as it was. An excellent job of caring for the children is being done by Miss Clara Nelson, and the children are well clothed, well fed, and well ordered. Missionaries closest to the ministry believe we are not taking advantage of our opportunities for a spiritual work with the children and their contacts. There is also concern that the children are not being properly related to Chinese life.... The field council wants Miss Nelson to retire in July. The responsibility will be turned over to Freda Rempel and Kathryn Merrill. Miss Rempel has been sent to Korea to spend several weeks at the Pusan Orphanage to gain insight into the successful methods used there.[3]

Radio Staff Rebuilt

The field council appointed Angeline Bernklau to head the radio work. Without experience in radio, Angeline nevertheless had spiritual gifts of working with the Chinese people. Later, Cam Willman was appointed missionary director and Elizabeth Albert was brought into the ministry. Jonathan Cheng was named national director and a new staff was assembled. Amazingly, much of the programming ministry, the correspondence courses, and the magazine were continued much as before.

In August 1961 I responded to a letter with questions about the radio ministry:

> Our radio work has been continuing at the same level as before and we believe that in the measure we relate this ministry to the local churches, in that measure we will see permanent fruit.[4]

Taiwan Radio had agreed to provide two hours a day of Mandarin programs for TEAM's new radio station, HLKX, at Inchon, Korea. This commitment was honored.

The radio ministry grew, kept up its correspondence course and gospel magazine ministry, and initiated a cassette distribution service. It reached out in evangelistic tours of Taiwan and Southeast Asia and on several occasions sent singing groups to North America. While these tours were quite successful in raising money to cover tour expenses and provide support for the radio work, they accomplished much more in that they were a soul-winning ministry in Chinese churches. Cheng led the earliest of these tours.

National Director's Change of Direction

Jonathan Cheng requested permission to study in the United States and to do representation work for Taiwan Radio. The radio board in Taiwan and the field council approved reluctantly, feeling that the result might be the eventual loss of Cheng to the radio work. While it was true that the Cheng family elected to stay permanently in the United States, they continued a very effective representation ministry on behalf of radio. They were also used of the Lord in evangelism. In fact, Jonathan and Margaret and their five high school and college-age young people formed the Grace Family Septet and traveled extensively in North America, Europe, Latin America, and Southeast Asia.

Heinsman, Lin Assume Leadership

William Heinsman, who went to the field as a radio engineer in 1962, became missionary director in 1974 and led the ministry through further development. Matthew Lin was appointed national director. Lin had been on the radio staff for many years and had a background of pastoral experience. By 1980 the studios and offices in Taichung, in use since 1958, were outgrown so radio moved to a new building—also in Taichung—constructed on the site of a missionary residence and church. The construction deal was an interesting one and of a type that was used on several occasions to improve mission facilities. A contractor agreed to build a multistory building on mission-owned land at his own cost and provide floors for the church and radio. His payment would be the ownership of several floors of the building.

Broadcast Target Area

At first, Taiwan was TEAM radio's broadcast target for programs both in Mandarin and Taiwanese. Then in December 1956, TEAM radio HLKX in Inchon, Korea, began broadcasting in Mandarin Chinese, later adding English, Russian, and Korean programs as well. Julius and Thyra Bergstrom, who were responsible for the Chinese division, originated Mandarin broadcasts from Inchon, but additional programs were needed and TEAM Radio Taiwan was asked to supply them. After the Bergstroms left Korea in 1959, Taiwan radio accepted major responsibility for preparing two hours of daily broadcasts, which were used twice for a total of four hours a day.

In time, the preparation of Mandarin programs became Taiwan's major responsibility, not only to meet HLKX's need but also much of the need of the FEBC stations in Manila and Okinawa. Later, about forty hours per week of Mandarin evangelistic and Bible teaching programs were prepared by TEAM Radio Taiwan and released over FEBC and Trans World Radio stations.

For the first twenty-three years of broadcasting toward China there was little solid evidence that Chinese people were permitted to listen. There were many questions. Was the signal reaching population centers without being jammed? Did the people have radios? If so, were they under such heavy restrictions that they dare not listen to a foreign broadcast and particularly a Christian program? If the people heard, would they dare write? If they wrote would their letters be intercepted and they be prosecuted? The few letters that got through were like a message from heaven to the radio staff.

After the death of chairman Mao in 1976, the waning of the Cultural Revolution, the normalizing of diplomatic relationships with the United States, and the settling of the power struggle within the Chinese government, some of the restrictions which bound the Chinese people began to be eased. Some restrictions, yes, but by no means all. Now the people were more free to listen to radio broadcasts, and also had more disposable income with which to purchase radios. Most significant of all, the strict interdiction of correspondence with outside radio stations was eased. The driblets of letters increased to a trickle; then, when the people realized that communication was beginning to open, swelled to a flow. (The name TEAM Radio Taiwan was changed to TEAM Radio China in 1989.)

Most of the responses to TEAM programs went directly to the stations which aired the programs and were included in their tabulation and publicity. Arrangements were later made to have reports of responses to specific programs and copies of actual letters shared with TEAM. A sampling of the hundreds of letters received reveals what an effective medium radio is for reaching over and beyond ideological barriers.

A Mr. Chen wrote:

Many of those who have heard your programs for a long time have come to the Lord. The young and old have come to the Lord in every season. Please pray for Mrs. Chang because her daughter-in-law treats her very badly. One young person, Mr. Liau, has believed only a half year. Please especially pray for him. His faith needs strengthening.[5]

A village evangelistic witness wrote encouragingly:

I have believed in Jesus for three years already, but I feel that I do not understand this faith very well.... At the beginning there were only two believers in my village. We have preached the gospel in this area for these three years. The church has grown to more than two hundred believers. I have a heavy burden to learn how to properly shepherd this church. There is no place to meet so we use my house to get together. At present I am the only preacher in the church and there is only one Bible. The believers want me to buy Bibles for them, but I can find no place to buy them. I hope you can help us.[6]

TEAM Radio China periodical No. 2 in 1989 reported that 2,107 letters had been received in response to all the FEBC China broadcasts in December 1988. Of these, 142 responded specifically to TEAM Radio China programs. Eleven writers requested studies in the Village Bible School series. The broadcasts have Bible training as a principal objective, in addition to evangelism.

Bible Institute Opened

As evangelism continued in the early years, many were being led to the Lord and the need for trained teachers and preachers became evident. Fred Nelson was one of the first to take steps to meet this need. The place selected was a small rural town by the name of Tachia in central Taiwan, not far from the large city of Taichung. The advantage was the potential of this farm home for remodeling into classrooms and other facilities needed for a Bible school. After initial remodeling the school opened in 1953.

Englund Again Training Workers

Though William Englund was seventy-two years of age, he and Anna were invited to come to Taiwan to participate in the Bible school ministry. With a rich background of Bible institute work in China, the Englunds were a great asset in Taiwan, where they served for three years until after Englund passed his seventy-fifth birthday. He continued active TEAM service for another ten years, with some public ministry and much time spent writing a Chinese commentary on the first eight books of the Old Testament. Though his hope was to complete work on all books of the Bible, weakness prevented his going farther. He passed away in 1970 at the age of eighty-eight, having been active in the Lord's work for most of seventy-two years.[7]

A Chinese Principal Appointed

While the missionary teachers at Tachia were proficient in

Chinese and experienced in working with the churches, they felt that Chinese leaders would serve better in attracting students. They were happy when Su Liang-I, a well-qualified Christian teacher from the mainland, joined the teaching staff. He was appointed principal and served until his death. His widow continued work at the Bible institute until it was closed in 1966 for lack of TEAM-related students. After teaching at another Bible school for several years, Mrs. Su accepted an invitation to become spiritual counselor at TEAM's Logefeil Memorial Hospital in Taitung, a ministry which she continued until after her eightieth birthday in 1985.

Three Noteworthy Graduates

Three members of the first graduating class at Tachia in 1956 were Jonathan Cheng, Joseph Chiang, and Ch'ih Shouen. Cheng served in the radio ministry for twenty years and also revealed God-given gifts of evangelism. Chiang became pastor of the Sung Chu Tang in Taipei and for a while was chairman of the church association. After serving the church in Hualien, where he had found the Lord, Ch'ih became pastor of the growing Mofantsun church in Taichung.

Training Outpacing Church Growth

A lesson learned rather slowly on some mission fields is that training of Christian workers and church planting must go hand in hand. Where training of workers lags, there is a shortage of pastors and teachers. True, some missionaries have a gift for selecting and training lay workers to serve as preaching elders and this meets the need for some time, but sooner or later the need for more formal training becomes apparent.

The other side of the coin is that difficulty surfaces if training of workers outpaces evangelism and church planting. Some believe that a school for training evangelists and pastors is a priority, and that if there is a supply of such workers they will somehow take the lead in planting churches. The problem is that those graduated from a mission-operated Bible school tend to expect the mission to provide work for them. If the churches have not matured to the stage where they can call and support their own workers these graduates turn to other groups, to parachurch organizations, or to the secular world for work. This may not be a loss to the gospel ministry in general, but it does not benefit the church planting ministry to which a mission such as TEAM is committed.

This was the problem encountered in Taiwan; training got ahead of the growth of individuals ready to go into service for the Lord and ahead of the maturity of churches which should be absorbing their service. For a period of ten or fifteen years other training institutions could supply the ones needed for TEAM-related churches.

Amis Tribespeople in Need of Help

Missionaries on Taiwan's east coast soon became aware of several tribal groups, many of whose villages in the mountain valleys between Hualien and Taitung were easily accessible. Most notable were the Amis, with a population of 100,000. Missionaries learned that there had been a remarkable turning to the Lord on the part of many tribespeople during the war years:

> Under Japanese occupation, the Christians were often severely persecuted, but "they ceased not to teach and preach Jesus Christ," and now there were at least 60 Protestant churches among them. Some of the believers had Japanese Bibles and had memorized verses of Scripture, even though it was a foreign tongue. Always they hoped that some day they would have the Word of God in their own language.[8]

Bereft of a Written Language

With the defeat of the Japanese and reimposition of Chinese control in 1945, there came a ban on the use of the Japanese language. The Amis and other tribes were seriously affected because their only written language was Japanese. They were cut off from their only source of reading material. When, ten years later, Ed Torjesen surveyed the Amis tribal area he was deeply moved by the desire of the Christians to have the written Word. He wrote:

> Can you imagine flourishing churches without a Bible? Chris-

tians fed on quoted bits of Scripture in a forbidden language? No hymnbook, no catechism, no Sunday school lessons? Yet this unique situation exists among believers of the Amis tribes in the hills of Formosa.[9]

Invitation to Work Among Amis

The Taiwanese Presbyterian Church was responsible for ministry among the Amis. It had not been able to do the linguistic work to give them a written language and gladly welcomed TEAM's offer of Ed and Jenny Torjesen for this work. The Torjesens selected the town of Chengkung on the east coast, about forty miles north of Taitung. Here, in the geographic and linguistic center of the Amis tribe, they set about to reduce the language to writing. About a year and a half later—in September 1956—I was with them and had opportunity to visit a number of villages and observe the beginning of Scripture translation.

The Village of Basongan Contacted

One memorable experience was our visit to the village of Basongan, which had no Christians and which gave permission for a meeting only because of the presence of a visitor from America. Dwana, an Amis evangelist, led the service and called on Oliver Olson and me for short messages. We spoke in Chinese while Dwana interpreted into Amis. I reported my impressions:

> Facing that crowd of people who were not only surrounded by the darkness of the night, but also submerged in heathen darkness, I spoke to them about Jesus, the Light of the world. Even as I spoke, my own heart was thrilled at the priceless privilege of proclaiming salvation's message to those who have never heard. Torjesen spoke next—in Amis. It was evident that the people were pleased to have someone care enough about them to learn their language. Then Dwana preached at greater length. He summed up all that had been said before and gave them a clear full outline of the truth of redemption in Christ.[10]

I learned later to my great joy that a number of the Basongan people expressed their desire to follow Christ. Yet, several years later there came a discouraging word. Because of a shortage of workers, no one had been available to go in to disciple the new believers. Though they had received the word with gladness, many had no root in themselves, and so endured but for a time; afterward when affliction and persecution arose for the Word's sake, they were offended (see Mark 4:16,17).

Torjesens' Continued Work

The Torjesens continued for several years to work on Scripture translation and prepare Amis literature. They were impressed with the need for more missionaries and their call for help was endorsed by the field conference. One need was for someone to hold literacy classes in the churches. Another was for assistance in Scripture translation. Yet another was for a doctor and nurses to meet the pressing physical needs of the tribal people.

Just at the time the Lord answered prayer in 1959 by sending Virginia Fey and Arthur and Alice Stejskal to work among the Amis, Jenny Torjesen began having health problems and needed a change of location and climate. Torjesen was drafted into the position of field chairman. Eventually, it was necessary for them to remain at home, where their gifts were put to good use in other phases of TEAM's work such as representing the Taiwan radio ministry, researching the life and work of Fredrik Franson, and writing valuable books based on that research. There followed nine years as representatives for TEAM in northern Europe.

Virginia Fey in Translation Ministry

It would have been better if the missionaries could have been more involved in developing tribal churches, but that remained the privilege and responsibility of the Taiwanese Presbyterian Church. Missionaries' participation in translation, literacy training, and Bible teaching was welcome. Virginia Fey continued working with a translation committee, which completed the New Testament in 1972. They finished an abridged version of the Old Testament in May 1980, which the Bible Society then published with the New Testament in August 1981. They also published a dictionary and books on Christian living. Virginia followed a regular program of visiting Amis churches to train the people to read their own language, to teach them the Word of God, and to counsel believers in their Christian walk. Her letters reveal a deep burden for the spiritual welfare of the Amis believers. Having the Word of God available to them in their own language will contribute much to their maturity in the faith. Under leadership of the Amis Presbytery, Virginia worked on further translation and revision of the Scriptures in 1989 and 1990, aiming for a completed Bible.

Dennises Come for Medical Work

An answer to prayer was the coming to the field of Dr. Frank and Sally Dennis in 1961. After several years of language study and a period of serving in a medical ministry elsewhere in Taiwan, they were ready to begin work on the East Coast with Taiwanese, Amis, and several other tribal groups.

Stejskals in Amis Literature

Art and Alice Stejskal gave themselves to the Amis literature ministry and later, when the hospital was opened in Taitung, followed up tribal patients who had been introduced to the gospel in the hospital. They were asked in 1986 to transfer to the Philippines to provide mature leadership for a field that was rapidly expanding with new missionaries. The similarity of the people of Luzon Island to the tribespeople of Taiwan helped them to adjust well in this new assignment.

Medical Work to Begin

The decision to locate the medical work in the southeastern part of Taiwan was based on need. This portion of the island was clearly the most lacking in medical services. In addition, it was here where most of the tribespeople lived. The Chinese were mostly Taiwanese, with fewer mainland immigrants than on other parts of the island.

After arriving in Taitung in 1965, Dr. Dennis used a mobile clinic to reach out to the people, but then realized that a base hospital was essential if their medical and surgical needs were to be adequately met. He noted the great incidence of polio victims and recognized that they needed help. Their care would also provide an excellent opportunity to minister spiritually during the longer stays in the hospital required for restorative surgery. The decision was made to establish a hospital in Taitung while continuing the mobile outreach into the tribal areas.

Dr. R. C. Logefeil, then medical director of TEAM, had a personal interest in the Dennises as they were members of the same church in Minneapolis. He directed interest and support to the proposed hospital project in Taitung. After Dr. Logefeil passed away in October 1966 it was decided that the 45-bed hospital to be erected should be a memorial to him. The field council invited retired missionary Oscar Beckon to come to Taiwan to supervise the building project. Oliver Olson designed a mural of Christ healing the sick for the main entrance of the building and provided other artistic touches to make it truly attractive. The hospital was dedicated April 22, 1969, with Mrs. Logefeil and two daughters present as guests.

To function well a hospital needs two doctors with surgical skills. In addition, there must be provision for necessary time away such as for mission committee meetings, conferences, vacations and furlough. The doctor, who manifests much concern for the physical needs of the people, is equally concerned for their spiritual need. In fact, the reason a mission hospital is established and skilled medical people assembled is to minister to the spiritual need as well as to the physical. The Lord provided a second spiritually concerned physician-surgeon in the person of Dr. Timothy Stafford, who with his wife, Marilyn, arrived in Taiwan in 1972.

In its first twenty years, the hospital was enlarged with two new wings, the latest being a pediatric care unit after Dr. Bob and Judy Long joined the missionary staff in 1976. Dr. Long is a board certified pediatrician with a background of medical service in Viet Nam and—of greatest importance—a deep concern for the spiritual and physical needs of children.

The local people were clearly in need of dental service. The

Lord's provision was seen in the coming of missionary dentist Dr. Marvin Hewlett and his wife, Patsy, in 1986. Stiffened licensing requirements for dentists were put into effect just before Dr, Hewlett was to install the dental clinic and begin a dental ministry. This necessitated taking the qualifying examination in Chinese. Through diligent study, careful planning, and hard work, Dr. Hewlett was able to qualify and launch the dental ministry in 1990.

Long-term Medical Personnel

Long term medical personnel at the hospital, in addition to Dr. and Mrs. Dennis, Dr. and Mrs. Stafford, and Dr. and Mrs. Long, have been Miss Bonnie Dirks, Miss Carol Gunzel, and Jack and Virginia Feenstra. Others assigned for chaplaincy or hospital administration have included Art and Alice Stejskal, Hugo and Mildred Johnson, and Morris and Janet Beck.

Timely Expert Assistance

The doctors maintained contacts with other doctors in the homeland and as a result there was a steady flow of short-term help from medical and surgical specialists. Chinese doctors from Taiwan and nearby Southeastern Asia countries rendered excellent service. Although there is one official language in Taiwan—Chinese *Kuoyu*—there are numerous tongues spoken in the Taitung area served by the medical work, Taiwanese being the most common. Some have said that seven or eight languages might be heard in the hospital over a period of weeks. To cope with this Babel-like confusion it is essential to have bilingual or trilingual people on staff. Employing a trained nurse of Taiwanese or tribal background guaranteed ability in the official language plus one or two others. Having dedicated staff members from the local area gave assurance of a positive testimony to all who came to the hospital. Field chairman Morris Beck referred to the spiritual results:

> For the last several years there have been more than 100 decisions for the Lord annually through the combined ministries of the hospital. The staff gospel team has been greatly used of the Lord in the outreach in the hospital, churches, and weekly jail

services.... The hospital staff has helped in the growth of the Taitung church as well as in the planting of a new work in that area.[11]

Door of Hope Phased Out

In 1972 the field council came to the conclusion that Door of Hope should preferably be a ministry of local churches. Because the TEAM-related churches were not yet strong enough to undertake that responsibility, the field council turned to a group known as the Mandarin Churches, headed by Pastor Wu Yung of Taipei. As a result, the Mandarin Church in Taipei agreed to operate Door of Hope for three years with TEAM making available the designated support received. Before the end of the three-year period, the Mandarin Church informed the field council that it did not wish to extend the agreement beyond March 31, 1975.

As the termination date neared, the field council and a special field conference spent much time studying alternatives for the future of Door of Hope and eventually adopted a minute which was referred to the board and received its approval:

> Having prayerfully considered various suggested alternatives, we notify our general director that it is our opinion that the best course of action regarding the Door of Hope is the phasing out of the orphanage ministry, with the ultimate goal of closing it down, and provision being made for a continuing [spiritual] ministry to the alumnae.[12]

This decision required several follow-up steps. Some girls were placed in other Christian orphanages with adequate support for their care. Some who had homes were released to their families. Donors in the homeland were informed about the changes. Plans were developed for a more adequate ministry to alumnae. Proper stewardship of the Taipei property also had to be considered.

The field council took seriously its responsibility to the Door of Hope alumnae and assigned Kathryn Merrill to this work on a part-time basis, with participation by Freda Rempel. Nor did it forget the needs of this ministry when making decisions about the future use of the property.

The Need for Graduate-level Training

The general educational level in Taiwan was higher than it had been on the mainland, with many church young people having completed high school and not a few going on to college or university. Several of the evangelical missions in Taiwan were facing the same need—for more highly trained pastors and teachers. No one mission or church group could supply enough students for a seminary-level school, nor could their churches absorb many graduates. The logical solution was a jointly operated graduate-level school.

TEAM was invited to participate in the planning of the China Evangelical Seminary (CES) but did not join until it was satisfied that doctrinal integrity would be protected by a strong evangelical statement of faith.

TEAM Joins CES and Gives Land

The choice location of TEAM's Door of Hope property was recognized by the board of CES, which approached TEAM in 1976 with a request that it donate about half of that property for the proposed seminary building. TEAM studied the matter carefully and agreed to contribute 500 *ping* (18,000 square feet) on a perpetual lease basis. TEAM had become one of the sponsoring missions and considered its long-term purpose of providing trained workers for its churches. This gift would cover TEAM's share of construction costs. The building erected was both beautiful and serviceable and soon was used to its full capacity.

Generosity Raises Questions

To TEAM's surprise, the gift of the Door of Hope property was given publicity in the Chinese religious press. To no one's surprise, the pastors and other leaders in the TEAM-related churches had questions. How could the mission be so generous to the evangelical work in general and yet deny much-needed help to its own churches? The obvious answer was that no money was involved in the transaction. The field treasurer did not have money to put into church buildings, even if the missionaries had believed that the churches should be relieved of their responsibility. Furthermore, the mission wanted the churches to take self-support seriously because this was one of the best ways to strengthen their work.

But still there remained the unanswered question: was there not some way in which to help the churches without removing responsibility from them? It would take further experience to find the answer to this question.

How Best to Use Door of Hope Asset?

When I was in Taiwan in 1980, the president of the China Evangelical Seminary, James H. Taylor III, expressed the hope that TEAM might give CES all or most of the remaining 871 *ping* (31,356 square feet) of the Door of Hope land. I explained that while TEAM recognized the seminary's need, it had urgent needs of its own in its radio, evangelistic, youth, and church ministries. The Door of Hope had been entrusted to TEAM because of confidence in its overall work and its faithful stewardship. I knew that the field council wanted this asset used to further such work in addition to following up on the ministry to the girls.

In 1985 the field council gave serious study to a more effective use of the remaining Door of Hope property. CES truly needed more classroom and dormitory space. Bethany campus of Morrison Academy, which was using the old Door of Hope building, also urgently needed a permanent home. Several TEAM ministries—a youth center for TEAM university students, Door of Hope follow-up, the church association—needed facilities. Could a multipurpose building be constructed on the Door of Hope site?

Evangelical Building Dedicated

When a request came from CES for additional space, the field council sought to balance the various interests and worked out a plan for a large building in which several organizations could share occupancy of the remaining 871 *ping*—the seminary (37 percent), Bethany Christian School (46 percent), and TEAM (17 percent).

They would divide building costs and share the benefit of this centrally located facility. The six-story "Evangelical Building," as it was named, was dedicated October 4, 1987.

Related Ministries

In 1958 when David and Betty Woodward joined TEAM after years of experience in other Chinese work, they requested assignment to the China Sunday School Association (CSSA). Because the CSSA was an excellent source of trustworthy Christian literature, it had not been necessary for TEAM to have a literature ministry of its own. After the Woodwards retired from the field in 1983, Janice White was assigned to that work.

Field Headquarters Staff

The Taiwan field had on average about sixty missionaries on the field at one time, with another twelve to fifteen on regular furlough. In addition, there were special short-term workers and members of summer teams. The record keeping, financial administration, visa arrangements, and other needs of this large family kept an office staff busy. In the earlier years the staff consisted of the field chairman, an accountant-business manager, a secretary, and a hostess. As the field grew, the staff was increased. The reports for 1988 and 1989 warmly commend the work of staff members Dorothy Holzwarth, Kathryn Merrill, Vergil and Kathleen Nelson, Janice White, and two Chinese young ladies—Penny Huang and Sherry Tao.

Morrison School System

Morrison Academy for the education of missionary children was an essential and important ministry to which a number of missionaries were assigned. In earlier years missionaries were often withdrawn from evangelistic and church work to meet the need for teachers and houseparents. Such has rarely been the case recently, because TEAM actively recruits staff for the children's schools. Rather than weakening other ministries, the availability of these missionaries provides extra summer staff.

Roughly 20 percent of the field staff has been assigned to the Morrison Campus in Taichung, its Bethany campus in Taipei, or its branch schools in Kaohsiung and Taitung. Some who have worked among missionary children over a longer period are Everett and Marcelyn Peterson, Paul and Ilene Peterson, Ruth Jobes, Fred and Julia Wentz, Eloise Harder, Bonnie Vander Zwaag, Bonnie Moller, and Patricia Foster.

Camp Work—Valuable in Evangelism and Discipling

Many of the missionaries who entered service in the post-World War II era were greatly influenced for Christ and His service in camping ministries. It should be no surprise, then, that this type of work would be done by them on the mission field.

> TEAM missionaries in Taiwan wasted no time in establishing camping as part of their evangelistic outreach. An island-wide young people's camp was held in 1952, only a year after TEAM's work began on Taiwan. The mission's Bible school was on the west coast. It had been opened in 1953 to train church leaders. But when the Bible school enrollment dropped to a point where continued operation was not feasible, TEAM closed the school in 1966. That's when the Youth Camp Committee decided to utilize the campus for camps, retreats, and conferences. Eventually, Chinese Christians took responsibility for planning the camp's programs.[13]

The first property devoted to a camp ministry was in premises at Neipu which had been used to house language students. Missionaries named the camp *Hsian Tsun* (Zion Village). Other camps were held in a number of different places.

Bible Institute Property Serves

When the Tachia Bible Institute campus became available, the Neipu property was sold and the camp committee expanded and improved the campus so it could accommodate as many as 200 campers at a time. Some camps were the full responsibility of TEAM churches and missionaries; others were sponsored by other Christian organizations, one of the most active being the Campus Fellowship, with which Dick and Florence Webster were working.

The Tachia property had a change in name and became known to the missionaries as the Iron Mountain Gospel Camp. Those most active in developing the camp facilities were Fred Nelson, Ernest Boehr, Vergil Nelson, Margery Moore, and Richard Olson. The activity over a number of years was tabulated by the committee:[14]

Conference Year	Days Used	Number of Campers
1978-79	95	2,109
1979-80	98	2,030
1980-81	102	1,813
1981-82	100	2,283
1982-83	109	3,249

The objectives of various camps included evangelism, deeper life with Christ, Bible training, and prayer retreats. Campers ranged in age from junior high through adult, sometimes including whole families.

> We continue to feel that the camping program is still one of the most effective means of winning young people to a definite acceptance of Christ as their personal Savior, and to help Christian young people make new commitments, and new progress in their Christian life.[15]

Church Growth Studied

The topic of major importance at the June 1970 field conference was *church growth*. A careful study had been reported to a special conference in December 1969, where decisions had been made which, it was hoped, would erase the last vestiges of dependency by the churches. The missionaries were conscious of the problem faced because churches were subsidized. The 1970 conference featured a series of lectures by the Rev. Allen Swanson, a Lutheran missionary, who had made a careful study of church growth in Taiwan in the post-war period.

> He had particularly studied Lutheran churches but for comparison purposes had surveyed all the work in Taiwan, Protestant and Catholic. What we had observed in TEAM's work—a rapid response in early years and a flattening off later—was evident in the work of every mission. Our problem was no different than the problems of others. There were, however, two groups which continued to grow—both fully indigenous. One was *Chen Yehsu*

Chiao [True Jesus Religion] and the other the *Chuhuei Tang* [Assembly Hall]. To him the reason seemed clear—no dependency upon foreign direction or funds.[16]

Missionaries felt some foreign direction had been justified as it was necessary to insure biblical integrity—which, in their judgment, was not always safeguarded in the indigenous groups, lacking as some were in adequate scriptural instruction. The question of dependence on foreign funds was another matter—and a sensitive one for both mission and churches.

Field chairman Morris Beck's report to the 1970 conference was not lacking in encouragement, however. Twenty-two of the sixty-six field missionaries were engaged in Mandarin, Taiwanese, and Hakka church work. That was one third. Good, but not as good as desired or as was true on other fields where more growth was seen.

Beck reported forty churches or regular meeting places, twenty organized churches, five ordained pastors, and sixteen evangelists. There had been 898 professed conversions and 184 baptisms in the year and 1,406 students were in the Sunday schools. Those figures gave much cause for rejoicing, yet the gap between the number of conversions and those following the Lord in baptism highlighted the problem of church growth. Either there was a weakness in discipling the new believers or a lack of attraction in the church bodies which should have drawn them into fellowship and retained their active participation.[17]

David Woodward, field chairman in 1971, pointed out that the welfare and progress of the churches was a constant concern to the field council:

> ...whose major decisions [in 1971] related to the decrease in subsidies to churches for the employment of pastors, the assistance of the Taichung Mofantsun Church, the Pingtung Shengli Church, and the Yuli Church with matching and other funds for land and building, and the working out of the stipulations by which matching funds would be provided or church land deeds turned over.[18]

These financial allocations marked a course correction that grew more pronounced as time passed. In part, the change answered the question of how to provide assistance to the churches without increasing their dependence on foreign support for their regular ministry.

> The general direction we are taking as a mission in Taiwan is toward an indigenous policy in the churches. This trend is the product of necessity. We are being forced along this line, whether we will or not. Chinese Christians have added confidence in their responsibility for management of their own church affairs and are proving that our financial handouts are no longer needed in the same way they were in the 50s.[19]

Each year it was the same—concern for the churches, yet recognition that there was progress even though slower than hoped for. Hugo Johnson expressed the same thought in 1973:

> Over the years one phase or another of our ministry has come under special stress. For a number of years the pressure lay in the area of the churches. Thank God for the pressures that keep pushing us back to Him. There are now encouraging signs in the churches—an open door to our missionaries for fellowship and service, young people sharing seriously in church life, a growing sense of stewardship, a search for means of fellowship among the churches, to mention a few. Let us join them in the pursuit of the much more that the Lord has for them and for us together. Certainly a strong and enthusiastic spirit of evangelism should have high priority in this.[20]

Decline in Church Planters

The following year, Johnson pointed out with some alarm that the number of field missionaries in church work had dropped from twenty-one to fifteen. Thus only 22 percent of the missionaries were spending full time in this central purpose of the mission.[21]

Why could TEAM not do something to change the percentage of those going into the direct church ministry? Christians in the homelands supplying missionary recruits are affected by trends in society as a whole. For about ten years young people in general— even Christians—had been influenced by "anti-establishment" thinking and were questioning the relevance of the church.

Many missionary recruits had experienced Christian fellowship in student groups, parachurch organizations, or on an individual basis, but had not been involved in a meaningful way in a local church. It was not that they were against the church; it was more a case of "benign neglect." Not until mission societies and Bible training schools reemphasized the central purpose of the redemptive message—the calling out of a people for the Lord and building the Body of Christ—did a change in emphasis became apparent among those offering themselves for missionary service. The other ministries on the field were good and necessary and often excellent means of evangelism, but without the planting and nurturing of the church they fell short of providing the permanence that was most essential.

No Lack of Trying

The field leaders did not give up in their efforts toward a stronger church ministry. The Church Work Committee spent much time in prayer, study, and discussion. Hugo Johnson took note of one aspect of the committee's work:

> I want to commend the work of the Church Work Committee in calling the meeting with the national church workers in February. Although the meeting was rather low key, it was a good start toward a better understanding and a closer working relationship between the churches and the mission. It is urgent that we make ourselves more available.[22]

Japanese Coworkers

As alluded to in chapter 29 on Japan, some missionaries were made available by the TEAM-related Japan Evangelical Alliance Church (Domei) and at least one other Japanese group. Their service with TEAM was covered by a formal agreement. The first in Taiwan, Miss Toshiko Suzuki, was not directly from the Domei but from *Cho No Hate*. The Domei sent Yoshihiro and Shimako Terada, Lydia Goeku (Habecker), and Mitsue Sasaki, a candidate. While they could have used the Japanese language to work among the older Taiwanese, they studied Mandarin to assure their wider usefulness. They became a part of the regular missionary staff and their service was greatly appreciated.

Hakka Chinese Hard to Win

The winning to Christ of any adherent of another religion is a miracle which only the Spirit of God can perform. Human agency is necessary but never adequate to break down barriers of suspicion, unbelief, superstition, and unconcern. Why does the Spirit of God choose people from among some groups more than others? This is a mystery that elicits many theories but no satisfying explanation other than the sovereignty of God. The Apostle Paul discusses this question in Romans 9, 10, and 11. In the Chinese setting there are two groups particularly resistant to the gospel— the Moslems and the Hakka people.

TEAM has no church planting work focusing on the Moslem minority but does minister among the Hakkas. Being Chinese the Hakka people are not considered a minority group. However, they are a distinct group in that they differ from most Chinese in customs, traditions, and—to a certain extent—language. The name Hakka is made up of two characters meaning "guest-people." The story is that Chinese from northern China migrated to the south, where they settled in the provinces of Fujian and Guangdong. Being surrounded by people of another language, their culture became isolated. Their language, too, took a turn which made it quite different from the northern Chinese of their ancestral province. As to religion, they were extremely superstitious and yet zealous and dedicated ancestor worshippers. Any perceived neglect of the ancestors created a serious barrier to communication with them.

Ernest and Barbara Boehr had been working at Miaoli for several years along the usual lines of preaching, teaching, and using literature, when they realized in 1976 that they were not effectively communicating with the Hakka—even though they spoke their language. So they sought the Lord's guidance about a different approach:

> Convinced by our own experience in trying to explain the gospel to the superstitious Hakka that it is necessary to begin where they are and in terms they understand, we began seeking the help of Christians to put the message in common language.... When it became clear that the burden was ours and not theirs, and being convinced in our own hearts that an explanation of the gospel in

terms they understand is necessary to make inroads into the 95 percent hard core idolaters and atheists, we embarked on the project by ourselves.... We have just finished the first draft in Chinese of the *Revelation of God from Creation to Consummation*. It consists of an introductory tract and eight tracts in a continuing series. Each tract also has a five or six verse poem expanding the teaching and complementing the teaching in the tract.[23]

Frank and Betty Ling, Chinese-Americans of Hakka ancestry, worked in Chungli among the Hakka people for several years.

University Students

High school graduates in the TEAM-related churches around the island competed for acceptance into university and many qualified. "University student work in Taipei was first begun by Lola Sunwall and Elizabeth Albert. Fruit from their work is very evident in several of our churches today," Morris Beck reported in 1990.

Those studying in Taipei—about 160, in all—became the object of joint ministry by the Chinese church and the mission. Bill and Ginann Franklin laid the groundwork for the Joy Church in the university district and were joined by Herbert SooHoo and Phil and Ann Schwab. The Schwabs wrote about this work in 1989:

The Lord has allowed us to be a part of the team of missionaries planting a new church—the Joy Church—in the center of Taipei's university district. We averaged twenty to thirty adults for the first month, along with a Sunday school of ten—plus, Joy Fellowship on Sunday evenings with twenty to thirty, and a kid's English class for about twenty (a chance to provide an important service to the community). Several are close to a decision for Christ.[24]

Outreach to New Areas

Kaohsiung, the second-largest city in Taiwan with a population approaching one million, was targeted as a church-mission project, beginning in the summer of 1976. A planning committee was formed which included Pastor Ch'ih of Mofantsun church of Taichung, Elder Chen and Miss Fu of Hsinying, Elizabeth Albert,

Phil Schwab, and Art Dickinson. Miss Fu and Elizabeth Albert, as full-time workers for one year, started the work. Janice White and two students from the OMS Bible school joined the group for the summer. Local churches supported Miss Fu and the students.

Team members visited 4,307 homes and distributed 17,617 tracts. They enrolled 313 students in correspondence courses and reported fifty-five completions. There were thirty-six conversions—twenty-nine through correspondence courses and six through personal witness. After the initial contacts Miss Albert and Miss Fu returned to begin the second phase, that of following up those showing desire to go on with the Lord.[25]

The report on the Kaohsiung project is of particular interest because it revealed progress in both principle and method. Two significant principles were followed—involving the churches as partners with the mission in the pioneering advance, and looking to the churches to support the Chinese workers involved. The progress in method was in the concentration of evangelistic approach by team members through personal contact, tract distribution, and correspondence courses, all with later follow up.

The group of thirty-six professed converts provided a nucleus to be discipled and was an important step toward planting a Taiwanese church. In fact, two churches grew out of the Kaohsiung project. Two of the younger missionary couples, Phil and Ann Schwab and Ross and Becky McKay, felt the Lord leading them to work in Kaohsiung, which they did until the churches were brought to maturity.

Kaohsiung Church Progresses

As the years passed, the Kaohsiung church with which Phil and Ann Schwab were working grew in strength and responsibility. One contributing factor was the Chinese coworker the Lord sent to share in the ministry, Jason Lio. Lio enrolled and was graduated from the Holy Light Seminary in Kaohsiung, where his wife had already studied. Lio was appointed pastor in 1985. Writing in September 1982, the Schwabs gave an encouraging report:

On July 4, the Kaohsiung Church celebrated its sixth birthday with a lunch after the morning service. The chairman of our TEAM church association had a part in the program. The young congregation is growing in responsibility as they now support their pastor, pay a healthy portion of the rent, and recently have taken on partial support of a TEAM Bible school grad, a young lady gifted in youth and children's ministry. Jason Lio shares the pulpit with two laymen, and heads up the overall spiritual ministry of pastoring. He also leads two discipleship groups with key members as well as cooperating with others starting two new churches in the greater Kaohsiung area.[26]

The Kaohsiung project initiated a movement toward opening new areas for evangelism and church planting. Much of the newer emphasis was on Taiwanese work. At the 1980 field conference Morris Beck reported on new places entered:

Since last conference the mission and several of our churches have begun new church planting efforts in Yungho, North Taichung, Hualien-Ganyuan, and Kaohsiung-Siaukang. Lydia Goeku and Anne Leland have been assigned to Taitung and Hsinchu respectively to begin a new outreach.[27]

Yungho, a church planting effort in the Taipei area, was started by David and Betty Woodward and followed up by Freda Rempel and Richard Olson. Later, Phil and Ann Schwab—after a period of Mandarin language study in Taipei—began a work in Wanfang, also a district of Taipei. What was significant in these new areas was that indigenous principles were followed from the very beginning.

Church-Mission Cooperation

A recommendation by Jack MacDonald on a visit to Taiwan in 1980 helped to focus the attention of the missionaries on the essentials of their work. He pointed out that a change in name from "church work committee" to "church work and *evangelism* committee" would keep before them the indispensable element in church work—evangelism.

Another step in the right direction was the formation of a joint church work committee with the formidable title of Chinese-Western TEAM Church Work Committee—or joint committee, for short.

By 1981 the church work and evangelism committee had called for thirty evangelism and church planting workers to come forward in the next two years. Beck reported that during the year 1980 there were 717 professed conversions through the combined ministries of the churches, projects, and missionaries, but only thirty-seven of these were baptized in TEAM churches. "We need to continue our follow-up of new believers." Church membership stood at 1,080.[28]

Church Association Reborn

An association of churches had been organized in 1956, but seemed to have been premature. It apparently did not arise out of the desire or initiative of the churches and, failing to prosper, collapsed. By 1977 the climate in the churches had changed as the believers in one place became conscious of their spiritual unity with those in another. Field chairman Hugo Johnson noted this fact:

> After years of waiting and after more than a year of study, discussion, and preparation, representatives from about half of the TEAM-related churches on the island used the occasion of the church retreat last August to organize a new church association. A committee of seven members was elected to serve on behalf of the association during the year. The association committee has had one meeting. From that meeting has come a strong recommendation to the mission that henceforth we consult with them in dealing with all questions in the churches.... The establishing of the church association and the program and goals which have been outlined for it clearly indicate that we are coming into a new era in our work on the island, first of all in our church planting activities, but ultimately in our supporting ministries as well.[29]

Fellowship Being Strengthened

The yearly reports reveal some latent difficulties in official communication between the mission and the church association. The fellowship on the more personal level seemed to have been very good. That is not unusual in the Orient, where personal and official relationships seem not to interfere with each other. Each is a separate sphere. Here are a few extracts from the reports that highlight the concern and also the way the Lord was answering prayer for genuine unity:[30, 31, 32]

> We long to experience a much-improved relationship with the executive committee of the church association [1981].

> I believe we are seeing answers to prayer in our mission and church association relationship. They desire to work with us in seeing some of the weaker churches revived and strengthened [1982].

> We are beginning to see answers to prayer. Part of their executive committee has met twice with representatives of the field council and the church work and evangelism committee. The mission is working with them in a new outreach to TEAM university and career young people in Taipei [1983].

> The renewed interest of the church association executive committee to work with the mission continued to grow and blossom into a very good working relationship throughout the year. We praise God for this. On six occasions representatives of their committee met with several of our missionaries for dialogue and prayer and the preparation of three papers: Organization of the Chinese-Western TEAM Church Work Committee; Helping Weaker Churches Call a Pastor; Matching Grants for Church Buildings and Land [1984].

> The most significant work the Lord has done in the last conference year is in the area of national-missionary cooperation [1985].

> We are grateful for the continuing excellent relationship with the church association [1989].

Concern Generates Intercession

An expression which recurs frequently in the reports over a period of twenty years is "concern for the churches." This is not an unfamiliar thought to those who follow the Apostle Paul's ministry. For him the concern for the churches was a heavier burden than his physical sufferings. Missionaries working with young churches know many of the heart burdens he bore. These concerns in Taiwan motivated many to faithful intercession, coupled with an earnest desire to find and do His will in the ministry committed to them. The Lord was faithful and answered prayer.

Anticipation and Thanksgiving

Writing this chapter on the Taiwan TEAM work has not been easy for me because of my own deep personal interest in the Chinese. The rapid growth of the first few years was exciting, the leveling off in the next decade disheartening, and the difficulty in establishing ideal working relationships with the leaders of the churches disappointing. But the concern was turned into anticipation and then to thanksgiving as I read through the annual reports submitted by Morris Beck and Phil Schwab for recent years, particularly 1987 through 1989.

Vision and Vitality

There is a return to the excitement of the earliest years in Taiwan. This was highlighted by Norman Niemeyer, area secretary for the Far East, in a 1985 report to the board:

> There has been tremendous encouragement coming out of Taiwan. The missionary family and the national church are working closer than they have in years.[33]

The number of organized churches remains at thirty, but the care of the churches is by thirteen ordained under-shepherds and thirteen biblically trained evangelists. Churches are supporting their workers; they are governing their own ministries; and they are reaching out to new areas on their own and in partnership with the mission. There is vision for the future, as also reported by Niemeyer:

> Last week the Taiwan field met in its annual field conference. As the missionaries and national church met together in strategy planning they came up with a goal of seeing 2,000 committed believers by the year 2,000. This will involve both evangelism and the planting of churches in urban developments throughout Taiwan.[34]

There is even a developing interest in foreign missions, as one of the young people in the church, Anna Hsiao, served a term in Africa with prayer backing and support by Taiwan Christians.

She expects to return there. Ten or twelve young people each year are in Bible schools and seminaries, preparing for the Lord's work. These young people have the assurance that their participation in the expanding work is needed.

The Taiwan churches also participated with missionary leaders in a survey of Macao in April 1990, in this way demonstrating a significant interest in outreach that might provide an open door to Mainland China.

Contact and Continuity

Matthew Lin, national director of the radio ministry, mentioned at the May 1990 centennial conference in Wheaton that the Taiwan Christians are conscious of and impressed by TEAM's history of one hundred years of ministering the gospel of the grace of God to the Chinese. They are increasingly burdened in prayer for the multitudes on the mainland and rejoice that through radio and occasional visits they can continue a century of God-honoring and fruitful ministry.

On a July 1990 visit to the mainland, one of the church leaders, Pastor Liu Hsingmin, made personal contact in Sian with Pastor Huang Hsingmin, inviting him to visit Taiwan to participate in the September 1990 centennial celebrations. Huang, the sole surviving ordained pastor and last chairman of the large TEAM church fellowship on the mission's first field, expressed his deep appreciation but was not able to accept due to old age (83) and physical weakness. The two major branches of TEAM's work among the Chinese had, by force of circumstances, remained isolated from each other for forty years due to political ruptures, but each was now learning of the grace of the Lord bestowed on the other.

KOREA, LAND OF OPPORTUNITY

Threat and Quick Response

"Quick response" and "mobility" are two concepts applied to the armed forces which can have significance for a mission society. But quick response and mobility may not assure long-term victory in the absence of in-depth planning. The experience of the United States in Korea at the close of World War II is a case in point. Soviet Russia's late entry into the Pacific war—just one week before Japan's surrender—gave her control over Korea north of the 38th parallel. Kim Il Sung was installed as communist dictator and for more than four years developed his own plan for reunification of North and South Korea. On June 25, 1950, when Kim considered the time was ripe, his forces launched a surprise attack on the South.

Kim Il Sung almost succeeded. Battling the weaker South Korean and hastily assembled U.S. and U.N. forces, he swept through much of the south until he had them bottled up within the Pusan perimeter in the southeast corner of the peninsula. There the battle raged but the southern lines held until Douglas MacArthur's well-planned and brilliant amphibious attack on Inchon harbor,

halfway up the west coast, completely confused Kim's forces and sent them into headlong flight toward their northern border with China.

When political planning took priority over military, MacArthur's long-range planning could not be implemented. The Chinese attacked and the forces of the South were driven back to a position midway on the peninsula where for almost forty years an armed truce has kept the belligerent forces apart—without victory and without peace.

Decades of Suffering

Under Japanese rule, the churches had faced tremendous pressure to compromise with national Shintoism. Many believers had suffered intensely for their faithfulness. The resistance of some Koreans to compromise may have had double motivation. They were a subject people with much of their lives being regulated by the Japanese. Their religious life should have been their own to choose. Shintoism, while a religion, was also a national movement designed to intensify the patriotism and militarism of the Japanese and would therefore be anathema to many of the Koreans.

For the Korean Christians the greatest motivation to resist yielding to government pressures was faithfulness to the Word of God. They correctly understood that the shrine ceremonies were more than patriotic; they were actually idolatrous. The churches became a rallying point for Christian fellowship and a lighthouse of testimony to faith in the one true God.

Communist Persecution

When the communists came into power they oppressed the Christians even more than had the Japanese. With the deliberate destruction of churches, execution of pastors, and scattering of congregations in the communist North, many Christians became impoverished refugees in the South where they fled during the years of war. These refugees promptly formed new congregations, some reportedly meeting in buildings constructed of rubble. There was a vitality that testified to the reality of faith and spiritual life.

TEAM's Quick Response

TEAM's experience in Korea has been conditioned by its initial quick response and mobility. This field was seen as a place of opportunity and all the early ministry was a series of taking advantage of one opening after the other. There is some value in opportunistic response but also serious disadvantage when it gets in the way of long-range planning.

When disaster strikes, Christians often respond with concern and help. News reports told of the dire need of the Koreans, whose towns and villages had been scenes of battle and where many were made homeless, with children bereft of parents. TEAM missionaries in Japan wanted to take a closer look at their neighboring country which had been under Japanese domination for forty years and now was experiencing another severe trial. Could the Japan field with its large number of missionaries be of help? George Martin, chairman of the field; Kenneth McVety, head of literature work; Tom Watson, interested in radio; and Fred Jarvis formed a survey party to visit South Korea in 1952.

The survey team's report to the board of directors and the Japan field council stressed areas of need that TEAM should try to meet. There was, first of all, the desperate need of displaced people and orphaned or homeless children. Opportunities for evangelism abounded. Gospel literature was an urgent need. Watson, the radio man, saw the possibilities in making Korea a base for broadcasting the gospel to communist-dominated countries.[1]

Johnson Gets a First-hand Look

On a tour of TEAM fields around the world in 1953, David H. Johnson arranged to stop in Korea, where he met Bill Garfield and Tom Watson and spent four days reviewing conditions. He was deeply moved by the extreme poverty and the plight of the refugees, especially the children. He wrote concerning these children:

> Approximately 200,000 children are without mother or father. Many or them are being cared for in orphanages, but multitudes live on the streets, caring for themselves as best they can. Thus many small children in Korea are growing up as beggars. As I saw these children in this pitiful condition, I said over and over again, "What if this one were my boy or that one my daughter?" What heartaches would we not have? Korea is far from America, so these scenes do not disturb the folks at home. However, they should move Christians to compassion.[2]

The availability of missionaries to address these needs was a key to decisions made by the board and the field council. The board in 1953 approved the opening of work in Korea as an extension of the Japan ministry.[3]

Missionaries ready to respond included a retired educator who felt the strong leading of the Lord to do something about the desperate need of the orphans. She was Miss Mabel Culter, founder of Culter Academy in Los Angeles and, more recently, short-term Bible teacher in Japan. William and Bertha Garfield, missionaries in Japan, wanted to undertake a literature ministry. Tom Watson wrote to President Syngman Rhee in 1952 making preliminary application for a radio station based in Pusan for the purpose of broadcasting the Christian message to Siberia and China.

Watson and Garfield were the first TEAM missionaries to enter Korea on a permanent basis, soon after the armistice between the North and the South in July 1953. Robert Livingston was an early candidate for evangelistic work, as was Claire Beckwith, who later became Mrs. Livingston.

History of Early Gospel Progress

In pre-war years the gospel had made outstanding progress in Korea. Several major groups had developed strong churches—the Presbyterians (Northern, Southern, Scottish, and Australian) the Methodists (Methodist Episcopal North and Methodist Episcopal South), and the Oriental Missionary Society. These missions had followed the Nevius principle of encouraging indigenous growth.

Yet there was another side of the story. The growing liberalism among the Presbyterians and Methodists had its unhappy effect on Korean theological students sent to America. Upon returning to Korea, many introduced liberal theology into the churches. That the churches should have continued faithful to God through trials of persecution by the Japanese and the communists and through the devastation of war, and then have many led astray by liberal theology and religious formalism is sad indeed.

Yet how encouraging it is that the "the Lord knows those who are his" (II Timothy 2:19, NIV). Throughout Korea, the nation with the largest percentage of Christians in Asia, there are millions who remain faithful to the Lord and actively evangelize their neighbors.

With understandable reaction to this drift there came a four-way polarization among the Presbyterians—extreme liberalism to the left and separatistic fundamentalism to the right. The large middle block of Presbyterians, mostly fundamental in doctrine, then divided on the question of relationship to the World Council of Churches. The non-aligned section was loosely called the "NAE" group, though this did not mean it had a relationship with the similarly named fellowship in the United States. It was with this latter conservative evangelical group that TEAM missionaries had areas of cooperation.

TEAM's Objective Questioned

Several missionaries of one mission expressed concern that TEAM might be planting churches, apparently feeling that the divided loyalties of local churches could result in some transfer of interest and loyalty to a new large mission such as TEAM. Though there is no record of any such promise by TEAM missionaries— and certainly not by the field council or board of directors—it was claimed that TEAM had promised to limit its work to special ministries such as literature, radio, and orphanage work, and not to establish any churches. When, in the 1960s, several churches were started in Kangnung, on the east coast, this criticism was raised again, but did not lead to any official study or consultation at any time.

Difficulties in Church Planting

Though there was no policy to avoid starting churches, difficulties were expected in developing such a ministry. First of all, TEAM missionaries were concentrating on special projects, whereas church planting requires all the time and dedication that a missionary can give, with a minimum of other interests.

Another difficulty was the ecclesiastical atmosphere in Korea, where comity agreements existed among missions and where

Christians were known by their denominational relationships to the extent that an independent church was often viewed as a cult.

Still another difficulty was in calling an evangelist or pastor to serve an independent church. Would his training be consistent with TEAM's doctrinal position and emphasis? Missionaries found, to their dismay, that some pastors invited to work with them had to be carefully screened to determine whether they knew the Lord personally and were not just depending on their "good works" and church credentials for their standing in the faith.

Yet There Was Sowing and Reaping

In spite of these difficulties as many as six couples carried on tent evangelism and other forms of outreach in the 1960s and saw groups of believers assembled in various places. Particularly active in this ministry were Bob Livingston and Larry Lunceford and later Jim Cornelson, Ray Pierson, and Bob Dignan.

The combination of these difficulties resulted in major church planting giving way to the other ministries, so that for a period of twelve years—1970 to 1982—only minimum missionary effort went into this vital work. It should not be inferred that the other ministries were not necessary or fruitful. In fact they were very important for their soul winning and discipling. Souls were continually being won to the Lord and built up in the faith through radio, literature, camps, conferences, Christian education activities, and personal witness.

TEAM's ministry in Korea was not much different from well-known parachurch ministries in the homeland. But it was not consistent with what TEAM was doing on its other fields. TEAM in Korea did not underestimate the importance of church ministry, but rather endeavored to strengthen the churches by the helps that it offered.

The Other Ministries

When the first missionaries entered Korea from 1953 to 1956 they developed work on four fronts—evangelism, literature, radio, and orphanage. Rather than trace the field history chronologically,

I shall deal separately with the major ministries from their beginning to the most recent record. This will cover about thirty-five years.[4]

Mountain of Blessing Orphanage

Miss Culter chose to establish the orphanage, which she called *Chuk Pok San*—Mountain of Blessing—in Pusan where there were more refugees than in any other part of the country. Orphans were first housed in temporary quonset huts located on a beautiful hillside overlooking the ocean. These huts were later replaced by concrete block buildings for which some of the blocks were made by the older orphan boys.

On a visit in 1956 I witnessed an example of Miss Culter's resourcefulness. She had learned that a Canadian ship was discharging cargo and reasoned that the dunnage used in protecting the cargo included good quality Canadian lumber. She contacted the appropriate ship's officer and offered to take all the lumber that might otherwise be discarded. Workers hauled several truckloads up to the orphanage where some of the lumber was used in the buildings; the rest was sold at a good price for other building needs.

Building a Work Team

Miss Culter was able to attract dedicated workers—another key to her effectiveness. Missionaries who responded to her invitation included Jim and Barbara Cornelson and Leo and Zarita Classen. Glen and Edith Reavis also joined the staff. A number of well-qualified Korean Christians were engaged for the varied functions of the home. When the baby home was opened for abandoned infants, the Lord sent Eleanore Pierson and Janet Moodie for the necessary nursing care. A refugee church elder and his wife from the North, Mr. and Mrs. Matthew Kim, became the senior Korean workers and served well for over ten years until they became the center of personnel difficulties in 1966.

Young Lives Transformed

It was a most satisfying experience for me to visit Mountain of Blessing on several occasions. Realizing that many of the children had lived by begging on the streets where they knew little of order and common courtesy, it seemed nothing short of miraculous to see well-ordered boys and girls in classrooms and dormitories and to observe how readily many of them had received the gospel message and allowed it to shape their lives. They had been under another kind of discipline on the streets—self-reliance and re-sourcefulness. Under the molding and shaping of the gospel as taught by Korean Christians and missionaries, they now seemed exemplary in conduct. That was how it seemed to visitors; though, as in many families, there must also have been testings and tears.

Reexamining the Orphanage Need

Over its first ten years the orphanage ministry expanded to care for 200 to 250 children at a time in Chuk Pok San and in its outlying agricultural branch at Tongnae. But with this growth came questions about its continuation after the most pressing needs had been cared for. What did the presence of an orphanage signal to some Korean people? According to one police official in Pusan, parents who were weighed down with the care of an infant could in conscience abandon it on the city hall steps, knowing it would be picked up and brought to the baby home to be fed and clothed. The children's refuge was seen by that official as contributing to a breakdown of family responsibility in the community.

By 1966 the Korean economy had largely recovered and Koreans were prospering. There were still needy children, but should not Korean Christians have the responsibility for their care? Was it necessary for foreigners and foreign money to be involved?

Another important question concerned the future of the children. Were they being prepared for life in Korea or were they becoming somewhat American in culture? Even the presence of Korean teachers and other workers did not overcome the foreign influence in the orphanage which, in the minds of some Koreans, left a permanent mark on the children. The greater the element of Korean support, control, care, and instruction, the less would be the foreign influence and the greater their ease in fitting into Korean life, which was what the children would have to do.

One more factor had to be considered. Some of the children were of mixed Caucasian-Korean parentage and as such had a very bleak future in Korean society. These children—as was the case with similar children in other orphanages—were made available for adoption in the United States where they would be welcomed and valued as individuals.

Phase-out Plans

Facing these questions, the field council decided that the mission's role in orphanage work should be cut back. In October 1966 the board approved the long-range purpose to shift the orphanage program to full Korean responsibility.[5]

The staff difficulties that same year surrounding Matthew Kim accelerated the plans already being made. Some might ask, "Why should the mission not continue to be directly involved in a labor of love to needy children?" When the involvement of missionaries is necessary and they are entrusted with the means to begin charitable work they should respond. But they must take a long-range view of their obligation and the results of the work they are doing.

Slowly Phasing Out

The phasing-out extended over about seven years. A Mr. Shim Moon accepted responsibility to administer the work. The assets were entrusted to the orphanage board, which continued to guide the ministry.

TEAM's spiritual responsibility did not end with the transfer to full Korean management. The mission continued to work with the alumni, providing college scholarships and, especially important, spiritual counselling.

The alumni tended to gravitate to the capital city, Seoul, and it was there that Eleanore Pierson had been transferred to work at the field office and in literature. Her apartment was often filled with young people who needed counsel and a temporary place to stay while in transition. Family is very important in Korea, as in all the

Orient. The missionary had become family to the alumni and this bore spiritual fruit in many lives. Field chairman Jim Cornelson commended Eleanore's work in his annual report for 1970:

> Ellie Pierson gives herself unsparingly to the 150 graduates of Chuk Pok San who come to her home at any time under varied conditions. She seeks to lead them to the Lord or into a deeper walk with Him. She answers all the letters in Korean, which number many.[6]

The orphanage ministry had met a real need for many years. The physical and educational needs were adequately cared for and, of greatest importance, the spiritual needs had priority attention. The orphanage provided vocational training to prepare the children well for useful lives. Many went on to attend college and not a few entered Christian service.

Applying for a Radio License

With encouragement from general director David H. Johnson and the board of directors, Tom Watson renewed the application for a radio license in more proper form in October 1952. He wrote to president Syngman Rhee again in December 1953 and named eleven prominent Koreans who had consented to serve on the radio board. This time he indicated the Seoul area as the location. Later he gave Inchon as the desired site for the transmitter.[7]

The Initial Radio Staff

The Korean government granted the license for station HLKX in May 1954. The initial installation was to be a 20,000-watt AM transmitter. Broadcasting would be in Chinese, Russian, English, and a minimum of Korean. William Winchell was appointed radio engineer. His wife, Edna, had gifts of secretarial administration, which proved extremely useful in the radio ministry. A second radio engineer, Herbert Korte, also served in the preparatory period.

A Site for Transmitter and Tower

The HLKX transmitter building and studios were located on a small knoll just off the salt water of the Inchon harbor tidal flats.

The engineers erected the 420-foot antenna on the flats so that with each rising of the tide it was standing in water. Engineers recommended this as a means of strengthening the signal toward the target areas of northern China and eastern Siberia. In addition to the radio buildings it was necessary to provide one duplex and five single-family staff houses. The builders and engineers completed the construction and equipment installation in the late summer of 1956. Testing and program preparation were finished in time for the initial broadcast to be made December 23, 1956—a live program in Chinese.

The Chinese Department

Julius and Thyra Bergstrom, who had a background of more than a quarter of a century of work in China, were asked to head the Chinese language division. Julius, born in China and a diligent student of the language, was one of the few missionaries who could speak Chinese with either the northwestern or official Mandarin pronunciation and without a trace of foreign accent. More importantly, he was gifted both in evangelism and in Bible teaching.

Slavic Gospel for Russian

Knowing that it would be difficult for TEAM to find and evaluate Russian-speaking missionaries for the Siberia broadcasts, Johnson approached the Rev. Peter Deyneka, founder and general director of the Slavic Gospel Association (SGA), with the proposal that SGA take responsibility for the Russian-language broadcasts including having Russian-speaking personnel at the station. Deyneka and his board agreed, with the result that Mr. and Mrs. Jack Koziol were appointed and served for many years. Peter Deyneka, Jr. took over the Russian work for two years and was followed by Mr. and Mrs. Alex Kushinikov.

English Programming

There were many American servicemen in the Seoul-Inchon area, which was very close to the demilitarized zone separating North and South Korea. Producers of some North American Christian programs made them available for airing to servicemen, and to Koreans who wanted to improve their English.

Taiwan Radio Participates

Bergstrom broadcast from the Inchon studios for about three years. When he and Thyra left Korea in 1959, TEAM radio studios in Taiwan accepted the responsibility to produce two hours a day of taped Chinese language material which, for the next fourteen years, included Bergstrom's messages. This Chinese block was broadcast at two different times for better reception in China.

Broadcasting in Chinese was truly a work of faith because for twenty-three years there was at most one or two letters a year in response. One of the first was from a Chinese listener in Alma Ata, Siberia, 2,300 miles distant. When missionaries at HLKX looked at the map they realized that many who lived much closer than Alma Ata were potential listeners and so the radio personnel broadcast in hope. It was not until 1979 that those who were sowing the Word in faith received abundant tangible evidence of many faithful listeners attracted to the life-giving message.

Russian Responses

It was much the same with the Russian broadcasts. For the Koziols, Kushinikovs, and Peter Deyneka, Jr. it was indeed a work of faith. An average of 15 Russian letters a year did get through by way of Japan and most of them asked for Bibles. Though these Bibles were sent out from Japan, there was little evidence that they were getting through. In fact, repeated requests from the same listeners provided convincing proof that the earlier mailings had been confiscated. However, the SGA office in Chicago reported correspondence from Christians in Siberia referring to these broadcasts.

Throughout Siberia were many ethnic Germans who had at various times suffered exile. Though many of them were born in Russia they had retained their German language and interests. Being also Russian-speaking, many had listened to Russian radio broadcasts from HLKX. Some became Christians. In one community these converts formed themselves into a congregation of believers. The leader secretly produced Scripture and other Christian reading material for distribution.

When Russia allowed the repatriation of ethnic Germans, this Christian leader and some of his congregation took advantage of the opportunity. Missionaries of SGA working among Slavic people in Germany came into contact with these returnees and heard the story of how the HLKX Russian gospel programs had ministered to them. Later, this leader was brought to North America by SGA and thus into contact with TEAM. Staff members were thrilled to meet this fruit of the work in Korea and through him to learn of many who had been won through the broadcasts.

Doubts Erased

There was a time when Jack Koziol questioned whether the HLKX broadcasts were being heard, seeing that letters were few and far between. Was the expenditure of effort and money really worthwhile? He had his doubts while still at HLKX, but even so kept faithfully at his work of broadcasting in Russian. The answer came a few years later after he and Mrs. Koziol had transferred to Manila to work in the Russian department of the Far East Broadcasting Company (FEBC). On a tour to the Tashkent area of Siberia he found large numbers of people who recognized his voice, having listened to the broadcasts. He found this true even in a government office. Needless to say, his doubts were erased.

In 1965 the director of Slavic Gospel Association gave TEAM the "encouraging information that HLKX is heard by large numbers of people in Siberia."[8]

Korean Broadcasts

Broadcasts in Korean were aimed principally to the people of South Korea. To avoid incidents the government did not want HLKX to direct its broadcasts to North Korea. For its part, North Korea was anxious that its people hear nothing from the outside.

According to *TIME* magazine for July 2, 1990:

> Radios have dials that cannot be tuned and loudspeakers broadcast propaganda 20 hours a day into every home.[9]

Yet news has leaked through by way of Korean intelligence officers that HLKX has a listening audience in the north, larger than might be expected, given the listening restrictions and counter-propaganda.

A number of radio pastors have served over the years and there have been positive results in souls saved and edified. A measurement of the growing listener interest has been the large radio listeners' rallies held from time to time.

A new transmitter was installed in 1964, increasing the power to 50,000 watts, and broadcast time was extended. In 1970 the radio compound moved from the original site to a new location, also near Inchon. By now broadcast time varied from 140 to 155 hours a week. Bill Winchell was named station manager that year.

Obstacles to Overcome

HLKX has not been spared hard times and difficult obstacles. In spite of this the Lord has always brought victory as He has shown the way out. One of the first major problems had to do with the radio compound. The government let it be known that it had eyes on the location bordering the tidal flats. Although this looked like useless land when the tides flooded it twice a day and the adjacent dry ground was not particularly desirable, a soda ash company was given permission to build its plant there. HLKX was compensated, but at a level insufficient to provide equivalent replacement of radio facilities and residences.

Another problem arose as the Korean economy continued to improve, allowing Korean radio stations to upgrade their facilities with the most modern equipment. Whether the government required HLKX to do the same or whether it was the Korean HLKX staff who continually left this impression is not clear. In any event, there were implied threats that it would be difficult to secure license renewal unless more money were spent on modern equipment.

Radio transmission requires a great deal of electrical power and its cost rose steadily until it took a gigantic leap at the time of the Mideast oil embargo in 1973. This put unbearable financial pressures on the station.

Proportionate Help from KLEF

A way of escape appeared on the horizon in 1972 and became more of a possibility in 1973. The Rev. Kwon Shin Chan, radio pastor, was active in a group known as the Korean Laymen's Evangelical Fellowship (KLEF). He and his associates in KLEF let it be known that KLEF would be happy to provide substantial financing if it could have a major say in the policies and operation of HLKX. On the positive side, pastor Kwon's messages on the radio were fully evangelical and strongly evangelistic. For the better part of a year, KLEF's administrative and financial help were greatly appreciated and seemed to promise good times for HLKX. But then a negative side became evident.

Parting of the Ways

Because pastor Kwon had been a pastor in one of the large denominations before he was converted, he tended to be very critical and judgmental of the church scene in Korea. General statements could be a source of embarrassment, but when specific names were mentioned with no real basis for criticism, the situation became intolerable to the point that church newspapers and even the daily press began to call attention to Kwon's criticisms. When Kwon and KLEF made unwarranted accusations against TEAM in 1974, it became necessary to sever relations. There followed a difficult period when KLEF took legal action against TEAM and sought to retain control of the radio station board. Difficult days for field council and station manager followed, during which time there was much prayer. At long last, there was light on the horizon as John Rathbun, field chairman, reported to the 1976 field conference:

> The KLEF problem is finally at the threshold of a solution, with TEAM controlling the juridical person (5 to 2) and $26,000

promised to be returned to KLEF in the near future.[10]

Bill Winchell, radio station manager, directed a restructuring of the HLKX administration, a necessary step after KLEF personnel were withdrawn from the ministry. But the urgent financial problem continued as power costs remained terribly high.

Partnership Talks with FEBC

In 1971 the Far East Broadcasting Company had expressed an interest in acquiring a station in Korea and staff officers of FEBC and TEAM met for preliminary talks. Though informative, the talks did not lead to any conclusion because FEBC apparently was going through some administrative restructuring.

After the radio situation in Korea was stabilized, TEAM renewed talks with FEBC and the two groups agreed on a partnership arrangement. TEAM committed to the partnership the assets being used in Korea under the control of the radio board: its license to operate; a history of twenty years of building a host of listeners; all the equipment of HLKX; certain lands and buildings; direct payments received from program suppliers; contributions from local listeners; and two TEAM missionaries to serve at HLKX—Pearl Rathbun and Dick Chase.

For its part, FEBC accepted full responsibility for the future development of HLKX: assumed all operating expenses; provided a manager—the Rev. Billy Kim—and other personnel; and continued to broadcast Chinese programs prepared by TEAM Taiwan Radio.

TEAM informed the supporters about the changes but retained its mailing list, hoping to provide funding for its share in the agreement and to encourage interest in the mission's continuing radio ministry.

The partnership became effective January 1, 1977, and continued for ten years with an initial review at the end of five years. At the end of the formal partnership there continued to be a harmonious working relationship. Looking back, it is clear that both missions were able to attain their objectives and recognized that their association truly had been directed and blessed by the Lord. FEBC, being a radio mission, was able to direct resources and interest to strengthen the station and enhance its outreach in Korea, while continuing its international broadcasts.

With all the uncertainties, problems, government pressures, and financial stringency, it is remarkable that the radio gospel ministry was maintained with almost no interruption and with most encouraging results—where they could be observed—for the more than twenty years that TEAM had sole responsibility. The many missionaries, Koreans, and contributors who made this ministry possible will undoubtedly have some wonderful surprises in eternity as they learn of thousands ministered to through HLKX.

Need for Christian Literature

When Bill Garfield visited Korea as a member of the first TEAM survey party, he was impressed by the urgent need for Christian literature. During the period of Japanese rule the Korean language was used only in the privacy of the home and in churches. Japanese was required in government offices and schools. The natural result was a lack of Korean Christian literature. With Korean sovereignty restored, the Japanese language fell into disuse, partly from official disfavor and partly because the people desired to use their own language. A great literature vacuum waited to be filled.

Word of Life Press, Korea

Garfield had an interest in literature that would serve the existing churches. He founded the Word of Life Press (WLP) in 1954 and served as its director until 1969. The early publications favored study books for pastors, rather than popular reading for the average church member. Garfield in 1962 negotiated with a large evangelical Presbyterian denomination to publish its authorized hymnal in a deal that for a while seemed to be of more advantage to the denomination than to WLP. Yet the years proved that it was a good contract to have.

Garfield was assisted by Larry Lunceford for a time and later succeeded as director by Neil Flippin. Flippin renegotiated the hymnal contract some years later so that it became not only self-sustaining but profitable. Flippin continued the work of publishing but shifted the emphasis to more popular and practical spiritual books. With his background in business, Flippin was able to change Word of Life into a self-supporting operation. One example was his move of both the publishing and retail operations from a suburb into the heart of Seoul for a better market.

Twenty-fifth WLP Anniversary

When Word of Life Press celebrated its twenty-fifth anniversary in 1979, Jim Cornelson reported on its ministry from its founding:

7.5 million gospel tracts.

1.8 million Korean hymnals.

3.5 million evangelical Christian books.

316 Korean titles in print.

118 graded Sunday school quarterlies in print.

337 church libraries (200 titles) placed.

1,600 Book-of-the-Month Club members.

50,000 Korean Living New Testaments sold since 1978.[11]

Recent Rapid Growth and Expansion

The most rapid and remarkable growth took place after this report was given. The Rev. Kim Jay Kwon came into the ministry in 1970 and was soon made managing director. Kim's background prepared him well for his responsibilities. Having lived in Manchuria (northeast China) where he attended a Japanese school, he was fluent in both Chinese and Japanese as well as in Korean.

A Prepared Instrument

After communism gained control of both Manchuria and North Korea, the Kim family was able to escape to South Korea. In the course of this exodus, Kim heard the gospel and received Christ. Drafted into the South Korean army, he served with a U.S. military unit where he learned English and served as language officer. His multilingual skills served him and the Lord's work well in later years.

TEAM missionary David Livingston came into contact with Kim during his army service and helped him get the seminary training he desired. Later Kim was invited to teach at TEAM's Kwon Dong College. While there he also helped Jim Cornelson plant and develop the Kangnung Evangelical Church which after more than twenty years continued to grow as a solid, evangelical, independent church. After five years at the college, Kim accepted a position at Word of Life.[12]

Kim and Cornelson—an Ideal Team

In 1985 Kim was appointed executive director and Jim Cornelson international director. Kim also became coordinator of the translation of both the Korean Living Bible and the Korean Standard Bible.

Word of Life Press was able to lease adequate space (8,000 square feet) in the Salvation Army building in downtown Seoul. Cornelson reported to *TEAM Horizons* about the move in 1985:

> We had our grand opening on April 10. Over 400 guests came to this occasion of praise, ribbon-cutting, and celebration. The staff worked hard to develop the whole facilities beyond our imagination. The more than 600 customers each day now have room to relax and shop in an atmosphere of excellent displays and the best in evangelical books in Korean and English.[13]

In the same report, Cornelson referred briefly to the expanded outreach of the literature ministry:

> Word of Life Press has a staff of 70 people at its offices in Seoul and Los Angeles. It publishes 75 new titles annually with many more reprints, totaling over one million books each year. These books are distributed through 63 franchise bookstores in South Korea and to Koreans all over the U.S. through the large distribution center in Los Angeles.[14]

International Outreach

With Southern California having a population of more than a quarter million Koreans and hundreds (reported to be 400) of churches, the demand for Korean Christian literature is so great that it is shipped in by large sea containers. In addition to the Los

Angeles wholesale and retail center, Word of Life has opened a bookstore in Chicago. It is a most interesting development that a branch of TEAM's foreign mission work in turn has a large and active division in the United States.

Christian Education Aids

A ministry of largely audio-visual material which developed separately for more than a decade—Korean Aids to Christian Education (KACE)—later was absorbed into Word of Life Press. In 1977, fourteen hundred cassettes were duplicated and sold, and two teacher training seminars were held.

Korea Christian Conference Grounds (KCCG)

A harvest field ready for reaping in the early years of TEAM service was among the youth. Recognizing their gifts for this work, Robert (Chris) and Helen Christopulous began a weekly Youth for Christ ministry. They also saw the possibilities in a camping and conference ground work in a country where this type of activity had broad appeal to children, youth, and adults. Chris found an area of about 13 acres on the outer edge of Seoul which had limitations on residential development because it was in the green belt. Here the KCCG ministry was developed in a picturesque setting of sparse pine forest, a bisecting brook, and huge cliffs on the upper outer border. With the generous support of "First Mate Bob" of the Haven of Rest Ministries and others, Chris was able to build dormitories, dining facilities, an all-purpose hall, and a large auditorium.

For the most part, the format was to rent the facilities and services to organized groups—many church-related, but some sponsored by a municipality or businesses. One requirement was that a representative of KCCG give a gospel message in at least one service for each group.

The annual reports of the KCCG ministry are quite similar from year to year:

> Over sixteen thousand people-days were recorded [in 1984] which makes it the largest number of people in one year. Five New Life Bible Camps, two English Encounter Camps, three

weeks of Mount-O-Pines and many other camps and retreats were held throughout the year. This year we had over 350 young people come to Jesus Christ and many more made real commitments to Him.[15]

After Chris and Helen left Korea, Glen and Edith Reavis became directors of KCCG. Barbara Chapman and Donna Dunlap worked with them for several years. After the death of Edith, Glen went into a church planting work and later married Donna Dunlap. Barbara became the director and continued in that responsibility after she was elected chairman of the field. Barbara's goals for KCCG included having much more of the activity be related to church-mission directed camps and retreats where the ministry would be more fruitful for the churches being planted.

Kwon Dong College Acquired

The field council wrote to general director Johnson late in December 1960 about an opportunity to take over a college in eastern Korea. Kwan Dong College was a project of local interests in the city of Kangnung. It had a large campus with all the buildings needed for its operation as a small four-year college. It also owned about 2,500 acres of mountain land from which trees could be harvested to provide modest income for the college. The school was also about $32,000 in arrears. Its board would be willing to turn it over to TEAM if the mission assumed the debt and promised to operate the school.

Johnson and the board agreed with the field council that this was an opportunity that should not be missed. Two voices of caution were raised. Delbert Kuehl and I pointed out that we had no established churches from which to draw students and to which to send the graduates for service. Furthermore, operating the college would require personnel, reducing the number of missionaries available for church planting. Though we did register our reservations we both supported the decision once it had been made. In March 1961, the board voted to "take over the Kwan Dong College, provided that it can meet our spiritual aims."[16]

Meeting TEAM's Training Goal

To meet the "spiritual aims" of the mission, permission would have to be sought from the Department of Education to add a Bible department to the existing commercial arts division. This request was granted. David Livingston was appointed president, and he went right to work to build up the Bible department and make other adjustments that would insure a strong spiritual emphasis in the school. After a visit to Korea in 1963, I reported to the board:

> The college ministry has taken a turn which is most encouraging, and therefore the future is infinitely brighter than it was when I was in Korea last July.... We now have an enrollment of 110 students, an accredited Bible division, an accredited commercial division, and an unaccredited Bible institute section. We have an excellent teaching staff of dedicated Christians. The school has already made a great impact on the community through evangelistic campaigns.[17]

Facing Government Obstacles

Just as the future for the school seemed most bright with the enrollment exceeding 200, and prospective students were showing interest, the government of Korea dropped a bombshell which adversely affected all educational institutions in the country. Research by the government had revealed that a large proportion of high school graduates were being accepted for college study while relatively few were taking technical training. A better balance was needed if Korea was to develop as an industrial nation. To accomplish its purpose, the Department of Education upgraded college entrance examinations and set quotas which would greatly reduce the number of new students permitted to enroll.

The area on the east coast where the college was located was under par in its high school training, so students from there were at a disadvantage when it came to qualifying for college. The result was to reduce anticipated tuition by $10,000, which seriously handicapped the college and jeopardized its future. It became a question of survival. The education department did grant permission to introduce an agricultural department, to which the mission assigned Ross Beach, who had a master's degree in that discipline.

428

Later, an English department was added which became popular because of the presence of American teachers.

College Viability Threatened

Over several years the enrollment restrictions became a more difficult problem, threatening the welfare of the college. In March 1969, George Martin reported to the board that new government entrance examinations had further reduced enrollments for the current spring term.

Then in July 1970, John Rathbun, who was then president of the college, informed the field council and the board that Myung Ji University of Seoul had expressed interest in taking over Kwan Dong College. The question was asked about the effect of the Department of Education regulations on Myung Ji. Would it be any easier for the university to function than for Kwan Dong? Another question related to the continuation of the Bible department. Would the college continue to provide sound biblical training for prospective workers? Would its transfer to Myung Ji University be the best long-term solution for Kwan Dong College?

Myung Ji Takes Over

The university president, Dr. You Sung Goon, anticipated no great difficulty with enrollments because its quota was more than the Seoul campus could enroll and some of its quota could be used in Kwan Dong. The transfer of the college was difficult for missionary faculty to contemplate. On the staff, in addition to John Rathbun, were Joyce Rathbun, Larry and Deloris Lunceford, Ray and Winnie Pierson, Janet Moodie, and Ross and Mary Beach. They had a wonderful ministry of building into the lives of choice young people, but the reality of the situation had to be faced. By the fall of 1970 the transfer was completed and within a few years TEAM missionaries were transferred to other ministries. Though cut short by this development, the service of the missionaries and their Korean associates in the college was not in vain, according to John Rathbun:

Yes, we did have some choice young people. Several became

pastors of large congregations; many became public school teachers; some found their way to Christian service with other agencies; one or two became foreign missionaries and became a channel of introducing hundreds to Christ through Operation Mobilization.[18]

A Question of Church Planting

Throughout its history TEAM has stressed evangelism followed by discipling the converts, then gathering the converts into local churches. It declares itself to be a church planting mission. Yet for most of its thirty-seven years in Korea, church planting had not been its most visible activity nor seemed to have the main emphasis. Why had this been true? There were two principal reasons.

First, the missionaries were deeply involved in projects—radio, orphanage, literature, conference grounds, college. There was soul-winning activity and much discipling in all these ministries but little church planting. It is true that evangelistic efforts resulted in congregations being formed in the vicinity of Seoul, on the islands off Inchon, in Choong Nam province and Pusan, and in Kangnung, but these congregations were mostly absorbed into other evangelical church groups and did not form a TEAM-related church fellowship. Someone has counted from twelve to fifteen such congregations.

Second, the presence of other live, growing churches caused missionaries to question whether it was not best to let the Korean Christians do what they were gifted to do and were doing—evangelizing and forming churches. In a field conference which I attended in 1956, Julius Bergstrom, radio minister to China and a veteran of extensive church work in that country, expressed his conviction that the best ministry in Korea was to work in cooperation with existing evangelical groups and not try to start what would be considered a new denomination.

A Decision to Assist Churches

After George Martin and I met with the Korea missionaries on the church question in June 1970, I reported to the board of directors as follows:

There are some very great encouragements in the church scene as indigenous, independent, evangelical churches are multiplying. This fact has a bearing on our TEAM objectives which, in the past, included the planting of local churches and bringing them together into a church fellowship. At the same time, TEAM has developed special projects of radio, literature, a conference grounds, and a college which should be of help to all evangelical groups but which are limited in usefulness because, as a church planting mission, we are viewed by others as forming a new denomination. The growing conviction of our Korea missionaries in recent months has been that we should not engage in planting local TEAM-related churches or form a fellowship of such churches but rather work with the many independent evangelical churches which are springing up, offering them spiritual assistance through radio, literature, and the conference grounds, and by evangelistic and Bible conference teams. After considering the total picture, George and I were inclined to agree.[19]

A New Look at the Objective

The result was that for a period of twelve years the emphasis on the field was ministering broadly through the projects—not a unique idea in the American scene. But the vision of the need and possibilities of church planting came to the fore again as reported by Barbara Chapman, field chairman, in 1983:

A new spurt of enthusiasm came through attendance at TEAM's first church planting school by Dick Hahn, Bob Dignan, and Barbara Chapman. In the fall we met as a field to try to pull together some of the ideas gleaned from this school and make plans for the future. We established some awesome goals: five churches organized by 1990; five branch churches begun by 1990; twelve new church planting units by 1990.[20]

Since that conference decision, four couples have been busy in the direct church ministry: Glen and Donna Reavis, Bob and Joyce Dignan, Richard and Julia Hahn (now retired), and Brian and Joyce Flickner. A good start has been made and the next decade should have the story of significant forward movement in the planting and growth of churches—all dependent on the Lord's making the seed grow and if Christ's return has not occurred by then.

For thirty-six years there has been earnest preaching of the gospel, faithful teaching, and consistent counseling. We join with the Apostle Paul in saying, "We continually remember before our God and Father your work produced by faith, your labor prompted by love, and your endurance inspired by hope in our Lord Jesus Christ" (I Thessalonians 1:3 NIV). Though it is impossible to count the full number of conversions, baptisms, and the present record of those taking their places in local churches, faith tells us that God has the record and knows the count.

Longing and Faith for the Future

What the next decade will bring to the Korean peninsula is known only to the Lord, but as Christians in Korea pray for their country, they continue to remember their long-held vision that North Korea and South Korea will be reunited; disrupted families restored to communication, fellowship, and unity; the gospel freely preached and accepted once again; and the church of Jesus Christ growing anew in the North. The liberating events in Eastern Europe in 1989 strengthened their faith and heightened their expectation.

The Reverend Fredrik Franson, who founded the mission in 1890. Truly a spiritual giant, Franson's evangelistic fervor and Spirit-blessed ministry influenced many well beyond his death in 1908. Today, some fourteen mission organizations and church fellowships still exist which were founded or greatly influenced by him.

The Reverend C. T. Dyrness, pastor of Salem Evangelical Free Church. Considered a "co-founder" of the mission, Dyrness was its secretary or chairman for almost forty-two years with only brief breaks. He and Fridolf Risberg were the mainstays of the home organization.

The Reverend Fridolf Risberg. Also described as a "founder" in the early literature, Risberg was a professor at the Swedish Seminary in Chicago.

Early Board of Directors, c. 1897. Front row (from left): Fridolf Risberg, August Pohl, C. T. Dyrness. Back row: H. Soderholm, E. Weleen, O. C. Grauer, J. A. Karlson.

The Reverend J. H. Hedstrom, general director from late 1921 until his tragic death in a train-car accident in September 1923.

Former Venezuela missionary T.J. Bach became the mission's third general director in 1928, ending nearly twenty years without a director except for Hedstrom's short service.

Board of Directors, 1940. Front row: Otto Hogfeldt, O. C. Grauer, G. Edwards, T. J. Bach, Charles E. Bodeen. Back row: Carl Gundersen, E. Johnson, David H. Johnson, M. Johnson, Enock C. Dyrness.

The Rev. David H. Johnson, 1958. An attorney who became a gifted evangelist and pastor, Johnson was general director from 1946 to 1961.

Administrators and board members, 1958. Left to right: David H. Johnson, Vernon Mortenson, Robert Van Kampen, Joseph Horness, Harold Lundquist, Carl Gundersen, Charles Bodeen, John Rea, Robert Cook, John F. Swanson, Enock Dyrness.

The author, Vernon Mortenson, in 1974. When the communist takeover ended his missionary service in China, Mortenson assisted Johnson in the home office for fifteen years before succeeding him as general director in 1961.

The Reverend Richard M. Winchell, 1972. From South Africa, where he led TEAM's Word of Life Publications ministry, Winchell was called to the home office in 1968. He became TEAM's sixth general director in 1975.

iv

Julius W. Bergstrom surveys bomb damage at the Sian Chapel, China, in 1941.

Oscar Beckon and Reuben Gustafson in Shanghai, China, in June 1946 with the truckload of Scriptures and supplies they would take inland. They were first to return to China after Japan's surrender.

China missionaries Anna and William Englund being taken to a
Hong Kong meeting in 1950.

Pastor Chiang
Tungchih of Sian,
China, in 1948.

China missionary Julius W.
Bergstrom, 1958. Though doors to
China closed, his ministry to Chinese
people did not end. Later service included heading the Chinese department of Radio HLKX in Korea.

Leaders of the church in Hwalien, Taiwan, with Oliver Olson and Pastor Ch'ih, 1956.

William G. Englund teaching at Taiwan Bible Institute.

Scripture translation in Taiwan: Edvard Torjesen checks translation of the first gospel literature in the Amis tribal language with Amis Christians, 1956.

Japanese Pastors Majima, Sugimoto, and Matsuda with Joel Anderson and C.E. Carlson, 1928.

Pastor Doi of Atami, Japan, with missionary Joel Anderson. Loved and respected by all, Pastor Doi intercepted and led to Christ many who tried to commit suicide at the high seaside cliffs.

Pastor Matsuda Masaichi, Nakano Church, Tokyo, 1956. Chairman of the Domei church fellowship from 1948 until a long fight with cancer forced his retirement in 1966, Pastor Matsuda provided mature and spiritually wise leadership.

Pastor Ando Nakaichi signing calligraphy, 1970. A former missionary to Manchukuo, Pastor Ando founded the Setagaya Chuo Church in Tokyo and succeeded Pastor Matsuda as chairman of the Domei church fellowship.

Word of Life Press building in Japan, Vern Strom in foreground, 1966.

The revision committee for the Mongolian New Testament, c. 1950. From left: Mattai, Erinchindorji, Stuart Gunzel, Gerda Ollen.

Mongolia Field Conference in exile in Hong Kong, 1951. From left: Stuart and Margaret Gunzel, Edna Heinz, Angeline Bernklau, Jenny and Edvard Torjesen.

Andrew Haugerud, leader of the first party of South Africa missionaries. He died of malaria less than eight months after arriving in Africa.

The Reverend William and Emma Dawson. From the Boer War until World War I, S.A.M. work in southern Africa centered around the activities of the Dawsons, Mr. and Mrs. Severin Bang, and Malla Moe.

Pastor John Gamede and Malla Moe, 1952.

David Greene and Bernard Johansson, former principals of Union Bible Institute.

Africans and missionaries working together at the Swaziland conference in March 1964. Front row: Dr. A. B. Gamede, Johanne Nyawo, Jonas N'debele. Back row: M. D. Christensen, Wesley Carlson.

Dr. Douglas Taylor waiting to check patient brought by mission plane to Mosvold Mission Hospital in South Africa.

Travel in Zimbabwe has its moments. Many hands together will solve this problem.

Meeting with Kandeya headmen who want schools for their villages, 1954.

Zimbabwe field chairman Norman Everswick with pioneer pastor Jordan, 1964.

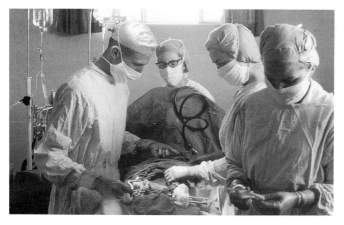

A much-needed hospital was opened at Karanda, Zimbabwe, in 1961. Surgeon Roland Stephens, assisted by nurse-anesthetist Beverly Nelson and surgical nurses Judy Gudeman and Wilma Gardziella, performs major abdominal surgery, 1963.

Pastor Frank Kakunguwo, Zimbabwe church leader, was killed in April 1974 by guerrillas who attacked Mavuradonha Christian School where he was chaplain.

Goulei Christians in Chad who suffered intense persecution from Chief Gabaroum. Pastor Noël Tissa, second from left, was the first convert in the Goulei tribe.

John and Anna Christiansen, 1939. With T.J. and Anna Bach, the Christiansens opened the Venezuela field in 1906. These humble servants of the Lord were still hard at work after four outstandingly fruitful decades in Venezuela.

Francisco Liévano, Venezuelan evangelist and Bible teacher, 1958.

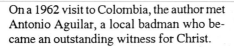

On a 1962 visit to Colombia, the author met Antonio Aguilar, a local badman who became an outstanding witness for Christ.

Converts in Polonia, Colombia, won to the Lord by Antonio Aguilar.

Bible Institute in Ocaña, Colombia; Jack MacDonald speaking.

In Anggi Lakes, Irian Jaya, Sougb church leaders baptize new believers, February 1971.

Meyah tribespeople in Testega, Irian Jaya, 1971. Work here was progressing rapidly by the early 1970s. In 1986 the Meyah church reported 888 adherents.

Dr. Burwell (Pat) Kennedy making a house call in the village of Al Ain, United Arab Emirates, 1961.

TWO NEW FIELDS
IN THE FAR EAST

THE PHILIPPINES

Bataan Peninsula, Leyte—these Philippine place names were deeply engraved in the minds of Americans during the years of World War II. Bataan represented a determined but losing fight against an overwhelming Japanese adversary. Leyte was a promise kept—that America would return—and the beginning of a great military victory.

In the intervening years the former U.S. dependency became an independent republic which has gone through various ups and downs and still is beset with severe economic and political problems. Its population has continued to grow rapidly and in 1990 is almost sixty-five million compared to an estimated forty-eight million in 1980.

Its people—largely of Malay origin, but under Spanish rule for 378 years—are 85 percent Roman Catholic, 4 percent Aglipayan (Independent Philippine [Catholic] Christian), 4 percent Protestant, 4 percent Islamic, and 3 percent other. Though there are 55 languages and 142 dialects spoken in the islands, an advantage is that there are only two official languages, English and *Pilipino* (based on Tagalog).

TEAM Looks at the Philippines

TEAM's interest in the Philippines developed in an indirect way. The mission had missionaries working in Irian Jaya, a

part of Indonesia, who needed a convenient place to send older children for high school training. Some had been sent to Malaysia, some to Taiwan, and others to the Philippines. Over time the Faith Academy near Manila became the favored place because of an agreement with the Academy to supply one or more teachers in exchange for reduced tuition for TEAM-related children.

Missionary Teachers Assigned to Faith

Ray and Cheryl Waterman were the first TEAM missionaries assigned to Faith, arriving there in 1978. Grace Peterson followed as a short-term worker in 1981 and returned for career service in 1983. Other TEAM workers served for shorter or longer periods including Jeanie Gerig; Keith and Terri Rascher, missionaries awaiting entry into Irian Jaya (1984 to 1986); and Linda Sommer, formerly of the North India field (1985). Dick and Karen Chase, who had worked with radio station HLKX Korea, were loaned to the Far Eastern Broadcasting Company in 1982 for service in Manila.

Visa Problems Prompt a Look

As the government of Indonesia began to restrict visas for missionaries, TEAM had a backlog of candidates waiting to go into linguistic and translation work. The Irian Jaya field council felt that the Philippines would make a good alternate field to which missionaries could go, either for short-term assignment while awaiting visas, or to enter linguistic work on a long-term basis.

In preparation for a visit to the Far East fields in March 1984, East Asia foreign secretary Norman Niemeyer shared his plans with the board of directors:

> I will spend a few days visiting Faith Academy. This will include prime time with our MKs studying there. Preliminary discussions will be held with the Ray Watermans concerning the possibility of entering that country as another TEAM field. With the critical visa situation in Irian Jaya, and the challenge of tribal work available in the Philippines, I will be investigating what possibilities there might be of entering that country.[1]

Upon his return, Niemeyer reported on his initial contacts in the Philippines:

> I met with Rev. Mauro Brion, executive director of the Association of Bible Churches of the Philippines, Inc. (ABCOP). Dick Chase accompanied me as we probed the possibility of TEAM coming into the Philippines under the Association.... Without committing ourselves to a decision, we discussed at length TEAM's burden for church planting, and tribal translation work. Rev. Brion shared the ten-year goal established by the Association to establish churches throughout the Philippines. These have now grown from 17 churches to approximately 128. I left the meeting with confidence that ABCOP was similar to TEAM in its doctrine, policies, and goals.[2]

Winchell, Niemeyer Survey

With indications that the Philippines was indeed a needy mission field and one open to missionaries, general director Winchell and Niemeyer made a survey in April 1986 to determine whether TEAM should consider entering. If so, they wanted to find an area and determine a strategy for church planting. The result was an agreement that TEAM missionaries could enter the country under SEND International, a mission of long standing in the Philippines, until TEAM was registered with the government. The church planting ministry would be in cooperation with ABCOP along with SEND International, Overseas Missionary Fellowship, UFM International, and RBMU International. TEAM's target area would be the provinces of Tarlac, with a population of almost 700,000, and Zimbales, bordering on the west, where there is still need for translation work.[3]

TEAM's Twenty-seventh Field

Having in hand the results of the survey made by Winchell and Niemeyer and looking to the Lord for guidance, the men of the board decided, at the May 1986 meeting, that TEAM should enter the Philippines as its twenty-seventh field. Following the policy of having experienced missionaries provide leadership for a new field, the mission asked Arthur and Alice Stejskal, who had served in Taiwan since 1959, to coordinate this new work. They had worked primarily among the Amis tribe, people quite similar to those of Luzon Island in the Philippines. The Stejskals, David and Kathy North, and Keith and Grace McCune arrived in Manila on October 29, 1986, and this date marked the official beginning of the Philippine field.[4]

Others followed in quick order, including Bruce and Jody Anderson, Bruce and Mitz Harrison, and Brent Preston. (The Harrisons and Preston later received visas for Indonesia and went on to Irian Jaya and Java.) The number also included short-term teachers for Faith Academy—Glenda Brumley, Jerry and Marybeth Filat, and Mark and Ginnie Scharfe.

After an initial period studying Tagalog, David and Kathy North began work in Tarlac. Niemeyer visited them there in early January 1989 and wrote encouragingly concerning their work:

> We spent some time talking about the work, their strategy planning for Tarlac and the compatibility of the missionary/national team working there. ABCOP leaders assigned Arseno and Ester Dayrit to work with the Norths in this church planting ministry. The Lord brought these two couples together in a beautiful relationship and it looks like it is going to be very successful. Dave and Arseno took Art Stejskal and me on a tour of Tarlac and the targeted area where they have concentrated their evangelistic efforts. We drove down some of the streets so Dave could show us houses in which decisions had been made for Christ. He said there have been 33 recorded decisions as a result of their house-to-house visitation. At present the greatest resistance is coming from the Iglesia Ni Christo cult which originated in the Philippines. They seem to have strong men who move in on visited families with warnings. In many cases the church owns the property of these families and uses that to keep them in line. To me it is very rewarding and exciting to see the first fruits in that area where Dr. Winchell and I had toured three years ago. We looked carefully at Tarlac and saw great potential. Now it is beginning to take shape. We have every reason to believe that the church is in the process of being raised up in Tarlac.[5]

Another early development in the Philippines was in Scripture translation, as had been envisaged when this field was first surveyed. Niemeyer also gave an encouraging report on progress in this ministry:

> I flew with Art Stejskal to visit Keith and Grace McCune in Cabagan which is located in the northern part of Luzon. After spending time with the family we made our way into the city to join a Christian fiesta.... Keith was the main speaker. He gave his testimony in the Ibanag language. He had only been studying it for six months, but seemed to have a good grasp of it. He spoke for about 30 minutes. It was reported that there were several decisions registered at the close of the meetings. It is in this language that Keith and Grace will translate the Old Testament. It is the sixth largest language group in the Philippines.[6]

Both Keith and Grace have doctorates in linguistics and are doing translation work primarily to further church planting in the mountains.[7]

When the Winchells visited the McCunes' work in Cabagan in 1990, they verified that Summer Institute of Linguistics workers had already translated the New Testament and having reached that goal, had moved on. They found some lively believers who had been saved in University campus ministries six or seven years earlier but who, at the time of the McCunes' arrival, had no thought of starting a church. With the McCunes' vision of a church, there was now a live, functioning congregation with seven preaching elders. Winchell preached at the commemoration of the first anniversary of their worship service.

The initial phase of TEAM's work has been successfully passed under the leadership of Art Stejskal with helpful guidance by the area foreign secretary. Niemeyer was able to report to the board in 1989 that the field was properly set up and functioning with career missionaries. The work was moving forward:

> The church planting effort in Tarlac continues to evidence growth. Dave and Kathy North, along with their national co-workers, have led more than 75 people to the Lord during these months. The nucleus of a church fellowship is now forming with 35 baptized so far. Keith and Grace McCune in Cabagan have begun to see their Bible translation team function. At present they are producing Christian books in comic format in the Ibanag language. This is an effective tool for evangelism because of the popularity of comic books in the Philippines. The purchase of

property in Quezon City for an office, guest house, and residence has been completed.[8]

HONG KONG

Many think of Hong Kong as a Chinese city. This is both true and not true. Its people—with very few exceptions—are Chinese, but have been under the rule of Great Britain. Hong Kong is a city but more than a city; it includes one large island off the southeast coast of China, many smaller islands, and a section of the mainland, for a total

of almost 400 square miles. The city of Victoria occupies most of the major island, and Kowloon and other growing cities the mainland portion. The area has been under British control since 1840 when China, the loser in the Opium War, ceded the island and Kowloon peninsula. In 1860, an additional area, known as New Territories, was obtained by lease which will expire in 1997.

Reclaimed by China

Though long asserting a claim to Hong Kong, China made no attempt to enforce that claim. However, when the People's Republic had consolidated its hold on China and firmed up its international relations, it entered into negotiations with the British government, as set forth in a publication by the Beijing government.

> Hong Kong has been part of China's territory since ancient times, but it was occupied by Britain after the Opium War in 1840. On 19 December 1984, the Chinese and British Governments signed the Joint Declaration on the Question of Hong Kong, affirming that the Government of the People's Republic of China will resume the exercise of sovereignty over Hong Kong with effect from 1 July 1997, thus fulfilling the long-cherished common aspiration of the entire Chinese people for the recovery of Hong Kong.[9]

A Steppingstone?

TEAM's interest in Hong Kong was secondary to its burden for Taiwan and the mainland, but when it perceived that its presence in Hong Kong well before 1997 could be a steppingstone to eventual ministry in China, it studied Hong Kong more carefully. In November 1985, Niemeyer presented a paper to the board of directors on TEAM's continued China responsibility, already being partially discharged through the radio programs prepared in Taiwan for broadcast to the mainland. He recommended that the mission "establish an evangelistic and church planting outreach in Hong Kong."[10]

Niemeyer continued to compile information through consultation with leaders of other organizations. He also arranged a survey in company with Jack MacDonald of the headquarters staff; Art Dickinson, Taiwan missionary serving as a representative; and Verner Strom, chairman of the Japan field at the time. Niemeyer's report included pertinent information about its history and people.

History and Population

At the time it was ceded to Great Britain, Hong Kong had a population of not more than 5,000. It grew slowly as a British colony, then increased more rapidly after the Chinese revolution against the Manchu dynasty in 1911. By 1915 the population had reached half a million. The second wave of growth came with Japan's attack on China in 1937. By the time Japan occupied Hong Kong in 1941 the count had reached 1,600,000. During the period of Japanese occupation the number dropped to one million.

As communism gained control of the China mainland there was continued emigration and by 1965 the Hong Kong population had reached three million. Vietnamese, fleeing communism in their country, added to the crowding of Hong Kong and by 1988 six million people were trying—and succeeding—to make a living in this confined area.

Its strategic location has made it a major economic and financial center for southeastern Asia.

People, Language, and Religion

Because the main immigration has been from Guangdong Province of China, the Cantonese language is predominant. It and English are the official languages. Other Chinese languages—Mandarin, Amoy, Hakka—are used by segments of the people. On my visits to Hong Kong, I have not hesitated to speak either Mandarin or English and have had no difficulty. There has always been a small but significant British population.

The Chinese generally follow traditional religions so Buddhist and Taoist temples dot the whole area. Christianity has made some impact and the recognized denominations are present, also many independent churches. Estimates, seemingly quite generous, are that evangelicals number 300,000.[11]

Positive Action by TEAM

In March 1988 the board of directors confirmed its November 1985 decision to take up work in Hong Kong. Dale and Lauri DeWhitt, who had long had a burden to reach the Chinese, were the first two missionaries assigned to this new field. They began studying Cantonese in July 1988.

Earlier TEAM Work in Hong Kong

But the DeWhitts were not the first TEAM missionaries to work in this British dependency. When the communists attacked China's northwest in 1948 and 1949, some TEAM missionaries evacuated to Canton and Hong Kong. Later, others who had relocated to other parts of China also came to Hong Kong, some to arrange transfer to Japan and others to wait in the hope that China would reopen to missionary entry.

The TEAM missionaries remaining in Hong Kong rented several small apartments in Kowloon and by arrangement with the Evangelical Free Church quickly made themselves available for ministry. Hong Kong was flooded with refugees from the mainland, many of whom spoke Mandarin Chinese. This provided many opportunities to reach displaced people who were quite open to the gospel message:

- Julius and Thyra Bergstrom had prepared gospel slide lectures for use in Shensi. These could be used to great advantage in refugee camps because Chinese characters had the same meaning in Cantonese as in Mandarin.
- Oscar Beckon had worked his way to southern China from the north, preaching from province to province from his truck equipped with a public address system and projector. He brought the equipment to Hong Kong, where he and coworkers used it for large outdoor evening evangelistic meetings.
- Missionaries without equipment made themselves available to work with Free churches in children's meetings and Bible classes where the Mandarin language could be used.
- William Englund was invited to teach in the Free Church Bible Institute where Mandarin was understood by the students, and where all, whether Cantonese or Mandarin-speaking, could read the characters he wrote on the board.

The ministry by a number of TEAM missionaries extended over two years. To the extent possible, converts were referred to Free churches for follow up. Believing that the Spirit of God does a deep and lasting work in the life of a convert, the missionaries had confidence that their service in Hong Kong, though for only a short time, was significant for eternity.

Dickinsons to Provide Aid

Arthur and Leona Dickinson, who began work in Taiwan in 1954 and ministered in both Mandarin and Taiwanese, let the mission know about their deep interest in Hong Kong and willingness to serve there. After several years representing TEAM in the homeland while Leona recovered from serious injuries received in a van accident in Taiwan, they accepted the challenge and spent several months in Hong Kong helping the DeWhitts to find housing, get started in language school, and begin the process of registering TEAM as a recognized organization.

Cranes Called to Assist

In keeping with the policy when entering a new field, Niemeyer sought an experienced couple to provide leadership and found David and Elaine Crane, pioneers of the Trinidad field, who had begun their work there in 1959. They were willing—and even eager—to accept this challenge, particularly because David was born to missionary parents working among the Cantonese-speaking people of Guangdong province. Furthermore, he had lived in Hong Kong in his youth. The Cranes went to Hong Kong in July 1990 and immediately plunged into Cantonese language study to gain at least a speaking acquaintance with it before beginning their work. For their specific work, conversational Cantonese would be sufficient.

Interest in Macao

Taiwan Christians became concerned about a possible ministry to Macao and sent representatives Stephen Wang, Sarah Chu, and Susan Lai to accompany Phil Schwab and Dale and Lauri DeWhitt on a survey trip in April 1990. Schwab's report contained interesting information:

> Macao is a peninsula jutting out of the China mainland. It can be reached by jetfoil in an hour and a quarter from Hong Kong. Macao is a Portuguese province and will return to total mainland control in 1999. Its population, which is 500,000, has doubled since 1979.[12]

Many Chinese dialects are spoken in Macao, but the principal one is Cantonese—fifty percent. About thirty percent use Mandarin and there are about eighty thousand Minnan-speaking people. (Minnan is the same language as Taiwanese.) The people are less settled as many move back and forth across the China border. With less Christian influence than in Hong Kong, it is felt the people will be somewhat harder to win.

Macao Approved as Part of Hong Kong Field

At its first meeting of TEAM's second century, the board of directors on October 15 approved a plan to begin missionary service in Macao, looking in faith to the Lord to also make this a steppingstone of return to the land where almost a hundred years earlier the missionary ministry of TEAM had begun.

IRIAN JAYA AND JAVA

THE ISLAND OF NEW GUINEA

New Guinea, located several hundred miles north of Australia, is the largest island on the globe after Greenland. Though known to geographers and historians for over four centuries, it remained a place of mystery except for the coastal towns. The Australian government administered the eastern half of the island before granting self-government to Papua New Guinea in 1973 and independence in 1976.

The Netherlands government took control of the western half of the island in the nineteenth century, but its Dutch East Indies Company had controlling rights beginning about the year 1600. Because of the approximate balance in the Catholic and Protestant power in the homeland, those two religious groups were able to divide Netherlands New Guinea into two spheres of influence and virtual control—the Catholics along the south coast, and the Protestants along the north.

Interior Almost Impenetrable

Because of the rugged mountains with elevations from ten to sixteen thousand feet, the vast interior did not come under the same control. The interior remained hidden until high-flying airplanes began to cross and the aviators observed that there were a number of broad valleys—one of them the Baliem—and evidences of large numbers of people with cultivated fields.

The C&MA at Wissel Lakes

The Christian and Missionary Alliance (C&MA) opened an inland station in the Wissel Lakes area in the 1930s, but did no work with the coastal tribes because of the prior entry of the Dutch Reformed Church in the north and the Catholics in the south. These powerful religious groups had virtual veto power over the granting of visas to missionaries.

East Indies Independent Except New Guinea

When the Japanese surrendered in 1945, Indonesian nationalists led by Sukarno and Hatta, who had been exiled in 1933 for political activity, proclaimed a republic. There followed four years of fighting as the Dutch tried to retain possession of the rich archipelago from which they had profited greatly by importing raw material for their factories. In 1949 the Dutch ceded sovereignty to the Republic of Indonesia over all their East Indies possessions except the western half of New Guinea.

A Possible Field in Indonesia

TEAM had not considered entering Netherlands New Guinea, but with the independence of Indonesia, general director Johnson responded quickly to the suggestion that the mission try to open a field there. While attending a missionary conference in Los Angeles in 1949, he met Mr. and Mrs. Henry Hotvedt, who had been Salvation Army missionaries in the Netherlands East Indies. Upon Johnson's recommendation, the board voted to begin missionary work there and accepted the Hotvedts as candidates. They diligently prepared to go out, but were denied visas.

Erikson Offers for Service

About the same time, a letter was received from Walter J. Erikson, a graduate of Columbia Bible College, asking about the possibility of serving in Dutch New Guinea. His reference to New Guinea was misunderstood to refer to Dutch Guiana in South America. TEAM had no plans to enter Dutch Guiana but invited him to consider the new field of Indonesia.

Walter had been a member of the United States Coast Guard and on a trip into the South Seas had used some weeks of leave to join a party which trekked into the Wissel Lakes area. When he had heard of many unreached tribes in the interior, he had felt the Lord would have him serve there. I talked with the Rev. A. C. Snead, foreign secretary of the C&MA, to learn if there would be any possibility of Walter and other TEAM missionaries entering Netherlands New Guinea under sponsorship of that mission. Though I did not receive a negative response, neither did I receive a positive one. I assumed that any available visas would be wanted for C&MA missionaries.

To Java on a Student Visa

One possibility was to send Walter to Indonesia as a student of the Indonesian language which the Dutch also used in New Guinea, calling it Malay. The Indonesian government granted Walter a student visa and he left for Java in the summer of 1950.

The Dutch who remained in Indonesia after independence were subjected to severe pressures, even threats to their safety. Other Caucasians faced similar difficulties because it was not easy for the people to distinguish them from the Dutch. The American Consulate strongly urged Americans to evacuate.

Walter did not readily accept a premature cancellation of his plans and so went to the Dutch Consulate to learn if he could get a visa to enter the remaining Dutch territory, New Guinea. It so happened—in the leading of the Lord—that the Dutch Consular officials were annoyed at the virtual veto power the Protestant and Catholic churches held over the granting of visas and so seemed to jump at the chance to allow a representative of another mission to enter during this emergency.

Approval to Enter New Guinea

When Walter learned that he could get the required visa, he telephoned me from Java (apparently the first overseas call ever received in the TEAM office) and requested approval to make a survey of New Guinea as a future field for TEAM. Dr. Johnson, general director at the time, was traveling by car visiting churches in the western states and could not be easily reached. I reminded Walter that a decision to enter a new field was the responsibility of the general director and the board of directors, but as a decision was needed immediately, I took it upon myself to give approval for him to proceed. Upon learning the situation, Dr. Johnson readily agreed and the board followed with its approval.

Walter arrived in Hollandia, capital of Netherlands New Guinea, on January 1, 1951. When he conferred with government and Dutch Protestant authorities he found mixed reactions to his presence. The government officers were very cooperative. The Dutch church authorities were the opposite and sought by various means to put obstacles in his way.

How Walter succeeded in getting around the interior is a bit of a mystery. He may have traveled some by government planes and probably also had the help of the C&MA pilot. He spent some time in the central highlands where C&MA was beginning work in the Baliem Valley. He also visited missionaries of the Australian Baptist Mission, the Unevangelized Fields Mission (UFM), and the Regions Beyond Missionary Union (RBMU) who were seeking to begin work in the highlands. Missionary Aviation Fellowship (MAF) had begun air service for these missions.

A Base for TEAM in the Bird's Head

By early 1952, Walter had concluded that the areas having the least opportunity to hear the gospel were the Bird's Head in the north—so named because of its configuration—and the South Coast. The Dutch government authorities—without reference to the Dutch Protestant leadership—authorized him to begin work in the Bird's Head with a base at the northern coastal town of Manokwari. Visas were to be granted for ten TEAM missionaries. Housing was in short supply but the government gave permission to import prefabricated aluminum houses as needed.

Official Approval, Religious Opposition

The Dutch Protestant leaders did not take kindly to the entry of another mission into Manokwari and the Bird's Head. They claimed exclusive right to Christianize both the north coast and the scattered tribes of the interior. Their contact with the inland tribes was apparently limited to having native teachers itinerate from time to time enrolling the people in the Dutch Protestant Church and baptizing the infants. Even with no real conversion and no understanding of the gospel or the Christian life, these tribal people were considered Christianized and not the object of any missionary work.

Though the government was favorable to the presence of TEAM missionaries, the tension with the religious authorities persisted until the Indonesians took control in 1963 and abolished all mission comity arrangements.

Open Door for Missionaries

When TEAM was approved for entry into the Bird's Head, Walter notified the mission office that waiting appointees should apply for visas without delay. He also asked that we file information about TEAM with the Chicago Consulate of the Netherlands. Appointees ready to leave for the field in the summer of 1952 were Harold and Muriel Lovestrand and Edward Tritt. Beulah Stapf, Tritt's fiancee, was an appointee working temporarily in the TEAM office in Chicago. Eleanore Johnson, a missionary of the Evangelical Free Church in Belgian Congo (Zaire), was engaged to Walter and was waiting for word that the way was clear to join him.

Tritt Joins Erikson

Tritt was the first to be ready. He arrived in Manokwari in July 1952. There he found that Eibrink Jansen, a local Dutch official, had invited Erikson to join him on a survey trip into the Kebar and Karoon areas of the Bird's Head, a potential field for TEAM. Would Tritt want to join the survey? Tritt's baggage and "prefab" would not arrive for several months so this would be a good time to become acquainted with a possible future area of service. Tritt was willing to go. He used the waiting period to begin a study of the Malay-Indonesian language.

Bird's Head Survey Undertaken

On September 10, the scheduled date to begin the survey, Jansen was delayed by government business but with five carriers hired and preparations completed it was decided that Erikson and Tritt should go ahead. After four or five weeks, when anticipated reports from Erikson did not reach Jansen, he became concerned. Then when he received a message from carrier Jeremias Waridjo that they had guided the men into the interior and had left them because of some difficulties, he became alarmed for the men's safety and prepared a search. At least two other patrols were active in the search at other points.

Local Concern for Men's Safety Deepens

Being suspicious that there was more to the story than Waridjo had told, Jansen asked him to serve as guide for the search party. Jansen's patrol started inland on October 27, following the planned route of Erikson and Tritt.

Meanwhile, the only details known to the TEAM office were that a survey was to take place. Knowing that the men would not be able to communicate for six weeks to two months there was no alarm at the silence.

TEAM Receives Stunning News

On the morning of November 6, 1952, Beulah Stapf was at the TEAM office switchboard when a telegram was called in by Western Union with the message, "Received telephone call. Bodies of Erikson Tritt New Guinea found." The news had come from Shirley Rose, a missionary of the C&MA, and was relayed by Duane Johnson who was serving temporarily at TEAM's West Coast Center.

Beulah typed up the message and delivered it promptly to Dr.

Johnson's desk. Who can tell the deep shock and emotion she felt as she received this word about Walter Erikson and particularly about Ed Tritt, her fiancé, whom she hoped to join in New Guinea within a few months? Her poise, calm faith, and acceptance gave eloquent testimony to her complete dedication to the will of the Lord. (Beulah did go on to the field and served at Anggi Lakes in the Manikion tribe. Later she married a missionary serving under another mission on a North American field.)

"Except a Corn of Wheat..."

I was attending a conference of the IFMA in Chattanooga, Tennessee, and was scheduled to speak at the forenoon session when I was summoned to receive a long distance call. Dr. Johnson was on the phone to give me the sad news of the death of Walter and Ed, two young men with whom I had worked in their preparations for the field, and whom I admired and respected highly. I felt led to change my message to one based on John 12:24: "Except a corn of wheat fall into the ground and die...." I shared the news I had just received and told something of the call, preparation, and dedication of these two young men.

After the service a young couple came up to speak with me. They said they had met Walter and now felt that the Lord would have them go out to help fill the vacancy the death of these two missionaries had left. They were Ronald and Charlene Hill, students at Tennessee Temple University. They were obedient to the heavenly vision and in the centennial year 1990 were continuing to add to their thirty-four years in the Lord's service on that mission field.

Lovestrands Receive News En Route

Harold and Muriel Lovestrand had left for New Guinea more than a month before the news of the death of the first two and only TEAM missionaries on the field. Knowing of their anticipated stop in Malaysia, I sent off a full letter with all the information I could give them. Conscious of the shock and consternation this news would cause I tried to give words of encouragement and support as they would be faced with an entry to their lifework now made doubly difficult. I also wrote to the Dutch official, Eibrink Jansen, about their expected arrival and asked that they be received representing TEAM. Mr. Jansen was very helpful and in time we learned what he had done to investigate the tragic deaths.

Dutch Official's Investigation

After picking up more information along the way as he approached the Kebar area, Jansen confronted Waridjo and got his confession:

> About four o'clock on the morning of September 27, Waridjo cut the ropes of the hammocks in which Erikson and Tritt were sleeping and with the other carriers fell upon the missionaries with machetes and wooden clubs. Tritt died at the place of attack but Erikson succeeded in freeing himself from the hammock and evidently crawled to a cave on the river bank, where he died. The bearers hid the supplies and took the more valuable articles of equipment with them. The Dutch officials believe the motive for the murder to have been robbery.[1]

Motive? Robbery or Fear?

While robbery may have been one motive it apparently was not the only one. When the effects of the missionaries were recovered, it was found that the journal kept by one of the men mentioned that the carriers, being men from the more civilized coastal area, were becoming increasingly fearful of encountering hostile tribes as they proceeded inland. They wanted to turn back and the day before had attempted to desert. At least one of the carriers had a gun in his possession. One of the missionaries took custody of the gun as a precaution. Robbery may have been the motive or at least an afterthought, but fear of the unknown may have been the strongest motive leading to an act of desperation.

Witness Given to Murderers

The carriers most implicated received prison sentences. When Dr. Johnson visited Manokwari in 1953, he asked to see the prisoners:

> Opportunity was given me, in company with brother Harold Lovestrand, to visit four of the five murderers at the prison in Manokwari. The following day we visited the fifth one, who was in the hospital. I sought to speak to them through interpretation. It was not easy. They were exhorted to turn to Christ. Only one of them can read a little, and he was given a New Testament by brother Lovestrand.... I told them that we forgive them for their murderous act and that I knew if Walter and Edward could bring them a message from eternity, it would evidence a forgiving spirit. I also told them that God would forgive them if they confessed their sin to Him and accepted His provision of salvation for them in and through the Lord Jesus Christ.[2]

Some thirty years later, one of the guilty carriers received Christ. He later was baptized and became a member of the local church.

Martyrs for the Gospel?

Paul Sheetz, editor of the mission's magazine, raised a point for consideration:

> We have applied the term martyrs to them in a general way, but now the question may be raised by some whether, in the light of this motive [robbery], we can rightly call them martyrs....[3]

The editor then discussed situations in which missionaries have lost lives and concluded that Erikson and Tritt willingly took risks to extend the gospel to lost and needy people even though in this instance they were not confronted with a choice of loyalty to the faith. They confirmed the faith by their obedience to the Spirit's leading. "Whatever reservations we may put on the use of the word martyr, we must generally agree that the Lord has set aside martyrs' crowns for Walter Erikson and Edward Tritt."[4]

Lives Offered Spark Wider Interest

The news of the deaths of Erikson and Tritt had a profound effect on students at the Columbia Bible College, where both had studied, and in particular on those who had known them. Scores of letters were received at the TEAM headquarters. Students at Columbia Bible College began collecting funds to finance purchase of a plane to be used by Missionary Aviation Fellowship in Netherlands New

Guinea in their memory.

Most noteworthy was the surge of young men and women applying to go to the unreached tribes in this primitive region. Within four years TEAM sent to the field no less than nineteen new workers in addition to the Lovestrands: Forrest and Dorothy Thorsby, Beulah Stapf, Charles and Bernita Preston, Calvin and Ruth Roesler, Henry and Marjorie Bock, Coral Tromp, Gladys Willems, Joyce Ratzlaff, Richard and Charlotte Griffiths, Jack Manly, Ronald and Charlene Hill, and Robert and Doris Frazier.

Dealing with Housing Needs

Preparations for serving in New Guinea were by no means easy. In addition to normal study of Bible and missions courses, each appointee was required to acquire training in linguistics and translation. Though the missionary outfit could be more modest in some respects, considering the primitive situation, it was more complex in another way. The major item for each couple to provide was a transportable house of prefabricated aluminum.

For one missionary who would be serving along the rivers of the South Coast the major piece was a shallow-draft river launch. All had to seek the Lord's supply of large outgoing transportation funds including the cost of setting up in some remote tribal area. The Lord set his stamp of approval by providing what was needed by these pioneering workers.

The Lovestrands were given a warm welcome and much help by the Dutch official, Eibrink Jansen. The prefabricated house sent out by Tritt was set up close to the small wooden building Erikson had erected. These two buildings served as headquarters for the anticipated growth of TEAM's staff and work. Jansen invited Lovestrand to accompany him on an inland tour to find the location of the temporary graves of Erikson and Tritt and to look for groups of people among whom TEAM missionaries might work.

Placement of New Missionaries

When the new recruits had completed their study in the Malay-

Indonesian language, the concern was to locate the best and most needy places to enter, reduce tribal languages to writing, and make beginnings in Scripture translation and evangelism. Accordingly, Lovestrand, Thorsby, Manly, and Preston made a seven-week trek through the mountainous interior not too far from the coastal towns of Manokwari and Ransiki.

Bird's Head Survey

The area surveyed may seem "not too far" on the map but reaching there on foot was another matter. Preston described the trek:

> Although we travelled from early morning until mid-afternoon, we covered only about five miles each day. All the terrain was rugged and rough. The trail led either straight up or straight down, and much of the time the path went over nothing but roots of trees. There were no plains in the valleys.[5]

The survey resulted in the selection of two sites for work: Anggi Lakes in the Manikion tribe, and Testega in what was thought to be the Meyah tribe. The Bocks, Beulah Stapf, and Gladys Willems were assigned to Anggi Lakes; the Thorsbys to Testega.

Initial Problems

After the Thorsbys had set up their "prefab" at Testega, two problems confronted them which resulted in their being transferred back to Manokwari. One was that they discovered that they were not located in an area of pure Meyah. The people seemed to speak a mixture of Meyah and Manikion. Obviously, if they were to reduce the language to writing as a basis for translating Scripture, they needed to be in the center of the tribe where there was little mixture of language. The second problem was a broken leg which Dorothy sustained and which made walking on the rough terrain out of the question.

A Need Met in Manokwari

The Thorsbys' transfer to Manokwari solved a problem for the mission. With a growing field there was an increasing amount of administrative work to care for. They were assigned to this work and yet could pursue an active ministry among the local people in the Malay trade language. According to the testimony of Doming-gus Major, a respected Irianese leader in the church ministry, it was the testimony and discipling by Thorsby that molded his life in service for Christ.

Four to Anggi Lakes

At Anggi Lakes Henry and Marjorie Bock began to reduce the previously unwritten Manikion language, while Gladys Willems and Beulah Stapf set about to minister to the people who from every appearance greatly needed much help.

When I visited New Guinea in 1956 and had opportunity to fly in by chartered single-motor plane over the high mountains to Anggi Lakes, I met people who impressed me as being the most depressed, diseased, and dirty people I had seen up to that time on any continent. One great problem was the widespread affliction with yaws, which Webster's Dictionary describes as "a tropical infectious disease caused by a spirochete and characterized by raspberrylike skin eruptions followed by destructive lesions of the skin and bones."

A second disfiguring affliction of many of the women and girls was their cosmetic use of resin or pitch on their cheeks which would often crack, splitting the skin and flesh with it, and opening the face to serious infections. Both yaws and the facial infections responded well to penicillin therapy.

One prescription for all who came to the simple dispensary was to go to the nearby brook and wash thoroughly before receiving treatment. That was not the easiest medicine to take in this high altitude with its perpetual chill, but it worked wonders for the outward appearance.

Four years later, when I visited this same tribe, I was amazed at the changed appearance of the people at Anggi Lakes. For the most part they were clean and free from visible sores. The medical help must be given great credit, but the look on the faces of new

Christians was a significant part of the change.

South Coast Survey

In 1955, Charles Preston and Harold Lovestrand made the long trip to the South Coast to survey tribal areas in the swampy marshes. The land south of the central mountain range is a vast area of low-lying, water-logged mangrove thickets, laced by many tide-level rivers. Native villages are to be seen along some of the river banks. The only communication is through travel by dugout canoe. The Dutch officials approved of TEAM's desire to develop a ministry among truly neglected people who had received little attention from either the government or the Catholic mission.

Asmats, Agats, and Mud

One of the major tribes encountered was the Asmat, about 50,000 in number, and scattered over a large area. The Dutch had established a small administrative post at the tide-level village of Agats on the banks of the large Eilanden river. I had heard that the village and administrative post were located in mud, but I did not understand the full significance of that description until I visited there in 1960.

There were only two ways to get around Agats. One was by dugout canoe in the few existing channels. The second was to use the elevated walkways connecting some of the buildings. To give me some idea of the mud, Jim Hyatt easily pushed a sixteen-foot pole deep into the mud and still did not reach a solid base.

Missionaries Assigned to Asmat Work

When Calvin and Ruth Roesler were assigned to the Asmat tribe to do linguistic and translation work, the place selected was the upstream village of Ayam, which stretched along a river bank for a mile and a half. Charles and Bernita Preston were assigned to Agats. Leaving Ruth and Bernita to come later, Calvin and Charles went ahead to set up their "prefabs" and begin work. Receiving a welcome from the chiefs of Ayam, the men went there in February 1956 to make a beginning.

A Rough Beginning in Ayam

One night soon after their arrival, Preston and Roesler heard an unusual commotion in the village. The mystery was solved when they learned the next day that the local residents had tricked several canoe loads of upstream villagers into believing that past animosities had been settled and welcomed them to find shelter for the night.

The Ayamers treacherously rose up against them in the darkness and killed twenty-nine. A cannibal feast followed. This was indeed quite a reception to hoped-for peaceful living and working conditions! Notwithstanding this gruesome introduction, the Roeslers settled in Ayam and the Prestons in Agats and have given thirty-five years of service to the Lord for these people.

Plane and Boat Transport

If missionaries were to get around the vast area of the Asmats, some provision of transport was necessary. This was solved in five ways. Missionary Aviation Fellowship (MAF), which already served several other missions, was invited to serve TEAM on the South Coast as it did in the north. Missionaries also used dugout canoes rigged with outboard motors, but these were tricky, with a tendency to roll over. Several had very close calls. Some used small boats with outboard motors for nearby trips. A larger freight boat, Mappi, was used for the inland rivers.

One other boat recommended by the field council was a thirty-foot shallow-draft launch suitable for longer river trips. Robert Frazier was asked to procure this boat, which he named *Pengindjil*—"the evangel." It went into service on the South Coast in October 1956 with Frazier in charge.

Territorial Expansion

Over the next seven years missionaries entered a number of new tribal areas. In the north, Richard and Charlotte Griffiths took up work among the Hatam people in the Bird's Head and opened a station at Minyambou. In the south, missionaries were stationed at

Kokenau and Amar in the Mimika tribe.

Dr. Kenneth and Sylvia Dresser began medical work among the Asmat people living along the coast at Pirimapun, on Cook Bay. Don and Joan Gregory began a station at Saman, several hours upriver by outboard motorboat from Pirimapun. Stations were also opened at Abahoi and Nohon in the Auyu tribe and Kawem.

One Asmat station was opened at Yaosakor on the Eilanden River. This station was also to double as a base for MAF planes serving the South Coast. At Yaosakor there was a stretch of land at about sea level which was out of water enough to permit development of an air strip. Wheel planes bringing people and supplies from the north could land there and transfer their passengers to a float plane to reach other river stations in the south.

Along the coast west of Agats, Larry and Shirley Rascher opened a station at Sumapero. The station at Kawem was later turned over to the Regions Beyond Missionary Union because of linguistic considerations.

Johnson Determines to Visit South Coast

David Johnson visited the field in 1957 and after seeing the work on the north coast wanted to visit the south. The missionaries mentioned that the *Pengindjil* was at Kokenau, quite distant from Agats. When Johnson asked why it could not travel directly across open sea to Agats, missionaries informed him that being of shallow draft the boat was not seaworthy and must be piloted through the interconnecting rivers, which limited travel to daylight hours. Trees in the water and overhanging branches were too great a hazard in the dark of night.

Johnson was eager not to miss that part of the field and offered to sit on the prow with a flashlight keeping watch for logs and branches. This he did for the two nights required for the round trip. He not only had opportunity to see the Asmats but also taught a lesson in determination and persistence.

Beginnings of a Bible Institute

In the coastal town of Manokwari lived several tribal groups, with people from the islands of Biak and Numfoor and others from the interior. Once in the town, many learned enough Malay to communicate in this trade language. When TEAM missionaries settled in Manokwari and nearby Sowi, they held Bible studies in Malay for adults and children.

Lovestrand began teaching some of the young men at a Bible school level of instruction, and these first classes developed into the Erikson-Tritt Bible Institute in Sowi. For some years no students from tribes where TEAM was working enrolled, but this changed when young people in the tribes began to get schooling in the Malay (later Indonesian) language and could be accepted into the institute. Douglas Miller and Robert Lenz were active in the training ministry in its early years.

Need for a Ministry in Depth

When I visited the field in 1960, I was impressed by the very real accomplishments of new missionaries going into primitive areas, establishing simple but adequate homes, learning a second language, and getting into linguistic reduction, literacy training, translation, and evangelistic witness. However, I was somewhat concerned that they had allowed themselves to be spread too thinly. In some instances a missionary couple bore the full responsibility in one tribal group.

I had prepared a series of Bible studies based on Acts 20 which I referred to as Paul's pattern of a "ministry in depth." I noted later that the field council gave serious consideration to placing enough workers in one tribe to care for linguistic work, translation, literacy, and evangelism, plus the important work of teaching the Word and guiding new believers into a biblical church relationship. Although it did delay expansion into new tribal areas, this emphasis bore fruit when mature believers from one tribe were able to serve as missionaries to another.

Indonesia Takes Control

The Republic of Indonesia continued to agitate against the Dutch presence in New Guinea and from time to time landed raiding parties to attack Dutch outposts. Indonesia claimed that Netherlands New Guinea should belong to it. Actually the people were more closely related by heredity and culture to Papua New Guinea than they were to those of Malay background in Indonesia. However, the trade language in the west was Malay, related to Indonesian, which gave it a close tie to the republic. Because of the continued pressure and agitation, Holland turned the territory over to the United Nations in 1962 and to Indonesia in April 1963.

From this time the territory known as Netherlands New Guinea went through several name changes: West Irian, Irian Barat, Irian Jaya, and is sometimes just referred to as Irian. Hollandia, the capital, is now Jayapura.

Foreseeing that this change in sovereignty could have a great effect on the work of missions, Dr. Louis L. King, foreign secretary of the C&MA, invited home and field leaders to meet in Hollandia at the time of the change. The missions represented were C&MA, MAF, UFM International, Australian Baptist, RBMU International, and TEAM. Henry Bock and Charles Preston represented the field and I, the home administration.

Positive Results of Consultation

Some important understandings came out of that consultation. One of the most important was comity. The missions working in the highlands stated that the Dutch Reformed national workers were coming into the highland tribes contrary to comity arrangements, but were objecting if the missions working there wanted to minister to people from the interior who had settled on the north coast.

The matter was easily settled when it was learned that the Indonesian government (probably its religious affairs bureau) had declared all comity arrangements non-binding. This was good news for TEAM because it was continuing to receive pressure from the Dutch Reformed workers even though its presence in Manokwari and the Bird's Head was by Dutch government permission and assignment.

On a second important matter, the problem of finding Christian primary teachers for tribal children, the mission leaders arrived at a joint solution. Under the Dutch regime, the only source of teachers was the Protestant foundation and it was almost impossible to find a truly Christian teacher. It seemed better to go without a school than to have the children come under the influence of an immoral teacher. With the government now being Indonesian, Christian teachers could be imported from Java or Kalimantan. It was decided to set up an evangelical school foundation to find, process, and place teachers with the missions having need. The education of Christian children could now continue, offering the promise of trained Christian workers in the future.

A third decision related to the Missions Fellowship in Irian Jaya. Agreement was reached on important principles limiting membership to evangelical groups only.

A fourth decision was to set up the Inter-Mission Business Office in Jakarta to serve the missions in visa applications, government relations, travel arrangements, etc.

A fifth decision concerned an elementary school for missionary children. C&MA agreed to take responsibility to provide a school, with other missions free to open associated hostels for their own children. High-school-age children would have to study elsewhere.

Entry Restrictions

Candidate secretary Delbert Kuehl reported in 1963 that nineteen appointees were preparing to go to Irian Jaya but were hindered by failure to obtain visas from the new Indonesian government. Many of these appointees eventually accepted assignments on other fields. In the years that followed, only a few new missionaries were allowed to enter Irian Jaya, so hopes for expansion to new tribal areas were realized to only a limited degree.

Evidence of Spirit's Working

After attending the missions consultation in Hollandia I visited most of the stations and was impressed by the very evident beginning of a work of the Spirit in several places. When I went with Charles Preston on Easter Sunday to visit some Asmat villages, I found that there were now a number of transformed people among these former cannibals. At one village located on a riverbank we were greeted and helped up the muddy slope by the old village chief.

Preston's introductory explanation was: "This fellow has eaten his share of people in his day."

My flash thought was: "I hope he doesn't care for an American dish."

But I rejoiced at meeting one for whom the new birth was indeed an outstanding miracle. As I shook hands with the old chief he was pointing to his heart while Preston interpreted his words. "Now I have the Lord in here."

With Cannibals Easter Sunday

I was asked to speak to the villagers crowded into one hut and I was glad to do so on this Easter Sunday. Who can say how much spiritual truth penetrated the hearts of these pagan listeners who yet seemed to give rapt attention. The glory of the gospel is that it truly does become the message of life to change darkened hearts—even some who hear it for the first time.

A stray thought which intruded as I looked out over this group of mostly naked people was the contrast with Easter services in our homeland churches, where many come dressed in Easter finery. What were the Lord's thoughts as He looked down from heaven? Surely—"man looks on the outward appearance, but the Lord looks on the heart."

Hospital Ministry Begun

Another stop was at Pirimapun with Dr. and Mrs. Ken Dresser. It had not been easy to give medical help to the Asmat people even though they had pressing physical needs. A wall of suspicion had to be surmounted. It was not until a very serious case of strangulated hernia was presented and Dresser operated with excellent results that the doubters were won over. By the time of my visit in April 1963 the people in surrounding villages had learned the value of the offered medical and surgical help.

Dispensary Building Erected

To better serve the many now coming for help, a moderate-sized hospital building had been constructed and was to be dedicated during my visit. As news of the dedication spread to the villages in the area, the people decided to celebrate the occasion in typical Asmat style.

In the late afternoon of the day before the dedication, hundreds of people—the men completely naked except for a few bone ornaments and the women with only skimpy grass aprons—began to assemble. They "danced" all through the night by jumping up and down while chanting endlessly in a monotone. How they could continue through the long hours even when rain showers fell was more than I could understand, especially as they looked so emaciated.

Medical Work and Gospel Explained

When the sun had been up an hour or two, the missionaries took advantage of the presence of so many people to explain the purpose of the hospital. Don Gregory from Saman gave a clear gospel message. Newly arrived local Indonesian officials attended and later invited the missionaries to visit their post to explain the mission's ministry, particularly what they perceived as the missionaries' reluctance to make common cause with Catholic teachers in the area. The missionaries' explanation of the distinctives of the evangelical message and their assurance that they had no desire to attack the Catholics seemed to satisfy the officials.

Ocean Waves Threaten

Over the next decade the hospital work, accompanied by evangelism and teaching, bore fruit in a congregation of believers being assembled in Pirimapun. The living church was built on a solid foundation and continued after the air strip was destroyed by the ocean waves and the buildings were threatened. Within ten years the waves had taken their toll and Dr. Dresser decided that the hospital would have to be moved before the waves finished their destruction—no easy matter when it seemed impossible to find land with enough elevation to avoid the tides.

Mass Movement Among the Hatam

I had heard of mass movements—or what some call community movements—among the central highland tribes and was not quite sure how to interpret the phenomenon. These movements involved most of the people within the community abandoning their former fetishes and confidence in magic. Were these movements an effort to gain some political or economic advantage, matters about which the tribes knew almost nothing? Were they a symptom of disillusionment with tribal religious practices by their witch doctors? Were they an indication of their weariness of inter-tribal fighting? Were they a response—mostly in ignorance—to some fragmentary information about Christianity? Or were they a definite moving of the Spirit of God on the people?

One suggested explanation seemed reasonable. It was observed that the people were weary of living in constant fear of evil spirits, which were thought to confront them at every turn. They wanted deliverance from the fear and futility that characterized their lives. The fragments of information they had heard about the God the missionaries were introducing seemed to offer them relief.

Though this may be the explanation, there must also have been the sovereign moving of the Spirit of God in these circumstances which brought large groups to a hearing of the message of life and encouraged a transformation which prepared them to become lights in a dark place.

A Firsthand View

My tour of April 1963 included the Minyambou station. The small MAF plane, taking off from Manokwari, had to circle to gain height as it neared the mountains so it could safely clear the 9,000 foot ridge. Looking down across the mountain there seemed to be only ridges and canyons but no place where a plane could land. Suddenly I became aware of an airstrip seemingly hanging on the slope of a mountain. The view may have been distorted by the banking of the plane as we swooped down for the landing. Dick Griffiths met the plane to help unload cargo.

Upon landing, my attention was directed to a group of people along the edge of the strip and others coming toward us. Dick explained that these were Hatam villagers giving up their fetishes. So many fetishes had already been brought in by others that Dick had set up a temporary shack of pole and bark into which these heathen objects of worship could be stacked, awaiting the time the people would gather together and consign the fetishes to the flames, completely repudiating their magic powers.

Not the First Such Movement

I learned that this was not the beginning of the mass movement among the Hatam. In their annual personal report for 1962, the Griffiths wrote:

> One of the most encouraging occasions took place on Christmas day when we witnessed scores of men from eleven villages bring not only their fetishes, potions, magic, and weapons, but also their prized poison plants, which are the source of their power. All these things were brought and discarded in an impressive manner, as they said they would no longer fear or follow the devil, but prepare their hearts to follow the Lord. Taking care to explain the gospel to them, and the origin and nature of sin, we encouraged them to individually ask forgiveness from the Lord, because only He could wash away all their sin and give them clean hearts. This whole movement, which has spread to sixteen other villages, seems to be socially motivated, in that each one wants to be sure that the other has given up everything, so as to make the area safe for all. However, we see an opportunity for

the Lord to work, and could wish we had a dozen lives that could go to work among the villages, pointing men to Christ.[6]

Need for Grounding in the Word

Griffiths did not make the mistake of assuming that this remarkable movement itself had power to carry the professed converts on to Christian maturity. He was fully aware of the need to teach scriptural truth, because growth and maturity would come only as the Spirit made the Word real to hearts. This need revealed a major problem. There were only scattered Bible verses in the Hatam language and the people could not read even these few.

Selecting Men to Study

Literacy classes were a high priority. With the mass movement affecting so many, Griffiths found village leaders among those who had given up their fetishes. As an example to the people, he selected leaders to learn to read, choosing the number three man in the village because he observed that the chief may have felt above becoming a learner, while the second man in line seemed too occupied with responsibilities delegated by the chief. The third man seemed the most logical choice.

The first class consisted of twenty-three of these third-level leaders. Griffiths worked with them to be sure they understood the gospel and were personally converted. He then taught them the mysteries of alphabet letters, words, and simple sentences, using newly translated gospel verses as the lesson material. His aim from the beginning was not just to teach these men to read, but to train them to teach others.

Beginning Readers Become Church Leaders

All or most of these twenty-three went on to become not only literacy instructors, but also spiritual leaders as the believers were formed into village congregations. Training enough leaders for the many village congregations posed a challenge. Leaders would have to qualify as elders and deacons as outlined in the New Testament. Pastors would be selected from among the elders. How would apt-to-teach men be found when the best were only pre-primary level readers and, furthermore, had little to read in the Hatam language? A Bible institute was out of the question.

The answer was found in what Griffiths called "witness schools." A beginning was made in 1963 and for the year 1964 he reported:

> In January, 93 men came from 62 Hatam and Manikion villages, representing well over 5,500 people. They enrolled in the second session of a witness school which lasted until July. Since enrolling, several of the men have moved their families to Minyambou and built their houses here. What used to be a little village with five houses and 74 residents has developed into a population center with twenty houses around the airstrip, bringing the census of our main valley to about 1,200. The advanced class which enrolled in the witness school were candidates for baptism.[7]

Witness Bears Fruit

The presence of these new Christians from outlying villages made an impact on those closer at hand:

> Minyambou and surrounding village residents also desired to enter the candidate class for baptism. After completing their eight-month candidacy satisfactorily, 59 local residents, including several from the witness school, publicly expressed their desire to be identified with Christ in baptism. This service was witnessed by over 1,000 of their relatives. In another area twenty miles away, 15 more men were baptized a week later while 750 looked on. All 74 who were baptized have not only passed the doctrine course but have also confessed that their old ways and habits have been forsaken and replaced by new life in Christ. These were organized to become the first national Hatam church in December. Two pastors were chosen, one for each language group, as well as four deacons.[8]

In the Pattern of the First Century

Some who read the reports may jump to the conclusion that the new Christians were being pushed too rapidly, but for these new believers the experience was much like that in the New Testament places where Paul preached, souls were saved, converts were counseled and instructed, and elders and deacons were appointed.

These Hatam people were truly born from above, had forsaken the old ways of life, and were demonstrating that their citizenship was now in heaven. Their later missionary outreach gave further evidence of the transformation that had occurred in the individuals, in the community, and in the tribe.

The 1964 the annual report showed continued victory in the tribe as a wonderful year came to a close:

> The third session of witness school was about to begin and over 500 inquirers were soon to enter the second baptism class.[9]

Feeding the Churches

The growth in the churches is told succinctly in Griffiths' annual reports:

> During the year [1965] our ministry involved teaching Bible lessons and courses mainly for the young church leaders. Charlotte presided over the revision of our literacy material as well as counseling the teaching assistants, and teaching her own class. Dick prepared lessons and courses, translating them for the school and the young church. The main translation accomplishment was a booklet entitled *Way of Salvation* containing about 175 Bible verses. The booklet was checked and revised four times before its publication. Various Hatam hymns were also compiled, edited, and incorporated into a short hymnbook for literate Hatam people. During the year the young church has grown numerically and, we trust, spiritually.[10]

Portents of Trouble

Griffiths alluded to a cloud on the political horizon in his report for 1965. "During June and months following, the government succeeded in putting down a local rebellion, the repercussions of which extended all the way to Minyambou."

In September 1965 the Indonesian military detained Harold Lovestrand for questioning in Manokwari (see chapter 23) on the false assumption that he was in some way helping the rebel cause. This rebellion affected the tribes in the Bird's Head and continued for about five years. Minyambou became a base for the army:

> These have been unusual months [in 1968] as we have lived in the shadow of a sweeping military operation which has caused needless disruption of the ministry here.... July, August, Novem-

ber, and December were the months when the church leaders came to Bible school where Dick teaches and counsels. Charlotte resumed direction of the literacy program for these men and other adults as well. Although some of the [tribal] leaders have sided with anti-government forces and have been killed or driven off, it was thrilling to hear the testimonies of those who have continued to work for the Lord during the difficult months of September and October. Many of them lived out in the jungles in caves and holes after seeing the churches burned down, their homes ransacked, and their gardens plundered.[11]

Rebel Action in Other Tribes

The Manikion and Meyah tribes were similarly affected by the rebellion and what has been written about the Hatam experience could be repeated for the work at Anggi Lakes and Testega. By the end of 1970 there was light at the end of the tunnel:

> The year ended after an uphill struggle that found us on a mountain top. The five-year anti-government rebellion drew to a close in November. The two and a half year military occupation of Minyambou ended in December. This meant that we could begin 1971 with an unobstructed view toward expanded outreach and unhindered evangelism and Bible teaching. Programs curtailed during most of 1970 could soon be restarted with the return of the Douglas Millers in early 1971. After seven years of short-term Bible schools for the church leaders, plans were under way to add a full-term course for six resident students and their wives.... Translation has progressed to Acts 18 in the Hatam language. In short, the whole Christian community—numbering several thousand—were experiencing a feeling of deliverance and freedom after years of oppression.[12]

Peace Allows Forward Movement

With the deliverance from the tribal turmoil the work could go forward as Griffiths hoped. Doug Miller took over responsibility for local students in the Bible school. The Millers' presence at Minyambou beginning in December 1966 made possible a sharing of responsibility in the ministry.

After a period of studying the Hatam language, Miller shared in teaching and counseling and in the outreach to all the villages in the Hatam tribe. Julie Miller, a registered nurse, took charge of the medical program, which included not only treatment of the sick who came to the clinic but also the training of medical assistants to work in the villages.

Pressing on with Translation

Health problems intervened from time to time and robbed the Griffiths of valuable time they needed for translation and literacy work. Yet they continued to press on:

> Dick has been greatly encouraged by the progress made in the translation program. The first drafts of Galatians and Mark have been completed and checked. Soon Mark will be in the hands of the Hatam church as Galatians has been since October [1974]. Two Hatam nationals have been a great help to us in this program. One is Alpons Iwou who continues to check translation drafts here at Minyambou and the other is Michael Iwou. Michael is a ninth grader in school in the central highlands who has attended the translation institute for nationals. He sends initial drafts for checking here.
>
> Charlotte also has been greatly encouraged by the progress made in the literacy program with the help of Petrus Nuham, her literacy assistant, who headed up the program during our recent furlough. No new primers have been undertaken since coming back from furlough, however, since we are facing a possible revision of the Hatam orthography. On top of this program she began teaching the church leaders' wives in regular Bible school sessions last fall.[13]

A Huge Spelling Problem

"Orthography" is a big word with a simple meaning: any style or way of spelling. Yet a change in spelling can present a huge problem to the linguist and translator. With Netherlands New Guinea having been under Dutch rule the phonetic values of Dutch were applied to the tribal languages. One example: "j" represents the "y" sound as used in English and Indonesian. What the Dutch designated as Mejah for the tribe became Meyah under Indonesia. Menjambo became Minyambou. The change had definite advantages but the changeover required a great deal of work:

> The Hatam language was upgraded with a new orthography early in the year [1975]. The results of this improvement have been

readily observable in the literacy program as well in the facility with which the Scriptures can be read both publicly and privately.... All the former literacy materials went out in the trash with the old orthography, necessitating an entirely new literacy thrust in the villages. During the year Charlotte conducted four short-term sessions to introduce the new orthography to around 40 village teachers as well as to about 30 church leaders.[14]

Concern for the Churches

When the Apostle Paul listed the burdens he bore and the hardships endured, he added, "Besides everything else, I face daily the pressure of my concern for the churches" (II Corinthians 11:28). His words are echoed in Griffiths' report:

Overshadowing all is our continuing task of planting churches in Hatam-land. For us this entails daily encouraging the believers, counseling the leaders, and desperately trying to steer the young church on a Biblical course to avoid both disruptive animistic hangovers and deadening western-oriented traditional practices. May the Lord help us to be sensitive and discerning![15]

The missionaries were not alone in bearing the concern for the churches. Of the many ordained pastors of the churches throughout the tribe whom the Word of God had transformed, one mentioned particularly as an example of a life changed and elevated to spiritual strength was pastor Habel Iwou.

Community Development

As the Hatam church grew, other events were taking place which impacted the work. The Indonesian government wanted the inland tribes to be "civilized" and had a few limited programs to accomplish that objective, but missionaries realized that these programs could also open the door to efforts to Islamize the people.

The Hatam leaders also began to think of the large number of children who sickened and died. They were grateful for the way they had been helped spiritually. Now could there be some help for their pressing physical needs? Seed thoughts planted by Dr. Winchell and a visiting friend of the Griffiths, Mrs. Dorothy Gorton, helped the missionaries become concerned that they lead the way in community improvements which would forestall the introduction of undesirable elements. When World Vision expressed interest, Doug Miller presented a detailed proposal which was approved in 1980.

The resulting Minyambou Community Development Project was an ambitious undertaking designed to meet major needs in the tribe, the greatest being to improve the nutrition of the people. Up to then, fifty percent of all children were buried by their parents. The project included agricultural development, animal husbandry, health care, family planning, sanitation, supply of pure water for the villages, gaining marketable skills, etc.[16]

Necessary Cautions

While recognizing the need to better the living conditions of the people, the missionaries were concerned that disproportionate time would be involved in upgrading the livelihood of the people at the expense of the spiritual ministries. Griffiths addressed this concern in his 1981 report:

> The Hatam church is sadly in need of a well-trained corps of leaders able to pastor their primitive flocks and preach Spirit-filled messages. May the temporal advantages of better living conditions not consume all our time and efforts in behalf of the Christian community.[17]

The concern was justified, as Griffiths sadly reported in the Minyambou station report:

> During much of 1981 the Hatam church was groaning under the attack of Satan due to a few key young people and church leaders falling into sin. Church attendance was way down and the leaders were very concerned. In September the church leaders had special times of prayer for revival in their lives and in the churches. Out of this came six weeks of special meetings throughout the tribe in November and December. As a result, 114 adherents were counseled for salvation and 550 believers for rededication. It was reported a few months ago that the churches were again full and there is evidence of revival among the believers. To date there are 10,889 adherents in 77 local congregations. There were 382 baptisms in the conference year. Active ordained pastors and evangelists number 157, and there are 105 unordained active church leaders.[18]

"To All Bird's Head Tribes by 1983"

Once Doug and Julie Miller had settled into the work in the Hatam tribe, Doug began to think seriously about the other tribes in the Bird's Head. He had heard of the Sebena (Moskona) people when he first came to Irian Jaya in 1960. It was rumored that they lived in trees, had tails, and were cannibals. Miller decided he would make that tribe a special object of prayer. In his annual report for 1971 he revealed that his prayer was more closely focused:

> We are praying that the elusive Sebena, who live 50 feet high in trees, will be reached with the gospel this coming year. Our personal prayer goal is that by next June the first trek will have been made into the Sebena.[19]

Initial Contacts

After a number of fly-overs to learn all that could be observed from the air and a period of dropping get-acquainted gifts, Miller, Doug Eager from the nearby Meyah tribal work at Testega, and several Hatam church leaders—one of whom spoke Moskona— made a survey trip in early 1973. One rumor was true; the people lived in houses about 50 feet up in the trees as protection from their enemies. The second was not; they did not have tails! As to the third, the human bone ornaments worn by some were an indication that they had been cannibals in the past.[20]

When the people learned that these trekkers were the ones responsible for the gifts dropped from the plane they showed friendliness and asked them to come back:

> About three years earlier they had heard what missionaries were doing for other tribes. Though most of the tribe wanted to remain isolated, eight chiefs decided to send word asking for mission-aries to come and teach—a tremendous breakthrough and an answer to years of prayer.[21]

Hatam Missionaries Ready to Go

For the next three years the missionaries were denied contact because of tribal warfare between the Meyah and the Moskona, but by 1977 some of the Hatam church leaders had committed themselves to go as full-time missionaries to other tribes and 76 Hatam churches were prepared to support them. Miller reported:

In January 1977 we began another trek to re-establish contact with the Moskona. Five Hatam pastors who were commissioned as evangelists and 17 Hatam volunteers accompanied me on the trip. On the third day out, we met Mersorjmem, a Moskona chief who had befriended us in 1973 when we made our first contact. A modern-day Cornelius, Mersorjmem told us he had been trying to follow the message he had heard nearly four years before, and now he had been on his way to look for us. He had never before been this far from home and here we met in the middle of the jungle—just when we needed him and he was looking for us.[22]

The chief led them back into Moskona territory where the five evangelists stayed for four months, learning more of the language, building their own houses, and starting gardens. Then the evangelists returned to their own Hatam villages to bring their wives and children to their new homes. Julie Miller trained five men to do medical work among the people. For these Hatamers, this was just as great a venture as it is for a missionary to go from North America to a country in Africa or Asia.

Desperate Physical Needs

These missionaries were there to preach and teach the gospel but they were prepared to minister to the physical needs they confronted.

The Moskona were in wretched physical condition. Many had yaws, an often fatal skin disease that can eat away the face. Usually one shot of penicillin could clear up this problem. Others, especially women, had huge neck goiters caused by iodine deficiency. Many Moskona had malaria or pneumonia. We saw very few children since most die before age six. Those who did live were usually malnourished.[23]

The Hatam missionaries worked in the tribe for two years before they saw the first indication of a desire to burn fetishes (not that they were prompting them to do so prematurely). About a year later the first believer was baptized. By 1981 Miller was able to report:

There are now thirteen Hatam missionary couples working in

the Moskona tribe where they have seen fetishes burned, close to 1,000 baptized, and churches established with lay leaders. There are now some twenty who are candidates for ordination as church elders. All praise be to God![24]

Meeting the Linguistic and Translation Need

While the Hatam missionaries did outstanding work and saw wonderful results among the Moskona, they were not prepared to do serious translation work. For this task the field council assigned John and Linda Price. John had the primary responsibility of reducing the language to writing and beginning Scripture translation. Family health needs interrupted and shortened their stay in the tribe. Linguists from the Summer Institute of Linguistics followed up on their work and are moving forward with translation.

Hatam Missionary Workers Conference

The Hatam missionaries were helped in their ministry in ways similar to the North American workers. One example was periodic Bible conferences for their spiritual encouragement. Miller reported on one such conference held in 1982 for thirteen Hatam missionary families working in the Moskona and Amberbaken tribes:

> What a wonderful time of fellowship it was! Amos Wonggor and I had the privilege of ministering to these choice servants of God. While there we put on tape the entire history of the opening of the work in the Moskona tribe. It was like listening to someone reading the Book of Acts. What God has done through these missionaries is perhaps unique in church history, in that one tribe has won another tribe to Christ, seen them burn their fetishes, as well as be baptized and gathered into local bodies of believers. They are teaching them to read and discipling them in the Lord. The first candidates for ordination as church elders are being considered. Though much of the tribe is reached, there are still Moskonas that have not been. Some of these pioneers are itching to go to them too![25]

It had not been easy to win the first Moskona, but the blessing of the Lord on this pioneer ministry led Miller to think of at least twelve other tribes in the Bird's Head peninsula which had not heard the true message of the gospel.

> Despite the obstacles—language difficulties, forbidding terrain, the anti-proselyting law that requires us to have an invitation from someone in the community before we can enter—it is our goal to reach them all, just as we were able to reach the isolated Moskona.[26]

A Wider Vision

Concern for the other unreached tribes in the Bird's Head led Miller to enlist a circle of intercessors to whom he sent information about all the tribes in the region, encouraging them to adopt a tribe to remember regularly in prayer. Knowing that the Lord had answered long-standing prayer for the Moskona, he believed that He would do the same for others if there was earnest intercession. He shared his prayer burden with Hatam believers and in the years that followed they sent missionaries to the Amberbaken tribe.

Bible Training Pays Off

The spread of the gospel by the Hatam people became a reality because of the Bible teaching they received. New readers were taught the available translated Scripture from their very first literacy lessons. Witness schools were the first step in organized teaching of the Word. Missionaries scheduled regular sessions for church leaders to teach Bible and train them in church leadership. Short residential sessions were gradually introduced for more extended training. Eventually a tribal Bible institute was opened. Walter Kennedy, who had joined the Hatam ministry, worked with Griffiths and Miller in the Bible institute teaching.

The progress made in preaching the gospel to the whole tribe of more than 12,000 is all the more remarkable when it is recalled that the people were entirely illiterate when the work started and had no verse of Scripture in their language. The preaching and teaching could proceed only as the Word was translated and as people were taught to read. The lesson to be learned is that a clear objective of evangelism and discipling with the aim of establishing reproducing, spiritual churches brought the desired results. The fruit of the work was seen by 1986 in 90 congregations with 10,803 adherents, of whom 6,269 were baptized believers. (The annual report for 1990 gave a total of 113 Hatam churches.)

Manikion and Meyah

The ministry among the Manikion and Meyah people was no less remarkable and rewarding. If it were to be related in the same detail as the work among the Hatam the account would be similar—initial sowing of the seed, mass movement of people disillusioned with their old ways, translation of Scripture portions, literacy instruction, teaching of the Word, training in witness schools, growth sessions for church leaders, and higher-level Bible training in preparation for Christian service in the tribes.

The Vanguard Among the Manikion

Henry and Marjorie Bock laid the foundation of the linguistic and translation work among the Manikion at Anggi Lakes and saw the first ingathering of souls. Beulah Stapf worked with them in literacy training and in teaching. Gladys Willems carried on the medical work. Patricia Fillmore came to the field in 1959 and was assigned to the medical work at Anggi Lakes to replace Gladys Willems. Later she became responsible for the Bible institute at Nenei, also among the Manikion.

Lunows Follow

Wolfgang and Barbara Lunow arrived in Irian Jaya in 1969 and after a short time on the South Coast were assigned to linguistic and translation work among the Manikion to replace the Bocks, who had to leave for health reasons. Bock had reduced the language to writing, had translated Mark and Acts, and had seen nineteen churches established. Lunow found that the Manikion numbered from ten to twelve thousand and were scattered over a wide area. He explained that the animistic background of the people presented a particular problem:

> The people are magic-oriented. They try, through giving of gifts and certain formulas, to influence the spirits into giving them

things and also not to harm them. When they saw the missionaries' outfits they thought they must have tremendous magic to acquire these things, so they wanted to know who their spirit was. When the missionaries told them about Jesus they wanted to know more, hoping Jesus would bring material abundance. When the missionaries protested that they had no magic formula there was disbelief. They surely must have magic, because there is no other way of obtaining such things. Later, when they translated Scripture and told the people they needed to repent and confess their sins, the people confessed everything that came to mind—perhaps that was the formula for obtaining things. When they heard about baptism, they thought that must be the magic needed. As I, with one church leader, tried to explain to the group what faith in Jesus really meant, the truth penetrated the heart and mind of this leader. His immediate reaction was that the church leaders had baptized many who did not really know the Lord. So we went around to teach and reexamine all those people, lead them to the Lord, and later rebaptize them.[27]

Pastor Yonahan's Maturity

When Dr. Andrew Karsgaard and I, accompanied by field chairman Ron Hill, visited Anggi Lakes in 1971, we were informed that Yonahan, the Manikion pastor, would like us to answer some questions. Most concerned how to deal with people who had involved themselves in the recent rebellion against the government. Yonahan had other questions which revealed an encouraging depth of spiritual understanding. He, for one, had been well taught by the Spirit of God.

Progress in Scripture Translation

Lunow continued translating the New Testament and by 1987 had a complete preliminary draft, which he then carefully revised with the cooperation of several of the young men of more advanced education. Barbara Lunow, a nurse, became responsible for the medical needs of the people after Pat Fillmore moved to Nenei to teach in the tribal Bible school. When Susan Moers joined the work in 1977 she was assigned to the literacy ministry.

By 1987 there were fifty churches among the Manikion and

6,000 baptized believers out of a 12,000 population. Lunow made trips on foot through the rugged mountains to forty-nine of the churches. The fiftieth was at Bintuni, eight days distant, along the south coast of the peninsula—farther than any of the others. To visit Bintuni, he called in the services of MAF.

No Longer Manikion (Dirty)

I recalled for Lunow my impression of the people on my first visit to the Anggi Lakes area—how dirty and diseased they appeared and how much better they appeared when I saw them later. He responded by giving me some fascinating information:

> They were called Manikion because they were so filthy. It was really cold up there because of the altitude so they never took baths. Last year the people sent a letter to the government asking not to be called Manikion because this was a derogatory name given them by outsiders. It means the dirty, black scum that is left after making coconut oil. They said, "We now know Jesus. We are clean on the inside. Please do not call us dirty people any more. Call us Sougb. We have always called ourselves Soubg. We are no longer Manikion; we are no longer black. We are clean on the inside and clean on the outside too."[28]

Meyah Tribe and Testega

Though circumstances had necessitated Forrest and Dorothy Thorsby leaving Testega, the work among the Meyah people was not forgotten. Doug Eager, who arrived in 1963, and his wife, Doris, who arrived in 1965, were assigned to the Meyah. The new Testega station—opened in 1964—was located more centrally in the tribe and at about the only place an airstrip could be prepared.

Rapid Growth of the Meyah Work

Chairman Charles Preston reported in 1973 that Testega was growing so rapidly that the work was too much for one missionary family. Paul and Teresa Rhoads joined the Eagers in 1974 and Vicki Lynn Hill in 1976. The Rhoads worked with the expanding church ministries. Vicki carried on extensive medical work and as part of that ministry trained medical workers for wider outreach into the tribe.

Eager reduced the Meyah language to writing and translated several New Testament books. Because of the load of work related to the churches, Eager accepted the help of a Summer Institute of Linguistics couple to insure a more speedy completion of the New Testament. Progress in the Meyah tribe has been encouraging. The total number of adherents reported in 1986 was 888, of whom 823 were baptized, active church members.

The South Coast

Earlier mention was made of missionaries assigned to work among the tribes of the South Coast in places such as Agats, Ayam, Yaosakor, Pirimapun, Saman, and Nohon. Some similarities existed between the people on the North Coast and those on the South Coast, but there were also great differences. Each area had its own special challenges.

Differing Working Conditions

Those working in the north had to contend with difficult travel through mountain terrain. There were no mountains in the south. There the physical hindrances were water, dense jungles, and swampland.

Tribal languages had little similarity. A translation of the New Testament into Hatam in the north would be of no assistance to a linguist working with the Auyu in the south. One common thread was the national language—Indonesian—but it affected only those areas where schools had been opened.

In the north there was no recent cannibalism, while in the south it had not only been a way of life in the past but there were also evidences of recent activity in some tribes.

Among the Central Highland tribes and in the Bird's Head there were mass movements of the people turning from their worship of fetishes and belief in magic, whereas none of this was experienced or observed in the south.

It is safe to say that there was no less dedication, no less dependence on the Spirit of God, and no less prayer, but the missionaries and national workers in the south saw only the tens—and in some instances, hundreds—respond, but not the thousands as in the Hatam and Soubg tribes of the north.

Comparing the North and the South

Comparative figures for the North and South Coast ministries for the year 1985 highlight the different results. Total adherents in the north that year were 16,392 and total active (baptized) members were 10,795, whereas the totals for the south were 9,426 and 2,255 respectively. In the north 66 percent of those attending or having a relationship to the churches were dedicated enough to go on with the Lord, but in the south that figure was 24 percent.

These figures explain why missionaries to the tribes in the south speak so much of the indifference on the part of many who hear the gospel and who make an outward show of interest. The response of the people in the north is not all that the missionaries long for, but by comparison they have much to encourage them.[29]

Asmat New Testament Translation

Cal Roesler is a highly trained linguist and translator, yet it required almost thirty years of diligent application on his part to produce a written Asmat language, to prepare literate readers, to complete the Asmat New Testament, and have printed copies delivered for use in the tribe.

Working as a lone couple at Ayam, the Roeslers had major responsibility for all aspects of the ministry in the tribe. This included literacy work, medical help, evangelism, training, preparing lesson material, and care of the churches. Add to that field council membership, construction, and upkeep of the mission station, and it is easy to understand why the New Testament was not completed in fifteen years as in some languages. The station work included operating a sawmill to supply lumber for mission building needs for the various stations on the South Coast.

MacDonald's Ayam Visit

On Jack MacDonald's first visit to Irian Jaya in 1982 he spent some time at Ayam and noted in his journal of the trip:

> Another ten minutes of flying brought us to Ayam where Cal and
> Ruth Roesler have worked since 1956. This is the main station
> and center for ministry to the Asmat people. Cal is a linguist and
> has just finished the New Testament in the Asmat language. It
> is an exciting time for the Roeslers now as they do the final
> checking and guide it through the revision and to the press. They
> hope to enter into a teaching ministry when this is finished. It is
> everybody's prayer that the availability of the Word of God in
> the vernacular will result in reaching many souls, who until now
> have been resistant.[30]

Asmat New Testament Published

Field chairman Marvin Newell made special reference in his
report of 1986 to the publication of the Asmat New Testament:

> A historic event took place with 5,000 Asmat New Testaments
> coming off the presses of the Indonesian Bible Society. We
> commend Cal and Ruth Roesler for their dedication to this
> momentous task over the past thirty years.[31]

While the Asmat tribe is large and spread over several hundred
square miles, the people speak basically the same language, but—
and here is the problem for the clear proclamation of the gospel—
they speak different dialects. Thus the Asmat idiom in Saman and
Yaosakor differs one from the other and from that in Agats and
Ayam—enough to make understanding difficult.

It is hoped that the New Testament will serve to unite the dialects
so that one standard of pronunciation and usage will prevail
throughout the tribe as has been the case in other language areas.
In the meantime—so that the people of Yaosakor will receive a
clear presentation of the gospel —Charles and Bernita Preston are
preparing a translation from the Asmat of Ayam to the Asmat of
Yaosakor.

Unfinished Asmat Task

Missionaries continue to manifest much concern for the Asmat,
as reflected in Chairman Ron Hill's report for 1984:

> Much prayer has gone up to the throne of Grace on behalf of the
> Asmat people. There is a continuing trickle of people in the tribe

coming to know the Lord. However, the trickle has become a small stream in the Saman and Pirimapun areas, as people respond to the witness of church leaders and evangelists. Recently more than one hundred people indicated a desire to receive instruction about the Lord. The churches in the two areas are filled with people hearing and trusting the Word of God.[32]

Other Tribes Responsive

Of the other South Coast stations the most significant growth has been at Senggo among the Citak people and at Nohon among the Auyu, with Miaro (Ayoub) third.

Jack and Annette Manly opened a mission outpost for a short time at a difficult area called Senggo among the Citak tribe. When I visited the South Coast in 1963 our MAF plane landed on the river in front of the simple mission house. A dozen or so men gathered on the bank to see what was happening. I saw immediately how lethargic their movements were and how their naked bodies were covered with sores.

Romans 1:27, 28 Exhibited

I thought I had seen the very depth of human misery when I first visited Anggi Lakes in 1956, but these people were in far worse condition, so malnourished and diseased that they were too weak to care for their dilapidated canoes—their only means of transportation—which lay scattered on the river bank.

These miserable men were no match for their enemies who had raided their village some time earlier, killing and kidnapping. According to Manly, the men seemed to reserve their meager strength for acts of depravity openly practiced within sight of the missionary house. Sensitive souls would suffer greatly in such surroundings. Annette's poor health made it necessary for the Manlys to leave that first Senggo station.

A New Location for the Hospital

When Dr. Dresser concluded that the ever-higher tides and the battering ocean waves made the Pirimapun location untenable for the hospital, a search located higher ground farther inland near

Senggo. An area along a river bank was selected where an airstrip for wheel planes could be prepared and where there would also be sufficient space for hospital buildings and staff residences.

Timely Provision

The new installation would be expensive but the Lord provided substantial help through CIDA, the Canadian government's agency for foreign aid. Dr. and Mrs. Dresser's Canadian citizenship was the key to open this door. Preston's annual report as chairman relates to this matter:

> Amazing things can happen even on the South Coast. We are thankful to the Lord and to the Canadian government for the large gift of $50,000 for the construction of the hospital complex at Senggo. We are also encouraged as we see the progress of the work in Senggo with the completion of the airstrip, Dressers' house, and the lesser buildings. A big boost to the construction to be done this coming year was given by the Clarence Gillett family working for three months at the Ayam sawmill. I have been personally encouraged with the cooperation of all the missionaries on the Senggo project.[33]

The chairman was able to announce the virtual completion of the hospital and its dedication on July 23, 1975.

Ministries at Senggo

Five major lines of work needed to be done at Senggo—medical, maintenance, linguistics and translation, evangelism and discipling, and church planting. This work required skillful and dedicated participants. With visas hard to obtain, the number of missionary workers was limited. Some Indonesian and Irianese personnel were trained and employed.

Missionaries in the work at Senggo were Dr. Ken Dresser; nurses Sylvia Dresser, Gail Vinje, and Ruth Dougherty; linguist and translator Margaret Stringer; and church planters Clarence and Twila Gillett. Other missionaries served for shorter periods, notably Bob and Amber Leland. Undoubtedly there was much mutual helpfulness and sharing of responsibility.

The poor physical condition of the Citak people gave ample

scope for medical service, much of it in preventative medicine. Available statistics do not give separate totals for the hospital, but the totals for the whole field show a marked increase after the hospital opened: 1974—46,206 outpatients treated; 1975—71,726; 1979—131,763; 1984—176,108; 1989—153,697. The increased emphasis on training village health workers among the Hatam and Meyah people may account for much of the increase but it is certain that the medical service at Senggo—a district with very evident physical needs—provided special commendation and help to the gospel message.

Linguistics and Translation

Another key factor to the spread of the gospel was the linguistic and translation work of Margaret Stringer as she prepared book after New Testament book to be used by missionaries and church leaders for evangelism and Bible teaching. In addition to the ministry in Citak, missionaries held regular services in Indonesian.

Remembering the dismal conditions—physically, morally, and spiritually—of the Citak people as the missionaries first encountered them, it is particularly gratifying to read about many being won to the Lord Jesus and progressing to the point of being effective witnesses to others outside of their own community. In an annual report Ron Hill stated:

> There was an increasing number of people in the Senggo area who have come to know the Lord—158 professions of faith in 1983 and 75 baptisms.[34]

Growth of the Citak Church

Within ten years of the beginning of the medical witness at Senggo, the Citak churches were ministering regularly to 3,445 adherents. Included in that number were 677 active baptized church members. Not only so, they also reached out to an unusually dark and backward group of people along the Brazza River.[35]

Brazza River People Visited

Missionaries working at Senggo became aware of Citak people

along the Brazza River some distance from the hospital. Margaret Stringer felt led to visit the area. She made an early trip to the village of Vakabuis in January 1983 in company with nurse Ruth Dougherty and a number of the Citak men—Pit Bakasu, a Senggo medical worker; Titus Fiak, translation helper; and Yakub Fiak.

This was not the first approach. Frans Isaka and Habel Kermek had earlier gone to Vakabuis to build a house for Frans and his wife, who were to be stationed among the people as evangelists.[36]

Getting Acquainted

A twelve-day stay in the village taught the visiting party much about the people. Cannibalism was still practiced. Chief Pau had six skulls to his "credit." They also learned much about the degradation and deceitfulness of the people and yet appreciated their outward friendliness. They found the people very eager to get material things, even the simple things the missionaries brought with them. The village people wanted them to leave all their personal possessions with them—even their clothing—when they left.

The visitors slept in a quickly built shelter which did nothing to protect them from heat and insects and offered only minor protection from rain.

> During the 12 days there we had a variety of interesting food— tree kangaroo, wild pork, jungle rat, lizard, fish, turtle, grub worms, sago, heart of palm, etc.[37]

Their principal concern was not the heat, the insects, the rain, or the food, but the spiritual need of the people they were meeting:

> Our main prayer concern now is for men from Senggo who are willing to make the sacrifice necessary to go and live among them.... We have learned to love these people in a special way. The women and children are no longer afraid of us and it was fun getting to know them better on this trip. We long for the day when some of these people will understand and come to know the Savior in a personal way. We believe it will be soon.[38]

Hazards of Loving Concern

Love for the people would be severely tested on the next trip

Margaret, Gail Vinje, Sahu Fiak, and Yakub Fiak took to Vakabuis in February 1983. They found the people more demanding and also more brazen in their attempts to steal from them.

The visitors soon sensed an uneasiness on the part of the people and noted puzzling changes in attitude. Sahu and Yakub became concerned and seemed to have some premonition of trouble. On Sunday most of the people refused to attend the meeting to listen to the Word of God. Instead, the village leaders and many of the other men went to the jungle to cut material for war arrows.

In the meantime Margaret and Gail had frequent radio contact with Dr. Dresser and the MAF pilot, John Forsythe, and were assured that these men were prepared to take emergency action to evacuate them, if necessary. However, the women did not think of themselves as being in danger of personal attack.

An Unsettling Turn
But the situation took a different turn over the next forty hours. On Tuesday—early in the morning—Yakub came to Margaret and told her that he woke up in the early hours in the long house and heard villager Dasawo discussing the visitors. Dasawo, a widower, was older than most of the others in the long house. He was saying that Sahu and Yakub had to be killed and Gail and Margaret would then be taken.

Facing danger of being killed by arrows the ladies had sensed fear, but that was minor compared with their feeling when they heard about possible kidnapping. Yakub said that he was not sure if the men were serious or only joking. Either way, it didn't sound too pleasant. They reported all this to Dresser by radio at the 7:30 scheduled time. The women decided to make a decision by 9:00 A.M. about calling for help.[39]

Reluctant Retreat
Turning on their radio before decision time they heard Clarence Gillett and Forsythe planning a way of evacuating them by helicopter, which would have to be done in two flights. They were

487

evacuated that Tuesday forenoon to Binam, where they were later met by Dominggus Major, hospital evangelist, who had come by outboard motor boat just before dark.

They spent a restless night in a palm-frond shelter. "I slept at the end of the shelter and got the worst part of a heavy rain storm in the middle of the night. I was glad when the night was over. We left about 5:30 A.M. on Wednesday and arrived home about 9:30," Margaret related.[39]

In Retrospect—a Wise Decision

While they were reluctant to cut short their visit, they were certain their decision to leave was wise:

> We may never know if they actually would have carried out what they were talking about. In retrospect, it looks very likely that they were indeed serious. With Sahu having been invited to go hunting on Tuesday with Dasawo, they could easily have killed him in the jungle. There was also the fact that the people were so nice and cooperative after Sunday and seemingly anxious that we not return suddenly to Senggo. Their culture of deceit and treachery all seemed to indicate that they had unpleasant plans for us.... Our most earnest thanks and love go to the Lord for his protection and sovereignty in this—for waking Yakub to hear the talk, for keeping Sahu from going hunting with them, for guidance in making decisions, and for making our evacuation peaceful and without incident.[40]

First Fruits

Missionaries continued to make visits to encourage Frans Isaka and his wife. Much prayer was also offered that these Brazza River people, so long bound by Satan, would be rescued from his grip. Niemeyer reported in 1986 that there indeed was fruit among these people:

> One year ago it was reported that three made decisions for Jesus Christ including the assistant chief. Now I am happy to report that another three have made those commitments to Christ. The Word of God is penetrating into this hidden people's group.[41]

Scattered Biak People

Biak is the largest of a group of sixty scattered inhabited islands lying to the north of Irian Jaya. It was a base of Japanese operations during the war years and was later conquered by General MacArthur's forces. After the war the Dutch airline KLM used Biak as its entry point to New Guinea. Its air terminal facilities were taken over by Indonesia in 1963.

Benefitting from contact with people from outside of New Guinea, the Biak people became more progressive and advanced in education than those from other tribes. Many were nominal Christians as a result of the German and Dutch missionary work in the late nineteenth and early twentieth centuries. Many of these nominal Christians, though apparently not possessed of true spiritual life, were nevertheless receptive when they heard the gospel message.

Tribal Mixture in Manokwari

The town of Manokwari has people from a number of different tribes, with those from the islands of Biak and Numfoor being most numerous. Missionaries in Manokwari used the Indonesian language to communicate with people from the various tribes as it was generally understood by the men and younger people who had gone to Indonesian schools. Those who had moved in from the Hatam area were ministered to in the Hatam language by church leaders from the tribe, and a number of churches had been established among them.

The work in Manokwari grew, as Preston reported to the annual field conference in 1974:

> Extensive changes have taken place in the Manokwari churches. Praise the Lord for awakening these formerly disinterested people. New churches are being formed, old ones are full and building additions are being made. The Rascher and Hill families are caring for this work. An evangelistic outreach from these churches has just been initiated with a Mujizat [mission boat] trip to Numfoor with thirty nationals going along and taking part in witnessing.[42]

Greater Interest in ETBI

With the conversion of many of the Biak people in Manokwari, there was a much greater interest by the youth in attending the Erikson-Tritt Bible Institute. Plans were made to take advantage of this interest by increasing accommodations and enlarging facilities. Missionaries were gratified to note that the school was filling up with young people from their own churches whereas several years earlier there were very few TEAM-related students.

> Each available space at ETBI was filled this year with a total enrolled of 44 students, 13 young ladies and 31 young men. Five students received diplomas.[43]

The institute underwent a number of changes during its more than thirty years of existence. When it began—about 1956—its academic level was low because its source of applicants was a pool of poorly educated tribal people of various backgrounds, most of whom were limited to a beginning knowledge of Indonesian. In time the level was raised so that students finishing the course were at a sixth-grade level. In 1963 a person having that level of training could qualify for a teaching position in primary school.

In 1971 when I visited the field I learned that few from our own churches were enrolled—or could be—because the requirements were too high. Some were questioning whether TEAM should have a Bible institute when we were not training workers for our tribal churches. It is a credit to the vision of those at the school—Bob and Shirley Lenz, Marvin and Peggy Newell, and Bob and Amber Leland—that they persevered in training those the Lord sent to them.

Graduates of ETBI could and did serve effectively in the Indonesian-language elementary schools that were set up for children in the tribal churches. They qualified to meet government standards as administered by the evangelical school foundation established by the missions at the time Indonesia took control.

Bible Institute Adds Seminary Level

Later, ETBI added an advanced course for a higher level of training to upgrade the preparation of earlier graduates. Some of these graduates, after years of experience in local churches, were being sent to seminary-level schools elsewhere in Indonesia. An advance came in 1983 when ETBI became ETBTS—Erikson-Tritt Bible and Theological Seminary—and later Erikson-Tritt Theological College (ETTC)—for training on a seminary level equivalent to other mission field seminaries.

A Christian education major was added in 1989 which proved popular, as the government was looking for teachers of religion in public schools through the high school years—a wonderful opportunity for evangelicals. Marvin Newell, principal, reported in September 1990 that progress toward accreditation by the Department of Religious Affairs in Jakarta was being made. This was important so that graduates could be qualified for placement in schools.

ETTC Enrollment Increases

Enrollment increased to seventy-five in 1990, part of which was in the theology major for preparation of evangelists and pastors. An important aspect of the training was weekly practical Christian work assignments. An excellent opportunity for such work was found in the transmigration camps near Sowi where thousands of people moved by the government from Java were located. Five churches have been planted among these formerly Muslim people.

Progress was made in transferring responsibility for the administration and teaching of the lower-level institute section to nationals. National participation in the training of Christian workers increased year by year. Akwila Baransano became a teacher at the school and president of the national church. Noakh Rombino was also given major responsibility. The national church began sharing in the support of the school.

Winchell Presents Diplomas

When Dr. Winchell visited Irian Jaya in 1986 he participated in the annual field conference and then spoke at the graduation exercises of the seminary, presenting diplomas to four Bible school and seven theological school graduates.

As one who has seen these people in the darkness of pagan tribal settings, I admit to being both amazed and delighted to learn of the results in able and qualified pastors and teachers for the churches. I should not have been surprised, because earlier I had seen young men of the same background working on extremely complex airplane motors. What was done to train men and women for secular work of great skill and responsibility could certainly be done in the church with even greater success, because here was the added factor of lives transformed by Christ and enlightened by the Holy Spirit.

Evangelism Team from Java Reaps Harvest

Romulo Maling, TEAM missionary working in Java, took a missionary-national evangelistic team to Irian Jaya:

> From October 6 to 26 [1988], I led a team of five evangelists to conduct a campaign in the Bird's Head region of Irian Jaya. We conducted a week-long campaign in Manokwari which resulted in the conversion of 471 souls, and a revival of one Hatam Tribe Church. After that we went to the transmigration project and five mission stations in the interior. On our way back to Jakarta at the end of our 20-day campaign, the Evangelism Committee told me that there were about 1,050 conversions, rededication of 511 believers, and 120 pastors and other Christian workers who renewed their commitment to the pastoral and evangelism ministry. We praise the Lord for using us in reaching thousands of Irianese for Jesus Christ.[44]

Biakkers and Numfoorese Won

Charles and Mary Sweatte had worked for several years on the island of Numfoor and had seen the work organized into a church. After they returned to the homeland, other missionaries, notably Larry Rascher and Marvin Newell, made occasional visits and the work there continued to grow.

The Raschers continued to have responsibility for the ministry in Biak. In 1983 chairman Ron Hill commented in his annual report that they had seen good response. The church group had doubled in size. Keith and Terri Rascher were the first TEAM missionaries to be placed there to work with the church.

The National Church

The organization which unites the TEAM-related churches is the Bible Christian Fellowship of Indonesia. This fellowship had its beginning in the 1950s in Netherlands New Guinea when missionaries and nationals applied to the government and received recognition as a church fellowship—*Persekutuan Kristan Alkitab.*

In 1973, the church fellowship was registered with the Indonesian government which now controlled Irian Jaya. The name was amended to include the word "church" and registered as *Gereja Persekutuan Kristan Alkitab, Indonesia (GPKAI)*. GPKAI thus became recognized as the national sponsoring body for all TEAM's activities.

While working under a loan arrangement with the C&MA in Java, Willem Hekman claimed that GPKAI was only a foundation without the privilege of organizing churches. He then proceeded to form a larger church body, *Gereja Kristan Alkitab, Indonesia (GKAI)*. This newer and larger body included—besides TEAM—AMG, *Berita Hidup,* and later, Torchbearers. These other missions were not related to TEAM but made some contribution to Hekman's work. This ill-advised linking of unrelated missions—each with its own goals and methods of work—would cause many difficulties over the next decade.[45]

Unsettling Influence

Though Hekman left the mission to work in wider fields, he continued to involve himself in GKAI along with former TEAM missionary Harold Lovestrand. This resulted in complicated relationships, as referred to by Norman Niemeyer some years later:

> This organization—GKAI—formed by the efforts of Bill Hekman was stated to be the only church planting organization including TEAM, AMG, and Torchbearers. This brought great confusion and discord over...ten or more years.[46]

Church Conference Takes a Stand

While attending the national church conference in Sowi in 1983, Jack MacDonald, then area secretary for the Asia fields, witnessed a firm stand taken by the national church leaders in response to one aspect of the continued interference of Hekman and Lovestrand through their relationship with Torchbearers and AMG. These men offered financial support to the TEAM-related pastors, which was contrary to TEAM's church policy. The churches had been wonderfully faithful in supporting their own pastors and all phases of their local work and missionary outreach. Neither they nor the mission wanted to see a lapse into an unhealthy dependence on foreign funds.

MacDonald related how one Hatamer told the conference that the Hatam churches wanted none of this money. They would trust the Lord for their own needs. "If we receive money to support our local churches, our churches will die." The crowd was nearly unanimous in applause and cheers. It was the most spontaneous of all responses. This was an answer to AMG and some of the coastals in Manokwari who wished to set salary levels and legislate money matters.[47]

By 1988 area foreign secretary Norman Niemeyer was able to report that the TEAM churches had severed their relationship with the organization formed by Hekman and had gone back to the original church fellowship established by TEAM. Both Irian Jaya and Java field councils had informed him that the Indonesian government recognized the Bible Christian Fellowship as the original and proper church planting organization formed by TEAM.

A Maturing National Church

When he was serving as field chairman in 1988, Marvin Newell wrote concerning the national church:

> In time, missionaries pioneered and opened isolated outposts in the interior, establishing a first-time witness among primitive tribes. The Lord blessed their efforts with many simple congregations brought into existence. In 1973 these churches were incorporated into one national body adopting the name of The Bible Christian Fellowship Church of Indonesia. Struggling through the normal growth process of childhood, then adolescence, and finally to adulthood, the BCFCI now stands as a

maturing national church. We of TEAM gradually changed roles through the years and now function as partners with the BCFCI, which is our official sponsor in Indonesia.[48]

In answering the question as to what kind of a church BCFCI is, Newell provided current information as of late 1988:

It is a Bible-believing evangelical church of 28,000 adherents, 15,000 of whom have qualified for membership. These believers are scattered in 275 congregations throughout the island of Irian Jaya and also a sprinkling located on the island of Java. Four Christian bookstores, 25 Christian day schools, and 4 vernacular Bible schools are sponsored by BCFCI/TEAM. At present 57 TEAM missionaries are engaged in an assortment of ministries such as Bible schools, Bible translation, literacy, evangelism, church planting, and medical work that help strengthen and expand the BCFCI.[49]

A Later Count

The official tally of the church, as submitted by the field office at the end of 1989, was higher than the chairman's estimate and indicated a church membership of 25,399 in 280 congregations. There were 501 ordained national pastors and evangelists and 670 non-ordained ministers active in these congregations. Baptisms of believers totaled 1,113 during the year. In the training ministries for service to this large, growing church body there were 82 in full-time residential study from the TEAM-related churches and 770 in part-time or non-residential studies.

Certain Types of Work Deferred

Some types of work often carried on in other fields were done in Irian Jaya to a lesser degree. For example, literature production and distribution, which is often a large ministry on other fields, is only in the beginning stages and for a very simple reason; there are not enough believers with advanced education who can write and publish needed material, and the level of reading is still so low that the market for literature is limited. Literacy training is addressing this problem as are day schools. The bookstore opened by the mission in Manokwari was transferred to the church for management, a good sign of its desire to progress in this field.

Not Finished but the Direction is Set

Much work remains to be done but the direction is set in pressing to the goal of having self-supporting, self-governing, self-propagating, and self-instructing churches. The proper development of the work is a constant concern of the field council and the missionaries:

> Every year at our annual conference we set aside the first day for strategy planning. Every missionary is involved, with several papers on relevant topics presented. Most discussions center on outreach and church development. Many times our priorities are evaluated then readjusted.[50]

God Really Made it Grow

There are several reasons for steady church growth in Irian Jaya. One is the openness and receptivity of an animistic people compared to those with an organized religious system. Another is the single-minded approach to mission activity which sees the church of Jesus Christ as the objective and evaluates other ministries according to their contribution to this goal. This is illustrated in the answer Newell gave to one question about field priorities:

> The emphasis in Irian Jaya has changed very little as church planting has been our priority since the beginning. But now with the tremendous influx of outsiders into Irian, especially through the government sponsored transmigration program, our emphasis will be to the cities, but also continuing our ministries in the interior tribes.[51]

New Opportunities

In line with the new look toward the cities, TEAM began work in Merauke, the largest town on the coast south of the Asmat tribal area. Ron and Charlene Hill were assigned to this ministry, which was carried on in the Indonesian language. As the Hills' ministry had been entirely in Indonesian they were especially proficient in the language and their work bore immediate fruit. A 1986 report listed 320 adherents and 65 baptized members.

General director Winchell took special note of the people yet to be reached when he visited Irian Jaya in 1985:

> There are about one million tribal people who speak about 200

languages. Now, however, the government has declared a plan to introduce transmigrants from other parts of Indonesia, which has hundreds of islands, some of which are very crowded. There is talk of bringing two to five million people into Irian Jaya. There is room for them, but they would completely overwhelm the local tribal people. Many thousands have come already and are being placed in transmigrant camps. In the Manokwari area we have one couple working with these Indonesians.[52]

Not Without Personal Cost

Hazards to the health of workers in Irian Jaya took a toll on many, with the South Coast region exacting a price of most who served there. Tropical illnesses abounded. This was true not only of foreign missionaries who ventured into this inhospitable climate but also of Irianese from other parts of the island. Many suffered from filariasis and a non-typical hepatitis which was elusive to diagnose and difficult to treat. Missionaries persevered through the various tropical ailments and many seemed to become "toughened" to the infections.

A danger that all faced was travel by air over high mountain passes, either to the Bird's Head or across the central mountains, and mostly in uncertain weather when cloud cover could build up quite suddenly and reduce visibility dangerously. No TEAM missionaries were involved in air accidents in spite of frequent trips over hundreds of miles of hazardous terrain.

Another hazard was travel on water, which was often necessary on the South Coast and to reach the ministries on Numfoor and Biak in the north. Jim and Margaret Hyatt escaped with their lives but not with much of their earthly possessions when their large dugout canoe capsized in one of the South Coast rivers. Being round-bottomed and without a keel, these canoes were difficult to control (though the local people could pilot them safely with six or eight men standing up and using paddles to propel them).

"In Danger at Sea"

The greatest water hazard was when travel by sea was necessary. One such trip brought tragic loss to Larry and Shirley Rascher when their boat was swamped by waves and two small children lost. It was in July 1971 that the Raschers with three children—Paul (Chipper), Gregory, and Karen—and an Irianese, Moses Kujera, left by boat from the South Coast station of Sumapero on what was to be a two-day trip to Kokenau to care for the work in the absence of a missionary. This trip would normally have been by MAF plane but MAF had recently had an accident and illness of personnel so the Raschers chose to go by boat. This usually would be through the interconnecting rivers.

After the first day of travel and a night spent anchored in a river, they went out to the ocean, which they needed to do to reach the next river. They found the ocean calm but with some rain clouds far to the east behind them. If they could go some distance on the ocean they would shorten their trip and save their dwindling fuel. To their complete surprise, a strong wind followed the rain clouds and churned up the ocean with large waves.

Two Children Lost to the Waves

Larry was able to keep control until one unusually high wave capsized the boat, trapping several briefly under the upside-down boat. When they freed themselves from this precarious position, they were still at the mercy of the waves. In the hours that passed, strength ebbed and survival seemed impossible. The two smallest children, Gregory and Karen, succumbed to the waves.

Chipper and Moses were urged to swim to the shore of an island. After many hours through the night Larry and Shirley finally were blown close enough to the island so they could touch bottom and, in spite of sheer exhaustion, reach a place of temporary safety. They, Chipper, and Moses were eventually rescued by mining company personnel working along one of the rivers. While they rejoiced in the Lord's intervention to keep them from being overwhelmed by the waves, they felt most keenly the loss of two precious children, as did the entire mission family. What missionaries have invested of toil, separation, health, and lives has been great indeed, but yet not so great compared with the price Christ paid in the garden and on the cross for the redemption of precious souls in Irian Jaya.

JAVA—POPULOUS ISLAND

With more than 100 million people, Java is the most populous island of Indonesia and, being small in area, its density is about 1,500 per square mile. Java has a homogenous culture with a major language—Indonesian—and several regional languages—Javanese and Sundanese. Islam is the most prevalent religion in Java and, for that matter, in most of Indonesia.

TEAM had no missionary work in Java when Indonesia took over control of Irian Jaya in 1963. Its ministry there began some seven years later as in indirect offshoot of the Irian Jaya work.

Hekmans Desire to Serve in Java

Willem Hekman, who with his wife, Verena, had served in Irian Jaya for a term beginning in 1960, wanted a wider ministry than among the tribal people and became active in evangelism among the more advanced people, with generally good results. While on furlough, Hekman approached the Christian and Missionary Alliance (C&MA) about the possibility of working with that mission in Java on a loan arrangement from TEAM.

George Martin, area secretary for TEAM's Asia fields, negotiated an agreement with C&MA for the Hekmans to serve in a church planting ministry in the capital city of Jakarta. This service with C&MA began in 1970 and continued for a term of four years. During that four-year period Hekman not only founded a C&MA church but initiated several ministries and relationships which would affect TEAM's future work, some positively and others giving rise to severe administrative difficulties.

Several Positive Results and One Negative

One positive result was to recommend that TEAM open its own work in Java, a recommendation approved by the board of directors. Another positive move was to work with the Irian Jaya field council in obtaining government recognition for TEAM and its various ministries and churches as a bona fide religious organization with the name Bible Christian Fellowship of Indonesia (BCFI). One move which was more negative than positive was the inclusion under the BCFI umbrella of several unrelated organizations which contributed to Hekman's work—the American Mission to the Greeks (AMG) and Torchbearers.

Initial Work by Hekman

C&MA leaders requested that Hekmans not do church planting for TEAM in Jakarta after conclusion of the loan arrangement in 1974 because they feared that C&MA church members would follow them to the new ministry. When the Hekmans returned from furlough in 1975, Hekman continued active youth work under the name of *Pamukri*, affiliated with Youth for Christ International, and newspaper evangelism and other literature work under the name of *Berita Hidup*. He also encouraged Harold Lovestrand, former Irian Jaya missionary, to work with him in a relationship with AMG.

Other TEAM Java Missionaries

TEAM sent Larry and Carol Fish to Java for language study and Bible teaching work with the C&MA in Kalimantan. Their loan arrangement ended in 1975 when the Hekmans returned from furlough. Because of the health needs of a daughter, the Hekmans left Java in May 1978; they resigned from TEAM to join AMG, which worked in several countries, and later changed to Torchbearers. Upon the Hekmans' departure Larry Fish became the leader of the field, a position he held for his remaining few years of service in Java.

Romy and Edna Maling became TEAM missionaries in 1975. They began a broad tract distribution work under the name of Every Home Contact (EHC), affiliated with Every Home for Christ, International.

The next reinforcements were Katsuhiko and Hiroko Seino, who arrived in 1976. David and Pamela Waldschmidt joined the work shortly thereafter in 1977.

The Hekmans' Legacy

Hekman's organizational arrangements left very little foundation on which later TEAM missionaries could build and much for them and the mission to unravel:

> Carl Davis, area foreign secretary [succeeding George Martin in 1974], worked hard to bring some measure of administrative order and direction to the field, but the ministries developed by Bill Hekman and the policies initiated made it very difficult to direct the work along the usual TEAM lines and, in particular, to establish it on a truly indigenous basis.[54]

Central Java Selected as Field

TEAM decided to concentrate its work in central Java, in and around the city of Yogyakarta. As a new TEAM field, Java did not have enough missionaries to form a field council and so was administered for several years by the area foreign secretary with a small provisional field council. After the death of Davis in 1979, Jack MacDonald—and later Norman Niemeyer—took over this post.

From Several Nations

The Java field has been quite international in makeup. Hekman was Dutch. Romulo and Edna Maling were Filipino, partially supported from their homeland. Katsuhiko and Hiroko Seino were Japanese, sent out and supported by the TEAM-related Domei churches. The Malings and the Seinos, being Asians, developed unusual rapport with the Indonesian people. Maling served as field chairman for six years and Seino for one year.

Seino was conscious of possible feeling by Indonesians against Japanese because of Japan's 1942 to 1945 occupation of the islands. When he began his ministry he publicly apologized to the people for Japan's past aggression and announced that he came as a bearer of the gospel of peace.

The Seinos were active in evangelism, teaching, and church ministries. They initiated a Bible study among Japanese living in Jakarta, travelling there from Surakarta once a month. The Japanese Domei church did not lose interest in Java when the Seinos were assigned to another ministry in Japan, but sent Mr. and Mrs. Tsutomu Osaka to Java to begin their language study in late 1989.

Indonesia began to restrict entry of new missionaries and limited visa renewals of others. This policy severely handicapped, though it did not entirely block, TEAM's ability to reinforce this small field.

TEAM missionaries in Java acknowledged that church planting was the most important activity but having two of the couples on loan to another mission for most of their years of service prevented their developing a TEAM strategy for church planting. They were not seriously limited, however, in other types of work—literature, training, and camp ministry—all of which could contribute to building strong churches. When the missionaries later could go forward in church planting some of the special ministries became useful tools to help them in their work.

Cooperation with ETSI

One relationship which was of great benefit to the TEAM/BCFI work was with the Evangelical Theological Seminary of Indonesia. This seminary was founded by an Indonesian graduate of Dallas Seminary, Dr. Chris Marantika. Located at Yogyakarta, the school not only had training as its objective, it also recognized the importance of actively promoting the planting and development of evangelical churches. One of its requirements for graduation was that each student develop a church of at least thirty baptized members from the results of evangelizing and discipling.[55]

TEAM agreed to provide a missionary professor for the school. David and Pamela Waldschmidt were the first to work with the seminary. When they left the field at the end of their term in 1982 they were followed at the seminary by Craig and Shirley Preston. The Prestons had worked in Irian Jaya since 1979—part of the time at the Erikson-Tritt Bible School and Theological Seminary. In 1987 Brent Preston joined in the seminary ministry at a branch in Madiun. Both brothers were active in church ministries.[56]

MacDonald Gives Encouragement

Jack MacDonald first visited and ministered in Java in March 1980, and sent a report to general director Winchell from Taiwan:

> Soon after my arrival in Jakarta I became aware of discouragement on this field.... The discouragement is due to several factors. Bill Hekman's—and now Harold Lovestrand's—continuing influence through AMG hangs over them like a great cloud. They still have to live with the unwholesome organizational arrangements set up by Hekman.... Actually the work is encouraging. Since 1977 they have the beginning of eight good [church] works going. I preached in four of them in Solo on Sunday. Romy has a solid group of 60 adults meeting each Sunday morning in one of the better hotels in Jakarta. He has a Sunday school in the afternoon. Dave has two works going in Yogyakarta. Seino also has one church moving along well. It just dedicated a new church building.... Using these facts, I was able to put things in some perspective through comparison with other fields that would rejoice if they could report eight new works in less than three years.[57]

Malings' Literature and Training Work

In addition to her involvement in the large literature distribution program of Every Home Contact, Edna Maling in 1986 began teaching Bible religious education classes in government and private schools in the Jakarta area. This led the Malings to initiate the Institute of Religious Christian Education, an ambitious program of training evangelical teachers for Bible classes in junior and senior high schools, with a goal of having 300 trained religious education teachers by 1995 and 300 more per year thereafter.

Introducing Christian Camping

Finn and Sandy Torjesen arrived in Indonesia in 1983 and have served in a discipling and training ministry in Surakarta/Solo.[58] After several years they observed the need for a camping ministry of a type so successful on other TEAM fields. Torjesen believed that youth would be best served if they could be under the influence of trained spiritual counselors for an extended period of days, as would be possible at a summer camp.

Torjesen began with a five-week "sample camp" in 1988, which established the framework for their program:

> Indonesian churches hold conferences and retreats every year, but until the sample camp, there were no programs using trained counselors to lead small groups. The churches had never seen a camp that was not speaker-centered or that offered a variety of activities.[59]

Successful Training Camp

Field chairman Maling reported enthusiastically on the initial year of camp activity:

> Last June we launched a Bible camp ministry, and have hosted one training camp for potential staff. It was attended by about 60 volunteer staff from various churches in Central Java and Jakarta. The training camp was then followed by three youth camps in which we reached about 500 youth. Now the program is being nationalized. A campsite has been bought and is being developed for next year's camps.[60]

Those who attended the camps spread the word through the churches about the interest, excitement, and inspiration of the camps. One result was that when a seminar on Christian camping was held more than ninety church and school leaders attended. The committee formed by Torjesen was asked to hold training courses in four cities. His evaluation after the first year:

> The Indonesian churches are ready and trying to reach their young people. They saw some of their youth come home changed after a week of camp and they saw youth excited about the next camping season. They have seen what Christian camping can do to reach the 70-plus million young people in Indonesia.[61]

Many Congregations Helped

The story thus far tells of literature, training, and camping—all aids in building strong churches. Because many of the churches were started by students of the seminary who then invited missionaries to share in the teaching of the converts, the work has taken a pattern different from most other fields. As of December 1989 there were eight churches where TEAM missionaries have primary responsibility, but as many as forty congregations in formation which will have significant spiritual input from national workers and missionaries. One of the early national leaders was pastor Foedikoa. Another was pastor Librek Anthony.

Discouragement Turns to Rejoicing

This section on Java started on a rather discouraging note but the Lord has brought victory and encouragement. The clarification on the registration of the mission, as reported under the Irian Jaya section (pages 493-95), was a big factor as it cleared up long-standing administrative confusion. The steady harvest of souls is always a major source of joy and satisfaction and that is being seen on the Java field.

One other source of great joy and promise for the future was mentioned in a 1989 report by Niemeyer:

> While I was in Java, Jeff and Gerri Miller arrived from the United States.... [It] was exciting to know that visas were granted for the Millers so that they could begin their first term of service in Java. We thank God for this answer to prayer.[62]

THE IMPACT OF INDIA'S INDEPENDENCE

Chairman O. E. Meberg spoke prophetically in 1945 when he predicted that current political changes would greatly affect missionary work. The political movement having the greatest effect was the transformation of colonial India into an independent nation—in fact, into two separate nations, India and Pakistan. The British government withdrew its rule August 14, 1947. The next day, August 15, became independence day. India was now a self-governing member of the British Commonwealth. Several years later, in January 1950, it became a democratic republic.

Hindu-Muslim Violence

Tensions had been growing between the Hindu and Muslim communities as agitation for independence increased. Open violence broke out in the districts with mixed Hindu-Muslim populations when the British withdrew. It is estimated that in 1947 twelve million Hindu and Muslim refugees crossed the India-Pakistan borders in a mass transferral of the two peoples. About 200,000 were slaughtered in the communal fighting.

The Western India field of TEAM was not greatly affected by this violence. What did affect it, however, was the developing nationalistic policies of the Indian government.

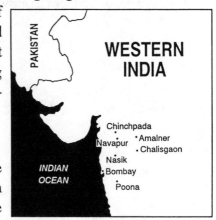

A Flood of Recruits

In the meantime, the large numbers of North American young people responding to the missionary call included many who wanted to serve in India. By the end of 1951, TEAM India had 102 missionaries, of whom 82 were on the field and 20 on furlough. This remarkable expansion of staff made imperative an outreach into new areas.

A new openness on the part of the people, more missionaries at work, and national independence combined to bring promise of a better day in the mission work. Writing about the 1952 annual TEAM conference in Chicago, India missionary on furlough Jane McNally shared the feeling of optimism among the India missionaries present:

> Continued receptivity in India since the withdrawal of the British makes that great land one of the most challenging of the fields where we must work while it is yet day.[1]

Entry Restrictions Begin

The years 1951-1952 were watershed years. The high point in number of missionaries serving on the Western India field was reached in 1951. And it was in 1952 that the missionaries learned they must obtain a "no objection to return" endorsement from the local authorities before leaving India if they hoped to be granted a return visa by an Indian Consulate.

Some had actually come home on furlough before learning of this requirement and so were refused visas to return. For the most part those who made application received endorsements. But it was a different matter for Americans seeking visas for the first time. Only British Commonwealth subjects were still welcome; so for the next eight or nine years it was mainly Canadians—and few in number, at that—who reached the field.

The effect of visa refusals can be traced in the annual reports. Dr. and Mrs. Albert Holt were the only missionaries to enter in 1954 and there were none in 1955. The Christian public considered India closed and consequently the number of new recruits declined, including Canadian young people who would have had no difficulty entering.

Johnson's First India Visit

David Johnson's first visit to India was in late 1948. When he arrived in western India he had already spent some time in Pakistan and along the Tibetan Frontier. The poverty and suffering in India impressed him deeply. Though the caste system was no longer legal, the results of the segregation were all too evident. The Outcastes, in particular, aroused his sympathy. Through this encounter with poverty and suffering Johnson gained great appreciation for the mission's medical work. He commented many times about the open door of ministry in the hospitals and dispensaries.

Johnson was also impressed by the opportunities in the village schools among the Bhil people and noted that many had first heard the gospel there. Many evangelists and laymen in the churches had received their initial Bible instruction in village schools.

A Move into Nasik District

Clayton and Lucille Kent were the first missionaries to take up work in Nasik District—at Satana. Their first step was to open a dispensary to give opportunity for loving service and witness. The Kents also learned, through having been called several times to help the sick in Kalvan, some twenty-one miles away, that the people there were eager to have missionaries among them. When they asked about opening a dispensary they found the whole village, including Kalvan's leaders, fully cooperative.

Though the Kents were alone at Satana and felt the strain of the heavy workload, they continued to be burdened about Kalvan. After prayerful consideration they decided to start work there also. A well-trained Indian nurse came to help them. The dispensary drew crowds of villagers, many of whom were afflicted with malaria. In time, evangelist Sasane came to work with them and to reach out to the surrounding villages. In this way, the large Nasik district was entered and a witness begun among its one million inhabitants.

Entry into Gwalior State

Johnson was never able to forget the sight of Indian multitudes like sheep without a shepherd and was eager that the expanding missionary force should meet the challenge of this need. He took the matter to the board of directors:

> The general director presented the urgent need for expansion into new fields in India and shared information about the unoccupied or poorly occupied areas. It was voted to ask him to correspond with the field.[2]

Indian independence had opened new areas for missionary entrance: the princely states. These states—592 in all—had maintained independence during the time of British rule, most led by hereditary rulers. Wanting to unify the country, the Indian government absorbed these states into the republic.

The field council considered Johnson's recommendation and agreed to survey an unoccupied area, but the field chairman was cautious and wrote to Johnson in a rather pessimistic tone.

> Humanly speaking, it is very questionable to start any new field in the Orient at the present time. I do realize your position in having so many candidates applying and the psychology of pushing into something new which always grips the imagination of the friends at home. In India we feel as though we are sitting on the top of a volcano expecting at any time an eruption. As far as I can understand, a change in government, either to the right or to the left, would just about finish the evangelical mission program in this land. The Congress party now in power keeps to the middle of the road, but if the socialists, or on the other hand, the orthodox Hindu party gets into power we fear the worst.[3]

The missionary heart of the chairman happily won the day and he continued his letter:

> Faith in God's overruling power disregards all human reasoning and we do plan to press on with this as if we were to stay here for good while the doors of opportunity to preach the gospel are still open. I also have to call to your attention that the starting of a new field does mean tremendous financial responsibilities.[4]

Encouraging Survey

The field council chose to survey the State of Gwalior, the sixth largest of the great feudal territories. (Gwalior is located about 400 miles north, between the western and northern India TEAM fields.) This state had been closed to missionary work and had few Christians among its four million people. Mr. and Mrs. Irvine Robertson, who spoke Hindi; Dr. and Mrs. Karl Klokke; and Mr. Meberg made the survey. Robertson's account of the trip is of interest:

> The land between the cities of Shivpuri and Guna in the center of the state was mostly under cultivation. Large and small villages were seen to be located two to five miles apart. Our hearts were filled with sorrow to know that these were places where the name of Jesus Christ had never been mentioned. These hard-working people were lost in sin but we rejoiced to think of the power of the gospel which is able to save such as these.[5]

The visitors were impressed by the crowds in Guna, which had a population of 20,000, and chose a place for an open-air meeting. People gathered even before the service began. Interest was high and there was a rush to buy gospel portions when offered for sale. The supply was quickly exhausted.

The board of directors received the report of the survey and the accompanying recommendation of the field council and on June 26, 1951, approved entry into Gwalior. The Robertsons arrived before the end of the year. This state was a hotbed of Hindu nationalism and consequent opposition to foreign influence. Missionaries experienced opposition in several ways—denunciations through news media and public demonstrations against them.

An Occasion for Hindu Wrath

A most unfortunate occurrence took place in 1961 in Guna, where Hindu opposition was particulary militant. Missionary Paul Kratofil saw that some cows had gotten into his garden and sent his dog to chase them out. One cow impaled itself on an iron bar in the gate and died. Passersby who saw the impaled cow immediately spread word that the missionary had "murdered" a cow, an object of Hindu worship.

A mob of 3,000 soon gathered and it was not long before they pushed down the gate and tried to break into the house, where the Kratofils had taken refuge in the attic. Deliverance came only when city officials sent police to disperse the mob. These officials had to satisfy the public clamor and so charged Kratofil with cow murder. Though the court exonerated Kratofil of this serious charge the incident effectively closed the door to his further missionary work in Guna. Others were able to continue their work.

Gwalior Expansion and Transfer

The Gwalior field staff later expanded to sixteen, including missionaries in the large nearby city of Jhansi. Their ministry continued under the direction of the Western India field until 1975. With some loss of personnel and few replacements, it was decided to combine the Gwalior and the North India fields, as both used the Hindi language and their ministries were similar.

Fiftieth Anniversary

The Western India field celebrated fifty years of history in 1955. Chairman Einer Berthelsen's report took note of the progress since the twenty-fifth anniversary observance. In 1930 thirteen missionaries were on the field, in 1955 seventy. Missionaries had worked from six stations then; now there were twenty-one. The number of organized churches in 1930 was not reported, but in 1955 there were forty-six. Baptized believers in the churches had increased from 581 to 1,879. Growth, though slow, was encouraging.

Light of Life Courses

One highlight in 1955 was the report on the Light of Life correspondence course ministry. The 24-lesson course on the Gospel of John had been authored by Don Hillis in 1949. Jane McNally made some later revisions and also wrote a similar course on Acts. The courses proved to be very helpful and other missions also began to make wide use of them.

The Light of Life office in Chalisgaon recorded the activity in India. In 1955, 20,947 had taken the English course on John and 5,052 had completed it. Five thousand had enrolled in Acts, of whom 1,671 had finished.

The Chalisgaon office was also responsible for the Marathi course and reported that 13,102 had enrolled in John with 1,074 completions; in Acts, 1,415 began and 392 finished. The courses in Hindi had a large enrollment paralleling that of the English courses. Since the beginning of the courses, 332,890 had begun with 56,158 finishing and obtaining certificates.

The continued rapid growth of this effective evangelistic Bible study makes it impossible to give an accurate account, but millions have been reached. Paul Sheetz stated in *The Sovereign Hand* (1971) that 2,010,516 students had been reached through various missions in twenty-one languages in India and Sri Lanka.

When I was in India in 1960, I asked questions about follow-up of students who clearly manifested an openness to the gospel. The answer was that the Light of Life staff held rallies at various places to which enrollees were invited and where there could be personal contact and more instruction. Of particular importance was the opportunity for lone students who had confessed Christ to come into fellowship with other Christians, a new experience for them. The new follow-up magazine, *Light of Life,* with which I was familiar, was pointed out as a useful tool.

> Early in the correspondence school's history, the staff realized that they soon lost contact with the students who had completed the courses, some of whom were still searching for the truth. So, in 1957, Miss McNally began an eight-page magazine, which included letters and questions from past and present students. This *Light of Life* magazine has since grown to a 32-page monthly English Christian periodical based in Bombay.[6]

Literature Ministry

Robert and Jean Couture laid the foundation of a literature ministry, Word of Life Publications, and started a Christian book club that had 895 members during the year. The book club was proving to be a good vehicle for distributing Christian reading material. Four books had been published and fourteen others were being prepared for publication.

Later, with cooperation of several other mission societies—the

Christian and Missionary Alliance, the Conservative Baptist Foreign Mission Society, and the Poona India Village Mission—Word
of Life Publications expanded its role in producing and distributing
Marathi Christian literature and moved its operations to Poona
(now Pune). In addition to Bob and Jean Couture, Earl and Jean
Conrad have had a large share in the literature work.

Hindustani Gospel Hour

Gwalior missionaries were producing a Hindi radio program—
the Hindustani Gospel Hour. This program, originated by Don
Rubesh of the Tibetan Frontier field, was broadcast over Radio
Ceylon in Sri Lanka. At that time it was said to be the only
half-hour gospel program in India's national language, understood
by 70 percent of the people.

Teaching the Word

Sunday school work was also in progress. Missionaries held
classes for teachers in Chalisgaon and Dharangaon and refresher
courses for pastors and evangelists. One hundred boys benefitted
from camps held in the Navapur district.

Bringing the Church into Focus

The missionaries' central concern was planting churches from
the fruit of the evangelistic work. District-wide tent evangelism
took place mostly in the cool season—November to February—
when missionaries and evangelists reached out for Christ to all the
villages. During this dry season, the farm families were not yet
busy in their fields and had more time to listen to the gospel.

The missionaries tried to encourage a growing sense of responsibility by the churches. They believed that when a church ordained
a pastor it should take on his full salary. The process was slow, but
in 1955 two churches paid their pastors' full salary and a third was
to begin the next January. The churches also assumed responsibility for spiritual uplift and teaching ministries. The church council
in each area arranged its own conference and quarterly day of
prayer. Berthelsen summed up his report with a look to the future:

The church still needs missionaries. The leaders are willing to admit this fact. In time, as the program of turning over progresses, there may be need of some readjustments and the work of the missionary may become more specialized, but the need still remains. There is much work yet to be done and much of this can only be done by the missionary. The great opportunity today is still evangelism, but equally important it is to get the church established so that she can carry more of the burden and responsibility. All that we can do in evangelizing and teaching is needed today.[7]

Concern for the Cities

Noting the streets crowded with people when I visited Delhi and Bombay in the mid-1960s, I asked our field leaders how much evangelical witness was in these two cities. In Delhi there was very little; TEAM had only correspondence course contacts. In Bombay, much the same—Light of Life enrollees, and one small effort near the airport where a West Khandesh Christian employed by Indian Air Lines gathered a few people together on Sundays.

Later, after a visit to India in February 1966, I reported to the board of directors:

Particularly gratifying to me was the action taken by both the Tibetan Frontier and India Field Councils to seriously consider ministries in the large cities of New Delhi, Bombay, and Nasik.[8]

The first move into an urban area in Maharashtra State was in early 1967, when work began in Nasik City, the capital of Nasik District. Lazarus Padale began holding regular church services on April 23, and reported an average attendance of twenty-one adults and twenty-three children. Christians were drifting from the villages to the larger cities and there was need for a spiritual ministry among them.

Bombay Targeted for Entry

About the same time, the field council decided to initiate work in the port city of Bombay, the populous capital of Maharashtra. Knowing that there were many in Bombay who had taken Light of Life courses, the council asked Jane McNally to develop a center and form a nucleus of those already contacted for the gospel. The

514

chairman's report for 1968 gave information about the first steps taken:

> Work in Bombay has now begun and numerous opportunities are before us. A great deal has been learned about the city through the willing help of Christians. Sion, a section of Bombay close to the main arteries of travel, has no Protestant work apart from a Malayalee Brethren group, and is the proposed district for locating a Christian ministry in the metropolis.[9]

Open Door and Threatened Obstacle

As is often the case in the work of the Lord on the mission field, when a door opens obstacles loom that threaten to halt the forward progress. This was evident in the plan to develop a church ministry in Bombay. The contacts made through Light of Life correspondence courses provided an opening wedge but a church planter was needed to develop a strong ministry. The problem was understandable. The missionaries were devoting their time and energy to preparing the Indian church leaders to take full responsibility for the 46 organized and 17 developing churches, so it was difficult to think positively of expansion into a new area. This would be a formidable task even if the missionary force were at full strength and expanding. But now the missionaries were down to 20 percent of their earlier strength.

It is not surprising that when Jack MacDonald made an official visit to India in 1975 he found an atmosphere of discouragement. The missionaries' energy was concentrated on transferring responsibility in the most orderly way to the Indian church leaders. His impression: "There was not the slightest intention of expanding to Bombay." MacDonald observed that three men were key to the situation—three who at various times served as field chairman and one of whom, Einer Berthelsen, was anticipating retirement. Earl Conrad had earlier asked to not be selected as field chairman. That left Ralph Hertzsprung as the only one available for the chairmanship. Yet, if the Bombay work was to be launched Hertzsprung was the one to undertake that task.

MacDonald went to Conrad, asking him to reconsider and take

the chairmanship for one year—if Berthelsen would agree to take over after a year of furlough. Conrad presented the plan to the conference, in session at the time. MacDonald's capsule report tells the outcome:

> The conference responded. Optimism was high, and it seemed that hearts became encouraged. Ralph and Lois Hertzsprung were contacted by telephone, and they accepted the assignment to go to Bombay to begin a church planting ministry. Earl Conrad will serve for one year as chairman beginning in July of 1976, until Einer Berthelsen comes back in July of 1977 to resume the post. Earl and Jean Conrad will return in July of 1978 after a year of furlough. God willing they will minister in and through the churches.[10]

A year later, Earl Conrad, as chairman, reported to the conference:

> Our Bombay work entered a new phase in 1976 when the Hertzsprungs went there in mid-August. Their industry and prayers are beginning to show results. Services are being conducted regularly in two places. In addition, a Bible study with an average attendance of fifteen and two Bible clubs, averaging eleven each, are also being held weekly.[11]

The churches established in Bombay adopted the name of Open Bible Fellowship. The chairman's report for 1981 had an update:

> Open Bible Fellowship has two departments, English, with an average attendance of sixty each Sunday morning and Marathi with thirty. In addition it has a youth group and a Sunday school with 110 students. Robert and Jean Couture filled in for six months while the Hertzsprungs were on furlough. Ulhas Raiborde is pastor of the Marathi department and James Salins assists in the English work.[12]

Norman Niemeyer, area foreign secretary, visited and ministered on the Western India field on a number of occasions. He was particularly impressed by the opportunity for further church ministry in the crowded city of Bombay. Upon his return from a visit in May 1983 he reported to the board of directors:

> In 1982 I stood with Ralph Hertzsprung on the top floor of a commercial building which was in the process of being sold. We asked God to give us one large section of that floor which could be used as both the Open Bible Fellowship church and a Word

of Life retail bookstore. One year later, I entered the same top floor on Easter Sunday morning. More than 200 people gathered to remember the resurrection of Jesus Christ. I cannot describe the spiritual excitement that filled my soul that morning. Here was undeniable evidence of God's working in Bombay.[13]

Closing Field—Open Doors

Over a period of twenty-five years the field chairmen's reports detail a wide spectrum of activity by missionaries who had matured in the use of the language and in their adjustment to the people and their culture. Each chairman in turn—Einer Berthelsen, Roy Martens, Earl Conrad, Clayton Kent, and Ralph Hertzsprung—reported on the work being carried out: village schools, boarding schools, hostels for school children, orphanage, medical dispensaries, hospital, literature work, correspondence courses, district evangelism, youth camps, radio work, church development, training for Christian service, lay training, women's classes, and vacation Bible schools.

Equipping Christian Workers

Conscious that they must prepare Indian Christians to take responsibility for maintaining and extending the gospel work initiated by the missionaries, the field leaders consistently emphasized training. As TEAM did not have a formal Bible institute, college, or seminary of its own, they did this largely through a program of scholarships.

The mission and the churches did not overlook the value of lower level training. The village schools and particularly the hostels for high school children provided opportunities for evangelism and Christian education. Scholarships assisted many high school graduates to attend Bible school or seminary. In 1957 the chairman reported sixty-six young people who were aided—thirty-three in high school, seven in teacher training, twenty-eight in Bible schools, four in college, and three in seminary.

The mission became a participant in the Maharashtra Bible College and in 1982 had fourteen young people enrolled. From time to time it provided staff for the Union Biblical Seminary at Yeotmal and had students in attendance. The growing number of churches thus had a source of supply for trained workers.

Training Lay Workers

An effective training instrument was the Berean Bible School, a short-term institute for laymen, which Leslie Buhler began about 1958 in Pimpalner. Part of the original objective was to impart Bible knowledge to laymen to raise the level of Christian life and testimony. It had been correctly observed that an untaught—and therefore weak—Christian was a negative testimony, rather than a shining light for Christ. The purpose was also to help laymen become effective in their witness and able to teach new converts.

That these aims were realized is clear from a response to an inquiry directed to Buhler:

> Especially in the Chinchpada area the trained lay leaders have done much of the evangelism leading to church planting, and the pastors have been able to include the lay workers in their church planting efforts. Most of the students at Berean have come from the Chinchpada area. At the annual and semi-annual meetings of The Evangelical Alliance Church the delegates from the local churches are up to 75 percent men who have studied at Berean. I think the Karanji church (Chinchpada area) has grown the most in the last 15 years. Today there are 3 or 4 daughter churches that have also been involved in evangelism and church planting. There are now Christians in over 20 villages surrounding Karanji.[14]

Medical Work Faces Restrictions

The medical work was a major means of contact with the people. Suffering people abounded and the missionaries took advantage of the opportunities for service in the name of Christ.

After India became independent the government increased its regulation of medical service. This might not have been a move to curtail mission activity as much as it was to control an increasing number of poorly trained would-be dispensers who were out to make money. In 1955 the government mandated that medicine be dispensed only by adequately trained personnel and it placed restrictions on the types of medicine that could be used in mission dispensaries.

The Pharmacy Act, in 1957, went a step further, requiring that "no dispensary be registered with the government unless it is under the supervision of a qualified doctor." These were reasonable requirements, but tended to limit the help that could be given by nurses. The saving feature was that the mission had a hospital at Chinchpada, with a doctor to take responsibility for general oversight of the dispensaries.

Keeping the hospital staffed with missionary doctors was not easy given the restrictions on the entry of foreign doctors. After Dr. Klokke left the field Dr. Albert Holt took over the work and served until he contracted polio. Dr. Alton Olson and Dr. Maynard Seaman rendered valuable help for a season and Dr. Ormond Uptigrove for a longer period. Dr. Chopde and Dr. Patil, who received medical training under TEAM scholarships, served very well for shorter periods.

Dr. Uptigrove realized that a more satisfactory long-term arrangement was necessary; therefore in 1970 he and the field council conferred with the Emmanuel Hospital Association (EHA) about affiliation. EHA was an association of Christian hospitals in India and could deploy Christian doctors to areas of need. This was especially important in a rural setting such as Chinchpada where it was difficult to obtain and keep qualified doctors.

Though TEAM no longer had direct control of the medical work it continued to have a spiritual ministry. The Chinchpada area reported the largest number of converts, year after year, which may have been due in part to the testimony of those who dispensed Christian love and the saving message as well as medicine.

Threads to Follow

Three threads began to appear in the reports of the 1960s and 70s and became more pronounced as time went on. One thread was the possibility of government action to limit the activity of missionaries, to restrict or prohibit their entry, to expel those presently in the country, or to make conversion to another religion illegal. National and state parliaments introduced bills by extreme Hindu partisans from time to time but the most drastic proposals failed to pass—undoubtedly because of the prayers of the Lord's people.

The constant drumbeat of low-key threats and the steadily shrinking missionary force began to impress the field leaders that time was short. They must involve the Indian people more and more in the essential ministries to strengthen the churches. They must also have a plan to safeguard the property for the benefit of the Lord's work.

Church Advance

A second thread evident in the reports was the steady advance being made in the churches. The chairmen continually urged that more responsibility be assumed by the churches. At the same time their reports tabulated the steady progress. To them the growth may have seemed slow but a comparison year by year gave reason for encouragement. Note some of the figures:

	Organized Churches	Not yet Organized	Baptized Members
1939			581
1955	46		1,879
1960	38		1,457
1963	38		1,769
1967	49		2,437
1969	46	14	2,614
1972	47	14	2,326
1975	46	17	3,281
1978	47	16	3,524
1981	53	22	5,622
1984	64	27	6,697
1989	73	30	8,645

Dealing with Property

A third thread was the matter of proper provision for the mission property. By standards of other countries, the properties were modest and not particularly valuable. Yet they were adequate for the mission's purposes and if their use were denied to the church, this would be a serious handicap indeed. With TEAM registered as a foreign organization, the law required that ownership revert to the government if the missionaries had to leave—which seemed a possibility. The churches would have no claim on the buildings they were using for worship or other related purposes.

Ralph Hertzsprung, in the chairman's report for 1968, reviewed the situation:

> We live in uncertain days. Missions and mission programs may not long continue in the patterns of the past. We do not bemoan these passing ways, but we must face the future, adjust to changing conditions, and consolidate the work which has developed during the past sixty-three years. The following are four priorities to which we must give our attention and, during this conference, initiate further steps necessary to insure the ongoing of the church:
>
> 1. Arrangements for turning over church properties and those institutions which will assist the church in its responsibilities.
>
> 2. Disposal of mission properties not being utilized or which might be considered superfluous to the church in the absence of the mission.
>
> 3. The Indianization of institutions and ministries which can be operated by the nationals and would be considered essential to the church.
>
> 4. Complete self-support and self-government of the Indian church.[15]

The first step toward implementing Hertzsprung's recommendations was to establish The Evangelical Alliance Ministries Trust in 1971 with a membership of missionaries and Indian Christians. The plan was that as missionaries would be reduced in number, their places in the Trust would be filled by Indians. Clayton Kent and George Martin, Asia foreign secretary, did major work on bringing the Trust into being. Though at first this arrangement made little difference in the actual conduct of the work, as time went by Indian Christians assumed major responsibility.

The Trust was legally responsible for property and finance, and became increasingly involved in the direction of the work. Vijay Khisty, for some years active in the Light of Life ministry, was named executive secretary of the Trust in 1983.

Village Churches Organize

Most of the village churches established by the Indian Christians saw the Trust as coming between them and the mission, and so formed their own organization of country churches—The Evangelical Alliance Christian Churches Trust. It seemed at first that having two separate church organizations could be divisive. Earl Conrad commented on this situation and was prayerfully hoping for the best as he gave his annual report for 1985:

> Fortunately, God led the missionaries in earlier conferences to form TEAM Trust and to give Indians leadership both in the para-church ministries and in The Evangelical Alliance Christian (TEAC) Churches, too. So, most of the ministries started by TEAM are prospering under the Lord's hand through the Indians' lives and ministries. The hostels, schools, Light of Life Bible Correspondence School, Berean Bible School, urban church ministries, and property matters are run by TEAM Trust. The village churches are organized independently as TEAC churches; and they voted in January 1986 to stay separate from TEAM Trust. The missionaries are cooperating with both trusts as the Lord leads and as there are needs to be met.[16]

Continued Shrinking of Missionary Staff

Earl Conrad gave this report in an annual conference of only five missionaries, including himself. These five, with two on furlough, were the full missionary body. By 1990 the number would be reduced to three, as missionaries retire and new recruits cannot obtain visas. While those who remain continue to be active in essential ministries, it is clear that the future of the entire TEAM-related work lies with the Indian Christians—the more than seven thousand who do not bow the knee to idols of wood or stone. They have been prepared for this day and the Holy Spirit who indwells them enables them to serve the Lord faithfully among people engulfed in spiritual darkness. The believers shine as lights in that darkness. Most of the growth in the churches in recent years has been through their witness.

In his report to the annual field conference for the year 1987, chairman Ralph Hertzsprung referred to the fast-approaching time when the last TEAM missionary would leave western India. He was thankful for both the fellowship of churches and a stable, functioning organization to carry forward many other ministries:

> Thus the western India field has brought into being two daughter organizations. It should also not be forgotten that there are two other well-established independent organizations that have had very solid roots through TEAM missionaries and are today functioning quite satisfactorily, namely, Word of Life Publications and Light of Life Society of India. We trust that under God these four organizations will perpetuate the work that TEAM missionaries have undertaken in the many decades of their ministry in India. While anticipating our departure, the pain is lessened by the realization that the work will continue under national leadership, and for this we give thanks to the Lord.[17]

The Sowers' Prayer

A poem by Olga Noreen, who spent many years as a missionary in western India, sums up the experience and aspirations of those who sowed the seed there:

The Sower

The sower of God's holy Word went forth his seed to sow,
On India's hot and barren plains, among the high and low.
As he beheld the needy fields, the sower voiced a prayer:
"May for Thy Name's own glory, Lord, this seed rich fruitage
  bear."

Some by the trampled wayside fell, and Satan's watchful eye
Was quick to see and snatch away, while some the passersby
Did stra'tway crush beneath their feet, till in that heart no trace
Remained of what was heard of God's redeeming grace.

Some fell on hard and stony ground, where was no depth of earth,
The hearts with joy received the Word, but failed to see its worth;
When winds of persecution came from relative and caste,
Their tender faith could not endure, but withered in the blast.

Some fell among the cruel thorns—the Word in truth they heard,
And to the better things of life their hearts within were stirred.
But filled anon with anxious care they failed to trust the Lord;
Enduring fruitage they had none, for lust had choked the Word.

Some fell on good and fertile ground—Lord give us eyes to see
Where Thou hast thus prepared the soil, that we who sowers be
May find the souls that wait to hear Thy sacred Word today;
Who long to meet and know Thee, Lord, the Life, the Truth,
   the Way.

The harvest time is coming soon, when sowing days are o'er,
When Christ shall come to claim His own, and time shall be no
   more.
Lord, grant that then from India's plains a ransomed host shall be
Assembled there to sing Thy praise through all eternity.[18]

FROM THE BORDERS OF TIBET— OUTWARD

The Tibet-Nepal frontier of northern India presents a spectacular mountain view. If missionaries responded primarily to the beauty, this area would indeed attract many. On the other hand, if their response was affected by travel difficulty or scattered population, it would attract few. For the first twenty years—1927 to 1947—the mission work was near the border of northern India and Nepal and along the pathways leading to Tibet. The next twenty years brought limited expansion among the scattered mountain people. Only in the last twenty-three years has the work spread down to the populous plains and crowded cities.

Pioneering in Bhot

The ministry to which TEAM succeeded in 1946 was the fruit of the pioneer labors of the Rev. and Mrs. Ezra B. Steiner, who after thirteen years of service with a Mennonite board in central India felt led of the Lord to begin a work close to the Tibetan border. This took them to the region known as Bhot, a mountainous triangle of northern India bordered by Tibet and Nepal. A blend of Hindu, Tibetan, Nepali, and aborigines stock, the Bhotiyas are Hindu, Buddhist, and animistic in religion.

Tibetan Frontier Mission

The Steiners came to Dharchula in 1927 and took over the work Dr. Martha Sheldon had pioneered from 1894 to 1912. Naming their work the

Tibetan Frontier Mission, they aspired to reach Tibetans beyond the 16,750-foot Lipu pass to the north and the Nepalis just over the Kali-Ganga River in front of their mission station. "The objective from the beginning was to open the closed doors of Tibet and Nepal."[1]

Tibetans in great numbers passed Dharchula on this main escape route from the frigid winters of Tibet to the warmth of India. Although the missionaries gave medical help, evangelism was the primary ministry. As a result Tibetans, Nepalis, Bhotiyas, and Indians believed on the Lord Jesus Christ. Though some remained scattered others were brought together to form churches or to join existing churches.[2]

Merger and Reinforcement

The Steiners' children, Bradford and Anita, left India after high school, completed their education in America, and returned to Bhot as Dr. and Mrs. Bradford Steiner and the Rev. and Mrs. Charles (Anita) Warren in April 1947. On the advice of and with the blessing of their parents, these young couples had contacted TEAM, not only to apply as missionary candidates but also to request that TEAM take over the Tibetan Frontier Mission field. After prayerful consideration, the board approved the proposal and received the work as the Tibetan Frontier field of TEAM at its October 1946 meeting and appointed the parents and younger couples as missionaries.

A Pilot but No Plane Service

This was a time when many young people were applying, and by 1951 fifteen missionaries were either active in four stations or at language school. Among the first were Don and Frieda Rubesh. Don, an experienced pilot, hoped to use a plane to transport missionaries and thus enable them to avoid the ninety-mile walk over steep mountain trails from Almora to Dharchula. This did not prove feasible. Not only was flying through mountain passes extremely hazardous, but the Indian government would not allow a foreigner to fly so close to China. Furthermore, any level land was needed for agriculture, and could not be spared for the many landing strips required for an effective aviation program.

Johnson Visits—the Hard Way

General director Johnson visited northern India three times, in 1949, 1953, and 1957. On his first visit he was eager to get to the frontier stations of Dharchula, Sirkha, Liktar, and Berenag. When informed that this would require long days of walking over precipitous mountain trails, he was not to be discouraged. Don Rubesh accompanied him a good part of the way. Don was able to get a horse for him, but this presented problems. Johnson found adjustment to the saddle difficult especially on the steep up and down grades. Johnson preferred to walk but had to endure the pain of poor walking shoes. A man of determination, weariness and pain did not stop him from completing his 180-mile round trip to the border. When he had opportunity to preach to people, such as at a local fair, he eagerly did so.

Enemy Hindrances

It is not surprising that the enemy tried to hinder this significant advance among people who had long been held captive by him. He had to challenge the quadrupling of the missionary body in six years.

Death touched the Steiner family in 1949 in the sudden passing of Mrs. Ezra Steiner and Cheryl Ellen, the infant daughter of Bradford and Martha Steiner. The health of Martha made it necessary that she and Bradford move out of the border area in 1950 to Landour, where a useful ministry awaited them at the Landour Community Hospital.

A new missionary, Marjorie Smiley, on her first trip over the mountains toward Dharchula on December 22, 1953, slipped from the trail (or was jostled by her dismounted horse) and fell directly to her death in the Gori Ganga River more than 50 feet below.

A brief hope in 1955 that the mission field could be extended into Nepal came to naught. The Nepal government required a signed agreement that those entering would not engage in religious activities. If this had been only in the law, and not part of the agreement, the board would have approved, but to solemnly agree not to evangelize, at a time when there were no witnessing Nepalis, was a promise that TEAM could not make in good conscience. This disappointed missionaries who had come to the border area hoping to enter Nepal.

Indian Government Restrictions

By the mid-1950s foreigners were no longer permitted in most border areas and by 1962, they were required to leave Dharchula. With serious border tensions between India and China, the Indian authorities were anxious not to provoke the Chinese. Happily, nationals working with the Christian groups could continue their work and had freedom of travel. The church at Dharchula remained strong and its day school maintained a fruitful ministry.

If Not Tibet or Nepal, Where?

Missionaries had come to this field with their hearts set on winning Tibetans and Nepalis. With much of this opportunity restricted, what were they to do? They entered every open door near at hand. They had studied language in Landour, high in the Himalayan mountains. This area was clearly related to the district they had left. Furthermore, the frontier call still loomed large, so to work here would ready them for the time the door to Bhot reopened. Those who could not serve at the border quickly found useful avenues of service here.

Dr. Steiner became superintendent of the Landour Community Hospital and was followed in that post by Dr. Zerne Chapman. Gordon Van Rooy began correspondence courses, which were organized into the Landour Bible Institute. Out of this grew the Leadership Instruction and Training (LIT) system of study which found wider usage in India and in other countries, TEAM's Trinidad field among them.

Charles Warren became chairman of the Hill Villages Mission, a local effort to reach the people in the hill country near Landour. He also pastored the Union Church in Mussoorie and answered many requests to teach Bible at conferences throughout India.

An opportunity came to develop a camping and conference ministry at Deodars. Olof and Helen Dubland were active in this work. Albert Bowdish served his fellow missionaries as field treasurer and took part in local ministries. His wife, Pearl, developed and published the Go-Tell series of Sunday school papers. Ralph and Nellann Seefeldt kept in touch with the frontier activities of national workers and received permission to make occasional short visits into this restricted area.

"A Doorway from Tibet"

Unexpectedly, a new door opened in 1959. Some of these missionaries had longed to go to Tibet; now Tibetans came to them. The DaLai Lama, the spiritual and political ruler of Tibet—revered as a virtual god—had fled the Chinese communist occupation and devastation of his capital, Lhasa, and had come to Landour to find refuge. It did not take the missionaries long to make contact with key people among the Tibetans and inquire how they could help them. These refugees, limited in language, needed a way to survive in this foreign country. They observed that the English language was spoken by many and so English seemed to be the key.

The missionaries took advantage of this opportunity and sponsored several Tibetan students in the English-medium Wynberg-Allen Christian School. Others were reached in tutorial classes. Some were welcomed into missionary homes. Many missionaries were involved in the Tibetan work, especially Ruth Stam, Irma Jean Wessels, Elcho and Millie Redding, and Dr. and Mrs. Maynard Seaman. No congregation of believers was assembled as a result of these ministries but individual Tibetans received a clear witness. Those coming to Christ are recorded in the Lamb's Book of Life.

Contrasting Pictures

My first visit in 1960 included New Delhi, Mussoorie, Landour, and the mountain preaching points of Saniodiar and Nag. Two vivid but contrasting pictures were etched in my memory. One was of the relatively few people in the scattered mountain huts, the other of the milling throngs in the cities. While I gained much respect for the dedicated missionaries—men and women—who climbed the steep mountain trails to reach isolated homes with the gospel message, I wondered who was reaching the urban crowds.

As I reviewed the missionaries' work, I felt led to emphasize the importance of follow-up. This was particularly important in the correspondence course ministry, because enrollees were often isolated, lacking Christian fellowship so essential for growth.

Some Pertinent Questions

My next visit was in late 1964 when I met with the field council in New Delhi. This stop gave me opportunity to review the ministries. As we conferred, my thoughts were continually going to the two pictures—the scattered homes in the mountain areas and the crowded city streets. As we drove along, I asked one of the men: "How many churches are there in this city of four million?"

"There are quite a few, maybe thirty or forty," was the reply.

"How many truly evangelical groups?" I questioned.

"Not many, probably five or six," came the answer.

"Should TEAM not be trying to reach these people? You have contacts here through the correspondence courses."

A Seed Germinating

That was the heart of our exchange, but the Lord caused it to lodge in the memory of the field council members. The Spirit of God allowed these few questions to become the springboard for a most remarkable work in this capital of India—the Delhi Bible Fellowship (DBF). That DBF is known throughout India is gratifying, but far more important is its impact on souls in that populous city and among people whose influence reaches far beyond Delhi.

The Flowering of a Vision

Delhi Bible Fellowship was conceived when missionary Murray Carter obeyed the vision of following up students of the correspondence courses offered by the mission.

> The words of Caleb came to me, "Lord give me this mountain" and I was moved to ask God for the multitudes of this great nation. I determined to live where our students lived and contact them. Delhi with the greatest concentration of contacts was the place to begin.[3]

Carter took his concern to the field chairman, Charles Warren, whose immediate response was, "The field council has wanted to send someone to Delhi for the past two years, but we have not had anyone ready to go."[4]

As it was clear that this was the direction the Lord was leading, Carter did a preliminary survey and in his report to the field council wrote:

> It is a safe guess that one church of a thousand members would not exist if all those in Delhi who have been born again by the Spirit of God were united in one body.[5]

Carter's vision was twofold: (1) to plant a large Bible-believing church in the south of Delhi "to reach the upper middle class... including diplomats from many nations," and (2) "to get the many correspondence students into Bible clubs which in time would become Bible-believing churches in all parts of the city." Warren approved the plan but counseled the Carters to first take their year of furlough to present their vision to a circle of prayer supporters.[6]

Recruiting Prayer Warriors

Coming back to India in 1968, Murray and Florence Carter looked forward to beginning the work. First, they wrote to those in the homeland who had been urged to pray:

> This letter goes to 1,000 people. Each of you represents a family and a church. Together you constitute a very large army of prayer warriors. If you will join with us and pray continually, I believe that we will see God do a great work in Delhi.[7]

"Get Started"

With Warren's help the Carters found a suitable house, which also had room for small meetings, and moved to Delhi in October 1968. Carter described his emotions after he began the challenging task of ministering in this capital city:

> I was frustrated and floundering around. Where to start and how to go about it? I asked fellow-missionaries and many other friends and received many answers. Finally John Dorsey, a Bible Presbyterian missionary from the other side of the city, gave me a word that got us started. "The thing to do is *start*. You won't ever accomplish anything as long as you continue running around the city talking about it!"[8]

The first English fellowship meeting was December 1, 1968, with thirteen present, including the family. Invitations were sent to 200 correspondence school students for the first Hindi meeting December 8. The attendance was eleven, including just two of the 200 invited. "That was our beginning!" The second English service had eighteen. By the fifth Sunday there were twenty-eight in the English and twenty-one in the Hindi service.

A Good and Right Decision

With the February average attendance going to thirty-one in the English and sixteen in the Hindi service, Carter began speculating what could be done if more help were at hand, so wrote to his prayer supporters, "We need an Indian evangelist to assist us full time and the money for his wages and housing."[9]

Carter had more to say on the same subject four months later in his next general letter:

> In our last newsletter we asked for funds for a national worker. Dr. Mortenson, our mission general director, suggested that we wait until the meetings can pay for a national worker in order to keep the work indigenous. God is answering prayer in this regard. He has brought several people to us who, though working at a full time job, have offered to help in their spare time with teaching, preaching, and visiting.... The second way God has answered is through the offerings. They are very good, in fact almost unbelievable.[10]

"Carter's Meeting" Grows

Word was getting around Delhi that the "Carter meeting" was where to go to find warm Christian fellowship and also a good place to take unsaved friends to hear the gospel.

> On August 31, [1969] we had a Youth for Christ team from Singapore with us. By opening the French doors and seating people in the front patio, using Laura's bedroom, and replacing all the furniture in our living-dining room with chairs, we were able to accommodate the 200 people who came. We were thrilled at the response. This showed us the potential we have in the work. Our Sunday school is also growing! We now have six classes—three Hindi and three English. Our highest attendance is 44, but if everyone would come at the same time, the classes would bulge. Our Bible Studies are growing, too. Murray has three—Tuesday, Wednesday, and Thursday nights.[11]

By the end of December 1969, the Carters could report that they were ministering to 100 different people in six meetings a week and that decisions for salvation and dedication were being made week by week. But stopping to consider the vast number of unreached in the capital city, they looked to the future and pleaded for more prayer.

"We Have a Name!"

By March 1970 the Sunday evening meeting had grown to between 60 and 80, which necessitated a move to a hall in the center of the city. There was growth, but Carter recognized a difficulty.

> Our problem was that we did not really have a name. The morning meeting was Family Bible Hour and the evening Bible Fellowship Hour, but to my embarrassment people continued to call it "Murray Carter's Meeting." One night Ben Wati phoned me and asked, "Who is speaking at the Delhi Bible Fellowship?" I said to my wife, "We have a name!" Everyone liked it and it has remained.[12]

Building Confidence and Strength

When Carter started the work he invited the leaders of several Christian organizations to meet with him for prayer. These leaders were in ministries whose outreach was generally beyond the borders of India but with some involvement within Delhi. These men brought spiritual maturity to the fellowship. They in turn welcomed a church home where they and their employees could find warm fellowship and to which to refer local converts.

Seefeldts Join the Delhi Work

Ralph and Nellann Seefeldt were assigned to Delhi in 1973 and the Fellowship committee asked them to serve in Kailish in the southern part of the city. The first need was to find a place to meet and Carter helped in this search. Florence wrote about the experience:

> In May, during the hottest week of the season, the Lord prompted Murray to visit a hotel in that area to see if it had a conference room which would be suitable. When the temperature outside was 112 degrees, Murray walked into an air-conditioned, fully carpeted conference room of the Vikram Hotel. This was the place God had for our new Sunday morning service. The manager told Murray and Ralph that the service was for a good cause and they could use the room each Sunday morning free of charge. We serve a God of miracles today! June third, in the middle of the hot season, we had our first service with 15 people and the next Sunday 35 were there.[13]

Fifth Anniversary of DBF

As the Delhi ministry neared its fifth anniversary in the fall of 1973, Carter reviewed what God had done in those five years:

> The Delhi Bible Fellowship is an organized church [registered with the Indian government under the Societies Act], meeting in four separate congregations, along with Bible clubs, ladies' meetings, and home Bible studies. We have some contact in most every part of the city. Week by week souls are being saved.... But what are five hundred in the light of five million? We praise God for the ones and twos, but multitudes are passing into eternity without Christ.[14]

Visit to Vikram

As I was to be on a visit to our India fields in October 1973, I was invited to participate in the Sunday worship at the Vikram Hotel. The conference room was filled to capacity. Afterward we all gathered around the outside swimming pool for a memorable baptismal service. There were twelve to fifteen candidates for baptism, mostly Indian. Of special interest was a teenage girl from Bhutan—one of the few to become a Christian—and a converted drug addict, a young man from England.

In the evening I attended the well-filled meeting at the YWCA hall. Here many who worshipped at the widely distributed Sunday morning services came together for the evening fellowship.

Warren Called to be Pastor

In May 1974, when Murray and Florence Carter were due for furlough, the church board, after seeking the Lord's will, extended a call to Charles and Anita Warren. Warren, a gifted pastor and Bible teacher, began his ministry at DBF in June 1974. A year later he reported on the progress:

> God is blessing with new people attending services each week. On Sundays, services are held in five locations. During the week Bible studies, women's meetings, and children's Bible clubs are conducted in various areas of the city. One large central meeting is held on Sunday evenings when as many as possible come together to worship. We had been renting a hall at the YWCA but it had begun to be too small and people were having to be turned away. A larger hall has now been rented in one of Delhi's large downtown hotels. This new location is drawing people who perhaps would not come to another place of worship, and God is blessing.[15]

Ten Years of Growth

The tenth anniversary booklet, *A Decade in Delhi*, lists a church board of nine mature Indian Christians, and additionally a deacon board of thirteen members, all nationals except one. The pastoral staff had three missionaries—Warren, Carter, and Robert Reid, and three nationals—R. K. Mala, C. B. Samuel, and Alexander Singh. (Reid had developed a similar strong work in the city of Jhansi.)

Mala, a movie star, had worshipped the snake god until his mother was bitten by a snake and became seriously ill. Mala cried out to God—not the snake god—and she recovered. Determined to find this God, he searched a Gospel of John which he had been handed. There he found Him in the person of Christ. Even without formal training he became a very effective evangelist and pastor to the Hindi congregations.

Objection to Return

When the Carters were due for furlough in 1979, they applied for the required "No objection to return" endorsement in their passport, and were shocked that it was refused. Their appeal to the Indian government for reconsideration was also denied. When they returned to Canada they applied for a new visa but it was not granted, even on appeal. So the door closed to further service in India where they had invested almost two decades of their lives. The Carters did not take this as a termination of their missionary service but entered another door that was opening for them—in Italy.

Missionary Interest Grows

As DBF matured a concern to share in a world missions outreach began to develop. In 1979 DBF held its first missionary conference, and as a result took on the responsibility of supporting three Indian missionary couples and a number of other individuals and ministries in India. In the following year DBF held vacation Bible schools with 250 children enrolled. Eighty young people attended the youth camp.

Planning to Build

In sixteen years of widening ministry the Fellowship had gotten along remarkably well in rented quarters, but there came a growing need for more space. After praying about this for some time the congregation launched a building program on Easter Sunday 1984. While the building fund was growing, government red tape blocked the way of the necessary permission to build a Christian church in Delhi. The hindrance had not been removed by 1989.

Objection to Remain

For some time the Warrens had indications that their residence permits would not be extended. It is possible that Hindu extremists were becoming conscious of the effectiveness of the Warrens' work and, having denied the Carters the right to remain, felt they needed to close off yet another Christian channel. On January 6, 1986, Warren wrote:

> Tomorrow we must leave Delhi and India. The appeal of our church, Delhi Bible Fellowship, to the Government of India for extension of our residential permit was rejected. We are grieved and disappointed but not disturbed. We believe God is sovereign in this decision and we willingly submit to His sovereignty.[16]

Robert Reid was then installed by the church board as the senior pastor. An able Bible teacher, Reid was founder of the Jhansi Bible Fellowship, a sister church about 400 miles from Delhi. The other pastors were Dr. Ramesh Richard, R. K. Mala, B. Johnson, and Alex Singh.

The Outward Reach

While the Lord's work in the Delhi Bible Fellowship was a center of intense interest, other ministries were also developing—in Landour-Mussoorie, in Gwalior, in Sri Lanka, and in Nepal—all outgrowths of the Tibetan Frontier work. Undoubtedly, the descendants of the Rev. and Mrs. Ezra Steiner, whose vision, dedication, and perseverance launched the frontier work, have viewed the broad scope and have been both amazed and gratified by the results. Let us briefly trace these other ministries.

Hindi-Speaking Fields Unite

It will be recalled that the Western India field opened a new area in Hindi-speaking Gwalior. With a significant part of the Tibetan Frontier field work being in Delhi, only 400 miles from the Gwalior section, and with the same language being used, the two field councils and the home office agreed that the Hindi work should be united under the name of North India field. This was approved by the board in January 1975.

Churches Planted and Growing

Church planting had gone on steadily in TEAM's North India work. In 1981 the annual report listed the following church ministries:

> Immanuel Church, Dharchula; Rajpur Bible Fellowship, Rajpur; Happy Valley Bible Fellowship, Mussoorie; Delhi Bible Fellowship, Delhi; Agra Bible Fellowship, Agra; Bethel Bible Fellowship, Shivpuri; Guna Church, Guna; Jhansi Bible Fellowship, Jhansi; Dandeldhura Church, Nepal.[17]

Contributing Ministries

In addition to the church work, missionaries and national coworkers were occupied in the following ministries: Jiwan Jyoti Bible Correspondence Center—a combination of the Landour Bible Institute and Hindi Light of Life Courses; Leadership Instruction and Training (LIT); Deodars Spiritual Life Center—a camp and conference ministry; Doon Medical Project; education of nationals through scholarships; and a Nepal medical work. Nationals active in these ministries included Nirmal Singh (Tibetan work), Swami Sundar Singh (education of nationals), L. G. Sacha (LIT), and Tashi Bahadur (Bible Correspondence Center).

Others Sharing in the Work

Recent retirees who spent a lifetime in the work are Albert and Pearl Bowdish, Olof and Helen Dubland, Dennis and Lillian Greenway, Robert and Geraldine Remington, and Margaret Vigeland.

Missionaries serving in 1990 are Carl and Marie Flickner, Iona Heppner, Robert and Ruth Reid, and Dale and Ruth Seefeldt. The Flickners are active in church ministries, as are the Reids. Iona Heppner has had a ministry in Christian education. Dale and Ruth (Warren) Seefeldt, after many years of working on a new Hindi translation of the Bible under the sponsorship of the Lockman Foundation, became full missionary members of TEAM in 1986. In a sense, they were always of TEAM because both are second generation missionaries.

Assuring Continuity

The same political pressures encountered by the missionaries of the Western India field were faced in north India. The government ceased granting visas. Some missionaries could not return for health reasons, some reached retirement age, and some, as we have seen, were requested to leave India when it became apparent that their work was effective in winning Indians to Christ. The solution to caring for the established work on the Western India field also had to be applied here. It was found that the work of the North India field could be brought under the same Trust. But more than a thousand miles separated the fields. The solution was to form a sub-committee of the Trust to administer the North India work.

George Samuel Serving

An Indian pastor, George Samuel, had been appointed strategy coordinator in 1981. According to the chairman's report his assignment was "to work with the field council to achieve our field goal of all ministries contributing effectively and efficiently toward church planting and nurturing church growth."[18]

His ministry was commended in Carl Flickner's 1986 report summing up the changes made:

> For the past several years the North India field of TEAM has been passing through a period of transition from missionary to national leadership. George Samuel, first as Strategy Coordinator and later as Director of Ministries, has played an important role in this change. The joint meeting of the Board of Management of TEAM Trust and the North India field council in November agreed to bring the ministries of the North India field directly under the management of the Trust.... We praise God for mature national leaders who will be able to carry on the ministries begun by missionaries with a vision for evangelism through camps, correspondence courses, schools, and medical work.[19]

Confidence for the Future

Those who spent long years to plant churches in northern India and along the borders of closed lands can take comfort that live, functioning churches continue to carry on a witness for the Lord in India. Nepal also has functioning groups of believers. Tibet has not yet been entered by a church planting team, but many Tibetans have received the gospel and some have been saved. These missionary pioneers look with confidence to the Sovereign Lord to bring in the harvest. They sowed and watered and God will cause the seed to germinate and grow for His glory.

SRI LANKA

The island nation of Sri Lanka (formerly known as Ceylon) has held TEAM's interest for 35 years; yet it is the field with the smallest missionary force. Its 15 to 16 million people, crowded into an area the size of West Virginia, are 72 percent Buddhist Sinhalese and less than 20 percent Hindu Tamils. Moors, Malays, and  mixed races make up the remaining 8 percent, and among them the Muslim and Roman Catholic religions claim about equal loyalty. Protestants are a small minority. TEAM's work here is an indirect outgrowth of the Tibetan Frontier field; a demonstration of God's sovereign opening of one door as another closed. The story is told quite fully in Paul Sheetz's book, *The Sovereign Hand*.

Don and Frieda Rubesh Enter New Field

Don and Frieda Rubesh, missionaries along the Tibetan frontier, anticipated a lifetime of service there, but were denied permission to remain. A radio ministry they had initiated in India was one means of opening the door to Sri Lanka.

> Don Rubesh began producing a series of radio programs with the hope of placing them on the powerful [Ceylon] station. While all other gospel programs for the area were in English, Rubesh chose to use Hindustani, a popular form of Hindi understood by 70 percent of India's people. He used Indian musicians and familiar Indian instruments and called it the "Hindustani Gospel

Hour." Radio Ceylon accepted Rubesh's weekly programs, and Back to the Bible Broadcast provided the financial backing.[20]

Agreement with Back to the Bible

Rubesh, a Nebraskan, enjoyed a long-term friendship with Theodore H. Epp, founder and director of Back to the Bible Broadcast, also based in Nebraska. When the Rubeshes were denied reentry to India, the Lord opened the way for them to represent Back to the Bible in Sri Lanka. Correspondence between Epp and David Johnson established a basis for Don and Frieda to have a dual relationship with Back to the Bible and TEAM. Most significantly, this arrangement qualified the Rubeshes to obtain one of the few visas granted to Christian organizations by this predominantly Buddhist nation.

Sri Lanka is the only country in which TEAM works where a visa is granted according to a ministry rather than to a named individual. The visa which the Rubeshes used could be transferred to a successor in their work. This enabled a substitute to serve when they went on furlough and it also provided the key for the entry of their son, Stanton, and his wife, Carol, in 1974 to carry on their church planting work.

English and Hindustani Programs

Don and Frieda began their Sri Lanka ministry in 1955. Not only did they put the Back to Bible programs on Radio Sri Lanka, they also were able to air the Hindustani Gospel Hour and several English language programs which they produced—"Quiet Corner" and "Children's Corner." Part of their time was spent in the follow up of the radio programs which Back to the Bible placed on the station. One effective tool they used was the Light of Life correspondence courses.

Government Restrictions

The year after the Rubeshes came to Sri Lanka, the government banned most Christian broadcasts but continued for a time to carry "Quiet Corner" and "Children's Corner" as sustaining programs.

541

Rubesh presented the gospel consistently through his choice of hymns and introductory comments. It was essential to "keep his foot in the door" hoping that Christian broadcasts would once again be allowed.

The programs that Don produced in Sinhalese and Tamil were sent to the Far East Broadcasting Company station in Manila to be beamed to Sri Lanka and India. Announcements concerning correspondence courses and literature received good response. When Radio Sri Lanka again accepted limited Christian programming, Don made arrangements for a Hindi language Back to the Bible program prepared in Delhi under the leadership of Bishan Singh. This program found wide acceptance throughout India.

Transition from Radio Work

Having allowed Stan and Carol to use their visa, the parents could no longer continue in Sri Lanka. This was timely for two reasons: Frieda's health was failing so she needed care at home and Don was asked by Back to the Bible to take on wider responsibility for its international broadcasts. Frieda passed away in 1979, and Don was ushered into the Lord's presence suddenly in 1985 when hit by a drunken driver.

The Rubeshes' ministry provides an example of vision and faithfulness. When they faced a closed door to service in India but refused to turn from their missionary calling, God honored their dedication and brought them into a place of greatly expanded outreach and blessing. Though much of their work is properly reported as the fruit of the Back to the Bible radio ministry, it did provide a foundation and much impetus for church planting in Sri Lanka.

Follow-through is Essential

In a paper about radio work, Bishan Singh made a significant statement concerning both its value and limitations:

> Through radio we can lead a listener to the point of decision, but we need someone to go to him and lead him to the Lord and to the church where he can have real Christian fellowship. Here

comes the work of the church.[21]

Whereas the first twenty years of TEAM's involvement in Sri Lanka were in radio and literature work, the next fifteen were concentrated on conserving the fruit through Bible teaching and church planting. Stanton Rubesh recognized the great value of what had been done before, but was also convinced that more was needed. Early in his ministry he wrote:

> Personal contact through the years has been limited to occasional follow-up rallies held in various central locations. For example, a concerted outreach was held this February in the eastern coastal city of Batticaloa. All six meetings were filled to capacity with people who had either taken the courses or listened to the radio programs. *The real problem is that there are very few solid evangelical churches into which converts can be channeled. Church growth in Sri Lanka has been very slow* [Italics supplied].[22]

Stan went on to explain that "international evangelistic organizations have made contacts in almost every corner of the island. But for all the effort, no appreciable numbers have been added to the church. This is true, for the most part, because the full cycle of the great commission has not been followed through"—that of making disciples.

Timely Counsel

The Lord directed in the timing of a visit to Sri Lanka by general director Winchell in February 1977 just as Stan and Carol were giving serious thought to how they should proceed in a church planting ministry. Winchell had only twenty-four hours for the Sri Lanka stop and wrote concerning that visit:

> Our most effective time was spent in studying goals for the future. The broad goal of a fellowship of evangelical churches with TEAM distinctives in the coming years was established. The immediate goal was to establish at least one weekly Bible study that can eventually become a church. This is to be done in the next two years before the Rubeshes' furlough.... The goal includes establishing churches in the Singhalese language, the major language of the island and a neglected area of current efforts in evangelism and church planting. I believe this basic

thinking has helped them to face the future with real encouragement.[23]

A Beginning in Kandy

With the goal of completing "the full cycle of the great commission," Stan and Carol searched out a concentration of correspondence course contacts in and around Kandy, the second largest city on the island. They began a Bible study in November 1977 with a group of these contacts:

> These were our first contacts and served as the nucleus of the group which we have come to call the Kandy Bible Fellowship. We have seen steady growth with someone new almost every Sunday. These are all new to the Christian faith, not people from other churches.[24]

A Brother's Timely Help

When Stan and Carol were due for furlough, Stan's brother, Ted, came out to continue the work and found it possible to extend his time. Carol expressed appreciation:

> Ted's assistance in the work here has been invaluable. He took our place while we were on furlough and now has a visa to stay at least until January and possibly longer. Many have prayed and God has answered. Both Ted and Stan have joined the faculty of the Lanka Bible College where we will send our own contacts for ministerial training in the future.[25]

A New Testament Church Founded

In addition to the Sinhalese service, the missionaries began work in English and reported in December 1980 that sixty-five people attended regularly every Sunday night. November 15, 1981, was the day selected to inaugurate the Kandy Bible Fellowship as a church with eighteen members. While the church was still very young, it and the missionaries had counsel and help from the outside. Dr. and Mrs. Walter Wilson of Renton, Washington, spent ten days in Kandy and from his rich pastoral experience Dr. Wilson taught church administration. Norman Niemeyer, area foreign secretary, shared insights from his church planting experience in Trinidad. The visitors brought great encouragement to these missionaries working very much alone.

Preparing for Growth and Permanence

By July 1982, the growth in maturity of the church members and the increased attendance convinced Rubesh that careful plans had to be made for the future.

> The church is now in a crucial stage of development, and it could go one of two ways. Either it could fizzle out as a movement, or it could stabilize and become a permanent fixture. It is the latter we are expecting and working for. Meeting in an inconvenient rented hall and other assorted places, as has been the case, does not contribute to the impression in the community that Kandy Bible Fellowship is here to stay. We have been able to build a strong and committed nucleus of believers intent now on expanding and becoming a center for evangelism and Bible teaching in the city of Kandy. At the beginning of this year the congregation set as a goal to find a central place for church activities. We have found just that place and this is the time to move.[26]

Sacrificing for a Church Home

The place the church committee found was ideal because of its accessible location. Though the owner had refused a previous offer of $100,000, he amazingly—and surely by God's intervention—accepted the bid of $65,000 from the church. The church members immediately began giving sacrificially, taking up an offering of $4,400 and pledging an additional $5,300 to be paid in the next year. This enabled the church to get the necessary financing to buy the building.

Two years later Stan reported the benefits of having their own permanent building:

> The Sunday school came alive. Regular services showed stability, and an evangelistic thrust put our new little church on the map. Our new facility gave us space for an expanded Christian resource center.... The church is still young and made up of new believers. But these growing Christians are assuming more and more responsibility, helping them to recognize and use their spiritual gifts.[27]

While Stan and Carol were busy in the church planting work,

they also produced a radio program called "Truth for Living." This was continued until 1986 when they set it aside for full-time church-related ministries.

By 1989 there was a membership in the Kandy Bible Fellowship of fifty-five. Average attendance was seventy with ninety in the Sunday school. No wonder that the missionary could joyfully exclaim, "God is committed to building his church and so are we. Under that mandate, our goal is to establish local churches in Sri Lanka."[28]

A New Door Opens

As 1990 opened, the missionaries were faced with a new and promising opportunity that would allow additional workers to come. A fourteen-bed hospital in the Digana International Village, Kandy, had been closed for about a year when TEAM was offered seven visas for personnel to reopen it. Dr. Andrew Rutherford, of TEAM's Oasis Hospital in the United Arab Emirates, investigated on behalf of the mission and joined with the Rubeshes in recommending that TEAM take advantage of the opportunity.

Lynn Everswick, area foreign secretary, visited Sri Lanka in January 1990 at which time an agreement was reached with the authorities. Dr. and Mrs. Maynard Seaman, whose visa to reenter Nepal was not renewed, agreed to take up the challenge of reopening the hospital and beginning this ministry, which has the potential of serving up to 50,000 people within three miles of the hospital.

The functioning group of believers in nearby Kandy enhances the opportunity for a fruitful spiritual ministry in this new location.

THE HINDU KINGDOM OF NEPAL

Nepal, a Hindu country of 56,136 square miles and a population of 17 million, landlocked in the Himalayan range, was long closed to Western influence and the gospel. The early S.A.M. missionaries had skirted its eastern fringes and the Steiners and others touched its western edges in a limited way. Dr. Bradford Steiner had presented the challenge of Nepal to the board of directors in his first letter in 1946:

> One of the great purposes of the [Tibetan Frontier] mission has been to carry the blessed gospel into the interiors of Tibet and Nepal. The Lord has been blessing and the doors of Tibet and Nepal have begun to swing open. Rev. and Mrs. E. B. Steiner have permission to enter at will and their native workers have been making regular evangelistic tours in these lands.[29]

A New Possibility for TEAM

To understand the readiness of the board members to consider Nepal as a new field, we must review the situation in the 1930s and 40s. The countries to the north of India seemed impenetrable. From west to east, Baluchistan in Iran, Afghanistan, Northwest Frontier Province in India, Tibet, Nepal, Sikkim, and Bhutan were all viewed as areas closed to the gospel. To now be presented with the possibility of entering Tibet or Nepal was exciting indeed.

Alert for an Open Door

Even when the missionaries in India were restricted from coming close to the borders they watched keenly for any opportunity to enter Nepal. In September 1955, Johnson reported to the board that permission had been received to send a survey team to investigate the possibility of having medical and agricultural workers serve within Nepal. However, the Nepal government made it clear that no religious activity or proselyting would be allowed. The board would not authorize the missionaries to go ahead on that basis, so for the time being the door to Nepal remained closed.

The Lord Prepares His Servants

While it did seem that nothing was being done, the Lord was

preparing his servants for this work. One of them, Maynard Seaman, while still in high school, heard a lady missionary tell that there was not one known Christian in Nepal. He began praying for this needy country and what he himself could do about the need. It would be twenty-two years before he reached the field of God's call. The Lord led him through medical school and later he and his wife, Dorothy, a nurse, applied to TEAM. When they arrived in India in 1960 they were asked to temporarily serve at the Chinchpada Hospital in western India. Later they proceeded to northern India for language study and work among Tibetans.

Seaman made an extensive survey of Nepal in early 1965, conferring with many key people. In his full report to the field council, the most important paragraph related to TEAM's possible action:

> I believe if we desired we could spearhead the medical work in Doti district some 60 miles east of Dharchula. The biggest barrier seems to be the question of a union with a group which has relations with the N.C.C. [National Christian Council, affiliated with the World Council of Churches]. I doubt that an independent entry would be met with a welcome unless we were to work as a government aid mission.30

Finally, a Viable Option

In the fall of 1965, Seaman received a letter from Dr. R. L. Fleming in Nepal with the information that Dr. Katharine Young, who was carrying on a medical ministry mainly to lepers in Dandeldhura, would have to retire to work in a less difficult location. Would Dr. Seaman be interested in taking over that work? This was of immediate interest to Seaman because Dr. Young was in Nepal under the terms of a direct agreement with the Nepal government. When Seaman learned that I was to be in Portland, Oregon, he arranged to meet me at the airport on November 2, 1965, where we reviewed his data on Nepal, considered both the difficulties and the prospects, and prayed together.

I asked him to write to Charles Warren, the field chairman, which he promptly did:

> It does seem like an open door which we should not consider

lightly. Should the field council, after prayer and further conference with Dr. Young, feel that we should enter in here, I would
be glad to attempt to spearhead this work.[31]

Two weeks later I wrote to Warren: "It may very well be that
this suggestion concerning Nepal may provide us the open door
that has been prayerfully sought for many years."

The Time is Right

Just over two years were to pass before entry became a reality.
In March 1968, Seaman and Albert Bowdish made a tour of the
western area of Nepal and came back with a strong recommendation that TEAM enter. Their report bore the probing title, "If not
now, when?"

With the Nepal government's approval of Dr. Seaman's request
to complete Dr. Young's ten-year contract, and the field council's
recommendation, the board of directors on June 14, 1968, approved the plan that Maynard and Dorothy Seaman and Peter and
Pauline Hanks be the vanguard of entry to Nepal. Thus the vision
and prayer of several decades had promise of fulfillment.

Dr. Young's clinic work was actually located in Pokhra, about
five miles from Dandeldhura, which was the administrative center
of a fairly populous area. The density was about 200 people to the
square mile. To get to Dandeldhura from India—whether from the
west or south or indirectly from the capital, Katmandu—required
five days of travel on foot over steep mountain trails. Later, a
"Jeep-able" road was opened.

The Vanguard, Seamans and Hanks

From the beginning, this was one of TEAM's most rugged
fields, yet the missionaries did not draw back from the challenge,
as Peter Hanks recounted:

In December 1968, Dr. and Mrs. Seaman and their four children
with Mr. and Mrs. Peter Hanks and their two boys made the
eventful move into Nepal. The clinic was one small room under
the Hanks' living quarters. Here the doctor examined patients,
the nurse gave injections, the pharmacist counted and dispensed
pills, and the record clerk kept his files. In one corner were a few

shelves on which were kept our stock of medicines. About five or six worked in this room, counting it a privilege to be there for Jesus' sake.[32]

A Foundation on Which to Build

Dr. Young's ministry had spiritual fruit as evidenced by a fair number of believers, particularly among the leper patients. No one had been baptized and there was no church body. This medical and spiritual work provided a good foundation on which to build.

The Nepal government required TEAM to build and operate a district hospital in Dandeldhura, while still maintaining the work at Pokhra. For a while there was no difficulty receiving visas for the medical personnel who applied. Short-term doctors and nurses rendered excellent service but the field was happy when career missionaries came with the promise of repeated terms of service. Among these career missionaries were Dr. Randy Loper, Kirk and Paula Dunham, Nancy Sturrock, Don and Margaret Grigorenko, Jere and Anita Kauth, Beth Pomeroy, Tim and Barbara Robertson, Patricia Ayres, and Ilse Wittal.

Nepal a Separate Field

The Nepal work was designated a separate field in March 1982 upon recommendation by the missionaries and approval by the board of directors. As the missionary family grew in number and as its work was in quite a different pattern than that in North India, the value of remaining part of that field was questioned. There was also the expense and difficulty of traveling to the annual field conference in India. Thus Nepal became TEAM's twenty-sixth field.

Government Restrictions

As time passed the government began to restrict visas for new personnel, and surprisingly in 1989 declined to renew visas for Maynard and Dorothy Seaman and Peter and Pauline Hanks, who had given more than twenty years of their lives to serve the people of Nepal. This refusal undoubtedly came because of their Christian testimony in the community. The limitation on personnel made it necessary to curtail expansion into two new medical ministries offered, one in eastern Nepal and one in the central area.

Forbidden to Preach

The work of the missionaries among the believers bore fruit in the lives of many and some were baptized and became part of the local church. The laws of the land decreed penalties for those who were baptized, thus signifying their change in religion, and even stiffer penalties on those who influenced the change. Many believers were arrested and brought to trial. Some spent time in prison.

When it came time to renew the agreement with the government, there were renewed restrictions which involved control of the medical ministry. The restriction on Christian witness occasioned the most heart-searching. Lynn Everswick, area foreign secretary, conferred at length with general director Winchell and having received his counsel reported fully to the board on this development:

> The final area of concern we have struggled with is the following requirement: *"TEAM and it members shall confine their activities to the achievement of the objectives of the projects to which they are assigned and shall not engage in any proselytizing and other activities which are outside the scope of their assigned work."*

> We in TEAM believe that our ministry is to share the gospel with every people in every land. Should we no longer be able to do so, then possibly it is time to leave.

> I looked back to past records of TEAM's involvement in Nepal and noted a reference by Dr. Mortenson to an earlier decision when we tried to enter Nepal, but because of this very statement which was in operation at that time we felt we could not sign and begin a ministry in Nepal.

> The natural question is, what difference is there between the situation we find in Nepal today and the situation faced by those early missionaries wanting to enter the country? I believe the key answer to this is the church of Nepal. In the early days when we were looking to Nepal as a field, there were virtually no believers in that land. Today there are many thousands gathering as

brothers and sisters in Christ. To enter a land for the first time and signing an agreement stating that we would not proselytize would have been a pointless exercise. However, today there is a church and they have requested of us that we continue in a supportive role.[33]

When the national church leaders learned about the government's demand they told Peter Hanks, "That is O.K. You do the medical work; we will do the preaching."[34]

Everswick stated further, "I believe it is a privilege to be in Nepal, even if it is simply to provide the spiritual support to the Nepalese church, especially in light of their having asked us to stay."[35]

Still, a Spiritual Work Goes On

Winchell and the men of the board registered full agreement with Everswick's convictions. The gospel work in Nepal has been continued by the Christians, having the quiet support of the missionaries. By early 1989 three congregations with a weekly attendance of ninety and a membership of sixty-two demonstrated the positive results of this decision.

With a keen understanding of the cost in spiritual concern, effort, and expense in ministering in this forbidding land, Everswick nevertheless considered it all fully worthwhile.

The TEAM hospital in Pokra in the far west of Nepal is truly a beacon on a hill and the light of it cannot be hid in terms of its spiritual impact on the community. What a delight to see missionaries and nationals ministering to the bodies and souls of those who come for help.[36]

The general director spent two weeks in Nepal in February 1989 studying the situation carefully and looking into some of the opportunities for increasing the outreach through medical work to be accompanied by a gospel witness. His report included a statement which was prophetic of future changes and open doors.

I am greatly impressed with what God has done in Nepal in these twenty years and even more enthused about the possibilities that are right around the corner. There seems to be a real possibility of an abundant harvest in this country, perhaps not in the open and obvious way in which it is taking place in the Philippines or other responsive nations, but certainly for a nation that has been so closed for so many years they are great. Our workers in Nepal, including the national workers, feel that the younger generation is not practicing Hinduism, and that, in fact, as little as ten percent of the population are truly devout Hindus. The younger ones are becoming modern, sophisticated, and materialistic, and an overthrow of the government would not be a surprise within a few years.[37]

A fruitful harvest field in Nepal seems assured because a foothold was maintained by wisely accepting some limitations without compromising the testimony.

EPILOGUE:

After the above chapter was completed, the Lord allowed events in Nepal to crystalize in a manner that gives great hope for more freedom for the gospel and lessening of persecution for the Christians. Everswick reported to the board of directors on June 25, 1990, about changes currently taking place in the ancient Hindu kingdom:

> Opposition to the old government by a pro-democracy coalition came to a head on April 7. There was a demonstration involving almost half a million people marching on the royal palace in Kathmandu.... The effect of this was to cause the government and king to make concessions toward democracy, which brought celebrations in the streets. It is hoped that some of the constitutional changes which have been promised will lead to new freedoms such as the freedom of speech and the freedom of religion.

> In evidence of the freedom of religion, a Christian assembly was held in the Royal Academy Hall in Kathmandu on May 7. An estimated 2,500 Christians were there and the experience was emotional and historic. Never in Nepal's history had so many believers gathered together to hear the Word of God and to sing praises to His name. We can only hope and pray that the church which TEAM has been a part of in Nepal will enjoy some of the freedoms that this change has brought. I am told that pastors are in the streets openly distributing Scriptures and debating with people in the market place. This somehow rings of opportunities like Paul and others had in the early days of the church.[38]

What would the pioneers who, with Franson, probed the borders of Nepal and Tibet from northern India almost a century earlier say to these remarkable developments? Their first response would be to bow in thanksgiving and praise to the Lord and the second would be to rise to their feet and press forward with the message of new life in Christ Jesus.

PAKISTAN—"LAND OF THE PURE"

Muslims living in India among people who bowed to a myriad of gods proudly repeated the confession, "There is no God but Allah and Mohammed is his prophet." Particularly offensive to the monotheistic Muslims was the worship of animals, among them the cow. On the other hand, the Hindus were enraged by the Muslim slaughter of cows for food.

I was first introduced to Hindu/Muslim hostility when our family spent several months in India en route home from China in 1945. There were frequent news items about clashes arising from "cow murder" by Muslims, on the one hand, and from noisy demonstrations by Hindus outside Muslim mosques, on the other.

How TEAM Came to Pakistan

The story of how TEAM came to have a work in Pakistan is told fully in two earlier mission histories, *Three Score Years...and Then,* by J. F. Swanson, and *The Sovereign Hand,* by Paul Sheetz. In short, TEAM was invited by a Presbyterian mission which felt it was not adequately reaching part of its assigned territory in Hazara and Northwest Frontier Province (see chapter 17). Dr. Andrew and Olive Karsgaard were the first TEAM missionaries, arriving in November 1946. Next to come were Carl and Agnes Davis and Marion Temple, who reached the field in early 1947.

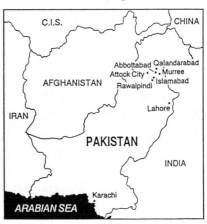

Partition of India

While the Hindus and Muslims of India were agreed in

1947 in their desire for independence from Great Britain, the Muslims were equally strong in their eagerness to separate from the Hindus. With Great Britain's withdrawal from India on August 14, 1947, Muslims, under the leadership of Mohammed Ali Jinnah, declared independence from both and named the new country Pakistan—"Land of the Pure." Jinnah thus secured a safe homeland for Muslims to practice their faith without Hindu interference—a dream he had since the Muslim League conference in 1940.

The basis for partition was that where the population was 50 percent or more Muslim, that portion became Pakistan; conversely, where it was 50 percent or more Hindu, that portion remained India. By the population distribution, Pakistan became divided into two sections—East and West—with a thousand miles of Indian territory in between. Large pockets of Muslims existed in India and many Hindus and other non-Muslims were to be found in Pakistan.

Uprooted Refugees

Whether motivated to leave because of fear or because they were expelled, the results were the same—a vast migration, in 1947 and 1948, of Muslims to Pakistan and of Hindus to India. An estimate at the time was eight to twelve million refugees uprooted from their accustomed surroundings and forced to seek homes in communities in which they were strangers. Compounding the tragedy was the communal rioting among Muslims, Hindus, and Sikhs resulting in the death of between one and two million people.

Protection Amidst Danger

The new missionaries assigned to the Northwest in what became West Pakistan were in India studying the Urdu language when chaos overwhelmed northern India and much of Pakistan. Writing in 1988, Agnes Davis recalled experiences of that time:

> It was March of 1947 when Carl and I arrived at the Indian mountain resort area of Landour, Mussoorie, to begin our Urdu language study. Rumors were already circulating of the possibility of India being granted freedom from British rule. It came

to pass in August of that year. At the outset, Hindus and Muslims marched together in joyful parade, celebrating their freedom. Forty-eight hours later, Muslims were being herded into concentrated areas and rioting began. All foreigners were advised to return to their stations on the plains. For us of TEAM that meant crossing the very volatile border between India and the newly formed country of Pakistan.... We evacuated the hill station in a pre-dawn exodus through the bazaar area. A few moments later stones were being hurled over our heads—not aimed at us but at opposing religious factions. Thus began our journey which normally took only 24 hours, but this time six days and six nights, during which God guided us through the rioting areas.... In the weeks surrounding our exodus thousands were slaughtered making the same trip.[1]

One missionary reported that some seventy missionaries from various groups rode rail cars across those "killing fields." They passed halted trains where every person on board—men, women, and children—had been slaughtered. When they arrived safely in the Lahore, Pakistan, station "the doxology was never sung with greater fervency by God's people."

Urgent Need for Medical Help
Though the missionaries' principal activity should have been language study, they could not be deaf to pleas for help. Dr. Karsgaard, Carl Davis, and nurse Marion Temple offered to join relief efforts among the refugees fleeing across the border. Their work was reported briefly by Karsgaard in the mission's magazine:

We have just spent a week in a camp of 175,000 which has been in existence for eight weeks. Most of these camps have no sanitary facilities, or arrangements of any kind—they are simply groups of people, the large majority of whom appear to be suffering from diarrhea, dysentery, cholera, and typhoid. Many have gone blind from eye infections. Signs of impending starvation are evident, such as swollen feet, etc.... In a few days' stay we managed to inoculate 25,000 people.[2]

The Country and Its People
Pakistan—cut to half size in 1972 by the secession of East Pakistan, which became Bangladesh—has Iran and Afghanistan

as its borders on the west, a bit of China on its north, Kashmir on the east, and India on its south. Though Kashmir is mostly Muslim, India moved first and claimed most of its territory, leaving to Pakistan only a small portion now called Azad (Free) Kashmir. India has never allowed independent elections lest the Muslim majority would vote for union with Pakistan. The Kashmir question laid the groundwork for continued ill feeling and tension that has led to armed conflict on several occasions.

While India's people are a blend of Aryan and Dravidian stock, Pakistanis are more Aryan and related to central Asia. The basic cultures of Pakistan and India are not greatly different except in religion.

A Nominal Christian Minority

Within Pakistan there is one majority religious group, the Muslims, and one significant minority, the Christian community. How did this Christian community come into existence? Many non-caste or low-caste Hindus, having been denied equality in the Hindu community, had searched for another identity. There were also thousands of genuine conversions, particularly under the outstanding spiritual ministry of John Hyde in the early 1900s. "Praying" Hyde—also called "Camel Knees" because he spent so much time in prayer—was responsible for moving the hand of God, when, in those years, God blessed the subcontinent with a mass movement to Christ.

Another reported movement to the nominal Christian community came at the time of partition. It was dangerous to be labeled a Hindu in a Muslim country, as the rioting in Pakistan proved. So when outcastes who were neither Muslim nor Hindu saw the legal acceptance of Christians, many declared themselves a part of the Christian community. The result was that many Christians-in-name-only knew nothing of a personal relationship with Christ. There was one positive aspect to this situation. Nominal Christians were more open to the gospel message than were Muslims.

Which Ministry to Emphasize?

From the earliest years in Pakistan, some missionaries were uncertain which ministry TEAM should pursue. Some felt a strong call to reach the Muslims, who were the least evangelized. Others believed they should win nominal Christians and help them grow in the Lord to become dedicated and effective witnesses. No rule was enacted to clarify this matter, but in time the Holy Spirit led certain missionaries to work more with the Christian community and others more with the majority. Both truly needed the life-giving message.

Early Workers' Assignments

The area assigned to TEAM was around the small city of Abbottabad north of the moderately large city of Rawalpindi and some 800 hundred miles inland from the large coastal city of Karachi.

Dr. and Mrs. Karsgaard were assigned to Taxila on loan to the hospital ministry of the United Presbyterian Mission of North America (UPMNA) for their first term of service. Though this was a general hospital, the high incidence of eye problems—particularly cataracts—required a concentration on eye surgery. For example, in 1949 Karsgaard reported that 864 of 1,000 major operations had been for cataracts. While on furlough in 1951 and 1952, Karsgaard enrolled in ophthalmology courses in Philadelphia and took additional studies in London to increase his skill in what obviously would be a major part of his medical ministry.

Carl and Agnes Davis were assigned to Abbottabad and there opened a reading room in the bazaar where he could distribute literature and converse with interested men. He also took advantage of opportunities to preach in market places and cattle fairs or wherever a group of listeners could be gathered. Muslim men seemed to be quite well versed in the Koran and prepared to challenge the message of the Bible. Davis saw the advantage of the printed page in leaving a message that could repeat its appeal again and again.

It was confidence in the effectiveness of gospel literature that led the Davises to work with the Christian Publishing House in Lahore, a Brethren publishing and distribution organization in which TEAM and several other groups shared responsibility. The Davises continued in that work for several years until 1965 when changes in the organization prompted them to request assignment to an evangelistic and church ministry at the Mangla Dam project to work with both Pakistanis and foreigners. That assignment continued until 1967 when TEAM asked them to serve its interests in Australia.

Medical Work Begins in Mansehra

When the Karsgaards returned to Pakistan in 1953 they chose Mansehra—some fifteen miles north of Abbottabad—as their center of work. Mansehra, the district headquarters, was strategically located on the edge of tribal lands previously closed to missionary entry. In these tribal areas the local *Khans* ruled with little regard for the central government. The spirit of fierce independence was evident in individuals asserting their rights with rifle or pistol. Karsgaard recognized the pressing medical needs along with the deep spiritual darkness on every side. He fixed up an adobe room, which at one time had been used as a cowshed, to serve as a treatment room.

Bach Christian Hospital Built

When general director Johnson visited Pakistan in 1953, he was impressed by the inadequate facilities and the pressure on the doctor, who was treating 100 patients a day. When publicity was given to the need, the first substantial contribution came from Mr. Garrett Veenstra in Racine, Wisconsin, who wanted to honor T. J. Bach; thus the name Bach Christian Hospital (BCH). Other funds came in over the next few years to allow the purchase of eight to ten acres of land closer to Abbottabad and to build several units of the larger hospital planned.

Carl Davis, having had some engineering training, saw the

initial stages of the hospital through to completion. It wasn't exactly an easy task. A local so-called contractor was hired to put a concrete roof on the clinic building. He put in much work of building a scaffold and mixing and pouring the concrete. When the scaffold was removed at the "proper" time the whole roof caved in! The builder had stolen and sold half of the cement intended for the roof.

In later years, additional large contributions were received, including grants from the government of Sweden, so the hospital could be expanded to the point of optimum effectiveness.

The care given at BCH attracted patients locally and as far away as the remote northern borders of Pakistan. Those visiting the hospital came from areas where—in addition to Urdu—the Punjabi, Pushtu, and Hindko languages were spoken.

Irwins Enhance the Ministry

The Lord answered prayer for a woman physician by sending Dr. Phyllis Irwin in 1956. In Pakistan—a particularly strict Muslim country—most women are covered by a *burkha* from head to toe and segregated from men. While male doctors can and do care for women, there is special appeal and advantage to having a female doctor at the hospital. Dr. Irwin's husband, Russell, is a seminary graduate whose ministry was also of great value to the field. For some years he served as administrator of the hospital. More recently Irwin headed up the work of TEE—Theological Education by Extension. TEE is a valuable tool in giving quality training to lay workers who cannot attend a resident Bible school for full-time training. At the end of 1989, thirty-eight students were enrolled in TEE courses.

Karsgaard's Changed Ministry

Dr. and Mrs. Karsgaard found it necessary to leave Pakistan permanently in 1962 because of Olive's health. Karsgaard went on in advanced ophthalmology training to obtain board certification. Upon the death of Dr. R. C. Logefeil in 1966, Karsgaard became medical director of TEAM, a service he rendered on a voluntary basis. Karsgaard traveled with me to visit mission fields in Latin America, Africa, and Asia between 1970 and 1973, where he reviewed the work in TEAM hospitals as well as advising on missionary health. In 1975 Winchell noted Karsgaard's desire to be relieved of the post and appointed Dr. John Bennett medical director and Karsgaard medical consultant. Karsgaard was elected to the Canadian board of trustees in 1965 and to the U.S. board in 1976. His interest in Pakistan remained high and on two or three occasions he responded to invitations to be present for special events.

Where to Give Priority?

On my first visit to Pakistan in 1960, I heard doubts expressed by several as to the wisdom of placing emphasis on medical work, which required a heavy investment in personnel and finance. Would it not be better to cut back on hospital work and reassign the personnel to evangelism and church work? One conscientious lady had serious doubts until she herself was assigned to do personal evangelism among women patients. I heard later that she realized her most fruitful work had been in dealing with women who were away from the intimidating environment of home or village where there was strong opposition to the Christian testimony.

A Key to Entry

Over the years it was seen that not only was the hospital a lighthouse for the gospel, it was also a springboard for entry by an evangelistic team from the hospital into many otherwise resistant villages. When a villager had spent some days in the hospital there seemed always to be a warm welcome to visit that home. Though professions of faith were slow—several hundred over thirty years—it was often in the home that a clear witness could be given and serious discipling done. For the women—so restricted in their outside contacts—the only opportunity they had for fellowship or to be instructed in the faith was the visit of the missionary-Bible woman team.

Community Health Project

In the late 1970s the field medical board authorized an experimental venture into community health. Betty Rairdan and a short-term worker set up a small outpost in Bararkot, Free Kashmir, and taught health, hygiene, water cleanliness, and sanitation in the area schools. They also held classes for women who had been contacted at Bach Hospital. The experiment was judged to be a success but was interrupted for two years. With the reinforcement of the medical staff by the arrival of new doctors in 1986, the program got needed development, particularly with the involvement of Dr. and Mrs. Rob Droullard and Dr. and Mrs. Jeff Moore. (The Moores had to withdraw from the field for family health reasons.)

After a period of study of the Hindko language and service at Bach Christian Hospital, the Droullards were assigned to the community health project. When asked in 1990 to summarize his goals for the project, Dr. Droullard responded:

> Our fundamental goal in starting the Community Health Project was to improve health conditions of a whole community—actually groups of communities. We wanted to see measurable changes in the level of health and, specifically, we were interested in seeing the infant mortality rate drop. We were also interested in improving the level of nutrition for pregnant women and children, and the level of sanitation, which is basically non-existent in rural ares of Pakistan; also perhaps improving the water supply in certain areas.[3]

Concerning the relationship of this ministry to TEAM's overall goals, Mary Droullard, a nurse, had an appropriate answer:

> We have continually felt challenged by the obstacles to sharing the gospel in a Muslim society, also the obstacles in trying to change tradition. But we feel they fit together and if we want to share Christ with people we have to get time with them. TEAM's goal is to plant the church and we feel the starting point for planting the church is just talking to people about Christ on a relational basis, spending time with them.[4]

A School for National Children

A day school for national children in Abbottabad begun by Presbyterian missionaries in 1923 was turned over to TEAM in 1951. Enrollments came from the Muslim and Christian communities and—before partition—even from Hindu and Sikh homes. Parents were willing to pay tuition to enter their children in a high-quality school even at the risk of their receiving Christian instruction. All went well until the 1960s, when the government took steps to require that all Muslim children be taught the Koran. Missionaries became concerned about government efforts to close Christian schools and in other ways limit or prohibit mission work. They were aware of mounting public pressures:

> For some eight months now there has been increasing pressure in the newspapers, rallies, etc., against Christian missionary activity.... Hardly a day goes by without serious articles about fantastic gains by Christian missions and pleas to have the government bring it to a stop. While the constitution guards freedom of the minority, the extremely vocal and powerful Islamic-centered voice seems bound to try and destroy this freedom.[5]

The government did not object that children from the Christian community were taught the Bible, but Muslim children must be taught the Koran—and by an Islamic teacher. This rule affected all missions which had schools. One local mission circulated a strong argument by a missionary in favor of yielding to the government's demand. This missionary—citing his experience in Egypt—felt there was much to be gained by winning the friendship of the people, as opposed to antagonizing them by refusing to honor the Koran.

In 1962, before the missionaries voted formally on the question of what to do about the Abbottabad school, the field chairman, Paul Lundgren, wrote me about the problem and also sent the paper prepared by the missionary to Egypt. In acknowledging Lundgren's letter I promised to present it to the board for review but also gave my initial reaction:

> My first reading of the paper leaves me with the impression that [the author] believes there is light in religions such as Islam.

Some are willing to say the same about Buddhism, Hinduism, and other religions of the East. We, on the other hand, hold that there is no true light in these religions. The "light" is actually darkness because it leads astray.[6]

After the board had considered the matter, I wrote to Lundgren giving its position:

1. For conscience' sake, and in faithfulness to the gospel, we cannot teach the Koran as a part of our curriculum, or on our premises.

2. It may be necessary to admit only students from the Christian community, and assume the increased cost.

3. If necessary, excuse Muslim students to attend Islamic instruction off premises but do not excuse them from Bible classes.[7]

It was necessary to give families adequate notice that the school would be changed into the Abbottabad Christian School (ACS) with enrollment from the Christian community. For the missionaries engaged in Muslim evangelism, this was a heart-wrenching move. They regretted the loss of opportunity to reach children of a tender age with the gospel, but agreed that an Islamic instructor teaching the Koran would seriously undercut the Christian instruction. It would also be an unacceptable compromise.

For the next two or three years the board directed some funds to ACS until the field could take the added expense into its budget. Missionaries were apprehensive about possible adverse community reaction and even official action against the mission for changing the school. However, all went well and the school went forward with a positive ministry to families of the Christian community, many of whom were as spiritually needy as the majority community.

A rather disappointing board minute is recorded the following year:

It was noted that TEAM was the only mission in West Pakistan that did not go along with the requirement of the government to teach the Koran in its schools.[8]

It would be a mistake to read this as judgment of other evangelical missions. In the first place, was this a correct perception? In the second place, did other missions have schools that would be affected by the requirement? TEAM did what it believed was right for its own ministry. Later experience with the school gave the missionaries assurance that the decision was right, as field chairman William Pietsch reported in 1964:

> ACS has continued to be a blessing to many Christian children. The fact that about 50 applications for admission had to be refused this last April points to the demand for such a school. Changed lives of children bear witness to its lasting spiritual value.[9]

Writing in 1988, principal Diane Evans gives information about ACS that reveals steady growth in the twenty-five years since the step of faith was taken to avoid compromise. The school now had 100 boarding students and an equal number of day students. Grades nine and ten were added in the 1980s and the high school section was changed to a girls' high school. Five ACS grads were on the teaching staff and the pastor of the local evangelical church is an alumnus. Half of the girls who were graduated in 1986 enrolled in a nursing program run by a Christian hospital in southern Pakistan.

> The goal of ACS is to assist Pakistani young people in coming to know Jesus as Savior and encouraging them to grow in their faith. It is exciting to see former students continue to walk with the Lord and to see them become involved in Christian ministries.[10]

At the end of 1989 there were 188 students in the elementary school and 12 in high school.

Local Presbyterian Churches

Under the terms of the understanding between the United Presbyterian Mission of North America (UPMNA) and TEAM which assigned responsibility for the Hazara and Attock districts, TEAM was to honor the existence of Presbyterian churches in Abbottabad and Campbellpur and minister to and with them. These churches had their primary relationship with the presbytery and were thus related to the Presbyterian national body. In a practical sense, this meant that TEAM had no strong influence in the local church, but it could and did have an open door of ministry.

Presbyterian Merger's Effect

The merger of the small UPMNA into the Presbyterian Church, U.S.A. (UPUSA), created a climate on the mission field different from what it was in 1946. Whereas the missionaries with whom the early TEAM people worked were compatible in doctrine and relationships, some of the newer UPUSA missionaries were understood to be more liberal in these vital areas.

Should TEAM be Limited by Agreement?

When I visited the field in 1966 I heard objections by some TEAM missionaries about the supposed limitations of the agreement. TEAM people in Campbellpur were having good fellowship with some warm-hearted believers who apparently were reluctant to join the local Presbyterian Church. I was asked if TEAM should still be limited by the agreement made twenty years earlier. I had never seen the wording of that agreement entered into prior to my time in the administration. When someone was able to produce a copy I read it carefully and found nothing that in any way limited TEAM missionaries from planting churches which would be independent of the presbytery.

When the field conference learned that there was latitude for TEAM to go ahead in a church planting ministry, it voted to proceed with establishing churches in Abbottabad and Campbellpur, and elsewhere as opportunity would arise. The missionaries as a whole felt greatly relieved by this decision as it would now be easier to push ahead in a church planting ministry.[11]

The chairman of the evangelism committee, Dick Thompson, reflected the satisfaction of that committee as he reported to the next annual conference:

> No doubt our biggest step this year was the decision to establish our own church work in Abbottabad.... This was finalized at our special field conference in February [1966] under brother Mortenson's guidance. Let us view this not as a riddance of old problems but as an acquisition of new responsibilities.[12]

In 1968, viewing the divisions in the Presbyterian Church, TEAM separated itself from all Presbyterian work in order to more fully pursue the planting of independent churches, which by 1990 totaled nine congregations.

The Direction Set

With this understanding of the direction to be taken, there began a slow but steady growth in the core ministry of the field—establishing Christian congregations in the New Testament pattern. Other ministries were increasingly viewed and evaluated in their relationship to this central objective. Still, among resistant people such as in Pakistan, church planting was difficult and slow. Missionaries had to be convinced in their own hearts of being in the will of the Lord when they could deal only with scattered individuals rather than with growing congregations. How true this was for those working with Muslims.

Retreats for Scattered Converts

Paul Lundgren, experienced as a pastor and evangelist, found that his main ministry in Pakistan was dealing with individuals. True, he was also invited to minister to large congregations in annual Sialkot conventions, but he, as others, took advantage of opportunities to find individual fruit among the Muslims.

In dealing with men who showed an interest in the gospel, Lundgren soon perceived a great need on their part to have fellowship with others of like conviction and experience. In their usual circles they could not easily open their mouths about any interest in Christ. Neither was it easy to associate with a church group, where—sadly—they might be viewed with suspicion as spies.

Lundgren's spiritual strategy was to call these inquirers together to some quiet place where for days at a time they could have fellowship and exchange experiences with those who were taking similar first steps of faith. Here they could have the Word of God opened to them. Here they could learn that prayer was more than the recitation of formulas; it was fellowship with the living God. Here they could find mutual strength to withstand the pressures of ridicule and persecution.

A Church but Not a Congregation

By the common definition of a church, these converts from scattered areas with limited opportunities for assembling could hardly be called a congregation. There were no elders or deacons. Some may have been baptized; others may not have taken that step. But here was a group that surely fit Christ's description of "two or three gathered in My Name." He was truly present!

I sensed the glory of the fact myself when—about 1966—Dick Thompson and I spent precious hours of fellowship in the Word and prayer with two converts, Inayat and Akbar, who eagerly opened up to the truth. We were fellow members of the body of Christ! We were the church in that place and members one of the other![13]

I could understand why I could detect no signs of discouragement among the missionaries who did Muslim evangelism. The ones and twos were precious jewels and therefore the source of much joy.

Others in Muslim Evangelism

Those who spent many years in Muslim evangelism had little to report by way of numbers but they were respected and appreciated by their fellow missionaries for their vision and perseverance. For most of Dick and Virginia Thompson's eighteen years in Pakistan, Virginia had a ministry in Abbottabad, while Dick visited remote villages and talked personally with influential *Khans,* seeking to lead them to an understanding and acceptance of Jesus Christ as Risen Son of God and Savior. He won a welcome in their homes, a polite hearing, possibly some secret believers, and a few open converts. Unsuspectingly, he also won the attention of Pakistan authorities, who were suspicious of his contacts with independent-minded *Khans.* When he applied for visa renewal in 1968 he was refused and he and Virginia had to leave the country. They went on to other Muslim work in western Asia.

Others engaged in patient Muslim evangelism included Caleb and Loretta Cutherell, Don and Garnett DeHart, Ed and Barbara Rasmussen, and Merle Hawton.

Literature Evangelism

With 25 percent of Pakistanis being literate, one effective means of communicating the gospel was through correspondence courses. Light of Life courses originated by Don Hillis in India were adapted for Muslim readers by a Miss Fran Brown of UPMNA, who began the Pakistan Bible Correspondence School in Abbottabad. Bill Pietsch, who reached the field in 1950, began TEAM's participation in this ministry. Others joined that work through the years, particularly Rodney Stent, Dave and Mary Davis, and Leroy and Beckie Nicholson. The ministry, based in Rawalpindi, had 1,384 active students enrolled in 11 courses at the end of 1989.

One student was Hamid, who saw the ad for the courses and began studying; after six months he visited the offices and for two days studied with the staff. Led to Christ, he returned home, only to be thrown out. He came back to the correspondence school office where he was helped and discipled further. When his father went overseas he returned home and sought to maintain a Christian witness, though he had no opportunity for Christian fellowship. His is just one example of the difficult pathway for converts from Islam.

The correspondence courses handled by TEAM are only part of the wider ministry of the Pakistan Correspondence School, which now operates four other centers, enrolling close to 10,000 students who use the same materials.

A Christian bookstore was opened by Vern Rock in the capital city of Islamabad. In addition to sales to the local people there were contacts with internationals. Of particular interest was the eagerness of Russian diplomats posted there to obtain Bibles in their own language.

Sales from the bookstore doubled when TEAM bought a small Suzuki pickup and put a display box on the back, modeled after a design used by TEAM in Taiwan. This mobile unit was found to be excellent for getting literature out to the people.

Vern and Wanda Rock spent over forty years in the service of the Lord among the followers of Mohammed. When a visa to return to Pakistan was delayed to the point of seeming refusal, the Rocks accepted an invitation to go to Trinidad to train pastors of TEAM churches to evangelize Muslims in that country.

Christian Camping Program

A camp ministry was first reported in Pakistan in 1967:

> For a number of years a camping program has been effective in bringing solid spiritual results in the lives of a goodly number in our area. Paul Lundgren has done much in regard to the development of the Jungle Dene site. This will lead to a ministry of far wider scope.[14]

When I visited Pakistan in 1973, Charles and Betty Burton showed me Camp Mubarak at Murree with the beautiful building that had been erected in a mountain glen. Camps of various types were held throughout the season. The report for the year 1989 listed 85 camp days with 640 participants. Professions of faith averaged 90 annually. In 1990, Lynn Everswick, area foreign secretary, shared the information that Camp Mubarak hoped to provide a year-round ministry, including a Christian counseling service.

Church Planting Started

After the watershed conference decision of 1966, a number of church planting efforts were undertaken. In Campbellpur—later renamed Attock City—an informal fellowship group already existed. Abbottabad was next to have a new assembly, as field chairman Lundgren reported "the imminent organization of our own church" in 1968. The following year he had a report of progress:

> The organization of our first Pakistani church has been a recent

highlight of our Abbottabad ministry. While we have small beginnings, the prospects are good. Actual organization was preceded by a series of Bible studies on the nature of the church and other related Biblical subjects.... Things moved slowly— more slowly than expected—resulting in sixteen members being welcomed into church membership on organizational night. Besides these, there are twenty-two more who desire to join our fellowship and will be giving their testimonies from time to time. Four officers were chosen and were dedicated at the communion service the following Sunday morning.[15]

Tarbela—Work Among a Transient People

The evangelism committee was alert to new opportunities for ministry and one such came into view in 1961 in connection with a huge public works project—the construction of the Tarbela Dam. Vern Rock reported for the committee in 1962:

> For five weeks our men have been able to carry on a ministry of personal work and literature distribution at the budding community of the Tarbela Dam project, while living in a tent recently purchased for such purposes. A log is being kept so that when advisable for someone to be located there, it will be possible for him to carry on. A few Christians have been contacted and they give promise of being a good nucleus for a ministry in depth.[16]

Pastor Barkat Parvais went to Tarbela and, beginning in 1968, traveled for weekly meetings in thirteen widely scattered labor colonies all around the dam-construction project, in the process wearing out three motorcycles. Over the years of his evangelism there more than 300 people made professions of faith. When their employment at the dam project was completed these believers scattered throughout Pakistan, undoubtedly bearing witness wherever they settled.

Evidence of the healthy condition of the Tarbela church was the note in 1972 that it provided a second worker and his financial support for a bookroom in Ghazi. In 1982 there were thirteen baptisms. A "practical" evangelism seminar was scheduled for the same year, indicating a live congregation interested in growth. Over a period of twenty-one years the Tarbela church developed into a functioning body—truly the objective of all church ministry.

572

Fellowship of Christian Churches

As individual Pakistanis were won to the Lord, missionaries became conscious of their need for mutual fellowship. In 1957, many years before there were TEAM-related churches, missionaries led the way in founding *Masihi I'tahadi Jamait* (MIJ). This was a step of faith, because the name really means Fellowship of Christian Churches. In the early years MIJ functioned as a meeting ground for TEAM-related individuals. It later undertook certain responsibilities in ministry, chief among which was evangelistic outreach.

Church Planting Gives Substance to MIJ

When, in 1966, the decision was made to move forward in planting TEAM-related churches, MIJ was seen in a new light consistent with its name—a fellowship of churches:

> It would seem that with this beginning, we need to take a thoughtful look into a more firmly organized situation, and then with one another into a stronger MIJ.[17]

"This beginning" referred to by Lundgren was the steps being taken by the Abbottabad Bible Church to bring believers into a body having spiritually qualified leaders. Other church ministries were progressing in Attock City (Campbellpur), Hasan Abdal, and Tarbela. By 1975, Bill Dalton was able to report:

> In the annual meeting of MIJ last February, I was thrilled to see how the nationals were taking the lead and moving ahead with definite membership, evangelism outreach, and working on the constitution.[18]

Dalton continued to be much encouraged as he reported in 1976:

> MIJ—the TEAM-created fellowship of churches—continues to show signs of leadership ability with nationals being at the helm and doing a better job than we could. Let us continue supporting them with our prayers, encouraging them, and believing God to do great things through them. They faced a major crisis with regard to their national missionary and came out on the victory side.[19]

The men who served as field chairmen from time to time—Bill Pietsch, Paul Lundgren, Bill Dalton, and Dave Davis—all held a clear vision concerning the centrality of the church.

Why the Slow Growth?

Why, then, did churches grow so slowly in Pakistan? First of all, there was strong Muslim resistance to the gospel. There were only scattered converts from Islam—too scattered to bring them together in a congregation.

Why did churches grow so slowly in the Christian community? When Dave Davis was field chairman he put his finger on one reason:

> With the emphasis we have had on institutions over the years, we need to ask God to help us keep perspective. We must never neglect evangelism and the institutions that provide us the opportunity for that evangelism, but we must also not neglect the church and the opportunities it provides for evangelism and discipleship. This is not our own work; it is God's work.[20]

The institutions and special ministries that TEAM established in Pakistan were excellent—hospital, correspondence courses, bookstores, Christian school, camping ministry, radio work, Bible institute, and Scripture translation. They provided opportunities for evangelism and discipleship. Many individuals were won to the Lord and discipled, but the weakness, if indeed there was one, was in not having the primary goal of building the church from the very beginning. The late start after 1966—when the entry agreement was correctly interpreted—nevertheless resulted in nine churches being planted, including one in the major city, Rawalpindi. Davis reflected on this in an annual report as field chairman:

> The church emphasis, that is, the emphasis on actively teaching and gathering believers into fellowships, is a definite step of progress. God has called us to evangelize (bear fruit) and to disciple (fruit that remains). We must bring people to maturity and into fellowship with one another. We have been active in evangelism; may we be equally active in discipling and gathering folks together that the church may be more visible and established in our area.[21]

If the Pakistan field conference made specific assignment of

574

missionaries to church planting and development in any given area, it does not have emphasis in the reports. As missionaries were assigned to various mission stations, evangelism was a top priority—as it should be—but the specific assignment of discipling the converts with the purpose of bringing them together in a local church may have been assumed but not specifically spelled out. It took several years for us in the administration to understand that definite church planting assignments and job descriptions were necessary if churches were to become a reality.

Radio Work Considered

Radio allows wide proclamation of the saving gospel and brings positive results in souls saved and built up in the faith. It may not, however, contribute directly to church growth unless there is follow-up to bring interested listeners into close contact with believers who can disciple them. But it is a wonderful tool in making men and women aware of salvation offered in Christ's name. This is particularly important in countries where political or religious oppression impedes personal witness or public proclamation.

An Opening in the Seychelles

Radio in Pakistan was government owned and operated so Christian programming was permitted only on Christian holidays for a brief time in the mid-fifties. Carl Davis, Earl Parvin, and a convert, Dr. M. A. Q. Daskawie, produced programs for over a year on a primitive tape recorder for broadcast on Radio Pakistan's A.M. frequency. A renewed opportunity to broadcast came when the Far East Broadcasting Association (FEBA), a British affiliate of the America-based Far East Broadcasting Company, established a missionary radio station on the Seychelles Islands in the Indian Ocean with the aim of broadcasting to India, Pakistan, and other southern Asiatic countries.

Growing Listener Response

Pakistan missionaries saw this as an opportunity to reach many who otherwise would never hear and were encouraged to take advantage of it by area foreign secretaries Carl Davis and Jack MacDonald. The official Urdu language was generally understood throughout Pakistan, but some programming was also done in other local languages. TEAM-sponsored broadcasts began in 1977 and during the first year three welcome letters came through to let the missionaries know somebody out there was listening. Letter responses kept increasing so that in 1987 more than 8,000 listeners to the program on family matters wrote in. Professed conversions increased from one in the first year to fifty in 1987.[22]

Missionaries and Pakistanis Involved

Douglas and Laura Snyder and Brent and Marie Jones worked in this radio ministry. The Lord provided choice nationals to help them produce programs and correspond with interested listeners. The husband and wife team of Ambrose and Crystal Gulzaman rendered outstanding service in programming and follow-up. As a counselor, Naji sent out an average of twenty handwritten letters a day. Staff missionaries commended his dedicated service:

> Confined to a wheel chair 20 years ago and now deeply committed to Jesus, Naji is a blessing to us all. He takes a keen interest in the spiritual condition of each listener who writes, and with the help of Urdu language materials and his own knowledge of God's Word, counsels them to find life's answers in Christ.[23]

Ammunition Explosion's Destructive Force

It seemed that the radio ministry would come to a sudden end when on April 10, 1988, an ammunition depot 300 yards from the studio building caught fire and began exploding. One visitor was killed and several staff members were injured. The interior of the studios was gutted by the blasts, which continued for about two hours. One unexploded live missile which penetrated the roof remained in a studio three days before being detected.

Liability payments by the government and contributions made it possible to restore the studios to full service again. A temporary concern was that the damage to the studios and its subsequent rebuilding would direct attention to the radio ministry and lead to some restriction of its work. But the Lord allowed radio to continue its fruitful ministry.

At Last, a Bible School

Although a short-term training program—the Frontier Bible Institute—had been held in Abbottabad in the early 1950s, a residential Bible school was a long time in coming. Field chairman Bill Dalton observed in 1982 that missionaries had talked for twenty-five years about starting a residential Bible school to train workers for evangelism and church ministries.

For evangelism, yes, that was understandable; but for church ministries such a move would have been premature before 1966. The only churches until then were the two tied to the national Presbyterian church by the UPMNA agreement. While some may have felt that a Bible school would hasten the evangelization of Pakistan, there actually was no adequate church foundation for such an undertaking. A lesson not learned in Pakistan at that time—and only belatedly grasped on some other fields—was that if a Bible school is to thrive, it must coexist with church planting. The churches must be the source of student enrollments and also the field where graduates will work.

After 1966, when missionaries recognized their freedom to begin TEAM-related churches, the desire for a Bible school took on meaning. As the churches in Abbottabad, Attock City, Rawalpindi, Hasan Abdal, and Tarbela developed, the need for trained workers grew, as did a pool of potential students called into the Lord's service. At the 1980 annual field conference Dave Davis commented:

> The decision to begin a Bible school in Attock City in 1982 is a profound move forward. It will require commitment on TEAM's part, but we will reap a harvest of trained Pakistani leaders for our churches and our ministries.[24]

This step of faith was matched by commitment and action. Don Stoddard and national church leader Barkat Parvais were ready and confident. The Bible school was started in 1982 and in 1984 Davis reported enthusiastically:

> Zarephath Bible Institute enters its third year and now is in a full
> program. May "giants" be trained for God's kingdom![25]

A prayer goal was set in 1985 to have ten students per class and that all be used in church work weekly. Even though those numbers were not reached, having the students become active in local churches paid dividends in their own lives and in the church ministries. Missionaries were thankful that the Bible institute was regularly training fifteen students by 1990. It was noted that a graduate currently served as pastor of the Abbottabad church. Good progress in the right direction, they agreed.

Bible Translation

Hindko, one of the local languages spoken in Pakistan's northwest provinces, had no Christian Scriptures, though it was spoken by four million people. Many of these people visited Bach Hospital where nurse Jean Sodemann came into contact with them. Without the Word of God in their language it was difficult to provide any type of follow-up.

Even though some did understand spoken Urdu, the Urdu Bible failed to communicate with them because most of the people are illiterate. Miss Sodemann became concerned that these illiterates, too, should hear the gospel. Her concern led to action and while on furlough she took special linguistic studies with emphasis on translation principles and techniques.

Hindko Translation Undertaken

Returning to Pakistan in 1976, Sodemann began translating the New Testament into Hindko, Betty Rairdan working with her. Two circumstances led to a different approach to translation. One was the widespread illiteracy, which would have required an extensive literacy campaign among people who lacked incentive to read. The other was that many Hindko speakers worked in oil-rich countries of the Persian Gulf and brought home cassette recorders for their families. Taking these circumstances into consideration they decided to read the translation onto cassettes.

Steps to a Hindko New Testament

The first step was to have an approved written translation, following all the principles governing faithful translation. Sodemann outlined the process in a report to the mission's magazine:

> When a book has been translated, the following process begins: (1) The material is checked to see if it will be readily understood by potential listeners. (2) A Summer Institute of Linguistics (SIL) consultant sees if translation principles have been followed and if the exegesis is good. (3) A recording session is set, and someone is found to read the script. (4) The cassettes are carefully distributed. (5) A committee of four missionaries advises on technical aspects of the project. After the entire New Testament is translated, a checking committee, of mainly Pakistanis, will be formed to make the final revision.[26]

The appeal of this procedure is that copies of cassettes are provided for immediate distribution.

The Hindko New Testament translation was completed in 1990. With written manuscripts on hand, publication of the Hindko Scriptures now becomes feasible to go beyond what the cassettes can provide.

Another Franson Mission Shares in Work

In 1968 Paul Lundgren consulted with the Swedish Alliance Mission concerning receiving some of its missionaries for service in Pakistan. Like TEAM, that mission had work in western India but was experiencing difficulty in getting visas for its missionaries. Lundgren was eager to bring in medical workers and the thought of their being supplied by a sister mission founded by Fredrik Franson was particularly appealing, not to speak of the interest engendered by Lundgren's own family roots.

As I was to stop in Sweden in February 1968 en route to TEAM fields in western Asia and Africa, Lundgren asked that I meet with the leaders of the Swedish Alliance Mission in Jönköping to discuss the harmonizing of requirements for missionary service with TEAM. The meeting was held in an atmosphere of mutual appreciation and understanding. When this was reported to Lundgren, the field carried forward the negotiations and in 1969 nurses Ulla Lindell and Irene Wernerhag arrived at Bach Christian Hospital. They were joined in 1978 by nurse Marita Wahlström. These nurses were still in service in 1990. Swedish Alliance also sent Bengt and Monica Svensson in 1979 for evangelism.

Not only did the Swedish Alliance Mission supply well-prepared, spiritually equipped personnel, but it also assumed a share of the financial responsibility for the hospital work. Particularly helpful was its assistance in securing substantial construction grants from the Swedish government to expand the hospital.

Growth of the Missionary Family

An often-heard statement is that the western Christian churches have little interest in countries where Islam is supreme. That might be inferred from a comparison of missionaries in these countries with those in the continents of Africa and South America. A closer look may change the impression. There are many Muslim countries where missionary entry is forbidden or seriously restricted, but in two of the Islamic countries—Pakistan and the UAE—TEAM missionaries have been granted visas with only minor difficulties. The total TEAM Pakistan staff on the field and on furlough usually is sixty to sixty-five. Undoubtedly, Bach Hospital's recognized service to the people is a strong point giving TEAM favor.

The presence of fifty or more missionaries in the country at one time means that there are usually twenty-five or more school-age children. When TEAM first had missionaries in Pakistan some children were sent across the border to schools in India. With mounting India-Pakistan tensions that became a less attractive option. TEAM started a small school in Mansehra in 1954 taught by Rachel Steeves and Rosemary Stewart. Later, a boarding school was operated for a short time in Abbottabad with Don and Garnett DeHart in charge.

Missions working in Pakistan recognized the need for a quality education on both grade and high school levels and organized Murree Christian School (MCS). TEAM's participation began in 1957 and all through the years the mission has had teachers and other staff members at the school. The present principal is TEAM missionary Stewart Georgia, who with his wife, Marlene, served at schools in Rhodesia. Long-term TEAM staff have been Eunice Hill, Marjorie Montgomery, Rosemary Stewart, and Marie Dalton Lehman. There is clear evidence that the children under their care have been both spiritually nourished and well educated. Especially impressive is the number who have gone into missionary service, many in TEAM.[27]

A Way Into Afghanistan

One of the closed central Asian countries long prayed for was Afghanistan. Staunchly Islamic, it permitted no Christian witness, nor would a local citizen be safe from assassination or execution if converted to Christ from Islam. After World War II a number of Christians were able to reside there as teachers or technical workers. One such teacher was Dr. J. Christy Wilson, who observed in 1965 that there might be an opportunity for Christians to enter under contract to render government-approved service in hospitals or schools.

Wilson met with leaders of a number of denominational and independent missions working in Pakistan to suggest that they form a joint mission which would serve in locally acceptable ways within Afghanistan and with the basic purpose of furthering Christian witness. He presented the organizational structure of the United Mission to Nepal as a pattern for the proposed International Afghan Mission (IAM). (The name was later changed to International Assistance Mission.) The home and field leaders of these missions meet in Kabul, the capital of Afghanistan, in February 1966 to officially organize the mission. Bill Pietsch, field chairman, and I were invited to represent TEAM.

Proposal for International Mission

We were given the proposed organization documents to study. TEAM registered initial approval in general, but felt that the doctrinal statement should be more explicit and stronger in regard to the inspiration of the Scriptures, have a stronger statement on the atoning work of Christ, and have safeguards against compromising relationships.

As the time approached, Wilson realized that the coming together of twenty or more foreign nationals in this closed society could raise serious questions in the minds of the security police, with whom all would have to register on entry. He requested that each mission send only one representative. Pietsch insisted that I be the one to attend and so it was.

Clearing Organizational Hurdles

Those who came together in Kabul were genuinely interested in winning Afghans to Christ. Our devotional times together were most refreshing. When we came to a discussion of the doctrinal statement we found that we were of one mind in principle but differed—especially between Europeans and Americans—on terminology to express certain views. The Lord cleared the way for agreement on a strong doctrinal statement but there remained one difficult problem, as I recorded in some historical notes in 1984:

> Those who met in Kabul were from a number of evangelical missions and there were also a number—personally evangelical—who were from old-line missions, such as Presbyterians and Anglicans. While TEAM would not be reluctant to enter into joint ministries with individuals of evangelical persuasion, there would be a problem of a direct working relationship with missions which were ecumenically related. TEAM's efforts—which finally prevailed—were to set up a board of governors of evangelicals without a direct involvement of their supporting missions.[28]

Related to Pakistan Field

As TEAM did not want to set up Afghanistan as a new field, it was decided that any who worked there would be members of the Pakistan field. Over a period of twelve years a number of TEAM short-term missionaries worked there. Gordon and Jeanette Stinson and Helen Petersen were there for longer service. Stinson was executive director of the IAM for several years and faithfully guided the work of missionaries from diverse backgrounds in accordance with the IAM constitution and consistent with his position as a TEAM missionary.

Bill Pietsch, Paul Lundgren, Rodney Stent, and Ed Rasmussen variously served as chairman or member of the IAM board of directors.

When I visited Kabul in 1973, I was delighted to hear the estimate of "several hundred" believers, whereas in 1966 it was stated that there were only five known Afghan Christians and three of them were outside the country.

Surmounting Obstacles to Witness

I found some diversity of views about Christian witness among the IAM workers. Some felt that the presence of a Christian rendering service was a witness in itself and verbal witness was not needed. They feared that verbal witness would stir up opposition and result in the expulsion of the workers. Others were convinced that verbal witness was essential.

TEAM missionaries believed in the necessity of verbal witness but also realized that in a Muslim country certain methods of proclaiming the gospel would stir opposition and close the door completely. In fact, the Kabul Protestant Church, which was a part of the IAM, was demolished by the government as it proved offensive to the Muslims. (Some observers felt that the church was far too ornate and unnecessarily called attention to the building. A more modest building might have escaped notice by the officials.)

Aggression Provides Opportunity

Pro-Soviet forces took power in 1978 and in late 1979 the Soviet army began a massive invasion. The invaders spread throughout the country where they encountered stiff resistance from Afghan guerrillas. When the last TEAM missionary was withdrawn in 1980, the mission ceased its participation in the IAM.

The Soviet aggression resulted in a vast migration of refugees from Afghanistan into Pakistan, which did not go unnoticed by TEAM missionaries. In his report as chairman in 1980, Davis gave some figures of the early influx:

> I believe an unprecedented opportunity in the form of Afghan refugees has enlarged our vision. One million people (42 percent children, 28 percent women, and 30 percent men, according to UN statistics) are now free to hear and read the gospel in our adopted homeland.[29]

The number of Afghan refugees in Pakistan swelled to over three million and missionaries found ways to minister to them. One of the earliest was to distribute 14- by 14-foot tents donated by World Vision, World Concern, and World Relief. Another project was preparing much-needed fuel by a method developed in Taiwan of compressing rice straw into briquettes.

Opportunity and Opposition

More important was the need for personal contact but that was difficult because of language differences. Then it was learned that the Afghans felt a great need to learn English as a second language. Here was a ministry that would bring personal contact and increase the opportunity for witness. An active English-as-a-Second-Language (ESL) program began under the direction of Arlene Dalton.

That ESL could be an effective channel for presenting Christ to the Afghans became evident through the opposition it stirred among the Afghan religious leaders, who then pressured the Pakistan authorities to restrict the missionaries' entry into the refugee settlements. Even so, Afghan men and women study English every day. Hundreds have accepted gifts of the New Testament or Bible. ESL has indeed proved to be a useful tool in reaching these people with the gospel—people who for so long have been sadly but effectively shielded from its life-giving light.

The Spiritual Battle Rages On

All missionary work involves spiritual conflict. Any invasion of enemy territory is met by intense opposition. It seems that certain sections of the battlefield are contested more vigorously than others. The whole Islamic world tenaciously resists the advance of the gospel of Jesus Christ and at the same time presses forward with determination to win converts to itself. Missionaries who see few results may work as hard and as faithfully as do those on more fruitful fields. No one should doubt their dedication and perseverance in prayer.

Could it be that Christians in the homeland feel that sending a missionary to minister to the Muslims is the extent of their support responsibility? What about the spiritual battle? Are there enough prayer warriors involved to spare the missionary from being overwhelmed? Where are the Christians who are eager that those for whom Christ died among these lost multitudes will be snatched from the brink of eternal destruction?

DESERT OASIS

What Comprises the Near East?

The year 1990 brought the Near East forcibly and graphically to the attention of the world. We took careful note of just where it was located and found names such as Kuwait, Iraq, Syria, Jordan, Bahrain, United Arab Emirates, Saudi Arabia, and the Persian Gulf. We may have learned that the Turkish Empire had extended over the whole area; but when the Turks were on the losing side in World War I much of the territory came under British control and later, after World War II, gained independence as separate nations.

The Missionary Situation

Studying more closely we also may have learned several additional facts: (1) this whole region was solidly Muslim—almost to the exclusion of Christian churches which once were present everywhere; (2) the number of Christian missionaries working in these Muslim lands was small indeed; and (3) Muslims were extremely resistant to the gospel message, which had apparently dissuaded many missionaries from attempting to win them and discouraged others who made the attempt.

Attention Directed to the Need

In mid-1953, Dr. Wilbur M. Smith, well-known Bible teacher and author, wrote to Dr. David Johnson stating that he had recently visited the Near East and learned that very few

interdenominational missions were working in the area. Would TEAM be interested in sending missionaries there? Johnson thanked Dr. Smith for the information and assured him that if volunteers should come forward TEAM would certainly give this matter careful study.

In September of that year I received a visit in the TEAM office from five experienced missionaries who spoke of their interest and burden for the Near East—Mr. and Mrs. Raymond Joyce, Mr. and Mrs. Merrel Callaway, and Miss Ethel Killgrove. Mr. Joyce later sent us factual material which put the emphasis on the Kingdom of Iraq—formerly known as Mesopotamia—which he said was very open to missionaries.[1]

Survey of the Area

As I was to be in Africa in the summer of 1954, Dr. Johnson approved my visiting the Near East en route. In early September I stopped in Egypt, Syria, Iraq, and Jordan. The most helpful information was received in Baghdad from the Rev. Harold Davenport of the United Mission in Mesopotamia, and from the Rev. Keith Stevenson of the Near East and Arabian Mission. Both extended TEAM a warm welcome to send missionaries to Iraq and offered assistance in getting started in the work.

Board Approves Near East Field

Upon my return to the mission office the board of directors took action:

Mortenson's recommendations for the Near East were heartily seconded by Dr. Johnson:

1. Raymond Joyces to proceed without delay.
2. Doctors Kennedy to follow.
3. After language study, personal evangelism, literature, and medical work.
4. Baghdad, Iraq, to be targeted.[2]

Kennedys to Iraq

During the time I had been in Africa and the Near East, Drs.

Burwell (Pat) and Marian Kennedy had applied to serve among the Muslims and the board tentatively appointed them to this new field. Ready to leave in 1956, they were sent to the Arabian Hospital in Amarah, southern Iraq. But then in July 1958 a leftist, Pan-Arab revolution established a republic which oriented its foreign policy toward Soviet Russia. Being away from the center of activity, the Kennedys were able to remain in Iraq for some months before it was necessary for them to withdraw to Lebanon.

Lebanon and Palestine

Meanwhile, TEAM received a request to take over responsibility for the Haven of Hope orphanage ministry in Beirut. Feeling that this might provide a stepping stone into the region, the board agreed to provide a missionary couple. Raymond and Mona Joyce accepted this responsibility as a temporary assignment. Miss Maria Mayer was the next to apply. She had the distinct advantage of having lived and gone to school in Lebanon as a teen-ager and so spoke the Arabic language.

The Joyces accurately judged that the Haven of Hope ministry could well be left to others engaged in the same kind of work but did not want to make that recommendation on their own. Miss Mabel Culter, founder of orphanage work on TEAM's Korea field, studied the situation. The board of directors concurred with her view that most of the children be turned over to another Christian home, thus freeing the TEAM missionaries to look elsewhere in the Near East for an open door.

After their withdrawal from Iraq, Dr. and Mrs. Kennedy accepted an invitation in 1959 to serve at the Berachah Hospital, administered by Mrs. Tom Lambie, near Bethlehem. This provided further orientation to the Arab people and assured more progress in the language.

The Lord Directs to Trucial Oman

Late in 1959, when no progress was being made in determining where TEAM missionaries should serve, they had a surprise from the Lord through a letter from Dr. Wells Thoms, of the Arabian Mission of the Reformed Church in America, with the news that the ruling sheikh of the Trucial Oman State of Abu Dhabi would welcome a mission hospital at the Buraimi Oasis. Could Pat Kennedy and Raymond Joyce come down, look over the situation, and talk with the sheikh? Believing this could indeed be the Lord's answer to their request for clear guidance on where to work, they readily agreed and made a survey trip in December 1959.

An Oasis at the Crossroads

Just where was the Buraimi Oasis? They learned that it was in the Sheikhdom of Abu Dhabi ruled by Sheikh Shakhbuut. Abu Dhabi, the largest of the seven Trucial States, was in the lower part of the Arabian peninsula bordering the Persian Gulf. The oasis was located 100 miles inland from the coast at about the point where Saudi Arabia, the Sheikhdom of Abu Dhabi, and the Sultanate of Oman came together. The oasis was made up of ten villages, three of which were in Oman. The other seven villages, of which Al Ain was the largest, were in the sheikhdom. These inland sheikhdom villages around the oasis were ruled by Sheikh Zayed bin Sultan, a brother of Shakhbuut.

In 1971 Sheikh Zayed deposed his brother with the justification that more aggressive leadership was needed to develop the economy of the sheikhdom. Contrary to common custom in the desert, he did not execute the deposed sheikh but instead provided him a palace and a position of empty honor. That same year—1971—the Trucial States joined together as the United Arab Emirates (UAE) and Zayed was made president.

The population of Buraimi Oasis ranged from 1,500 to 2,000 for most of the year, but in the extreme heat of the summer when temperatures rose to as high as 130 degrees, the population multiplied five to eight times with those who were fleeing the high humidity of the coastal towns. Buraimi Oasis sustained its people on its abundance of dates, its camels, and its goats, with a minimum of imported food. One reason for the existence of the oasis was a system of underground water conduits, made of stone, leading from the mountains in the south. Whether or not the origin of these conduits has been actually determined, the general understanding is that they were constructed by Persians about 1,500 B.C. They are truly life-sustaining waters.

A Close-up Look and an Invitation

Kennedy and Joyce reported a most satisfactory survey tour in December 1959 which included contacts with British political and military officials. Of foremost importance to them was their meeting with the absolute ruler of the sheikhdom—Sheikh Shakhbuut. The ruler was most cordial and, when he learned their errand, stressed that it was a mission hospital that he wanted. He took them to an open space outside the village of Al Ain and indicated that the hospital should be located there. On this property was a solid adobe building which he suggested could be a church. He even suggested that his people were free to believe the Christian message.

As missionaries of the slowly growing Near East staff received word of this new field, they rejoiced to have a focus for their prayer and preparation. The board of directors approved the plan at its meeting in February 1960. Kennedy and Joyce made a second trip to the oasis in April.

The First Permanent Entry

When I was on an extended tour of the Far East in the fall of 1960, I received word from the TEAM office that the first permanent party was to move into Buraimi in the third week of November. Could I change my flights to join that first group? I could. Changing planes at Bahrain, farther north on the Persian Gulf, I flew in a small fourteen-passenger plane across desert sands to Sharjah, about two hundred miles from the oasis. Here in Sharjah, on the morning of November 20, 1960, I found Dr. and Mrs. Kennedy and four children, Maria Mayer, and Land Rover driver Ali all packed and waiting. The desert road followed the coastline for a hundred miles to near the town of Abu Dhabi. At that time the town was a collection of native palm-frond and adobe huts. Visible were several large, sprawling, prominent white buildings where Sheikh Shakhbuut lived and held court.

Across the Sands

From the town of Abu Dhabi, our desert road—actually just the tracks of other vehicles—led eastward for the next hundred miles through an area of sand dunes. The British explorer and naturalist, Wilfred Thesiger, D.S.O., had traveled through the sheikhdom and adjacent "Empty Quarter" of Saudi Arabia and described what he saw:

> ...mountainous dune chains, sometimes 400 to 500 feet in height running for hundreds of miles, or crescent-shaped dunes...the color of which varies greatly from silver, cream and gold, to rose and brick-red.[3]

We did not have to cross hundreds of miles but even so sand dunes were there to confront us. Being new to the desert we wondered how we would get over the beautiful but awesome barriers. But others had done so and Ali showed no particular concern. How good it was that the Land Rover had compound lower gears and these were used—all but compound low. That gear would not have allowed us the momentum to plow through the sand on the up grade. Several times we had to lighten the load as we got off and trudged up the steep mountain of sand while the vehicle plowed through to the summit.

A Start in Make-do Quarters

We arrived at Al Ain about 11:00 P.M., located the new empty guest house which had been promised, and found places to spread our sleeping bags. I doubt that in our weariness any of us heard the pre-dawn Muslim call to prayer from the nearby minaret. This adobe guest house was to be the missionary residence and medical dispensary until more suitable and permanent quarters could be provided.

Looking out in the morning from the veranda of the guest house,

I could see parts of the village of Al Ain. There were stretches of open sand, a number of adobe houses, and many palm-frond enclosures. Several women clad in black flowing robes were walking nearby and I could see that they wore black masks so only their eyes were visible. When they came closer they used part of their outer robes to cover their faces more completely—either because they thought strangers might be in the guest house or they saw me on the veranda.

While men moved about freely, women were truly prisoners of their Arab culture. Surprisingly, the women had no fear of me when I was with the doctor or the lady missionaries. They would be wearing the mask but would not cover their heads with their robes. When an Arab man came into view they would immediately veil themselves.

Word got out early that doctors had come to the oasis and both Marian and Pat decided they should tell the people whose cases were not urgent to wait several days until they had unpacked their medical supplies. In the afternoon, a driver came to the door and told Pat that he had come a long distance and desperately needed help for his ailing wife who lay on a mat in the back of his pickup. After a quick examination Pat decided that it was necessary to give the woman an injection of penicillin, which required unpacking supplies, sterilizing needles, etc.

Confirming a Policy

Some hours earlier we had been discussing what the policy should be in regard to charges for medicines, shots, and other services. Pat questioned whether the people could afford to pay anything. I pointed out that charges would be necessary to enable the dispensary to keep up its work and, besides, the people would judge the value by its cost.

When the doctor had given the injection, he asked if I thought a five-rupee charge (about 70 cents at the time) was too high. I did not think so and Pat quoted that amount to the husband. To our surprise, the husband angrily protested that he wanted his wife to have the ten-rupee injection! Pat apparently was able to make him understand that his wife had received the proper dosage at half price. This was a timely experience at the beginning of service to these people, as it enabled the doctors to value the medical help in the same light as did the people themselves.

Resort to Prefab Buildings

It became clear to us immediately that housing would need to be provided when more staff arrived on the field. Palm-frond houses were too flimsy and temporary. Adobe houses were expensive and also too temporary—given their being built of crumbly sun-dried brick. The solution seemed to be prefabricated "Cosely" houses from England.

While I was present the doctors decided that the medical ministry should in faith be named the Oasis Hospital.

When the Joyces arrived, Joyce was asked to be field leader. He, therefore, handled most of the correspondence that was needed to care for the details of getting a ministry underway. Maria Mayer's proficiency in Arabic was a great asset and she, though not a medic, was a great help in the medical ministry.

Preparing the First Hospital

Over several years a number of missionaries with building skills helped to erect residences on the plot which the ruler had allotted. The most challenging task was to provide a prefabricated hospital building. The medical personnel set forth the requirements and Clayton Kent, on furlough in Chicago from India, designed the building and placed the orders along with specifications to the suppliers in England. That building with several satellite structures had to meet the needs for over twenty-five years.

The Medical Need

In addition to the usual ailments in a subtropical climate—malaria, dysentery, etc.—the great problem was child mortality at a rate of 50 percent. This problem had a prenatal beginning in the care—or lack of care—of the mother. All too often, the second child was stillborn. This was a concern not only of the poor Bedouin; it touched the wife—or wives—of the ruling family as well.

It soon became apparent that a major portion of the medical work would be obstetrics and here God's special provision was to have Dr. Marian Kennedy at the hospital. Her work in this field soon won the confidence of the women and afforded countless opportunities for witness. The work of both doctors, Pat and Marian, became widely known, with the result that patients came from across the desert from many miles around.

Auxiliary Staff

A hospital ministry is very dependent on auxiliary medical personnel, particularly nurses. One of the early nurses was Gertrude Dyck, who arrived in 1962. Other early nurses were Janice Shafer, who came in 1966, and Nancy Brock who arrived in 1970. Miss Shafer had a tendency to overwork in her nursing duties and eventually she was transferred to much-needed administrative work, where she also had opportunity to overwork but apparently not to the same extent.

Among the early missionaries were Gerald and Marjorie Longjohn, who had a versatile ministry. After the main clinic building had been erected, Longjohn planned and developed much of the rest of the physical plant with a small crew of workmen. Both had many local contacts for witness and for the needs of the ongoing ministry. Longjohn also served as field chairman from time to time.

Replacement and Volunteer Staff

When the Kennedys had to be at home for a while, Dr. and Mrs. Norman Streight served for a term. Then for several years the hospital depended on short-term doctors. Their help—usually at their own expense—was greatly appreciated and enabled the hospital to continue to meet the needs of the people. Few of these doctors were obstetricians, but their medical and surgical training enabled them to serve well. Dr. Joseph Schoonmaker, who had been a medical missionary in India, helped for repeated short terms. Some of the nurses had special training in midwifery and were able to handle all the cases except Caesarean sections. There were enough other illnesses and injuries (camel bites included) to keep the doctors fully occupied.

A Government Hospital Opened

The Oasis Hospital had been in existence only a few years when the government of the sheikhdom opened a large public hospital at Al Ain where the people could receive free care. It was staffed entirely by doctors from other countries, some of whom were reported to have little interest in the people. At first the missionaries were concerned that patients would stop coming to the Oasis Hospital, which continued to charge a modest fee for treatments and medications.

Statistics Remove Cause for Concern

The missionaries were reluctant to give up any of the opportunity they were having to serve and witness to these people. They need not have worried. If there was a reduction in patient load it was hardly noticeable. The people soon revealed their appreciation for the Oasis Hospital missionaries and their loving concern and attention. The missionaries realized, of course, that with the population of Al Ain growing so fast their patient load would otherwise have increased dramatically.

Oasis Hospital continued to have a steady load of both inpatients—3,244 in 1980 and 3,259 in 1984—and outpatients—42,489 in 1980 and 44,783 in 1984. Expectant mothers accounted for more than 75 percent of the admissions. The number of deliveries remained quite consistent at 2,500 to 2,800 year after year. Delivering 210 to 230 babies month after month kept the doctors and nurses extremely busy.

Admitting one patient soon involved the care of two—mother and baby. Twins arrived as often as twice a month and triplets once a year. All the supporting services of laboratory tests, x-rays, ultrasound exams and treatments, immunizations, and prescriptions were in proportion. For the year 1982 these procedures totaled 251,737. Just keeping the record was a major undertaking, not to speak of the time and effort involved.

One other statistic is more difficult to pinpoint. It is the number of family members who accompanied the patients. There would have to be one or more to provide the meals, so over the course of a year there might be three to five thousand family members for stays of four to seven days just for the inpatients alone. What a wonderful opportunity to let the light of Christ shine for multitudes to see! And with the staff's aim of giving verbal witness to all it was clear that the people were receiving a testimony. That most were resistant to the Word was a matter for concern and prayer but the mandate of proclaiming the Word was still clear.

The Purpose is Witness

Right from the start, missionaries and other workers in the Oasis Hospital took advantage of opportunities for witness. People usually came in quite early to the daily men's and women's clinics, so there were always numbers waiting. When the waiting room was most crowded, the doctor would stop and have a portion of Scripture read with brief comments, followed by prayer. There were opportunities for witness and prayer on an individual basis as patients were being seen. Missionaries and staff regularly held ward meetings. The 1978 annual conference evangelistic committee report is of special interest:

> Faithfulness is a highlight, with a steady testimony radiating through the lives of our staff as they minister to the physical needs of people. Indian staff quietly share in more than six languages with those who come for treatment. Arab staff—along with missionaries—minister to women and children in hospital visitation, in meetings held in the hospital, in our bookroom, through administrative duties, and in many other ways make indelible impressions through life, word, and print. The Urdu people are no longer left out because now we have staff who have Urdu as their native tongue reaching out to these people in

the same ways as the other language groups. Our hospital has been able to minister in at least six native language groups through keen evangelistic-minded missionaries—both staff and career.[4]

The hospital contacts also opened the door to another encouraging type of outreach—home visits:

Faithfulness in home visitation, discipling, and friendship are also keys. One convert of over ten years has been faithfully taught every week—almost continuously—for that time by several of our missionary ladies. Other missionaries and staff have started launching out in home visitation and have been warmly welcomed. Reports from these visits have encouraged our hearts many times to praise the Lord for the opportunity.[5]

Sensitivity and Restriction

The local government became sensitive about Christian witness and, over a period of years, it first limited then restricted witness in the wards. The bookstore, which had a good supply of Christian reading material, was investigated by the authorities and samples were taken to determine whether any derogatory statements about Islam were in the material. Later, they closed the bookstore even though they did not find any objectionable material.

Naturally, these restrictions brought disappointment but not to the point of discouragement. A great source of encouragement was the realization that here at one of the few populated spots in the Arabian desert—where total spiritual darkness had reigned for countless generations—there were now Christians living for their Lord and serving in His name. This was indeed an open door and a privilege not to be viewed lightly.

Oil Flow Beckons Immigrants

The Trucial Oman States began developing their extensive oil reserves about 1962 and many petroleum experts, business people, craftsmen, and laborers came into the country. Among them were workers from other Arab-speaking countries—Egypt, Jordan, Lebanon, Syria, Oman, Iraq, and the West Bank (Palestinians). In addition, there were people from Iran, Pakistan, India, Bangladesh,

Somalia, and European countries.

The number of foreign workers (expatriates) increased year by year until in 1985 it was reported that they made up 80 percent of the total population of the United Arab Emirates. Though oil production brought them there, they were involved in many lines of work in support of the oil industry and the population growth:

> A majority of the expatriate population is there for employment. Broadly speaking, the *Iranis* and *Omanis* tend to be manual laborers; the *Pakistanis*—skilled craftsmen as carpenters, etc.; the *Indians*—clerks and shop assistants; the *Palestinians*—government officials and primary school teachers; and the *Egyptians*—secondary school teachers and more senior government officials. There also is an increasing number of Americans and Europeans in the Emirates with the oil industry and other companies.[6]

I recall going with Dr. Pat Kennedy to the royal palace in Abu Dhabi city in the mid-60s to pay a courtesy call on Sheikh Shakhbuut. The armed guards recognized Kennedy and ushered us in without challenge to the spacious reception hall. Seated along the sides were scores of Western businessmen each hoping to be called for an interview. The sheikh looked up, saw Kennedy, and motioned us to come up to sit by him. He evidently was being pressed to the limit by insistent commercial representatives seeking a share in the development money being rather lavishly spent. The sheikh seemed relieved to have a conversation with the doctor whose requests, if any, were modest in the extreme.

Beginning of Group Ministries

Among the Arab expatriates there was a sprinkling of Christians, both evangelical and nominal. George Awad, one of the Palestinian male nurses, was a zealous witness and began services for Arabic-speaking people. The hospital administrator, Samuel Zayyat, and his family were also active in this ministry. These services were held near the hospital in the adobe building that the sheikh had first pointed out to Kennedy and Joyce.

Missionaries also began services in English to reach Indian and Pakistani people in the area, many of whom understood English.

Then Bible studies were started among other groups in languages as varied as Urdu, Telegu, Malayalam, and Bengali. The service of Richard and Virginia Thompson, who spent eighteen years in Pakistan—and several years in Iran—was a great help and blessing to the Urdu congregation.[7]

Lebanon Not Forgotten

The continued open door for service in Lebanon was not forgotten as Harry and Carol Genet, who felt a call to Muslim literature work, were assigned there for the benefit of the gospel outreach in all the Arabic-speaking world. On a visit to Beirut in 1970, area foreign secretary George Martin commented on Genet's excellent work with the Arabic Literature Mission. He was training national leaders and anticipated that within two years that mission's entire ministry could be carried on by them. When that goal was reached, Genet was invited to join the home staff as editor and publications secretary.

Church Development Begins

While never losing sight of the primary purpose of bringing loving service in Christ's name and the gospel message to the local people, missionaries began to realize in the 1970s that a marvelous opportunity was opening among the growing expatriate population. From that time forward the church ministries assumed increasing importance. With few exceptions, those who worked in these ministries—both missionaries and employed staff—were also involved full-time in some part of the medical ministry. Their entry into the UAE was under Oasis Hospital sponsorship and they were faithful to that designation. Later, some were able to receive visas under sponsorship of one of the church groups.

Planning the Spiritual Work

It was in the early 1970s that missionaries recognized the need to plan the evangelistic activities as carefully as the medical personnel planned and carried on their work. The reports of the evangelistic committee outline the steps taken so that missionaries could coordinate their ministries and work with clear goals in witnessing and discipling. An outreach committee was responsible for looking beyond the medical work to the many other witness and church development opportunities in the growing communities of the UAE.

Looking back from the year 1985, the field editor commented:

> As we look back over 25 years of ministry in the United Arab Emirates, we praise the Lord for the opportunity that has opened up since the early 70s for church development. All this church work is done among the expatriate community, having begun with the expansion of our TEAM outreach into the coastal area of Abu Dhabi City. The key was a building project that included a chapel facility—recently expanded to provide a main-floor meeting room to seat 200 and a second floor meeting area to seat about 100, plus Sunday school rooms and nursery. This allows more than one group to be meeting at a time. With seven groups using the facility, it is kept very busy.[8]

The groups using the Abu Dhabi chapel in 1985 were Arabic, English, Brethren, Korean, Telegu, Malayalam, and Filipino. In addition there were five language groups meeting in facilities at the Oasis Hospital—Arabic, English, Malayalam, Tamil, and Urdu.

Only a sampling of committee reports to the annual field conferences on this growing activity can be given:

- 1975—Samuel Zayyat, hospital administrator, and 'Issa Fakhoury, bookroom manager, share responsibility for the weekly Al Ain Arab Sunday evening preaching service and the Tuesday evening Arab Bible class.
- 1975—Indian staff members Mr. Jacob, Mr. Samuel, and Mr. Ninaan, and Mr. E. B. Mirza of Pakistan divide responsibilities for the Al Ain Friday evening worship services held in Indian languages and Urdu.
- 1975—Shafiiq Haddad of Jordan and Safwat Girgis of Egypt do most of the preaching for the Friday evening Arabic Fellowship meeting in Abu Dhabi. There is also a Monday evening Bible study.
- 1975—Carl Sherbeck preaches at the Sunday English worship service in Abu Dhabi and other missionaries, with the cooperation of Fellowship members, care for Sunday school activities. Women's Bible study is led by Barbara Sherbeck. Youth and

children's activities. Follow up of names referred by Oasis Hospital.

- 1977—Abu Dhabi Arab Fellowship calls Pastor Nicola Abdu and family from Syria.
- 1981—Al Ain English Fellowship board taking more responsibility. Developing Awana Bible Club program. Friday evening worship service and Monday evening Bible institute program provide regular Bible study opportunities.
- 1981—Al Ain Bible Church is the congregation of Pakistani believers. Church leaders meet twice weekly in a structured leadership training program in addition to regular Bible study and prayer times.
- 1984—Al Ain Bible Church (Urdu) sent one of its teaching elders to Pakistan to attend seminary. Church supports a number of missionaries in Pakistan.
- 1985—Evangelical Church of Al Ain (English) reports average attendance at weekly worship service of over one hundred.
- 1985—Al Ain Bible Church (Urdu) reports elder Barkat Masih was imprisoned in March on false charge of speaking against Islam. Case being appealed.
- 1985—Evangelical Church of Al Ain (Arabic). Pastor Ameal Haddad reports the regular services are: Sunday night worship, Tuesday Bible study and prayer, Friday family fellowship, Sunday school, young people's meeting and ladies' Bible study. Over 180 attended Christmas program and gospel message.[9]
- 1988—Sherbecks move to Dubai to begin Arabic Ministry in Dubai and Sharjah.[10]

Of great help to the Arabic church work was the fact that four missionaries spoke Arabic as their native language and had first-hand knowledge of the culture: Dr. and Mrs. Salem Barghout, Nadeem Serhal, and Ameal Haddad.

Growth of the Filipino Work

The work among the Filipino community was particularly noteworthy. It started in Abu Dhabi City and spread to Al Ain, Dubai, and Sharjah. In time, the Abu Dhabi Filipino Christian Fellowship was able to call and support pastor Elmer M. Tandayu (of Conservative Baptist background) from the Philippine Islands. The pastor's report to the 1986 annual conference revealed the scope of the work:

The Filipino Christian Fellowship (FCF) has grown greatly from its struggling beginnings to the healthy mission-minded church that it is now. To God be the glory! The reason for the existence and functions of FCF is discipleship. Since the time I arrived in Abu Dhabi, it has been my desire to balance our ministry activities according to church functions and discipleship as stated in Acts 2:41-47. The church's growth can be measured in several areas [condensed below].

Worship: Average attendance—80. Five to seven visitors each week. Worshipper participation. Lives being changed.

Instruction: Eleven Bible study groups. Thirty members in TEE courses. Discipleship for potential leaders. Christian education for children.

Fellowship: Concern for others—prayer, visitation, counseling, burden-sharing.

Evangelism and Missions: Reaching people through personal witness and Bible study groups. Outreach to Dubai and Sharjah. Support of two Filipino couples for church planting in the Philippines.

Music Ministry: Choir of 35 members. Sextet for outreach.

Prison Ministry: Each Monday in men's and women's wards.

Correspondence Course: Correspondents in UAE, Saudi, Kuwait, Qatar, Muscat, and Libya.[11]

Most of the Filipinos were of nominal Roman Catholic background and many, on hearing the evangelical message, were led into a personal relationship with Christ.

Expansion of Filipino Work Continues

At a meeting of the TEAM board of directors in November 1988, area foreign secretary Lynn Everswick reported continued progress by the Filipino groups:

We continue to marvel at the growth and development of expatriate groups and Bible studies. The Filipino Christian Fellowship in Al Ain has nine Bible study groups now operating, with expansion in the near future. A new group is now meeting in Ajman, and the largest group is in Sharjah. Dubai and Abu Dhabi round out the five cities in which the FCF is now expanding. The FCF held its first missions conference, October 19 to 28. All five groups met together on the 28th in Dubai with a special concert and guest speaker Dr. Gilbert Vitelez from the Asian Seminary in Manila. More than 300 were in attendance and their goal was to raise support for missionaries who would go to remote, unreached parts of the Philippines.[12]

The news of this work during the next year was equally encouraging as the Filipino Fellowship reported 270 conversions and 51 baptisms in 1989.

Theological Education by Extension (TEE)

A ministry used to excellent advantage was TEE—locally called Church Leadership Training Program—adapted for the UAE by Moses and Nancy Jesudass. These two Americans of Asian background—Moses being Indian and Nancy Vietnamese—could work well in a cosmopolitan setting. With this background and with good theological training, Jesudass was a logical person for this program, which served a wide cross-section of people. Conducted in Arabic, English, and several Indian languages the program trained mature Christians in Al Ain, Abu Dhabi, Bahrain, Kuwait, Dubai and Sharjah. The goal was not only to enhance the witness of local Christians and train them for leadership in the churches, but also to prepare expatriates for the day of their return to their own homelands.

Many expatriates were in the UAE on two-year contracts so there was great turnover in the congregations. This created an urgency in training while the opportunity existed, and it also provided means to affect the home areas of these people as they returned quite well equipped to communicate the gospel in their own culture.

What is the Greatest Need in the UAE?

As Gerald Longjohn considered this question in 1981, he did so out of an intimate knowledge of the country and its people from the time it was a typical Bedouin sheikhdom through its transformation into a modern cosmopolitan state. In answer to the question concerning the greatest need, he stated his convictions in a paper presented to the 1981 annual field conference:

> The need today is the same as it was when the mission first came here, the need of sharing Christ. True, some may say they really do not need our hospital today in the same way they did then, but the primary need is as great today as it ever was—and even greater, with the many expatriates—the need of accepting Christ. We praise God that He has allowed the hospital to stay as a witness for Himself and to give us the opening for the development of churches. It is our prayer that from the open door given the hospital we might see active, vibrant, witnessing churches that would by all means share Christ in word and deed. The hospital has been and continues to be a key to reaching out in a country that has over 100 mosques and less than 10 churches.[13]

Longjohn recommended that the mission continue to develop churches that have a common understanding of and are faithful to evangelical doctrine, and that also have sufficient uniformity for there to be easy association—even with language and cultural differences. He stressed the importance of the churches being able to present a clear witness to the community and a unified stand before the government.

Several years earlier, the government had recognized "The Evangelical Church of Abu Dhabi" and later extended this recognition to include "The Evangelical Church of Al Ain." Government recognition proved helpful in securing visas for missionaries and pastors who were not linked with the Oasis Hospital but worked primarily with the church groups. The security officials who approved visas seemed to have increased confidence in groups linked with a government-recognized church. Longjohn looked forward to the day when there would be an umbrella organization, "The Evangelical Churches of the UAE."

Should the day ever come when the authorities would consider the Oasis Hospital redundant because government medical facilities were taking full responsibility, it was his fervent hope that the Evangelical Churches would be able to sponsor the entry of missionaries.

Outreach Committee Appraisal

The outreach committee presented a perceptive report to the 1983 annual conference which highlighted several features of the church situation in the UAE, including its ministry along language lines and its constantly changing constituency. A third feature was that the church is a minority under attack:

> The Christian Church in the Middle East, even by its broadest definition, recognizes itself as a minority, and is accustomed to being treated with varying degrees of discrimination. For example, evangelical Christians in the UAE may regularly hear or read attacks on their faith in the local media, which are based on caricature and misrepresentation. Since there is virtually no recourse open for response, a believer is forced to go on in silence simply ignoring the injustice. The situation calls for a resolute refusal to entertain an attitude of helpless defeat on the negative side, and on the positive side the prayerful development of approaches to authorities to exert legitimate pressure for recognition and respect.[14]

Doctor Liddle's Evaluation

Doctors on the mission field are generally so pressed in caring for the physical needs of the many who come seeking help that the missionaries in conference only rarely ask them to take on responsibilities such a field chairman position. An exception was made in the UAE when Dr. Larry Liddle was elected to that position about 1984. Dr. Liddle and his wife, Marilyn, originally intended to go to Taiwan but were requested by TEAM headquarters to serve for a time at the Oasis Hospital which then had no regularly assigned doctor. After several years in that work, the Liddles felt the Lord was leading them to become career missionaries in the UAE.

In his first year as chairman, Liddle made a careful study of the issues the missionary body was facing and presented his findings in a paper to the 1985 annual field conference, titled "Church Development and Church/Mission Relationships in the UAE." Apart from the hospital, the planning and development of which was on course—being slowed only by official red tape—the other major mission responsibility related to the churches. On this important subject he found a record of field conference decisions and a number of thoughtful and important papers by previous field chairmen, and by Gerald Longjohn, Arif Khan, and Moses Jesudass. All recognized the need for progress in church-mission relationships and in the development of fellowship among the churches.

Viewing the progress to date, Liddle recognized that insufficient action had been taken to implement earlier recommendations and decisions. His question: Are we in danger of thinking that decisions alone can bring the churches to full health and vigor?

Liddle then gave the analogy of a doctor facing an ailing patient. The doctor must learn the patient's history, make a physical examination, obtain the results of laboratory examinations and x-rays, then correlate the findings and come up with a diagnosis. When the diagnosis has been determined the next step is to plan the treatment. In doing so the doctor does not consider that his diagnosis and treatment instructions will of themselves be sufficient to bring health. The patient must additionally be an active participant in the whole process "so that both he and the doctor reach their mutual goals—healing of the disease."[15]

Liddle indicated that the conference had studied and examined the church question and agreed on a diagnosis, therefore:

> Now is the time for action, not just another paper or more committee meetings and discussion. We now have pastors in each of our churches and it is time to make progress in continuing to develop our present churches. It is time to make progress in the areas of church recognition and requests for land. It is time to make progress in formalizing the relationship among our churches and between them and the mission. Certainly, there needs to be much prayer, thought, and work, but first there must be the will to work together and face the hard questions honestly and trust God to show us how to develop and carry out plans that will advance His Kingdom in this country.[16]

Liddle gave credit for the solid work already accomplished:

> We now have six churches in various stages of organization that have resulted from the direct involvement of TEAM in the UAE. They are all basically structured around different language groups. Each is unique in its needs and concerns. Each is at a

different stage of organization and in a different place on the road to becoming an independent church.[17]

According the TEAM *Principles and Guiding Rules,* the goal is to have the churches become self-propagating, self-supporting, self-governing, and self-instructing. How had the churches progressed?

Liddle reported that the English church in Abu Dhabi was covering all its expenses and was not dependent on the mission. The other churches were still dependent on the mission to a greater or lesser degree, principally through the supply of a missionary as pastor.

In most churches there had been solid progress in self-government and most now had a written constitution and a functioning board. As for self-instruction, Liddle was encouraged to see pastors teaching their people to study the Word for themselves in discipleship classes and through the TEE program.

As far as self-propagation was concerned, he noted that the mission could suggest and encourage by teaching and example, but it ultimately depended on the pastor and his board and their vision for development in this matter.[18]

Liddle then addressed the need for a visible fellowship of the churches and quoted a recent letter from Lynn Everswick, area foreign secretary:

> For some time I have sensed that there is a real need for the churches which have come out of direct TEAM involvement to in some way be linked by a common doctrinal statement and constitution.... This would in no way take away the autonomy of the local church. However, it would provide a loose fellowship of churches, irrespective of their cultural and language backgrounds. I believe the churches in the UAE need to band together for prayer, and financial and moral support.[19]

The Church Fellowship Becomes a Reality

The Lord answered prayer in bringing about unity of purpose so that the churches were able to establish a fellowship. Everswick reported on this development in 1986:

> This fellowship of evangelical churches is now a reality and last

month they met for their first meeting to select pastors to hold office for the coming year. We are greatly encouraged by this move and feel it will bring about a greater spirit of unity and strength in terms of outreach into the community.[20]

Later, Everswick reported that there were eight churches, of which five had full-time pastors. These churches joined together in what was called "The Evangelical Church Trustees Committee" to encourage one another and present a united front to the government when requesting visas for their pastors.

Soul-winning Continues

While it was important for the future of the work that wise decisions be made on the relationship of the churches to each other and to the mission, the really important work of bringing men and women to Christ must be paramount. And it was. One important group of about 15,000 in the UAE came from the former Portuguese colony of Goa, now a part of India. Many Goans of mixed Portuguese and Indian heritage are Roman Catholics. Moses and Nancy Jesudass were able to reach many of these Goans for Christ. Nancy taught a group of fifteen teachers in a Bible class and all fifteen accepted Christ. These and other contacts among the Goans were brought together in a worship service:

> The worship service attendance grew larger each week. The conversion of Wilfred D'sousa, a music teacher deeply rooted in yoga and Hinduism, brought additional inspiration to all of us. Through his personal contact with people in the music institute, he kept bringing many to the worship services. His brother Stan accepted Christ last week.... Our number has grown from 15 in the early days to about 45 now. The Lord is adding to our number and there is a growing awareness of the need to witness more. We are sure the Lord is leading us to new dimensions.[21]

A Pastor for the Goan Church

That the Goan Christians now have a pastor to serve their growing congregation is a source of satisfaction, but who he is and where he is from adds special interest. C. S. Dutt was a fellow student with Moses Jesudass at the Union Biblical Seminary in India. Later when he moved to the capital city, New Delhi, he became active in the Delhi Bible Fellowship. It was here that he learned of the need for a pastor of the UAE Indian Christian Fellowship. He and his wife, Ruksanna—a medical doctor—responded to the need and went to the UAE as missionaries of the Indian Evangelical Mission, supported by the Delhi Bible Fellowship, and loaned as regular missionaries to TEAM. Thus, one mission field of TEAM shares in the ministry of another.

Oasis Hospital Still a Key

To be sure that the Oasis Hospital would continue to have the approval of the government and attract patients, and thus be the basis for continued Christian witness in the UAE, some serious thought had to be given to renewing and updating the hospital facilities. As early as 1981, Dr. Larry Liddle prepared a study for the attention of the annual conference in which he recalled efforts already made and shared the thinking of the medical staff on the future of the Oasis Hospital. He first restated the long-range goals previously set:

> As always, the main purpose of the Oasis Hospital will be ministering to the physical and spiritual needs of each patient. It is the desire of the whole staff to have each seeking soul followed up and led to believing faith in our Lord Jesus Christ and included in a local New Testament church.

> Oasis Hospital will make all efforts possible to improve and update the medical and surgical facilities, care, and treatment within limitations of staff, budget, and our approximate 50-bed capacity.[22]

Hospital Planner Needed

Several years earlier the hospital administrator had sought government approval for remodeling or reconstructing the hospital building. Preliminary approval was long in coming—at least three years. When it did come, the medical staff got busy in earnest to plan the new facilities. It was then they realized that this was a bigger assignment than limited time and experience would make possible. But the Lord had a solution:

> It was becoming obvious that we needed more expert help in

planning a new and/or renovated hospital, and we were beginning to inquire in the States for someone to help in this area. But
God, through circumstances that only He could have arranged,
sent us two of Britain's top hospital architects. It was even more
thrilling to see Brian and Ceri [Hitchcox] come to a saving
knowledge of our Lord Jesus. Brian has been most involved and
has devoted himself with enthusiasm and sensitivity to our needs
and peculiar situation. He has donated literally thousands of
hours to drawing and redrawing plans and has visited here
personally several times.[23]

Alternate Plan

With further delays in obtaining approval for a new hospital
building and later rejection of the application, alternate plans were
prepared for renovation and some face-lifting. Hitchcox provided
invaluable help in this work as well. The renovations were undertaken and resulted in better medical care and vastly improved
working conditions.

Though the medical personnel were frustrated by the negative
government response they still aimed to make the Oasis Hospital
ministry one that would truly honor the Lord. With all the mod-
ernization in the country, they keenly felt that as one of the few
Christian institutions and as representatives of Christ, they should
not be faulted because of outdated and antiquated facilities:

> Our guiding principle should be—what we do, we do well, in
> Christ's name. In light of this, I believe it is important that we
> eventually have a new hospital building. The renovation is an
> excellent transition stage and will give us the time we need to
> build but it is not adequate to fulfill the patients' expectations
> nor is it an adequate expression of our desire as Christians that
> the quality of our facilities reflect the quality of the medical care
> we deliver.[24]

New Hospital Building Approved

After years of uncertainty about the possibility of rebuilding the
hospital there came sudden approval. At least that is what it seems
from the available reports. In 1985, field chairman Carl Sherbeck
referred to the good news:

> The long-awaited hospital building project is now under way.

This is surely a sign that we are an acknowledged part of this community. Even the process of working through the unexplained "hold" on the 1982 building permit has kept us in significant contact with key people in the local government.[25]

The missionary family and staff celebrated the ground breaking on October 7, 1984, and excavation began November 6. Construction went ahead in four phases, extending over several years, because the hospital work had to continue without hindrance. Missionary Scott Anderson supervised the building process and had the assistance of a number of volunteer construction workers from the homeland. Larry Liddle, who had a two-fold interest in the project as doctor and as field chairman, made rather jubilant reference to the project in his 1986 report:

Certainly one of the major reasons for rejoicing this past year is the obvious progress on the new hospital building. We rejoice that the Lord, in ways we did not anticipate or plan for, brought the needed skilled workers and laborers at just the right time. Even as we rejoice at the progress of the physical building, we rejoice even more that this project is contributing to the building up of the spiritual body of Christ.[26]

Hospital Completed and Dedicated

The various steps of completion of the hospital were celebrated with appropriate dedication services:

Phase I—Surgery, Obstetrics—May 26, 1988

Phase II—Inpatient and Nursery—January 26, 1990

Open house to celebrate completion of new hospital and Thirtieth Anniversary—November 27, 1990

It was fitting that Doctors Burwell (Pat) and Marian Kennedy could be present. They laid the foundations of the Oasis Hospital medical ministry and invested so much of their lives in the service of the Lord among the people of the United Arab Emirates.

With the hospital construction complete and equipment in place, medical staff members eagerly anticipated more effective ways of serving the people. They prayed for an enhanced testimony among those whom they had come to love and whose eternal welfare was of even greater concern than their physical betterment.

Doctors Offer for Service

In comparison with the early years of the Oasis Hospital, there was now no serious shortage of doctors. Dr. Larry and Marilyn Liddle joined the work in 1975 and, as earlier mentioned, Larry doubled as field chairman for three or four years. Dr. Andrew and Ruth Rutherford joined the staff in 1976. Dr. Rutherford had previous experience as a hospital administrator and this was of great value to the Oasis Hospital until another missionary could replace him. Dr. Salem and Farideh Barghout of Syria joined the work in 1978. They had the special advantage of being Arabic-speaking and well-versed in the culture. In addition, Dr. Barghout was an able preacher of the Word and had a special advantage in the spiritual ministry.

Drs. Michael and Muriel Bah came to the work in 1983. Though both were doctors, they were of different disciplines. Michael was a Ph.D. and Muriel a D.O.—Doctor of Osteopathy—which profession is recognized in many countries alongside the medical profession. Among his responsibilities, Michael included hospital administration. Dr. Gregg and Kathy Donaldson joined the work in 1984, Dr. William and Holly Campbell (on loan from Arab World Ministries) in 1987, Dr. John and Joyce Hart in 1988, and Dr. Paul and Marie Schroeder and Dr. Chris Homeyer in 1989. Dr. and Mrs. Rutherford found it necessary to remain home for an indefinite time for family health reasons.

If it should seem that the hospital was oversupplied with doctors, it must be borne in mind that time for study of the difficult Arabic language had to be provided as well as rotation away from the pressures of the medical and surgical work, particularly during the extremely hot summer. Then there is the need for regular furlough every four years, during which time medical personnel must have a specified amount of continuing professional education to retain their licenses to practice.

Nurses a Necessity—Also

But the availability of nurses was another matter. They seemed always in short supply. Even with five or six in 1990, there was a call for at least twelve more. In addition to Gertrude Dyck and Nancy Brock, mentioned earlier, there were—as of 1990—Bernita Missal, Sharon Mossbarger, Marilyn Niewoehner, and Margaret Paisley, and a number of expatriates on direct hire.

A problem faced by the earlier missionaries was the insular situation of the Buraimi Oasis. Missionaries lived and worked, as it were, on a small island in the sand with no place to go except the desert or a two-hundred-mile round trip to the cities on the coast. When the missionary family was small and the workload far too heavy, the need to get away for a change and rest was urgent but hard to arrange. For several years a vacation in Lebanon afforded the desired break. Later when the older children went to school in Pakistan that was the place of choice for parents.

Is it Worth the Cost?

A question is sometimes asked whether there should be so great an investment of missionary time and money in a resistant field. This objection was made by a few in regard to missionary work among Muslims in the Arabian desert. One generous contributor at the time the UAE was entered asked that his contributions be used where there was the most favorable response. The mission was asked to list such areas and indicate the level of response. This information was provided and his contributions were designated according to his preference. We agreed with this friend that his assistance should be given where it would speed a ripening harvest.

Contributions Terminated

In the course of time the contributor noticed a news item in the mission's magazine that the missionary force in the Arabian desert was being increased by a certain number—possibly thirty percent. He wrote to the mission challenging what he thought was an unwise action. We tried to explain that we were not diverting missionaries from the more responsive fields but sending out those who felt a strong sense of call to win Muslims to Christ. Our explanation was not acceptable and our friend terminated his giving to TEAM.

This disappointing experience to both the contributor and the mission took place about 1970. For a while it would seem to a careful observer of the work in the United Arab Emirates that our friend's evaluation of the situation was correct, that the time and money invested there could have been better spent in a more fruitful field where the count of souls won to Jesus Christ would have been greater. The Lord will have to judge which course of action glorified Him more, the faithful proclamation of the gospel by those obedient to His call to these followers of the prophet for whom also Christ died, or the sending of reapers into a field where the harvest was easily gathered.

An Unanticipated Harvest

Then came the surprising five-fold increase in the population of the UAE as workers arrived from at least fifty different nations. With this influx of people and the raising up of a testimony among many of them, TEAM's entry into the UAE must be viewed as God's providential leading. The majority of the people reached here return to their own countries in two to five years. Many have been won to Christ and taught His Word. They have also been taught to witness for Him. This has been an unanticipated dividend from an investment of missionaries and the gifts of the Lord's people in a desert place.

Does this not remind one of the fruit of the obedience of Philip the evangelist, who was directed by an angel to go down to the highway leading from Jerusalem to Gaza *"which is desert"?* According to tradition, the Ethiopian eunuch he met there planted the church in Ethiopia and for centuries that nation had some influence by the gospel of our Lord Jesus Christ.

Plans for Sultanate of Oman

Just as a new century of TEAM's ministry was beginning, the UAE field, with thirty years of history, anticipated expanding into another country—the Sultanate of Oman. At the board meeting of October 15, 1990, Lynn Everswick reported that Tim and Martha Hatch were hoping to take over a small language institute in a somewhat heavily populated part of Oman called Nizwa.

This was by no means TEAM's first ministry to the people of Oman. As Al Ain is right on its border and an average of forty percent of the outpatients seen at the Oasis Hospital are from Oman, there has been a continuing witness to many who cross the border for medical help. The Hatches enter that ministry with a background of more than a decade of experience in the UAE and an earnest desire to see the gospel extended to more of this area's one million people.

Desert Oasis

The Near East is still largely a spiritual desert. This is true wherever Islam holds sway, as it does throughout this region. But the Living Water has caused certain spots to flourish as a garden. As the desert people are attracted to an oasis for safety, refreshment, and comfort, even so have many sin-burdened and weary wanderers found safety for their souls, refreshment for their spirits, and the comfort of Christian fellowship at the Oasis Hospital and one or more Evangelical Church Fellowships. Hundreds have come to the Arabian desert seeking a share in its prosperity, probably with little thought that here they would find an oasis whose refreshment is eternally satisfying— *"a spring of water welling up to everlasting life."*

CHANGES IN SOUTH AFRICA

The first half century of work in South Africa and Swaziland had been among people in a tribal setting. The next half saw great changes. Though gospel work continued among the Zulus and Swazis in their traditional home areas, this was carried out more and more by the African Christians themselves. What had been strictly a rural ministry widened to include cities, reflecting the population shifts of the country.

After World War II ended in 1945, the government of South Africa turned its attention from the war effort to pressing internal matters, the foremost being the migration of many Africans from their tribal lands to the outskirts of the cities.

Life Around the Cities

The Africans built shantytowns in crowded "locations" around the metropolitan areas—hovels made of lumber scraps, poles, tar paper, flattened tins, and straw mats. Having left behind them the orderly life imposed by the tribe, they came under new authority—municipal law and its enforcement arm, the police—for them an unnatural arrangement. They were drawn to the cities by jobs. Mining and other labor-inten-sive industries had advanced greatly during the war years and laborers were needed.

The shantytowns lacked mu-nicipal services and it takes little imagination to understand the conditions under which the peo-ple lived. Coming from primi-tive tribal areas, they were not accustomed to modern sanitation and other necessities of urban life. Their living conditions—partly of their own making—were deplorable in comparison with the homes inside the city.

The government was not unaware of the problems faced by the tribal Africans in this migration, nor was it totally unconcerned about the welfare of the black people. However its foremost concern was the potential effect on the lifestyle of the white population. When the National Party came to power in 1948, it responded to the concerns of the white people by codifying into law what had already existed unofficially: apartheid—separate development.

Separate but Not Equal

Though the races—black, white, Indian, and mixed (Coloured)—were each very much dependent on the others, they were not allowed to associate closely in residential areas, social contacts, education, or work status. Most of all, they could not intermarry. Living areas were assigned to the various races according to the supposed worth of each.

Even so, there was a measure of concern for the Africans. For those working in manufacturing and commerce in the cities, the government built huge sprawling townships with tens of thousands of small single-family and duplex rental cottages. Although this housing was a tremendous improvement over the shantytown slums they were forced to vacate, and possibly better than the kraals they left behind in the bush, the crowded conditions and lack of any personal share in the ownership insured rapid deterioration.

How Mission Work Was Affected

During the forty years that followed, this migration to the cities created both problems and new possibilities for mission work. Rural churches suffered with the movement of people, mostly men, from their tribal areas. As the congregations in Swaziland and Zululand were already 75 percent women, this further weakened the churches. Yet the concentration of needy people in urban areas opened a new door of ministry. People congregating around Johannesburg and Durban presented a new field for evangelism and church planting.

"When He Saw the Multitudes...."

When M. D. Christensen returned to America in 1948, he came with a new vision of reaching the urban areas for Christ. Having obtained the concurrence of the Africa field conference, he presented the project to the board of directors at home. What he wanted was approval to appeal for four or five young couples gifted in evangelism and Bible teaching who also had practical construction skills to work with him in the urban ministry. In addition, he wanted a builder to do major building on a school and a church. The board gave its blessing on meeting this "challenge of the native locations at Johannesburg, Vereeniging, and Odendaalsrus (Orange Free State), as the Lord supplies the workers and the funds."[1]

Soweto Township

The Lord did supply funds and workers in the next two years. Among these workers were Ralph and Helen Christensen and Richard and Marjorie Winchell. The M. D. and Ralph Christensen families, a father and son team, developed the work in Jabavu, a huge location outside of Johannesburg which is now part of troubled Soweto township. They opened a school for primary children and used it as a means of contacting the parents, winning them for Christ, and beginning a congregation. Their work spread to other concentrations of Africans in the vast suburban area which stretched for twenty miles beyond Johannesburg city limits. It was necessary to work in two major vernaculars, Zulu and Sotho. Trained workers were available among the Zulus but it became necessary to open a Bible school to train Sotho converts who felt led to serve the Lord. This school in time became the Evangelical Bible Institute and was moved to Rustenburg, about seventy miles outside of Johannesburg.

Orange Free State

A major gold discovery had been made in the Orange Free State, several hundred miles to the southwest of Johannesburg. This area was predicted to become more rich in gold output than the mines around Johannesburg. To exploit the wealth, the government opened its doors to laborers from Angola, Malawi, Mozambique, and Zambia as well as from the South African tribal areas. The men who worked in the mines were provided living space in large dormitories and furnished good meals and excellent medical care, but were not permitted to bring their wives to these facilities.

Winchells' Pioneer Post

The Winchells were assigned to plant a church in Welkom, one of the new mining centers. They had learned Zulu but now had to study an additional tribal language—Sotho. The white population spoke mostly Afrikaans, based on Dutch, so the Winchells also studied this language to enhance their communication. When I visited Welkom in 1954, Winchell took me to see the large compounds housing thousands of miners. It was to these compounds that he went regularly to preach the gospel. In order to communicate, miners from several different areas used *Fanakalo,* a pidgin language somewhat related to the major tribal tongues and other minor dialects. Winchell found it necessary to gain a working knowledge of *Fanakalo* in order to make the gospel clear to many. So with three native languages plus Afrikaans and English there were few indeed he could not reach with the spoken word.

Post-War Missionary Influx

In the six-year period following World War II about fifty new missionaries arrived in South Africa. Over time, they became deeply involved in the various ministries: the (Bantu) Evangelical Churches and the Evangelical Bible Churches (Coloured and Indian); Franson Christian High School, Evangelical Teacher Training College, Durban Bible College, Union Bible Institute, Florence Christian Academy, Evangelical Bible Institute—

Rustenburg, and Swaziland Evangelical Bible Institute; Mosvold Mission Hospital; Word of Life Publications; and field administration.

Some would be used in outstanding ways to shape the course of the ministry. Serving as chairmen at various times were Wesley Carlson, David Greene, Irl McCallister, Dalmain Congdon, and Stewart Snook. Many were active in the Bible training ministry: Nolan Balman, Ruth Hall, Lydia Rogalsky, Elizabeth Bromley, Wilfred Hart, Ralph Christensen, David Greene, Roberta Tromp, and Malcolm MacKenzie. When the African churches became autonomous in 1956, the number in the African church planting ministry was reduced but some had continued direct responsibility: Wesley and Norma Carlson, and Charles and Beverly Smith. Church planting in the Coloured and Indian communities had the participation of Harold and Lydia Johnston, Marlin and Gladys Olsen, and Charlotte Payne. Others served in medical and literature ministries which contributed directly to evangelism and the growth of the churches.

Malla Moe and the King

Though Malla Moe was in her late eighties when the many new post-war missionaries arrived in South Africa and Swaziland, she had not retired from responsibility as an active witness for Christ. She was as concerned for the "high and mighty" as she was for the poor and weak. An example was her concern for the Swazi ruler. King Sobhuza Dhlamini, though a university graduate, maintained traditional Swazi customs including having a large number of wives, even while Swaziland was a protectorate of Great Britain. Malla had won the king's mother to the Lord and continued an ongoing deep friendship with her. In November 1947, at the age of 84, she wrote to the king about her concern for his soul. This was not her first witness to him.

> I have a photo of your own dear mother, my good friend, when I visited her. We read the Bible together and we prayed. Now she is at rest, home with Jesus. We had a good time together.... Now you, too, need to get saved, and your wives and children.

You will be sorry if you lose your soul. Dear King Sobhuza, seek the Lord God now. Make ready to meet your dear mother again. She loved you. She prayed for you. Together we prayed to God for you to get saved. I am yours in Jesus' service in Swaziland for lost souls. —Malla Moe[2]

A Few Disenchanted Ones

There also were several who came to the field—and returned home. For some it was a question of health. For others it might have been that the work and adjustments demanded too much and they could not take the pressure. But there may have been a mission reason as well. After the resignation of three or four young couples in 1954, and with understandable questioning by others, it became apparent that weakness in administration was a contributing factor. The field needed help from an outside objective viewpoint. I had been invited, as early as December 1953, to spend some time in South Africa. With the approval of the board of directors, I accepted the invitation and planned the trip for July 1954.

The Lord's Gracious Response

As the time approached, I became more aware of the need for a healing ministry and some constructive adjustments in field administration, such as in the deployment of personnel, guidance in their work, and more equitable financial distribution to the various ministries. This seemed like far too great a challenge for the most junior member of the home staff but assurance came from the promise in John 14:14, "If you ask anything in my name, I will do it." My attention was drawn particularly to the clause, *I will do it.* If anything was to be accomplished, the Lord would have to do it.

This is what the Lord did for the South Africa field in 1954 when the field council and I prayed, counseled and planned together: He brought a renewed spirit of tenderness, love, and unity in the missionary body; He clarified administrative and work relationships; He brought whole-hearted agreement on a workable financial plan; and He brought to the missionaries a sense of victory and an anticipation of blessing in the work ahead. As in the early church experience of Acts 6, the work went ahead with the Lord's blessing when the administrative problem was recognized and the Spirit's guidance followed for the solution. Christ's promise, *I will do it,* was fully honored.

A Field Headquarters

When the number of missionaries on a field increases to more than twenty or thirty, their service is enhanced by some very practical arrangements, such as having a center where necessary administrative matters are cared for. South Africa's first headquarters was at Vryheid. It was later moved to a suburb of Johannesburg.

As the number of workers grew, it became necessary that the field chairman be freed from other regular assignments to devote full time to the spiritual and administrative leadership of the work. Those who served as field chairmen have been mentioned elsewhere. Their role was vital but the headquarters ministry could not function without able secretarial and clerical help. The one who served the longest in that capacity was Virginia Kearney, whose work extended over thirty-five years. There were shorter periods of office assistance by Claire Christopherson and Dorothy Vust.

Urgent Need for a Hospital

The physical needs of the Swazis and Zulus were much in evidence. Nurses opened and operated dispensaries at various places but recognized the need for a doctor. The lower elevations of Swaziland and Zululand were particularly malarial. When stations were opened in low-lying Tongaland at Ekuseni and Tshongwe, missionaries were right in the heart of fever country.

Ingwavuma village was situated at an elevation of 2,300 feet overlooking the malarial lowlands and had a more healthful climate. Here, in 1937, missionaries set up a dispensary and an eleven-bed hospital. This met the need of many patients for a time but there were serious cases to be dealt with as well. These cases needed a doctor's special skills.

Bites and Burns

Not only were there cerebral malaria patients from the lowland, there were also injuries that required surgical attention. Crocodiles continued to be a hazard in the streams and the few who survived an attack by the huge reptile had terrible injuries requiring extensive repair and treatment.

Burns were another major problem. A fire of coals was kept alive in a typical African hut, providing warmth in the cool season and discouraging mosquitoes in the hot. It was also a handy spot for cooking. For all its benefits, the fire presented a hazard for children and tiny tots were often seriously burned. Adults did not always escape this hazard because after a beer drink they could easily roll into the fire and receive third degree burns.

For years the missionaries had prayed for a doctor and an adequately equipped hospital. The doctor was provided first when Dr. and Mrs. Douglas Taylor responded to the Lord's call in 1948. By then the provision of the hospital was assured through the initial contribution of the Mosvold family of Norway. Before the hospital could be built another doctor was also available. Dr. and Mrs. Don Morrill were appointed in 1950.

Hospital Built and Dedicated

The crowds which gathered for the hospital dedication, March 4, 1952, were a testimony of its importance to the Ingwavuma district and the African villages in a wide area. The mission periodical of May 1952 carried a report:

> The Mosvold Mission Hospital in Ingwavuma, South Africa, the vision of many years, is now a reality. Its occupancy became official with the dedication ceremony on March 4 in the presence of representatives of the mission, the government, residents of the area, and visitors from other missions and mission hospitals. Gathered on and around the wide front veranda of the new building, the happy throng evidenced the appreciation of the groups for the new, modern, 57-bed structure which promises to minister to the physical needs of a wide area. Present from TEAM and other missions were approximately 200 missionaries. There were Europeans, Eurafricans, and a thousand Africans. The local chief sent a detachment of his warriors. Some of

the African schools were closed for the occasion, 200 or more students arriving en masse.[3]

Of the many in attendance at the dedication, special mention was made of the presence of Mr. and Mrs. Torrey Mosvold; a sister, Esther Mosvold Haanes and her husband, Christian; Mr. and Mrs. Carl Gundersen and Mr. and Mrs. Joseph Horness, who represented the TEAM board of directors; the Rev. Tom Olsen, chairman of the TEAM South Africa field; pastors Johanne Nyawo and Jonas Mndebele, representing the African churches; and Magistrate Craig of Ingwavuma.

Training of Nurses

By the time of the dedication, the training of twelve auxiliary nurses had already begun under the direction of Nurse Louise Troup. The students, recommended by their churches, received a high level of training prescribed by the government. In addition, they were given elements of Bible Institute training—becoming well equipped for both nursing and spiritual service. Others who served later in the training of nurses were June Salstrom and June Lewers. Of the young ladies thus trained, some stayed with the hospital as staff nurses, others worked in outlying dispensaries, and some went farther afield in a combined medical and spiritual ministry.

Helping the Needy Come for Care

It is one thing to have doctors and a hospital located in a modern city with adequate transportation facilities, but another matter altogether to serve those needing help in a bush area of several hundred square miles. Some patients can and do walk great distances. Others come by primitive conveyances. Some may be able to purchase space on a crowded bus or truck. However, without transportation provided by the hospital, some would die not having received the necessary care.

Part of the solution was a carryall van which served as an ambulance. Problems remained, however, in getting a message to the hospital and defining the location where the patient could be picked up. Two dispensaries down in the lowland at Ndumu and Opondweni, closer to people at risk, solved the problem in part. These lifesaving outposts were staffed by missionary nurses who could give preliminary care and notify the hospital by radio—often asking that a doctor come, even if it meant several hours of rough traveling. Eleanore Erickson, Enid McKenzie, and Fern Larson were at Ndumu; Lois Cox and Doris Moore at Opondweni.

As the hospital work expanded, the help of another doctor became an urgent need. This need was filled with the appointment of Dr. John and Betty Bennett in 1958. As the doctors had to take regular furloughs, having three doctors assigned to the hospital was not a luxury but a necessity. All had to be prepared for both medical and surgical service.

How About Air Service?

The time doctors spent on trips to the dispensaries and responding to emergency situations soon caused overload and it was not long before they thought of the possibility of air service. Dr. Morrill took steps to help provide that service. While on his first furlough he took flying lessons and became qualified to transport passengers, as would be necessary for the hospital ministry.

When Morrill presented this matter, the board of directors was reluctant to give approval, even though there was great appreciation for his vision and initiative. Although Morrill had been checked out on his training and flying skill the key question was: would the doctor put the patient's need ahead of his own safety? If a call came at dusk to fly to a remote bush landing strip to save the life of a seriously injured person, would the doctor-pilot put the patient's welfare over his own? This is a risk a non-medical pilot would be taught to refuse.

Whether or not the board was fully satisfied that Dr. Morrill would make the safe choice for himself, they did regard very highly his purpose and zeal and so approved the project. Through that term of service and for several terms following, Dr. Morrill flew his plane to visit outlying dispensaries, and often picked up patients at remote points to bring them to the hospital. His was indeed a worthwhile project.

A Second Pilot

At the time the doctor's flying was under discussion, an application for service came in from John and Janet Snavely. Snavely was a pilot trained at the Moody Bible Institute missionary aviation division. The field council determined that there was enough need for ambulance and taxi service to justify the addition of another pilot and a plane which would not be restricted except by the pilot's own judgment. Snavely was kept busy, though sometimes in non-aviation engineering and mechanical duties. The last plane he used was a Helio Courier which could take off and land on very short airstrips. The hospital's aviation program continued until the government takeover of the hospital seemed imminent in 1977.

Preparations were made over a period of several years for the national government to take over the hospital. The medical ministry in Pretoria took responsibility for capital improvements and determining the personnel needed. About the same time—in the late 1970s—the government was working out its policy of separate homelands for each tribal group. The Zulu people were the most numerous and for them the government specified the KwaZulu homeland. While the homelands would enjoy internal self-rule, their economy was very closely linked to and dependent on the government of South Africa. Because the Mosvold Mission Hospital was in Zululand, the KwaZulu government took over its control and operation.

In anticipation of the day of government takeover, the missionary and senior African personnel prepared well for the continued outreach of the gospel, not only through the hospital ministry itself but also in a widened evangelistic and Bible teaching ministry to the community. Among those involved were the pilot, John Snavely, and the nurse matron, Shirley Preece. African hospital personnel were not only trained in their medical duties but many of them became effective witnesses for Christ and remained active in the evangelistic outreach. An interesting development was noted when the government took over control. Military doctors were often assigned to the outlying hospitals and it was noted that Christian doctors asked assignment to the former mission hospitals, where they could build on the foundation laid by missionary doctors.

Reaching the Coloured Community

The early missionaries to South Africa and Swaziland worked primarily among the Africans but there was another people group right at hand—the Eurafricans (Coloured). Malla Moe had not overlooked soul-winning opportunities among them, and William Dawson had reached out to them quite early by means of the Florence Christian Academy. Bertel and Agnes Pagard followed in that work as did a number of other missionaries. A small congregation of believers came into being. But many of these people were also to be found in the metropolitan areas.

Remembering the Forgotten

When Marlin and Gladys Olsen first came to Swaziland they worked at Florence. Later they moved to Johannesburg, desiring to reach Coloured people in the segregated living areas. Many of these people were suffering under the apartheid policies which relegated them to poor living conditions.

Though the Indian population around Johannesburg was not large, their living conditions were much the same as those of the Coloured group. The soul-winning work among Coloreds and Indians progressed well and they found places to meet for worship—some in sub-standard buildings.

Don and Eva Aeschliman were also assigned to this work and gave these converts further encouragement by getting their church groups properly organized and housed in better buildings. The Johannesburg Bible Institute, for which the South Africa General Mission (now Africa Evangelical Fellowship) had responsibility, and in which TEAM personnel assisted, was a source of trained workers for the Coloured churches.

Indians Imported for their Labor

The Indian racial group in South Africa was descended from people brought to Natal province from India as indentured workers in the sugar cane fields. They came from a number of different language areas and mostly Hindu communities. As one generation followed another, the Indian languages fell into disuse and English became the common language.

As soon as the Indians were free to do so they left the cane fields and moved to the towns and cities. By natural aptitude, many became merchants and business people and most did well. The Indians were in a rather difficult position. Because they were non-white, the government assigned them to a lower status than whites. Being quite energetic and progressive they tended to advance steadily and thus incurred the resentment of many African workers. Even so, there was a measure of affinity with the Eurafrican people and their children went to the same schools.

Harold and Lydia Johnston were the first to begin a sustained work among the Indians. Indians were employed to oversee the African laborers in the Hlabane and Coronation mines in northern Natal, near Vryheid, and had their families nearby. When Johnston asked the mine operators about the possibility of doing children's work among the Indians, he was warmly welcomed and told that in the fifty years since the mines opened, he was the first to want to do something for the Indian children. When the Johnstons went on furlough, Malcolm and Ruth MacKenzie followed them in the work.

Upon the Johnstons' return to South Africa they began work among the Indians in Ladysmith. I visited them there in 1963 at the time of the dedication of their church building. I was impressed by the warmth of the testimonies I heard and by the quality of the singing. Having musical gifts, the Johnstons trained singers comparable to a choir in the homeland.

"A Brand Plucked from the Fire"

A baptismal service was held that dedication Sunday. The testimony of one man being baptized impressed me greatly and I spoke to him later. Learning that he had been a fire walker I asked him, "Did you really walk on red-hot coals?"

"Yes, I really did," he replied.

"Weren't you terribly burned?"

"No, not at all," the man assured me.

"How could you avoid it? If I took one step on the coals, I would end up in the hospital."

"Well, it was this way, I invoked the demons to take possession of me so I would not be harmed," he explained.

Our further conversation revealed that Christ had delivered him from demon control and he was now trusting fully in Him as his Savior. Any dependence on demons was totally a thing of the past. Many Indian Christians had been similarly delivered from demon worship.

The Johnstons later moved to the large coastal city of Durban where extensive Indian communities were located and where the Durban Bible College trained Coloured and Indian Christian workers. The Marlin Olsens also transferred to Durban to work among Coloreds and they, too, saw fruit from their witness.

Evangelical Bible Churches Formed

A spirit of fellowship developed among the Coloured and Indian churches being planted in four separate areas—Swaziland, Johannesburg, northern Natal province, and Durban. With the assistance of the missionaries, they formalized that fellowship in the Evangelical Bible Churches. Though united in this organization the two groups recognized the distinctions and designated two branches, Coloured and Indian. The Evangelical Bible Churches developed good leaders and the work continued to strengthen with the inclusion of churches in Cape Town.

Autonomy for the African Church

TEAM's stated purpose is to gather the fruits of its evangelism into local churches. A second related purpose is to encourage local churches raised up through the ministry of the mission to form fellowships for mutual encouragement, assistance, and united witness. The organization of a local church, as set forth in the New Testament, is simple and suitable for Christians in any culture. An organization or fellowship of churches is somewhat more involved and may not fit various cultural patterns as easily as does the local church. Yet there is teaching in the Acts of the Apostles and Paul's epistles, by way of inference and example, that reveals the fellowship enjoyed among the New Testament churches.

The early churches in Swaziland and Zululand were linked primarily through the mission. Later, the pastors and evangelists met quarterly in their various districts for study, fellowship, prayer, and discussion of the work. Even though the quarterly meeting began to assume more and more responsibility, missionaries still had the final word. This control was not in line with the mission's goal of an indigenous church fellowship—at least not after sixty-five years of work in Africa. Some African Christians and missionaries of vision realized that definite visible steps must be taken to give the churches responsibility for their own work and to demonstrate this to others.

Bantu Evangelical Church Announced

On July 25, 1956, two African church leaders—the Rev. Abner Mndebele and the Rev. Johane Nyawo—accompanied by Irl Mc-Callister, called on King Sobhuza II of Swaziland to announce the formation of the autonomous Bantu Evangelical Church. Abner Mndebele was chosen to be the first general superintendent and Johane Nyawo his assistant. Mndebele, son of a pastor and graduate of the Union Bible Institute, was a very able man—gifted as a teacher—who had taught at the institute for eight years. Johane Nyawo's father was the second ordained pastor—right after John Gamede—who, upon becoming a Christian, had renounced his right to lead the powerful Nyawo tribe.

Mndebele's Untimely Death

Mndebele and Nyawo were to be formally installed at the annual meeting of the churches in 1957, but, sadly, before this could take place, word came that Abner Mndebele had passed away unexpectedly on May 25, 1957, as the result of a heart condition. He was just thirty-eight. One missionary wrote concerning him, "I have never seen an African Christian near Abner's caliber. His salvation was real to him. Whenever he said *Baba* (Father) to God, one could feel just what he meant. His death has been a great shock to us."[4]

The Bantu Evangelical Church included African churches in Swaziland, Zululand, Durban, and the Johannesburg area. Quarterly meetings with local authority were still convened in these districts. Somewhat later, at the request of the churches, the official name was changed to Evangelical Church.

STRUGGLE AND PROGRESS

Uncertainty and Questions

The granting of autonomy to the African churches made a difference in their relationship to TEAM which took several years to fully understand, appreciate, and adjust to. This relationship had both its joys and its tensions. Independence was implied but how was independence to be defined? Was it an admission of weakness by a church to still need missionary help? Would the field council assign missionaries or would the church take the lead to invite them? If invited, who designated the missionary's work? What was his or her authority and responsibility vis-á-vis the church leaders? Who had the ultimate responsibility for church expenses, including paying the pastors?

A Time of Mutual Learning

Even though the African Christian leaders were well taught in Scripture, some have suggested that they received insufficient teaching on practical church administration before the churches were publicly acclaimed to be on their own. Although there is a great deal of this kind of teaching in Paul's epistles, it may have been considered less "spiritual" than salvation, sanctification, and glorification and so overlooked. The next few years were times of learning for both church leaders and missionaries.

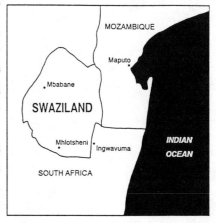

During this period there were inevitably some losses in the African work. Some missionaries, not sure of their full welcome and yet desiring to serve the churches, turned to special projects. These projects were valuable and brought great benefit. But when the churches were ready for the help missionaries could offer in Bible teaching, counseling, etc., these workers were not available to them, being already involved elsewhere.

Another problem—when churches wanted help they wanted it from mature missionaries who were fluent in the language. However, they seemed not to realize that the only way workers could be thus prepared was to be plunged into the work while they were still untaught and less than helpful.

One result was that for a twenty-year period the churches experienced little or no growth—due to the combined effects of migration from the tribal areas and weakness in missionary evangelism and teaching. However, there was another side to the coin as missionaries turned to other work; the ministry in the Coloured and Indian Churches went forward. Medical, literature, and Bible School work expanded and progressed.

Slowly Attaining Self-support

Though decisions had been made about self-support as early as 1934, progress was slow. The country churches did quite well because the pastors and evangelists could support themselves in part. Self-support in the urban-area churches was more difficult. Here living costs were higher and pastors had no fields to till or cattle to sell. Although having wage-earners in the urban congregations should have helped, African Christians were slow to commit themselves to tithing. It was hard for the church leaders to understand why the mission could not easily give support when it seemed to have money for literature and medical work.

But there was progress. By 1960, the field chairman could report that services were regularly held in 175 places. Among these were 145 organized churches, of which 137 were self-supporting. "When we speak of self-support we do not mean that all the preachers are paid a full cash salary by the churches they serve. Most of the national workers have to supplement their income through such means as sale of cattle, hides, produce from their own fields, or Christian books, or from part-time jobs near their homes."[1]

The Mission Also Learning Lessons

For its part the mission may have been slow in sending the proper signals to the church. After a visit to South Africa late in 1970, I reported to the board on my observations:

As recently as 1968 when I met with the church council, the African leaders felt there was still a tendency on the part of the mission to consider the church a subordinate organization. During the past three years there has been progress so that the church leaders are quite aware that the mission means business in turning over responsible control of the church to African leadership. Instead of mission-appointed representatives on the church council or even church-selected advisors to meet with the council, there are now two responsible groups—the church council and the mission field council—which meet together from time to time as mature responsible partners.... There are challenging areas where the mission and the church should join in partnership of evangelism and church planting. The mission has been waiting for the church to take the leadership but now it seems there is an understanding that the group best able to launch a work should go ahead. It is understood, of course, that with the establishing of any churches the full responsibility will then pass to the church. If there can be this partnership directed toward a church planting ministry there are certainly vast areas in Africa where the Evangelical Church ministry can go forward.[2]

A Small Cloud on the Horizon

In the same report to the board I touched on the generally healthy relationships with the Evangelical Bible Churches (Coloured and Indian) and also on one problem that was just "a cloud the size of a man's hand."

The relationship with the Evangelical Bible Churches has been very healthy through the years. The control of their own work is so complete that the leaders need to be reminded from time to time that the mission's views need to be considered if there is to be the strongest type of partnership relationship. This has become apparent recently in regard to the Bible Institute ministries which the church leadership seems to want to develop along narrow sectarian lines.[3]

Most of the Coloured pastors had been trained at the Johannesburg Bible Institute, which was not a TEAM school. One very influential former teacher was not only strongly committed to the dispensational interpretation of theology, but considered the traditional interpretation to be heresy. This teacher, though no longer resident in South Africa, made occasional visits and kept up correspondence with many of his former students. His strong plea to them was to defend the dispensational view as being worth giving their lives for.

A New Bible School and a Question

A problem of major proportions had its unexpected beginning in 1971 when Don Aeschliman opened the Cape Evangelical Bible Institute (CEBI) in Cape Town—though it was with the full approval of the field council, and initially of the national council of the Evangelical Bible Church. In formulating the curriculum he planned that the school should be wider in its teaching to include traditional views generally held in conservative evangelical groups. Aeschliman was willing to have dispensational theology taught by a TEAM missionary committed to that view. Yet because he was not willing to have the school limit its stand and its teaching to the dispensational view alone, the national council of the Evangelical Bible Church voted to have nothing to do with it. This meant that any of its pastors invited to teach at CEBI risked censure and, further, that no recommendation would be given to students to attend nor would they be welcomed in the churches upon graduation.

While many TEAM missionaries preferred a dispensational interpretation, they were not ready to brand as heretical the views held by many conservative evangelical Bible scholars. At the same time, there were strong convictions that this question should not be allowed to drive a wedge between the Evangelical Bible Churches and TEAM. Discussions went on in 1972 and 1973 with the result it was finally decided that CEBI should be continued outside of TEAM, in association with the Bible Institute of South Africa, Kalk Bay, Cape Town.

An EBC School in Cape Town

Subsequent to this development, the Evangelical Bible Church (Coloured) opened the Evangelical Bible College in Cape Town in 1978. A 1984 report showed an enrollment of 17 full-time day and 70 to 80 evening students. While the church carried the main responsibility, TEAM missionaries assisted and helped with finances.

The Evangelical Bible Churches, both Coloured and Indian, have been zealous in reaching out to new areas. During 1986, according to a report by Stewart Snook, field chairman, the Coloured churches opened seven new preaching points with the expectation that these would be developed into organized churches. The Indian churches were planting three new congregations. It was a significant step forward when one of the leading Coloured pastors, Wilfred Matham, went to Port Elizabeth, a major city on the south coast, to begin work among the large Coloured population.

Widening Literature Outreach

The literature work begun by the Richard Winchells and Irl McCallisters in 1956 grew steadily and from a modest beginning developed into Word of Life Publications, a gospel enterprise that played a significant role in furthering Christian literature in southern Africa for a quarter of a century. To meet the needs of its expansion it was organized into three divisions: publication, wholesale, and retail.

Several other missionaries joined Word of Life for various periods including Claire Christopherson, Enid McKenzie, Ruebena Peters, and Len and Nina Buck. Winchell brought in a number of local Christians as bookstore managers and clerical personnel. It was truly a multiracial staff with African, Coloured, and white members.

636

Bretts Brought In

One move with far-reaching benefits to TEAM was finding Ronald Brett, a businessman and active Christian layman in Benoni, Transvaal, and inviting him, in 1961, to become a bookstore manager. When the Winchells were called to home office duties in 1968, the field council placed increased responsibility on Brett and in time he became general manager of the whole literature ministry. In 1972, Brett and his wife, Pat, were commissioned as TEAM missionaries.

Retail Bookstores Purchased

The scarcity of gospel literature in the African languages had led Irl McCallister to publish small booklets in Zulu for sale at a few pennies. A bookstore which limited its sales to vernacular language material could never pay expenses. This led to the purchase of the Christian Book Room in Durban where the sale of English Christian literature would carry the load and also make possible a wider distribution of vernacular material. Later, Word of Life Publications purchased the Heart Bookroom in Johannesburg and, still later, the Calvary Bookroom.

TEAM literature personnel promoted the sale of books aggressively on both retail and wholesale levels. By carrying large inventories of evangelical books from such publishers as Moody Press, Zondervan, Baker Book House, and Tyndale, the wholesale division made it possible for smaller bookstores to obtain supplies with ease.

The retail operations—TEAM Bookstores—expanded to smaller cities: Roodepoort, Benoni, Manzini in Swaziland, and Empangeni in Natal. Africans did not limit their purchases to tribal language material; a growing number bought English or Afrikaans books as well. The bookstores became a great place for personal evangelism and counseling. Some of the stores set aside a separate small room for counseling in privacy. Ron and Pat Brett promoted Christian reading in local churches through seminars, bookfairs, and teacher training courses.

Transferring WLP to Local Responsibility

By 1980 great changes were taking place in the bookstore scene in South Africa. Other organizations opened Christian bookstores and it seemed less necessary that a foreign mission be involved in supplying the general Christian public. A program of scaling down began. The wholesale ministry was sold to another Christian organization. Four of the six bookstores were transferred to other Christian groups that would continue the same emphasis. The literature center which had been developed by McCallister in the town of Unified was leased and eventually sold to yet another Christian group.

Parceled out in this way to others, including Africans in Christian work, this broad and effective literature ministry took on new life under a wider group of promoters. With these changes, the Bretts were invited to join the home staff in Wheaton in 1980.

Providing a Key Bible Study Aid

One outstanding vernacular publication was born of individual initiative and perseverance—the Zulu Bible Concordance. It was prepared by Gertrude Kellogg with the help of at least one Zulu-speaking African—Mavis Shezi. Begun in 1957 while Miss Kellogg was teaching at the Franson Memorial Bible School, the New Testament portion took seven years to complete for publication by Word of Life in 1964. Miss Kellogg devoted an additional thirteen years of intense application to the Old Testament portion. The complexity of the project can be grasped if a characteristic of the Zulu language is understood. The *root* of the word, not the initial letter, determines the alphabetical order. Note an example from the book of Job—"out of the whirlwind": *esesikhwishikhwishini*. This word is listed under "K," the initial of the root. The concordance lists 5,800 individual Zulu words with 262,000 references. For those who think a tribal language is on a child's simple level, here is the title of the concordance in Zulu—*Ikhonkodensi Yebhayibheli Elingcwele*.

Swaziland Gains Independence

Swaziland and Zululand had many similarities. Their tribal languages were close enough so that the Zulu Bible and Zulu literature could be easily used by the Swazis. Missionaries tended to deal with both groups of people as if they were one. Not so with the governments, however. The Swazis were proudly conscious of their nationhood even during the sixty-five years of British rule as a protectorate. Their king traces his dynasty back over 400 years. Swaziland obtained its independence from Great Britain in 1968 but remains in the British Commonwealth.

Someone once likened the relationship of the Soviet Union and Finland to that between the elephant and the flea in Noah's ark. The flea's plea: Don't shove, big boy! The relationship of the Republic of South Africa and Swaziland was similar. South Africa is large—about seventy times the area of Swaziland. It has about sixty times as many people. Swaziland, too, has had to cooperate to a measure to keep from being stepped on.

Though there was unofficial separation of the races in Swaziland under British control there was no legal segregation. After independence was gained, Swaziland took steps to insure that there would be no trace of apartheid within its borders.

TEAM's Social Influence

There is no country in which TEAM works where it has had more social influence than in Swaziland. This has not been because of any political action program. It has been the result of establishing the church of Jesus Christ and obeying the biblical injunction to teach the gospel. Evangelizing has brought thousands out of animism into the Kingdom of God. Teaching the Word of God to tens of thousands of school children in village classrooms and to thousands in the Franson Christian High School has made a Christian impact on the nation, which continues to have a policy of Scripture teaching in its school curriculum.

Franson Alumnae of Influence

Consider the Franson Christian High School graduates who

have been brought into influential posts in the church and Swaziland government, as reported by Miss Beth Bromley in 1980:

> The late Prince Makhosini Jameson Dlamini, first Prime Minister of Swaziland.
>
> The late Rev. Abner Mndebele, Bible teacher and first chairman of the Evangelical Church.
>
> Bible institute administrators: the Rev. Barnabas Lusekwane Mndebele, the Rev. Albert Xaba.
>
> Diplomats and other government officials: James Dlamini, Mboni Dlamini, A. B. Gamedze—first minister of education in the Swazi cabinet, Norman Malinga, George Mamba, Elijah Nhlabatsi, John M. Simelane, Timothy Zwane, Mrs. Abel Lukhele, Mrs. Isabelle Shongwe Khatamuzi.
>
> Education officials: Themba O. Dhlamini, Petros Dlomo, Elmoth Dludlu, Henry Khumalo, Abel Lukhele, Miss Glory Mamba, Ambrose Maseko, Paul Nhlengethwa, Solomon Simelane, A. Busa Xaba.
>
> Doctors: Dr. Petty Dlamini, Dr. Lilly Shongwe.[4]

The royal family has received much gospel witness. King Sobhuza II, who passed away in 1982, made no profession of faith. The present king, Mswati III, son of Sobhuza, has been under gospel influence but his personal commitment to Christ is not known.

Still a Spiritual Battle

While the Evangelical Church in Swaziland is strong in its loyalty to Christ, there were other strong influences that vied for supremacy, one of the strongest being worship of ancestors. Long a basic feature of animism, ancestor worship has infiltrated some so-called Christian groups on the African continent in the developing of an African theology. While conservative missions and churches have not drifted as far as incorporating ancestor worship into accepted practices, other trends caused alarm. An example of this was seen in Swaziland about 1971 to 1972.

Missionaries of a number of organizations, with the cooperation of their African church groups, wanted to sponsor a nation-wide evangelistic effort. This was a worthy goal, but not so worthy was the plan to include Adventists, Roman Catholics, and theological liberals in the sponsorship, some of whom were reportedly quite accepting of ancestor worship. To target such groups for evangelism was one thing, but to invite them to be the evangelists to win Swazis to their non-biblical positions was quite another. TEAM and its Evangelical Church of Swaziland refused to participate. To complicate the matter, the national committee invited a very able TEAM missionary to be the coordinator of the campaign.

The field council requested the campaign committee—to no avail—to limit sponsorship to those of fully evangelical belief and practice. TEAM would not approve the request for its missionary to be the coordinator and also asked that any missionaries contemplating cooperation would devote their energies rather to a strong evangelistic outreach in cooperation with the TEAM-related churches.

TEAM Pays a Price for Principle

The missionary in question viewed the situation quite differently, feeling that a nation-wide campaign with wide sponsorship would make a great impact for the Lord in Swaziland. I was in Swaziland when this matter came up for decision and joined with the field council in the position that a sponsorship which included preachers of a faulty gospel would dishonor the Lord and be potentially disastrous to the church. To our regret, the missionary chose rather to withdraw from the mission and link with a group not having a similar stand on broad cooperation.[5]

What About Race Relations?

Can there be a story about mission work in South Africa without mentioning the political pressures on all races with whom the mission works? Missionaries traditionally have not been silent about their views, yet they have not been particularly vocal—as contradictory as that may sound. Most have spoken clearly by their attitude toward other races, but have not joined demonstrations to shout their protests aloud. They have been there long enough to see the true progress the Africans, Coloreds, and Indians have made in the last four decades. They have appreciated the sincere efforts of many South Africans of good will to change the relationships. They are also conscious of the many who oppose changes which would benefit the non-white races. Some missionaries, it is true, have wondered if they, themselves, have been too accepting of the status quo.

A basic principle they have observed is to demonstrate by personal contact that Africans, Coloreds, Indians, and whites are all alike in God's sight and equally the objects of His love and desire to save. They want to preserve the right to work in the Republic of South Africa and so have not flaunted their principles to the point of being excluded from the country. It is on the grass-roots level that they have demonstrated their oneness with the people.

As far back as 1963 when I attended the Indian church dedication at Ladysmith, I was delighted to note that it was a multiracial gathering as members of all races were represented.

More recently, women of the churches and missionaries have joined in annual multiracial retreats for devotional inspiration, Bible study, and fellowship. There have been many testimonies of the practical and spiritual benefits experienced in the Christian life. The trend holds promise. People of the different communities may now prefer to associate with their own race, but many look forward to the day when it will be personal choice that can bring people together and not law and tradition which separate. The time may yet come when churches—white, black, and brown—will be places where people are received as potential objects of saving grace and citizens of the Heavenly Kingdom.

Statistics for 1988

With churches gaining autonomy, the mission cannot always keep current on the statistics needed for accurate annual reports. Record-keeping presents a difficulty for some. A few national churches misunderstand the reason for reports. Nevertheless, the field office seeks to provide information—sometimes by report received, sometimes by count, and sometimes by estimate—so that the tempo of growth can be understood.

At the end of 1988, there were 185 fully organized congregations and 68 in the process of formation. Baptized membership totaled 8,617. There were 75 ordained pastors and evangelists and 36 non-ordained preachers. These churches are lighthouses still surrounded by a great deal of pagan darkness.

Goals Set by Church and Mission

In 1981 the missionaries and the African church agreed on a *Partnership Policy* to extend the work into new areas. In 1982 definite goals were set up by which the progress of their work could be measured. Several of these joint undertakings were in the native homelands established by the South Africa government. The first was an outreach by the Evangelical Bible Institute (EBI), Rustenburg, in the independent area of Bophuthatswana. In a creative plan, the whole curriculum of EBI was designed around an actual church planting effort.

Ray Shive wrote in 1986 about the beginning of that work:

Things are moving so fast it is almost scary. Prior to the opening of school, [Paul] Hayward, [Pastor] Tselapedi, and I surveyed potential church planting areas. Although we found them all about equally needy, the Lord seemed to guide us to begin with Tsitsing. *Total spiritual darkness! NO believers!* Using the usual contact techniques and open air meetings, we found openness, interest,—and converts! Follow-up has been almost impossible; so many are receiving Christ but only we and a few staff and students to continue the discipling process. We are holding cottage meetings now at mid-week; there were 63 present in one little hut last Wednesday. We are beginning to move toward Bible studies, etc., with a view to consolidation. Meanwhile, open air services continue on Sunday afternoon.[6]

Paul Hayward gave further information about this new ministry:

What is thrilling is our church planting ministry in Tsitsing, a community in Bophuthatswana. It has grown amazingly and many (over 50) have received Christ and are being followed up twice a week. This is new to the three of us staff members and we are carefully analyzing each move prayerfully. He has given us a tremendous unified spirit.... Johannes Tselapedi, a fixture at the school for some years now and the chairman of the Evangelical Church in Transvaal, also is a man with big designs for EBI. He is a man of the Word and has a heart for evangelism and now church planting. Like us he wants the school to be more than just an educational facility but to be known as a church-planting school where the main thrust would be exactly that.[7]

When M. D. Christensen first started the Evangelical Bible Institute in Johannesburg almost forty years earlier, he had involved the students in evangelistic outreach. From those won to the Lord came the growth of churches in the Johannesburg area. What was different in the recent forward movement was that leadership was in the hands of an African pastor. Whereas in the past the church would have looked to missionaries to lead the way, the Africans now felt the responsibility to move forward.

Transkei and Other New Areas

As part of the outreach into new areas, Wilfred and Ruth Hart were assigned to work in Transkei, one of the "homelands" of South African government policy. The first months of ministry, in 1988, in Ngangelizwe, near the capital city of Umtata, were encouraging as the Harts opened a Sunday school for children and began adult services. They welcomed three new missionaries for Xosa language study—Jenny Martin and Eric and Susan Binion.

Other areas for expansion have been considered, including Lesotho and Namibia. The Evangelical Church has also been discussing the matter of a foreign mission outreach.

A New Century—New Open Doors

Looking back over ninety years of TEAM history in South Africa, David Greene, field chairman, was impressed by change. In a 1983 presentation to prospective missionaries, he reviewed the past and looked to the future:

Winds of change have indeed swept across Africa during this past generation. Not one country has been left untouched. With some it has been a violent change.... As the political and geo-graphical change has come it has deeply affected the way missionaries do their work and their relationship with national believers. Because of this, the South Africa field has taken a new direction in its strategy to reach its objectives.... A new beginning is in the making. A few years ago the annual conference approved a paper which re-emphasized field objectives and set out a strategy for attaining these. This has pushed the field in a new direction of church planting and world-wide missionary outreach in partnership with the national church. We have pledged ourselves to share spiritual gifts, personnel, and finances in order to evangelize, not only this part of the world but everywhere. There is a new spirit of cooperation.[8]

Goals, and Progress

Goals set in 1982 in consultation with the churches were a good yardstick to measure current progress:

1. Plant 30 new churches by 1990.

2. Train 500 workers for our national churches and the church at large.

3. Encourage the national churches to develop their own mission structures.[9]

The churches caught the vision and moved steadily forward. By the year end of 1987 the picture held much encouragement. Of the thirty churches envisioned, twenty-three had been organized and were functioning well. That left seven to go by 1990. Three more started during 1987 were expected to reach the established stage in the near future.

Regarding the goal of training 500 national workers, the chairman reported: "This year we graduated 103 students. Of these 69 were day students, 34 extension or evening students. This brings our overall figure since 1983 to 404. We need 96 more graduates to make the goal."[10]

The stage is set for new and higher goals to be established—and reached—as the churches and mission, working together in their God-appointed ministry, enter their second century.

MOZAMBIQUE

The people of Mozambique in southeast Africa—now numbering almost fifteen million—have been a prayer objective of TEAM missionaries for nearly sixty years. Mozambique shares a common border of about sixty miles on its west with Swaziland, where TEAM work has flourished, and a border of fifty miles with Tongaland on its  south. All of the bush stations of the mission's Zimbabwe field, farther north, were near the Mozambique border. There was enough movement of people across borders so that those of Mozambique were thought of as neighbors.

No other country has been looked at and prayed over for so many years with entry still being either very difficult or entirely denied. The first official action to enter Mozambique (known at that time as Portuguese East Africa) took place at the South Africa field conference of 1933. This resulted in two couples undertaking the study of Portuguese. One of the couples—Magnus and Clara Foreid—opened the Portugal field. The other couple—Rudy and Mary Danielson (along with Orval and Helen Dunkeld)—began the work in Southern Rhodesia when entry into Mozambique was denied.

Andrew Friends Find a Temporary Opening

Another serious attempt was made in the early 1970s and for several years Andrew and Barbara Friend were able to live in the capital, Lourenço Marques (now called Maputo). They established a working relationship with the Portuguese Evangelical Mission which assisted them with visa guarantees. The Friends had plans for a type of extension seminary training for Christian workers that also would be useful to other evangelical groups in the country.

There were pressures for independence from colonial rule throughout all of Africa and Portuguese East Africa was no exception. The war of independence, begun in 1965, continued until Portugal gave up its hold almost ten years later. The 1974 revolution in Portugal paved the way for the orderly transfer of power to Frelimo (Front for the Liberation of Mozambique). The Friends left the country prior to its becoming independent and later served in Portugal.

Frelimo was Marxist-Leninist in its orientation and its leaders vowed to remake Mozambique into a communist state. In the following ten years, the Mozambique economy declined so drastically that the country became one of the most impoverished nations of the world. Finding that the expected aid from the communist bloc was little more than empty promises, Mozambique began looking to the non-communist West for help. The most recent step was the Fifth Congress of the Frelimo government in July 1989 abandoning Marxist-Leninism and declaring its intent to develop a capitalistic state encouraging free enterprise. With this turn of events came increasing openness and new tolerance for religious groups, even to the extent that the government is said to encourage the church ministries.

Four Ready and Willing

While four TEAM missionaries, Lee and Sandra Comly and Don and Kyla Lester, completed Portuguese language study in 1989, they were obliged to wait to enter Mozambique because of lack of housing to rent or buy. In late October 1989 word was received of recognition of TEAM, which opened the way for the Comlys to proceed to the field.

This delay has not closed the door to gospel outreach by churches in neighboring Swaziland. Evangelist Mahlalela, a member of the TEAM-related church in Mbabane, Swaziland, is looked upon by the Mozambique government as the head of a group of thirty-six newly planted churches.

The South Africa field council is directing efforts to gain a foothold in southern Mozambique. The Zimbabwe field council committed itself to do the same in the northern sector when personnel are available. When that door opens no one will rejoice more than the pioneers who paid a high price to open stations along Mozambique's Rhodesia border. Mary Danielson, widow of Rudy who laid down his life along that border, returned to spend thirty years more in the same tropical region. Orval and Helen Dunkeld, who left the graves of two children near that border, served for over thirty years.

Revelation 5:8 has a word about the "golden bowls full of incense, which are the prayers of the saints." Some interpret that to mean that prayers offered through the years and for which there seemed to have been no answer are nevertheless stored up and will yet bring glory to the Lamb that was slain. Certainly, the many prayers that have gone up for the needy souls in Mozambique have not been in vain but will bear fruit in a harvest, some of which is already seen in the thirty-six congregations of believers looking to Swaziland churches and TEAM missionaries for spiritual help.

ZIMBABWE—TOWARD MATURITY

Post-War Reinforcements

With the close of World War II, missionary recruits waiting at home could more easily obtain passports and passage overseas. Southern Rhodesia appointees Norman and Thelma Everswick and Orla and Marguerite Blair sailed in 1946. Russell and Margaret Jackson and Lillian Nelson (Austin) were the next, entering this pioneer field in 1948. They joined Orval and Helen Dunkeld, Mary Danielson, and Eunice Ott, who were already on the field.

With TEAM's work being in the inhospitable Zambezi Valley, the Everswicks and Blairs stocked up on supplies to help them through the rainy season and traveled to the Valley to build their own mission stations—the Everswicks at Rukumitchi and the Blairs at Hunyani.

These new missionary men soon learned how to make mud bricks and burn them in a kiln. Whether they had ever done any building before, they now had to become builders, enlisting the help of Africans to the extent possible. A problem they faced was how to build in such a way that termites could not make short work of their dwellings.

Mozambique Not Forgotten

They were about as close to Mozambique as they could be without crossing the border. By this deployment it is clear that Mozambique was still on the hearts of these missionaries. Their mission stations were near enough to make short trips into that closed land. They

could also contact some who crossed from the other side. The vision and prayers of the missionaries at the 1933 South Africa conference were beginning to bear fruit.

The people of the Zambezi Valley seemed distant and hard to reach when the missionaries tried to communicate simple gospel truth. But their interest increased when missionaries and Africans worked together on the buildings. Missionaries at times tended to view the necessary manual work as a waste of precious time that could otherwise have been spent in direct gospel ministry, but then they learned that some can be won only through this type of contact. They were reminded of the Apostle Paul making tents and took courage.

Living Off the Land—in Part

For meat the men went out into the bush to shoot antelope or guinea fowl. They raised chickens and goats but had to carefully protect their pens from leopards. They planted gardens but these also were in danger from wild animals, particularly baboons and elephants. Wild animals often presented a hazard when missionaries traveled and had to camp at night along the way. Some hair-raising stories are told about encounters with leopards, lions, and elephants, stories which I fully believe because I had an exciting brush with a lion in 1954 when I was traveling in this same area with Norman Everswick, Orval Dunkeld, and Charles Pruitt.

Southern Rhodesia—a Separate Field

The work in Southern Rhodesia was at first part of the Africa field, which also included Swaziland and the Union of South Africa, a thousand miles to the south. When T. J. Bach visited both areas in 1947, missionaries spoke to him about the difficulty of administering such a broad expanse of work. With recommendations from both areas, and Bach's added word, the board of directors designated Southern Rhodesia as a separate mission field.[1]

Enough Missionaries?

Missionaries were now placed at Msengedzi, Rukomitchi, and Hunyani in the valley, and word came that more were applying for service. Thought was therefore given to the future development of the work. Where would new missionaries be placed?

> In the early 1950s, the field chairman informed the home office that the field had all the missionaries needed and could not absorb any more because its intention was to limit the work to the bush area of the Valley. One reason was that the missionaries felt keenly that it would be easy to be dissuaded from the very difficult ministry in the Valley if stations needing personnel were opened in more favorable living areas.[2]

Dr. David H. Johnson believed that if the Lord was raising up missionary recruits for Southern Rhodesia, other areas would open up for them. I was working with the many recruits at that time and agreed with Johnson that the Lord of the harvest understood both the needs of the field and the availability of laborers and would bring them together. And the Lord did just that.

Expansion Becomes Possible

The Zambesi (British spelling) Mission, headquartered in England, was having a difficult time getting recruits for its Southern Rhodesia field. Its assigned area of work was in the higher elevation just above the escarpment forming the rim of the valley. TEAM agreed to take responsibility for two districts—Mavuradonha and Rusambo. Accepting that it was the Lord's will that other needy areas be considered, missionaries found that there were many concentrations of people who should be reached. Within five years work was begun at the rather remote area of Kapfundi and at a number of farming areas where there were concentrations of farm laborers.

Importance of a Capital Location

Though the missionaries' vision for the more remote unevangelized areas remained undiminished, they were forced to consider the capital city of Salisbury for at least four reasons. First, they needed easier contact with government offices. Second, required supplies were not available in the outlying regions. Third, they must consider the education of their children. Fourth, believers from the bush areas who were drawn to the big city for work needed spiritual care. Required by racial segregation policies to live in crowded, sin-choked township locations on the outskirts of the city, they faced difficult living conditions and new temptations.

A Place for School Children

In 1950, TEAM was given a five-acre plot with a home on it in the suburb of Hatfield. This served as a center where missionaries could park their trucks when they came in from the bush. It was no hardship for them to camp for the days they needed to be in town. An adjoining plot of five acres was later purchased and on it the missionaries built dormitories, a dining hall, and an assembly room for children who came in from the bush stations to attend the local school. Orval and Helen Dunkeld were asked to live and serve there.

Over a period of time, various missionaries served as houseparents and counselors of the many missionary children (MKs) who made Hatfield their home for three-quarters of the year. Some children from other missions were also accepted and their presence enriched the fellowship. It has been particularly gratifying to see how many MKs from this field have gone into missionary service.[3]

Evangelism in the Townships

Missionaries in the city also had opportunities to minister to people in the crowded locations and found many hungry hearts. Some were able to help young Christians who had attended church at home in the bush but when in the city had been swept into a sinful lifestyle by new and tempting allurements.

Schools and Bush Clinics Required

When missionaries were granted permission to set up a mission station in rural areas, it was only as they agreed to open elementary schools and care for basic medical needs of the people. This caused no problem as long as these schools were small and missionaries were available to teach, but sometimes it was difficult to find enough teachers to meet the great demand for education. Some teachers trained by other missions were available, but in time missionaries decided that it would be best to have a TEAM-related training institution near at hand.

Qualified Teachers Needed

The need came into sharper focus in 1954. At the request of the village of Tsenguve in the Kandeya Reserve, a young evangelist, Frank Kakunguwo, was sent to open a school. He was not trained as a teacher, but as a zealous Christian worker he won the children to Christ and some of their parents as well. When the education authorities found out about the school and its untrained teacher they demanded that it be closed. The word of this closing came as I was visiting the field in 1954.

Norman Everswick, who was then stationed at Mavuradonha only about twenty wilderness miles from Tsenguve, intercepted my escort, Charles Pruitt, and me along the road and told us that we should stop overnight at Tsenguve in order to meet with the village leaders to explain why they could no longer have a school. Darkness had fallen when we arrived but the men had a big bonfire for us to sit around while we talked.

A Villager's Eloquent Plea

The village headman, Bveke, spoke for the group: "When you took away the teacher and closed the school, God left our village. When can we have our school again?"

Everswick explained the problem and then asked for the villagers' help. The mission needed to find a place to begin a school to train teachers, he said, and had considered the Kandeya Reserve. Would the men help find a place close to a good supply of water and large enough for school buildings, demonstration classrooms, dormitories, workshop, soccer ground, and missionary residences?

Maranatha Teacher Training School

The villagers responded positively and within six months a suitable location was found at Chironga. The district commissioner gave permission and the Maranatha Teacher Training School was established.[4]

Missionaries who served at the Maranatha Teacher Training School included Clifford Ratzlaff, William Warner, and Donna Kahlstorf. For the eight or ten years of its existence the training school graduated many teachers who were well enough trained for their vocation. They also had enough Bible training to give spiritual leadership and instruction in the schools where they taught and be active in community outreach. In Chironga, itself, grade school classes were held for as many as 300 children from the surrounding villages.

Community Responsibility for Schools

The government later made a change in the administration of schools, relieving missions of responsibility for education and instead charging community school boards with this task. While in one way the change resulted in less opportunity to reach children of tender age with the gospel, the door certainly was not closed for contact.

Missionaries and qualified African workers were given the right to enter the schools to offer religious instruction. That right of entry existed not only under the white government but also later under the black government with its Marxist orientation. Missionaries could not help but be struck with the irony of American Christian teachers, who would not be permitted to tell a Bible story or even teach a Christmas carol in an American school, being encouraged to teach the Bible in a systematic way under a Marxist system. One of the most active in this ministry for many years has been Marian Wilterdink.

Urgent Need for a Doctor

Because TEAM had no doctors in the early years it assigned

nurses to care for the medical needs of the people. Some who had only paramedic training also worked in the clinics. Betty Mason (Wolfe), one of the early nurses, wrote about her experience when faced with serious medical conditions:

> A few weeks ago a man was brought in who couldn't walk. He had a pain in the lower portion of his back which had gone down to his leg. His leg was very edematous and painful. We did not know what was wrong with it. The leg became paralyzed. The man gradually became weaker and weaker and lost weight rapidly. The road finally dried up enough so that we could have taken him out the long 65 miles to the nearest doctor, but the man had never seen a doctor or a hospital and refused to go. Finally we just had to take him home, worse than when he came in.[5]

Hospital Facilities Also Needed

As early as 1952, the annual field conference appealed for a doctor. That appeal was repeated in following years until at last, in 1958, Dr. Samuel Wall and his wife, Emily, responded.

There clearly also was need for a hospital. When the district commissioner was approached at the time of my 1954 visit, he stressed that water must be readily available and plentiful. Drilling wells would not solve the problem as this whole northeastern part of the country was like a self-contained saucer with no underground streams. Normal seepage of rain provided some ground water but not sufficient for heavy water usage. He could not give permission for a hospital which needed large quantities, unless it could draw from a river with good year-round flow. That requirement provided the guidance in selecting the site. Only two miles from Chironga there was an area sloping down to the Ruya River at a place named Karanda.[6]

Hospital Dedicated in 1961

The chairman of the TEAM board, Carl Gundersen, and the vice chairman, Joseph Horness, agreed together to contribute to make possible the basic structure of a 69-bed hospital. Dedicated April 21, 1961, as the Gundersen-Horness Hospital, the name was later changed to Karanda Hospital when the new government frowned on European names.

Dr. and Mrs. Wall served for one busy term during the construction of the hospital and the initiating of its ministry. They were joined in 1961 by Dr. and Mrs. Allan Clemenger, whose time on the field was shortened by health needs. Though Dr. Clemenger left this field, he continued to provide much help to the mission, including short terms of obstetric service at the Oasis Hospital in the United Arab Emirates.

Nurses' Training Begun in 1962

From its beginning, missionary nurses served at the hospital as well as at outlying mission station clinics, but they clearly needed more help. The solution was to establish a nurses' training school at Karanda to prepare African nurses up to a level dictated by the government medical authorities. Wilma Gardziella (Anderson) was the first to serve in this training program, which began in 1962. When she went on furlough, Patricia Mortenson succeeded her. Others in the training program included Cherith Till, Ann-Britt (Byrmo) Smazik, and Karen (Holritz) Drake. The nursing school was moved to the capital in 1978 because Karanda had by then become a center of guerrilla activity. One year later the school was closed and students were placed in other schools to complete their training. It reopened in March 1985 under the direction of Karen Drake.[7]

Training of nurses provided help for the hospital and bush clinics, but it had a greater purpose: that the young women—and a few young men—be equipped as witnesses for Christ by life and word as they dealt with many ailing and sin-sick individuals. Nursing students were drawn from different parts of the country—though preference was given to qualified local applicants—and it was not easy to follow them after graduation. Where their work was known, their instructors were satisfied that spiritual as well as professional objectives were, on the whole, being reached.

A Surgeon's Central Role

Dr. Roland Stephens, a board-certified surgeon, and his wife Katherine, came in 1962 and served until 1978. Stephens, doing outstanding surgery, attracted to the hospital many who would otherwise have been viewed as hopeless cases. I watched several hours of an eight-hour intestinal operation and marvelled that the patient came through in satisfactory condition. In our homelands, surgery of that kind would have required one or two additional surgeons to assist and a supporting staff of surgical technicians. Beverly Nelson, nurse anesthetist, had been on duty much of the previous twenty-four hours. How she stayed awake, I will never understand. Judy Gudeman had assisted in so many operations that she was able to care for certain procedures. Wilma Gardziella handled all the necessary instruments and had them in the doctor's hand in order and on time.

The hospital and staff deservedly earned a good name for the excellence of the surgery. But field leaders had to think of the overall effect. With the shortness of staff and their being so continually overworked, was it wise or necessary to put on them the burden of supporting major complicated surgery that could have been referred to a hospital in the capital? Were opportunities for closer patient contact and witness being missed?

Beginning Churches

Missionaries gathered converts into small congregations as they ministered in their local areas. Missionaries did most of the preaching and teaching until those who were trained locally or in the new Bible school could share in this responsibility. One of the first church buildings was at Msengedzi. Dedicated in 1954, it was named the Rudy Danielson Memorial Church in memory of the pioneer missionary who laid down his life for the Lord in the Zambezi Valley. Though missionaries were concerned that the congregations care for their own expenses, including the support of their pastors, self-support was difficult to attain.

Many men from the bush areas went to the city to work. Their wages were low, their expenses higher than expected and they had little to send back to their families. Their women planted maize, harvested the crop, pounded out the grain, and cared for all other necessities—none of which required cash. Where people are not on a cash economy, the traditional way of supporting the church by cash offerings is generally not successful. Some learn to contribute produce of one kind or another to support the work, but this method seemed not to have caught on in Rhodesia. The result was that the churches were at first almost completely dependent on mission support.

A Church Fellowship Organized

Under leadership of the early missionaries the churches were organized into a fellowship—the Evangelical Church. Africans, comparing it with other church groups, tended to call it a denomination. They felt it was an honor to be a member and even designed an identifying pin so members could reveal their association with the Evangelical Church—a step which caused some concern by missionaries who feared that the emphasis could be on externals rather than on the heart relationship.

The churches valued the relationship that existed among them and met in annual conferences. At the 1967 conference one of the subjects for discussion was the matter of self-support. Attending the conference as a delegate was a promising graduate of the Maranatha Teacher Training School of Chironga, Pius Wakatama, who was working in the mission's literature ministry, Word of Life Press. He apparently presented a strong argument for self-support by the churches—which was certainly in line with TEAM's goal. Along with that argument he stressed other aspects of independence which tended to foster a rift between the churches and the mission. The outcome was that the churches voted to receive no more mission support. This action was premature and too abrupt and brought on strain that took several years to overcome. While there were steady gains in self-support, this question failed of complete solution for the next fifteen years.

Training Christian Workers

The need for trained Christian workers became apparent. The first step in that direction was taken by Norman Everswick who began the Evangelical Bible School (EBS) in Mavuradonha in 1953 with six students. Some of the men were already experienced in witnessing and preaching but needed much greater depth of understanding of the Scriptures. In 1955 EBS was moved to the remote station of Kapfundi where Wilfred and Dorothy Strom served. Under Strom's leadership the enrollment increased and instruction was given in both Shona and English.

To be more convenient for students and to provide more opportunity for Christian service, the school was relocated to Sinoia (Chinhoyi) in 1968 and the curriculum was upgraded. The school appealed more widely than just to students from TEAM-related churches, some of whom served in TEAM ministries upon graduation. Roy Eichner and Carl Hendrickson led the school in turn until it was time to appoint an African to the position, at which time Isaiah Chiswiti became principal.

Higher Training for Africans

Missionaries on the field adopted a far-sighted policy of assisting local Africans of dedication, ability, and promise in their desire for higher education. Those who went for such training also had the endorsement of the church council. One of the first to take advantage of the training opportunity was Isaiah Chiswiti, a qualified and experienced school teacher. Chiswiti completed undergraduate work at the Grace College of the Bible in Omaha. Upon return to Rhodesia, Chiswiti was appointed principal of the Evangelical Bible School, where he served until he returned to the United States for graduate work in 1990.

Other Africans who taught at EBS and had training overseas included Edgar Bumhira, Fanuel Chandomba, Onesimus Ngundu, and Julius Mberego. These young men were dedicated Christians and gifted teachers. Missionaries on the teaching staff over a period of years included Donna Hendrickson (Correspondence School),

Orla Blair, Bronson Sherwood, Stewart Georgia, Armond Fritz (Extension), Donna Kahlstorf, Patricia Mortenson, and Richard McCloy.

Toward the end of 1990, the Evangelical Bible College, with Dr. Onesimus Ngundu as its head, was preparing to move to the former mission headquarters plot in the Hatfield suburb of Harare and take a new name—Harare Theological College. Dr. Ngundu took his doctoral studies at Dallas Theological Seminary.

Twenty-year EBC Summary

How can the work of the Evangelical Bible College be evaluated? An available summary of its training and long-term results is found in a study prepared by Carl Hendrickson in 1976. The study gives a picture of the first two decades of ministry, which may also accurately reflect the more recent results:[8]

    Gross attendance: men–156, women–86, total–242
    Graduates: men–82, women–40, total–122
    Known active: men–64, women–30, total–94
    Pastors, TEAM-related churches: 19
    Pastors, other churches: 17
    Bible college teachers: 6
    Other Christian ministries: 13
    The other 39 were active laymen in their local churches.

Homecraft School

Church leaders and missionaries recognized that pastors and evangelists could serve much more effectively if their wives were able to provide spiritual and practical support. Some of the men were married to illiterate women who lacked understanding of what a Christian home should be or how they could help their husbands apart from such things as bearing children, carrying water, tilling the fields, and pounding the corn into meal.

Mary Danielson had taught school at Mavuradonha much of the time since the death of her husband, Rudy, in 1943. She had learned of a type of instruction which would benefit the wives of the workers—a Homecraft school. With the enthusiastic approval of both missionary and African leaders, Mary began such a school in

Rusambo in 1962.

The young women were taught such basic skills as reading, care of the home, sanitation, child care, sewing, and nutritious cooking with locally available foods. While the spiritual dimension of the training was not included in the name it was very much present in the daily program. The husbands were so convinced of the value of the training to their wives and consequently to themselves that they were willing to allow them to be away from home for the school year.

War Closing In

By 1974, when it was becoming difficult to carry on any ministry in the area most affected by civil war hostilities, Mary had begun to realize that the higher level of schooling available to both men and women was reducing the need for Homecraft-type training. She had considered closing Homecraft in September or October 1974 because of furloughs and lack of replacements. The emergency military situation in April 1974 brought the matter to a head and Homecraft began phasing out in June. Homecraft truly gained the well-deserved appreciation of the churches and their leaders.

Background for Civil War

At the close of World War II, Africa had only two independent nations: Liberia and Ethiopia. Over the next fifteen to twenty years, most African territories gained independence from the European colonial powers. One exception was Rhodesia, whose white minority foresaw and feared the granting of rule to the black majority by the British government. White-ruled Rhodesia declared unilateral independence from Great Britain on November 11, 1965, under the leadership of Prime Minister Ian Smith. Great Britain and many other nations resisted this move and imposed sanctions and embargoes but did not intervene militarily. Portugal, which had two colonies adjoining Rhodesia—Angola and Mozambique—and the Republic of South Africa did not join the sanctions but maintained communication and trade with Rhodesia. After these two colonies gained independence in 1975 they provided no further help to Rhodesia.

Independence and sanctions had one beneficial effect in that Rhodesia became less dependent on imports and more self-sufficient in supplying its own needs. But the net result was suffering and death to many, both Africans and whites.

Raids by "Freedom Fighters"

Efforts on the part of Africans to force majority rule consisted mainly of raids by "freedom fighters"—as they called themselves—or "terrorists"—as they were called by the minority whites. This was civil war along racial lines. Civil war always engenders intense bitterness and cruelty and this was no exception. The security forces used drastic measures to counter guerrilla activity and the guerrillas employed equally extreme tactics to force uncommitted Africans to assist them or join their cause.

Beginning at a low tempo in 1968 the fighting increased in frequency and violence until, after several unsuccessful attempts, the British arranged a cease-fire in 1979.

The Impact on Missionary Work

General director Winchell commented on the effects of the war on missionary work:

> A severe challenge to church growth in Zimbabwe was the recent war that raged for eight and a half years or more. Limitations on travel by national workers and missionaries because of danger in rural areas made evangelism and follow-up difficult. Mission stations in these areas were closed. The hospital continued its ministry of mercy for a time until, finally, the situation deteriorated to the point that it, too, had to close. The church suffered a great deal during that time. General upheaval in daily life made even the conduct of normal church life difficult. Many people of the meeting places and church groups in the affected areas of the north and northeast were scattered. Large numbers were removed to fenced villages for protection, but some ministry could be carried on among them. A number of the teachers in mission schools were killed, either as a result of land mines on the roads

or from direct action by the guerrillas.[9]

Missionary Aviation

Located in the northeast where most of the guerrilla action took place, the Karanda hospital was in a vulnerable spot militarily and politically. With many of the local roads mined, there were many casualties among the local people. When a bus detonated a mine, as happened from time to time, there were deaths and serious injuries. Many of the injured were brought to the mission hospital for life-saving care.

With road travel so hazardous, the Missionary Aviation Fellowship (MAF) plane based at Karanda was used to transport missionaries to outlying areas for preaching, teaching, and medical work. MAF also brought critically ill patients to the hospital. The pilots accepted the hazards of flying in a war zone where missiles or even rifle shots could easily have brought a plane down. Pilots and others prayed and were as cautious as they could be. MAF also chose a color for its plane quite different from the Rhodesian military. Of the MAF pilots who served there, three are especially remembered for their flying skill, willing service, and their help in the evangelistic outreach—Dave Voetmann, Gordon Marshall, and Dave Richardson.

Two Christian Leaders Slain

A sad message reached TEAM headquarters in Wheaton in mid-April 1974 with the news that pastor Frank Kakunguwo and teacher Richard Tsinakwadi had been slain by intruders thought to be associated with the rebel activity. Kakunguwo was currently serving as chaplain of the Mavuradonha Christian school, which had both elementary and high school grades. Prior to his work at Mavuradonha he had been chaplain at the Gundersen-Horness Hospital. Kakunguwo was a recognized leader in the Evangelical Church, having served as chairman. His assailants felled him with a gunshot or two.

Several missionaries may have been at Mavuradonha at the time, but the one sought out by the intruders was teacher Stewart

Georgia. They demanded that Georgia lead them to boarding master Tsinakwadi. Knowing what they had done to Kakunguwo and suspecting that they had the same intention regarding the boarding master, Georgia offered himself in his place. The murderers refused that offer and sought out Tsinakwadi, whom they then beat to death with a heavy tree limb.

These shocking events quite naturally brought consternation to the missionaries, the African staff, the large group of students, and their parents who had entrusted them to the school feeling it was a safe place. Students who could return to nearby homes did so. Those from more distant places in Rhodesia were taken to Salisbury and many were enrolled in other Christian schools.

It is not known whether any motive for the killings was established. The two men were not the type who had personal enemies, nor were they involved in the political struggles of the day. Some wondered if there could have been lingering resentments arising from some disciplinary action in the school, or if the deeds were for the purpose of getting back at some relative who may have offended the killers at some other place and time.

When I arrived on the field ten or twelve days later at the request of the field council, I found the prevailing thought that this tragedy was a part of the human cost of the struggle between the African advocates of more liberty and independence and the white government. There seemed little feeling that the attack was directed at the mission work of TEAM.

But targeted or not, the field council was responsible to deal with the effects. It called a special field conference over the end of April and the beginning of May 1974 to face prayerfully and squarely the question of what to do with the vulnerable mission stations of Mavuradonha, Rusambo, Chironga, and Karanda, where upwards of twenty-five missionaries worked. The decision was made to close Mavuradonha and Rusambo, which were most in danger.

Guerrilla War Intensifies

As the war continued, it became apparent to the white government that much of the northeast region of the country was infiltrated by guerrilla fighters or sympathizers. The seriousness of the military situation was recognized by the international press as reporter Lee Griggs wrote in the March 28, 1977, issue of *TIME:*

> Much of the countryside—particularly in the eastern districts that face Mozambique—is subject to attack by increasingly well-armed guerrillas who terrorize black villages, assault sand-bagged and floodlit farmhouses with rockets and mortars, sabotage the two rail lines to South Africa, and plant mines on paved as well as dirt roads.[10]

In a move to blunt the effectiveness of the guerrilla infiltration, the government moved the scattered African people into protected villages (Keeps) which were fenced, controlled, and guarded.

MAF Eager for a Ministry to the Keeps

Within thirty minutes' flying time from the MAF base at the Karanda hospital, the government had established twenty-six Keeps with a total estimated population of 175,000. Gordon Marshall, MAF pilot, was eager to have MAF help minister to these Keeps. When I was in Rhodesia in 1977, he took field chairman Russell Jackson and me on an air tour of the area so we could see many of the protected villages, including the large Mukumbura Keep situated along the Mozambique border. We talked with those in charge and when the possibility of Christian work was mentioned, we were given a warm welcome to begin.

When Jackson brought the matter to the field council he found real interest but was also informed that, sadly, the evangelism account was depleted. I promised to ask general director Winchell to contact a potential donor to see if money could be given for this strategic ministry. I considered it strategic because of the unique opportunity to reach people from previously unreached villages, to follow up with biblical teaching, and possibly to organize some congregations which would later form the nucleus for local churches when the hostilities were over.

Involving the Evangelical Church

We did not want this ministry to be solely a mission project so took the question to the joint church-mission council. Automatic approval by the church council was not assured. The men evidently wanted to determine whether this was a mission project like certain others which might compete with the church ministries. Jackson noted the question in the minds of some church leaders:

> During your recent visit to Rhodesia I shared with you something of the opposition we sensed from the church council in connection with an evangelistic outreach to the Keeps. I rejoice to tell you that this opposition seems to have melted away and, although the church council has not offered any support for the program, yet they have given their official permission and full approval so we are moving ahead together. But the actual challenge of the outreach into the Keeps is being taken up by the church at the grass roots level.... The Evangelical Church on a local grass roots level is alive, vibrant, and prepared to go forward.[11]

How to Support the Undertaking

Funds promised by the missions department of Back to the Bible Broadcast would go far to cover the cost of necessary air service to transport the evangelists and Bible teachers to the various Keeps.

To avoid direct hiring, the joint committee for the Keeps ministry chose evangelists and pastors who could be spared from their regular assignments and offered them their expenses and an honorarium. Africans engaged in this ministry included evangelists Magwojo, Madzika, Madyekadye, Jeke, Piroro, and Chadereka. Jackson described the latter two as older evangelists of "tremendous vision and potential." Both had sons who had been abducted and taken across the border into Mozambique for training as guerrillas. Neither man knew anything of the whereabouts of his son or if he was still living. The zeal of these fathers was truly based on a desire to "avenge" these acts—not by force or bloodshed, but by service of love to the Lord and to the people.

Careful Scheduling

The committee worked with MAF to arrange a schedule that

would enable the men to minister in a large number of Keeps. They visited in the temporary homes, did personal counseling, and also held larger meetings. So they would not be mistaken as having any association with the administration of the Keeps, they declined to use the public address system over which the officials made announcements and gave orders.

Timeliness of the Campaign

The committee members sensed the urgency of taking advantage of opportunities to reach many people at a time when they might well be more receptive than usual to the gospel. This is reflected in the reports sent back by Jackson, such as the one of March 24, 1977:

> Gordon Marshall and David Richardson spent a couple of hours with me yesterday discussing the results of the first series of meetings in the Keeps. Reports from the three team leaders were very positive.[12]

The Effect on Church Morale

It is evident that this new outreach and fresh contact with receptive men and women, coming at a time when the military situation was placing great pressure on Africans and missionaries alike, brought great encouragement and with it much stimulation in the ministry. This is indicated in the chairman's correspondence:

> The most thrilling aspect of Evangelism in the Keeps is that should the Keeps dissolve, the people involved will still remain in the very near vicinity, because most of the people living in the large protected villages come from within a radius of a few miles. Should small churches be planted in the Keeps there is no reason why they should not continue.[13]

My touch with the campaign was only at its beginning. Winchell and area secretary Delbert Kuehl maintained close communication as long as the program continued, which was until the government allowed the people to return to their own villages. There was general agreement that the effort and expense were amply rewarded in terms of the spiritual harvest.

Hard to be Neutral

Members of the military wounded by gunfire or land mines would often be brought to the hospital. Doctors and nurses tried to demonstrate neutrality by giving care as needed and without prejudice, but the movement of military personnel—and undoubtedly some of the guerrillas—through the hospital for medical care seemed to compromise neutrality. Hospital personnel—both African and missionary—continued their service to all having need long after Karanda had become one of the major hot spots of the conflict. The maimed and wounded under their care brought vivid reminders of what could happen to them. The torching of a nearby Keep by guerrillas proved that the same could easily happen to the hospital. As if that were not enough, the incursion of armed bands from time to time confronting Norman and Thelma Everswick and Dr. David Drake demonstrated the vulnerability of the staff and the ease with which the hospital could be occupied and taken over.

A Most Difficult Decision

General director Winchell provided counsel at just the right moment in 1978 by visiting Rhodesia to help reach decisions about continuing the ministries in the face of the mounting danger. The question of the hospital's future was certainly the most pressing and also the most difficult. Dr. David Drake, who was then on furlough, made a special trip to the field to help in reaching a decision. Missionaries—almost without exception—are accustomed to serving regardless of personal cost to themselves. If this is true generally of missionaries, it is particularly true of health professionals. Long days, late hours, and personal inconvenience are considered necessary components of missionary medical work.

Even the matter of avoiding personal danger is secondary to meeting the needs of suffering people. When the staff at Karanda Hospital faced the possibility of having to leave because of surrounding dangers their reluctance was entirely predictable. Were the dangers actually as threatening as people were saying? Would the guerrillas not understand that the hospital was there to help the people and therefore consider it no threat to their revolutionary aims? Who would meet the pressing needs of wounded and sick people if the hospital closed? Didn't the Lord send us here and won't He care for us now?

Winchell could easily see that if the decision about the hospital's future were left to the personnel at Karanda or even to the field council there would be too many subjective factors involved. Whatever would be decided would affect the local people, including many in the churches. Winchell and the field council therefore conferred with the church leaders and found them reluctant to advise. They suggested that the decision be made by the board of directors, so no action was taken at the time. Instead, the matter was referred to the board. A few days later Winchell was back at headquarters and without delay brought all the board members together in a conference phone call. He gave a comprehensive report on the situation and presented various views as he had heard them expressed. The board members took time to raise questions and share points of view and when a vote was called for it was unanimous for a temporary closing of the hospital. This "temporary closing" stretched out to almost two years.

A Greatly Welcomed Armistice

The armistice arranged by the British in 1979 was followed in 1980 by transfer of power to a majority government with the Shona leader, Robert Mugabe, becoming prime minister. Majority rule brought many changes: Rhodesia became Zimbabwe; Salisbury, the capital, was renamed Harare; universal franchise was attained; racial laws were abolished; the government declared itself Marxist in orientation; and, in general, the people spoke of being liberated.

Medical Work After the War

Another long-term member of the hospital staff was Dr. David Drake, who came to the field in 1966 and continued until 1990. To Drake fell the responsibility of reopening the medical work in 1980 after peace had come to the country. One of his first tasks was to survey the Karanda area to evaluate the medical needs of the people and determine the condition of the hospital facilities:

> Dr. Drake reported that the medical condition of the people in the rural area is deplorable. Malnutrition is present everywhere because the people were not able to plant fields or keep their cattle. Diseases such as measles, polio, tuberculosis, and leprosy which were beginning to be controlled are now rampant.[14]

The hospital plant had been vandalized during the time it was closed and much rebuilding and repair were required. With only one doctor and the need to rebuild the auxiliary staff, it seemed at first that the hospital could only be an outpatient facility. But that changed of necessity and by 1986 it was reported that the 150 beds for inpatients were filled most of the time. The maternity ward had twenty beds and sixty to seventy-five babies were delivered each month.

As if the war experiences were not enough, the people had to face famine conditions because of drought. The hospital therefore became a base for famine relief under the direction of George Smazik. Able-bodied people were given work around the hospital and paid with food. When that program ended, a new one was opened with seed and fertilizer being distributed for the work done.

Community Health Project

In keeping with recent trends in missionary medicine, the Karanda hospital staff in 1980 shifted its emphasis from a curative approach to primary care and preventative medicine. This program included the development by nurse Lorraine Waite of a nutritional teaching center and an outreach to surrounding communities. Miss Waite shared something of the extent and impact of this service in a 1987 letter:

> Community nursing consists of doing immunizations in different outreach places, teaching health in schools, doing community analyses and diagnoses by visiting all the homes, and doing hospital and nutrition village follow-up. My student nurses and I take the results back to the community for them to act on. The people themselves decide what they want to do with our results. They actually make changes in their ways for better health. It is

very rewarding to me and my students as they see what can be done through community based nursing care. We deal with physical, spiritual, mental, and social health, and draw medical, church, school, political, and many other groups into our team.[15]

Spiritual Healing and Life

There is, of course, a dual purpose in community service—doing good for the body and also for the soul. The same letter had a paragraph which reveals the fruit, in part, of this loving service in Christ's name:

> During the whole month of March the Evangelical Church had a huge tent at the town of Rushinga, 15 miles from Karanda Hospital. Four evangelists were there and many people from all age groups accepted the Lord. The Jawana family, strong Christians in the town for many years, joyfully received each new Christian and took him or her under their care. When the evangelists finished their work, they left one pastor and also the tent for three more months. When the people heard this they clapped their hands loud and long for joy. I expect this group to grow quickly into a strong sending church.[16]

The shortage of doctors was alleviated with the coming in 1987 of two doctors sent out to serve with TEAM by the German Missionary Fellowship (DMG)—Dr. Gisela Roth and Dr. Elisabeth Zeulsdorf.

Difficult Choice Between Two Cultures

Missionaries realize that in order to work effectively they must adjust to local culture. When they live in a colonial country—such as Rhodesia was—adjustment is complicated by the existence of two side-by-side cultures—that of the indigenous people, and that of the colonial power. The basic culture of the majority of the people is Bantu-African. The culture of the minority—which was for so long the ruling class—is British-European. Some American missionaries undoubtedly were delighted to find British people with whom to associate during their initial months—or even years. Almost without realizing it, their bonding was with the British or Rhodesian, rather than with the African. Yet they may have thought they had adjusted to the African people when, in fact, their adjustment was to the minority culture. Happily, this was not universally true.

Dale Everswick, field chairman in 1982, looked back over the experience of missionaries in this colonial setting and made some perceptive observations:

> When the gates of racial segregation were finally broken in 1980, we faced quite a revelation. The barriers were down and though we had known each other for years, we were still strangers. We found it hard to identify. It was hard to weep with those who weep because of all we didn't understand. We felt little solidarity with national Christians. Our lives hadn't touched at enough points.... Now the challenge that lies before the church and the mission is to show the country the kind of love and reconciliation which only Jesus can bring. [17]

If the changes brought about by independence were traumatic for those who understood the Shona language and culture and knew the people well, how much more so for those who had made only superficial adjustment.

Walking a Fine Line

During the years of civil strife, missionaries were torn between the conviction that they were responsible to be "subject to the higher powers"—*i.e.* the government—and their desire to share more fully in the aspirations of the people. They succeeded quite well in walking a fine line so they did not draw the ire of the Ian Smith government, nor were they expelled when the majority black government came into power. As long as their actions could demonstrate that they were non-political and their motives and activities centered on service to the people they were allowed to work in the country.

The Meaning to the African of Independence

It became evident later that the more politically zealous youth thought that missionaries had not been sufficiently supportive of the independence movement and this had its effect on relationships in the church. Another effect of independence was the example of the colonial governments surrendering authority and privilege to the African governments which succeeded them. In a typical government department, the authority was understandably transferred to a national as head minister. Certain former colonial officials might be retained as advisors but with no authority for decision. All property—from a large headquarters building to a small pencil sharpener—became the property of the new black government. Applying this concept to relationships between the mission and the national church, as was true in some countries and with some missions, it was easy for some church leaders to assume that missions in the new Zimbabwe would turn over all property to the church and become one organization under the authority of the church. How this affected church-mission relationships became painfully apparent later.

Individual Re-evaluation

The coming of independence to Zimbabwe required missionaries to rethink their relationship to the people. A small number, who allegedly could not imagine themselves working under African rule, withdrew from the field. They apparently believed, in all sincerity, that their spiritual ministry would be diminished by the necessity of submitting to African leadership. Most faced the issue squarely and in the spirit of the Apostle Paul adopted as their guideline his word in I Corinthians 9:22, "I have become all things to all men so that by all possible means I might save some."

Church Planting During the War

Of the work carried on during the war, Bindura presented an interesting case study. Begun in the town and adjoining farm area by Russell and Margaret Jackson, it included ministry to African farm laborer families and European farmers. Warren and Lois Bruton worked there for a shorter period and were followed by second-generation missionary Lynn Everswick and his wife, Judy. Later, George and Pat Dee were assigned to Bindura and continued to see the work go forward.

The farmers who became Christians began to take a new interest in the many Africans working on their extensive farms. Separate congregations were formed of farmers and laborers, not primarily because of the segregation policies of the country, but more because of language differences and the preferences of the people. (It seemed strange to an outsider that these two—black and white—living in close proximity and involved in the same farm work had only the minimum of common language necessary for the requirements of manual work and little by way of genuine communication. Bindura was by no means an isolated example but quite typical of black-white relations. It took the missionary with his spiritual interest in both to bridge the gap.)

The Bindura area proved to be one of the hottest centers of guerrilla activity. Both the farmers and the Africans had to take special precautions for their own safety. It was not unusual for farmers to bring firearms for their own protection on the way to the meetings. But through all the trouble—and probably because of it—several strong churches were planted. Furthermore, the missionaries learned much of dependence on the sure promises of God and His protecting power.

Ministry After the War

With the coming of peace to war-torn Rhodesia-Zimbabwe, the missionaries and African Christians looked forward to a time of fruitful work. But there must first of all be an inventory of losses and gains. Down in the Zambezi Valley where churches were first planted, there was little visible church life. Christians had been scattered.

In centers such as Bindura, Chironga, Karanda, Sinoia, and Harare there were good foundations on which to build. Though the mission station and schools at Mavuradonha were devastated and in ruins, there was strong work going on in the Chiswiti village area. Of the supporting ministries, there was still the Word of Life Bookstore in Harare, and the Evangelical Bible College, the Light of Life Correspondence Courses, and Theological Education by Extension in Chinhoyi (Sinoia).

Field council members and church leaders spent much time reviewing the work and seeking the Lord's will for the future course of the ministry, both for the churches and the mission projects. Tom Jackson, another second-generation missionary, who was field chairman in 1986, responded with encouragement to a question about the African church in the post-war period:

> Over the last three years, in particular, we have seen new health and vigor in the national church. Part of this has been the result of new leadership that has come into the church—a group of men who are committed to ministry and who have a vision to see their church multiply and grow. This has given us such delight because the church has a vision for development, for church growth, and for missions.... This has shown itself in their desire to hold evangelistic campaigns on the local church level, to encourage local churches to hold evangelistic campaigns, as well as to organize and plan for evangelists to go into areas and work with the church in community life campaigns. Then there is the desire to follow these campaigns with a church planting effort.[18]

But less than two years later Jackson expressed concern about mission/church relationships:

> A series of events this year that calls us to thought and prayer has been communication from the leaders of the Evangelical Church (EC) that there is dissatisfaction with areas of mission/church relationships. There have been significant areas of blessing in TEAM/EC cooperation. On the personal level there are numerous examples of excellent mutual interest, concern, and a spirit of working together. Yet there are areas that need further consultation and planning.
>
> The EC leadership is asking for significant and radical structural change. This request grows out of a variety of root issues: there is the desire to see the task of evangelism and church growth maximized with the very best coordination and cooperation; there is the desire that TEAM "look right" in the Zimbabwe context—that it lose its expatriate and foreign appearance; there is also the basic difference of opinion and understanding of TEAM's relationship with the EC. The big question: Is TEAM primarily or solely committed to working with the EC?[19]

Church Relationships Over the Years

In a meeting of the EC council which I attended in the early

1970s, one of the topics for discussion was self-support by the churches. Several council members commented that the mission seemed to be diverting money from the support of the churches to parachurch ministries, such as the Bible college, Light of Life Correspondence courses, radio work, and bookstore. Some EC council members did not share the missionaries' enthusiasm about the value of these parachurch ministries, which they viewed as being in competition with the churches. They also observed that the struggling churches could not match the salary these projects were giving to their employees, which put the churches at a great disadvantage. How could the churches compete in calling a pastor? Of what benefit to the EC were the correspondence courses and radio? Was not the mission weakening rather than strengthening the churches through its outreach and support policies?

These were good questions deserving an answer, but quick answers from the mission's point of view did not easily satisfy the concerns of the churches. The EC leaders were of the opinion that the mission had resources it could divide at will. If less was being given to church support it must be because more was being given to these other less-important ministries.

What Was Really Good for the Churches?

Explanations which seemed logical to TEAM were not so to the church council. Missions and their supporters were convinced that self-support by the churches was the best way to strengthen them and assure their long-term stability. Dependence on foreign support would only weaken the churches. The other ministries were meant to be either evangelistic tools to aid church growth or means of training to insure spiritual growth. Contributions intended for churches were not diverted to these ministries, which had to depend on designated giving.

These explanations were true to the facts and yet there was a deeper truth that needed to be considered. Were the ministries designed in a way to encourage the interest and participation of the churches? More than that, were they developed to meet the felt needs of the churches? Had they, instead, been essentially the projects of missionaries who wanted fulfilling ministries? Some of these questions might seem judgmental, but were of the type that the church believed needed to be asked—and receive answers.

The Need for Wider Church Vision

On their part EC leaders needed vision to see beyond their immediate work and its problems. They had commendable zeal for the EC, but needed to more clearly see the possibility of bringing others into the church and reaching out through evangelism and teaching even where the organized church might not gain immediate advantage. Their background of tribal loyalty—and more narrowly to clans within the tribe—made it difficult to see wider needs and appreciate ministries that reached outward. Problems of this kind were not unique to the Shona people. The first century church had the same problems. It took the scattering of the believers through the persecutions following the martyrdom of Stephen to open the eyes of the early church leaders to the wider field among the Gentiles.

Insufficient Cause for Break

While questions in the minds of church leaders created tension they were not serious enough to disrupt the fellowship in the early years. Nor did the pressures and tensions of the war cause a break. The church members and the missionaries suffered together during that period and, indeed, shared suffering tends to unite hearts. However, it became evident in time that there were several major matters in the minds of some younger EC leaders that went beyond attitudes and incidents. One major matter was control and another property.

A Small Spark Ignites a Flame

The mission property in Hatfield, a suburb of Harare, had clearly increased in value as Harare continued to grow and develop. When acquired, it was merely some rural acreage on which to place necessary buildings for serving the needs of the mission and the missionaries. Now in the new Zimbabwe it seemed to thoughtful missionaries attending the field conference in January 1988 that the spread of fifteen acres of suburban residential land gave a wrong signal of the dominance of the foreign mission even though the facilities were also being used by Africans in the ministry. The headquarters needs could be adequately cared for on much smaller property; missionaries could be housed elsewhere; and money could then be freed to assist other ministries having pressing needs—including the churches.

Winchell reported the church reaction:

> News of this proposed sale reached the ears of some of the Zimbabwean leaders and they protested strongly, writing to me as well as communicating with the mission in Zimbabwe. They insist that the property rightfully belongs to them and that if we should sell they would sever their relationship with us "forthwith."[20]

The church leaders requested that Winchell come out to Zimbabwe to "bring us together." He made the trip in October 1988 and spent the better part of a week consulting with African and missionary leaders. Though Winchell observed that field chairman Wilfred Strom led the way in asking forgiveness for past attitudes and actions, he did not sense that there was a reciprocal spirit by the African brethren, who accused the mission of having prejudicial racial policies.

Misunderstandings and Hasty Actions

There undoubtedly were some unfortunate judgments expressed by missionaries and equally unfortunate actions by the church leaders. One such action was the "excommunication" of TEAM missionaries. They were no longer to be allowed to attend or fellowship in the local churches of the EC, an action which greatly saddened missionaries and many—if not most—of the members of the local churches.

Under Winchell's leadership the field council and the EC negotiating committee worked on a plan to integrate ministries which should have gone far to create a good working relationship. The plan, however, was not fully acceptable to the missionaries as it seemed that the church leaders' action was an attempt to coerce the mission. Nor was the plan acceptable to the church negotiating committee which seemed satisfied with nothing less than full control of ministry and property. Though communication continued, the matter dragged on for several years without solution. In the meantime, the missionaries—and undoubtedly many in the churches—prayed earnestly for true reconciliation.

Further Efforts to Reach Understanding

In a July 1990 meeting between the TEAM field leaders and the EC negotiating committee, field chairman Ray Williams reviewed the historical relationship between the two:

> In the past, TEAM has worked extensively with the Evangelical Church. We helped to start local churches that established their own identity as the Evangelical Church and we have continued to assist and encourage that ministry. As the church developed, our role changed until in August 1980 a special ceremony was held at Karanda to recognize the "coming of age" of the Evangelical Church. Since that time it has been our desire to work alongside the church as two cooperating organizations, but with neither having direct control over the other. From 1982 to 1988, TEAM had been under the impression that there was a good relationship with the church and that the structures then in effect represented the aspirations and expectations of both groups. The Joint Council provided a forum for planning and coordination without requiring either to relinquish its particular distinctives. In 1988 there was a decided shift in attitude of the EC leadership with regard to this arrangement.[21]

Changed Attitude

That there was indeed a shift in attitude by the EC leaders was made clear in Williams' outline of the situation:

> From 1988 to the present, there has been consistent pressure from the Evangelical Church for TEAM to become something we are not prepared to be.... Because TEAM was not willing to accept an arrangement such as this [being only a support group solely under the control of the Evangelical Church], a number of harsh measures were pursued by the church. A letter was lodged with the immigration department denouncing TEAM, the

Central Intelligence Officer was called, the newspaper was brought in, letters were written to the city of Harare opposing some of TEAM's projects and signed by church members claiming to represent TEAM, and delegations consisting of the leadership of the church regularly visited both missionaries and nationals with the intent of ensuring cooperation even if it required coercion. TEAM was not and is not willing to "negotiate" with this type of leadership. Currently, TEAM missionaries have been barred from attending any Evangelical Church functions. This was done in spite of the fact that several TEAM missionaries had actually joined the EC and were full voting members of various congregations. TEAM was excommunicated summarily without any acknowledgment of Biblical procedures for excluding someone from fellowship. As a result of the excommunications, the TEAM missionaries who have been involved in Evangelical Churches have sought and found other avenues of ministry in Zimbabwe. Our emphasis is still on the local church bodies and our missionaries are all a part of such bodies of believers.[22]

Door to Fellowship Kept Open by TEAM

Chairman Williams' statement to the EC leaders left the door open for a resumption and continuation of fellowship in the work. He pointed hopefully to the future:

> We want to continue to work with the Evangelical Church on specific projects and church planting ministries. These would be at the invitation and under the direction of the Evangelical Church, subject to the availability of personnel and resources. An example of this type of relationship would be the current situation at Mavuradonha Secondary School. TEAM would continue to accept invitations from other groups in Zimbabwe in the same way.[23]

Continued Hope

Though the results of the July 1990 consultation with the EC leaders were not particularly encouraging, the TEAM field council members felt that there had been a clear statement of what the ministry of the mission should be in Zimbabwe. The situation was not entirely hopeless because they saw encouraging signs on the local level as many expressions of good will toward the missionaries were received. In the meantime, missionaries continued working in many local churches and ministries outside of the EC.

Encouraging signs of answered prayer began to appear later in 1990. Lynn Everswick, area foreign secretary, reported these developments to the board:

> At the most recent annual conference of the Evangelical Church, the Negotiating Committee—which to this point has been dictating the agenda—was dissolved, and some of those who are being given responsibilities within the EC are those of a more moderate stance. We need to be praying that the Lord would continue to bring about changes that would lead to a God-honoring settlement and understanding of one another's ministries so we can complement one another and effectively serve the Lord together in Zimbabwe.... I believe earnestly that both the mission and the church will be refined and strengthened as a result of the difficult experiences we have gone through during the past two years.[24]

Tension is Not the Whole Story

The recounting of unwelcome church/mission tensions has taken too much of this story but it is a part of the field history that cannot be bypassed, occasioning much concern and prayer. Its telling has resulted in under-reporting other vital ministries—ministries which have been both necessary and fruitful in transforming the northeastern section of Zimbabwe from a dark unevangelized area into one with numerous gospel lighthouses where the Shona people may hear the message of salvation and participate in sharing the good news.

One such ministry is the Word of Life Press (WLP), begun in 1962 in Salisbury, transferred several years later to Sinoia to be administered by the Evangelical Bible College. With English being one of the official languages and secondary education being carried on in this language, there was English Christian literature available for WLP to distribute.

Another ministry greatly valued by the Christians was Mavuradonha Secondary School. Closed after the slaying of Frank Kakunguwo and Richard Tsinakwadi in 1974 and with its facilities vandalized during the war, its future was in doubt for some time. However, the Christian community felt the school was vital to the welfare of its families and so urged the rehabilitation of the property and resumption of high-school-level education. Isaiah Chiswiti and his brother took the initiative to rebuild the school. Though TEAM was not to have responsibility for administration it provided some of the money for rebuilding and a missionary couple—Dick and Ruth Regier—to serve at the school. The school is a good field for evangelism in addition to its educational function.

Broadcast Evangelism and TEE

Word of Life Radio, which was given an excellent start by Paul and Helen Smith, has been carried forward for over fifteen years by two young ministers, Stephen Bapiro and Hamad Chashaya. Up to two and a half hours a week of Shona gospel programs, prepared in studios in Harare, are released over Trans World Radio in Swaziland and to a lesser degree over the national radio of Zimbabwe. One notable result of these broadcasts has been the salvation of listeners in Mozambique. There has been fruit in Zimbabwe as well.

The goal of Theological Education by Extension (TEE) is to train leaders in the context of their local church involvement and ministry. In Zimbabwe, TEE has been an important arm in church planting, helping to establish on a sound footing various churches which have been started. Steve Agriss and Naboth Mtangadura, who were active in this work, had the goal of helping the Harare area churches to reach out and establish daughter churches.

Smaller Force but Gospel Work Goes On

In the last ten-year period the number of missionaries on the Zimbabwe field—including those on regular furlough—varied from 55 down to 35. The government was continually tightening its visa and work permit policies, which limited the number who were allowed entry and also their length of stay. The men who in turn served as field chairmen had no easy task in dealing with government regulations, in addition to their other responsibilities

682

of administering the varied ministries. Men who served in this position in earlier years were Orval Dunkeld, Norman Everswick, Orla Blair, and Wilfred Strom. More recent chairmen have been Dale Everswick, Tom Jackson, and Ray Williams.

Good Reasons for Encouragement

Though there have been recent difficult experiences, missionaries who have invested their lives in meeting the spiritual needs of the people of Zimbabwe are greatly encouraged as they contemplate the impact of the gospel in this area. In the mid-1850s, missionary-explorer David Livingstone traversed the Zambezi Valley and found unrelieved spiritual darkness. Through the work of a number of missions—TEAM included—there are now hundreds of churches and tens of thousands of believers led by dedicated and capable pastors and laymen. Though missionary forces in TEAM's area are reduced, there is confidence that the gospel work will continue to expand.

Some younger workers—most of them second generation missionaries—have initiated new church planting ministries, independent of the Evangelical Church, in urban or suburban areas and have seen encouraging results. These ministries have been much on the pattern of the Bindura work developed by Lynn and Judy Everswick. These new church efforts are at Mvurwe, Rusape, Gateway-Harare, and missionaries involved are Paul and Mandy Jackson, Tom and Lois Jackson, Doug and Nancy Everswick, and Chris and Joyce (Everswick) Goppert.

As the mission's second century was opening there was ample evidence in these new churches that the Spirit of God was still at work bringing men and women to the foot of the cross. Chris Goppert's report on attendance at the Gateway-Harare church from mid-1990 to mid-1991 showed an increase from an average of 40 to an average of 106. Giving by the people was in proportion.[25]

Long-term Goal Reached

A goal often declared by missions—TEAM included—is to

leave viable churches which can function effectively without missionary presence and support. It has long been recognized that world conditions may prevent missions from continuing their work in certain countries—and, indeed, that has been the situation in China and some other countries. That such situations should arise from political pressures was anticipated, but to have doors closed because of relationships between the mission and churches it planted was neither anticipated nor welcomed. What is important is not the reason for the closed door, but whether there remains a live, functioning organism to continue the work of evangelism and nurturing the believers.

While the field council in Zimbabwe remains confident that there will be a good future for mission-church cooperation and partnership in the gospel work, there is satisfaction that the basic goal of church autonomy and responsibility already has been reached. There are live, functioning evangelical churches in Zimbabwe which are maintaining and expanding the gospel work.

CHAD, A DESERT BLOOMING

Identifying the Location

Having prided myself that I was quite familiar with worldwide geography through reading and travel, I was somewhat humbled in 1968 when I had to ask Sudan United Mission representative John Russell the exact location of the Republic of Chad. I had an idea that it was somewhere in or close to that broad geographical area in Africa referred to as "the Sudan." I thought of the whole Sahara desert area of northern Africa as one vast empty space of sand dunes, barren mountains, dry wadis, widely separated oases, and with only a scattering of nomads. I had flown the length of Africa several times and what I had seen from the air was extensive open spaces with little evidence of human habitation.

Initial Inquiry

Russell had come to our TEAM office in Wheaton to talk about SUMNA—the North American Branch of the Sudan United Mission (SUM). I knew, of course, that SUMNA was a member of the IFMA and much of what I had learned was through Russell's efforts in the IFMA meetings to have people understand that the Sudan *United* Mission (SUM) was not the larger and better known Sudan *Interior* Mission (SIM) then working in Ethiopia, Nigeria, and certain other north central African countries. He wryly referred to SUM as the Sudan *UNKNOWN* Mission.

As we talked, I found I had much to learn about Africa's geography and the SUM. SUM was a large mission with home bases in the United Kingdom, France, Switzerland, and Australia as well as in North America. The branch in North America had its principal office in Toronto, Canada, and smaller offices in Brooklyn, New York, and Chicago.

Why SUMNA was Seeking Merger

Russell informed me that the North American branch had recently taken official action to separate from the international body of the Sudan United Mission, the principal reason being that one or more of its other branches had links with the World Council of Churches. Missionaries on the field were similarly concerned, according to SUMNA's Chad field chairman Stewart Weber:

> For a number of years under the leadership of Mr. Victor Veary [general director of SUMNA] the North American branch had sought to bring into clearer focus the original aims and structure of the Sudan United Mission. There was growing concern over the misunderstanding caused by the wide divergence of the attitude of the various branches regarding the ecumenical movement. There were denominational branches whose churches were members of the World Council of Churches.[1]

The SUM North American Council was not complacent about this complicating relationship but diligently pursued the question with other branches.

> Mr. Veary finally prevailed upon the British Branch to call an international meeting in 1966. At that meeting he and Rev. Alex Stein suggested that the denominational branches withdraw from the SUM fellowship and permit SUM to continue as a non-denominational faith mission. However, no action was taken at that meeting to help us solve the problem that was confronting our branch in North America. From that time on our home council sought another solution.[2]

The SUMNA council was seeking the Lord's will about whether to form a new mission or to join an existing group in which it had confidence. Would TEAM want to be considered a prospect for merger? Russell's inquiry was only exploratory.

Extent of the Work

TEAM needed to know more about SUMNA. First of all, where

did it work? The Republic of Chad. And where was Chad? We learned that it was one of four countries carved from French Equatorial Africa in 1960 and granted independence. Chad was located in the center of the northern half of Africa, south of Libya, west of Sudan, north of the Central African Republic, and east of Niger, Nigeria, and Cameroon. Its population was about three and a half million, one half of whom were Muslim. About three percent were Protestant Christians and two percent Roman Catholics, while the other forty-five percent were animistic, divided into dozens of tribes.

Beginnings of the Work in Chad

SUMNA began work in Chad in 1926 when Mr. Herbert Wilkinson, first SUM appointee from Canada, and Mr. Harry Ferrant of the British SUM made their way by dugout canoe and on foot from Nigeria to southern Chad in search of the Laka tribe. Not able to locate the Laka, they pushed on to Koutou in the Ngambai tribe. Wilkinson remained there while Ferrant returned to Nigeria. Shortly afterward—in January 1927—Victor and Florence Veary joined Wilkinson. The Vearys came prepared to settle in and reach the Ngambai tribe which they found in Koutou and its neighboring larger town of Moundou.

Not long after the Vearys' arrival the governor-general of French Equatorial Africa came through Koutou. He was amazed to find white people deep in the bush "without protection" and told them that they "had come too soon to this wretched country. The people are still savages. Give us time to educate them. You may stay but at your own risk." They assured him that the Lord was their keeper and they would stay.

The Vearys' first task was to learn the Chadian Arabic trade language and the next, the Ngambai language, which they did by mingling with the people and asking questions. They had significant help in Ngambai from a young man named Boimbase who later became one of the first Christians.

A Base at Beladja

The Vearys' work base was changed to Beladja—also in the Ngambai tribe—and there in 1932 the first Ngambai baptism was held with eleven men and five women entering the sluggish waters of the Logone River. Response continued good, as Veary later recalled:

> Two years later eighty-eight baptisms were registered in the district, and from that time till this [1948], the stream of baptisms and conversions has flowed on, growing deeper and broader as it flowed.[3]

Other missionaries joined the Vearys, among them George and Frances McAlpine and Jack and Madge Brotherton. The missionaries very early committed responsibility to the new Christians by sending them out to witness, training them in short courses:

> From 1927 when the first missionaries arrived to 1942 when they started the first residential school, they were training by calling people for three months, sending them out to do the work, calling them back, training them, and sending them out again.[4]

Growth in First Twenty Years

Twenty years after the missionaries began their pioneer work the growth of the ministry was revealed by Veary's report on the Church of the Logone in 1947.[5]

Congregations with full church status—36
Congregations, mission churches—85
Baptized believers, men and women—2,727
Believers, not yet baptized—12,172

A group was counted as a church whose baptized membership numbered twenty or more, which had a full complement of elders and deacons, and whose offerings sufficed to support a local church—or in some cases showed a surplus to help others.

(It should be noted that there is a wide numerical spread between the reported number of believers and the number of those baptized. From the outset of the Chad work, the policy was to baptize only those who could read and were thus in a position to grow in the faith through the reading and study of the Word. Though the objective is commendable there is a question as to whether this restriction is supported by Scripture. At least, this policy provides strong motivation for promoting literacy in the churches.)

Training Made a Priority

Work in 1947 was carried on in the Ngambai, Goulei-Mbai, Nanjeri, Kabalai, and Ngambai-Gagal tribal areas.

During 1947 a new training program was undertaken. Ninety-six families were enrolled in an elders' course between December and February—three groups each for one month. This extra teaching was made possible by the help of Jeremie Njelarje and Zacharie Yangar with the men, and Verité Bainar with the women.

Other advances in the work were also reported in 1947:

> The Bebalem Bible School completed its eighth year and six couples were graduated. The classes helped us complete the translation of Romans, First Corinthians, Galatians, Ephesians, and First and Second Peter. This is a big step towards the completion of the New Testament. Other stories were also translated, notably a full story of Creation, the Fall, and the Flood. During the eight years of its ministry the Bebalem graduates have planted churches in most of the strategic centers of the district. From those churches, infant churches have been planted in many of the neighboring villages and leaders have given elementary instruction to the new converts.[6]

Formal Request for Merger

After the SUMNA council in Toronto formally approached TEAM on the possibility of merger, officers of both missions and several furloughed SUMNA missionaries met to exchange information. SUMNA decided to send board member Alex Stein and Canadian secretary Gerald Morehouse to the Chad field conference in December 1968 and invited TEAM to send its general director and one other representative.

Because French is one of the two official languages of Chad (the other is Arabic), and because some of the missionaries from other European missions participating in the conference spoke French but not English, I requested the chairman of our France field, Arthur Johnston, to accompany me. Not only would he be able to explain TEAM's policies in French but he could do so from the field point of view. His help was most valuable. In addition, he testified to the inspiration he received from contact with so flourishing a mission work as he found in Chad.

Johnston's presence was helpful for another reason. Normal contacts by Chad missionaries with overseas countries—apart from North America—are with France and Switzerland. New missionaries studying the French language would do so in France and be guided by the France field council. African church leaders taking advanced Bible training would probably do so in France. Certain financial arrangements such as remittance of support could be made more advantageously through France. It was therefore reasonable to have close ties between the Chad and France fields of the mission. Another reason became apparent later. Some missionaries' health suffered in Chad's tropical climate but they would not face similar difficulty in France's temperate climate. France gained several valuable missionaries because of this circumstance.

Chad Field Conference Adds Recommendation

The field conference was held in Koutou at the Palmview School for missionary children. Johnston and I were given ample opportunity to minister, explain TEAM's principles, and answer questions. In a business session from which we were excused, the subject of merger was brought to the floor for vote. Johnston and I were in a room some distance from the conference room—so far that nothing of the proceedings could be heard. After an hour or so, we did, however, hear the familiar strains of the doxology. I remarked to Johnston, "They are rejoicing, either because they escaped from being absorbed by TEAM, or because they agreed to join us."

After a few minutes we were called in and informed that the vote to join TEAM was unanimous, with no abstentions. Much of the groundwork of negotiation had already been completed so it did not take many months to finalize the legal formalities of joining the ministries of two Canadian corporations and two U. S. corporations. The merger became effective on April 25, 1969.

Seasoned Missionaries Available

The number of SUMNA missionaries was not large, but considering that about thirty workers with outstandingly fruitful ministries were made available to continue the work in Chad, TEAM felt amply rewarded for the work involved in the merger negotiations and the incorporating of SUMNA into TEAM. The Chad field chairman at the time was Stewart Weber. His wife, Marion, served as his secretary. The two of them handled a great load of correspondence with the TEAM office before all the details were in place and the field was operating in the pattern of other TEAM fields. In reality, we suggested that certain procedures remain as before until changes would come about naturally. Richard Winchell had to work through some of the adjustments several years later.

Extent of the Work in 1969

The fruitfulness of a field ministry is commonly measured by the professions of faith, the number receiving believer's baptism, the growth of the churches, and the number of active national pastors and evangelists. At the time of the merger in 1969 the Chad field reported the following:

Church congregations—421
Number receiving baptism the previous year —1,183
Baptized believers—17,117
Believers not yet baptized—25,032
Average Sunday morning attendance—61,786

These 421 congregations were ably led by national pastors, evangelists, and lay leaders.

The Broad Benefits of Self-Support

The ministries in Chad were self-supporting, with only a minimum of financial help from the mission. Here are some examples:
- When village believers meeting under a sheltering tree wanted a better place to meet they put together a small building of poles,

sun-dried brick, mud, and thatch. As attendance grew they needed a larger building. When the people had completed the main structure, the mission offered help with the one building material that required cash expenditure—the galvanized iron or aluminum roof. That was the extent of financial help provided.

- Vernacular Bible institutes operated in each tribal area. Students recommended by their local churches came prepared to support themselves by caring for their own garden plots, with some assistance from their churches.
- Scripture translation required the expertise of a missionary plus the cooperation of a committee of Chadians who knew their own language well and were also familiar with other languages which already had some Scriptures. The churches which spoke the language into which Scripture was being translated provided the support of the Chadian committee members.

These examples reveal the sense of responsibility the Chadian Christians had for the support and extension of their own work. Self-support, self-government, and self-propagation form a triple cord that is not easily broken. Since the three go together, it is not surprising that these self-supporting, self-governing churches were also diligent in evangelism.

Smaller Tribes Also Reached

By 1969 the tribes being reached and having functioning churches included Goulei, Lélé, Marba, and Mesme as well as Ngambai and Nanjeri. Victor Veary had completed the Ngambai New Testament. Jack Brotherton was progressing rapidly toward the completion of the Nanjeri Bible. Brotherton's Nanjeri students in the local Bible institute helped with the translation work.

Persecution by Chief Gabaroum

The Goulei people were not as numerous as either the Ngambai or the Nanjeri. In some respects they were harder to win. One factor was probably a stronger Muslim influence, but the greatest hindrance was the opposition of paramount chief Gabaroum.

Gabaroum ruled with a vicious heart and hand. He was physically big and politically powerful. No one dared question his judgment or decisions. He could be kind but he was brutal more often than charitable.... When missionaries planned to open a work at Ter among the Goulei about 1937 Gabaroum was the greatest obstacle.... Christianity...must be blocked, and block it he did. Anyone who accepted Jesus Christ would be punished—whipped and imprisoned. In spite of his persecution and frightening threats quite a few Gouleis heard the message of redemption and accepted Christ as their Savior. They paid the price, though, in hardships and banishments as Gabaroum's wrath descended on them.[7]

"A Valiant Missionary"

To speak of the Goulei tribe and the mission station Ter but not mention Ella Hildebrand would be a serious omission. Miss Hildebrand had retired before the merger so never was a part of TEAM. Even so, she demonstrated a warm interest in the Chad ministry carried on under TEAM, attending mission functions in Canada as she had opportunity.

Ella left Canada for France in October 1929 to study French and then traveled to Chad to begin work with Mr. and Mrs. Veary at Beladja. She became Veary's "right hand man" in overseeing the unmanned Ter station. She later volunteered to live at Ter to carry the work forward, very much alone. Chief Gabaroum's opposition and cruel persecution of believers did not discourage or intimidate her. In fact, she gained his respect and admiration even though she constantly opposed his pagan practices, especially in the initiation of girls, as was then the custom in the Goulei tribe.

When Mr. Veary learned of Ella's death, October 26, 1988, he wrote a glowing tribute to the life and service of "a valiant missionary":

> Ella not only had a willing heart to bear the burdens of others, but she had a stout heart to bear her own burdens, and when the going was rough, a believing heart to cast all her burdens on the Lord.[8]

A Wake for Pastor Yangar

On my first trip to Chad I was happy for the invitation to visit

Ter. The special occasion was to attend the wake for Zacharie Yangar, senior pastor of the Ter congregation, who had passed away just as our missionary conference was concluding in Koutou. The trip to Ter required a drive of more than two hours. Gerald Morehouse, Arthur Johnston, Bill Cameron, and I made up the visiting party.

A Christian wake in Africa is different, at least as far as I could understand. It seemed to me that people just came and sat silently in the dust of the yard. I did not see them talking with each other or going to the widow with condolences. Apparently their presence was eloquent enough.

Meeting Pastor Noël Tissa

When we were free to move around I had opportunity to speak with some of the people. Here is an excerpt of my report to our mission magazine:

> Many impressions remain. One such is a conversation with Pastor Noël Tissa, the first convert of the Goulei tribe, and three of his early converts. He related how a missionary came telling them about Christ and how he received Him as Savior. He then won these three friends. For years they stood alone in the face of threats, beatings, and other forms of bitter persecution.
>
> "How did you hold out?" I asked.
>
> "I knew the Lord had changed my heart," Tissa answered. "I couldn't disappoint Him. I also knew these friends had become Christians because I won them. I couldn't desert them."
>
> The three friends volunteered, "We held firm because Tissa was taking so much punishment and staying true. We couldn't let him down. The Lord used us to strengthen each other."
>
> Thirty-six years have passed and these four have been stalwarts for Christ ever since.[9]

Simultaneous Interpretation

A service was held in the Ter church with Bill Cameron as main speaker. Since he and his wife, Jean, had worked among the Goulei, he was fluent in that language as well as Ngambai. As Cameron spoke, he held a New Testament in his hand and appeared

694

to be reading from it. I learned that after the service some of the Goulei people came to him wondering how it was that he had the New Testament in their language but had not let them know it was available. Cameron had to show them the New Testament he was holding—the Ngambai version. Being fluent in both languages, he could look at the Ngambai words and interpret directly into Goulei.

Field-wide Church Organization Formed

The churches organized the *Eglise Evangélique au Tchad* (EET)—the Evangelical Church of Chad—which was registered with the government as an autonomous organization. Jeremie Njelarje was chosen president. Because of the size and tribal diversity of the membership, the EET recognized certain "annèxes" or districts, which bore local responsibility for their churches. I was impressed by the spirit of unity in spite of tribal and language distinctions. Many of the people were fluent in several tribal languages in addition to the official French and Arabic.

The Strength of the Churches

After my second trip to Chad in early 1970 I wrote to supporters of the Chad work commenting on the strength of the churches:

> The growth of the churches has been particularly outstanding so that the believers are now meeting in 421 congregations under the leadership of their own pastors, evangelists, and lay leaders. Churches are responsible for Bible schools in vernacular languages and participate in many other areas of the work.[10]

Unfinished Work in the Churches

There sometimes is a tendency to be satisfied with the progress made and not see what still should be done. In 1970 the Chad missionaries were very conscious of much unfinished work.

> There is still much work for missionaries to do. One of the outstanding challenges before them at the present time is a three-fold program which begins with a literacy campaign to insure that as many of the believers as possible will be able to read the Scriptures and other Christian material for themselves. The second aspect of the program is an intensive evangelistic

campaign for Chad in which both church leaders and missionaries will bear heavy responsibility. The third aspect will be an intensive instruction campaign so that the new and present believers will be more thoroughly grounded in the Scriptures and thus given the possibility of steady growth and increased usefulness.[11]

Church leaders and missionaries were understandably concerned about the large number of genuine believers who had not been baptized and taken their places as church members. Because ability to read was required as evidence of their intent to grow in understanding the Christian life, the key was instruction in literacy. Literacy training is not a simple matter. It is much more than recognizing written symbols and pronouncing them correctly. It is reading linked with understanding. To read with understanding requires practice with a wide variety of material that covers much of the tribal vocabulary. Although the people may have had a large spoken vocabulary, there was comparatively little in writing—at least in the smaller tribes—and thus not much on which to practice reading.

To meet this need, the missionaries—with the encouragement of the churches—initiated a two-pronged approach. They set up a print shop in Koutou and began to print material for evangelism and spiritual growth. They initiated a literacy campaign as a second step. Doreen Barrie was given the responsibility of training literacy teachers, who would in turn train other literacy workers in their local districts. In this way thousands were taught to read simple material. The literacy problem was also partially overcome by the increase in primary education in the French official language. Many of the young people were learning to read and, once literate in French, could make the adjustment to the tribal orthography. Yet even so, the leaders were concerned about the many believers who were not sufficiently literate to study God's Word for themselves.

Saturation Evangelism
Missionaries in Chad were impressed by the effectiveness of the

New Life for All Campaign developed by SIM missionaries in Nigeria and wanted to adapt it for use in Chad. They were careful to avoid diluting of the gospel message by having non-evangelicals take part, as reportedly had been the case in similar campaigns elsewhere.

Jack Brotherton was appointed to coordinate the campaign, which they called Saturation Evangelism. The first step was to explain the program to leaders of the EET. They approved enthusiastically. The next step was to prepare instruction material in several languages which could be used to train participants.

Daily Prayer Cells

The program started with the organizing of small daily village prayer cells of about ten believers each. The 4,000 daily prayer cells which functioned throughout the campaign were instrumental in much of the effective evangelism that took place. Some people came to the Lord simply through the testimony of a prayer cell in action.

> Picture a functioning prayer cell of about ten people seated under a tree. They are so intent in speaking to God that they are not aware of numbers of unbelievers who have crept up quietly, sitting just a couple of yards behind them, and listening in amazed silence to their names being pronounced before God. Something or Someone had drawn them to that circle. In one village, the result was thirty of these people making profession of faith in Jesus Christ.[12]

One man who had never set his foot inside the church at Beladja came to the evangelist and said, "I want to give my heart." Immediately he asked that a prayer cell be established at his house.[13]

By the autumn of 1972 there had been a reported 6,366 new converts and 1,624 backsliding Christians restored to faith and fellowship.[14]

Less than a year later, Stewart Weber wrote that reports from 214 villages throughout four language areas recorded 13,970 converts in a period of ten months. Though reliable statistics are not easy to secure in a primitive society, it is abundantly clear that God was doing a great work in the hearts of thousands of Chadians. Large congregations experienced a 25 percent increase in attendance. Some smaller groups doubled in size. The New Life for All program indeed had a multiplying effect on soul-winning and church growth as new believers became witnesses and brought family and friends to Christ.

Lake Chad Evangelism

Lake Chad lies between Chad and Nigeria and is extraordinary for several reasons. According to *Colliers Encyclopedia,* "It is one of the few shallow lakes whose waters remain fresh without the circulation of an outlet." Several rivers flow into it—including the Chari from Chad and its main tributary, the Logone. It is assumed that the water is absorbed into the sands of the Sahara Desert with the fresh-water inflow being enough to forestall salinity.[15]

Another characteristic of Lake Chad is the constant change in its size and shape. *Colliers Encyclopedia* gives the area as 7,000 square miles and the average depth five feet. (*World Almanac* of 1982 says 6,300 square miles and maximum depth 24 feet. Other sources give the area as being as much as 15,000 square miles.) In the 1980s the drought in that region shrank it to a fraction of its usual size and so shallow that much of the earlier boat traffic became impossible.

Islands that Float

The floating islands on Lake Chad, a characteristic when the water is high, attract great interest. Large clumps of intertwined reeds along the bank, some many acres in size, become detached and float away from the shore. As the reeds continue to grow and as wind-blown silt accumulates, these clumps grow into islands, some quite extensive. Many fishermen live on floating islands and use them as bases for fishing and preserving their catch. I recall a visit to such a floating island. At first glance, the island seemed no different than any other but I soon discovered I had to be alert lest

I step on a weak spot that would let me down to a drenching or possibly a watery grave beneath the island. These floating islands occasionally ground on sandbars, become fixed in position, and grow into regular islands.

In its desert setting, the lake became a center of attraction with the result that an estimated two hundred thousand people lived on its shores and islands. Two of the tribes were the Boudouma and the Kanembou. These people were Islamized Africans who, though counting themselves Muslims, were not as steeped in Islamic doctrine and tradition as were Arabs. Even so, they were far more resistant than the people of the southern tribes.

Dr. David Carling of the British branch of the Sudan United Mission in Nigeria believed that the SUM had a responsibility to bring the gospel to these people. His earlier experience convinced him that medical help would be an effective tool to gain their interest. He accordingly had a five-ton, thirty-one-foot diesel launch built to serve as a floating dispensary and base for minor surgery. He named the launch *Albishir* (Good News). Some ten years later, a larger launch, the seventeen-ton, forty-one-foot *Al-barka* (Blessing), joined *Albishir*.

Medical Mission Outreach Proposed

Because Lake Chad was as much in Chad as in Nigeria, Carling believed that the SUM North American branch and the EET should share in the ministry. Two of his trained male nurse-evangelists were from the EET area in Chad—Paul Kagdombai and Joel Bealoum.

When he presented this opportunity to the missionaries in Chad they, in turn, challenged the church. Prepared by the Spirit of God, Church president Jeremie led the churches in responding to the call. To give focus to the mission outreach, Jeremie recommended that the churches form a mission society. This was done in 1967 and nurses Paul and Joel were appointed as medical missionaries. Eventually, eighteen couples were commissioned by the Chad church for Lake Chad missionary service. The local churches provided their support, while the mission promised to cover the cost of necessary transportation by Missionary Aviation Fellowship to reach Lake Chad and for major moves during their service.

Ben Strohschein, who was located at Fort Lamy as a counsellor to the seven city churches, was asked to work with the Lake Chad project. He and Freda were already extremely busy in the church ministry and in serving the interests of missionaries on loan to TEAM from a number of European missions. For a period of time he also served as field chairman. His work with the Lake Chad project involved not only purchasing supplies and arranging the transport of missionaries and materials, but also encouraging and counseling the African missionaries.

Help from European Missionaries

While Mr. Veary was still active he was concerned about many personnel needs in Chad. One means of meeting this need was to put the challenge before French-speaking young people in Europe. Young men faced with compulsory military service in France could be placed with a recognized mission organization for a set term of service overseas instead. Through this arrangement a number of workers came to Chad, serving mostly in the capital, Fort Lamy (N'Djamena), where there were several types of ministry—a school at the high school/junior college level, Muslim evangelism, and a French-language church for people from the various tribes. These missionaries were from SUM branches in France and Switzerland and from EMEK, a Mennonite mission. Though their terms were quite short their service requirements were similar to those who came through regular TEAM channels.

On my visits to Chad I did not have frequent contact with these European workers but I learned that their ministry in the French language was much appreciated. Many of them spoke no English and this was one reason that the annual field conferences were held in French. There was one Swiss missionary—Jacques Baumann— who worked with the French-speaking "Foyer" church in the capital. Baumann could understand English though he could not speak it. I found that he was fluent in German, which I could understand to a fair degree but could not speak. So our fellowship as we met at various times would have sounded unusual, being quite successfully carried on in German and English with no interpreter.

Essential Help for the Medical Work

Another phase of the ministry which was greatly helped by European missionaries was the medical work. SUM missionaries had done a great deal of medical work in the various tribes and had established a hospital at Bebalem with Dr. Gordon Carter in charge. When Dr. Carter was not able to return to the field after his first furlough (which was prior to the TEAM-SUM merger), outpatient and maternity services were provided by missionary nurses with the help of Chadian nurses and paramedics, who had been trained both by Dr. Carter and by Dr. David Seymour at the Baptist (Mid-Mission) hospital at Koumra. For three or four years the need of a doctor for the Bebalem hospital was a constant prayer request. The Lord answered in a most satisfactory way.

There was in France a group of doctors and other medical personnel associated together in *l'Union Evangélique Médicale et Para-Médicale* (UEMP) who were greatly interested in medical missions, particularly in French-speaking Africa. Gerald Morehouse, Eastern Canada Secretary and former missionary to Chad, was visiting Chad in early 1972 when the possibility of a relationship to UEMP came up. He and field chairman Bill Cameron arranged to meet with UEMP leaders in France to discuss joining hands in the Chad medical ministry. Through their efforts and those of Chad missionary Ben Strohschein, a mutually satisfactory cooperation agreement was worked out which has guided and safeguarded the relationship for two decades.

Dr. and Mrs. Bernard Geffe were the first to serve at the Bebalem hospital under this arrangement. Subsequent medical staff needs have been largely met by others who came under the auspices and support of these European doctors and nurses, who formed a new organization called *Médicament Pour Afrique (MEDAF)*.

Expansion of the Bebalem Hospital

The medical work has expanded greatly to meet local needs, making the Bebalem hospital the largest such institution in TEAM and the largest private hospital in Chad. It includes an extensive outpatient program carried on at the hospital and at sixteen district dispensaries. One interesting feature is the official involvement of the Chadian church. Those who are given medical training for work in the dispensaries must also have Bible training and be under church sponsorship. This assures that the medical work has an adequate spiritual component through the witness of the dispensary workers.

Expansion of the hospital facilities was made possible by various grants: from the Canadian International Development Administration through the representation of Gerald Morehouse; from the Swedish government through the help of the Swedish Alliance Mission, which sponsored the service of Margareta Jönsson at the hospital; and from the French government.

When general director Winchell returned from visiting Chad in January 1990 he reported that the hospital now had 250 beds and that 40,000 patients a year were ministered to in the hospital and dispensaries. Because family members accompany patients to care for their meals, it was estimated that at any one time a thousand people come onto the hospital property.

Another item of special interest was that two outstanding Chadian doctors were on the staff—Doctors Manassé and Toralta. Both were trained in Russia, where they faced a severe test of their faith but came through victoriously. Dr. Toralta was led to Christ in Moscow by Dr. Manassé, and together they share a particular concern for the spiritual ministry of the hospital.

Reaching the Youth

Several of the missionaries saw growing possibilities for reaching the young people of the tribes. Now that children were taught in French-language schools, it was possible to move forward in coordinated programs for girls and boys. Beulah Carpenter initiated and guided a girls' ministry under the name *Lumieres*, patterned after Pioneer Girls in the U.S. Bert Baskin, who left Chad before the merger, and Nelson Bezanson organized the boys' work with the name *Flambeaux*, following the pattern of Christian Service Brigade.

The purpose of these ministries was to win boys and girls to Christ, teach them the Word of God, and train them to take responsibility as capable leaders or faithful followers.

McAlpines Return for Special Ministry

In January 1973 pioneer missionaries George and Frances McAlpine accepted an invitation to return to Chad to teach Bible in the churches. The McAlpines had come home from Chad because of serious health needs and remained for twenty-two years in mission representation and pastorates. McAlpine prepared a series of mimeographed lessons which would be of long-term value to church leaders and, in spite of a long absence from the field, was still able to communicate Bible truth in the Ngambai language. Their ministry continued for two years.

Independence and a President

When Chad gained its independence from France in August 1960, it became a republic with François Tombalbaye as president. He presided over a one-party system with all its possibilities for misrule. Tombalbaye had been under Christian influence in the Sarh region of the country where Baptist Mid-Missions worked. It was reported that he had been a teacher in a Christian school and was reasonably well informed about Christian doctrine and practice. It was also reported that he had been disciplined by a local Baptist church. If so, this may, in part, explain his later vindictiveness toward Christians.

Turning the Clock Back

With his early Christian influence, Tombalbaye was—for a

while—assumed to be sympathetic to Christians and the work of missions. However, they received a rude awakening. With but little advance warning, Christians were dealt a devastating blow in a presidential action which turned the clock back to pagan times, as Victor Veary explained:

> On the 27th of August 1973, with flaming fanfare and brilliant oratory in the French language, le MOUVEMENT NATIONAL pour la REVOLUTION CULTURELLE et SOCIALE—[MNRCS] was launched in N'Djamena, capital city of the Chad Republic.... All the long speeches by members of the Chad government left no doubt as to who started the "revolution." The one formerly referred to with deference as Monsieur le Président François Tombalbaye, was now crowned with glory: Le Grand Compatriote N'Garta Tombalbaye, Founder and General Secretary.[16]

Even a person with little or no knowledge of French can understand that what was being introduced was a national movement of cultural and social revolution:

> This movement whose central interest is the CHADIAN MAN, among all its objectives proposes: to reconcile all Chadians with themselves...revive the true value of our national culture...have recourse to our roots for help and protection...discover our real and profound identity...continue our efforts to consolidate our NATIONAL UNITY.[17]

Initiation Practices Revived

Buried in the flowery language was a not-so-subtle call to return to the pagan tribal initiation practices—called Yondo or Lao—which, in some tribes, the Ngambai included, had not been required for thirty years. Now, initiation was required of all men and adolescent boys. Included was a call to a return to spirit communication and ancestor worship.

Foreign Names Outlawed

One requirement of the movement was that all who had foreign or Christian names were to change back to Chadian names. To aid in enforcing this rule, the post office in some areas refused to deliver letters addressed to Chadians with Christian names. Cities and towns with foreign names must change them. The capital, Fort Lamy, was renamed N'Djamena.

Initiations Begin in Southeast

It was in November 1973 that the long-awaited signal came for the initiations to begin. These were to start in the southeast part of the country in the Sara clan known as *Majingai*. This was Tombalbaye's birthplace where, as a youth, he had been initiated according to the decrees of his ancestors. This was also the area where Baptist Mid-Missions worked and had flourishing churches. The Baptist church leaders were of the same clan as Tombalbaye. Knowing the secrets of the initiation to be non-Christian or anti-Christian, they refused to obey the presidential decree.

That same November three missionary couples of Baptist Mid-Missions were arrested and driven 300 miles in an open truck under a scorching sun to the capital and deported from the country. One week later three other couples and six single ladies were expelled. The doctor at the Baptist hospital and four nurses were allowed to remain to do medical work.[18]

Persecution of Pastors

General director Winchell was on a tour to Chad while some of these problems were developing. His perceptive reports kept the headquarters informed and made it possible to enlist much prayer for the steadfastness and safety of the Chadian Christians and for wisdom for missionaries faced with many uncertainties. Winchell made clear the seriousness of the threat to believers in the Sarh region where initiation had started and the anticipation that those in the Ngambai and Goulei tribes would face the same persecution:

> There are many stories of persecution and death in the Sarh region. What takes place is that a boy, or young man, goes off [with the initiators] to the initiation camp and becomes their boy. He comes back beaten into submission with scars on his face. He has been completely taught the morés and traditions of the tribe. He learns a new language which only the men speak. When they return they are supposed to have forgotten everything and everyone. They are now men and must be treated so by all the

women. They do not remember people, but have gone through a completely new birth.[19]

What happened to the pastors who refused to bow to the president's order? Though much is not known, one thing is sure: in resisting the presidential decree, the church leaders and their followers would suffer the grisly penalties for disobedience decreed by their *Majingai* ancestors. Thirteen senior pastors were arrested and never came back. Some time later their clothes were returned in bundles to their wives. We now know that the pastors joined the illustrious company of heroes of the faith who became martyrs.

Persecution Pattern Spreading

Having started the initiations in the southeast, the government began making the same requirement of tribes farther west. The Goulei tribe was the farthest east in the TEAM work and it was from there that the first reports of difficulty came. Winchell wrote concerning sufferings of Christians in the Goulei tribe:

> Nelson Bezanson and I had a talk with pastor Andre Mbogg-dengar from the Goulei area on Sunday, November 25, [1973]. He says that two evangelists and twelve of the Christians are in prison in his area. It is understood that [the government] intends to exile these Christians out into the desert. The man who is pushing this matter is the government minister Djidengar, the son of the late chief Gabaroum who gave Christians such a hard time over many years.[20]

Impact on Evangelical Church Leaders

Seeing the approaching storm threatening to engulf the Christians in the tribes where TEAM worked, the missionaries working most closely with them naturally expressed their concern. The church leaders, who felt they understood the implications of the government's demands, asked the missionaries to leave any consultation with the government to them. Having seen that the counsel given to the Baptist church leaders resulted in the missionaries' expulsion and the arrest of the leaders, they were understandably cautious about a repeat of that tragic experience.

Christians who had gone through initiation before conversion understood full well the idolatry and occult practices involved. They also recognized that some of the ritual amounted to a denial of their faith and a renunciation of Christ.

Withstanding the Pressures

How did the believers as a whole withstand the pressures and temptations, most not being mature in the faith and grounded in the Word? There was no consistent pattern. Many examples were given of men who accepted persecution and suffering rather than participate in a pagan exercise. How good it would be if we could say that all believers steadfastly resisted temptations to compromise; that no one was overcome by fear or yielded to government pressures; and that none went through the pagan initiation. But as was true of the Lord's disciples at the time of the crucifixion, there were some who were too weak to remain steadfast when threatened with loss of livelihood, physical suffering, or possible death.

Jack Brotherton, a missionary who was close to the situation in both the Ngambai and Nanjere tribes, reported:

> The initiation rites, set aside over thirty years ago as a direct result of the gospel of Jesus Christ, have been reinstated in a search to establish a true African identity. The initiation ceremonies include rites of separation and atonement, penitence, lacerations, and reintroduction to daily living. This reintroduction is necessary because the initiated person has died to the old life to be resurrected to a new life. He must be reintegrated into society, but this time with the stature of a perfect man—a new man. Initiation is the "way which leads to God," says the leader of the Chadian people. This comes into direct conflict with the Word of God and Christian conscience. While the church is united against this practice, some Christians have not taken a public stand against it due to fear and intimidation.[21]

To the great disappointment of church leaders and missionaries, the president of the church remained silent. The original decision of the church leaders was a courageous one—that they would stay true to the Lord even at the cost of their lives. Jack Brotherton sorrowfully reported a weakening of the stand:

> Since our church leaders met here at Bebalem and declared that

they would hold to their original decision to stand firm, some changes have taken place. Unfortunately, there is not a unified stand. Pastor Njelarje has deeply disappointed us and given no leadership whatever. In fact he allowed two of his own to go to initiation and said nothing when other relatives went. He even remained silent when elders of the Beladja church went.[22]

A Courageous Voice

One who did not remain silent was a young Christian government employee, Elie Ndoubayidi, who bravely circulated a letter addressed to pastors, evangelists, and other church leaders in which he gave scriptural grounds for refusing to go through initiation. It was, indeed, a brave act on his part because he made himself doubly vulnerable; first, by his own refusal to go through the pagan rites, and second, in his position as a government employee whose opposition could be considered treasonable.

I visited Chad in February 1975, in part to be better informed and in part to encourage missionaries who entered so emotionally into the victories and defeats of the believers. My report at the time reveals some of the uncertainty:

> In spite of many inquiries, I could not get a complete picture of what has actually happened in the churches. I learned of many who had suffered under great pressure. I learned of others whose courageous stand up to this point made it possible for them to avoid the demands of the government. Some others had apparently weakened under pressures too great for most of us to imagine.[23]

Several missionaries took early furlough at that time, believing that their views on initiation might endanger some believers. Most felt, however, that they should remain to be of help in any way possible. They certainly believed they would be needed once the storm had blown over.

A Timely Intervention

As the difficult year 1974 ended and the potentially more difficult 1975 lay ahead it was not easy to detect any weakening of the storm of persecution. Just when the situation seemed darkest the Sovereign Lord intervened in a remarkable way:

Early Sunday morning, April 13 [1975], the military, under the leadership of General Odingar, launched an attack on the security forces camp and the presidential palace in N'Djamena. In a few short hours it was all over. Having refused to surrender, President Tombalbaye lay dead in the shambles of his palace.... General Odingar, acting commander of the armed forces, went on Radio Chad later the same morning and announced, "Our armed forces have exercised their responsibilities before God and the nation." General Odingar is a professing Christian and frequently attends one of our churches. It is reported that several months ago pressure was put on him by President Tombalbaye to go through initiation but he refused on the basis of Christian convictions.[24]

That this *coup d'état* was indeed a providential act of the Lord—particularly as to timing—was confirmed by information revealed later:

It was soon learned that prior to the coup another widespread persecution was being secretly planned by the president and his government. The very day of the coup a large number of Christians were to be forcibly taken to initiation on the pretext of taking them to the cotton fields. Churches were to be closed. Missionaries were to be expelled. It is reported that by the end of May every Christian was to have been initiated or put to death.[25]

What About Those Defeated?

This sudden delivery from danger naturally brought rejoicing and relief to the Christians but it also left church leaders with a dilemma. Many of the sheep had been wounded and needed to be healed and restored, but to maintain the biblical standard of discipline, action must be taken about those who willingly went through the pagan initiation or encouraged and aided others to go. Soon after the April 13 coup, the general assembly of the church met in N'Djamena. It is interesting to note that the Chadian Christians had the maturity to deal with this situation and did not call on the missionaries to impose a course of action. They promptly set up a committee of six laymen plus some pastors "to deal with discipline of Christian leaders in Chad whose conduct was reprehensible."[26]

This committee took courageous action and prepared a strong

letter addressed to the whole church but more particularly for the attention of pastors and evangelists who failed to keep faith:

> You pastors and evangelists who were servants of the Lord: We fellow servants of yours write this letter to remind you of the true way of God so that you may see it clearly and walk in it. From the beginning of the time when heartache and heartbreak surprised the Chad Church, making it halt and lame, we have never ceased to pray for you. God heard our prayers and has answered us and we thank Him. We ask you, who were followers of Jesus but returned to the beggarly rudiments of your forefathers' ways and were initiated according to the idolatrous rites of *Lao,* to lay down your office for a season.

> You pastors and evangelists who told men to go and perform those idolatrous rites: We write to you also. You ordered men and boys who were Christians to go, saying that it was by order of the authorities and promised them that they could return to their places in the church.... You are the ones who threw fire on the church that could have destroyed it and put shame on God. You sought the glory that comes from man and today God refuses to honor you. Therefore, leave your office in the church, for as we see it now, if a greater trial comes to our church you would do it even greater harm. Repent of your sins and let us see the intent of your hearts. God called you to be shepherds of His sheep to keep them from all evil, but you deceived them and led them deep into sin. We know your names and could call you, but we leave it to you, whoever you may be, to arise and obey your God. Do not boast of being God's shepherds for He no longer sees you as such.[27]

The letter referred to ten Scriptures which were applicable to the situation and the responsibilities of shepherds of the flock.

Pastor Jeremie's Confession

Pastor Jeremie prepared a full letter to the council of the church "to explain the things that have affected me." In it he dealt with two matters in which he had been misunderstood and misquoted. One was the letter circulated by Elie Ndoubayidi and the other was the letter from the "Committee of Six," both of which directly condemned the initiation rites as idolatrous. Jeremie stated that he had been falsely accused of criticizing the letters and the writers. Not so, he countered, and emphasized that he had strongly commended those letters to the attention of the church and had not criticized the writers. Why, then, had he not spoken out or written letters to give guidance to the church?

Jeremie confessed three fears that affected his actions:

(1) When I told the missionaries to keep their mouths closed, it was because I was afraid they would be sent out of Chad like criminals, as were the missionaries of Sahr.

(2) I called pastors and evangelists and told them that if they had not been initiated they should not go of their own free will, but if they were forced they should not resist lest they be murdered.

(3) My own three children came to me from Moundou and N'Djamena and I failed to advise them not to go to the camp because I was afraid that if they refused they would be murdered.[28]

An Act of True Humility and Courage

When Jeremie had opportunity to speak to the general assembly of the church in February 1976 he showed true humility and personal courage. Charles McCordic recorded the memorable scene where it was evident that the Spirit of God was moving in the hearts of all:

After the devotional message on the second day, president Jeremie Njelarje rose from his seat and very humbly and sincerely began to confess his failure during the church's tribulation, and we could see that this was costing him dearly. When he finished speaking he took from his pocket the seal of the church president and laid it on the table, saying, "I can no longer lead you."

There were missionaries present who in thirty years had never seen a Chadian man weep. Yet when the delegates saw this great man of God humbling himself before them in evident obedience to the Holy Spirit, that same Spirit began to work in their hearts and ours. All of us, missionaries and Chadians alike, began to weep. Many were sobbing unashamedly with shoulders shaking. Jeremie had asked pastor Thomas Kaye to pray, and he began to pray but kept breaking down, "We are all guilty. We were all afraid," he repeated over and over.

Pastor Jeremie, in those few minutes, had preached the greatest sermon of his life. Then he left the hall and went home to his village. A missionary who visited him there soon after found him busy in the work of the local church, and gloriously happy.

We have learned a great lesson through these experiences. Had we yielded to the impulse to speak out we would never have known what blessing God wanted to bring upon the church in His own time and way.

So now we know the direction the church is going. It is on the road to repentance and renewal. Already it is stronger than ever before. Past illusions are gone, the church knows its own weaknesses, and the new leaders believe firmly that God will help them to overcome them.[29]

Smoking Flax Not Quenched

As Jack Brotherton reviewed what had taken place during the difficult years of persecution he noted that the troubles had effectively interrupted the great harvest that was taking place in the Saturation Evangelism program:

By the spring of 1974 our program of Saturation Evangelism in the church of Chad, with its excitement, its challenge, and its effectiveness, had been stalled by the blanket of fear that swept over the country.... The prayer cells, and there were some 4,000 of them representing 40,000 Christians praying daily for souls, the parades through the cities and villages, the special evangelistic meetings in local churches, and the house-to-house witness which [all together] produced some 20,000 professions of faith, gradually petered out under the pressures of a decree that said, "Conform or take the consequences."[30]

Brotherton tried to evaluate the long-term effect of the persecution:

The church was shaken to its very foundations. Many learned through this experience what true loyalty to Christ involves. When the cloud lifted, and the sun began to shine again, there was much soul-searching. For those who compromised through fear, the way back was humbling and painful. Those who had been faithful had to learn how to forgive the weak in love. It took time—a long time—but the healing touch of God's Spirit was felt and the rebuilding began.[31]

In the Steps of Simon Peter

In this difficult situation there is some comfort in the record of the Apostle Peter whose fears kept him from standing by his Lord during His trial and crucifixion and who even denied the One to whom he had protested his undying faithfulness. How encouraging to read Peter's later history and his outstanding apostolic ministry.

Abel Ndjerareou's Evaluation

A young potential leader—Abel Ndjerareou—was absent from Chad during the initiations because he had been sent overseas by the church for advanced theological studies. He first studied at the evangelical seminary in Vaux, France. He followed that with studies in North America to improve his English, attending Trinity Evangelical Divinity School in Illinois and finally Dallas Theological Seminary where he earned his doctorate. He was in Chad briefly during the time of initiations and so had opportunity to observe their impact on the churches. The church council later appointed him to serve as administrator of the widespread church organization with over 700 churches in seven or eight tribal areas.

When Ndjerareou was in Wheaton in 1987 I had opportunity to speak with him at length about the work in Chad. I asked him in particular about the effect on the church of the cultural revolution. Did it weaken the churches or make them stronger? Here was his answer:

> I think it has rather strengthened the church. When the cultural revolution happened it really hurt so many people and families. But on the other hand, it was something which really made the church stronger because for the first time we had to choose the Lord or something else. There were so many people who really stood up for Jesus Christ. It has strengthened the church. Even those who fell—when they came back to the Lord, they came back stronger.[32]

A New President for the Church

Thomas Kayé was named the second president of the church organization in 1976 to succeed Jeremie Njelarje. Kayé was from the Kabalai tribe but was associated more with the Nanjere where he pastored the Bere church and taught at the vernacular Bible institute. He had also served in the Lake Chad mission work of the church. About 1970 he and another promising church leader, Elie Reoukilla, had been sent overseas for further training by the church council. Because they were fluent in French they had enrolled at the Nogent Bible Institute in Paris. This was an enriching experience, not only because of a higher level of schooling than they had been able to obtain in Chad, but also because of their opportunity to fellowship in the TEAM-related churches in France. The fellowship advantage was reciprocal because the French Christians could learn much from Chadians about zeal in evangelism and assuming responsibility in the church.

Two strong vice presidents were also selected: Elie Reoukilla and Moise Mbaitellel, pastor of the large Bebalem church.

Scripture Translation

Though French and Arabic were official languages, the language of the heart for the people was their own tribal tongue. For many years the Ngambai and Nanjere churches had the New Testament, but not the Old. Jack Brotherton worked on the Nanjere Old Testament, and Thomas Kayé headed the translation team. Doreen Barrie was given responsibility for the Ngambai Old Testament with the assistance of a committee chosen and supported by the Ngambai churches. Elie Reoukilla headed the Ngambai translators.

Translation work was done on the Lélé and Zimé Testaments by Pamela Simons and Ruth Hufnagel.

Koutou Printing and Publishing Work

As the level of literacy in the church slowly grew, the mission sought to make Christian literature available to the believers in their own tribal languages—either by translating existing material or by writing original material. With seven or eight tribal languages plus Arabic and French, providing an adequate range of literature in all languages would have been an involved undertaking. Since some tribes had only a smaller number of believers, the problem was reduced to trying to meet the needs of the Ngambai, Nanjere,

Goulei, Lélé, Marba, and Arabic language groups—still a formidable undertaking for a printshop and distribution center.

A number of missionaries were active in the printing work in Koutou, among them Sam Clark, David Whitfield, Carl Hodges, Jack Snyder, Jurg Fisch of the SUM Swiss Branch, and several other European workers. Missionaries working in the various languages were called on to provide lesson material for use in vernacular Bible institutes and Sunday schools. Stewart Weber did much work on such material even after retirement from the field.

Literature Distribution

It is one thing to write and print suitable material, but another to distribute it to those who should read it. An effort was made to set up bookstores but that was not found to be successful. During the saturation evangelism campaigns in the 1970s and '80s, evangelistic literature was produced and distributed in an organized way as part of the campaign.

Of particular interest was the development of the Literature Distribution Center in Moundou. Before the temporary evacuation of missionaries in 1979 due to civil war dangers, most literature distribution had been financed and managed by TEAM. This task was then transferred to the administration of the Evangelical Church. The Center sells literature to as many as twenty-two regional centers.

The Church Requests Agricultural Help

As early as 1969, TEAM received a request from the Chad church for the assistance of a missionary qualified in agricultural science. Chad remains one of the poorest countries in the world. Being short of natural resources and lacking industry, its economy is dependent almost entirely on the soil.

Because cotton, the principal cash crop, is Chad's main source of foreign exchange, its growth, processing, and sale are strictly controlled. It does not provide significant income for the families, so the people must grow grain for their own needs and for additional cash. The farmer must contend with climate, pests, and wild animals. Once the grain is harvested—be it rice, sorghum, or other cereal crop—storage is a problem where termites, rats, and other vermin abound. One response to these difficult circumstances is to sell the grain as soon as possible before it has been ruined. With much grain being offered for sale, the price is low. Later when grain is needed for food and for seed, it is available only at a high price.

Qualified Help Made Available

One advantage of a multi-field mission such as TEAM is that when a door closes in one country there can be open doors elsewhere. In Korea, the mission planned to develop the agricultural ministry of Kwandong College but the circumstances related in chapter 31 made it necessary to withdraw from that work. Ross and Mary (Inky) Beach had studied the Korean language and were active in the college's agricultural program when they were told that the school would be turned over to other management. They were immediately presented with the opportunity in Chad, for which they were fully qualified.

After having spent two years studying the Korean language it could have been discouraging to face several more years of studying French and Nanjere, but sensing the Lord's leading through this open door, they willingly accepted the mission's assignment.

Chad Christian Cooperative

As soon as possible the Beaches, with the full approval and cooperation of the Evangelical Church, initiated a project to help the people:

> In 1975 the Beaches launched a Christian Cooperative on a trial basis in the Bere area where they were located. The basic goal of the program was to help the farmer market his grain at a greater profit. This was to be done by purchasing the grain immediately after harvest and then storing it for resale when the prices are higher. At the purchase time each farmer's grain is individually weighed and marked and he is given the current market price. When the grain is resold, any profit realized is paid

to the farmer in direct proportion to the quantity of grain he sold to the cooperative.[33]

The church leaders had been informed that the program depended on North American Christians giving to provide the capital for the project. When pastor Thomas Kayé saw what came in he was overwhelmed and exclaimed, "We can hardly believe that our Christian brethren in America care that much about us and our daily needs. We thank God for His answer to our prayers."[34]

Famine in Africa

Chad was seriously affected by the widespread drought across sub-Saharan Africa in the 1980s. Though not as severe as in some other countries, famine in Chad caused great suffering. Farmers had even been forced to use their seed grain to save lives of family members. Missionaries and the church were greatly concerned and sought to provide some relief. TEAM's Christian Concern Fund was able to channel some assistance. World Relief organization also gave help through the mission.

One bold program to cope with the results of the famine was for the Chad Christian Cooperative to buy 220 tons of seed rice to give to farmers who were too impoverished to have seed for planting their fields—a formidable task indeed. Each farmer accepted in the program was given a quantity of seed deemed sufficient for the area to be planted. His one requirement was to return that amount of seed at the next harvest. Ross Beach felt the program was a marked success. The yield was high; farmers repaid the amount advanced to them and had seed for the next planting.

Hospital Staff Active in Relief

Jack MacDonald, area foreign secretary, was enthusiastic in his commendation of the seed grain project and also another extensive famine relief project by Bebalem hospital personnel:

> At one point this last summer [1985] our hospital staff, along with a number of volunteers from France, distributed 1,200 tons of rice and millet to around 80,000 people. They did all this and kept the 200-bed hospital and ten dispensaries functioning. In

addition they vaccinated 15,000 children against seven diseases. It is almost impossible to realize the amount of work this represents for so few people. While this was going on, Ross [Beach] and his few people at Bere were busy in a nutrition project of another sort. He had received cereal, powdered milk, and sugar. One of his men cooked up 2,500 liters of this food each day for many weeks. Mothers would bring their children to the dispensary across from the cooperative and there they were fed. Many little lives were saved through this effort.[35]

Training Servants for the Church

Bible training for church leaders was a prominent part of the work in Chad from the very beginning. The training advanced from level to level as the church developed and the believers grew in maturity. At first training was informal—giving basic instruction to converts who could go out alone or with the missionary to preach the gospel in new areas. Then training became more prolonged, as vernacular Bible schools were set up in the various tribes. The first vernacular school began in Bebalem in 1942. There were eventually seven schools with over 300 students operating on a three-year cycle. With no educational opportunities for village people in the early years, the students came without any previous training but with intellectual capacity and a desire to learn. Many useful servants of the Lord received their basic training in the vernacular Bible schools, which have been the backbone of pastoral training for fifty years.

As French language schools expanded and people became more interested in educating their children, a larger number were literate in French. To take advantage of this potential, the church and mission opened a French Bible institute in Bebalem. Jack Brotherton, Charles McCordic, several other missionaries, and some of the Chadian church leaders were the teachers.

It began to be realized that some Christians were receiving more advanced French schooling and should have Bible training on a more challenging level. Also, the pastors needed to be able to minister intelligently to the more educated young people. As these needs became apparent, the mission and church took a forward step and established the Evangelical Bible Institute in Moundou in September 1977. Missionary personnel included Paul Cochrane, Charles McCordic, and Lorraine Green from TEAM, and several associate European missionaries. Students were required to have at least two years of high school for admission. The course included two years of introductory-level instruction followed by two years of more advanced theological training.

On some fields the training ministry gets ahead of church development, with the result that there is a very limited source of students on one hand and, on the other, very limited work opportunities for the graduates. That certainly was not the case in Chad. If anything, church growth was ahead of the training ministry. The churches were growing rapidly and needed trained leaders. There were also many potential students for a Bible school.

Civil War and its Effects

The Chad field missionary experience has many similarities to that in mainland China. Both presented physical challenges in travel, disease, famine, encroachment by expansionist neighbors, civil war, political turmoil, official persecution, and antagonistic ethnic religions—all of which were potential hindrances to the work and some of which made temporary retreat from the arena by the missionaries necessary.

Chad's desperate situation has been well described in the September-October 1990 issue of *Africa Report:*

> A few numbers speak volumes about the suffering Chad's people have experienced in the last three decades. One out of every four children dies before the age of five. The calorie intake for the average Chadian is tied with Mozambique for lowest in the world and Chad's per capita GNP of $150 is the second lowest in the world after Ethiopia. Only one-quarter of the population has access to safe water, and there is only one doctor for every 100,000 people. UNICEF reported recently that health care facilities in Chad—where they exist—have crumbling walls, no beds, and no equipment. Pharmacy shelves are bare and many health personnel have had little or no training, leaving them unable to recognize or treat common illnesses.[36]

It is a matter for thanksgiving that the Evangelical Church and missions, working together, have been able to meet some of these dire essentials plus many of the urgent spiritual needs.

Chad and China were alike in this also, that outstanding response to the gospel followed times of determined opposition. In all the history of TEAM's mission work, these two countries have seen the most abundant harvest. Both fields demonstrate the truth of the Scripture quoted by pastor Huang of China to us after thirty years of communist suppression of the church: "He that goeth forth and weepeth, bearing precious seed, shall doubtless come again with rejoicing, bringing his sheaves with him" (Psalm 126:6).

Attacks on Major Cities

The church's deliverance from the satanic attack of the cultural revolution did not bring with it guarantees of a smooth pathway ahead. For much of the time between the 1975 ending of the cultural revolution and 1990, Chad suffered aggression from Libya or internal civil war—much of which was apparently fomented by Libya. The result was that N'Djamena and Moundou were repeatedly involved in armed attack. To avoid being repetitious I quote only brief reports giving some details of recent war conditions:

> In August 1978, President Malloum, head of the military government that had ruled Chad since 1975, established Mr. Hissen Habre as prime minister. Habre was the recognized leader of a guerrilla group from northern Chad, and this was an attempt for political reconciliation with the largely Muslim north. Seven months later, February 12, 1979, open fighting broke out in N'Djamena between Malloum's forces and Habre's army. Sporadic fighting also occurred in other centers.... Because of the political unrest, some of our personnel moved to Cameroon while others left on early furlough. As the situation became more tense, the remainder of our staff in southern Chad crossed the border into Cameroon in early May. The Hodges family stayed on in N'Djamena. Those located in Cameroon have been involved primarily in literature production for our churches and Bible schools in Chad.[37]

Carl Hodges, who served as field chairman for a number of years, shared information on experiences he and Sandra and their sons had in N'Djamena:

> N'Djamena has been in a state of tension and unrest since last year's war. On March 21 this year [1980] severe fighting broke out again between two major forces in the government. By the 23rd, the fighting was increasingly violent and most white people, including American Embassy personnel, began leaving for Cameroon along with tens of thousands of Chadians. Despite earnest suggestions that we leave, we remained at our house along with another couple and a single lady, hoping the fighting would stop or that it would not be in our area. It became worse, with heavy fighting on the main street two hundred yards from us. At least two large stores were hit by mortars and destroyed. By the end of the week, and after three mortars had exploded on our property near our house, each of us felt that the Lord wanted us to leave. For four nights we had been sleeping on the floor in the boys' room under tables and mattresses in case anything came through the roof. There were so many bullets and mortars whizzing through the trees that we could seldom allow the boys outside.[38]

Pressure Felt by Pastor Kayé

The civil war put great pressure on many, even those who were not directly involved. An example of this was reported by Jack MacDonald after his 1983 visit to Chad. It concerned pastor Kayé, president of the EET, whose oldest son was involved in the military opposition. When the pastor was called before the government military at both the local and district levels, Ross Beach accompanied him to support him. Ross's involvement truly moved the people, who were surprised but genuinely pleased that he would stand by the pastor in this way. They attributed the relatively kind treatment Kayé received and perhaps the sparing of his life to Ross's faithfulness and loyalty to him.[39]

Growth Continues

Yet fifteen years of war have not quenched the spirit of the church in Chad. When general director Richard Winchell visited Chad in January 1990, he took special note of the church's continued growth in spite of the hindrances of the political situation. In the capital city he counted fourteen congregations, some of which had suffered great property losses due to the fighting. The larger city churches enjoyed attendances exceeding 1,000 on Sunday mornings. He reported that there were about 800 churches in the EET and that Sunday morning attendance in these churches totals "in excess of 200,000 people."

Tribes Yet Unreached

Although TEAM missionaries rejoice at the wonderful response to the gospel in Chad and the EET's continued growth, they are still concerned about the many tribes remaining unreached to the east and the north. Surveys conducted by missionaries of the Africa Inland Mission (AIM) in the east have found evidence of thirty to sixty tribes without Christian witness and with no written language or Scriptures. By agreement with the EET and the field council, some AIM workers are seeking to reach a number of these tribes, meeting with TEAM-EET annually to coordinate their efforts.

The field council is seeking to move into the north beyond Lake Chad to reach more of the Islamized tribes. Rick and Monica Haberkamp and Rob and Vicki Anthony have moved back into Bol on Lake Chad. With the anticipated arrival of Steve and Tosha Godbold, the field council is looking more closely at the northern towns of Faya-Largeau and Nokou. The goal is to reach the Teda people, many of whom have now migrated to the Niger Republic, which has lead to an interest in beginning a work in Niger.[40]

PORTUGAL—SLOWLY GROWING

A New Field to the Southeast

The spiritual needs of Portugal impressed Magnus and Clara Foreid anew when they returned from furlough in 1946 after the end of World War II. As the churches at Alges and Queluz were doing well, they felt it was time to take a serious look at the province of Baixo Alentejo. Beja, the capital, with a population of more than 12,000, was located about 100 miles southeast of Lisbon and had many towns and villages surrounding it. The area was without any known gospel witness, which led Foreid to make an urgent appeal for missionary recruits.

After several visits to Beja, Foreid located a suitable hall and had it ready for dedication by T. J. Bach on his return from a trip to South Africa in August 1947. In the next few years he also reached out to neighboring towns and opened preaching posts in Cuba, Serpa, Ferreira-do-Alentejo, and Penedo Gordo.

Nineteen Recruits

Prayer was answered for new workers over the next five years with the coming of Margaret Hartt (Grewell), Marjorie Ruth Hawes, Herbert and Alice Goertz, August and Lillian Ramsland, Sarah Snead, Dean and Lorraine Fredrikson, Luke and Ruth Boughter, Rolf and Phyllis Egeland, Jim and Helen Pietsch, J. C. and Barbara Gholdston, and Albert and Mary Lee Bobby. After language study, these new missionaries began preaching and

teaching in the Lisbon area, and in Beja, Sines, Vila Nova de Milfontes, Santiago, Cercal, and Portalegre.

Eight Early Losses

The earliest of these arrivals were granted residence permits, but after the government entered into a concordat with the Vatican in 1952, those who had not obtained such permits had to leave the country. Not wanting to return to America, the Egelands, Pietsches, and Gholdstons crossed the border into Spain to renew the process of visa application. Their efforts were not successful, but for each of these couples the Lord had another open door—the Gholdstons in Spain, the Pietsches in radio work in Tangier, and the Egelands on the home staff. Herbert and Alice Goertz made a good beginning in Sines but left the field before the completion of their first term. The field force was thus reduced by eight workers.

Medical Emergency Removes Two More

The missionary force was reduced further in 1959 when August and Lillian Ramsland had to return home because of Mr. Ramsland's critical health situation due to a combination of tropical diseases contracted in Portugal. Major surgery corrected the condition to a degree, but the mission's medical director forbade a return overseas. The Portugal field's loss was gain for mission headquarters. Ramsland had training and experience which fitted him for service in the publication department, where he filled an important role for almost thirty years.

Hard To Close the Gap

The Ramslands' departure was keenly felt for several reasons. Both had become fluent in the language, and they were church planters. Most of the churches they began in the Santiago area have continued through the succeeding thirty years, with only occasional help from missionaries—proof that they were established on a solid base and with sound principles.

The Ramslands also served in the bookstore *Livraría Alegría*, which was at first in a third-floor Lisbon office building. In

724

December 1958, it was moved to a strategic downtown street-level location where eight to ten thousand people passed daily. Its first display window had an attractive Scripture quotation which people noticed: *Porque Deus amou o mundo...deu o Seu único Filho* (For God loved the world...He gave His only Son).[1]

Divergent Methods of Work

Another reason the Ramslands' departure was a loss had to do with methods of missionary work. They were among those who had provided a balance between two commonly held work methods. In brief, the two differing views could be described as "hands on" and "hands off."

In the first approach, the missionary took full responsibility for all phases of the ministry and maintained personal control of the church planting process. In the second approach, the missionary taught and counseled, but exercised little control, expecting the converts to grasp the principles which would result in their coalescing into visible church bodies.

Although it is doubtful that the Foreids saw themselves as representing the "hands-on" principle or that the Boughters and Fredriksons felt that they were fully "hands-off," an experienced observer could discern these divergent principles at work in Portugal over a period of years.

All concerned were diligent, hard-working missionaries with genuine concern for the salvation and spiritual progress of the Portuguese. People were won to the Lord. Many were taught the deeper truths of the Word. But the pattern of New Testament-type self-propagating, self-governing, and self-supporting churches did not develop.

The Stanley Foreids Join the Force

When the younger Foreids—Stanley and Francisca—joined the field in 1962, with their intimate knowledge of the Portuguese culture and wonderful facility in the language, it was natural that they would follow the methods of the senior Foreids. (Francisca was a convert of the work in Beja.) Their assignment was in Beja and surrounding towns where they joined forces with Stanley's parents. They worked hard, held many meetings, actively led the congregations, and saw men, women, and children come to the Lord.

Lack of Common Field Strategy

Thus the work of TEAM in Portugal took two separate approaches. For several decades the senior Foreids carried on the work in the Beja area following—whether consciously or unconsciously—the "hands-on" method. When the parents retired in 1970, the younger Foreids succeeded them in this responsibility.

At the same time, the Lisbon work of other TEAM missionaries continued to develop its own distinct pattern of youth work, Bible studies, radio programs, and assistance to several established groups.

These approaches, while good in themselves, were not similar enough to allow a common field strategy for evangelism and church planting. As a result, by the mid-1980s—after forty years of TEAM work—there were just nine small congregations, though many other Portuguese had heard the gospel and of these a fair number had accepted Christ as personal Savior.

Warm Personal Relationships

In spite of the divergent methods, there was a high degree of spiritual unity and fellowship among the missionaries. They were cordial and helpful to each other. They met in annual field conferences and enjoyed interaction in their ministries—except in the question of adopting common goals and planting churches with similar organization, structure, and purpose. They also worked together in field council meetings to discuss matters of general interest.

Common Ground at Camp Caravela

Another common ground was in the ministry of Camp Caravela. This camp, located near the ocean and close to the town of Vila

Nova de Milfontes, was started in 1957 by the Ramslands. All the missionaries worked together coordinating program planning, spiritual counseling, camp direction, and the practical duties related to dining hall and facilities.

Camp Caravela continued as a vital ministry year after year. Reporting to the annual field conference in 1986, the chairman spoke approvingly of its ministry:

> Camp Caravela once again proved to be a very vital part of our field. Several people were saved and many Christians were strengthened as they spent several days of fellowship with other believers and under the teaching of the Word. All the missionaries participated in some way to make the three [camping periods] a success.[2]

Hawes, Hartt, Grewell

Margaret Hartt and Marjorie Hawes teamed together in Lisbon in children's and women's work until, in 1968, Miss Hartt was married to Russell Grewell. Grewell was in Portugal studying the language in preparation for service with the Africa Evangelical Fellowship (AEF). Due to the revolutionary movements in the Portuguese African territories, the AEF released Grewell to TEAM. He was a welcome addition to the recruit-starved field. The Grewells chose to work in and near Porto, the second largest metropolitan area in Portugal.

About the same time, the field benefited further as a result of the tensions in the Portuguese African colonies. Peter and Ruth Muir, who had served in Angola, were loaned by AEF to TEAM for the bookstore ministry in Lisbon. They served as managers there from 1965 to 1971.

Growth in Beja

The response to the gospel in Beja had been very encouraging during the senior Foreids' active ministry and continued when Stanley and Francisca were in charge. The preaching chapel which had served for over twenty years became too limited for the church activities. Conscious of the Portuguese emphasis on quality buildings, the missionaries planned for more suitable and attractive facilities. Stanley wrote to the mission office about raising the needed money.

The mission policy was that assistance from foreign funds be in proportion to the giving by the local congregation, though part of the congregation's share could be obtained through a loan. It was important that the congregation, and not the missionary alone, make the decisions about building and financing so that the members would sense that the building was truly their own. The Beja missionaries felt that since the believers were poor, many would be unable to give. The field council, however, insisted that they assume some responsibility rather than look to the mission for all the needed money.

Member Participation Essential

In planting a church the believers must be involved early in the process—caring for the meeting place, contributing, caring for the offering, leading meetings, giving testimonies, going out with witness groups, teaching Sunday school classes, serving on a committee or board, and preaching when able. The Apostle Paul refers to this process in Ephesians 4:16 (NIV): "From him [Christ] the whole body, joined and held together by every supporting ligament, grows and builds itself up in love, as each part does its work." Through the teaching of the Word and sharing in responsibility, believers in mission field churches grow to maturity and churches become strong.

Even with the concern that the churches had not developed self-leadership, there was satisfaction that the missionaries were preaching the gospel widely in the Beja area. Church attendance in Beja and outlying preaching points kept up quite well. It seemed to be the most successful part of the Portugal work. What, then, of Lisbon?

Special Ministries in Lisbon

Livraría Alegría was functioning well, its outreach extending far beyond downtown Lisbon as mail order coverage widened its ministry. An upstairs room also served as a meeting place for counseling and Bible study.

The bookstore was also a key factor in a radio outreach, even though evangelical preaching on radio was not permitted. Luke Boughter thought there might be a way around restrictions by reviewing books on vital subjects of current interest which presented scriptural values and answers to problems. While the dramatized weekly program "Pages of Fire" contained the clear gospel, it skirted restrictions because it was not classified as a sermon. Aired over a Lisbon commercial station and using Portuguese voices, it was the only evangelical broadcast in Portugal for nine years.

Benfica (Lisbon) Chapel Opened

The mission was particularly eager that a church ministry be started in Lisbon, so when the bookstore lease expired in 1971 and the key money deposit of several thousand dollars was returned, the missionaries prepared a meeting hall in Benfica, a nearby suburb of Lisbon. Several participated in that ministry—Luke and Ruth Boughter, Dean and Lorraine Fredrikson, Marjorie Ruth Hawes, Chris and Sherill Lubkemann and—for a brief period— Richard and Elaine Wischmeier.

Even with the changes of missionary personnel, the Benfica attendance kept quite steady at forty to fifty. Sunday school teachers were drawn from among members of the church (1979) and the people themselves led the mid-week prayer meeting. Marjorie Hawes' work with the young people, such as with singing groups, helped keep them active. In 1981, the Stanley Foreids were assigned to work in the church. Their ministry resulted in an encouraging increase in attendance.

Europe Secretary's Report

Reporting on the Portugal work in 1982, Jack MacDonald, who began to serve as area secretary for TEAM's Europe fields in 1974, had a good word about Benfica:

The church has experienced significant growth by transfer and conversion. The work is still far from large, but is taking on its own personality as national leadership develops. It is seeking its own pastor.[3]

The annual field conference in 1983 also heard reports of continued growth:

> Weekly attendance has been around sixty, including youth. About fifteen women regularly come to the ladies meeting. Several men have been showing good spiritual interest and promise. Giving has increased fifty percent over the last year. The youth did one service a month and some went regularly with the Foreids to Milfontes to help in the Sunday school program.[4]

The Area Secretary's Concern

MacDonald became concerned that there be more unity of purpose in the missionary body in the specifics of planting spiritual congregations. He worked with the missionaries on this vital matter, as he reported in 1982:

> Another encouraging item is the development of a solid ecclesiology and strategy for the churches and field. A lot of work has gone into this and I believe the Lord will glorify Himself.[5]

A Bold and Effective Move

In 1983, MacDonald observed that missionaries had become few in number and lacked administrative experience. Furthermore, they were all fully occupied in their own spheres of activity. So he moved to put the field administration on a better basis—a move that had no precedent on any other field of TEAM. It is revealed in his report to the board of directors, November 4, 1983:

> The Spain field chairman is to be shared with Portugal for the next three years. Gary Bowman is to assume chairmanship of Portugal, January 1, 1984, while still holding the chairman position in Spain.[6]

Gary Bowman had served as chairman of the Spain field for over ten years, and had led the missionaries in working together to expand the ministry and plant new churches. Dale Vought, who had fifteen years of church planting experience in Spain, was asked to become a regular member of the Portugal field council.

730

Porto, Northern Portugal

Russell and Margaret Grewells' work in Porto and nearby communities was slow and demanding, but they kept right at it, having a definite goal of seeing a church planted and functioning. A review of reports given at the annual field conference reveals that the fruit was mostly among young people. The teaching and counseling of this group contributed to growing maturity and responsibility in the church. Excerpts from the reports reveal progress:[7]

> The young people are showing zeal and taking responsibility in the church. A training program will begin in the fall. Plans continue for a church building [1976].

> A number of young people have made professions of faith. There is good leadership by two young men of the congregation. The young people have held street meetings. There is also good growth by adults [1977].

> Sunday school attendance is increasing. The youth group continues to be active and faithful. Two key young men are growing spiritually. Each preaches monthly. The church has overcome difficulties in getting the building plans approved by the government [1978].

> Between 150 and 200 people attend showings of gospel films every fifth Saturday [1979].

> Five young people are active in visitation and door-to-door evangelism [1981].

Strong-man Rule Ends

Political changes in Portugal between 1968 and 1976 affected missionary work. The nature of these changes is given in capsule form in the *World Almanac:*

> Portugal had been a republic since 1910.... From 1932 a strong repressive government was headed by Premier Antonio de Oliveira Salazar. Illness forced his retirement in September 1968. He was succeeded by Marcello Caetano. On April 25, 1974, the government was seized by a military junta led by Gen. Antonio de Spinola, who was named president. The new government reached agreements providing independence for Mozambique, and Angola.... Spinola resigned in September 1974 on pressure from leftist officers. Free elections under a new

constitution were held in 1976 with the Socialist party gaining a parliamentary plurality. Three years of turmoil left the economy and political life in disarray.[8]

Preoccupied with Politics

Stanley Foreid had observed in 1975 that the people's interest in politics occupied their minds to the point that they did not have ears open to the gospel. He was glad to note, however, that the young people of the Beja church were now taking greater initiative. In 1976, ten decided for Christ and five were baptized. The Sunday school ministry was the highlight of the Beja work. One special activity the young people sponsored attracted 200 young people to the church. They were also helping in the Cercal and Milfontes meetings.

Andrew and Barbara Friend to Beja

When Andrew and Barbara Friend could no longer remain in Mozambique after the 1974 independence move, the mission invited them to consider Portugal, where their knowledge of Portuguese would fit them for a teaching ministry. Upon arrival in 1978 they were assigned to Beja. They undertook a teaching ministry but also spent time in the outlying churches, trying to build them up. Church attendance dropped to a very low point when the Friends went on furlough but the Sunday school grew under the leadership of two Portuguese—Jacinto Rodrigues and Manuel Martins—which was part of their strategy of committing responsibility to others.

Herb and Linda Gregg Take up Work

When Herb and Linda Gregg arrived in 1981, the Beja church was probably at its lowest point in years. The transition from a missionary-centered ministry to one where the local Christians bore the major part of the load was not easy, but with patience on the part of both missionaries and people it was a successful transition. One result was that elder Rui took major responsibility in the Beja church and even guided the smaller churches of the area. Gary Bowman was able to report in March 1986:

732

The Beja church has its constitution and governing body now, and is moving ahead quite well. I had the privilege of speaking at the installation of the elders and was really encouraged with what I saw and sensed. Herb and Linda Gregg have worked hard and been very patient to bring the church to this point.[9]

Lessons to be Learned

Lessons can be learned from TEAM's experience in Portugal where many heard the gospel and a fair number professed conversion, but where after forty years there were just nine small congregations. The local church must function as a body if it is to grow, mature, and make spiritual progress. The missionaries working on the same field must also function as a body if a strong church fellowship is to become a reality. It is not enough to draw people into a preaching hall or even into an attractive church building. It is true that those who come to church have common interests, but Christians need to recognize a bond stronger than common interests and concerns.

The Church—a Living Body

One New Testament description of the local church uses the figure of a living body. "In Christ we who are many form one body, and each member belongs to all the others" (Romans 12:5 NIV). "Now the body is not made up of one part but of many" (I Corinthians 12:14 NIV).

The born-again, baptized members of a local church must recognize the special bond uniting them in Christ. That link is stronger than that of brothers in the flesh. The body truly needs the individual member; each individual member truly needs the whole body. Until the believers recognized this spiritual bond and took steps to appoint spiritual leaders as directed in the epistles, they lacked the cohesion and permanence that should be evident in the local Christian church.

The first practical steps in establishing the basic New Testament church organization in Beja and Benfica were taken after Gary Bowman became chairman of the field. The leaders in the churches came to recognize their responsibility for the local body and understand that it was they, not the missionary, who must lead. They also gained a better appreciation of their relationship to the believers in the other churches.

The Missionaries, Also a Body

It was not enough that missionaries enjoyed good fellowship, not enough that they were diligent and worked hard, not enough that they had a variety of ministries. Unity of vision and purpose was essential. Coordination of church planting and development activity was also necessary.

Upswing in Work Observed

It was Bowman's emphasis on missionaries working together as a body that brought definite change in the work. In his first report to the Portugal field conference in August 1984, he reviewed the concept:

> I believe the field is looking with real anticipation to doing things together and trying to work out a common strategy and direction for the field. I believe we are at a point where we will work together and get some things set down so the new missionaries will have something to fit into and sense a common purpose and strategy for the field.[10]

When Bowman reported in 1986, he mentioned specifically the Benfica church as an example of encouragement:

> The church in Benfica has made great strides this year and has a committee which helps Stanley Foreid with the direction of the church. The final step of a church board has not yet been taken, but that will come soon, and we certainly do not want to make that move too quickly.[11]

At the same conference he reported advance toward meeting the goals set in 1985. He also turned to some of the goals yet to be met and the need for progress toward a unified purpose:

> There are still some areas that need to be worked out and some of them will be dealt with at annual conference, such as guidelines for camp, how to provide for national pastors, a more developed strategy, and how to finance church buildings. *We really need to move ahead as a field in these areas, rather than*

as individuals. [Italics supplied.] We also need to pursue the idea of an association of churches. And we must be ready to accept and place new missionaries coming to the field in such a way that our field strategy will be effective and efficient, thus reaching people with the gospel and establishing churches for the glory of God. But with all our planning, organizing and efforts, we must remember that it is Jesus Christ who builds His church. It is His work, but we must be faithful to serve Him.[12]

The Portugal missionaries gladly accepted this administrative arrangement and saw it as an answer to their prayers for more purposeful progress in the planting of live, functioning churches, dedicated to winning the many unreached around them.

When Bowman was asked to join the home staff in 1987, Dale Vought, the Spain field chairman, also became chairman of the Portugal field. Two new missionary couples—Clark and Yvonne Malone, in 1988, and Ron and Cindy Elder, in 1989—joined forces with the other missionaries to press forward unitedly in the church planting ministry.

Viewing the harvest fields all around them in cities, towns, and villages, the missionaries in annual conference voted to appeal for twelve new workers. They looked expectantly to the One who had commanded them to pray for laborers for the field and who also had promised, "I will build my church."

FRANCE—CHURCHES EMERGING

When general director David Johnson returned from his 1950 survey of several countries in Europe, he reported: "A person born in France has less opportunity to hear the Gospel and be saved than one born in the heart of Africa."[1]

My own visits to France in the early years of TEAM's work and the experience of our missionaries have confirmed his assessment. Although a majority of the French people are nominally Roman Catholic, few practice their religion and even the Catholic church considers France a mission field. When field chairman Arthur Johnston and I were riding on a train in France during my 1963 visit, we met a middle-aged professor of history who, though well-educated, had never before seen a Bible. Johnston summed up the situation several years later:

> France now has a population of over 50 million.... Of this number only six or seven million, at the most, are considered to be practicing Roman Catholics.

Liberal theology held sway in the vast majority of the 895 towns and villages served by resident Protestant pastors, while another 36,000 towns and villages had no Protestant church of any kind.

The result of the invading materialism and secularism into the traditional church of France is a religious vacuum into which many of the sects are entering.... It is quite true that the average man has never seen a Bible. Adults and children in France have never even heard the name of Jesus.... Truly evangelical works of all kinds are exceedingly few and very widely scattered.[2]

France Targeted by TEAM

David Johnson's burden for Europe and his vision of TEAM work there made a strong impact on the board of directors, who voted unanimously at their March 1951 meeting in favor of TEAM's expansion into this part of the world. Then in June and July the board approved France as a TEAM field, with Arthur and Muriel Johnston its first missionaries. Two other couples, David and Geraldine Barnes and John and Ethel Jesberg, were accepted as candidates.

Language Study and Service

The Johnstons sailed to France in January 1952 and were joined by the Barneses in July. The Johnstons' first task was intensive language study but, as missionaries often do, they found opportunities for service even during this important and difficult phase of their work. Art taught two courses in English at the European Bible Institute and Muriel helped him with a Sunday school class at the American Church in Paris. They also worked with American youth in a Young Life club.

David Barnes had already studied French and so was able to begin his ministry right away. He taught church history in both French and English at the European Bible Institute and used his music training to help students minister musically in local churches. Personal evangelism, literature distribution, hospital evangelism and open-air meetings were among the Barneses' activities that first year.

More Workers

By August of 1953 this fledgling field had doubled in size as two new couples joined the ranks. Burdened for the young people they had met, the Johnstons encouraged Art's brother to join them in France. Rodney and Fran Johnston, who had been contemplating missionary service among teen-agers in the Orient, arrived in April. They were followed four months later by John and Ethel Jesberg.

Then in December, TEAM missionaries John and Betty Aerni were expelled from Franco-controlled Spain and brought across into France by secret police. After spending several months in their native Switzerland, the Aernis returned to France to begin work in the Spanish-speaking community at Béziers in the south.

First Steps in Ministry

Though working in a highly civilized and cultured nation, these first missionaries were truly pioneers. While learning the language and surveying ministry possibilities, they reached out in many forms of evangelism.

During Easter break in 1953, Arthur and Muriel Johnston took twenty American teen-agers to Wengen, Switzerland, for the first-ever camp held by TEAM France. Another first for TEAM was an evangelistic tent campaign held in May 1953 at St. Germain, near Paris. David Barnes preached and other evangelical mission groups cooperated to make the campaign possible.

David Barnes spent some time in itinerant evangelism and used his musical gifts to further the gospel cause. With their burden for training national leaders, he and his wife, Geraldine, devoted themselves more and more to the work of the European Bible Institute.

Though still in language study, the Jesbergs distributed tracts in many areas, following through on their vision of using literature as an evangelistic tool. John also helped in the Young Life clubs.

Art and Muriel Johnston had by now developed their work among French young people through contacts in the American Young Life Club. By June 1954 fifteen teen-agers were attending discipleship classes.

While they studied French, Rod and Fran Johnston helped Art and Muriel with the American Young Life Club and at the Easter camp, and found other opportunities for witness as well.

Focus Needed

I was privileged to join these five couples in September 1954 for the second France annual conference and also to travel through France to Spain and Portugal with Art and Rod Johnston. To them I stressed that missionary work should have as its prime focus the creation of churches in the New Testament pattern. Art Johnston would later say that these conversations had greatly influenced the thinking of both Rod and himself. In these first years, however, the work did not have church planting as a clear overall goal.

In his valuable history of TEAM's first twenty-three years in France, missionary Robert Vajko describes the basic problem in these early years as the lack of a strategy effectively integrating the workers and the work. "There were differing views as to how to most effectively evangelize resulting in a lack of concentration with a resulting lack of direction."[3]

A Resistant Field

While the need in France was great, response was discouragingly slow. Fran Johnston described their first efforts in an article in the mission magazine:

> As we set up housekeeping and contacted people on the street, in the shops, and in the market place, we learned to appreciate the warmth and charm of the French people.... And we learned more and more the reality of their casual indifference toward "religion." God was passed off with a shrug of the shoulders, referred to as "Fate" or the "good God," and considered as a rather indulgent grandfather.[4]

Though a number professed new faith in Christ, it was not until December 1954 that the first convert requested baptism. Art Johnston baptized this sixteen-year-old boy, whose bold action separated him from the religion of his family.

Two Fronts

Missionaries were now working in two main areas: the Aernis at Béziers in southern France and the others in the Paris area.

The Aernis began evangelistic work in Béziers with the goal of establishing a church among Spanish-speaking immigrants, and soon obtained a hall to serve as an evangelistic center. Some of the

Paris-area missionaries visited to help with special meetings and follow-up.

Emphasis on Youth

Although missionaries were using many methods to try to reach people for Christ, as we have seen, work among young people became a focus. As TEAM's magazine reported in 1955:

> France, perhaps, presents a perfect example of the specific importance of youth work when we are attempting to reach a nation for Christ. Because of the prevailing apathy among adults, TEAM's missionaries to France concentrated their efforts on young people.[5]

Through the Young Life clubs, ski camps, regular Bible studies with young converts, and children's clubs, missionaries were winning young people to Christ and discipling them: "Our objective is to see them established in the Word of God, to lead others to Christ, and to see them established in an indigenous church."[6]

Disappointment and Resolve

When Art and Muriel Johnston left for furlough in May 1955, they left behind in Paris a promising group of about thirty-five young people. On their return a year later, they learned disheartening news: only one young person had remained faithful against the counterattacks of the Devil. And since they had not really begun to reach the parents, there was no stable group of believers left with which to build a church.

Heartbreaking though it was to find no lasting results from more than three years of committed work, the missionaries gleaned from this disappointment a lesson which would change TEAM's direction in France: an effective ministry cannot be built upon youth alone; rather, planting a local church which encompasses all generations must be the central aim.

Another principle adopted during these years came to be known as the "cluster principle." Though it proved to be of great benefit to the work, it actually came about through mixed signals from the home office.

With the marked increase in the number of missionaries coming to France in the 1950s, their studying language in Paris and then entering into ministries there, general director David H. Johnson became aware of the potential concentration in the metropolitan area to the detriment of outlying towns and villages. He therefore wrote the field recommending that the missionaries scatter out across France.

About the same time, I received a question from the field council about how close or how far apart these church ministries should be established. My answer was that they should be close enough so believers could fellowship together from time to time and participate in joint activities such as baptismal services and ordinations. Their closeness would avoid the feeling of isolation which affects many Christians in a resistant population.

In the leading of the Lord, my advice was followed. After forty years of experience in France, it is the testimony of the missionaries that the cluster principle has been a means of strengthening the believers and the churches.

Beginnings in Vitry

While studying French and helping with the Young Life clubs in Paris, Rodney and Fran Johnston developed friendships and shared Christ with neighbors in Vitry-sur-Seine, the industrial suburb where they lived. They began a child evangelism class in their home, led by a French Bible school student, and befriended several teen-agers on their block, whom they at first took to the Young Life club in Paris. Later they started a club in their own home. By now, John and Ethel Jesberg were also living in Vitry.

One day they met Monsieur and Madame Kahan, a Jewish family who had become Christians some years earlier, who asked, "Where do you hold your Sunday services?" And with this prompting, a Sunday afternoon service for adults was started in Vitry. By March of 1957 at least six families were attending regularly.

Prayers Answered in Orly

About seven kilometers away, in Orly, a middle-aged woman

named Madame Dufour had been praying for more than seven years that God would send someone to teach the Word of God in her area. As Robert Vajko tells the story:

> One Saturday [in July 1956] Art and Rod Johnston were on their way back from a picnic with their families. They arrived at a railroad crossing in the city of Villeneuve-le-roi, just below Orly. A train was passing and the gates had been lowered—suddenly they noticed a sign in the little building next to the crossing. It said something that is rarely seen in France: *"Réunion évangélique ce soir sous la tente"* [Evangelical meetings tonight under the tent]. It was a handmade sign and was rather badly written, but it communicated its message.[7]

They parked the car and Art went back to the building, where Madame Dufour invited him in. Through her he met the small group of Christians in the area, and her home became the meeting place for a thriving Saturday evening evangelistic service. Thus just about two months after the Johnstons returned to France to find that their work among French youth had dissolved, God led them to prepared hearts and a new and exciting beginning.

Planning a Strategy

By September 1956, TEAM missionaries in France numbered fourteen. The Barneses had resigned to continue their work at the European Bible Institute under Greater Europe Mission, which directed the Institute, but three new couples had just arrived. As workers increased, it was more important than ever to develop common goals.

In the months before the September annual field conference, Art and Rod Johnston and John Jesberg had met many mornings and prayed together many evenings to develop a plan for the TEAM work. This guide plan, a first for the France field, was presented to the conference and adopted as the work's guiding principle. Titled "TEAM Guide for an Indigenous Church in France," it identified the France field's goal as evangelism for the purpose of establishing an indigenous church, with other institutions and programs contributing to that goal.

A National Association

Another decision which would have tremendous implications for the work in France came at the following year's conference, when field chairman Arthur Johnston presented a plan for a national association. Its purpose: to weld new believers together under a common statement of faith, to allow newly forming churches to purchase property in the name of the association, and to provide a French identity. The goal was to have the association ultimately under full French leadership. Missionaries agreed wholeheartedly, and the association became a legal reality on May 29, 1958.

The name of the new association was *l'Alliance des Eglises Evangéliques Indépendantes* (Alliance of Independent Evangelical Churches), known as AEEI. The Reverend Jacques Blocher, co-director of Nogent Bible Institute and a prominent French evangelical, had suggested the name and agreed to serve on the governing committee.

Forming the AEEI was a true step of faith, in that there were as yet no organized TEAM churches; but missionaries looked ahead to the day when the forming groups would indeed be full-fledged churches. Having the AEEI in place as church groups developed set a healthy pattern for church-mission relationships and provided encouragement to developing works.

A Building for Vitry

As the Sunday afternoon service in Vitry grew, believers began to look for a permanent meeting place. A former shoe factory, now empty, became the answer to prayer as this first TEAM church building in France was dedicated in May 1959. The building was purchased under the AEEI with money borrowed in faith from TEAM headquarters. Repayment of the loan would come from offerings of the Vitry believers, missionaries' pledges, and a few gifts from TEAM supporters. It was intended that the repayment would become a revolving church loan fund.

A Sunday School in Orsay

Orsay, a suburb southwest of Paris, was the site of TEAM's field headquarters. Property had been purchased there in 1957 to accommodate offices and housing for language students and a resident family.

Now, in 1959, Wanda and Wallace Geiger were assigned to develop a church there. They and Muriel Johnston had begun a weekly Sunday school, rejoicing in a beginning enrollment of fifteen children, and planned to start adult services in the fall.

A Call to Tarbes

In December 1958 David and Norma Halvorsen independently opened a new area of work when they answered the call of a group of recent converts in Tarbes, near the Spanish border in the Upper Pyrenees.

Missionaries rejoiced at this evidence of hearts open to the Word of God, but some doubted the wisdom of beginning work in an area so far removed from the rest of the TEAM ministry. The Spanish ministry at Béziers was already some distance from Paris (where Vitry, Orly and Orsay were all southern suburbs). How would the mission back up pioneer work in yet a third area?

Sowing the Seed

In June 1959, six and one-half years since the first TEAM missionaries arrived in France, field chairman Arthur Johnston reported the scope of TEAM's ministry: twelve baptized believers; no organized churches; six meetings held weekly and three others held biweekly or monthly; three Sunday schools; and six children's clubs.

> It seems as though we are clearly in the period of seed sowing and evangelism, although we do praise the Lord for some saved and for one baptism during the year.... Obviously, this period of preparation seems long and we grow impatient for greater quantities of fruit and individuals baptized. Building a national church under indigenous principles requires greater patience, but, we trust, produces hardier and more abundant long-term results.[8]

First Bible and Missionary Conference Held

The church association took a big step in June 1960 when it held its first Bible and Missionary Conference. There were now church groups forming in five areas: Béziers, Vitry, Orly, Orsay and Tarbes. Held at Vitry, an obvious choice because Vitry was the only group with its own building, the conference featured several French pastors as speakers and included a youth rally and reports of mission work in the Ivory Coast.

French Co-laborers

The story of TEAM's early years in France would not be complete without mentioning the contributions made by local evangelical leaders. The advice and support of respected French Christians were invaluable to the missionaries and the AEEI. Pastor Jacques Blocher of the Tabernacle Church and Nogent Bible Institute served on the AEEI committee and helped in many other ways. Professor Jules Marcel Nicole, a noted evangelical scholar and teacher at Nogent Bible Institute, joined the AEEI with his wife in 1960 and provided students to help in TEAM Sunday schools. André Adoul, an evangelist and Bible teacher, helped in Vitry and then preached on Sunday mornings at Orly for a time, as well as at special meetings. Pastor Christian LeFlaec and his wife took responsibility for the work at Tarbes while the Halvorsens were on furlough. Richard Douliére assisted in youth camps and conducted special meetings with TEAM in Vitry, Orly and Paris. The list could go on.

Sacrificial Giving in Orly

The church in Orly was growing—and outgrowing the home in which the believers were meeting. An adequate church facility of some sort was becoming necessary. At its annual meeting in January 1961, the group was asked to decide about the purchase of a piece of land. When all the money on hand plus gifts and loans available were counted, the church was short 300,000 old French francs (about $600), with the deadline two weeks away. Finally it was decided to hold a *Journée de Victoire* (Victory Day) in two weeks. If the money came in on that day, the church would take this as a sign of the Lord's approval and buy the land.

Missionary Louise Lazaro reported what happened:

> The people came to the morning service with expectant hearts, each bringing his offering in an envelope. There were many sacrificial gifts. One woman had no money left to buy coal for the winter. A young engaged couple gave money they could have used for their wedding. After the six families and several young people had contributed, the total was counted.

> What rejoicing there was in the hearts of the French believers and missionaries when they learned that the goal had been reached—with $8.00 over! God had done the impossible![9]

So the land was purchased. In late September 1961, a three-week evangelistic tent campaign was held on the new land. The believers requested a permit to build a temporary wooden chapel, but without success. Then in November 1962, the church decided to build a permanent church building.

Reaching out to Youth

France missionaries continued their keen interest in seeing youth won to Christ, but now the emphasis clearly was on channeling young converts into a church home. Youth clubs in Orly, Orsay, and Vitry met bimonthly in Vitry's building, with an average attendance of about thirty-five in 1961.

Summer and winter camps proved an excellent way to touch the lives of young people. Said field chairman Rod Johnston in 1961, "The camping program has been one of the most fruitful ministries in our work. Most of the missionaries have participated either in recruitment or camp work itself."[10]

A year later he reported a marked increase in both camp attendance and in achieving the camps' spiritual goals. "God has given us contact with many needy young people who would never be touched by another means of evangelism," he said.[11]

During 1961 the missionaries also held an excursion on the Seine River in Paris for 195 young people. A French guitarist entertained and shared the gospel. Similar excursions and other special events would touch the lives of thousands of young people over the years.

Film Showings Provide Contacts

John Jesberg showed Christian films and distributed the Gospel of John in and around the areas where TEAM worked. This seed-sowing ministry was a source of new contacts both for the TEAM church groups and for the few other evangelical churches.

New Work in Fresnes

Early in 1962, Ivan and Donelda Peterson arrived to help Rod and Fran Johnston in Vitry. New to TEAM and to France, the Petersons had served under the Berean Mission in the Belgian Congo until rebellion broke out there. Unable to find anywhere to live in the Vitry area because of a severe housing shortage, the Petersons finally settled in Fresnes, about four and a half miles southwest of Vitry.

"Although it seemed that a problem provided this housing in Fresnes," Bob Vajko recounts, "it turned out to be very much God's hand." For Fresnes was only four or five miles from Orly and was halfway between Vitry and Orsay. "It was an ideal place to start a new church in line with the developing policy of concentrating on an area and planting churches that could be of mutual help."

Besides helping at Vitry, the Petersons immediately began a Bible study in Fresnes. Intensive evangelism was aimed at developing this, in time, into a church as well.

Training Lay Leaders

Work was progressing steadily on two of the three TEAM fronts in France. At Béziers by 1962 there were thirteen baptized believers and an average of twenty-seven attending the weekly meeting, in addition to a thriving Sunday school and children's clubs.

The church groups clustered in the Paris suburbs—Orly, Orsay, Vitry and now Fresnes—were also progressing well.

Only the work at Tarbes presented a problem. The Halvorsens, who had been TEAM's only representatives there, resigned while on extended furlough. Disagreements among the believers had caused serious problems. In view of this and Tarbes's great distance from the rest of TEAM's work, the field council decided in late 1962 to turn responsibility for the work over to the lay preacher there. Its later development is not known.

But as churches were taking root and growing steadily in TEAM's main work areas, there came a pressing need to train French leaders. The solution was to develop a training program for lay preachers. The Lay Preachers Institute, launched on October 14, 1962, benefitted greatly from the cooperation of Jacques Blocher and Jules Marcel Nicole, the co-directors of Nogent Bible Institute. Missionary Louise Lazaro also began training classes for Sunday school teachers and child evangelism workers.

A New Guide Plan

At their 1963 annual conference, missionaries adopted a new guide plan setting the direction for TEAM's work in France. Building on the work of previous years and based on counsel from French colleagues and the home office, this document clearly placed church planting as the missionaries' central objective. As field chairman Arthur Johnston said: "Our progress in the Lord's work should be measured in terms of the churches of the AEEI."

He also suggested that since more and more of TEAM's activities were being coordinated with those of the church association, regular council meetings should be held with the French pastors—for in this way "we will obtain the best counsel from them and cooperation with them."[13]

The Fruit of Careful Sowing

After eleven years of hard work and slow progress, 1963 was a landmark year. "God has visibly blessed His Word and His work...," reported Arthur Johnston. "The groundwork is established and we are privileged to see the fruit of careful sowing."

The reasons for this rejoicing were many. There had been twenty-eight baptisms during 1963—truly a moving of God's Spirit since only thirty-one others had been baptized since the beginning of the work. Overall attendance in nine areas of work had increased 32 percent from 1962 to an average of 205. The first two young men from TEAM churches were attending Bible school. A first French coworker had joined them under the auspices of AEEI. Marc Atger, a former military chaplain, worked primarily with youth camps and the *Jeunesse Ardente* young people's clubs, but also preached, conducted Bible studies and assisted in other ways.

Another reason was the steady advance in collaboration between TEAM and the AEEI. Arthur Johnston reported that the field council had integrated almost all field activity with the AEEI. Quarterly committee meetings were now being held with the French pastors. "All business not concerned with our personal missionary problems is transacted with French counsel. Their confidence has been manifested by requesting missionary help and association in the Nogent Bible School."[14]

Victory in Orly

On the land bought so sacrificially in Orly was built a modern church building—the first such AEEI building constructed in France. The first worship service in the new church was held December 20, 1964, climaxing eight hard years of work in this Paris suburb. Fran Johnston described that victorious day:

> Tears of joy glistened in the eyes of those in the congregation (close to 70 people in a sanctuary built for 150). The first to respond to the invitation at the close of the message was a much-prayed-for husband whose slavery to drink had made life a living hell for his wife and six children. This man was Andrée's father, and it was her mother who had put up the sign at the railway crossing. A forty-year-long prayer was answered that December morning.[15]

In the years that followed, this new building would play a key part in the evangelization of the Orly area. As Robert Vajko pointed out, it allowed the church to double its attendance. Average attendance during 1963 in the Dufour home was fifty-one. In 1965, it doubled to ninety-eight. The Orly church also served as a rallying center for other developing churches—holding united baptismal services, annual AEEI conferences and other special events. And it gave a permanence and an image to Bible studies which, as we will see, developed into branch churches.

A Permanent TEAM Camp

For many years missionaries had been praying and searching for a permanent TEAM camp site—while a steady schedule of summer and winter camps continued to reach scores of young people each year in rented facilities.

At the Christmas 1964 ski camp, almost all of the TEAM workers in France pitched in to host seventy-six campers at the Hotel Praz de Lys, which was near Taninges in the French Alps. Impressed with the facilities, the TEAM missionaries decided to purchase the property in cooperation with Young Life—with whom they had been working since the early years. The *Jeunesse Ardente* young people's work would now have a permanent camp base. The final purchase papers were signed in June 1965.

The impact on the camping program was not long in coming. "The whole camp ministry has been revolutionized by the purchase of the camp in the French Alps...," exulted Rod Johnston. "We not only doubled the camp attendance from 1964 to 1965, but over a month in advance of the Christmas and Easter ski camps this year our quota was filled." But such success brought its own problems: it was frustrating indeed to have to turn away spiritually needy would-be campers. "Prayer is requested for wisdom in either expanding our present facilities or launching another camp in rental facilities," he added.[16]

Camp leaders rejoiced to see lives transformed and Christian faith strengthened, as teen-agers heard the gospel presented daily for a week, ten days or even two weeks. Camps were a unique and enjoyable way to give teen-agers prolonged exposure to the claims of Christ.

750

More French Workers

Marc Atger had been the first national worker supported by the AEEI when he joined the work in September 1963. Now two other men were added to the team.

Marc Descheemaecker, also a former French Army chaplain and a graduate of Nogent Bible Institute, began helping the Petersons at Vitry and Fresnes in September 1964. When the Vitry church organized officially, it called Descheemaecker as its first French pastor in June 1965. Then at the Fifth Bible and Missionary Conference in February 1966, Marc Descheemaecker became the first French worker to be ordained by the AEEI. These were the beginnings of a long and fruitful association.

Marcos Flores, a Spanish national, was the third man to join forces with AEEI when he and his wife took responsibility for the work in Béziers in May 1965, replacing the Aernis during their furlough.

God was raising up national leaders, and the churches were responding with financial support.

A Conference Grounds at Houlgate

An unexpected development in 1965 expanded TEAM's sphere of ministry even further. TEAM was offered a beautiful summer conference grounds at Houlgate on the Normandy coast, which could be purchased on an annuity-type program. The owner, Mme. Chaland Klutchko, could no longer operate the grounds on her own because of advancing age, but she wanted to see the program her father had built up continue its evangelical doctrine and evangelistic spirit.

A provisional contract was signed, and TEAM board member Robert Van Kampen generously offered to make the monthly payments. A new association was formed in 1966 to operate the grounds—*Les Amis de l'Alliance des Eglises Evangéliques Indépendantes,* or Friends of the AEEI. Legal details and complications delayed the final signing for the property until February 1968.

Field chairman Arthur Johnston spoke for the missionaries when he said, "...[T]he Lord provided both the opportunity and the funds to purchase by monthly payments the English channel seashore property at Houlgate. We trust that this property will provide not only a much needed rest area for us, but will also develop into a program to compliment the other ministries God has given us."[17]

In the decades ahead, the ministry at Houlgate would grow under God's blessing far beyond what missionaries could have envisioned in 1965.

Three New Beginnings

Two small Bible studies begun during this period are particularly interesting because they were led from the start by French leaders under the auspices of an AEEI church.

The first began when a family asked the Orly church to start a Bible study in the city of Morangis, where they lived. Jacques Lang, a student at Nogent Bible Institute, had been converted through the ministry of the Orly church and the camp in the Alps. He agreed to lead the Bible study, which met in his apartment.

The second Bible study was begun by Marc Atger in his home in Longjumeau, under the auspices of the nearby Orsay church.

Then in 1966 TEAM opened up a completely new area for church planting: the metropolitan area of Lyon, a city second in size only to Paris. Rod and Fran Johnston wanted to move closer to Camp Praz de Lys and Lyon was a strategic area nearby.

Developing Momentum

Slowly but surely momentum was developing. By the end of 1966 there were five organized churches:

> In *Vitry* the believers with a French pastor were meeting in a remodeled shoe factory. In *Fresnes* believers were meeting in a newly-acquired house in a remodeled living room. In *Orsay* the believers were meeting in a remodeled garage, in part of the headquarters building. In *Béziers* the believers were meeting in a small hall on a little street of the city. And in *Orly* the believers were meeting in a brand new building....[18]

Combined membership of the five churches now totaled one

hundred.

In addition, there were two areas with regular Sunday services and seven Bible studies. In all areas combined, about 300 were meeting for Sunday services each week and 466 for Sunday school.

But as the work grew, missionary numbers had remained relatively stable. Though some new workers had arrived and others had left for different avenues of ministry, the year 1967 began with thirteen missionaries in France and two on furlough—only five stronger than the ten missionaries of July 1954. The workload was heavy, including as it did administrative responsibility for a church association, camp and conference grounds. National workers were also busy—Marc Atger at *Jeunesse Ardente* and Marc Descheemaecker adding to his job as pastor at Vitry the part-time directorship of Houlgate Conference Grounds.

Joint Evangelistic Campaigns Held Yearly

At their semi-annual conference in November 1965, the missionaries decided to hold united evangelistic campaigns—one per year—in the areas where AEEI was developing churches. French believers from sister churches and missionaries would together concentrate their efforts on a two-week campaign. Vitry was the first area to be targeted. "Vitry for Christ" in 1966 was followed at yearly intervals by "Orsay for Christ," "Orly for Christ," "Fresnes for Christ," "Morangis for Christ," and "Houlgate for Christ."

In terms of professions of faith and new people added to the developing churches, these campaigns did not bring the hoped-for results. Although some were converted and a few continued on in fellowship, results were disappointing given the massive efforts, which included distributing thousands of handbills and hundreds of posters for each event. But there were other benefits: lay people were mobilized for prayer and evangelism, and believers were blessed as the AEEI church groups supported each other in a common cause. As Arthur Johnston reported after the Vitry campaign:

The united Alliance [AEEI] evangelistic campaign, Vitry for Christ, was both a heart-warming reality, a success in seed-sowing, and a source of unity for both the Vitry Church and the Alliance.[19]

Church Association Strengthened

A weakness of the AEEI was that its administrative structure did not allow adequate representation from the growing number of churches. The church association had been formed before any TEAM churches were even officially organized and was led by missionaries and French evangelicals. It had served well to bind the new believers together under a common statement of faith and to give the work a French identity. Now was the time to give the churches a direct voice. As I had written to field chairman Wallace Geiger in 1967, "...I believe that the AEEI will eventually have to come under the control of the churches. There is no church membership at present as far as I know but in time that will be a reality."[20]

Thus at the Seventh Bible and Missionary Conference in February 1968, the AEEI general assembly decided unanimously to open membership in AEEI to delegates from churches having twelve or more members. This step, allowing as it did greater involvement by lay people and direct representation from each church, could only strengthen the association.

The following year, Arthur Johnston reported encouraging progress. Lay delegates had represented their churches at the Eighth Bible and Missionary Conference and subsequently taken part in an AEEI administrative session. The results had been "renewed interest and participation" in the work of the AEEI. This had also sparked a new interest among the laymen in the AEEI's financial needs. "We praise God for this step forward."[21]

A Geographic Guide Plan

In February of 1968 the TEAM missionaries adopted a plan to guide outreach into new areas. The two previous guide plans had set church planting as the central aim of TEAM's work in France.

Now missionaries answered the question of where, geographically, TEAM should set its sights.

First they studied the current situation in France. Where were other evangelical works? What were the strategic centers? Where were people most receptive? The French government was planning new satellite cities. Should TEAM move into these new urban areas? In a land where the need for gospel witness was almost overwhelming, the missionaries believed in careful planning toward specific goals, steeped in prayer and combined with a flexible spirit open to the Holy Spirit's guidance. The result was a plan pointing out logical extensions from their current work as well as new key targets.

A Web Movement in Orly

In late 1968, a chain of events began in the Orly area which was like nothing missionaries had seen before in "resistant France." A young member of the Orly church invited his neighbor to an evangelistic weekend. Charles Siounath, a native of the island of Guadeloupe (one of the four overseas departments of France), was impressed by what he heard and began to attend a Bible study. In time he accepted Christ and began to make changes in his lifestyle in obedience to God's Word, including marrying the woman with whom he had been living.

Charles asked an officer of the Orly church to come witness to his family, particularly his mother, who followed a mixture of Catholicism and Hinduism. Robert Vajko, who with his wife, Noreen, was working with the Orly church at the time, picks up the story:

> [The Orly church officer] was warmly received and through a "bridge of God" the gospel penetrated into the mother's heart. She was the key to the whole family. She came to the Sunday morning service at Orly and gave her heart to Christ. She destroyed the Hindu idols that she possessed declaring that she no longer needed idols now that she had come to know the living God. The transformation in her heart and home was both biblical and radical.[22]

It was not long before other family members trusted Christ as well. By June of 1969 nine adult members of the Siounath family had been baptized. The movement would spread even more until it included family members living in Guadeloupe as well as on Charles' wife's side of the family. In all, more than sixty individuals in this extended family became Christians, all the adults and teen-age children being baptized.

Missionary Reinforcements

Missionaries were still burdened by heavy workloads. By the end of January 1969 the missionary force had grown to twenty-three in France, but of these almost half were in full-time language study. Missionaries were grateful for these new arrivals and prayed for more. As field chairman Ivan Peterson said:

> As we see the tremendous high-rise apartments around us, filled with thousands and thousands of people, and think of new areas opened up, we seem at times like a chicken scratching at a mountain. For these new ventures of faith, we need more workers in the harvest field, both national and American....[23]

The work in Lyon received welcome back-up when Kenneth and Lois Beach joined Rod and Fran Johnston there after completing language study in the summer of 1969. They were the first reinforcements to this TEAM post since the Johnstons had moved there four years earlier.

Self-supporting Leaders

It was exciting indeed to see French leaders taking charge of new ventures while supporting themselves in secular work.

Claude Jarrin was leading a Bible study group at Crosnes.

And the Bible study Jacques Lang and his wife had begun in their Morangis apartment was now thriving. By 1968 a worship service was held in the Langs' apartment every two weeks, with the believers attending the Orly church in between. A year later field chairman Ivan Peterson reported a weekly Sunday morning service in addition to children's clubs and youth clubs.

Supporting himself as a sales representative for a company

which made paper products, Lang spared the group the burden of a leader's salary in the early years. In time, the members gradually began to assume his salary and the church moved out of the apartment into a hall in Chilly-Mazarin. Lang had by now become the second man to be ordained as a pastor by the AEEI. The group then constructed its own building in nearby Longjumeau, where a vacant lot had been purchased at a very reasonable price.

This was the first AEEI church to be developed entirely under French leadership. Though a number of missionaries assisted in various ways—including Norman and Sue Kapp, Evelyn Ericson, Ron and Linda Kidd, Tom and Mickey Hurshman, and Sarah Page—they did so under Jacques Lang's direction and leadership.

It is interesting at this juncture to take a look ahead to 1986, when I asked field chairman Wallace Geiger for an update on the work. By then the Longjumeau church was one of AEEI's largest. Its three-story building could seat more than 200 in the sanctuary on the main floor, with classrooms, activity area, and an apartment upstairs. Regular church ministries included the church service, Sunday school, young people's and children's activities, a ministry to singles, and a weekly prayer meeting. A telephone ministry gave callers a three-minute message with music. In addition to a strong preaching and teaching ministry, Lang also had outreach through radio. Another source of new contacts was a program through which he directed about a hundred local young people and children to camp each year. Truly God was blessing this work.

Training Programs Launched

Back in 1971, the addition of the Morangis church under Jacques Lang's leadership brought the number of AEEI churches to six. As churches grew, so did the need for trained leaders.

The Theological Education by Extension (TEE) method seemed ideal for the French situation, with its emphasis on better equipping those who were already showing leadership in the churches. The first course offered in 1971 was New Testament Survey, with more courses becoming available each year. Missionaries Robert Vajko,

Kenneth Beach, and Tom Harris worked to adapt the program to the French situation. Roger Lefevre, the third pastor ordained by the AEEI, helped to teach the courses. Within several years the responsibility for TEE was assumed by the church association.

Educating believers in this way met a growing need, as Robert Vajko would say in 1974:

> In just five years, our churches could double; we will need trained leadership—pastors and elders. A certain number can come through residence training, but we will never meet the need only by this means. Let us, therefore, move forward as the need becomes more and more evident and the Spirit of God leads.[24]

Another type of training was also offered for the first time in 1971—this to equip believers for personal evangelism. In cooperation with Campus Crusade for Christ, a Lay Institute for Evangelism was held at the Orly church. Well-attended by people from more than fourteen churches in the Paris area, the three-day course taught believers how to live a Spirit-filled life so that they would be motivated to witness, and then gave specific training in how to do so.

An Ending and a New Beginning

When John and Betty Aerni retired in 1970, TEAM faced a difficult problem in Béziers. Who could take responsibility for this Spanish-language church so far from either Paris or Lyon, the other two areas of TEAM ministry? Tom and Gayle Harris moved to Béziers for a time, but it was apparent that to be effective in the work they would need to learn Spanish. After much prayer and discussion of the options, TEAM withdrew from Béziers at the end of 1971, giving responsibility for the church to a Spanish-speaking pastor.

Across the country in the Paris suburb of Créteil, a new church was forming. It had begun as a Bible study in the Siounath family home. Now nine members of the Siounath family plus several others from the Orly church joined to form the core of this new branch work led by missionaries Roger and Julie Lehner.

Extremely high rents and property costs in the Paris area have been a major hurdle for new churches. But now a hall was obtained in a huge apartment complex for the symbolic rent of one franc per year. This was indeed a miracle, and one which TEAM would see repeated in the years ahead.

By the end of 1971, average attendance at Créteil was twenty-five, a most promising start. Just one year later, the Sunday attendance had doubled and Créteil was officially organized as a church.

Landmark Events in 1972

The year 1972 saw progress on many fronts.

National AEEI leaders were growing in number and taking on more responsibility. Pastor Willy Lehnerr and his wife joined the *Jeunesse Ardente* staff and began a Bible study and Sunday morning service in Cluse in the French Alps. Jacques Lang, leader of the Morangis church, was ordained by the AEEI. Roger Lefevre became pastor of the Vitry church. By summer, the AEEI had eight workers, the most ever.

In March, the Fresnes church inaugurated its beautiful new building. I was invited to speak at the dedication service, joining a crowd 350 strong to share in this joyous culmination of ten years of work in Fresnes.

The ministry at Houlgate was growing by leaps and bounds under the part-time directorship of Marc Descheemaecker. A piece of adjoining property had been purchased and work done to upgrade the premises. From 200 guests in 1969, the conference program had expanded to accommodate 500 in 1972. It was time for a full-time director. Thus in July 1972 Marc Descheemaecker and his wife were commissioned as a team to direct the conference grounds full-time. At the same time, a local church was inaugurated at Houlgate under their leadership.

Last, but not least, the miracle of a rent-free hall in Créteil was repeated in the city of Brunoy and led to the development of a church there. Eugene and Priscilla Cox headed this work, which was inaugurated in October by a visit of believers from other AEEI churches in the area. In December a Sunday morning worship service began. And in the adjoining city of Epinay-sous-Sénart, a third hall was contracted to AEEI for the symbolic rent of one franc per year. Would a church begin here as well?

A Turning Point in 1973

A long-held goal became reality in February 1973 when Pastor Marc Descheemaecker was elected the first French president of AEEI at the Twelfth Bible and Missionary Conference. Missionaries still made up about half of the AEEI membership, but control was gradually shifting and it was exciting to see this most able man of God take on the responsibility of leading the association.

At this same conference, Charles Siounath was ordained as the first evangelist of the AEEI, and a French medical team from Alsace was committed to the Lord as it prepared to go to Chad. The French believers had a heart for missions, both at home and abroad.

Changing Church-Mission Relationships

Several days after Marc Descheemaecker was elected president of AEEI, I met with the missionaries for their annual study and planning sessions. We discussed work strategy for the years ahead and the changing relationship between church and mission.

A common pitfall in areas of pioneer evangelism is that missionaries can come to dominate the work. Because there are no other Christians, missionaries at first naturally lead the new converts—teaching, taking the initiative, making the decisions. But if this pattern becomes entrenched it can be very difficult to change.

TEAM's early years in France certainly held the potential for a mission-dominated work. This was pioneer evangelism in an area of very few Christians. What spared the field from an unhealthy pattern was the missionaries' vision of seeking fellowship with and counsel from recognized French evangelical leaders. Men such as Pastor Jacques Blocher and Professor Jules Marcel Nicole addressed missionary conferences, spoke at special gatherings of the

760

converts, conducted baptismal services, and so on. When they were asked to join the AEEI—which was at first made up mostly of missionaries because no churches had yet been organized—they did so as members of influence, and their advice was heeded.

But now, in 1973, what direction should the church and mission take? Should they aim for fusion, with the mission merging into the church's organization? This was the goal of the ecumenically related churches, based on their understanding of John 17:21 and Ephesians 4:1-6. Or should they aim for two independent organizations—mission and church association—collaborating in home mission outreach?

Experience has shown the dangers of complete merger. As missionaries come under the complete control of the churches, tensions can lead to discouragement and resignations. The missionary whose vision for pioneer evangelism is not shared by the church, for example, must forego that work or resign. The opposite problem occurs if the church does not take control and missionaries dominate from within the structure. This has been branded as neocolonialism.

Far better is a pattern which maintains the distinctions of mission and church, and yet joins both in a voluntary cooperation that recognizes the particular gifts of each member of the body. And it was along this path which the France missionaries decided to go, adopting changes to their field organization to give AEEI responsibility for its own affairs.

Just over a year later, Arthur Johnston would report:

> The leadership of the AEEI has firmly and graciously assumed the responsibilities that the Mission once essentially held. Last year at this time, there was a rather hesitant transfer of authority that had been legally adopted; but this year has marked the real transition and has revealed the wisdom that the Lord has given in making this change.
>
> A spirit of love and mutual confidence has characterized the relationships with both the Councils of the AEEI and the pastoral meetings.[25]

761

Two New Churches

Seven years after TEAM missionaries had moved to Lyon, a church was finally started. Under the guidance of Kenneth and Lois Beach, the church began Sunday worship services in a member's home in September 1973 and then rented a meeting place in Tassin. Average attendance was soon in the twenties.

Meanwhile, back in the Paris area, a third branch work of the Orly church was developing in the new satellite city of Epinay-sous-Sénart under the leadership of Charles Siounath. Christians in Epinay had remodeled the rent-free hall there and in December 1973 they began a regular Sunday morning service. Just one year later the church at Epinay was officially organized.

Thus by the end of 1974 there were eleven AEEI churches in various stages of organization, seven of which had national leaders.

Headquarters in Chilly-Mazarin

The need for better administrative facilities was finally met in 1973 when TEAM purchased two apartments in Chilly-Mazarin to be remodeled into offices, missionary housing, and guest rooms. David Nelson took care of much of the remodeling.

Administrative work was growing along with the number of missionaries and ministries. These behind-the-scenes tasks can have a great impact on the effectiveness of a mission's work. With inflation and France's extremely high cost of living, good financial management was critical. And careful planning and coordination bear fruit in many ways. As area secretary Jack MacDonald would say after his visit to the 1984 France annual conference:

> Whenever one visits the France field he is made aware of good organization and good field administration. The conferences show that much work has been done prior to the meetings.... This, of course, makes it easier to minister in the Bible and prayer hours because everyone is in a relaxed attitude.[26]

The same principle holds true for the work of the field as a whole. Good organization behind the scenes by the field chairmen, office staff, and field committees contributes to a smooth and coordinated effort. Those working in administration generally do so part-time, carrying on a church ministry as well.

The France field also assisted in the work of other TEAM fields. When TEAM entered Austria in 1964, the work there benefitted from a consultative relationship with missionary leaders in France for several years. Then in the mid-1970s, a special relationship with TEAM's Chad field began. Chad missionaries coming to France for language study received help and fellowship from the France missionaries. They, in turn, contributed their gifts to the churches and other ministries during their temporary stay.

Preparing for Even Greater Growth

Believing that TEAM should be a catalyst for growth among the AEEI churches, missionaries held a one-day conference in June 1974 to introduce the basic principles of church growth. At the end, participants were asked to set goals for their own churches that were made by faith and yet reasonable in light of the principles they had learned. The results were amazing—projecting a growth rate of 28.8 percent for the next year and more than double the number of AEEI churches in five years.

This was the beginning of a series of church growth conferences, which helped to share practical knowledge and generate enthusiasm for the possibilities of building Christ's church in France.

Camping Ministry Grows

At Camp Praz de Lys in the French Alps, more and more young people were being reached through summer and winter camps. In the first five years at this permanent site, annual camp attendance grew from 55 to 490. Rod Johnston reported that Praz de Lys had been "the spiritual maternity ward of many French young people." Some camps emphasized evangelism while others concentrated on developing leadership skills among Christian youth.

But growth was not without its pains. Building and remodeling were the order of the day for several years, as facilities were upgraded and expanded to meet the needs of a fast-growing program as well as to conform to local fire-safety and other building regulations. Two new dormitories, the David Koop Memorial Building and Bethany Chalet, were being constructed. For two winters and three summers, camps had to be held in rented facilities or in tents because of the construction and delays in obtaining approval from local authorities. Short-term work crews from the United States gave a much-needed boost to what sometimes seemed like never-ending construction.

With these difficulties, the camping program slowed down during the early 1970s, but by the 1973-74 season the number of campers was back up to 482, with an all-time high the following year of 556.

Jeunesse Ardente Changes its Focus

Changes were taking place in the *Jeunesse Ardente* youth program, as Rod Johnston worked with French leaders to form a new *Jeunesse Ardente* Association under full French leadership in October 1975. Roger Lefevre was chosen as its first president.

For many years, the *Jeunesse Ardente* program had benefitted from the ministries of both TEAM and Young Life, with French leaders gradually assuming more and more responsibility. Now came a change in focus as Young Life and the new *Jeunesse Ardente* Association decided to target the masses of unchurched young people by means of youth clubs, rather than using the local churches as their base.

As so often happens, one change led to another. Rod and Fran Johnston decided in 1977 to continue their ministry under the auspices of Young Life. And the AEEI churches now had to begin a new youth program, as field chairman Wallace Geiger reported in 1977:

> The withdrawal of *Jeunesse Ardente* as the youth movement of our churches by the decision of Young Life leaders...in June of 1976 necessitated the development of a new youth program which took the name of *Jeunesse Agapé* (Youth with Love). Good interest and attendance at club meetings have indicated an encouraging potential for the future. French leaders are carrying the responsibility.[27]

Disagreement Over Praz de Lys

Now disagreements arose over the future of Camp Praz de Lys, a focus of the *Jeunesse Ardente* youth work. Diverging paths made it difficult for the smooth cooperation of past years to continue. Young Life and *Jeunesse Ardente* were now working outside the local church, while to TEAM and AEEI the church was central. But there were other difficulties as well. Young Life wanted to include Roman Catholics and other non-evangelicals as camp leaders and speakers, for example, while TEAM and the AEEI could not agree to this departure from sound principles of evangelism. Misunderstandings grew as the French leaders of *Jeunesse Ardente* took control of Praz de Lys, mistakenly believing Young Life to be majority owner of the property because of past contributions made to the program.

Much prayer and discussion on both sides was aimed at resolving the differences in a way which would honor Christ, and it was finally agreed in August 1978 that TEAM would sell its share of Praz de Lys to Young Life.

Planning Together for Church Growth

Since the first field guide plan in 1956, France missionaries had regularly set goals to direct the focus of their work. Now, in 1976, TEAM missionaries and AEEI leaders developed the first joint guide plan.

It was with a spirit of humble thanks for what was being accomplished and excitement about future possibilities that the Joint AEEI-TEAM Five Year Guide Plan for Evangelism and Church Multiplication was written in mid-1976. AEEI now had thirteen churches in various stages of organization, two of which had begun during the past year at Evry and St. Quentin. The number of baptisms showed growth as well—110 people had been baptized during 1975 and another fifty by July 1976.

The joint plan for 1977-1981 set out goals by faith and specific plans for how to achieve them. Its tone is captured in the final paragraph:

Finally, the weight lies heavy upon the AEEI-TEAM councils, AEEI pastors, TEAM missionaries and all involved in the AEEI to catch the great vision before us and to overcome any tendency to self-centeredness, unbelief, or unwillingness to sacrifice. We can possess the land if we will move ahead by faith. His grace is sufficient and He has said, "I will build my church...".[28]

AEEI Modifies its Structure

Looking back on twenty years of AEEI history, field chairman Wallace Geiger could say in 1978 that forming the church association had "proved to be a very wise move." He outlined its benefits in his annual report:

- The AEEI had united the groups of believers formed in various places. Combined or coordinated baptismal services, missionary conferences, evangelistic efforts, annual picnics, and youth clubs had made a significant contribution to church growth and multiplication.
- The association was a key factor in excellent church-mission relationships. Because it allowed churches to develop on property owned by a French association rather than on mission property, many potential tensions were avoided.
- It gave a solid base to the national churches and a positive image of churches working together under a common doctrinal statement. French pastors could join the work with confidence.
- It had helped to develop national leaders through teaching programs and TEE.

Geiger also reported that the AEEI Council was now made up of five French leaders and three missionaries:

Two of the missionaries, I[van] Peterson and myself, were re-elected for a six-year term, upon the insistence of the French brethren. In our thinking, we envisioned our positions being filled by them. We are grateful not only for the confidence that has been expressed, but also for the desire to work together. In due time and in keeping with the Lord's timetable, a total French Council will be leading the AEEI.[29]

Later that year, the AEEI modified its legal structure to become a union of churches rather than the "association of persons" it had been—a necessary change at this stage of its development. A leading advisor in this process was Daniel Bordreuil, a French pastor who had recently joined the AEEI after twenty-one years as a missionary to Indochina and France. Some years later, in 1987, Bordreuil would succeed Marc Descheemaecker as president of the AEEI. By-laws of the restructured union of churches were adopted at the AEEI annual meeting in 1981.

A Time of Slow Growth

During the final year of the joint five-year guide plan for church growth and multiplication, field chairman Wallace Geiger could report only that "Some of the goals have been partially achieved." There had been progress, but with only months to go until the end of 1981, results were far short of the goals.

Qualitative goals had been achieved to some degree, although many were difficult to measure. They included such aims as a greater emphasis on prayer and Spirit-filled living, a renewed thrust in leadership development, and greater fellowship among the AEEI churches.

The quantitative measures were clearly falling short. One new church had begun, but with the loss of an existing one the AEEI entered 1981 with the same number of churches as in 1977. Active church members were only five above those in 1977, while the number of communicants had actually dropped. Of the 900 baptisms projected, only more than 200 had taken place so far.

On the plus side, the churches were maturing. Three more had become legal associations, doubling the number to achieve this highest level of organization. Four other churches had moved up to the second-rung status of being officially organized with more than twelve members. Three new pastors had joined the AEEI. And the groundwork had been laid to begin several new works in the very near future.[30]

The destruction of the Lyon church building by arson in January 1981 had been a major blow. Over a period of several months, four Protestant churches in Lyon had been burned or vandalized. But

Robert Vajko reported that "Romans 8:28 applies to church buildings. [Steve and Donna] Niles shared recently that attendance has increased and apparently the result will be a building that will be even more functional...."[31]

A new program showing great promise was the AEEI's pastoral internship program, where new workers—national or missionary—would serve under an older pastor for one year of on-the-job training. Roger Piaget interned at the St. Quentin church; then he and his wife, Elvire, were called to serve the Epinay church.

Though the work was deepening and maturing, this was a period of slow growth for the AEEI.

A New Permanent Camp Site

With the loss of Camp Praz de Lys in 1978, the camping program continued on a smaller scale while the members of the TEAM camp committee searched for a new permanent site.

Terry Regnault reported that the Christmas camp in 1978 had been excellent, with some professions of salvation and Christians rededicating their lives to the Lord. "At this camp," he said, "as well as the camp last summer, we were able to see the importance of a camping ministry in evangelism, church planting, and in unifying our young people into a cohesive youth program that is honoring to the Lord."[32]

Jeunesse Agapé, the new AEEI youth organization, asked TEAM to continue organizing camps until the end of 1981, when it was expected that they would take over this responsibility.

Camps were held at a variety of rental facilities—with the many frustrations of locating and promoting different sites—while the search for a permanent camp continued. A great deal of hard work was finally rewarded when Terry Regnault and Steve Niles found Le Belledonne, a hotel at Chamrousse in the French Alps. Snow sometimes lingers into the early summer months in this lovely ski resort area, situated at 4,954 feet above sea level on the same slopes where Jean-Claude Killy earned five gold medals in the 1968 Olympics.

Later a second hotel, the Choucas, was purchased and an ambitious remodeling and reconstruction program was begun. With accommodation for 50 campers in the Belledonne, capacity could be increased to 130-150 once major refurbishing of the Choucas was completed some years hence. Volunteers and teams from the United States were among the many who worked on this project over the years.

The Friends of the AEEI, the association which ran Houlgate Conference Grounds, was responsible for operating the new camp grounds. TEAM continued to assist by providing directors—Terry and Elaine Regnault—and helping with financial management and fundraising to pay off the camp loan and construction costs.

In 1986 field chairman Wallace Geiger reported that the Belledonne Camp Grounds were contributing greatly to the church planting ministry:

> Believers are being edified and stimulated in their Christian life and return to their churches with renewed zeal to serve the Lord. The program is also an excellent tool for evangelism.[33]

An added benefit, and not unimportant, was that the Belledonne was also a place of relaxation and renewal for missionaries and pastors.

Growth at Houlgate

In 1972, the year Marc Descheemaecker became full-time director of the Houlgate Conference Grounds on the English Channel, 500 guests had come under its ministry. A church work was just beginning.

Three years later the conference grounds were serving more than 800 people year-round in five buildings. An historic sixth building was added when a crusade to save the large Protestant church on the beach nearby was successful and the conference grounds obtained a ten-year lease for its use. Geiger reported:

> The response to the save-the-building campaign was excellent, providing funds to carry out the necessary improvements to make the edifice functional on a year-round basis. An additional image and dimension has thus been added to the impact of the ministry in that area.[34]

During the summer holiday season which followed, Sunday services at this church on the beach were reaching capacity crowds of 150-180. Also noteworthy was a telephone ministry, where people could call to hear a short Bible message. Because of increasing calls, with a high of 500 logged one week, another phone was added.

A number of TEAM missionaries helped at the conference grounds and the developing Houlgate church, notably Eugene and Priscilla Cox and Sarah Page. Among the others who assisted were Norman Kapp with the finances and David Nelson and Terry Regnault with physical improvements. But from the first this ministry was primarily in French hands under Marc Descheemaecker's directorship. Gradually the Friends of AEEI, which was responsible for operating the grounds, gained more and more French members. And by 1981 field chairman Wallace Geiger could report that a national staff was assuming the responsibility for this ministry.

The church at Houlgate continued to grow as the core group of members and year-round attenders increased. The year 1979 was especially encouraging, as several new families strengthened the nucleus of believers and the church was officially organized. These families also became vitally interested in the conference grounds and began to share in the ministry there.

A step of faith was taken in January 1984 when Michel Breyne was hired as full-time administrator and maintenance engineer. His wife, Anne Marie, was an accountant and volunteered to take on the bookkeeping, another answer to prayer. The Breynes were a providential addition to the staff at a time when growth had made their services truly necessary.

Though TEAM and the AEEI had only been involved for the past two decades, Houlgate celebrated 120 years as a Christian conference center in 1984. The report for that year was most encouraging:

> The spiritual ministry has been very rewarding with sixty decisions last year. People are receiving spiritual help and being nurtured in the Word. They are exposed to good music and

Christian fellowship and are returning along with newcomers.[35]

During 1985, more than one thousand people were guests of the conference center. Its challenges for the future included a need to upgrade the buildings in light of the greater comfort offered by newer vacation facilities. An ongoing concern was to remain financially viable while keeping rates as attractive as possible. But as God had led in the past, so would he direct in the future.

Revival in 1983

TEAM's second All-Europe Conference was held in Belgium in August 1983. Missionaries from all of TEAM's Europe fields came together at the GEM Bible Institute in Louven, meeting separately by field for the business sessions and together for Bible hours under the ministry of Ray and Anne Ortlund. The conference theme was renewal, and area secretary Jack MacDonald, who was there, reported that renewal did indeed take place:

> The conference came to a climax on Friday. In the morn-ing...missionaries shared what the Lord had been doing in their hearts. Several asked forgiveness of others, openly confessed areas of need and shortcomings, requested prayer, etc. The same followed the brief evening message.... The testimony of a num-ber was that they did not see how they could be the same ever again.[36]

A year later, MacDonald attended the France annual conference in Holland. "It is quite evident that the results of the revival we experienced in 1983 in Brussels are still very much affecting the lives and ministries of our missionary families," he said. "The work is moving forward."[37]

Theological Education by Extension

From small beginnings when the first course was taught in 1971, TEE grew over the years to become an important training tool for lay leaders and potential pastors.

By 1977, TEE courses were being taught in both the Paris and Lyon areas to a total of twenty-four students. Three missionaries and two French leaders made up the teaching staff for the next fall.

Houlgate joined the program three years later with an Old Testament course taught by Marc Descheemaecker. By now enrollment had grown to forty-five. Music courses were added to promote this area of church ministry.

Missionaries and French pastors devoted a great deal of energy to preparing and teaching the classes, which by 1985 were reaching students from thirteen of the twenty-three AEEI churches. Led by missionary Tom Blanchard, TEE expanded greatly that year: in comparison to 1984, the number of courses had doubled and the number of students had increased to seventy-nine enrolled at the beginning of 1985. This training in music and sound doctrine would benefit the churches for years to come.

Churches Growing and Multiplying

At the end of 1976, thirteen AEEI churches had been dotted across the map of France in the Paris, Lyon, and Houlgate areas. The number had remained at thirteen in 1981 as the end of the first AEEI/TEAM guide plan for church growth and multiplication was approaching, even though goals had been much higher.

But the decade of the 1980s saw tremendous growth as the work of many years bore fruit. By the end of 1985, there were twenty-one churches in all, an increase of eight. Compared with 1976, church membership had grown from 348 to 514, and the total number attending the various churches had nearly doubled, increasing from 726 to 1,308.

And the outlook for the future was indeed bright, both for the AEEI and for evangelical works in general. Wallace Geiger told the annual conference in 1986:

> There have been a good number of evangelistic campaigns in France over the past thirty years. None, however, have produced the expectations and momentum as [the Graham Crusade] in 1986. The evangelical impact and growth of churches have been steadily increasing over the years....

> This has all come about because God's people, with much perseverance and a bold faith, have patiently moved onward with the message of the cross. Churches have been planted one by one to where they are now literally dotting the map of the Paris

suburbs and the capital itself. The next ten years have the potential of being the most fruitful in the expansion of the church since the Reformation. Let us pray and labor to that end.[38]

In March 1986 area secretary Jack MacDonald summarized the situation in France for the board of directors. "God's hand of blessing continues to be on this field," he said.

Growth is evident in every area. Twenty-four churches are functioning in various stages from beginning to fully organized. Five more are developing from Bible classes as outreaches from existing churches.[39]

New Work in a Satellite City

Behind the bare statistics of new churches formed are many rich stories of God's faithfulness as well as of difficult and sometimes discouraging work by missionaries and French leaders. Unfortunately, space does not permit their telling. But a brief account of one of these new churches, Savigny-le-Temple, helps to give substance to the numbers.

In the early 1980s, four families from the Orly church moved to the new satellite city of Savigny-le-Temple, about fifteen miles south of Orly. Buying homes there, they also planned to start a new branch church. Bible school graduate Claude Jarrin became leader of the group, though others shared in its development.

The believers found a suitable meeting place and were encouraged in their new venture when several hundred people from neighboring AEEI churches attended its inauguration and took up an offering to give them a financial boost as well.

After some time the group was forced to find new meeting quarters, but in the process made contact with city officials and shared their long-term vision for the church. As a result, the officials found a piece of land which they made available at a price far below its normal commercial value. Because Jarrin and his wife supported themselves in secular work, the group did not have to pay a pastor's salary and began saving money from the beginning, enabling them now to purchase land.

One element of the church's outreach was a bookstand in the

city marketplace, which gave the believers contact with people who were spiritually open but would otherwise never have known about the church.

By 1985, weekly attendance was averaging about sixty and the church had voted to go ahead with construction of its own building. They had saved sufficient funds to receive a loan for the first phase of the building project. Savigny-le-Temple was a key location for a church building, as TEAM and the AEEI sought to increase their evangelistic thrust as well as begin new works in the area.

Ministries Supporting Church Growth

This narrative would not be complete without describing at least briefly some of the other ministries which have contributed to church growth and development.

Youth work has already been mentioned. Ron and Linda Kidd were among those who worked with *Jeunesse Agapé* to strengthen this vital ministry. Many other missionaries assisted in the youth groups of their local churches. In December 1984, the association *Maranatha* was formed to function along with the AEEI in ministering to youth. The *Maranatha I* program targeted the junior-high and high-school levels, while *Maranatha II* reached the college, career, and singles groups.

Women's ministries were another vital area. In a highly developed country such as France where friendship evangelism is one of the main methods of sharing the gospel, day-to-day hospitality plays a major role. Also, as Wallace Geiger pointed out:

> Frequently some of the first contacts in a home are made through ladies and children. Bible studies, coffee hours, Christian Women's Clubs and retreats have been fruitful in the conversion and spiritual growth of a good number. Many of our ladies have been involved in these ministries and hold key positions in Christian Women's Clubs.[40]

In their homes and in the churches, missionaries and French believers made a tremendous contribution to the work as a whole by reaching out to the women of a community.

Christian films have been used extensively by the churches over the years as a means of evangelism and finding new contacts who are open to the gospel message. Tom and Mickey Hurshman spearheaded the audio-visual ministry for a time, which by 1986 was being transferred to full AEEI responsibility.

Music also contributed to church growth and development, though this ministry was something of an uphill struggle. Because music took very low priority in French public school studies and even in general usage, this aspect of worship was not well developed in the churches. Dale and Sherrilyn Anderson devoted many years to music evangelism and assisting with music programs in the churches. Many other missionaries used their musical gifts as well. Music courses were added to the TEE course selections, and in 1981 the field chairman could report that music students outnumbered those enrolled in other TEE courses, indicating good interest in this discipline.

With a growing interest in music, particularly among young people, this gift of God carried great potential for enriching worship and transmitting a message to believers and unbelievers alike.

Short-term workers have also been used effectively in France. Besides the construction crews which worked at the camp and conference grounds, summer workers and associate workers have contributed to a variety of evangelistic and church development ministries.

Why Has the Church in France Grown?

By 1990, the France field had grown to fifty-three missionaries, and there were twenty-five AEEI churches with some 1,600 members among them. In the Paris area, the churches in Vitry, Orly, Orsay, Fresnes, Longjumeau, Créteil, Val de Yerres (formed when the Brunoy and Epinay churches merged), Evry, St. Quentin, and Savigny-le-Temple had been joined by others in Vigneux, Arpajon, Paris, Les Trois Villages, St. Germain, Bretigny, Rueil Malmaison, Franconville, and Nogent. To the northwest on the English Channel was the church at Houlgate. At Chamrousse, a church was growing along with the Belledonne Camp Grounds work. Bud and Nancy Pedersen were starting a church in Orleans, 100 kilometers south of Paris. In the Lyon area, there were churches in Lyon, l'Arbresle, and a new work beginning in St. Foy under the leadership of Mark and Sarah Anderson and Stewart and Beth Webster. The AEEI now included several churches started by missionaries of the Greater Europe Mission.

Why this remarkable growth in a country where every step forward is hard-won? The fact that in Europe all mission work has been very difficult and slow—church planting particularly so—makes these churches' steady growth and vitality all the more extraordinary.

Answering the same question in 1978 about the growth that had taken place by then, Robert Vajko stressed three of the many factors which could be cited: the guidance of the Holy Spirit, the strategy of planting churches in a cluster, and the creation of the AEEI in 1958.[41]

Norman Kapp elaborated on the benefits of the cluster principle in 1982:

> Fourteen of our seventeen churches are clustered in the southern Paris suburbs. The close proximity of these churches serves as real encouragement and strengthening to each other, especially the smaller ones. Pastors get together frequently for prayer and to share burdens, problems, needs, suggestions and blessings. We work together on evangelistic campaigns. Baptismal services each month bring our churches together, so that those who may normally number 30 to 60 people find themselves part of a group of 200-300 people. It is amazing what that can do for the morale of a small church.... As we expand the work, we seek to move out so that no new church is isolated from fellowship with other churches.[42]

The early creation of a church association has played a key role in giving the work a French identity, helping young churches grow, and providing the means to develop and integrate French leaders. Its creation set up the distinction between church and mission that is so necessary for healthy growth. Wallace Geiger attributed the excellent working relationship that TEAM and the French leaders of AEEI have enjoyed largely to the "modified dichotomy" structure adopted in 1973:

> In this structure TEAM and the AEEI, as separate organizations, each carry their own responsibilities and also stimulate one another with the vision and call God has given to each one in church planting.[43]

As separate organizations working closely together, neither TEAM nor the AEEI is swallowed up in the other. Both exercise their unique gifts and encourage each other in carrying out a shared ministry.

Two other methods used in France are well worth emphasizing. One is the creation of daughter churches—branch works of an existing church. A major benefit here is that the church planter starting a new work is not alone. A nucleus of Christians from the mother church will be there to attend the new church and help in the work.

The other is the use of teams, where two missionaries, two nationals, or a missionary and a national work together to develop a church. This has been especially helpful to first-term missionaries or new leaders who benefit from working with an experienced pastor, but is also a real bonus when moving into new areas. Geiger pointed out that teams only function well "if the people can put their gifts together, harmonize their working relationships, and clearly define their responsibilities. Heading up a team requires tremendous skills and know-how." Though some missionaries and nationals work in teams better than others, "teams are essential if we are to see churches developed," he said, "since it is difficult for any couple, whether national or missionary, to do the work alone because of its difficulty and because of all that is involved."

Besides teamwork at the local level there is the teamwork at the regional level afforded by planting churches in clusters. "From this we have seen tremendous fruit," Geiger told me. "As a church grows and calls a national pastor, quite often he is the sole worker. He really needs the fellowship and help of the other pastors and the other churches."[44]

And finally, as Robert Vajko pointed out, of utmost importance is openness to the Holy Spirit's guidance. Without His help and direction all efforts are fruitless.

SPAIN—AFTER THE DICTATORSHIP

In France, missionaries had found indifference and something of a religious vacuum, but neighboring Spain presented a completely different picture. A virtual theocracy since the fifteenth century, Spain described itself as being more Catholic than the Pope and considered itself the defender of the one true faith.

During the Spanish Republic, from 1931-39, religious tolerance allowed the growth of some 200 Protestant churches. But when General Francisco Franco came to power at the end of the Spanish Civil War, Protestant churches were prohibited and believers were scattered. Because of the close ties between church and state, Protestant disagreement with the Roman Catholic Church was seen as opposition to the government. The churches remained closed from 1939 to 1945, when a law of religious tolerance was passed, but even then Protestants faced many restrictions and some persecution.

When TEAM entered Spain in 1952, the mission's magazine reported that there were twenty to thirty Protestant churches plus scattered groups of evangelicals, an estimated 20,000 believers in all—this in a country of 29 million people.

John and Betty Aerni Join TEAM

During his 1950 tour of Europe, David H. Johnson visited Spain and there met John and Betty Aerni, Swiss nationals who had worked independently since the early 1930s in the southern town of Archena. During the severe persecution of

Protestants after the Civil War, the Aernis were imprisoned and then expelled from the country. After ten years of ministry in Switzerland and France they returned to Spain. The Aernis had been praying for the backup that affiliation with an American mission would give and, with Dr. Johnson's encouragement, they joined TEAM in September 1952.

But their ministry with TEAM in Spain was shortlived. Just a year later, in December 1953, the Aernis were escorted to the French border by secret police. Their expulsion from Spain climaxed several months of opposition from the Archena mayor and Roman Catholic priest, who had made a concerted effort to stop the work, restricting their activities and charging them with holding illegal meetings.

The Aernis joined TEAM's France field and developed a church among Spaniards who had emigrated to Béziers, France, until their retirement in 1971.

Visa Problems Bring Gholdstons to Spain

While this drama was unfolding in Archena, J. C. and Barbara Gholdston were having difficulty obtaining residence visas in Portugal. After two denials, it became clear that they would have to serve elsewhere. Thus in January 1954 they traveled to neighboring Spain and settled in Madrid.

God led them to a small Brethren Assembly church a block and a half from their home which had been praying for a pastor. As they worked with this church they found open doors to other Brethren Assemblies throughout the country. It was virtually impossible to start new churches during this time due to government and social restrictions, but the Gholdstons carried on a fruitful teaching and evangelistic ministry in these already established churches and saw many come to Christ.

"Persecution has borne fruit in Spain," J.C. Gholdston said at TEAM's 1958 annual conference in Racine, Wisconsin. Although Christians faced many restrictions, precious souls were coming to Christ.

Now, we don't have mass evangelism in Spain, but fruit growers know that hand-picked fruit is always the best. It's prettier and sweeter. So, in Spain the fruit has to be hand-picked, but it's precious. And He gives the increase.[1]

Surmounting the Obstacles

Person-to-person evangelism was of necessity the method used. Protestants and other non-Catholic religious groups were prohibited from identifying their churches by any outward sign, advertising their services by press or radio, publishing or distributing evangelical literature, or renting halls for special gatherings.

Sharing Christ with friends and neighbors was therefore key. Yet this was not done without cost. As the Gholdstons wrote in 1955:

> You are no doubt aware of the impossibility of speaking of the things of Christ outside the churches here. This is considered proselyting and is forbidden by law. However, who can stop the mouths of the true children of God so that they do not speak of their Savior and Redeemer? Although it costs many of the Christians their jobs and being hated by their neighbors they continue to speak.[2]

Reinforcements and a Bible School

The Gholdstons were TEAM's only Spain missionaries for seven years until Larry and Margaret Allmon arrived in 1961, soon joined by Ernest and Mary Hickman. Together the three couples prayed about beginning a Bible school to train young men and women. Investing in the lives of national workers seemed a critical focus in uncertain times.

The school opened in Madrid in October 1962 with sixteen students. Ten of these were resident and the others attended as many classes as they could. Representing five denominations, these first students came from several provinces of Spain. The Madrid Bible Institute offered a two-year program of Bible training combined with practical work, equipping these young men and women to serve Christ in their home churches.

The Bible school continued until 1969, when it had to be closed for lack of personnel and insufficient support. It left a legacy of graduates serving the Lord in Spain as well as farther afield.

Restrictions Easing

Restrictions on Protestants were beginning to lighten, as the era of Vatican II brought more liberal attitudes toward non-Catholics. When I visited Spain in February 1963 I found an air of expectancy. Liberal laws giving recognition to Protestants had been proposed and evangelicals believed they would soon be allowed to print Christian books and open new places of worship.

Meeting together in conference, the missionaries decided that the field would begin focusing on church planting in 1964 when the Gholdstons returned from furlough. Even with fewer restrictions, starting a church would not be easy. As one missionary wrote: "God evidently is leading in this direction and we must follow in spite of opposition and lack of workers."[3]

Church Planting Begins

On my next visit to Spain, at the end of 1964, I found the Gholdstons beginning a small study group in their Madrid home with the help of Ernest and Mary Hickman. At the same time I learned that government restrictions were tightening again after a period of relaxed pressures.

In April 1965 the Gholdstons could report slow but healthy growth. Sunday afternoon meetings had been started and attendance had reached as high as twenty-six adults and eleven children. Three had accepted Christ as Savior.

> ...[O]ur hearts cry out for more fruit, but God is trustworthy and will answer in the way that will glorify His name most. In Spain we have experienced that slow growth is healthier and creates less opposition. Yes, we still have opposition here. The freedom that we had hoped for is still not to be found in Spain, but there are means of working, and perhaps more freedom than we are taking advantage of.[4]

The 1967 Religious Freedom Law gave additional leeway but required Protestant organizations to file with the government an annual list of their members' names and addresses, a financial

782

statement, and a statement of belief.

By 1970 word from Spain was that "the vision for a church planting ministry has been enlarged and great possibilities lie before us."[5] The work the Gholdstons had begun in Madrid was now the Canillejas Evangelical Bible Church, the field's only established church. The nucleus of another church was growing in nearby Guadalajara under the leadership of John and Ellen Johnson. Work had also begun in Vicálvaro and Aranjuez. Other vast areas with no gospel witness awaited the arrival of additional missionaries. The Spain field was praying for thirty-six new missionaries to join them by 1974.

Reaching out Through Correspondence Courses

In January 1969, Dale and Anne Vought's first assignment after language study was to begin a correspondence course ministry. The government granted permission to print and distribute "Light of Life" courses on John, Acts, and Galatians, and a small offset press was purchased.

The purpose was evangelism leading to church planting. Courses were advertised in selected areas where missionaries or local Christians could follow up or where missionaries hoped to begin a new church.

In 1970, Ernest Hickman took on Word of Life Press—the literature work—full-time, printing the correspondence courses along with evangelistic tracts and flyers. The Voughts continued to administer the correspondence courses while trying to start a church in a Madrid suburb.

For most of the students, this was their first experience with evangelical ideals and the Bible itself. Prejudices were being overcome as they studied God's Word for themselves. In 1971, there were 259 correspondence students, of whom fifteen accepted Christ.

The literature ministry continued until 1976, when the printing press was sold.

A Start in Alcobendas

Missionaries David and Sharon Esau began laying the ground-work for a branch church in the Madrid suburb of Alcobendas in 1971. Its official opening was marked in November of the following year by an evangelistic street meeting, held with government permission after minor opposition by the mayor and others.

By February 1975 Ernest and Mary Hickman reported that a solid foundation of several families was attending the regular Sunday service. "The work in Alcobendas has been the uniting of believers in that area, rather than a number of conversions," they wrote. "We long to see souls saved and the church growing."[6] Their immediate strategy was to visit door-to-door offering a packet of free material, show a series of films, and hold special meetings.

Gary and Sherryl Bowman joined the work in Alcobendas a year later. Besides the Sunday services, regular ministries in this young church included Sunday school, a young people's group, and a weekly women's meeting. Members were beginning to take on more responsibility, partially paying the meeting-place rent and witnessing in the community.

The missionaries' hard work continued to bear fruit in the years ahead. In 1984 Phil and Elaine MacDonald accepted the leadership of the Alcobendas church and within two years it had an associate national pastor. In 1988 this man assumed the pastorate and within a year the church was independent of TEAM.

Two Decades of Slow Progress

By the early 1970s, Spain had been a TEAM field for two decades. During these years a small number of missionaries had worked against great odds. For the first eight years there was no more than one TEAM couple in Spain. Others had begun arriving in 1960, and by February 1973 there were five couples and one single woman. These were welcome additions to the team but a far cry from the thirty-six new missionaries for whom the field had been praying.

Government restrictions and opposition had made it impossible to plant new churches at first, but even when the laws were eased growth was slow and hard-won. Efforts to start churches did not always succeed. In early 1973 Canillejas was still the only fully established church, doing well with a congregation of ninety people. The much younger church in Alcobendas was also growing and had received government approval, while congregations were forming in three other areas.

Why the Slow Growth?

Looking at the broad evangelical scene in Spain in early 1973, Dale Vought suggested a number of reasons why evangelical churches were growing so slowly. Vought felt that the usual answer—government restriction—was not the main problem, since growth rates appeared to be higher during the years of restriction than during the last four years of relative freedom.

Rather, he saw most of the problems as arising within the evangelical church itself. One problem he called a "catacomb complex"—the feeling by evangelicals that they were not quite up to par with the rest of society, an attitude which came about because they had been a minority and legally suppressed for so many years. Although the 1967 Religious Freedom Law had eradicated much of this, it remained a problem particularly in small villages.

One of the greatest hindrances to growth, Vought said, was the concept of clergy with an uninvolved laity, drawn from the Catholic system and supported by past missionary practice. This belief that "the clergy is to minister and the laity is to be ministered to" meant that people in many evangelical churches felt little sense of responsibility for outreach. The traditional concept of a "good church" was one with a large congregation, a nice building, and a full-time, paid pastor. Because few evangelical groups could maintain such a church on their own, there was much foreign subsidizing and frustration. Tied to this view of the "good church" were the ministerial training institutions in Spain, which prepared men to pastor an existing church, not to plant churches.

As a result, said Vought, the Evangelical Church of Spain was irrelevant in Spanish society because it had not related itself to the people.

> In many cases it is considered too foreign or at least a tool of foreign interests and not Spanish. This creates many barriers that ought not to exist and can only hinder their growth.

Those few churches which were growing rapidly emphasized home visits and evangelistic activities carried out by the whole church, he said.[7]

Though TEAM's missionaries worked to plant churches where lay people were active in outreach and gradually assumed full responsibility, their progress was certainly affected by these prevailing attitudes.

Theological Education by Extension

To teach laymen to be leaders in the churches, TEAM decided to begin Theological Education by Extension (TEE). After several years of planning, the program began in January 1976. Five evangelical churches in Sevilla sent students, and Dale Vought and a Spanish pastor taught the first two courses.

TEE was much less costly than full residential training and had the added benefit of equipping laymen who showed leadership potential to take more responsibility while remaining in the churches.

Joining a Church Association

Rather than beginning its own association of churches, as the mission has done in many countries, TEAM in Spain decided to affiliate with an existing Spanish group, the Federation of Independent Evangelical Churches of Spain (FIEIDE). All churches started by TEAM missionaries were encouraged to join FIEIDE as soon as admission requirements were satisfied and to be active in its programs. Canillejas was the first TEAM-initiated church to join FIEIDE.

Evangelical Christian Academy

As missionaries slowly increased in number, so did missionary children. The need for affordable, suitable schooling led Ernest Hickman and other parents to start a Christian day school in Madrid. In the fall of 1973 Evangelical Christian Academy opened for its first year of service to missionary children with twelve students.

TEAM In Sevilla

Except for the Aernis' work in Archena to the south, the first two decades of TEAM's work in Spain centered around the large capital city, Madrid, in central Spain.

Then in 1974 the field decided to open a second area of work in southern Spain, assigning the Voughts to assist a church in Sevilla which had its own national pastor. Soon after the Voughts arrived, five evangelical churches sponsored a city-wide campaign featuring Luis Palau, the Argentine evangelist. The results were exciting indeed. Said Vought:

> We were able to get all of the permissions in time to distribute 100,000 tracts, post several thousand notices along the major streets, and buy time on two radio stations. The fact that we were able to buy time on the Catholic radio station is in itself a major accomplishment. It was the first time since 1932 that Protestants have been able to have public meetings of such proportions in Sevilla. The impact on the entire city has been fantastic.[8]

In all, he said, there were about 125 decisions for Christ—amazing results when the entire evangelical community of Sevilla numbered only 300 before the crusade.

As an outreach of the Sevilla church, the Voughts began Bible studies in the village of Utrera in August. By January 1975, the group numbered six families and had outgrown the home where it met. Encountering unwillingness to rent a meeting place to Protestants and unable to afford the purchase of a building, their prospects at first were discouraging. But the Lord overruled, and by March they had rented a building on a main street and begun the long process of requesting government recognition.

The Sevilla church itself was growing in numbers and maturity. In November 1977 Vought reported that the youth group had grown to fifty from twelve when they first arrived. The young people were now completely responsible for a Christian youth center which offered programs four nights a week. The church facilities had been enlarged twice in the past four years and were due for further expansion. And a team of church members was visiting homes in a new area of the city three nights a week, hoping to start a new church there.

The TEE program to train church leaders was also progressing, with twenty-nine people studying a course on personal evangelism. When other churches learned of TEE and asked for help, Vought travelled south to Algeciras every two weeks to teach classes.

Canillejas Church Calls a National Pastor

The Gholdstons had been hoping to turn the Canillejas church over to a national pastor for a number of years, but as their furlough approached in 1975 the matter became urgent. Prayer was answered in the form of Roque Sanchez, a pastor from southern Spain who had attended the TEAM Bible institute for a semester in 1962. TEAM agreed to provide part of his salary until the church could assume it in full.

A Growing Field

At the beginning of 1976, TEAM's work in Spain was still relatively small. The Bowmans and Hickmans led the small church at Alcobendas, assisted by Don and Denise Tucker who were studying Spanish. The Voughts worked with the churches in Sevilla and Utrera while starting up TEE. Debbie Laws taught at Evangelical Christian Academy and worked with young people in the church at Canillejas. The Gholdstons were on furlough.

But the next years brought tremendous growth. From eleven missionaries at the beginning of 1976, the number of workers had more than tripled by 1982. And many new areas saw concentrated church planting efforts. Near Sevilla, missionaries moved into Alcalá de Guadaira, Coria del Río, Morón de la Frontera, and Dos Hermanas; near Madrid they worked in Colmenar Viejo and Hortaleza.

Their methods included literature, films, children's work, musical programs, and many home visits. Films played an important role in the churches but also in drawing unsaved people to hear the gospel. Many who would not enter a Protestant church attended film showings in public buildings. Films were also shown in schools, providing opportunities to talk with staff and students and to distribute literature.

Evangelistic methods unheard of in TEAM's early years in Spain were now also used successfully. Following General Franco's death in 1975, King Juan Carlos I had ushered in a new parliamentary democracy which guaranteed human rights and removed the official status of Roman Catholicism. This paved the way for such methods as tent campaigns and street meetings, which could be held year round in many areas because of the warm weather. In Sevilla, time was purchased on a local radio station for a gospel program which offered listeners an attractive edition of the New Testament.

Field chairman Gary Bowman reported in 1982 that all areas of work had seen spiritual growth and most of them numerical growth as well. In all, there were 165 members of organized churches at the end of 1981, with an average of 377 attending church weekly. Sunday school attendance was 220. During the year there had been eighty-three professions of faith and forty-five baptisms.

Growing Pains

With the increase in missionaries and a field divided in two—Madrid and Sevilla are 325 miles apart—the need to work toward common goals became important. Thus in 1980 the Spain field adopted a Ten-Year Plan of Evangelism, aiming to plant twenty new churches by 1990 in the lower half of Sevilla province and the northern half of Madrid province. "Goals that are realistic, flexible, and challenging make us all work harder," said field chairman Dale Vought. "We need to become more committed to a Field Plan. Individual goals should be set in light of field goals and not vice versa."[9]

There was also the tension between reaching out in evangelism and helping believers to grow. Vought found that although the field had identified evangelism as its top priority, most missionaries were actually working primarily with believers.

> It appears that, contrary to what we say is our emphasis, we are very much church-development centered and weak in evangelism. Most of our time and energy are being devoted to small groups of Christians and the development within the group.[10]

Achieving a balance in ministry is always difficult, and it was also difficult for missionaries caught up in the heavy demands of their own work to feel at one with work carried on in another part of the country. "Both districts have made progress in considering each work as a part of the whole and not something off by itself," said field chairman Gary Bowman in 1982.

> We still have a long way to go and we must continually look at our fellow missionary and his ministry as a vital part of our own. With this attitude we will be more open to helping one another and our prayers will take on more urgency. As we develop this relationship we will experience God's blessings in our TEAM family and see the Lord's Church established in Spain.[11]

Legal Recognition for TEAM

With Spain's changing political scene, TEAM was now able to receive government recognition as a legal religious entity. Papers signed on January 28, 1981, gave TEAM the Spanish name *Misión Alianza Evangélica*. As a religious entity, TEAM could now open mission points and provide them with legal recognition and protection. The churches in Coria del Río and Dos Hermanas were the first to come under the legal sponsorship of the mission, a temporary step until they progressed to the point of becoming legal entities in themselves.

During this same period, the church in Utrera developed to the point of buying property. Under the leadership of Phil MacDonald, the congregation built its own place of worship and a new stage of ministry outreach was underway. When MacDonald went on furlough the work was left totally in the hands of Spaniards.

A New Outreach Through Literature

In 1983 Bob and Barbara Newman began a literature ministry, *Selecciones Cristianas,* to share Christ through the printed word. The Newmans were newcomers to Spain but had been missionaries in Latin America for nearly thirty years. Based in Sevilla, they sold Christian books in marketplaces, schools, and book fairs, as well as on consignment in churches.

In 1987 the Newmans reported that TEAM's sale of literature to the six provinces of southwestern Spain had doubled in the last year. A Christian bookstore had recently been established in Sevilla, and two Spanish workers were travelling throughout the provinces selling Christian materials.

Closer Relationship with FIEIDE

For a time missionaries had questioned the wisdom of continuing to have new TEAM churches join FIEIDE—the Federation of Independent Evangelical Churches of Spain—thinking that perhaps TEAM should begin its own church association. But in 1984 Gary Bowman reported that TEAM had been greatly blessed in not breaking its affiliation with FIEIDE. The Federation now wanted not only a closer relationship with TEAM but also an official one.

> They have complete confidence in the mission and will stand behind us even in legal matters.... [It] is a tremendous encouragement to see that the foundation that TEAM has been laying for many years is now being built upon, not just by the missionaries but by the Spanish leadership as well.[12]

In September 1983 Dale Vought had been elected to the executive council of FIEIDE, an honor for a missionary and a benefit to TEAM in allowing it direct input into the Federation's policies and planning. Now TEAM and FIEIDE formalized their relationship, remaining independent from each other but agreeing to work together to establish new churches. FIEIDE also agreed to represent TEAM before the government to facilitate obtaining residence permits for missionaries.

TEAM had recently begun planting churches in three new areas—Carmona and Marchena, both in the south, and Córdoba, a major city eighty miles north of Sevilla. Although the ten-year plan had not anticipated work in Córdoba, an increase in the missionary staff made it possible for TEAM to assign Don and Paula Cabeen to Córdoba when a group of believers there requested help.

And it looked as though TEAM's work would expand further in the coming years. A strong missionary force and cooperation with FIEIDE boded well for new ministry opportunities.

TEE Revitalized

During 1983 the theological education by extension program was revitalized. Groups in Coria del Río, Utrera, and Dos Hermanas were studying pastoral theology, while seven young men in Morón de la Frontera were learning how to preach. In Utrera, three men were doing projects to develop spiritual maturity and leadership.

Although many individuals benefitted from the program, TEE had not achieved the scope missionaries had hoped for. In 1987, Daniel and Susan Batlle accepted TEE as their main ministry, planning to develop it into a training program for the entire field. Sadly, Daniel Batlle passed away shortly after receiving this assignment, succumbing to a long-standing kidney ailment.

A New STEP in Education

In Madrid, TEAM continued to assist Evangelical Christian Academy, the school which many TEAM missionary children attended. In 1987 TEAM had four teachers and a secretary serving at the school, plus five missionaries on its board of directors. Gary Bowman was president of the school board, which gave even more TEAM influence in the school.

In Sevilla province to the south, most missionary children

attended local Spanish schools. Though this pleased many parents, there were problems in several areas and some children were not learning adequate written English skills.

Thus in 1986 a new program was introduced: the Spain TEAM Education Program (STEP), taught by missionary Katherine Koehn. Its purpose was to offer English schooling to TEAM's missionary children in Sevilla province. Missionaries could choose either extra help with English for children attending Spanish schools or a full English school program. At the end of its first year, the field decided to continue STEP and build on the good foundation laid that year.

The full program had to be discontinued when Miss Koehn left the field in 1987, but mothers carried on a partial program for another year. Plans exist to reinstate the program when the next group of missionary children reaches kindergarten age.

Providing Administrative Help

Beginning in 1983, Spain missionaries provided administrative help and guidance to TEAM's work in Portugal. Spain field chairman Gary Bowman served on the Portugal field council as its chairman also. This arrangement provided leadership to a small neighboring field for a number of years.

Then in 1986 another mission—SEND, International—asked TEAM to sponsor its entry into Spain and give its missionaries orientation and direction. The two groups agreed that SEND would work under TEAM's leadership for at least three years. Though this gave additional responsibility to TEAM, it allowed another mission to begin a fruitful ministry in Spain.

Progress in the Churches

In 1985 Gary Bowman reported that the Coria del Río church had joined FIEIDE, making a total of six TEAM churches which were now members. Though the Canillejas church was no longer a TEAM ministry, having been fully independent for some time, missionaries rejoiced that after several difficult years the church had financed and built a new church building while continuing to pay the pastor's full salary. Few churches in Spain had accomplished what Canillejas had.

Though attendance at all TEAM-related churches had almost tripled over the past decade, increasing from 125 in 1974 to 370 in 1984, the numbers had levelled off and even dropped slightly over the last three years.

Said Bowman in the annual report covering 1985:

> Again this year much of our missionary efforts have been directed to the edification and training of the believers. This type of effort must continue, but we need to direct more of our prayer and activities to the evangelization of the Spanish people. Some of this can and should be done through the preparation and sending of the national believers, but there needs to be more of a commitment to this on the part of the missionaries.[13]

But by the end of 1986 the picture was changing. Professions of faith were up 10 percent, baptisms were up 33 percent, and church attendance had increased 33 percent.

Missionaries and churches had been trying new avenues of reaching unbelievers. In Sevilla, a recorded telephone message offered words of hope to those who called. The church in Coria del Río was on the air "live" each Sunday morning with a one-hour radio program and opportunity for people to call the studio with questions. Musical groups from three churches had recorded cassettes during the year, providing an on-going ministry in homes around the country. The Hortaleza church was reaching out with puppet shows in parks. And the Coria del Río church continued to make new contacts through its Awana program, while the group in Lantejuela followed suit.

Developing a Camping Ministry

Christian camps were a good opportunity to spend concentrated time with believers and unsaved friends. As the camp grounds available for rent became busier every year, missionaries began to discuss the need for a permanent TEAM site. After years of study and trying to raise funds, a camp property was purchased north of

Sevilla in 1990, giving the promise of a new thrust in the Spain field's ministry.

Reaping a Harvest

Behind the statistics and names of towns entered are the individual stories of hundreds of lives changed by the gospel. One of these was Mariano Canestro, who attended the Awana club at the Coria del Río church as a ten-year-old. He left the church but returned to accept Christ during his teen years. Mariano's changed life became the open door to his unsaved family. Over several years, twenty-three of Mariano's relatives became Christians, including some burdened by drug addiction and one who had dabbled in the occult.

Similar stories could be told from other TEAM churches. Consistently, churches grow as they reach out to the believers' extended families. Another area of fruitful ministry has been helping drug addicts and their desperate family members. The Coria del Río and Puebla churches and the Nueva Vida Church in Sevilla have also reached out to families through preschool programs held in their church facilities. Both the children and their parents have heard the gospel, and some have found new life in Christ.

One thrilling measure of the harvest being reaped in Spain is that three of the young people saved and trained at the Alcobendas church are now pastoring churches started by TEAM missionaries in Alcobendas, Colmenar Viejo, and Hortaleza. It is exciting indeed to see God calling Spanish men and women to build his church—and to see him finding ready hearts and willing spirits.

AUSTRIA, ITALY, AND TURKEY— THREE SHADES OF RESISTANCE

AUSTRIA

After visiting TEAM's work in France, Spain, and Portugal in early 1963, I travelled on to Germany with France field chairman Art Johnston to confer with Christian leaders about the needs in Germany and Austria. Nationals and missionaries alike told us that the gospel needs in both countries were tremendous. In Austria, with 90 percent of its population Roman Catholic, only 6 or 7 percent were Protestants and very few of these were evangelical.

The situation described to us was graphically illustrated in a Stuttgart restaurant when we spoke in halting German to our Austrian waiter, a young man of about twenty-seven. We asked what he knew of the Bible. He had studied it in school. Did he believe it? "Who believes it any more?" was his reply. "Isn't it pretty much a collection of myths?"

Returning home, I urged that we give Europe new emphasis in our prayers and recruiting:

> In proportion to the need the Christian church is doing less to evangelize Europe than any other area in the world. TEAM's efforts are commendable, but far too limited. We could put in 100 missionaries over the next five years and still barely touch the need. Now is the time for TEAM to give Europe new emphasis.[1]

The board of directors responded promptly, approving Austria as TEAM's twentieth field at their April 1963 meeting.

First Workers Arrive in 1965

Richard and Elsbeth Baarendse were the first TEAM missionaries to reach Austria, arriving and beginning their German language study in 1965. By 1967 they had been joined by Don Silvis and Barbara Archer (who married each other in 1968) and by Lloyd and Val Benton. One of their first ministries was among students at the University of Vienna. During these early years the Austria field worked under the guidance of the France field council.

Focus on Vienna

In 1968 the Baarendse and Silvis families moved to the Tenth District of Vienna, an area with no evangelical churches. They began to reach out to the community in every way they could think of: home visits, outdoor film showings, poster campaigns, and Bible studies. At parks and outdoor markets, they attracted listeners with music and testimonies, giving them tracts and inviting them to meetings.

These efforts fell mostly on skeptical ears. Said Elsbeth Baarendse:

> Most Viennese...have one goal: living the good life. That means material possessions, a prestigious position in society, and the privacy to enjoy a few intimate friends. They respond to the gospel with innate distrust and skepticism. Their nod to religion consists of paying yearly dues to their traditional church.[2]

Yet the missionaries did find some prepared hearts. After an evangelistic tent crusade in September 1968 they began regular Sunday meetings in a rented hall. By 1972 the Tenth District Fellowship had grown to include thirty-nine Austrians. Among those helping to lead its healthy program—Sunday worship, five Sunday school classes, two Bible studies, and a youth group—were two Austrian university students, Wolfgang Frey and Robert Janscha.

The second area to be targeted was Vienna's Twenty-third District. By 1972 regular Sunday morning services were held alternately in Jim and Rosemary Brubaker's home and David and Bonnie Rinehart's home.

That same year saw many evangelistic ventures. In cooperation with Greater Europe Mission, TEAM held its first camp for teen-agers in Annaberg, Lower Austria. Though TEAM had assisted in a children's camp for the past three years, this fourth year it was directed solely by TEAM missionaries for the first time. A tent crusade and several weeks of outdoor film showings reached many adults and children.

More Workers and Administrative Independence

When I visited Austria in March 1972, the field had grown to fifteen missionaries, nearly half of whom were in language study or on furlough. The others were busy in evangelism and shepherding the two young church fellowships in Vienna. We decided that it was time for the Austria field to operate on its own; beginning with the 1973 annual conference, Austria would conduct its business independently of the France field.

On March 15, 1972, a corporation was formed which gave the mission legal status to buy, sell, and possess property. Its name, *Freunde der Evangelikalen Allianz Mission,* translated to "Friends of the Evangelical Alliance Mission."

A Third Area for Church Planting

In early 1973 TEAM moved into a third area, suburban Mödling District. Many good contacts made in the early months of the work encouraged Deno and Julie Elliott and the Brubakers in their prayers that a church would soon be established here.

The two church fellowships were making good progress. In late 1973 the Tenth District Church took a step of faith when it purchased its own meeting place—two rooms which had been a tire sales and service center. After the believers renovated and redecorated, grand opening celebrations for the new chapel were held in May 1974. In the year which followed, the Quellenstrasse Church became fully organized, adopting a constitution and official membership.

In the Twenty-third District, the church group outgrew the

Rineharts' home and rented a meeting room. By spring 1973 sixteen to twenty people were attending the worship service regularly.

Setting Field Goals

The Austria missionaries set measurable field goals toward which they prayed and worked each year. One goal set in 1973 had been to write a doctrinal statement which could be adopted by the forthcoming TEAM-related churches. This had been done by annual conference in 1974—and wisely so, forestalling the problems which can arise if young church groups do not share a statement of faith. Another goal had been to trust the Lord for thirty-three conversions and eleven baptisms during the next year. Though the results fell short—only seventeen were converted and one baptized—the missionaries were thankful for each one and were not deterred in setting high goals for the year ahead. Said field chairman Richard Baarendse:

> These statistics indicate less numerical growth than in previous years. We have learned to beware of cheap, meaningless professions. Indeed, pulling on unripe fruit or pressuring premature conversions for the sake of statistical growth does more harm than good. On the other hand we must ask the Lord for a faith which *daily* expects to see people personally committing themselves to Jesus Christ.[3]

Besides annual goals, the missionaries agreed on a challenging long-term faith goal: 400 baptized believers gathered into seven churches by 1985.

Two New Beginnings

By mid-1977 TEAM was working to start or develop churches in five areas in and around Vienna. Twenty-six missionaries were assigned to the field; though, as usual, furloughs and language study meant that the number actually engaged in church planting was less. Two new areas had been entered: in September 1976 Herbert and Lorelei Apel had moved to Vienna's Eleventh District and the Elliotts settled in Perchtoldsdorf the following May.

Strengthening the Core Group

In the Twenty-third District, missionaries were concerned because the Sunday worship service, which had been held in a rented hall for several years, was seeing very little growth. After prayerful analysis, they concluded that the church needed a larger and stronger core group, and that they should build up this nucleus in a home gathering before meeting as a formal church. The Sunday service was therefore discontinued and missionaries put all efforts into personal evangelism and home visits.

A Miracle in the Tenth District

The Tenth District Church was growing steadily, averaging a full house of sixty-five at Sunday worship by February 1977. When the church had moved into its two-room facility in 1973, the missionaries had by faith reserved the adjoining unit with the Lord; it would be ideal when the church needed more space.

One day in October 1976 Richard Baarendse noticed that the tenant was moving out of the movie theater complex next door. But when he checked with the building's owner, the situation seemed hopeless. Three large businesses had already made bids for the space at amounts far above what the church could offer.

"All in the church prayed fervently," said Baarendse, "and for several weeks we vacillated between great faith in the Lord and fear that the project was too much to tackle."[4] Finally the church decided unanimously to make an offer that was one-third that of the highest bidder.

That December a miracle happened: the owner accepted the lowest bid, and the church became the new tenants. Once the new unit was renovated, there would be room for 150 people, Christian education rooms, and a basement youth center.

Miracles continued as a Christian architect from the United States donated his time to draw up renovation plans and one roadblock after another to successful renovation was removed.

Money came in through the sacrificial giving of many, including a retired woman who gave her savings to pay the plumbing bill.

800

Discouraging Statistics

Studying their work at the annual conference in 1977, the missionaries concluded that the seed of the Word should be sown on a broader basis. Together they decided to emphasize evangelism. The next year tract distribution increased 775 percent—from 4,000 to 35,000. A new telephone ministry was also begun. Newspaper ads, tracts, and posters encouraged Viennese to call for a two-minute gospel message, after which listeners could leave their names and addresses for literature and follow-up visits. In its first three months 1,507 calls were logged.

Though a strong emphasis on evangelism continued in the years which followed, only small numbers came to Christ each year. In 1981 field chairman Stephen Stutzman wrote:

> As we read together the annual reports from the different areas and ministries and then come to the statistical summary, the contrast between so much activity and so little measurable results is striking. The picture appears even darker when it's pointed out that the total of professed conversions [thirteen] this year is lower than at any time since 1967.[5]

Missionary numbers were down as well. From twenty-six assigned to the field in 1977, now in 1981 there were eighteen.

Yet there was some progress, as the churches in the Tenth District and in Mödling District matured. In the Tenth District, responsibility for the church had passed from missionaries to Austrian believers, freeing the Baarendses to begin work elsewhere. Elders had been installed, a church council was functioning, and Austrians had taken full charge of the Sunday school. David and JoAnne Harthan continued to assist in an advisory capacity.

In Mödling, the believers had moved from a home to an auto repair garage which they rented and renovated, doing much of the work themselves. Led by the Brubakers and Pat and Dick Worden, the group drew up a constitution and incorporated as a church. Sunday attendance had increased to thirty-five by 1981 and church members were beginning to share in the leadership.

Work in the other areas was largely difficult ground-breaking, though the Baarendses were encouraged with their start in the

Nineteenth District. A Bible study they held in an Austrian home had grown to ten people. Wondering how to reach city apartment dwellers who rarely opened their doors to unknown visitors, they thought of a telephone crusade. After recording the testimonies of ten Austrian Christians on the telephone answering system, they distributed brochures and placed newspaper advertisements encouraging people to call to hear them. During the ten-day crusade, 845 people listened to the testimonies and thirteen people requested a book that was offered.

In Alt-Erlaa in the Twenty-third District, Rob (Butch) and Shirley Hammond were working hard to make new contacts. In the Rodaun area of the Twenty-third District and in the Thirteenth District, Don and Barbara Silvis and Ed and Dorothy Moehl were visiting homes, distributing tracts, and working with a small group of contacts.

Encouraging Progress

Two years later, in mid-1983, field chairman Richard Baarendse could report progress in all areas of work. Twenty-eight people had accepted Christ during the year, and thirteen had been baptized. Both organized churches were growing: average Sunday attendance in the Tenth District was ninety and in Mödling, fifty. The three home Bible studies had also grown: Rodaun to six people, Alt-Erlaa to six people, and the Nineteenth District to fifteen.

Though the field had fallen short of its earlier long-term goals, the missionaries were now working towards a new ten-year goal: having nine churches and four missionary starts by 1993. An ongoing goal, that of encouraging fellowship among the TEAM-related believers, was achieved in part when members from the various groups met together for baptismal services. And during the past year, church and mission leaders had met three times for prayer and planning.

Another step forward came in September 1983, when the group in the Nineteenth District began a regular Sunday worship service, meeting in two rented rooms of a civic building. The Baarendses and Brent and Annette McHutchinson were excited to see twenty adults and six children becoming the core of a new church fellowship here.

Mission to Yugoslavians

Some 85,000 Yugoslavians live and work in Vienna, and it was to serve this group of people that Mike and Shelley Cochrane came to Austria in 1982. After German language study, they began studying Serbo-Croatian and joined the only Yugoslavian church in Vienna.

They were soon involved in many aspects of the church's ministry, including music, preaching, and Bible studies. They were joined in 1987 by Frank and Anna Dragash, two TEAM missionaries whose mother tongue was Croatian. "It's been exciting to see the Yugoslavian work moving into high gear and the encouraging responsiveness this work is experiencing," reported field chairman Steve Stutzman that year.[6]

Through literature, personal visits, and discipleship camps held in Greece, the missionaries also worked to help the struggling church in Yugoslavia, whose communist government did not tolerate open evangelism.

Bringing Young Adults to Christ

Missionaries and Austrian Christians together reached out into several large housing complexes in Vienna. Students and young adults from outlying provinces lived in the complexes, which contained hundreds of apartments. Believers found these young people more open to the gospel than the average population, and many of those who accepted Christ joined the churches.

Reaching Out to Hungarian Refugees

The Mödling Church began a ministry among Hungarians living in a nearby refugee camp. Missionary Martin Van Horn started a Bible study for Hungarians in 1983. Two years later about twenty attended the Bible study and a number had accepted Christ as

Savior.

Vienna Christian School

Limited educational options for missionary children led TEAM and other missions to investigate the possibility of establishing a Christian school. TEAM became a partner in Vienna Christian School (VCS), the first evangelical school in Austria. Primarily for missionary children, it would also serve other international students.

VCS successfully completed its first year in 1987. By 1988 it had already outgrown its facilities and moved to a new and larger location in Vienna's Fifth District.

TEAM's contributions as a partner mission were amply repaid when missionary parents could continue their work confident that their children were receiving a caring, Christian education.

Celebrating Twenty Years in Austria

The year 1985 marked TEAM's twentieth year in Austria. From one couple, the missionary family had grown to thirty adults and twenty-seven children. And in a culture resistant to the gospel, clear advances had been made in Christ's name. Field chairman Steve Stutzman looked back over two decades:

> From a small international student group, our work has grown to encompass five church fellowships holding Sunday worship services, audio-visual and telephone ministries whose impact reaches beyond the TEAM fellowship, a developing Yugoslavian church, and teaching ministries for national workers and missionary children. The Lord has indeed blessed us and the people of Austria.[7]

During the past year, camps for teen-agers and children had brought an excellent response, and the telephone ministry had received its 100,000th call. And it was exciting to see a growing sense of cooperation among the TEAM fellowships. Joint projects by the women's groups had spurred thoughts of other joint activities. A TEAM-wide men's meeting had been scheduled, and the groups were discussing a cooperative evangelistic thrust. "We are seeing the Austrians themselves becoming aware of the vast potential our groups represent—not only singly, but in support of one another...," said Stutzman.[8]

This spirit was evident in a joint offering taken by the Austrian church groups to help the TEAM-related churches in Chad. This led to plans for a cooperative missions weekend, and in November 1985 the Austria churches held their first missions conference.

Administrative Help

Over the years, the Austria field provided administrative help to missionaries serving in nearby countries. TEAM's teachers at Black Forest Academy (a missionary children's school in West Germany) came under the wing of the Austria field, as did Rich and Carol Shultz, who served at Freie Theologische Akademie in Giessen, West Germany. For a time TEAM's work in Turkey was also affiliated with Austria.

Don and Marie Bauer and, later, Howard and Nancy Dmytro helped the field chairmen and the work of all missionaries by providing capable administrative assistance at field headquarters.

Moving Out into the Provinces

It had long been a field goal to begin work outside Vienna in the smaller provincial cities. Surveys and part-time efforts had been made earlier, but finally David and JoAnne Harthan were assigned to Micheldorf, where a group was forming in 1985 even before they arrived. Working with an Austrian couple, their goals were to teach, counsel, and bring a church fellowship to maturity.

Faithful Seed-Sowing Continues

As the end of the decade approached, missionaries faithfully continued to evangelize, teach, and build up the church groups. Besides the new ministry in Micheldorf, lives were being changed in five areas of Vienna:

- The Tenth District Church, assisted by the Stutzmans and Ed and Joanne Lewis, became completely independent and carried on a vital ministry.

- The Mödling Church, where Martin and Sharon Van Horn worked, had passed through some tests which brought it to greater maturity. Believers there were holding evangelistic Bible studies as a first step toward starting a daughter church.
- In the Nineteenth District, the Döbling Church suffered setbacks when some members dropped out, but by June 1989 more than forty people were attending worship services regularly. Many of the newcomers were university students. Here the Baarendses and McHutchinsons were assisted by Andrew and Cheryl White and Melvin and Valerie Jenkins, two families loaned to TEAM by UFM International.
- In Southwest Vienna, the Rodaun church group was still in the early stages of church life, but the Silvises had helped the believers to find a regular meeting place in nearby Liesing and were thankful to see the core group becoming stabilized.
- In Alt-Erlaa, where years of difficult work produced few results, the Hammonds reported that the Bible study group now averaged eleven people, with real spiritual growth taking place among its members. Their prayer goal was to see a church officially organized by 1992.

And in the Yugoslavian work, opportunities for outreach were increasing both within Vienna and in neighboring Yugoslavia. Mike Cochrane told of a Yugoslavian customs official, a woman in her late thirties, whom Shelley Cochrane had led to the Lord at TEAM's discipleship camp in Greece. Frank and Anna Dragash visited her regularly on their travels in Yugoslavia, and reported that she was hungrily reading the Word and growing in faith even though she had no Christian fellowship in her city.

ITALY

As an army chaplain during World War II, David H. Johnson visited Italy many times and came away deeply burdened for this spiritually needy land. His prayers for Italy bore fruit more than three decades later when TEAM chose that nation as its twenty-fourth field.

In deciding whether or not to enter a new country, TEAM has generally looked for certain benchmarks. One is that a genuine need be presented to the mission. Another is that Christians and other missionaries working in the country confirm the need and welcome TEAM's assistance. The third is that people touched by the Lord for service in that country come forward. So it happened with Italy in the late 1970s.

While speaking at Columbia Bible College, general director Richard Winchell was approached by three or more people who were interested in TEAM but felt God's call to Italy. Returning to headquarters, Winchell learned that candidate secretary Michael Pocock had just had a similar experience at another school. Said Winchell, "Do you think the Lord is trying to tell us something?" It seemed only right to investigate the other factors: Was there a genuine need? What other missions were working in Italy? Would they welcome TEAM?[9]

Results of their research led the board of directors to declare Italy a TEAM field in November 1979. A survey team was dispatched the following October to choose areas of possible ministry. Michael Pocock and Europe area secretary Jack Mac-Donald were joined in Rome by Wallace Geiger, chairman of TEAM's France field. Since most evangelical missions worked south of Rome, the three men focused on northern Italy, visiting cities and interviewing missionaries and national pastors.

Needy but Indifferent

When David Johnson had visited Italy in 1950, he saw a country which had "Catholicism but not Christ. It has an abundance of religion, but knows practically nothing of regeneration."[10] Now the three men found that although Italy is indeed steeped in Catholic tradition, religion in any form has lost ground to massive spiritual indifference. Though 99 percent of the population is nominally

Catholic, government statistics showed that only 5 percent practice their faith. Evangelical missionaries faced no overt opposition, but rather struggled to make some advance in a society where secular interests had crowded out hunger for the spiritual. At the political level, Italy's government had changed hands forty times in thirty-four years. Though communism was a powerful force, it was not publicly atheistic and, in fact, some communists even welcomed evangelical activity as a help in breaking the grip of Catholic ideology.

Missionaries interviewed by the survey team warmly welcomed TEAM's entry and confirmed that the spiritual need was immense. Of the 32,000 cities and towns in Italy, 31,000 had no known evangelical witness. The country's 58 million people had only 114 church-planting missionaries serving among them. Italy was without doubt the least evangelized country in western Europe.

Following Proven Principles

The beginning of the work in Italy benefitted from TEAM's experience in other parts of the world, as several proven principles were brought into play.

One was the thorough on-site survey which chose target areas for the work and made contact with local Christians and missionaries. Also, the survey team selected two areas which would lend themselves to the cluster method of church planting already proving successful in France, Spain, and Austria. Working in towns close to each other, missionaries could share responsibilities in each place and use their particular gifts to the full. At the same time, developing churches would be close enough to support and encourage each other.

Finally, TEAM's aim of having seasoned missionaries begin the work in any new country was marvelously achieved when Murray and Florence Carter, who had served with TEAM in North India for twenty years, agreed to spearhead the work in Italy after their visas for India were refused. They courageously undertook to learn an entirely new language and culture for the second time in their missionary careers.

Beginnings for TEAM

In September 1981 the Carters settled in Florence, Italy, for a year of language study and then moved north to Ravenna to care for a small congregation while missionaries of the Bible Christian Union went on furlough.

The survey team had suggested two possible locations for TEAM to begin planting churches, but it was left for the Carters to make the final choice. After months of consideration they decided to begin work southeast of Bologna in an area which had no evangelical work of any kind.

In December 1982 the Carters were joined by the first of a healthy stream of young missionaries preparing to serve in Italy. Jim and Kathy Haglund, who had previously served in Irian Jaya, and David and Julia Hines were soon busy with language study.

Early the next year the Carters established TEAM headquarters in a villetta in Castrocaro Terme, a town just outside the city of Forlì, and began the lengthy process of registering the mission with the Italian government.

TEAM's Work Officially Inaugurated

TEAM's ministry in Italy was officially inaugurated on August 13, 1983, at the headquarters in Castrocaro Terme. Among those attending the opening service were missionaries from six other missions, Italian Christians from the neighboring town of Cesena, and assistant director Jack MacDonald.

Going In to Possess the Land

Several days later the Carters, Haglunds, and Hines met in Belgium at TEAM's second All-Europe Conference. Though their numbers were small, it is clear from the long-term field goals that their vision was not: by 1990, they aimed to have thirty missionaries in Italy, a Christian radio station that would reach the area where they were working, and three fully organized churches plus ten others in the process of being developed.

Field chairman Murray Carter reported that they were already well on the way to reaching the goal of thirty missionaries. Stephen and Cindy Thompson and Bruce Gregersen were expected to arrive in September 1983, four couples and a single woman had completed candidate school, another couple was in seminary, and a number of others were interested in joining the work.

The radio station was also close to a reality. With virtually no restrictions on FM broadcasting in 1983, missionaries felt that radio would give TEAM valuable exposure and contribute directly to church planting by reaching new contacts and preparing hearts. The format would be round-the-clock easy-listening music interspersed with short gospel messages designed to catch attention, challenge, and encourage people to call or write. Steve Thompson, a radio engineer, would head up the work, and finances were in hand to begin it.

The church planting goal was, however, ambitious indeed. As Murray Carter said: "To fulfill this third goal we will need to see the walls of Jericho fall and we will face the giants in the land."[11] At present in this area of several hundred thousand people, the missionaries knew only one Christian Italian couple: Ivan and Maria Trianni. The Carters' daughter, Annette, had led their two children to Christ and was discipling them. The Carters planned to start a home Bible study with the Triannis in October. It would be a long road from this one family to the goal of three churches and ten preaching points.

The Carters hoped to add to this small beginning by visiting a list of contacts they had received from Back to the Bible Broadcast and from churches in neighboring Ravenna and Cesena. Recognizing the difficulty that lay before them, they were not discouraged. Said Carter: "Let us go in and possess the land!"[12]

A Start in Forlì

New churches come into being only with great effort. Thus it was almost three years after the Carters arrived in Italy that TEAM held its first Sunday morning worship service.

A Bible study with the Trianni family and a Sunday school with their children had been held earlier in the Carters' home, but now the missionaries decided to rent a ground-floor apartment in Forlì to provide a base for their work. On May 20, 1984, this became the site of the first Sunday morning worship service. Forty people attended the service, nine of them Italians from the Forlì area. Believers from the Brethren Assembly of Cesena also came to encourage this new beginning.

In June the Haglunds and Hines completed their language requirements and prepared to give full time to the work—the Haglunds in Forlì and the Hines in nearby Faenza.

Mid-week Bible studies and regular Sunday services continued in Forlì and by August the few Italians attending now also included two children from the Haglunds' neighborhood, an interested Catholic woman who peddled ten kilometers on her bicycle to attend on Sunday mornings, and a family who drove fifty kilometers to the service. Every new contact was hard-won and precious.

In August 1984 the Italy field held its first official annual conference, electing a field council under the continued chairmanship of Murray Carter.

Radio Luce On the Air

On December 27, 1984, all the connections were made and the power was turned on to begin the first evangelical broadcast in Forlì.

After two months in makeshift facilities, a 500-watt transmitter and better antenna were installed and TEAM's Radio Luce ("light") was broadcasting a program of music, light conversation, and encouragement from the Bible on the FM band. Eight tape recorders and a computer-automation system allowed the station to operate around the clock under the direction of one missionary family.

As the first year of operation was ending, director Steve Thompson reported that the station was receiving three to six calls each week from people wanting to know more about Radio Luce. As a result, one woman had begun attending the church in Forlì and another, though she did not come to church, listened regularly with Bible and notebook to look up the Scriptures mentioned.

By 1986, Radio Luce was reaching all of Forlì and Faenza and the new recording studio TEAM had built in Forlì allowed local programming to round out the station's offerings. Two years later, Jack MacDonald reported that the station's fine signal now gave it a potential audience of 300,000. A little more power and the new antenna under construction would nearly double the potential listeners.

> Several have come to Christ through the station and a few Christians have learned about the churches because of it. Half of the attenders in Faenza are there because of the radio.[13]

Slow Beginnings

The rented church facility in Forlì was a central place to which missionaries could bring contacts and new believers, but in spite of much prayer and hard work—including distributing tracts and church invitations to every home in Forlì, Faenza, and the surrounding towns—the church in Forlì did not grow. Said Carter in 1986:

> The work in Forlì continues to be discouraging. One young lady professed faith in Christ, but has not continued on. Other than our missionaries and a couple who attend a Pentecostal church in Rimini, we do not know of any believers in the city of Forlì.[14]

Yet the team there—Carters, Haglunds, Thompsons, and Bruce Gregersen—continued faithfully to lead Sunday services, Bible studies, and evangelistic meetings; distribute literature; show Christian films; operate Radio Luce; and befriend neighbors and shopkeepers.

In Faenza, progress was also slow but more evident. David and Julia Hines had, with help from the Carters, brought their contacts together for a regular Sunday morning service, a Sunday school, and an evening evangelistic service. By mid-1986, two people had accepted Christ and been baptized, while another two new converts were being discipled by David Hines.

Camp Maranatha

In 1986 TEAM became a participating mission in Camp Maranatha, a camp in Badia Tedalda owned by Bible Club Movement. Formerly a farm, the camp's buildings were being renovated in 1988. Though still in the development stages, Camp Maranatha was showing great promise as an enjoyable setting where children and young people could hear the gospel and grow in their faith. Fifteen people accepted Christ during the five camps held that year.

Young, but Growing in Numbers

Only rarely has the number of missionaries on a new TEAM field grown as quickly as in Italy. The Carters had arrived in late 1981. By the third annual conference in 1986 there were fifteen TEAM missionaries. Two years later the number was twenty. And during 1990 it seemed certain that the goal of thirty missionaries would be achieved by year's end: twenty-nine missionaries were in Italy and five appointees were preparing to go.

All except the Carters and Haglunds were first-time missionaries; and all faced the struggles of learning a new language—which some found extremely difficult—and adjusting to a new way of life. So many new workers entering an unresponsive area made for a difficult situation, eased immensely by the Carters' mature leadership. Also evident in the annual reports are hard and faithful work and a strong emphasis on prayer.

After visiting Italy in June 1988, Jack MacDonald told the board of directors that the work there was off to a very good start. He added, "It has been and will be the target of Satan."[15]

Expanding to New Areas

Though it often seemed that missionaries put out a great deal of effort for little or no results, the picture began to change in 1987 and 1988. Though the group in Forlì remained small, new people began to attend. In Faenza, the group rented a hall for their church services. And TEAM expanded its church planting work to Bologna, Ravenna, and Alfonsine—taking over two existing works and beginning a new Bible study in Alfonsine, an outgrowth of the Ravenna work.

In May 1988 field chairman Murray Carter reported encouraging statistics for the past year:

> We have had 12 or more people accept Christ and we have baptized 5 people. Our overall church attendance on the field has risen from an average of 25 to 70 people counting missionaries.[16]

A year later there was more good news. Sixteen people had been baptized during the year. The Carters had seen the Ravenna church grow and the Bible study in Alfonsine expand to include a Sunday worship service. The Forlì missionaries—the Haglunds, Thompsons, Raney Brown, and Bruce Gregersen—rejoiced in five new believers, the first since the work began. Though plagued with illness, the Faenza workers—Craig and Mary Conner and Beth Wrenn—reported that the church there continued to grow. Missionaries in Bologna felt that a second church could be started there, growing from a Bible study held on the opposite side of the city. Radio Luce continued to provide new contacts in Forlì and Faenza; and the developing ministry at Camp Maranatha was a blessing, especially to young people.

General director Richard Winchell and assistant director Jack MacDonald were able to visit Italy on a number of occasions to confer with the missionaries and give guidance. For Dr. and Mrs. Winchell this was of particular interest because their son Barry and daughter-in-law Dawn were serving as missionaries in Bologna.

Setting New Goals

As 1990 was approaching, Murray Carter reviewed the field goals set six years earlier. Two out of three were achieved or nearly so: Radio Luce was on the air and there were almost thirty Italy missionaries; but the goal of three organized churches and ten preaching points had fallen short. It appeared that there would be one organized church and four, possibly six, preaching points by the end of 1990.

At the 1989 field conference, the missionaries met to plan goals for the decade ahead and to refine their team strategy of church planting, possibly enlarging the teams and aiming for each team to plant several churches. "I believe that we can face a new year with joy and much expectancy," said Carter. "Let us believe God for the harvest."[17]

TURKEY

In the first centuries of the Christian era, the area known today as Turkey was strongly influenced by the gospel. The Apostle Paul travelled extensively here during his missionary journeys; such familiar Bible places as Ephesus and Antioch are located in present-day Turkey. This area was also home to the Seven Churches addressed in the book of Revelation.

Once the majority religion, Christianity was all but wiped out when the Turkish peoples conquered this area in the tenth and eleventh centuries, militantly imposing Islam. Today 99.2 percent of Turks are Sunni Muslim.

When the Republic of Turkey was formed in 1923, President Kemal Ataturk began a series of major reforms which aimed to make Turkey a modern, secular state. Though Islam is no longer the official state religion, it remains central to Turkish life. Veteran missionary Thomas Cosmades described the prevailing attitude as this: "To be a Turk, one must be a Muslim. If I give up Islam, I cease to be a Turk."[18] Freedom of religion is provided by law, but it remains difficult to practice another faith. Believers have suffered for their faith, not least in being disowned by their families. Others have lost jobs or been imprisoned. Missionaries report some easing of difficulties in recent years.

Unique Among Ministries

The work in Turkey is unlike TEAM's ministry in any other part of the world. Turkey does

815

not grant visas for missionary work as such: most missionaries there are either "tent-makers" like the Apostle Paul, engaged in a profession such as teaching English; or tourists, remaining in the country for the three-month maximum before exiting to return again. Because Christians are so few and Christianity so suspect to most Turks, TEAM's work in Turkey has deliberately kept a low profile. For fear of reprisals against them, believers and interested contacts were never named in TEAM's publications in a way which could allow them to be identified.

In 1985 it was estimated that there were only 150 to 200 believers in the entire country of more than 51 million people.[19]

TEAM Begins Ministry to Turks

TEAM first considered work in Turkey because of the interest and availability of Thomas and Lila Cosmades. Tom was born in Istanbul of Greek parents; his language skills and local contacts gave hope of an effective ministry in a land which was without missionary workers.

Because he had been naturalized as an American citizen, Cosmades was not allowed by Turkish law to live permanently in Turkey. He and Lila therefore established residence in Greece and entered Turkey in 1960 as tourists—the first Christian missionaries to serve in that land in the modern era. They were joined in the country within the next year by two Operation Mobilization missionaries who were shortly imprisoned and their literature confiscated.

In the years which followed, the Cosmades regularly visited Turkey to evangelize and disciple isolated believers. They also learned that many Greek and Turkish workers were being employed in Germany. Away from home in a country where the gospel could be freely proclaimed, these migrant workers presented a clear opportunity.

A Base in Germany

During their furlough in 1967-68, the Cosmades visited West

Germany. The open door among Turkish and Greek guest workers there, combined with the Cosmades' need to establish a home base outside of Turkey, convinced them to settle in Siegen, West Germany.

From here they carried on a varied ministry. Between regular visits to Turkey, they developed an extensive Turkish-language literature ministry. Christian literature—particularly God's Word itself—was a powerful tool in a land where opportunities for witness were limited.

They also worked among Turkish workers in Germany, especially during 1968 to 1972, which Cosmades termed "the golden years of evangelizing Turks." During these years Turkish men were in Germany without their families, with nowhere to go and little to do outside working hours. They gladly attended gatherings where Turkish was spoken and people were friendly. Slides, literature, tea, and coffee attracted many who had never heard of Christ. In later years, as the families and more Turks arrived, the Turkish community established its own schools and mosques, and leaders warned against attending the meetings. Thus it became necessary to find new avenues for witness.

The Cosmades also carried on an itinerant ministry in a number of Eastern European countries, including Yugoslavia, Romania, Bulgaria, and Hungary. They were able to encourage Christians in these countries during years when Christian contact from the outside world meant a great deal to faithful believers there.

Radio Outreach

Using yet another approach to reach Turks, the Cosmades began a fourteen-year association with Trans World Radio, writing and recording gospel programs which were beamed into Turkey. When the broadcasts began, the weekly fifteen-minute program brought in five letters a month from listeners. In later years the broadcasts increased until they were aired daily, with a high of 400 letters being received in a month. Many people heard the gospel for the first time in this way.

First Resident Missionaries Arrive

In October 1971, James and Karan Romaine arrived in Turkey as TEAM's first resident missionaries there, settling in Istanbul for language study and to teach English as a means of staying in the country.

After more than four years of witness with no tangible results, they met Hasan, a merchant seaman who had lost his job because of his interest in Christ. While Hasan's ship was docked near New York City someone gave him a Turkish-language Gospel of John. Through reading God's Word he put his trust in Christ—but then had to return home, thrown off the ship by the Muslim captain.

Jim began studying the Bible with Hasan every week, carefully discipling him in his new faith. So strong was Hasan's desire to know God that he would often rise at 3 or 4 A.M. to read the Scriptures and pray.

A House Church Begins

As the years passed, the Cosmades and Romaines continued to share the gospel through literature, radio, and personal contact—a slow and demanding task where each interested person or new believer was a "pearl of great price," worth much prayer and labor. Extending hospitality was also a major avenue of ministry. Said Karan Romaine:

> In this culture entertaining is important. And God has used this means to bring many who come here to himself. Guests don't always come when they are invited; in fact, most seem to come uninvited. But it is very important to make each guest feel a warm welcome and a freedom to stay as long as he likes. In one year I counted over 300 guests who came for a meal or stayed over-night.[20]

By the late 1970s, the missionaries knew a number of converted Muslims who were interested in studying the Bible. When they asked Hasan if he would like to begin a small worship service in his home, he agreed enthusiastically.

But after several months of twice-weekly meetings for Bible study and worship, it became apparent that these frequent visits by foreign missionaries were drawing unwelcome attention and suspicion from the authorities. The group would have to find another meeting place. After much prayer, God led them in 1980 to an ancient church building in the Kadikoy area of Istanbul.

This building met the need for three years, though it was less than ideal. A very large and unheated stone building, it was so cold that jackets had to be worn even in summer. Only a few men attended the meetings because it was too cold for the women and children.

Growth and Heat

By the fall of 1983, the church had grown. Now twenty people were attending, including some women and children. The group appointed two national elders, both Muslim converts, to lead the church with Jim Romaine. They would help direct the ministry and share the teaching and preaching. Said Romaine:

> We now had a "family church." But another winter was approaching, and we knew the women and children would not be able to come unless we found another meeting place. God gave us a wonderful small building with heat and two rooms for church and Sunday school before winter really set in.[21]

By 1986, more than thirty people were attending services each week. The church had adopted a set of standards and beliefs, and its ministry included a Sunday school, where eight to ten national children were taught by a former Muslim girl.

Translating the New Testament

Thomas Cosmades believed that it was time for an updated Turkish translation of the New Testament based on the early Greek texts. The last revision of the Turkish Bible had been produced in 1941, and all previous revisions were based on a translation made in the seventeenth century by Ali bey, a Polish expatriate in the Ottoman court, but never produced.

Using his knowledge of Greek, Cosmades had been hard at work translating the New Testament into modern Turkish for ten years when the United Bible Societies adopted his translation project in

1980. Continuing as chief translator, Cosmades now had the help of others in bringing the New Testament to publication.

By 1989, the revised New Testament was being distributed widely at book fairs and by Christian workers. It was also reaching Turkish hands in Germany and, by mail order, throughout the world. A new translation of the Old Testament from Hebrew was underway, with Cosmades serving as a reviewer.

Enduring Hardships

By the early 1980s, so many listeners were responding to the radio broadcasts prepared by Cosmades and aired by Trans World Radio that TEAM hired a Turkish Christian to help the Romaines follow up on each person. This man's ministry was to send personal replies to those who wrote letters to the radio station and to visit as many of them as possible. Visiting listeners was no easy task, requiring difficult travel as well as tact and bravery. Local authorities were often deeply suspicious of strangers who visited their area, fearing terrorists or propagandists. Many believed that anyone who professed Christianity must be anti-Turk. Jim Romaine described this man's ministry in 1983:

> During this year he has traveled over much of the country and visited about 300 contacts. He has been arrested, beaten and endured many traveling hardships. But he has also seen the Lord save several contacts he has visited and he has been able to bring several new believers to the meetings in Kadikoy.[22]

On one occasion this worker and a radio listener he visited were imprisoned and questioned for two days by the village police. During this time he was beaten repeatedly and hung blindfolded by his arms while being hit on the soles of his feet. Finally brought to court, he was released and ultimately declared not guilty of anti-government activity.

Missionary Reinforcements

For more than a decade the Cosmades were TEAM's only missionaries to the Turks until James and Karan Romaine arrived in Istanbul in 1971. Another decade would pass before any new helpers joined them.

TEAM Austria missionaries Herbert and Lorelei Apel became burdened for the needs in this Muslim land, and by 1983 they were studying Turkish in Istanbul. Sadly, their ministry here was cut short when medical problems forced them to return to the United States two years later. In later years they were able to return to Europe, where their knowledge of German made it possible for them to serve as TEAM representatives.

Then Howard and Claudia Williams, who had served in Turkey with a youth mission, joined TEAM in 1986. Howard taught English as a second language at Marmara University in Istanbul, while both he and Claudia worked with the church and extended hospitality to Turks, some befriended through Howard's job.

Opportunities and Dangers

When I visited Izmir (Smyrna) in 1963, there were no known believers in that city. Now there is an active church fellowship, made up primarily of young people, which meets every Sunday. It came about through the combined work of the Cosmades and missionaries from other missions. Thomas Cosmades spent a week there in 1990 teaching the qualities of Christian leadership, and reported that the church included zealous and ardent believers, not afraid to declare their faith.

My 1963 visit also included Istanbul, where I preached at the morning service at Bible House Church, with Tom Cosmades translating for me. This church—a heterogenous group of Assyrian and Armenian Christians, Turks converted from Islam, and a few Christians of Greek background—remains today. Cosmades preaches there during his annual three-month stay in Turkey.

These two churches plus the TEAM church on the Asiatic side of Istanbul are among a handful of Christian churches in the country. The other few believers are scattered, discipled whenever possible by national Christians or missionaries. When Tom and Lila Cosmades visit Turkey each summer, a large part of their ministry includes teaching and encouraging young Christians from around the country who come to stay with them for this purpose.

Area secretary Jack MacDonald described TEAM's work in 1987:

> Ministry in Turkey is almost entirely on an individual basis, visiting in homes and meeting people in tea houses to talk about the gospel. While the work is mostly carried on in Istanbul, much travel is required and our folk will go anywhere in the country to follow up a contact or to encourage a believer, if they cannot find a missionary of another organization who resides in the respective area.[23]

He reported that TEAM's church fellowship in Istanbul was one of four, possibly six, known assemblies in the entire country.

Yet doors for careful witness remained open. Said MacDonald:

> Opportunities for tent-makers abound. This kind of missionary going out under TEAM has much more opportunity for witness than one going as a fully self-supported worker. Therefore we need to do everything possible to recruit people for this highly specialized ministry.[24]

New missionaries Joel and Susan Persson took up the challenge of work in this needy land in 1989, and Jim and Renata Bultema followed in 1990.

Thomas Cosmades told me in January 1991 that Turkey is without doubt more open to the gospel now than in earlier decades. He warned, however, that the worldwide upsurge of Islam was strong in Turkey and was making its presence felt in every walk of life:

> So while we see definite encouragement and progress in the field of missions, we cannot be too optimistic.... The religionist element is becoming increasingly more vocal, more effective, and is making its presence felt. [We must] pray to God that the effectiveness of the Islamic segment will be subdued.[25]

Though the work in Turkey remains slow and difficult, pin-pricks of God's light are scattered across this vast country, growing brighter year by year.

DEVELOPMENT IN VENEZUELA

Surprising Urban Growth

Just before our airplane touched down at the Maracaibo airport in late April 1983, I looked out over the broad expanse of a city of two-thirds of a million people. I could see clusters of large office and apartment buildings distributed quite evenly across the area and a larger, more dense cluster along the waterfront of Lake Maracaibo. This was not my first visit to Maracaibo. I had been there six or seven times between 1953 and 1973. But I was truly surprised by the remarkable growth in the ten years since my last visit.

I thought back to my first visit in 1953 and the Spanish colonial town that was just beginning to take on some modern appearance. I also thought back in imagination to the time, seventy-seven years earlier, when the T. J. Bachs and John Christiansens had first disembarked at the small lake-front wharf. What remarkable growth and development had taken place over the years!

Equally Surprising Church Growth

City growth was not the only surprise awaiting me. As I began talking to TEAM missionaries about El Salvador Church and its outreach, the figure of eleven stuck in my mind. Had there been continued growth beyond the eleven branches I knew in 1973? Indeed there had. Now, in 1983, there were twenty-nine branches. By 1988, thirty-nine branches had grown from that first evangelical church planted

in Venezuela's second largest city. I learned that similar growth was taking place in other centers across the country. At the annual field conference in January 1984, the chairman, James Carmean, had reported with thanksgiving:

> One of the greatest blessings this year is to see the way God is working in a number of churches across the field. There are more churches enthusiastically involved in evangelism and discipleship than at any other time in Venezuela's history. There have been many conversions, discipleship classes, and baptisms, which have contributed to new congregations being formed. A number of churches are in building programs in an attempt to accommodate the growth. Our missionaries involved in other ministries have participated in planting and watering a number of churches. Others are involved full time in planting a new church, such as in Puerto La Cruz, Barquisimeto, Cana de Azucar, Coro, La Mesa, and Trujillo. We have reason for much rejoicing as we reflect on what God has done in this past year in the churches with which we work.[1]

By the end of 1989 there were 180 TEAM-related organized congregations and 178 others in process of formation. Sunday attendance averaged over 19,000. When this history last referred to the Venezuela work in 1946 (see chapter 16), missionaries and national coworkers could point to fifty places where gospel services were being held. What brought about this growth in four decades from 50 to 358 lighthouses for the gospel?

Growth in Missionary Staff

In 1946, the world was just beginning its recovery from World War II. Venezuela had been only indirectly affected by the war—part of that effect being in economic gain to its oil industry.

Venezuela also gained spiritually because of the war. The book of Acts records how when Paul and Silas confronted closed doors in Asia Minor, the Lord opened another door for them in Europe. Similarly, when missionaries faced closed doors to Japan, China, and Mongolia, the Lord held the door to Latin America more widely open. During and immediately following that war, twenty-three new TEAM workers went to Venezuela, Colombia, and the Netherlands Antilles. Among them were some who had planned to go to the Orient. Upon arriving they found—as had Paul and Silas—that the new open door was a promising place for fruitful missionary work.

Still Facing Opposition

Although opposition to the evangelical message was less severe in the 1940s than it had been when Bach and Christiansen pioneered in Venezuela, there was ostracism of converts and sometimes outright persecution. Those who chose to follow Christ as all-sufficient Savior rather than the blind shepherds of the Roman Catholic church invariably faced opposition. Evangelical missionaries were still described as being worse than heretics and the Bible was a forbidden book. But people in general were much more accepting of both missionaries and the Bible. Evangelical believers had, by their changed lives and upright walk, won respect in the circles where they were well known. However, social and cultural barriers were still evident. A person who became an evangelical was accused of breaking with his religious and cultural background and this put strains on family and social relationships. To receive Christ, and by that decision turn away from the Catholic Church, brought the wrath of the priests and the scorn of many Catholics.

Pre-Evangelism

Several mission ministries had contributed to increasing acceptance of evangelicals. Colegio Libertador—the Christian day school—became known throughout Maracaibo and surrounding Zulia state for its excellent education in the elementary grades. The Venezuelan schools of that period were far behind in training and discipline. Many parents, including some in government service, were glad to send their children to the Colegio even if it brought them some criticism. It was still not socially acceptable to be too friendly with evangelicals, but the growing church, the periodical *La Estrella de la Mañana*, the school, and the lives of the believers combined to create a powerful testimony for good in the community.

Assignment of New Workers

The various ministries—magazine, bookstore, print shop, day school, and Bible institute—were functioning well when this influx of new missionaries took place, and the established churches were mostly self-governing, self-supporting, and self-propagating.

So although some new missionaries were assigned to the special ministries or to existing churches, most were sent to pioneer areas. Names of different Venezuelan cities and towns began to appear on reports, correspondence, and the mission's prayer list: Los Puertos, Bachaquero, Carache, Ciudad Ojeda, Cabimas, Barinas, Sabaneta, San Antonio, Guasdualito, Machiques, Tiá Juana, and Quisiro. It was a period of rapid territorial expansion.

Key Points to Consider

The battle for souls on the foreign field faces challenges common to other enterprises. If either planning or harmony is weak or lacking, the ministry suffers. When I visited Venezuela in 1953, I was impressed that there were needs along both lines. The rapid growth of the missionary body, the orientation of many toward individualistic work habits, the lack of strong field council leadership, and an absence of unified strategy combined to create a spirit of discouragement. This discouragement was by no means justified in light of what the Lord was doing in the various areas. The new missionaries were actually seeing fruit in their work even after only a few years on the field.

My efforts to be of help were only partly successful. I tried to define quite carefully the roles of the annual conference, the field council, and the leaders of project ministries. This did not immediately solve the problem, though some benefits were evident. There was also a spiritual component that needed to be addressed.

Spiritual Refreshing

It was the general director, David Johnson, who on a visit in 1955 was used to bring about a genuine revival in hearts and a re-direction of purpose. While in Venezuela he made it a point to talk personally with each missionary in whom he sensed there were unanswered questions or problems. This personal approach had a profound effect on many, with the result that the missionary body as a whole felt a spirit of revival. Johnson wrote about this memorable manifestation of the Lord's work in hearts:

> It was my privilege to meet with the missionaries at their annual field conference in San Cristóbal, Venezuela. The Lord was present in power to bring blessing to us all. A real melting spirit was in evidence. Tenderness, unity, and harmony prevailed and we all left the conference refreshed in spirit, and with a desire and determination to be our best for Jesus.[2]

The administrative adjustments of two years earlier were not in vain. With changes in attitude and renewed harmony of purpose, it was helpful to have guidelines to clarify responsibilities. Just one example: The field council had no clear understanding of its role. It met to set the agenda for the annual business meetings and only one more time—right after the conference. An initial improvement was to schedule its meetings no less than once each quarter and, later, once in six weeks. It began to take an active role in guiding the work of the missionaries. The chairman became a full-time leader and administrator—a necessity on a field with several score missionaries serving in two countries. The improvements were ably administered, and vision and purpose promoted, by succeeding field chairmen over a period of thirty-five years: Duane Johnson, Harold Lake, Jack MacDonald, J. L. Morris, William Horst, Elton Dresselhaus, Kenneth Larson, James Carmean, and Dan Tuggy.

Extended Evangelism

Evangelism is at the heart of missionary work. Without it missions would be little more than social service. Evangelism can take many forms: personal conversations, Bible study groups, formal church services, outdoor preaching, sound-truck with films, literature distribution, radio messages, etc. Missionaries and national workers used all these various methods effectively and saw the mission work grow.

827

Jim Savage in 1954 noted new open doors that made widespread evangelism imperative in Latin America:

> After more than half a century of missionary activity, which in the main was seed sowing, South America is now prepared for a glorious harvest of souls. This is not a mere theory, but rather my conclusion after months of traveling with an evangelistic team through many parts of the continent.... Until 1948, mass evangelism, though occasionally conducted, was little known in South America. Now, however, this method is being used of God to awaken a continent to its spiritual need. Almost anywhere today where a special effort in evangelism is sponsored, one can expect from fifty to a hundred to manifest their desire to accept the Lord in a week's campaign.[3]

Evangelist Francisco Liévano

The Lord called and equipped a young man, Francisco Liévano, and used him greatly in evangelistic campaigns in Venezuela, Colombia, and more widely throughout Latin America. Liévano was a native of the hill country near Cúcuta, Colombia. As a boy he came to the market in Cúcuta where he heard the gospel and was led to Christ by Irene Garrett. TEAM missionaries helped him study his grade school lessons and he took Bible courses at night. Because it was clear that the Lord had His hand on him for special service, the missionaries encouraged him to attend the Ebenezer Bible Institute in San Cristóbal, Venezuela. This he did and after four years was graduated in 1953. His call to evangelism is related by Jim Savage, who was director of the Bible Institute:

> Two years ago Francisco Liévano was studying in the class on evangelism at Ebenezer. One day after class he went to his room and promised the Lord that if He needed evangelists, he was one who was willing. The Lord answered by giving him gifts along that line, and since graduation in July of last year, his ministry has been in demand all over the continent. Right now he has enough appointments to keep him busy through all of 1955 and 1956.[4]

After several years of fruitful evangelistic activity and further academic training, Liévano was appointed assistant director of Ebenezer Bible Institute.

Some Years in the Desert

There followed a period when Liévano was limited in travel away from San Cristóbal because of difficult family circumstances. This "desert" experience was used by the Lord to prepare him for a key role in training evangelists and pastors. In addition to completing university-level education, he translated many theological texts from English into Spanish—a means in itself of post-graduate training. He also pastored a growing church. When his family circumstances changed in 1986 he was prepared to accept the call to become rector of the United Evangelical Seminary in El Limón, a joint undertaking of TEAM, the Evangelical Free Church of America (EFCA), and their national church bodies.

Evangelism Goes Public

Political conditions in the country had some effect on the methods of evangelism. In many Latin American countries outdoor meetings would provoke counter-activity by the priests, even to mob action. In the interest of keeping the peace, the local police were usually unwilling to permit a public meeting in a town plaza, even where no law prohibited it. TEAM missionaries' evangelistic activity was a factor in clearing the way for a more open and aggressive public evangelism—of a kind that would have been out of the question in the first fifty years of the work in Venezuela. The 1950s and 60s marked the beginning of this open evangelistic effort. The Youth for Christ Congress in Caracas in 1956 and the Graham crusades of 1962 had an impact and made the evangelical message more widely known. An evangelistic team made up of both missionaries and Venezuelan Christians grew out of the Caracas crusade.

Giving Leadership to Evangelism

One missionary with a burden and gift for evangelism and a background of evangelistic church ministry was Jack MacDonald, who, with his wife, Miriam, arrived in 1956. During his eighteen years in Venezuela—part of that time as field chairman—he was a leader in broad evangelistic outreach. In 1958 he conferred with Kenneth Strachan, general director of the Latin American Mission, and was impressed by his vision of an evangelistic effort that would mobilize the whole Christian community in a country. Strachan called it Evangelism-in-Depth.

With the assurance that the program could include only evangelical groups, MacDonald convened a meeting in Maracaibo to determine whether the method could be adapted by the evangelical churches and missions in Venezuela. The result was a nation-wide evangelism program in 1964 which reached into virtually every major city and region of Venezuela. The Rev. Asdrúbal Ríos, editor of *La Estrella de la Mañana*, was named national coordinator, and MacDonald shared in the administration. Churches that could whole-heartedly subscribe to the evangelical position were invited to participate and these churches reaped great benefits. The initial benefit was a training program where volunteer workers were taught to give spiritual counsel to seekers. The foremost and eternal benefits were the souls saved and brought into the body of Christ.

MacDonald also invited several musical groups from Wheaton College and Moody Bible Institute to come to Venezuela. Their ministry was particularly effective in winning a hearing for the gospel. He reported to the annual conference in 1962 on the impact of the Wheaton College Brass Ensemble:

> The visit of the Wheaton Brass Ensemble more than fulfilled our expectations. The music was of the best and the blessing received in many places has nothing from the outside to compare with it. We believe the Lord did a real work through this ministry of music and the preaching of the Word. We saw some souls saved and are thankful. But we believe the real effectiveness of their ministry was seen in the breaking down of prejudice and disinterest. We ministered to more than 30,000 persons, figuring conservatively. This does not begin to estimate the multitudes reached through the many broadcasts. More than 75 appearances were made, including two in the universities of Mérida and Caracas.[5]

Directed Purpose in Evangelism

Evangelism is the central activity of missionaries, no matter what their assignment. Realizing, however, that it needed special attention if pastors and missionaries in any local area were to have the help they needed, the annual conference appointed a standing committee on evangelism. In 1972 the name of the committee was changed to *Evangelism and Church Planting*. The chairman of the committee for that year, Charles Belch, reported to the annual conference on the reasons for this change:

> New philosophies and goals of the Evangelism and Church Planting Committee have been elaborated during the year that spell out the direction evangelism has taken on the TEAM Venezuela field. Basically, it has to do with evangelism in two areas: church growth and new church planting. While there remains the old goal of evangelism for church growth, there comes a new impetus for evangelism that should result in the founding of churches in metropolitan and capital areas where the great masses of people live. This will give greater return for our investment, the feeling being that evangelism of the smaller and rural areas should be the responsibility of the established churches, while evangelism of the more populated areas should be a united effort on the part of TEAM and OVICE [the national church association—pronounced *oh-vee-say*].[6]

Expanded Printing Ministry

Printing the gospel was a significant TEAM ministry from the very earliest days in Venezuela when Bach used wedding gift money to buy a small press. In addition to printing tracts, a magazine, and small books, Bach did some job printing for others. This service continued through the years in a limited way. The print shop's single largest regular project was the magazine *La Estrella de la Mañana*. When a professional printer, Duane Johnson, responded to the need of the field in 1948, he immediately proposed upgrading the equipment with a linotype and an automatic press.

Robert Van Kampen, member of the board of directors, owned publishing and printing firms in the U.S.A. and was a great promoter of Christian literature. On a visit to Maracaibo he studied the needs of the print shop. The modern equipment the mission was requesting had far greater capacity than TEAM could utilize, so he conferred with the leaders of the Evangelical Free Church Mission (EFCA), which worked in central Venezuela, and proposed a joint printing ministry based in Maracaibo. This would serve not only the two missions but also a wider evangelical clientele, including the Bible Society and the Billy Graham Evangelistic Association.

Inaugurated in 1960, *Tipografía Evangélica Asociada* (TEA) was jointly operated for nearly a quarter of a century, printing scores of Christian books, magazines, tracts, and other material. In 1983 TEA was sold to *La Estrella* editor Asdrúbal Ríos and his son, Rigoberto, a TEA employee. This private company continued to serve the evangelical community.

Several TEAM missionaries worked with TEA, but Jim Carmean served the longest, nearly half of the time as director. He and his wife, Annette, were also active in church ministries and Carmean was field chairman for two years.

TEAM and EFCA also jointly developed a publication and distribution ministry, *Editorial Libertador,* which served for many years. Distribution to all of Latin America from the northern extremity of the South American continent had its problems so that joint ministry was terminated in 1983.

How Should Responsibility be Passed?

Missionaries are often heard to say: "Our job is to work ourselves out of a job." That is partially true, for the missionary will not always be available. Serious illness may intervene. Political upheavals can and do occur. Most important is a wider whitened field to enter, so staying too long on one job precludes a forward advance. In the words of the Apostle Paul, it is the missionary's responsibility to "entrust [the teaching] to reliable men who will also be qualified to teach others" (II Timothy 2:2 NIV). The dedicated missionary does not try to finish a limited job and then go home. He wants to be able to turn the work over to a qualified national successor to free himself to repeat the process elsewhere. He is anxious to multiply the number of workers in the field.

From their earliest days in Venezuela, Bach, Christiansen, Holmberg, and others followed that sound mission principle and the results are evident in the many indigenous churches they established.

The more difficult question concerned the institutions and special ministries. By 1962—in addition to the many churches in process—TEAM was responsible for a gospel magazine, a bookstore, a Christian day school, a Bible institute, a Christian education office, several camp ministries, a correspondence course outreach, a radio recording ministry, an evangelism extension team with sound truck and films, and pioneer work in the Yaruro Indian tribe. Missionaries were assigned to each of these ministries. Much of their work depended on mission money, and TEAM was fully responsible for progress in these ministries.

(At this time Venezuela and Colombia were combined in one field, so there was also the responsibility for a day school, a normal school, and a Bible Institute in eastern Colombia. Colombia began to be separately administered in 1970, as is related in chapter 48.)

In addition, TEAM and the Evangelical Free Church Mission had recently entered into an agreement combining their printing and publishing ministries and were exploring the possibility of a joint seminary.

The Need to Entrust Responsibility

When I visited Venezuela in February 1962, I asked Dr. Enock Dyrness, secretary of the board of directors, to accompany me, thinking that personal contact between board members and missionaries was mutually beneficial. The time we selected for the trip happened to be a time of political ferment. Castro had brought Cuba under communist domination in 1959 and in the years immediately following undertook subversive activities in Venezuela, which had just voted in a democratic government. When we arrived in Venezuela it was easy to see the effects of Cuban propaganda. Graffiti such as *"Castro sí, Yanqui no!"* were scrawled on many walls. America seemed to be losing ground.

We were escorted to the various mission stations and institutions by Harold Lake, chairman of the field. When we came to San Cristóbal, where Ebenezer Bible Institute is located, we learned that there had been a minor insurrection some weeks earlier provoked by Castro sympathizers. All was quiet when we arrived but both nationals and missionaries had become much more aware of possible serious trouble.

Francisco Liévano, assistant rector of the Institute, spoke to me about a matter of some importance, as he saw it. He said that several missionaries had disturbed some of the pastors by saying, "You national brethren will soon have to take over Ebenezer. We don't know how much longer we will be here. Our consulate could order us to leave because this could turn into another Cuba."

Liévano went on, "We know that the mission has encouraged the churches to support the Institute and wants more national participation, but the churches are not ready to take this responsibility. What concerns me is that we have not had any official word from the mission about this possibility."

As soon as I had opportunity, I suggested to Lake that he and Jack MacDonald—who was scheduled to become field chairman in March—arrange a meeting with Liévano and me to discuss his concerns in a preliminary way. The question could then be brought to the field council and, if recommendations were forthcoming, to OVICE and to the annual missionary conference.

A Workable Plan Designed

It became clear from our discussions that TEAM had done some thinking about transferring responsibility for the Institute to OVICE, but that no official word to that effect had been communicated. It was also clear that the leaders of OVICE were afraid they would suddenly find themselves shouldering a burden that they were not prepared to assume, lacking both finances and qualified personnel.

834

The current unsettled conditions suggested that it might be wise to have a plan that could be activated on short notice, but the need still existed for a long-range plan.

When would OVICE be ready for complete responsibility? That might be ten years. I suggested that the year 1972 be tentatively set as a target date and outlined certain biennial progress steps leading up to that date.

What was significant about this meeting was that a workable procedure for transferring responsibilities for ministries was fashioned. The field council, field conference, and OVICE later adopted the plan with some revisions. (The Bible Institute was transferred to OVICE in 1977, five years later than first planned.) This plan also became the agreed-upon procedure for handing over other ministries to the churches.

Mother/Daughter Church Principle

From the earliest days of the church, El Salvador members reached out in evangelism both inside and outside Maracaibo, opening preaching points and Sunday schools. A second Maracaibo church was organized—*Iglesia Evangélica de la Cruz.* As this church grew it became the focus of attention of some newly arrived Pentecostal workers. Somewhat later, some Venezuelans convinced of that persuasion won the vote to sever the TEAM relationship and join the Assemblies of God group.

About the same time, missionaries linked with a large North American denominational mission entered the field. It seemed that some of the newer churches might be influenced by promises of financial help to join that group.

El Salvador church leaders were eager to preserve the integrity of their work and consequently adopted a plan which they felt would be a safeguard. They tightened their organization so that El Salvador was in full control of the preaching points and branches. This control extended to a common treasury, common boards, and even to the appointment of Sunday school teachers and speakers in the branch congregations.

This control did indeed protect the newer branches from being taken over by proselyting groups, but it also stifled initiative and growth and there was understandable reaction within some branches. Although El Salvador did establish a procedure for branches to gain independence, it was purposely cumbersome in the interest of safeguarding them from a raid by a proselyting group.

Parent-Child Relationship Has Limits

The plan of centralized membership and control served a purpose, but then outgrew its usefulness. It could be compared to a family situation. Children need the support, protection, and guidance of parents during the formative years, but the time comes when they must become fully responsible for their own lives, even though close family ties and mutual concern should continue. Some branch church leaders felt that El Salvador was continuing the parent-child relationship too long—to the detriment of the branches—and took steps to separately organize. I commented on the question in 1965.

> Three years ago [1962] the Sierra Maestra Church group organized independently of the central church and this caused quite a stir. At that time we took the position that we would stand with El Salvador Church in requesting our missionaries not to further the break in any way through giving encouragement to this independent movement. We did indicate, however, that if Sierra Maestra Church would become a member of the Western Convention of Evangelical Churches (OVICE) it would have our cooperation, and this has taken place. At that time we requested that the Maracaibo Church take steps to allow branches a greater degree of independence.[7]

The Maracaibo church was completely self-governing and had been for years. TEAM did not control it. Missionaries were working in some of the branches, and were sympathetic to their position. They were advised not to involve themselves in delicate relations between churches. The field council was able to represent the concerns of the missionaries and in due course El Salvador set in motion its plan for the more mature branches to become independent.

Growing Maturity of the Churches

Latin Americans are quite independent by nature and church members are no exception. The thoughtful missionary welcomed this independence because it led the converts to take responsibility for the conduct of church affairs and to be more zealous in outreach. All in all, church/mission relationships were excellent because the mission recognized the growing maturity of the church leaders and their right to control church affairs.

The field council even supported the right of the church to restrict a missionary, as in the case of one who took it upon himself to preach against communism. The missionary saw communism as an atheistic philosophy, as it indeed is. The church considered it a political movement, since it was a legal party, and had a rule that there be no political activity—pro or con—in the church. His strong opposition to the communist party was construed as political promotion of one of the other parties.

As they studied the Word, exercised their spiritual muscles in witness and service, and dealt with internal affairs in the congregations, the church leaders were gaining the spiritual vigor and maturity they needed to meet the opportunities and challenges of the decades ahead.

VENEZUELA CHURCHES MATURING

Strengthened Field Administration

As the number of missionaries increased and the work grew in extent and complexity, the earlier decisions concerning the function of the field council and role of the field chairman began to prove their worth. The field was working more and more in a coordinated way with definite goals to be met. Several factors gave further impetus in the same direction.

One was the appointment of an area secretary at TEAM U.S.A. headquarters. Until 1963 the general director had responsibility for liaison with all the foreign fields, then sixteen in number. In September of that year the board of directors approved my request that Delbert Kuehl be given responsibility for liaison with the Latin America fields, of which Venezuela-Colombia was the largest. The value of this arrangement was that one man could concentrate on a limited area and keep more current on field goals, plans, personnel, and progress.

With this new responsibility for Venezuela-Colombia, Kuehl was in regular communication with the field chairman and in frequent touch with furloughed missionaries. He attended the annual field conference at least once every two years and made other visits as necessary. Kuehl had a background of missionary experience in evangelism, church planting, Bible teaching, and field administration in Japan. This experience and his current work as candidate secretary prepared him well as counselor to individual missionaries and the field council as together they reviewed the work of the field.

Outgrowing the Headquarters Building

A second factor of great value in promoting field coordination was the development of an adequate headquarters building in

Maracaibo. There was a sense in which La Estrella bookstore in Maracaibo served as the business center. Bookstore personnel handled necessary purchases for missionaries, made overseas travel arrangements, saw baggage through customs, helped with financial transactions, dealt with government offices, and served the missionaries in other ways. But all of this was administrative work that should not be imposed on a bookstore ministry.

Until Duane Johnson was elected field chairman in 1955, the chairman might live anywhere in western Venezuela. As Duane and Freda were stationed in Maracaibo, the chairman, for the first time in many years, was located there and able to devote full time to the leadership of the field. When Harold Lake was elected chairman in 1959, he and his family moved to Maracaibo from Barinas, one of the more remote mission stations. When Jack MacDonald succeeded Lake in March 1962, a stable headquarters in Maracaibo had been established. This may seem to be a minor matter, but the positive results in promoting coordination and field unity were soon appreciated.

The word "headquarters" probably conjures up a vision of a large, well-planned building. No such thing here. A visitor would have come first to a small overcrowded bookstore and some overcrowded storage space, then would be directed down a long, narrow hall to several offices where La Estrella de la Mañana magazine was edited and mailed. Out the back door was a galvanized iron building, a portion of which accommodated the print shop. That was all there was, except for two small apartments situated up one level to catch any available cooling breeze.

There was a sentimental attachment to this place on the part of many because it was here that the Bachs and Christiansens persevered together in faith through those first difficult years. Hundreds of stones had been thrown at these simple premises, and here countless verbal bricks had been hurled at the evangelical ambassadors of Christ. The original building width measured only twenty feet, but that had been doubled by the purchase of another strip of similar size.

Plans for a New Building

When MacDonald became chairman he took a thoughtful look at the situation. He recognized its historic significance and strategic location close to an important plaza. Could this place be rebuilt to meet the needs of bookstore; editorial office; print shop; offices for field chairman, treasurer, and business manager; Christian education center; a meeting area; and several apartments and rooms? He thought so and in 1965 took his recommendation to the field council and conference, where it won full approval. This was a real step of faith because, apart from the value of the lots, the only building fund was another property which could be sold to cover about 15 percent of the construction cost.

With much faith, diligent representation by MacDonald and others, and some financial assistance from headquarters, the project was launched, the building constructed, the ministries installed, and a new headquarters dedicated April 8, 1967.

Children's Classes as Church Feeders

From informal classes of street kids in a dusty section of Maracaibo to formal institute classrooms in San Cristóbal has been the pathway several women missionaries have followed. From small beginnings has grown a ministry reaching far beyond small children—as important as they are—to teenagers, Bible school students, and churches both small and large. While many have served in this vital ministry, it is possible here to trace the experience of just a few individuals.

When Clara Carlson was invited to work in El Salvador Church, Maracaibo, in 1948 she asked to work with one group that she perceived to be losing interest in the church—the teenagers. There was much activity in teaching the smaller children. Adult classes were well attended and adults were often involved in evangelistic outreach. Something was needed to keep the youth under the ministry of the church. Otherwise its work would be handicapped for years to come by the loss of potential leaders, as was experienced by many churches at home and abroad.

Involving the Youth

Clara's purpose went beyond holding Sunday school classes and other typical youth activities. Her vision was to get the youth involved in evangelism and teaching, so she began teacher training classes. The field at hand for their work was the vacation Bible school classes held at El Salvador and branches. Teachers and helpers were needed. The church board was glad to assign willing adults, but Clara wanted it to demonstrate confidence that the youth could be motivated and trained to do significant spiritual work with youngsters of the city.

Central Christian Ed Supplies

Up to that time the missionary women involved in children's work had to search far afield for suitable material. Clara felt it would be useful to have one center where material could be evaluated, gathered, translated if necessary, and distributed. Some limited space was found in the old crowded La Estrella center above the print shop, with just enough room for small teacher training classes and some literature storage. This convenient, centralized location for obtaining material and counsel helped to promote the Christian education ministry.

Seguidores Founded

The first group of youthful workers chose *Seguidores*—"Followers"—as its name. In 1958, the first year of the plan, these workers were busy in twenty of the thirty-five classes held in the city. Year by year their involvement increased. A layman, Ciro Gutierrez, took a real interest in work among the youth and served as sponsor of the *Seguidores.*

Teran and Osborn

A recent graduate of the Ebenezer Bible Institute, Miss Eulalia Teran, was brought into the program, as was Phyllis Osborn, a missionary who arrived in Venezuela in 1959. Clara Carlson was transferred to San Cristóbal in 1964 to initiate a similar Christian education and youth program and to assist in Christian education courses taught at Ebenezer Bible Institute. She later became a regular member of the faculty of the Institute where a center of Christian education material for the San Cristóbal area was set up. EBI students and other lay women were directed in their practical work outreach from that center.

When Clara retired in 1977, Phyllis Osborn was chosen to succeed her as Christian education teacher at Ebenezer and to head up the child evangelism outreach.

Eulalia Teran had previously been made head of the Christian education office in Maracaibo.

> Today she is in charge of the Christian education program of the national church [OVICE]. Her work involves preparing materials for Sunday school, Bible clubs, and vacation Bible schools, conducting teacher training classes, and conducting Bible clubs in detention centers.[1]

Seminary Founded

As the first director of *Seminario Evangélico Asociado* (the United Evangelical Seminary), Jim Savage gave the background to this new venture in his report to the annual field conference in January 1968:

> As early as 1950 conversations were being held with members of other mission societies about the possibility of a cooperative effort. The "Seminary Project" has been discussed at regional and national church conventions. During the United Convention held in 1965 official encouragement was given to our fellow missionaries of the Evangelical Free Church [EFCA] to take the initiative in the establishment of the seminary.[2]

The seminary opened in El Limón, a suburb of Maracay, in the fall of 1969 with seventeen students, on property loaned by the Free Church Bible Institute. EFCA and TEAM were jointly responsible. Both mission groups wanted their national church bodies—ADIEL for the Free Churches and OVICE for the TEAM-related churches—to share in the direction, support, and benefits of the school. Each mission provided professors—at first only missionaries; later, several Venezuelans. Over a period of twenty years—1969 to 1989—Earl Blomberg and Wilford Anderson from the Free Church and James Savage, Kenneth Larson, and Francisco Liévano from TEAM/OVICE served as directors. EFCA supplied more than half of the teaching personnel. Both missions provided financial subsidy and Venezuelan churches also helped. Efforts made to enlarge the campus struck snags, particularly in dealing with unscrupulous real estate operators.

Cumbersome but Harmonious Administration

The seminary administration was cumbersome in that it involved four organizations: EFCA, TEAM, ADIEL, and OVICE. With major decisions by the seminary board having to be referred to the field councils of both missions, to the joint EFCA-TEAM seminary board in the homeland, to the two home boards, and also—in Venezuela—to the boards of ADIEL and OVICE, the word "cumbersome" is indeed justified. Participants undoubtedly pondered on how much easier administration would have been if only one mission and its church organization had full responsibility.

This cumbersome arrangement could have caused major problems had it not been for the high level of good will that existed among those involved. It was largely the wisdom, dedication, and grace of the men most involved that kept the project on course and doing well. They were the area secretaries—in succession—for Latin America: Delbert Kuehl, Elton Dresselhaus, Michael Pocock, Jack MacDonald, and Gary Bowman of TEAM; and Lester Westlund, Vernon Anderson, and Larry Schlotfeldt of the Free Church, along with the seminary directors listed earlier.

The Seminary's Good Fruit

The seminary's perennial struggles with shortage of funds and scarcity of classroom and dormitory space seemed not to lessen its appeal to students or the dedication and perseverance of professors and staff.

After an initial slow start, the seminary attendance maintained a consistent level of fifty to seventy students in the four-year course, with twelve to fifteen being graduated each year. Many congregations in OVICE and ADIEL reaped the benefits of having better-prepared spiritual leaders.

In recent years, however, TEAM and OVICE began to question their continued participation in the seminary. After more than a year of careful study, and consultation with the national church organizations and members of the Free Church Mission, the field council recommended to the annual field conference in January 1990 that TEAM/OVICE withdraw from the project. The reason given:

> The conditions which were set forth at the last annual conference have not been met. The school is not meeting the needs of TEAM or of OVICE and ASIGEO, the two national church organizations with which TEAM works. They do not feel they can or should continue to support a school which does not offer a higher level of education than do the two Bible institutes which TEAM has been supporting for quite a few years.[3]

The recommendation included an offer to allow TEAM staff at the school to continue and to give limited response to staffing and support needs in the future.

Better Communication, Better Understanding

Latin Americans in general tend to view North Americans as being somewhat domineering. This conception is unwelcome enough in international relations and business dealings. It is even more unwelcome in mission/church relationships, and it is unnecessary for those who are one in Christ. But the feeling can grow unless there is conscious effort to eliminate causes of misunderstanding. Careful communication and consultation do much to enhance spiritual unity, harmony, and cooperation.

The larger and more complex the mission's work became and the greater the growth of the churches, the greater the need for such communication and consultation. Not only were there many churches where missionaries had direct personal contact, there were also programs and institutions in which both missionaries and Venezuelans shared. The question: were all working toward common goals?

The field chairman conferred often with individual church leaders and officers of the church convention. Joint meetings between church leaders and field council were initiated in 1966 and continued for a while on an irregular basis. When Elton Dresselhaus became chairman he felt the time was ripe to begin regular meetings in order to keep each group informed of the thinking and plans of the other. Best relationships could be assured where there was this close consultation.

Joint Board (DEA) Set Up

In his chairman's report for 1971, Dresselhaus told of the steps taken at a men's retreat in 1970 at Esnujaque to enhance consultation. Attending this retreat were pastors and workers of the churches and men of TEAM:

> Very much in evidence throughout the entire retreat was the desire for improved working relationships with our national brethren. One of the concrete results of our time together was the formation of *Directiva Evangélica Asociada—DEA*. A real sense of unity was evident during our entire stay in Esnujaque, and in a number of ways the retreat seems to have signaled a real turning point in our relationships with the national church and a new awareness of what our role as a mission organization should be.[4]

A second retreat was held in Barinitas later in 1970. Once again a spirit of real unity prevailed:

> Perhaps the most concrete result has been the formation of DEA. After a full discussion of the advantages and disadvantages of a joint committee whose purpose would be to foster better understanding and a more effective working together, a vote was taken in which the overwhelming majority responded positively to the idea. It is too early to evaluate DEA. I believe, however, that a note of cautious optimism should be sounded. One national pastor said to me, "Something like this should have been done long ago." I believe that God establishes His own timetables, and that this time of drawing together was accomplished by Him and Him alone.[5]

In a 1975 report, the field chairman referred to the continued cordial and productive relationships existing between the mission and OVICE.

> For several years the Venezuela field council and the national church board plus the president of the ministerial union have met at three-month intervals to exchange ideas, discuss problems, review general progress, study the placement of missionaries, and formulate plans. The arrangement is informal. Neither group has lost its identity since decisions are valid only if the national board and field council individually approve. For us, the answer has been partnership, not amalgamation.[6]

Evidences of Partnership

In response to a questionnaire in July 1986, the field chairman, Dan Tuggy, noted three things as evidence of the partnership in evangelizing Venezuela: (1) there is always consultation between the field council and the church in placing missionary workers; (2) a missionary and a national worker supplied by OVICE serve together in a pioneer work; and (3) in planting a new church the missionary and the national church worker unite their efforts.[7]

With so much territory yet to be possessed—in spite of the progress made in eighty-four years of mission history in Venezuela—the united dedication of nationals and missionaries is not only commendable but absolutely necessary. And with that unity and dedication there is still the realization that it is God who makes the church grow.

AVANCES '76-'77

The response of OVICE to TEAM's worldwide "Target 7" program of evangelism and church growth was most encouraging. The churches in Venezuela adapted Target 7 to the observance of the seventieth anniversaries of the beginning of the work in 1906 and the founding of the magazine *La Estrella de la Mañana* in 1907. One part of that program was concentrated prayer for evangelism and revival. Delbert Kuehl reported a conversation with Asdrúbal Ríos, who indicated that there were as many as 1,000 prayer cells in the churches. Two courses had been prepared for the participants, one on personal evangelism and one on stewardship.

Bill Horst, field chairman in 1977, stated that the evangelistic emphasis of *AVANCES* had been outstanding:

> Over 1,000 people made professions of faith in the 91 local campaigns which were held and about 600 professions were recorded in 11 zonal campaigns. Some of the results were startling —there were about 100 professions in the campaign in Pampanito near Trujillo and almost 200 in Las Piedras near Machiques. The year 1977 is dedicated to special efforts and will need our support and prayers. Special mention should be made of Mr. Rios' untiring efforts in behalf of *AVANCES,* and it is no exaggeration to say what success we have had is largely due to his planning and persistence.[8]

Orinoco River Mission Merger

In 1979 an official committee of the Orinoco River Mission (ORM) approached Richard Winchell and Delbert Kuehl about a possible merger into TEAM. ORM was founded in 1920 by Van V. and Gara Eddings and had a fruitful ministry for sixty years in eastern Venezuela. Eddings first arrived in Venezuela in 1915 and worked as an independent missionary selling Bibles in the eastern part of the country. He became impressed with the lack of any evangelical witness in that area and along the large Orinoco River—the principal thoroughfare in the east. With a vision of the possibilities he returned home to recruit workers for a new mission—the ORM.

The ORM ministry grew and matured in the six decades of its history. The 116 churches planted were joined together in the Association of Evangelical Churches in Eastern Venezuela—*Asociacion de Iglesias Evangélicas de Oriente—ASIGEO* (pronounced ah-see-hay-o). A common meeting ground between the ASIGEO and OVICE churches was in the United Convention, held every five years, bringing churches of OVICE (west), ADIEL (central), and ASIGEO (east) together for fellowship, discussion, and certain limited joint activities.

Why ORM Sought Merger

Five internal problem areas were recognized by ORM: (1) Many of the missionaries were close to retirement age, so a shortage of missionary staff was imminent. (2) ORM had not been able to make retirement provisions for its missionaries. (3) Very few new missionaries were joining the mission. (4) Uncertainty existed regarding relative authority of field and home board. (5) ORM did not have a large enough missionary force from which to draw leaders for the work.

The discussions—in which I also participated—proceeded smoothly and in time it was felt that Winchell and Kuehl should visit Venezuela to get a firsthand look at the ORM work and give the missionaries an opportunity to ask questions about TEAM. It was also necessary to give the TEAM missionaries an equal opportunity to learn the facts and express themselves.

Missionary approval came quickly, but there was one further important step that must be taken—securing the wholehearted approval and cooperation of the ASIGEO church group. This was not to be taken for granted. Although ASIGEO leaders knew many of the OVICE church leaders, the churches were in separated areas and neither organization had ever suggested merger of the two church groups. ASIGEO leaders also knew some of the TEAM missionaries, but to commit the church fellowship to a long-term working relationship with TEAM required more detailed knowledge of working principles.

ASIGEO Church Leaders Agree

To Elton Dresselhaus, field chairman, and Al Lewis of ORM went the responsibility of meeting with ASIGEO leaders to describe the working relationships that existed between TEAM and OVICE and that could be expected between TEAM and ASIGEO. Dresselhaus brought OVICE leaders into the discussions as well. When the leaders of ASIGEO learned of the close fellowship and coordination between the missionary and church bodies they saw that this same kind of relationship could exist in this new grouping. With some further clarification having to do with properties, approval was not long in coming.

Coordination with ASIGEO Established

It was indeed good that in 1970 field chairman Dresselhaus had invited the *directiva* of OVICE to hold regular joint meetings with the TEAM field council. It was when ASIGEO observed this cooperation that it decided to approve the merger and enter into a working relationship with TEAM. An understanding was reached that there would be a TEAM/ASIGEO committee for coordination, and schedules would be determined to transfer the Las Delicias Bible Institute and Buenas Nuevas bookstore to ASIGEO.

United in Spirit and Purpose

In anticipation of the agreement between the two mission boards being signed by January 1, 1980, missionaries of ORM were invited to join the approximately 100 TEAM missionaries holding their annual conference in Rubio at the Christiansen Academy during the first week in January. From the first it was clear that the missionaries were quickly united in spirit and purpose. Once again, in the experience of TEAM, a merger arrangement which had been prayerfully and carefully worked out produced a harmonious result that preserved and enhanced the work of a sister mission.

A Field as Wide as Venezuela

With this merger, TEAM's field now extended from east to west in Venezuela, a distance of 800 miles. Thirty-three missionaries were brought into TEAM and with them many going ministries in eastern Venezuela. The 116 churches reported a total of 4,000 believers having been baptized and a total community of 18,000 Christian worshippers. There was a bookstore, a ministry to the deaf, work among Indian tribes, and the Las Delicias Bible Institute which had trained 400 national workers through the years.

Of the thirty-three missionaries, ten still remained active in 1990 and one served on the Wheaton staff. Thirteen others were retired, six were deceased, and three had resigned. Two of the active missionaries—David and Joan Coots—led the way in opening a new field for TEAM at the southern end of the Baja California peninsula in Mexico in 1988. Coots had served as the last general director of ORM. In Venezuela, some TEAM missionaries in the west were reassigned to the east and some from the east to the west—a healthy blending of experience. The two church organizations—ASIGEO and OVICE—remained distinct, but recognized a growing unity of purpose and fellowship.

Ministries in Transition

Ebenezer Bible Institute, the first mission operation scheduled to be turned over to OVICE, began a ten-year transition in 1962. OVICE, however, requested a lengthening of the period so that the churches could prepare more adequately for financial support and administration. The first Venezuelan director appointed by OVICE was Alvaro Pérez, who was installed September 1, 1975.

The transition pattern for the Institute was adopted for the other ministries which the mission turned over to OVICE. Rather than trace the step-by-step process, let us take a look back from January 1985 when field chairman Jim Carmean reported to the annual conference:

"The five ministries that OVICE received from TEAM are in the same or better condition than they were when we received them."

This statement was made by an OVICE leader as we discussed the transition the other day. After he left I made a quick review of the ministries and concluded that he was pretty nearly right.

- Ebenezer Bible Institute is doing well, has expanded its curriculum, and is involved in building more units for married students. Several of our [missionary] professors will be retiring in the next five years and that is a matter of concern.
- Maranatha Camp is being used considerably and looks better than I have ever seen it.
- The Christian Education department continues under the able leadership of Eulalia Teran. Increased printing costs have been a problem to them but they continue to have a vital ministry to the churches.
- *Radiofonía* had its setbacks but it is now on its feet and has vigorous plans for an increased ministry, including an FM station in San Cristóbal.
- Even though La Estrella Bookstore has been in the hands of

850

OVICE for nearly two years, it was under the very capable leadership of Emelia Friebel until June 1st. We trust that the store will continue to have a fruitful outreach.

- *La Estrella Magazine* is the only other ministry still in transition. We agreed to turn it over to OVICE in December 1985. Subscriptions are up to over 3,000 and the magazine has been able to sustain itself financially even though OVICE has not been able to help much.

  Out east, we have turned over one ministry and are in the transition process with another.

- Buenas Nuevas bookstore is presently going through a period of testing. In addition to severe financial problems, ASIGEO is in need of a competent manager for that ministry.
- Las Delicias Bible Institute is scheduled to be turned over to ASIGEO in July of 1987.[9]

Other Important Ministries

More than one hundred missionaries are regularly assigned to the Venezuela field. Only a score are mentioned in these chapters, which is regrettable but unavoidable. More than thirty percent are busy in evangelism and church planting. About a fourth are in training ministries to provide Christian workers for the rapidly growing churches. Five percent are in administration; six percent are in other ministries, one of them being correspondence courses; thirty-four percent are involved in the education of missionary children. Some of these ministries have not had any special mention here but their value to the missionary work in Venezuela should not be underestimated. One such is the education of missionary children at Christiansen Academy in Rubio.

Suppose someone's suggestion were to prevail that the mission spend no more money operating the school. What would be the result? The fall-out of such a decision would seriously affect TEAM's evangelism and church planting work. Consider some of the losses that would be experienced:

- Families with children would have to devote much important time to home-schooling, or would have to leave the field so their children could attend qualified schools.
- The teachers and houseparents who help in church summer

programs or in camp work would no longer be available.

- These missionaries who go out in part-time evangelism and church work would no longer be there to assist.
- Students who are imparted a missionary vision while in the missionary children's school might not be influenced for the Lord's work.
- The cost of sending missionary children to schools for American business people would be greater than the present method.

All in all, Christiansen Academy is a necessary ministry. Its benefits extend not only to the Venezuela missionaries but to Colombia, Netherlands Antilles, and Trinidad missionaries as well. Missionaries on the field do not hesitate to describe the work of school administrators, teachers, and houseparents of the Academy as essential to their service for Christ.

The Challenge of Caracas

In the first sixty years there was enough work in western Venezuela to keep the missionary force fully occupied. Central Venezuela had other missions at work, so in those early years TEAM gave little thought to beginning a ministry there. It was not that there was no need. Caracas, being the capital of the country, was a Mecca for thousands in rural areas who wanted to improve themselves economically. The poor and disadvantaged were not the only ones drawn to the country's largest city. Industry, commerce, and education all beckoned those who wanted to forge ahead.

One result was that many evangelical believers were drawn to Caracas. There were good churches in the city but many of the believers from western Venezuela longed for the fellowship they had enjoyed in OVICE churches. They also noted that with only one evangelical church per 20,000 people there was a great field for evangelism. So it happened that in the late 1960s OVICE encouraged TEAM to begin a church planting ministry there. OVICE and TEAM cooperated, and soon there were several churches under way in the capital.

After the merger with ORM, TEAM's field was nationwide and Caracas was right in the middle. That tremendously increased its importance as an objective for church planting. One goal of the evangelism and church planting committee, as reported in 1983 by committee chairman Charles Davis, was to plant clusters of churches in major cities from west to east. One of the cities targeted was Caracas.

Davis returned on furlough in 1986 with the purpose of recruiting a team of church planters for Caracas. The Elmbrook Church in Waukesha, Wisconsin, was host that year to the TEAM annual conference. In the leading of the Lord, the church missions committee had been considering how it might have a definite part in a church planting ministry in an urban mission field of need and promise. It was announced at the conference that the committee had chosen TEAM as the channel and the church and mission were jointly developing plans to send out a team to Caracas. By the fall of 1988 these missionaries were in Caracas.

An added indication of the importance Caracas and the vast expanse of eastern Venezuela were assuming in TEAM's plans was the moving of the field headquarters from Maracaibo to Caracas in 1988 under the direction of Dan Tuggy, field chairman.

Why Have Churches Grown?

In the opening pages of chapter 46 we expressed the hope that we could discover reasons for the growth in Venezuelan churches. Simply put, it was the application of time-honored missionary principles, as old as those set forth by the Apostle Paul, who advised Timothy, "And the things you have heard me say in the presence of many witnesses entrust to reliable men who will also be qualified to teach others" (II Timothy 2:2 NIV).

Entrust Responsibility

The key to this growth is undoubtedly that it has not been the work of missionaries alone. From the earliest days, missionaries emphasized that new believers were responsible to witness to family, friends, and neighbors—even if they themselves had not had the opportunity for formal training. The believers were provided with tools that made their message clear and convincing: the gospel magazine *La Estrella de la Mañana,* simple tracts, Scripture portions, the Bible, and evangelical books.

"Preach the Word"

An important element in winning Venezuelans to Christ was public preaching, even in the face of opposition. As opposition lessened, public proclamation increased and proved to be fruitful. Evangelism was never a secondary activity. Missionaries and nationals alike maintained a proper emphasis on this vital ministry.

Understand the Place of the Church

The believers had a proper understanding of the church and their relationship to other believers. They knew that they were bound together in a spiritual body, and that the members of the body were to exercise their Spirit-endowed gifts.

Teach Stewardship

The churches learned early not to depend on the mission or missionaries for their expenses, such as for meeting places and support of workers. They met happily in simple thatch, adobe, or concrete-block buildings, biding their time until they could afford better facilities. This was true even though the example of the Roman church was ornate buildings and not a few cathedrals.

Relate Training to Level of Service

Missionaries gave proper emphasis to training but on a level related to the general educational level of the people. The Bible institute level, without strict entrance requirements, was sufficient for many years. As the educational level of the people grew the institute raised its standards. Later the higher level of seminary training was made available. The mission did not train a group of workers who would be out of touch with the people.

Have A Plan of Transfer

Then the field began an enlightened process of transferring ministries to the church organization, with the dual purpose of getting the churches even more involved in the work and of freeing missionaries for more extensive church planting.

Involve Spirit-appointed People

The provision of Spirit-gifted laymen, ministers, and teachers cannot be overemphasized. Only a few names can be included here but mention must be made of Asdrúbal Ríos, Francisco Liévano, Antonio Mendoza, Candelario Acosta, Francisco Rojas, Ismael Arenas, Jorge Montenegro, Rafael Pino, Señora Rincón, and last— but certainly not least—Señorita Eulalia Teran. These are choice workers who responded to the Lord's unmistakable call and commission.

Ninety-five Percent Unfinished

The believers in Venezuela are estimated to be about five percent of the population. There is much territory yet to be possessed for Christ. Working hand-in-hand as partners, missionaries and national believers have witnessed much progress. In faith they look forward to a multiplying of the fruit in the remaining years until Christ returns.

OPPOSITION AND OPEN DOORS IN COLOMBIA

Our last glimpse of the gospel work in Colombia ended with the martyrdom in 1946 of José de la Cruz Bolívar, a leader of the congregation at El Páramo de la Paz. Unrestrained violence against political liberals and evangelical believers mounted rapidly in the following years.

Ten Years of Violence

The story of the ten years of violence and its effect on the gospel work in Colombia was strikingly related in Paul Sheetz's eightieth anniversary book, *The Sovereign Hand*, published in 1971.

> For ten years terror reigned in Colombia. In the first five years (1948-1953) alone, 43 church buildings of all evangelical mission groups were destroyed by fire, dynamite, or bombs; 110 primary schools sponsored by Protestants were closed; and 52 evangelical believers were martyred. Thousands more were stoned, beaten, jailed, fined and driven from their homes.[1]

TEAM's work was mostly in the state of Norte de Santander, reaching out from Cúcuta to smaller towns. With local town authorities under the control of the Conservative political (Catholic church-related) forces, the evangelical work in these small towns was particularly vulnerable. The mission had twenty-two missionaries in Colombia in 1946; by 1954 the number was reduced to six. Most TEAM-related churches were closed. Missionaries able to remain through all of those diffi-

cult years were Elof and Isabel Anderson, Arthur and Mary Louise Bakker, Irene Garrett, and Minnie Waage. Joe and Verda Butts and Cora Soderquist were on the field through part of the violence.

A Microcosm of Persecution

It will be easier to understand the reality of the persecution by taking a closer look at what happened in the case of one believer. Olav Eikland described the pressures on this evangelical youth and his caring church in Ocaña in 1948:

> A young man, Félix Flores, became a Christian and demonstrated always the meekness of his Lord and Master, Jesus Christ. We never saw him in vocal contention with his fellow men, and never did we hear an angry retort to those who reviled him for being an evangelical Christian. For several years he suffered the burden of a sickly body without making audible complaint to his Maker for permitting his soul to be carried about in an infirm body. But when he finally came to his deathbed—fighting the last enemy—enemies of the gospel came and like vultures hovered around the corpse and the house where he lay....
>
> In Latin America an evangelical funeral is still the most hated religious service in the minds of Catholic leaders and their followers. Its proclamation of an open heaven for all souls saved through the blood of Christ, where they may enter immediately at death, is a false doctrine to those deluded Catholics who look for purgatorial torment at the end of their earthly journey. In fact, the doctrine of purgatory, with pretended need of paid masses for the dead, is the most profitable business of the priestly profession....
>
> Because this was to be the first adult evangelical burial in Ocaña, it was to be expected that our program would not go unchallenged. And indeed, they turned out with the most formidable weapons. First came a man offering a considerable sum of money for calling a priest to take charge of the funeral. Then a detachment of officers of the law, one of whom, with candles in one hand and a revolver in the other, demanded that the candles be placed, according to Catholic custom, around the corpse resting in the casket. It required all the courage the evangelical believers watching over the body could muster to refuse this demand. Another agent of the law sent off several shots from his revolver in an attempt to scare off attendants at the funeral.

When we arrived at the house for the service we found a third officer with revolver in hand, sitting near the casket. He had previously told one of our deacons that if any service were held he would shoot the one attempting to hold it. When we saw a hundred faces out in the street wondering what we would do, we felt constrained by higher powers to proceed with our intended service. Reading of the Word of God, prayer, and song initiated the service, with splendid attention on the part of all. Bible exposition followed, revealing Christ as the only One able to open heaven to man, Himself being the Way to that glorious place.

In spite of the silence of the audience we did not fail to notice hostile movements here and there. The man near the casket representing "law and order" lifted his hand several times as though he were to shoot the preacher, but he was held back by some friends beside him, and no doubt restrained at the same time by Divine powers. Out in the doorway a man in civilian clothes, with a big revolver in hand, tried several times to enter. In spite of these ominous disturbances we felt the presence of a powerful Hand staying the powers of darkness from getting control of the meeting.[2]

Missionaries Also Targeted

Missionaries were not immune from attack. Elof Anderson, Arthur Bakker, Joe Butts, Olav Eikland, and Edward Nilsen all experienced the dubious thrill of peering into the muzzle of a gun, feeling the brush of a bullet, or dodging a brandished machete. While many were threatened, none was wounded, taken captive, or held hostage as was the experience of some in other missions.

First Assembly in Four Years

My first visit to Colombia was in August 1953. The Association of Evangelical Churches was holding an annual conference—the first in four years. It was a demonstration of courage and devotion that so many came together for this significant gathering. Meeting places had been destroyed and many believers scattered. Yet they desired the fellowship and biblical instruction which had been denied them in many of the country places. Conference meetings were held in the Cúcuta church, the scene of mob attacks against the evangelicals at the dedication twenty-five years earlier. Elof Anderson brought the Sunday morning message.

As guests of the conference at the large Sunday afternoon praise and testimony service, Charles Bodeen, TEAM board member, and I were invited to sit on the platform along with Colombian and missionary leaders. The believers filling the sanctuary impressed me as being in an expectant attitude—as well they might be after being denied this fellowship for so long.

Eager Testimonies

When the leader gave opportunity for testimony, so many rose to their feet at the same time that he asked all who wanted to speak to stand at once. I estimated that several hundred stood. He then asked them to ring the inside of the auditorium and come to the podium one by one with a time limit imposed on each. With my meager knowledge of Spanish I could understand only snatches of what was said, but I had the help of one of the missionaries who gave brief background bits on many.

I remember two individuals in particular. One was Señora Candelaria, who, with a sister and a young girl of the family, had been attacked with machetes by a priest-led mob. She had been terribly wounded, with the flesh of one arm slashed away. Her testimony did not refer at all to her suffering but to the joy she experienced in the Lord and her delight in being able to witness for Christ.

The second was Vicente Gómez, described to me as an unpromising student while at the Ebenezer Bible Institute, but transformed by the Lord into a fearless witness as persecution grew. Beaten, spit upon, reviled, threatened, and jailed, yet he kept on with his zealous witness for Christ. I heard that he alone had been responsible for starting thirty-five congregations of believers.

Listening to the testimonies and thinking about the persecution experienced by many, my feeling was of great unworthiness in the presence of these heroes of the faith, who knew much more than I about the cost of faithfully following Jesus. I could understand that the body of Christ was growing through the multiplication of witness by individual believers as much as through formal church ministries.

Repression and Terror by Rojas Pinilla

In that same year—1953—a Conservative Party leader, Rojas Pinilla, seized control of the government:

> Again the situation worsened. Rojas became a tyrant to preserve his own power, concurring thoroughly with the plan of the clergy to exterminate the evangelicals. Having failed to destroy the church through persecution, enemies of the gospel now concentrated on outlawing it. A 1902 law which gave the Catholic Church exclusive rights in "mission territories" was now interpreted to include any area where missionary priests were working. This was arbitrarily extended to three-fourths of the country, including vast areas where evangelical churches had long been established. This gave legal basis for closing chapels and schools, breaking up families, dissolving meetings, denying marriage licenses, burning Bibles, and expelling foreign missionaries.[3]

The Gospel Fire Spreads

The more the opposition raged, the greater was the response to the gospel message. One zealous witness in Santa Inez in 1955, Marcos Franco, was targeted for death. Enemies surrounded his house when there was a gathering of family members. Wielding torches they set fire to the house, thinking to trap the whole family. In a marvelous way every member escaped—truly the protecting hand of the Lord. Three years later—marvel of marvels—there were nine new congregations of believers in this very district!

Antonio Aguilar, Fighter

When I visited Colombia in 1962, I spent a week in an area of great violence and outstanding growth. Joe Butts was my escort as we spent memorable days among believers whose suffering had borne such remarkable fruit. One man traveling with us part of the way was Antonio Aguilar, who had been converted after living a life of dissipation and violence. I noted that his right arm was useless, the result of his battles.

Butts and I went with Aguilar to Polonia, high up on a mountain ridge, to have a meeting with a group of thirty new Christians whom Aguilar had won to the Lord. One of the men in the group had spent time in prison for murder. We enjoyed heartwarming fellowship with the believers. We also enjoyed a tasty meal of chicken soup. Butts cautioned me to not look too closely at the contents of the soup bowl unless I relished chicken heads and feet. It was not the soup and the climb that were most memorable but rather the fellowship with precious believers who were sincerely devoted to Christ.

An amusing remark was made by a man of Polonia after Butts introduced me as the director of TEAM: "This is special," he muttered, "the Catholics in this mountain area never get a visit from their bishop."

Mushrooming Church Growth

Some of the reports the TEAM office was receiving at the time seemed hard to believe. Having heard that the open churches had been reduced to six, we began to hear of twenty, then thirty, then fifty churches. Before the violence was over there were as many as seventy congregations of evangelicals. Elof Anderson recounted many of his experiences in visiting outlying mountain areas where lay witness was bearing fruit. Some places to which he was invited for the dedication of a chapel had never had a visit from a missionary. He and Isabel were active throughout the years of violence, ministering in many areas of danger.

Evangelism in River Communities

Missionaries had been working in the mountain areas but were also conscious of the greater concentration of people along the River Magdalena. In 1948 Joe Butts built a forty-five-foot launch, *El Anunciador*. This launch was used by the Butts and several other missionaries and Colombian evangelists over a period of several years to reach many communities along the river and its tributaries.

Crisis in Schooling

Even before the period of violence, the literacy rate in Colombia was low, with only fifty percent of the primary-age children being in school. Missionaries were concerned about the children of church members and also considered that primary schools could provide an evangelistic opportunity in the community. They had opened six primary schools but these were closed due to the violence. From 1948 to 1957 the children of evangelicals were prohibited entry into the Catholic-dominated schools. To enter they would have had to renounce their evangelical faith. The solution seemed to be once again to open schools in connection with the churches, but there were no teachers to be had. Consequently several of the lady missionaries—Minnie Waage, Edith Platt, and Irene Garrett—operated a teacher training school.

The method of training suggested the Laubach literacy slogan, "Each one teach one." Girls even with minimal schooling were welcomed, taught for six months, and then sent out for six months to teach the lessons they had learned. They then came back to study at a higher level for six months and were again sent out to teach. In this slow way a corps of teachers was gathered. When restrictions were lifted, the new teachers could raise their level of training in government schools.

How To Find Trained Leaders?

With the multiplication of believers and congregations, leaders became a pressing need. Ebenezer Bible Institute was not far away across the border of Venezuela but there were problems for any Colombian young people who might want to attend, such as their inadequate academic background, great differences in living standards, and difficult border crossings. Missionaries and pastors also feared that those who went to Venezuela for study might not return to the hardships of Colombia.

Arthur and Mary Louise Bakker in Cúcuta were not only concerned about this need of training, but were willing to do something about it at considerable inconvenience to themselves. They turned their own home into a combined dormitory, classroom, and eating facility, and invited young men from the country churches. Here the Bakkers taught them for three to six months, providing basic training which would give them a measure of preparation for later entry into a Bible institute. Over a period of ten years they welcomed a total of ninety young men into their home for this training.

More In-depth Training Needed

This informal arrangement served well in a limited way but the Bakkers recognized the need of doing more. Having moved to Ocaña, they prayed about the next step:

> We knew that we needed more than these preparatory courses.... We needed a school right here that could do two things: (1) take in Christian boys at age 16 or older who lacked formal education and prepare them in a two-year course as lay workers in the churches, and (2) from among them find the ones whom God was calling into full-time service and train them in an additional two-year Bible-school course.[4]

National pastors and missionaries encouraged them to start a Bible institute, and so they launched out:

> In faith we made 24 desks and 26 beds for the course starting in March 1963. We asked God for 25 boys, another house, a cook, and so forth. God gave us more than we asked—and even greater spiritual blessings! While teaching a lesson on the Holy Spirit in the Bible Synthesis class, God's presence became so real to all of us that we had to forget the schedule and spend the forenoon in prayer.[5]

The Bakkers worked in an overcrowded situation with one additional group and then announced a six-month Bible institute course to begin in February 1964, which would launch them into a regular training program.

Ocaña Bible Institute Founded

National pastors located and purchased a seven-acre plot of mountain farm land on the edge of Ocaña with a brook for water supply and potential for a Bible institute and conference grounds.

Buildings were built as funds were available. The acreage made possible the cultivation of certain crops, thus providing work for the students for their school costs. Definite principles concerning the project were set forth in advance:

1. The institute property, control, and direction should be indigenous as far as possible and should fit with the customs and standards of the people.

2. Churches should provide for the operation of the school.

3. National teachers should be used whenever possible.[6]

During the next twenty-five years these principles were followed quite closely. Missionaries active in the school over a longer period—in addition to the Bakkers—were Charles Sheers, Marleen Beck, and Sherman and Patty Walker.

National Teachers Involved

The goal of having national teachers in the Institute was reached quite early and more than fifteen taught over a period of two decades. Santos Millán, Pedro Quintero, Julio Esteban, and Elain Arevalo served for the longest period. The Coordinating Committee (of national church and the mission) appointed Santos Millán director in 1978, a position he still held in 1989.

The enrollment reached a high of fifty-one in 1971 and maintained an average of thirty-two. Additional students were working in churches for their assigned year of practice. With the reopening of Colombian schools, better prepared students were enrolled, the course was lengthened to three years, and the preparatory course was discontinued. The Institute supplied pastors and other workers for many of the Colombian churches and contributed greatly to the spiritual maturity of the Christians.

Extension Training

Theological Education by Extension (TEE) was another means of preparing leaders for the churches. Charles Sheers was particularly active in preparing study material for these courses, taught by both missionaries and nationals to several hundred participants. He also conducted a two-year advanced study program for leaders.

Bookstore Ministry

Tim and Lynn Anderson in Cúcuta developed a bookstore in a strategic market location and later a second at a place where riders of city buses found easy access. They also worked to reach the more educated classes in the city and this led to the planting of a second large church—El Salvador. Tim also served as field chairman for many years.

Colombia, a Separate Field

From the time the first TEAM missionaries in Venezuela visited Colombia in 1923 to gain a foothold for the gospel, and through almost fifty years of itineration, literature distribution, sale of Bibles, preaching, teaching, planting churches, training converts, and working with church leaders, these missionaries were a part of what was called the South America or Venezuela-Colombia field. Though the missionaries of both countries met together in annual field conferences, the varied concerns and ministries made it advantageous for each country to have separate business and planning sessions at the conferences.

There was much of mutual interest to keep these two groups meeting at the same place and time, but the reality of the distinctives of each field led to a discussion with Richard Winchell on the matter when he visited Colombia in January 1970. The Venezuela-Colombia field council concurred in March. Winchell brought the question to the board of directors and added his recommendation. The result was that on May 1, 1970, the board approved the division of this large Latin America work into two separate fields. Administrative coordination between the two was not needed, but since fellowship and consultation would still be beneficial to both, interfield consultations were held from time to time.

Widened Consultation

Interfield meetings had their beginning in 1963 in Rhodesia. I had spent several weeks among the South Africa missionaries and was due to go to Rhodesia as well. I had proposed that the two field councils meet at Bulawayo, about half-way between the two centers of work, and spend several days discussing prepared topics of mutual interest and concern in the African work. This recommendation found immediate acceptance and the responsible leaders of the work had a very profitable time together.

This idea of interfield consultation was carried to the Europe, Far East, Western Asia, and Latin America fields. Consultations were arranged about once in three years, usually with the general director or an area secretary participating. When Jack MacDonald became the senior area foreign secretary he developed the idea further into occasional joint spiritual life and field business conferences in Europe.

CADAL '86

Impressed by the value of the missionary interfield consultations, the Colombia field council proposed that not only should the missionary leaders of the six Latin America fields—Colombia, Venezuela, Brazil, Peru, Trinidad, and Netherlands Antilles—meet, but also representatives of the church groups. When the idea was approved, the Colombia field council served as host for a conference held in Bogotá, March 3-7, 1986. Of the thirty in attendance, three were from North America, eleven were missionaries, and the rest nationals. The conference chose the name *Congreso Aliancista de América Latina (CADAL)*. Jack MacDonald and Michael Pocock from the staff attended, and MacDonald reported to the board:

> The information and exchange of ideas during the sessions were very helpful. However, of no less value and perhaps even greater, was the opportunity this afforded the national leaders to be together from the different fields. From the beginning it was clear that they thoroughly enjoyed one another. The good fellowship was mutually appreciated and stimulating.[7]

The participants proposed holding another such gathering in Trinidad in 1989. This was actually held in the spring of 1990.

To the Cities

In the 1980s TEAM's Colombia focus shifted from rural ministry in the eastern provinces to ministry in major population centers, following the demographic changes in the country. Mac-Donald called attention to this shift in a 1986 report to the board:

> The church planting ministry of TEAM missionary personnel has shifted almost entirely from our old territory in eastern Colombia to the region around Bogotá and Bucaramanga. In both places it is very encouraging. Several new works are growing well in both cities. Bogotá will have five organized churches belonging to the association by the end of 1987. The field headquarters continues to be in Cúcuta along with the literature work. The Salvador church has just moved into its new three-story building. New works are coming into existence in that region but largely under national leadership and effort.[8]

The Colombia missionaries had discovered what had been observed on other mission fields—country people were moving to the cities. The population shift affected the work in at least two ways. The first was that young people in search of employment and a better standard of living were relocating. Thus, potential leaders were lost to the older congregations. The second was the thinning out of the rural population in comparison with the cities.

The need of the unevangelized multitudes in the cities was seen to be much more urgent than that of the many smaller towns which already had congregations of witnessing believers. The population of the whole state of Norte de Santander, in which most of the older TEAM work was located, was only a quarter of that of the city of Bogotá with its two million. Cúcuta made up almost half of Norte de Santander's population and the mission had thriving church work there.

To Bogotá, the Capital

Dan and Alice Harder were the first to be assigned to Bogotá—in 1978. Their efforts were directed toward reaching the higher class residents, so often bypasssed in missionary work. Sharon Harder, Sandra Salomon, and Joyce Varlack were also assigned to work in the capital city. The Lord prospered the witness and it wasn't long before several churches were planted and reaching out in evangelism on their own.

Vision and Vitality

Missionaries and national church leaders in Bogotá did not lack vision or faith, as was discovered by Richard Winchell and Gary Bowman in 1989. Bowman, who had recently been appointed area foreign secretary for Latin America, reported to the board:

> It was a challenge to see the opportunities of church planting in Bogotá. The field has set a goal of having 100 churches in the Bogotá area by the year 2000. Although there are only five TEAM-related churches at present, this seems like a feasible (and very stretching) goal since the Colombian believers are also excited about starting churches and are helping to do so.[9]

Bucaramanga

Irene Garrett started a church planting ministry in Bucaramanga as early as 1974. This city had a population of more than a quarter of a million. Charles and Cathy Sheers began work there in 1976. The Sheers used Bucaramanga as a base for Theological Education by Extension and for a leadership training program in the churches. The Arthur Bakkers and the Robert Archers also served in this area.

Church-Mission Cooperation

The difficulties and opposition that Colombian Christians and missionaries faced together forged a bond of understanding and close working relationships between them. Nothing binds a family together more than shared suffering. This bond made it natural to confer and plan together. A coordinating committee consisting of leaders of the Association of Churches and the field council made decisions about entry into new territories, placement of missionaries, operation of special ministries such as the Bible Institute, etc. The cooperation grew as the work grew. This was not something that had to be thought through and worked out only after each group had gone its own independent way. It was the accepted way of working.

One example of this cooperation was seen when, in 1970, the churches were invited to share in the support and direction of the Bible training ministry in Ocaña. They entered into that partnership fully and wholeheartedly.

Churches continued to grow through the combined witness and work of missionaries and Colombians. As 1989 began there were 98 congregations with average Sunday attendance of 4,211. There was a baptized membership of 3,843 believers. The determined efforts of the Catholic hierarchy to crush the existing evangelical churches and block all future planting and growth had not only failed, they had actually opened the way for the Lord to bring great victory to the churches. Truly, the believers had become more than conquerors.

Taught and Used by the Spirit

The missionaries wisely did not make the Colombian Christians dependent on them when they were going through times of persecution. The believers thus learned valuable lessons of dependence on God; He was their shield and buckler; He could provide for them when all earthly props were torn away; He could motivate their witness even in the face of threats to their lives; and He could empower that witness and make them fruitful.

In some mission situations there is a tendency to expect the believers to first mature as Christians and only then begin to take on the responsibilities of an indigenous church—self-support, self-government, and self-propagation. The Colombian Christians manifested these graces right from the first. They were quickly taught by the Spirit of God to bear witness, provide their own meeting places, and work together guiding the affairs of the congregations.

In the 1960s, after the believers had come through years of harassment, Elof Anderson gave a message on Colombia at a TEAM annual conference in the homeland. What was particularly memorable was his listing of all the supporting ministries the Colombian Christian did *not* have. Missionaries from other fields had told of aids used in proclaiming the gospel—radio, films, medical care, Christian magazines, etc., all very worthwhile.

By way of contrast, Colombian Christians had nothing apart from the Word of God—only their hands, feet, ears, eyes, and voices to dedicate to the Lord as instruments in evangelism. They walked the mountain pathways, visiting villages and farm homes, witnessing to individuals. Many of them had been known for their former sinful lifestyles but now their cleansed lives were a convincing testimony to the power of the Risen Christ to transform.

Though health problems and widespread poverty abounded, the believers were not dependent on medical and welfare programs to open the way for their witness or to help them plant churches. To the hypothetical question, "How can you expect a hungry man to listen to the message of the gospel?" their answer could well be, "Give him the gospel first and when his life is cleaned up, he will meet many of his physical needs with the money he formerly spent on liquor, tobacco, gambling, and a corrupt lifestyle."

The response to the gospel did not stop or significantly slow down with the halting of the persecution. The evident hunger found among the multitudes in the great capital city of Bogotá gives evidence that the harvest will continue unabated.

The lesson of Colombia is that God is sovereign. The enemies of the gospel sought desperately to destroy the evangelical Christian testimony, but their efforts to put out the fire served only to spread it. God won the victory and His people are joined in that victory. The Colombian Christians can certainly echo the words of the Apostle Paul, "But thanks be to God, who always leads us in triumphal procession in Christ and through us spreads everywhere the fragrance of the knowledge of Him" (II Corinthians 2:14).

NETHERLANDS ANTILLES AND ARUBA

When the post-World War II period began, the ABC islands—Aruba, Bonaire, and Curaçao—lying to the north of Venezuela in the Caribbean Sea, were enjoying more than usual prosperity because of the huge oil refineries on Aruba and Curaçao. Political changes altered their relationship to the Netherlands government over the next several decades.

Religion and Language

What was most apparent to the missionaries was the religious background. The predominant religion is Roman Catholicism (85 percent), with the Dutch Reformed Church far behind in numbers. The language spoken throughout is Papiamento, with only some slight differences in word usage on the separate islands. Dutch continues to be the official language.

Becoming a Separate Field

From the beginning of TEAM's work on the ABC islands in 1931 until 1953, the missionaries were part of the South America field organization along with Venezuela and Colombia. With different languages in the two areas, the expense of traveling between Venezuela and the islands, and the growth in the work in Aruba and Curaçao, the board of directors approved that the island mission work become separately organized as the Netherlands Antilles field.

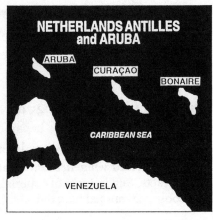

Increase of Missionaries

Two missionary families were caring for small congregations on Aruba and Curaçao in 1946, but they saw opportunities for evangelism all around them. In the decade after the war came an influx of missionaries who would make an impact on the evangelization of the islands: Robert and Marge McClain, Edgar and Ruth Martens, Earl and Ruby Ressler, Betty Ratzlaff, Lillian Mikkelson, Richard and Betty Cowser, Wilbur and Grace Chapman and, later, the staff of the radio station. Many others present for shorter periods shared in the planting and growth of the churches.

From two regular meeting places in 1946 to nine organized and three developing churches in 1988 may not seem to be outstanding growth, but in proportion to the missionaries involved and in the variety of ministries required it compares favorably with other older fields.

Lack of Literature

The Antillean culture presented an anomaly with nearly 100 percent literacy but an almost complete lack of reading material in Papiamento, the common language of the people. The official Dutch language was the medium of instruction in the schools but was not generally spoken by the people. Papiamento was not taught in the schools, did not develop a literature, and was used by only a quarter million people. There obviously was no local source of Christian literature to draw from. This made it necessary for the missionaries to translate or write and produce all that was needed. Good evangelical literature was available in English and Spanish but it was Papiamento, not those languages, which spoke to the hearts of the people.

Threefold Literature Program

The literature ministry became a growing department of the work, developing along three lines:

1. *Editorial Evangélica.* Preparation, printing, and distribution of tracts, Sunday school material, literature for discipling, song books, devotional material, and Bible studies.

2. *Boekhandel Evangélico*. Bookstore for retail sales and an excellent place for personal evangelism and counseling.

3. Old Testament translation.[1]

In the first area—preparation, production, and printing—the missionary/national team members active over the longest period were Betty Cowser, Iris Bradshaw, Marita Petrona, and Wilbur Chapman. Bookstore responsibilities were carried by Grace Chapman, and earlier by Betty Weiser, Corrine Drury, and Peter Steneker.

The Papiamento New Testament published by the Bible Society, with a recent revision, was adequate for its time. The great need was for the Old Testament books, and TEAM missionaries worked many years to complete this major translation project. Most active were Ruby Ressler, Lillian Mikkelson, and Dean Ressler. With local differences in the language, the translators set up review committees on each of the islands and a determined effort was made to establish a standard. This did much to stabilize the spelling and pronunciation. The Bible, which gave stability to the English language and to so many others through the centuries, promises to do the same for yet another.

Completing the Old Testament

The latest translation report available (1986) indicated that all 929 chapters in the Old Testament had been translated, 652 chapters initially published, 500 revised, and 437 entered into the computer. Lillian Mikkelson handled the project as a whole, monitoring the progress toward completion. The churches eagerly received the portions as they were completed. One Christian lady on Bonaire, Rosa Julia St. Jego, although able to read Dutch, said to Ruby Ressler when the Papiamento Book of Isaiah came out in print, "Now this speaks to my heart!"

An Opportunity through Radio

TEAM's first opportunity to proclaim the gospel by radio came in February 1955 when *Voz di Aruba* offered a free hour of broadcast every fourth (or fifth) Sunday. Bicento Henriquez, a deacon in the Oranjestad, Aruba, church, was pressed into service as the radio speaker. After the second broadcast, the radio station stopped the program because neither TEAM nor the church was a member of the World Council of Churches. The Lord overruled and kept the program on the air. When the missionaries heard that many were listening, the field council decided, in February 1957, to apply to the government for a license to establish and operate a radio station on Aruba. On September 5, 1957, the government granted the license.[2]

Radio Victoria Dedicated

David H. Johnson, general director, gave the address for the dedication of Radio Victoria PJA-6 on November 2, 1958, to a large audience of Christian friends, community leaders, and other interested local citizens. Carl A. Gundersen, chairman of the TEAM board of directors and a generous contributor to the radio project, also participated in the service.

Johnson's address presented three propositions:

Man needs a remedy for sin.

Man must have knowledge of the remedy.

Man needs to appropriate the remedy.

God has provided the remedy—the Lord Jesus Christ. It is man's responsibility to appropriate the remedy. The key question, then, is: "Does he have knowledge of the remedy?" The purpose of this radio station, Johnson said, is to give the people of Aruba, Curaçao, Bonaire, and northern Venezuela an adequate opportunity to hear about God's remedy, so that they can appropriate it.[3]

Mydske, Bedard Appointed

Norman Mydske was appointed station manager and Robert Bedard station engineer. Both had originally applied to work with TEAM in a hoped-for radio ministry in Uruguay—which failed to materialize. Though these men and their wives had finished Spanish language study, they willingly agreed to serve in Aruba for several years to assure that Radio Victoria would get off to a good start and be able to progress smoothly. Mydske, Bedard, and Edgar

Martens constructed the radio facilities, including the erection of the 425-foot antenna. The station went on the air with an initial power of 1,000 watts.

Mydske built up a small Aruban staff, including two men from the Oranjestad Evangelical Church—Bicento Henriquez for Bible messages and Leo Tromp for announcing and other duties. These two maintained a long-term relationship with Radio Victoria and served with sincere dedication, as did other local Christians. Norman and Valerie Mydske and Robert and Juanita Bedard reminded the general director that they considered their assignment to Radio Victoria to be temporary, pending the finding of other permanent personnel. The Lord had been preparing a future manager, Paul J. (Jim) Pietsch.

Jim Pietsches Drafted

Having been refused permission to remain in Portugal, Pietsch and his wife, Helen, accepted a temporary assignment to work at Radio Tangier in Spanish Morocco. After several years in that work, they were approached about a long-term relationship. David Johnson learned of this about the same time the need at Radio Victoria was recognized, and accordingly asked them to return to a direct TEAM ministry. They accepted his invitation, serving with the station in Aruba and representing it in the homeland for much of the next twenty years.

Immediate Needs for Development

Pietsch soon recognized that more Papiamento programming was needed in order to be effective locally, but that could become a reality only if local Christian talent were prepared to serve. The limited facilities in the studio building would not allow for group participation. A larger radio building was needed.

To send a strong signal throughout the three ABC islands and to reach Venezuela and Colombia, a more powerful transmitter of 10,000 watts was essential. In addition, there was one need for equipment replacement that had not been anticipated. The engineers had expected the 425-foot antenna to last for years in the dry atmosphere of Aruba, but inspection revealed widespread corrosion, evidently caused by fine ocean salt blown by the ever-present trade winds. Replacement by a stainless steel tower could not be long delayed.

These three property and equipment needs—studio building, transmitter, and tower—presented a difficult financial challenge, but with the necessity of protecting the broadcast license, there was nothing else to do but to go ahead, looking to the Lord to provide through His people. His provision did come in time and was the occasion for much thanksgiving.

God's Solution to a Serious Problem

When the stainless steel tower had been erected and was put into use, the engineers were faced with the serious problem of dismantling the old corroded tower. It was judged to be too dangerous for any worker to climb and dismantle section by section. In good conscience they could not ask a local contractor to take the job at the risk of the lives of the workmen. This was a problem with no clear answer and all they could do was to pray and "sleep on it" a while. One morning, after "sleeping on it," Pietsch drove to the site of the old antenna and found that it had collapsed of itself—shaken, as it were, by the hand of God. By His gracious protection it had not injured anyone or crashed into the radio building. Its collapse solved the dilemma and saved much expense for the station.

The new studio and office building for Radio Victoria was dedicated January 19, 1964, "in memory of T. J. Bach, whose pioneer ministry reached many in South America and the Netherlands Antilles for Christ."[4]

Daily News and the Good News

The broadcast of news received by radio teletype from a major international news service attracted many listeners. The newscasts were in four languages and the schedule was designed to allow short evangelistic appeals right after the news. Papiamento and English programs occupied most of the broadcast day, with shorter periods devoted to Spanish and Dutch. The radio ministry made the evangelical work widely known, and the radio personnel rejoiced as letters and phone calls told of the impact of the programs. The providers of English and Spanish programs received letters direct and often shared this information with Radio Victoria.

Less than three months after the dedication of the new studio building, the missionary family and the radio station suffered a great loss in the accidental death of radio engineer Charles Jobes, who lost his life in a fall from an antenna pole he was erecting for ham radio operations at his own home. Charles, Ruth, and two children had been on the field only two and a half years. For Ruth the missionary call was still strong and she went on to serve as a teacher of instrumental music at Morrison Academy, a school for missionary children in Taiwan.

Other long-term missionaries at Radio Victoria have been Dennis and Pat Christensen, Wayne and Alicia Gandre, Robert and Anne Catteau, and Robert and Nan Childs.

Early Impact of Broadcasts

By 1966, field leaders were noting the impact of Radio Victoria in making many aware of the gospel message. Richard Cowser, field chairman that year, included welcome information in his annual report to the field conference:

> Effectiveness of our radio work is being seen by the fact that many homes are opening up where in previous years it was impossible to get into them. During the year in Curaçao, two families started coming to church through listening to Radio Victoria. As a result, six members of these families have accepted Christ and are now attending church regularly. Four contacts from Back to the Bible broadcast have been forwarded to Curaçao. Two of these have been baptized and are now members of the Salina church.[5]

Missionaries and church workers doing visitation evangelism often found it to their advantage to introduce themselves as from Radio Victoria. Rarely were they turned away when they identified themselves with the message of this station.

The staff of Radio Victoria celebrated its twenty-fifth anniversary in 1983 with Richard Winchell as special speaker. Supporting friends in North America had been invited and also joined in a tour of TEAM ministries on the other ABC islands, Venezuela, and Colombia.

Resslers Begin Bonaire Work

The ABC island smallest in population is Bonaire and it was the last to have attention from TEAM missionaries. Earl and Ruby Ressler, who arrived in Aruba for language study in 1951, moved to Bonaire in 1952. They immediately began visiting homes and distributing tracts and encountered opposition much more intense than had been true on the other islands. Five years after the work was started they were able to report a small but stable church work at North Salina, with an average of twenty-one in the Sunday school and thirty-five in the evening services.

Evangelistic preaching was a regular feature of the ministry. One such campaign in May 1957 had Vondal Martin, TEAM missionary on Curaçao, as the speaker. Ressler singled out those meetings for mention:

> At the close of the first week, the local priest began to oppose, coming to the church personally and visiting the homes in the community repeatedly. The opposition did not greatly affect the attendance. Three years ago we would have had to close the service.[6]

Trials and Triumph in Rincón

After being sure that the church at North Salina was on a good footing, the Resslers began work in other village centers on the island, Nikiboko and Rincón, thus requiring a spread of attention to three areas. We trace the investment of effort, time, and concern in Rincón as an example of diligence and perseverance in the face of active opposition over twenty years. A sampling of the annual reports of the work in Rincón tells the story:[7]

> 1963—The last six months of the year we realized a gradual increase in attendance at Rincón, climaxing with the Christmas program. That night the local priest came along as the crowd dispersed. "To kill, to steal, and to destroy," accurately describes

what took place that night and the following months. Except for a couple of saved young men, our Rincón congregation disappeared. Since Easter we have had a gradual increase in attendance again. In the battle that continues our hearts often cry out, "How long, Lord, how long?"

1964—The work at Rincón has suffered much opposition; nevertheless the Lord has raised up a nucleus of believers there during the past year. Many of them are faithfully out witnessing in the face of much persecution. We have been working with them to encourage, establish, and build them up in the faith.

1965—Every Home Crusade was completed in Rincón, mostly through the faithfulness of the Christian young men. Five believers from Rincón were baptized.

1966—An evangelistic campaign was conducted with the Richard Cowsers. During the campaign and the month following, a number of souls accepted Christ as Savior. While some of those have not gone on with the Lord, others have shown Christian growth. Among them are a husband and wife, representing the first couple in the Rincón church.

1967—It was a real joy to have fellow workers Alehandro and Irene Martínez with us during the year. Alehandro assumed the responsibility for the church in Rincón.

1968—The work at Rincón suffered a stunning setback. A number of Christians had backslidden. Others who had been interested in the gospel consequently lost confidence; the congregation fled. The Rincón church is built on "devil's hill," and he does not easily retreat. First the attack was from without, then from within. "What the palmer worm hath left the locust hath eaten." We hardly had the heart to pitch in again after the battles encountered there, but we had less heart to throw up our arms and quit when we were convinced as ever that the Lord has his chosen ones in Rincón. All but one of the backsliders are back in the services, although not fully surrendered to the Lord.

1972—Alehandro Martínez: In 1966 I returned from Ebenezer Bible Institute [San Cristóbal, Venezuela], to my home on the island of Bonaire. I was placed in the Iglesia Evangélica in Rincón at that time to work for the Lord. I was never a stranger to my countrymen in the village of Rincón because they all knew me. Yet, why did I appear to be a stranger in their eyes? The Lord told me, "If you were of the world, the world would love its own, but you are not of the world, therefore the world hates you." In Rincón, the enemy did not want me to preach the gospel of salvation to my people. I had to fight face to face with him using the sword of the Lord. I do not want to tell you all that happened to me in the past six years. I want to thank God for those who are coming to the services regularly—about twenty in number.

1974—The gospel has gotten a toehold on "devil's hill." We pray and persevere that it may gain a foothold, with many turning to the Lord and standing for Him. Nikiboko, which some years ago seemed so very hopeless, is now a prospering work. Can we not trust the Lord for Rincón? It took 20 years in Nikiboko, and we are grateful we did not give up there. We determine to remain faithful in Rincón, trusting the Lord to accomplish whatever He desires.

1975—The regular services have continued throughout the year with increased attendance and good interest. There is a good spirit among the believers. Gradually they are taking more active part in the services. Also they are having a more active witness throughout the week.

1979—There has been good interest and a good spirit in the church. The attendance is up approximately 20 percent over a year ago. The people are generally eager to help in whatever way they can.

1982—After much study and definite leading of the Lord, the church was formally organized with 25 members. Children's classes continue in two districts taught by two ladies of the church. The men have begun meeting biweekly for Bible study, emphasizing spiritual maturity. The ladies continue meeting once a month.

1985—It is encouraging to see the church maturing spiritually. In general, the members are enthusiastic about helping where they can.

Steady Growth on Curaçao and Aruba

While the difficulties and opposition were not as pronounced in the work on Aruba and Curaçao, the same degree of dedication and perseverance was required. The Curaçao work went forward well under the short ministry of Vondal and Roberta Martin and the first church building was erected. This gave more permanence to the work. Richard and Betty Cowser came to Curaçao in 1955 and worked in the Salina church for some time and later in establishing the Montaña, Palu Blancu, and smaller churches. With gifts of evangelism, Cowser was often called upon to minister on the other islands. He also served as field chairman from time to time. During periods in the homeland he represented TEAM in the southeastern states.

Aruba was the second of the islands to have a church. The group was formed from the ministry of Paul and Charlotte Sheetz. After the Sheetz's transfer to Venezuela, the Aruba work was continued by Robert and Margaret McClain. When the congregation in Oranjestad grew, the people felt the need for a suitable church building. This building continued to serve—with some enlargement—for over thirty years.

The Oranjestad church carried major responsibility in developing and operating a camping and conference ministry at a location on Aruba with the unexpected name of Camp Washington. Betty Ratzlaff, who spent many years working with the Oranjestad church, was a leader in this camp ministry.

Because the Lago oil refinery employed many English-speaking West Indians, a settlement of these people grew not far from the refinery in San Nicolás. Edgar and Ruth Martens were among the first to work among them. Through the years members of the Radio Victoria staff whose preference was to work in English participated in the San Nicolás church.

Another Papiamento church was planted at Pos Chiquito using the old radio building. Robert and Mildred McClain were leaders in this work. (Margaret McClain passed away in 1966. Bob married Mildred Sawyer, a member of the Radio Victoria missionary staff, several years later.)

Children's and Youth Ministries

From TEAM's earliest years on the islands, a great deal of evangelistic activity was directed to children and youth. Literature for this purpose formed an important segment of the production of *Editorial Evangélica*. In his report as field chairman in 1982,

Richard Cowser summed up this ministry:[8]

> Klub Saforma begun in Curaçao some ten years ago by Corrinne Drury plays a key role in providing activities for children 8-14 years of age. Practical and spiritual guidance given to these boys and girls is helping to build stable Christians as well as providing a Christian-oriented atmosphere for their boundless energy. In this ten-year period the program has been nationalized. Leaders, including the director, are Christians from local churches.
>
> Another plus in the Lord's work in the Antilles is the ministry of Word of Life Clubs for young people fifteen years and over. These youth clubs are under the direction of Mr. Calvin Varlack, a school teacher in Curaçao, and his wife Silvia, graduates of Word of Life Bible Institute, Schroon Lake, N.Y. In cooperation with the local churches, these young people are making an impact on the unsaved, and are a real encouragement to the local churches as well.
>
> There are training programs going on in most of the local churches in Curaçao and Bonaire under the direction of Antillean pastors. Simple courses in song leading, Bible studies, and personal evangelism taught in these classes are building up the body of Christ in these churches. There are frequent reports of conversions and blessings from this emphasis. We are grateful also for the renewal of child-evangelism with a full time worker on the Island of Bonaire, Felicia Emerenciana, under the auspices of Child Evangelism Fellowship.

Home-grown Leaders

In the early years of planting churches, missionaries served as pastors but kept before the congregations the desirability of having men called of God from the local groups to serve the churches. One of the earliest to become a pastor was Bicento Henriquez of the Oranjestad church. Others serving in other island churches included Hipólito Zievinger, Tony Green, Eusebio Petrona, Clevis White, Alehandro Martínez, Calvin Varlack, Carlos van Langeveld, and Wilfred Antersijn.

Coordination—a Necessity

With the influx of missionaries in the 1950s it was necessary that they coordinate procedures. This was on the minds of some as they met in annual conference on Bonaire in 1957. Several of the missionaries in newer churches were ready to appoint elders and anticipated the ordination of pastors. Should the missionaries not agree upon procedures to guide such matters? I recalled this as I wrote historical notes on the Netherlands Antilles work in 1984:

> Though the tendency of the believers on the separate islands is to consider themselves independent of others, it has been possible for them to get together in an association of churches. This was first suggested to the field when I was at the conference in 1957 at a time when the churches were formulating their constitutions and beginning to consider problems such as ordaining of workers. It was recognized that an organization could not be imposed upon them, but we recommended that they begin to develop areas of communication and fellowship. This began to take place in some short-term Bible schools and in some youth activities. In recent years a very good organization has developed with the churches participating in an excellent way.[9]

Moving Toward Fellowship

The missionaries were wise in the way they proceeded toward the ultimate goal of linking the churches in a mutually beneficial organization. They were aware of the insularity of the people of the three islands, yet they recognized the elements which drew them together—their new life in Christ and their interest in the Word of God. As churches called workers from another island to help at times, they began to develop common interests. Radio Victoria broadcasts and the growing availability of mission-produced literature were also factors. But it was only in 1964 that a move was made by the missionary leaders to present the concept of a church fellowship to the churches:

> The initial step was made toward the formation of a national church fellowship, in conjunction with the ordination of Hipólito Zievinger in Curaçao. Approximately fifteen church leaders met in an afternoon session of explanation, discussion, and fellowship. While a few expressed enthusiasm, it is entirely new to the majority. It will take time to promote a realization of the need and advantages of having such a fellowship.[10]

There was enough interest so that a conference of the churches was called the next year:

> The first organized meeting of the National Church Fellowship

met in Curaçao during a three-day weekend, June 5-7. It was a profitable time of fellowship, with Aarón Espinoza as main speaker. Three national men, including two pastors and one layman, were elected to head the National Church Fellowship the coming year.[11]

Espinoza was a leading pastor in *OVICE*, the church fellowship in Venezuela, and it can be supposed that he was very positive about the advantages of a church fellowship as was experienced in Venezuela.

Development of the Fellowship

Over the next two decades a fellowship of churches developed and matured. These brief excerpts from annual reports trace the progress:

1967—The meetings reached over the two hundred mark in attendance.

1969—The organization shows more maturity. It is hoped that in due time it will be able to assume more responsibility for the direction of the Lord's work in the Netherlands Antilles.

1971—It is recommended that the national organization take the initiative in future ordinations, and serve as examining body.

1972—The Fellowship of Churches has drawn up incorporation papers which will give it recognition by the Antillean government as an indigenous body. This will greatly aid them in future expansion of the Lord's work in the Antilles.

1973—Of the eleven regular meeting places with services, nine are being ministered to by nationals. The short-term Bible school program is now being directed completely by the fellowship, with Hipólito Zievinger in charge. Over 100 students participated in the program last year.

1980—The Fellowship met in the Montaña Church in October. Approximately 350 present. This was probably the largest evangelical gathering in Netherlands Antilles history.

1984—Board of the Fellowship of Churches met with the annual field conference to discuss formation of a National Missionary organization.

1986—There has been a good working relationship with the Fellowship of Churches. There is one joint meeting of the field council and the Fellowship. It is good to see the national church committee seriously assuming responsibility for churches without a pastor.[12]

Training for Christian Service

Missionaries were eager to encourage young people to enter Christian service, recognizing the need for Christians prepared to minister in the local churches and elsewhere. When the work first began on the ABC islands the tendency was to recommend study in North America. After several disappointing experiences which seemed to bring no benefit to the local work they began looking elsewhere. There was no available Bible institute in Papiamento or Dutch, but with many of the young people fluent in Spanish or English the solution was to recommend Ebenezer Bible Institute in Venezuela and the Jamaica Bible Institute in Jamaica, West Indies. Several went to the Word of Life Institute in Schroon Lake, New York.

Short-term Training

These formal school experiences were valuable in preparing for pastoral service, but more in-depth training was needed for lay workers. Earl Ressler, in his annual report for 1963, made a plea for a thorough study of the possibility of training Christian young people locally. A year later he renewed the recommendation that "we plan a periodic, concentrated short-term Bible school program on our islands of possibly two weeks duration for those who cannot take formal training."[13]

In 1965 Ressler was able to report a satisfactory beginning:

A two-week concentrated Bible school was conducted in Cura-çao in May with 14 students from the three islands. Two missionaries and one national assumed the teaching responsibilities. Students participated in the services of the island, and in visitation and tract distribution. It was a time of real challenge and blessing.[14]

The short-term Bible school became an annual affair under the leadership of missionaries until in 1973 when Richard Cowser reported:

The short-term Bible school program is now being directed completely by the Fellowship of Churches, with Hipólito Zievinger in charge. Eusebio Petrona, Tony Green, and he were the teachers this past year. Over 100 students participated in this program last year.[15]

Aruba Chooses a Different Status

When, on January 1, 1986, the Netherlands government granted home rule to the islands, Aruba chose a special status independent of Curaçao and Bonaire. Aruba then became a country distinct from the Netherlands Antilles. Historical and demographic differences provided political reasons for this division. Similarities were greater than differences, in the viewpoint of TEAM missionaries who had worked on these islands in the years following the mission's entry in 1931. While ethnic backgrounds were not particularly important to missionaries, they were probably of some concern to the people of Aruba and were likely a factor in Aruba's desire to separate from the other islands. Aruba also clearly desired to avoid domination in a parliamentary vote by the more populous Curaçao. TEAM's ministry was not affected by this change.

Where are the Dividends?

With more than fifty years of gospel investment in the Antilles, the question could be asked as to the results. While missionaries are still active—and needed—in literature, radio, and some church work, nationals are clearly leading local ministries and extension into new areas. Over a period of more than ten years, missionaries have been preaching foreign missions with the result that a number of young people have gone into foreign service. TEAM has benefitted from this appeal in the persons of Ingrid (Mrs. Dean) Ressler in Bonaire and Joyce Varlack in Colombia.

What Remains to Be Done?

With an active membership in the churches of 509 baptized believers and an average Sunday attendance of 1,023, there is still much work to do to reach the unreached on these islands and to make them a base for a foreign mission outreach.

TRINIDAD, PERU, BRAZIL, MEXICO— FOUR LEVELS OF OPENNESS

TRINIDAD AND TOBAGO

The Republic of Trinidad and Tobago lies just off the northeastern coast of Venezuela, its tropical climate moderated by the breezes of trade winds. The islands have been colonized by the Spanish and French as well as the British, who governed Trinidad and Tobago from the early nineteenth century until independence in 1962.

Most of the people of Trinidad and Tobago are of African or East Indian origin. The Arawak and Carib Indians who once lived on the islands died out after the European colonization, and today's Trinidadians are descended from black slaves brought to the islands in the seventeenth century, East Indians and Chinese who came to work the sugar cane plantations in the nineteenth century, and the European settlers.

Trinidad's mixed cultural heritage is reflected in the religious scene. Sixty-one percent of the people declare themselves to be Christian, chiefly Roman Catholic or Anglican. Of the Protestants, a mere one to two percent are evangelical. Hinduism claims another twenty-five percent of the population and Islam six percent. Visitors to Trinidad see ample evidence of these latter religions. Prayer flags flutter on tall bamboo poles outside many houses and there are numerous Hindu temples and Muslim

mosques.

TEAM Enters in 1963

TEAM's interest in these small islands was sparked in 1963 when the Caribbean Broadcasting Company (CBC) asked about a possible merger. CBC had applied for a radio license, so far without success. Their missionaries David and Elaine Crane had served in Trinidad since 1959, busy in camp work and evangelism while waiting for a radio license which never did materialize.

The TEAM board of directors approved Trinidad as a new field in June 1963 and the agreement to absorb CBC was finalized in December.

Formative Years

TEAM gained two experienced missionaries in David and Elaine Crane. In 1960 they had begun developing a hilltop thicket of thirty acres in mountainous northern Trinidad into a youth camp. Located near the capital, Port-of-Spain, the camp was named Victory Heights. The Cranes and other TEAM missionaries who joined them worked in close cooperation with the West Indies Mission.

In the early years of TEAM's involvement, the field was administered directly from TEAM headquarters and Dr. Delbert Kuehl and I made a number of visits to help lay down guidelines for this developing work. By 1967, at its second annual TEAM conference, Trinidad and Tobago was officially organized as a regular field, electing a full field council under the leadership of chairman David Crane.

"Trinidad is open as wide as it ever will be for the spreading of the Gospel," Crane reported at the end of 1967. "In speaking with each of our missionaries, we are all covenanting together to make [1968] a Church Planting Year."[1]

Planting Churches in Northern Trinidad

Missionaries were working to start churches in a number of areas in the northern part of Trinidad. Since Trinidad and Tobago together total only 1,980 square miles, about the size of Delaware, the distance between towns was not too great for missionaries to meet regularly. The men of the mission met weekly for an early morning prayer meeting, while all met together monthly for Bible study and communion.

By the late 1960s and early 1970s, chapels were forming in Five Rivers, Trincity, Port-of-Spain, St. Augustine, Maracas Valley, Caroni, Cascade, and St. Anns. Church planters such as the Cranes, Davis and Ruth Hopkins, Norman and Sue Niemeyer, LeRoy (Bud) and Audrey Johnson, Forrest and Dorothy Thorsby, Guy and Karen Storm, and Isaac and Dorothy Brown were helped by a number of associate and summer workers. Because English is the predominant language in Trinidad, this field more than many others was able to make good use of short-term workers.

Growth at Victory Heights Camp Grounds

Harold and JoAnne Kendall, who had served with TEAM in the Netherlands Antilles, joined the Trinidad field in 1967 and were assigned to Victory Heights, which was growing steadily year by year. More than 2,000 attended camp in each of 1968 and 1969, and many young people made decisions for Christ.

Besides its ministry with young people, the camp also performed another important function. It was the central meeting place for the young church groups. As I reported to the board of directors after my visit in the first months of 1973:

> All of these groups are interested in the various camps and also use the camp site for their baptismal services and other special gatherings. About 2,100 campers were enrolled during 1972, and there is steady gathering of spiritual fruit as a result of these camps.[2]

Gradually what began as a youth camp expanded to attract many adults as well, establishing itself as a vital arm of the field's church planting work.

Riots and Martial Law

In early 1970, "black power" pressure and an army mutiny

brought severe political unrest. Riots erupted in Port-of-Spain and numerous fires blazed over many days. Then, on April 21, the government imposed a martial law state of emergency. Field chairman David Crane reported:

> For thirty days, being pretty much confined to our immediate area afforded each one of us time for personal prayer, intercession, and personal work with those nationals closest to us. This was a profitable time in bringing us closer to the Lord and closer to those nationals who had a burden for souls.

The curfew was relaxed after thirty days but for the next five months missionary activity continued with some limitations. Said Crane:

> There is an air of uncertainty and expectancy in Trinidad which means that the opportunities are greater than ever. We face a national election year which may mean more problems, but we stand firm that *our* calling and election is sure.[3]

Progress in the Chapels

During 1971 Brother Alfredo George became the field's first national pastor, taking full-time responsibility for Trincity Chapel. In the year that followed, Trincity purchased a lot and began building its own facility.

Five Rivers Chapel was making great strides under the leadership of Norman and Sue Niemeyer. The believers there, too, were constructing a building, and Five Rivers would soon become an organized church—the first of the chapels to take that step. During my visit in February 1973, the Five Rivers-Khandahar Evangelical Bible Church was officially organized with a charter membership of seventy-nine. The organizational service was a thrilling event, with the building crowded to capacity and scores of people standing outside. The elders who had been elected were installed at the service and deacons were chosen subsequently.

"What do 1973 and the years ahead hold for TEAM Trinidad?" asked field chairman David Crane early that year. The answer:

> Unanimously we have agreed and covenanted to press for an early establishment of the chapels into local churches, operating autonomously in every respect….[W]e have dedicated ourselves to more effective and concentrated church planting.[4]

One problem, however, was training for national leaders. There was no local training institution to which believers could be sent, and although missionaries were teaching laymen informally in the churches, it would be a long time before many could bear the main responsibility for teaching and preaching—a major impediment to forming autonomous churches.

Visa Problems Begin

For the first time, the government refused to grant visas to several new missionaries in 1973. In one day rejections were received both for Joe and Olga Reimer, who were already in Trinidad, and for Ralph and Lila Bauer, who planned to come in August. Written appeals and many hours in prayer and at the Ministry of National Security followed. After a first appeal the Bauers were granted visas, but nine months of appeals were to no avail for the Reimers, who finally had to leave Trinidad. In their last weeks on the island, the Lord opened a door for them to continue their camp ministry with TEAM in the Netherlands Antilles.

Correspondence Courses and a Bookstore

Closing doors across the world in India brought a new ministry to Trinidad, as Henry and Marion Goertzen, veterans of three terms there, arrived in 1973 to begin a Bible correspondence course ministry.

A new TEAM office was opened in St. Augustine that same year, centrally housing the field chairman's office, correspondence courses, and the extensive film library that was used so effectively over the years.

Then in September 1974 a bookstore was opened, also under the leadership of the Goertzens.

National Leaders Step into the Gap

Missionaries in Trinidad were feeling the pressures of a depleting staff as health problems, visa problems, and furloughs reduced their numbers. Though more missionaries were needed, acting field chairman Guy Storm reported at the end of 1974 that some good was coming from these difficulties:

> Through lack of foreign missionaries we have seen many of our national brethren step in to fill the gap and most of them have done an excellent job. This has certainly caused us to make greater progress toward indigenizing our six congregations which are still not officially organized.[5]

Believers were taking added responsibility in a number of different ways. When the nationals helping in the work full-time faced support problems, the faith promise program was introduced to the believers in 1973. "The Lord used that time to burden hearts," said Norm Niemeyer, "and the result was that all of our workers were totally underwritten by promised pledges."[6] One such worker was Edna Nicholas, whose many ministries over the years included discipling women, teaching Sunday school, teaching religion in the public schools, and directing women's camps. Another worker was Indra Soodeen, a Hindu convert who was discipled by Dave and Elaine Crane and then attended Jamaica Bible College before returning to Trinidad as a worker in TEAM's national missionary program.

At the Cascade-St. Anns and Caroni Chapels, councils were formed in 1973 as a first step toward local leadership. And at Victory Heights, a board of missionaries and nationals was appointed to oversee the camp grounds. Besides greater spiritual outreach, their ultimate aim was to bring the camp under full national leadership.

Church Association Incorporated

A goal of several years came to pass in January 1976 when the Association of Evangelical Bible Churches of Trinidad and Tobago (AEBC) was officially incorporated and registered with the government.

That year two successful mini-conferences were held for missionaries and church leaders, at which they prayed together, shared ministry needs, and discussed methods and goals. Over the years, missionaries had held regular "think sessions" on specific topics or to plan for the future. Now in 1976 two of these sessions brought nationals and church planters together to discuss many facets of chapel operations.

This was a time of change for Trinidad as a whole. The effects of the oil boom on its petroleum-based economy had ushered in a time of prosperity and high prices. And in 1976 Trinidad became a republic, electing a new president and voting a new constitution into force.

National believers recommended that government recognition of the AEBC would be better assured if its unlimited incorporation were passed by parliament through a "private members bill," thus making its way into the statute books. Missionaries and believers alike rejoiced when the bill was successful in 1978.

Now came the challenge of activating a joint TEAM/AEBC committee to direct the work of the churches, chapels, and ministries. This committee would be chosen from the AEBC board and the field council. Said field chairman Norman Niemeyer, "We need to be very sensitive to this new phase in our church planting ministry so that it will meet with success from the very beginning."[7]

Leadership in Training

The need for trained leaders was becoming acute. Some young people left the country to attend Bible school, but this was not feasible for many of the laymen who showed promise.

Then in 1975 the Niemeyers began Leadership in Training (LIT), a program of Bible and leadership training offered in the evenings and on weekends. Field chairman Guy Storm was happy to report some months later that "Many of God's present and future leaders are now taking evening classes while still holding down jobs and providing for their families."[8]

By 1980, the first four-year cycle of courses had been completed and four students were graduated in an impressive ceremony at Victory Heights. Fifty-four students were enrolled that year, with classes taught in four locations. Missionaries Armond (Bud) and

Lolly Fritz and David and Gwen Broucek had by now taken responsibility for LIT School of the Bible, with Bud Fritz as principal.

Among the national Christians who served on the LIT committee during this time were Joe Caterson, Jr., an elder of the St. Augustine Church, and Kendra Sharmasingh, a young man from Dinsley Chapel who attended Jamaica Bible College and then returned in 1977 to become the pastor at Dinsley.

The LIT program also sponsored workshops in practical leadership training. Since in 1980 only one of the eight AEBC churches and chapels had a full-time pastor and the others relied on elders and deacons, training lay leaders was critical indeed. As Dave Crane said, "LIT is the petrol in the motor of church planting that keeps the machine advancing forward."[9]

Trials and Burdens

Guy Storm wrote of 1975 that it had been a very challenging year for the small missionary force. "The spiritual battles that we have faced clearly show us that we have penetrated deep into enemy territory."[10] The accounts of the years which follow show that growth in the churches and progress in ministry were not going uncontested.

During 1976 and 1977, three new missionary families arrived in Trinidad only to leave the field in less than a year for medical reasons. Another family whose arrival was eagerly anticipated could not come for lack of funds. Ralph and Lila Bauer and Henry and Marion Goertzen left for furlough in 1977 with no one to replace them in their work, and when the Goertzen's visa extension was refused this made their departure permanent.

Two new families who applied to come as missionaries in 1977 were at first rejected by the government, and then given visas on appeal. But one couple, John and Diane Garvin, had been in Trinidad for only about six months, working at Trincity Chapel, when a tragic automobile accident seriously injured John and killed Brother Ali, one of the Trincity members. After some anxious days, the Garvins were flown back to the United States.

And there were other difficulties as well. "There have been many critical times in 1978," wrote Norm Niemeyer at the end of the year, "but we have seen the Lord move into each situation so that glory came to the Lord Jesus Christ."[11]

Outreach in Lopinot

It was encouraging indeed to see national believers stepping out in ministry. In early 1977, K.K. Bachew became a full-time evangelist, reaching out with the support of Five Rivers Church into Lopinot, a village of 1,500 which had a history of numerous clashes between its Roman Catholics and other groups who had tried to evangelize there.

Under K.K.'s leadership, the first step was a detailed study of the village, followed by three months of prayer and fasting to discern God's will for the church-planting effort. Finally, members of Five Rivers went from house to house, visiting again and again. Said Bachew:

> This attempt to befriend individual villagers worked in their favor, for the villagers began to trust them. They even started to ask for special prayer. This growing relationship was in stark contrast to another group who had attempted to infiltrate the village at an earlier date. That attempt resulted in a stoning.[12]

A day-long picnic climaxed by an evening film showing was the next step. Then Five Rivers members again went house to house, inviting villagers to a tent crusade. During the three-week crusade, Five Rivers members were divided into three groups, two of which would attend the meetings while the other prayed.

Although the local priest had warned people to avoid the Protestants, 250 crowded into the tent the first night. Opposition continued, however, and about half of those who made decisions for Christ returned to the Roman Catholic church within two months.

There was spiritual opposition as well. "Demonism was a real problem in the village," said Niemeyer, "but the Five Rivers believers stood with K.K. all through those hectic hours until total deliverance was given by the Lord."[13] Bachew reported that in every home where someone had been demon possessed, the one possessed had been saved along with at least one other person.

By early 1981, about forty adults were meeting regularly in Lopinot and praying for land to house a church building. They, with believers from Five Rivers, were reaching out to share the gospel in Surrey, a village about four miles away.

Religious Instruction in Schools

One area of tremendous opportunity was in Trinidad's public schools, where forty-five minutes a week was allotted for religious instruction. Ralph and Lila Bauer were challenged by the possibilities this presented when they arrived in 1973, and Ralph began by teaching Bible in a nearby junior high school one day a week.

From this small beginning, the Bauers initiated an exciting new program. By 1980, fifty national Christians were teaching Bible in forty public schools, and Bauer was organizing a massive follow-up program for children who had responded. Less than two years later, the program had more than doubled in scope, with 100 national Christians teaching Bible in 112 public junior high and high schools.

"The phenomenal growth of this ministry is due in large part to the vision God gave to a young, enthusiastic Trinidadian named Steve Paul," reported the mission's magazine. "He is an excellent children's Bible teacher, recruiter, and teacher trainer."[14] Besides teaching classes, the religious instruction team was also invited to hold special counseling days at many schools.

Soon plans were made to send Bible teachers into the primary schools as well. By 1986, 123 Christians were teaching God's Word in more than sixty primary schools in Trinidad and Tobago.

Linda Alexander, a Trinidad national supported by the churches, became the Bauers' full-time coworker in 1986 and took over complete responsibility for the ministry in 1987.

Progress on Many Fronts

By the end of 1979, field chairman David Crane could report

encouraging news on a number of fronts. Though one new missionary family's visa had been rejected, visas for four other families had been renewed. Visa troubles were beginning to come to an end.

Nationals were assuming more leadership. The AEBC board met many times, setting goals to strengthen and challenge the church groups. A national workers committee was, with the help of Bud Fritz, taking full responsibility for the collection and distribution of the national workers' funds. It had also taken charge of the annual TEAM Family Day at Victory Heights, when about 500 people from the churches and chapels met for fun and fellowship.

Though there were ups and downs in the various churches, overall there was much progress. Caroni Chapel became a fully organized church in 1979, while Lopinot organized as a chapel. Members from Trincity Chapel reached out to share the gospel in Caparo Village:

> Every week a delegation would travel the twenty miles (some of it fairly rough) to "keep services." The faithfulness paid off. Today Ralph and Lila Bauer are living near to the Village and holding Bible classes in several homes to the end of establishing a church. [15]

The camp, LIT program, and religious instruction in the schools were all experiencing solid growth. The bookstore, which had been difficult to maintain after the Goertzens' visa renewal was denied, was sold to a Christian businessman. The correspondence courses were continuing a strong outreach under the leadership of national worker Sister Edna Nicholas. Said Crane:

> When we look back ten years and take inventory, there was not an organized church then. Now there are four [Five Rivers, St. Augustine, St. Anns, and Caroni]. The past five years, baptized believers have doubled. Membership has tripled. This has been good. God is working. However, we must look at the overwhelming percentage of unsaved yet unreached. Just the forty villages between Caroni and San Fernando without a consistent witness should put us on our knees.

He also pointed to the tremendous surge of Islam in Trinidad in recent years. "Will the evangelical church keep pace?" he asked. "Our nationals are determined to meet this need."[16]

National Directors at Victory Heights

Freddie and Charmaine Canode, associate workers who had directed Victory Heights since 1977, completed their assignment in July 1981 when they handed over responsibility to Ashoke and Stephanie Bachew. At a special service on July 12, a new chapel was dedicated and the Bachews were inaugurated as the first national coordinators of the camp grounds.

During the previous year, more than 6,000 campers had attended Victory Heights and hundreds had received Christ as Savior. Under the Canodes' leadership, the camp had become self-supporting.

Church Association Strengthened

Although the Association of Evangelical Bible Churches (AEBC) had been incorporated in 1976 and a board of directors began actively leading its affairs some years later, it was not until 1981 that a constitution was finalized and a representative council was elected from all the churches. The council met for the first time that year and chose an executive committee, electing lay leader Joseph Caterson as its first chairman.

In a stirring service at Victory Heights in September, the members of the new representative council were committed to the Lord. That same afternoon there was much rejoicing as three men—Carroll Connor, K.K. Bachew, and Kendra Sharmasingh—knelt for ordination as pastors.

At the beginning of 1982, the TEAM field council met for the first time with the AEBC's representative council. Through the year, TEAM and AEBC met several times on items of mutual interest. AEBC was taking shape as a maturing body making decisions in its own right.

AEBC held its first missionary conference in November 1981, a success with good attendance and participation by the churches

898

and chapels. Seven people dedicated their lives to the Lord for Christian service and healthy faith promise pledges were made on the last day.

Crossing Cultures for Christ

Over the years, many evangelistic teams, special speakers, and summer workers came to Trinidad from North America. Trinidad's proximity and common language made such visits both possible and useful.

Of special interest are visits from other TEAM fields. In 1977 the Endigeri family from India spent more than a month in Trinidad under the TEAM REACH program, which encourages cross-cultural evangelism. Speaking and singing in both English and Hindi, the Endigeris were greatly used of the Lord among East Indians. In 1981, the Jonathan Cheng Musical Family came from Taiwan. Twenty-two meetings and eleven days later they were on their way, having touched the hearts of many.

Teams from Trinidad also traveled internationally. In 1978 a team of young people from the St. Anns and Five Rivers churches shared Christ in Europe for six weeks. Then in 1981 a six-member musical group brought their steel pans to Peru for a month of evangelistic meetings under the direction of Joe Caterson.

K.K. Bachew brought a thirty-four-member team, *Los Conquistadores,* to Colombia in 1987. They returned the following year with fifty-six delegates ranging in age from four to forty. *Los Conquistadores* presented the gospel enthusiastically, using the lively music of steel pans, a children's choir, and an adult drama team. Missionary Karen Johnson, who toured with the group in 1988, reported that about 200 people responded to invitations during the three-week trip, perhaps half of them making a personal commitment to Christ. An added benefit was a growing interest among the team members and their home churches in missions.[17]

Growing Churches

During 1981, Dinsley Chapel was formally organized as a church, electing elders and deacons and extending a call to K.K.

Bachew as pastor. Dinsley Church was busy in an ambitious building program, envisioning an auditorium and balcony which could seat 600.

In 1982, St. Augustine Church dedicated its new facilities, a former shirt factory which was renovated into a lovely edifice seating several hundred with room for expansion. Another renovated building became a parsonage plus offices for the audio-visual and correspondence course ministries, ably run by Sister Edna Nicholas and her assistant, Patricia Lewis.

That same year Five Rivers called one of its own elders, LIT graduate Carroll Connor, as full-time pastor. Expanding both spiritually and numerically, Five Rivers was renovating its building to meet the needs of growth until it could build a new one.

Doctrinal Disagreements

One difficulty not easy to solve was doctrinal disagreement among the churches. Field chairman David Crane said at the end of 1982 that both he and AEBC chairman Joe Caterson sensed that not all was well with the AEBC.

> ...[M]any churches and ministries have grown tremendously. Several have new facilities, others are on the verge of expansion. All have reported numerical growth. Many have enthusiastically rejoiced in what God has done. However, we sense a need for togetherness. We feel that division is very possible. The enemy, as weeds or tares in the garden, will come in and proceed to destroy and devour the fruit. We must be on the alert.... Division, dissension, doctrinal misinterpretations and differences creep in. We must stand firm and strong in the Word with love, "...rightly dividing the Word of truth...."

Crane stressed the importance of the weekly Thursday 6:00 A.M. prayer time for men and the bimonthly prayer time for women. "These two regular events must be preserved at all costs."[18]

By the end of 1986, field chairman Ralph Bauer could report growth toward unity in doctrine. During 1985 the AEBC had held many meetings on this subject, out of which had come a statement concerning the baptism of the Holy Spirit agreed to by all organ-

900

ized churches. Said Bauer:

> I believe that this statement, along with tremendously changed attitudes on both sides, is why 1986 has been a year of united church development. There probably will be more occasions in the future when other areas of conflict will arise. I believe that through much prayer, face to face discussion and study of God's Word, the Holy Spirit will continue to bring us together.[19]

United Evangelism in Chaguanas

One example of this new unity was a massive joint evangelistic crusade held during 1986. TEAM and all of the AEBC churches and chapels joined together in this venture, which had as its aim the starting of a church in Chaguanas, Trinidad's fastest-growing town. Home to 40,000 people, Chaguanas is located in the heart of the island's sugar belt.

The ten AEBC churches and missionaries prayed together for months before the two-week crusade. They worked together visiting homes, publicizing the crusade, planning the program, and following up afterwards. Most of the cost was paid by the AEBC churches, which also provided the evangelist, people to give testimonies, musicians, and counselors.

Attendance ranged from 300-400 each night, with 700 one evening. Scores of people made decisions to follow Christ, and the goal of the crusade—a new church—was met.

In nearby Edinburgh, a group of thirty believers had been meeting regularly in a home. They joined the new Chaguanas believers to form the Chaguanas Evangelical Bible Church. The St. Augustine Church sent two of its leaders and their families to help develop the new church, and by the end of the year more than seventy people were meeting regularly in a rented hall. Missionaries Walter (Dub) and Susan Ludwick, who oversaw this new ministry, were working to develop a team of leaders. Truly the new Chaguanas church was a united effort.

Progress in Santa Rosa Heights

Santa Rosa Heights, a middle-class bedroom community eighteen miles from Port-of-Spain, had been targeted for church planting by AEBC in 1980. When Dave and Gwen Broucek moved there in late 1983, they found a thriving Sunday school and two weekly Bible studies which had been developed by Bud and Audrey Johnson and a Trinidadian couple, Monty and Betty McDonald. Assigned to transform these elements into a local church, Dave wrote in the mission's magazine:

> We soon discovered what the other couples already knew: this task was not easy. In most Santa Rosa Heights families, both husband and wife work. They leave home at 5:30 A.M. and don't return until after 6 P.M. Then they retreat behind fences and locked gates into comfortable homes.... We also quickly learned that the residents of this community—whether Roman Catholic, Hindu, Muslim, or Anglican—share the same philosophy: "All a' we is one." They believe in the validity of everyone's religion. This belief conveniently sidesteps the question of truth and makes religious affirmation a matter of family heritage or personal preference.[20]

Slowly, individuals began to come to the Lord and a church service held on the Broucek's front porch grew in attendance.

In May 1987, a second united AEBC tent crusade was held, this time in Santa Rosa Heights. Members of the local group volunteered their time and gave testimonies. Sixty people made decisions or rededicated their lives to Christ, and some joined the church.

By late 1987, a church council had been formed and was meeting monthly. In September the congregation bought land, a major step toward a permanent church building, and elders and deacons would be chosen in the new year.

Other Advances

Under the guidance of missionaries Paul and Karen Johnson, the small group of believers in Chickland purchased land in Chorro in 1987 and laid a foundation for a permanent church building. The newest member of the AEBC was Grace Chapel in Pasea, a small but enthusiastic church led by pastor David Maharaj.

LIT School of the Bible had a record high of seventy-seven students registered for the fall term in 1986, increasing to ninety-two the following year. Led by David and Elaine Crane, David Broucek, and a committee chosen by the AEBC churches, the program had grown and expanded tremendously. Serious consideration was given over many years to beginning a full-time Bible school, but so far this remained a hope for the future. In 1986 Bud and Audrey Johnson were teaching a new Christian education course, while Dub Ludwick was piloting a leadership training course and Dave Broucek a Greek course. They were assisted by four national teachers.

Another advance was targeted outreach to the Muslim community. Answering AEBC's call for a missionary couple to take this on, Vern and Wanda Rock arrived in Trinidad in 1987, veterans of twenty-eight years with TEAM in Pakistan and four years working among Muslims in New York City. One of the AEBC churches also commissioned several people, including three converted Muslims, to begin a church among Muslims. Many Muslims heard the Christian message through these efforts and a number made decisions for Christ, but the vision of a church among Muslim converts has not yet been realized.

A final area of advance was in the Joint Council meetings—"the functioning heart of TEAM/AEBC," as David Crane described it—made up of the AEBC executive and the TEAM field council. "These quarterly meetings have done more to bring us working together than any other field activity," he said.

> We now sense an air of accomplishment in the ongoing of the ministry. The unanimity is excellent.... It has been a joy for the field council to work that closely with the executive of the AEBC in planning joint crusades, missionary placements, distribution of revolving fund requests...and setting goals for the body.[21]

Opportunities for a New Decade

Concern for Muslims, united crusades, evangelistic trips overseas, outreach to neighboring areas—the church in Trinidad had a heart for sharing the gospel. And this concern to reach out continued to grow as the decade of the nineties approached.

In October 1988 eleven AEBC churches—three with missionary pastors, four with national pastors, and three under the leadership of an elder board—met together for a week-long World Missions Conference. Part of AEBC chairman K.K. Bachew's challenge to the churches was this:

> I charge every church to "lift up your eyes and look on the fields. They are white unto harvest".... It is the very heartbeat of God that men be saved. It is the supreme task of the church. It is the heavenly mandate given to every child of the living God.... Let us now pray, prepare and give sacrificially. Let us open our visions, hearts, and pockets to materialize this great commission of our gracious Master.[22]

And the challenge was taken up, as the AEBC decided at the end of the conference to form its own missions agency. By early 1989, AEBC was working out details of the agency's constitution and hoped to send out its first two missionaries by the end of the year.

At home in Trinidad, another door for ministry was opening as the government asked TEAM to help staff a new hospital. By 1990 a team of medical personnel was being assembled, with the prayer that this new ministry would open the door to church planting among the professional classes.

PERU

A vision of what could be accomplished for Christ through radio led TEAM first to Uruguay and then to Peru in the 1950s and 1960s.

TEAM entered Uruguay in 1953 with the specific aim of establishing a Christian radio ministry. Charles Ward and Marvin Steffins of TEAM worked with World Radio Missionary Fellowship for several years in a joint attempt to purchase a radio station, but this proved impossible due to exor-

bitant costs. TEAM therefore withdrew from Uruguay in 1957, turning the work of preparing programs for broadcast on existing stations over to local Christian groups.

Interest in radio ministry continued strong, however, and in September 1960 the board of directors directed Norman Mydske and Robert Bedard—who together had established Radio Victoria in Aruba—to survey possible areas for radio work in South America. I was on an overseas trip visiting eleven of our fields when I received minutes of the September board meeting. I wrote to general director David H. Johnson from Nasik, India:

> If a radio work is undertaken...I believe that we should also go into church work. I note that when radio is tied in to the church work we can expect results, such as is true in Japan. In Formosa [now Taiwan] where no efforts were made in the past to co-ordinate the radio work with the church activities, or to have the churches follow up on the radio contacts, we do not gain the fullest benefits.[23]

In Uruguay, missionaries had announced that TEAM would not be establishing churches. I considered this a serious mistake which should be avoided in any new radio work.

In December Bob Bedard reported the men's findings to the board of directors: Lima, Peru, had the greatest potential for a TEAM radio station in connection with church planting. Santiago, Chile, was also recommended.

On the Air in Lima

In January 1961 the board of directors voted to enter Peru for radio and general missionary work. Norman and Valerie Mydske and Bob and Juanita Bedard settled in Lima that year, their goal to start a Christian radio station. Local evangelical leaders favored the project enthusiastically, and a group of laymen organized a cultural association called *Ondas del Perú* which officially sponsored the station.

After a great deal of hard work, Radio del Pacífico went on the air in 1962. Attracting listeners through a program of music and newscasts, the station also offered short Bible messages and longer gospel programs at various times throughout the day. From the beginning the missionaries kept a low profile, hiring Peruvian staff to assist them and using local evangelical speakers.

TEAM's radio work in Lima was truly pioneer: when Radio del Pacífico began broadcasting it was one of the very few AM radio stations in the city; its FM transmitter (added in 1964) was the third to be installed in Lima.[24] A shortwave transmitter, built largely by missionary James Newing, began broadcasting in 1969, allowing the station to beam its message to scattered listeners in the Andes Mountains and remote jungle areas.

Operating a radio station proved to be a larger task and certainly more costly than was envisioned at first. Salaries for the non-missionary staff, rent, and operating expenses were only partly offset by obtaining a commercial license so the station could sell advertising. In addition, missionaries wanted to improve programming to better reach Lima's masses for Christ. This, too, would cost money. The financial situation and heavy workload challenged the missionaries year after year.

Yet many listeners were won to Christ, both through the station's programs and through the evangelistic crusades, film showings, and Christian books the station promoted. One such listener was Rosario Rivera, a young woman whose compassion for the plight of Peru's many poor people led her to become a communist guerilla. Fueled by hatred for the privileged classes, she smuggled weapons and felt no remorse about those she killed in her revolutionary activities. While listening to classical music on Radio del Pacífico one day in 1971, Rosario's curiosity was aroused by an announcement of a meeting featuring evangelist Luis Palau. At the meeting, she began an encounter with God which transformed her life. Since then, scores have come to Christ through her witness and the lives of many have improved dramatically through her Christian love and social concern.

In 1973 Radio del Pacífico moved from rented quarters to a new location purchased by TEAM. The three missionary families in Peru at the time—Barry and Elieen Hancock, Lorne and Caroll

Kliewer, and Charles and Barbara Cousens—worked long hours until the station was finally up and running at the new site.

The following year, 1974, TEAM turned Radio del Pacífico over to a Peruvian board of directors. TEAM missionaries remained on staff for several years until the station was completely nationalized. Operating on AM, FM, and shortwave, the station has continued to experience God's blessing on its gospel outreach.

A Start at Church Planting

Though area secretary Delbert Kuehl and I had stressed that church planting should accompany the radio ministry, this did not come to pass for some time. For nearly a decade, the small missionary force concentrated on the demanding day-to-day operations of Radio del Pacífico. Missionaries assigned to the station did assist in local churches, however, and helped to start one church which became a congregation of *Iglesia Evangélica Peruana*—the Peruvian Evangelical Church.

Finally new missionaries arrived who could devote their time to following up the many leads from radio listeners. Herb and Carolyn Samworth came to Peru in August 1968, Barry and Elieen Hancock in 1971, and Charles and Barbara Cousens in December 1972. Many lives were touched through their ministries and, in time, a group of believers was formed in Pueblo Libre. This church, which fellowshipped with Plymouth Brethren congregations, later purchased its own real estate and continued as a vigorous work, periodically inviting TEAM missionaries back as guest preachers.

Yet during the early 1970s this difficult church planting work was not yet a major thrust for TEAM in Peru. The field and its leaders focused instead on radio as it supported the broader evangelical community. TEAM also supplied teachers to Penzotti Christian School for missionary children, a cooperative effort of several missions. Not until the late 1970s, when Radio del Pacífico was in national hands, did TEAM Peru begin to emphasize church planting in earnest.

Evangelical Seminary of Lima

TEAM gained three experienced missionaries and a new ministry at the end of June 1975 when the board of directors gave final approval to a merger agreement with the Peruvian Gospel Fellowship. TEAM now had missionaries participating in the Evangelical Seminary of Lima, where Gladys Linthicum and John and Dawn Boice were on the staff. These missionaries had worked in Peru for more than a decade, teaching and counseling young men and women who felt God's call to Christian service. They continued this valuable ministry under TEAM.

Targeting the Middle Class in Santa Felicia

In 1977 Charles and Barbara Cousens headed up the field's first concentrated effort to plant a church. A team of missionaries studied the Lima area for six months, held a church-planting retreat, and prayed for wisdom and guidance. They chose Santa Felicia, a middle-class suburb of Lima which had no evangelical witness. Targeting the middle class posed a challenge; such people do not readily respond to the gospel, hindered as they are by material success, their apparent self-sufficiency, and peer pressure.

For the first six months the missionaries knocked on doors, gave out portions of the Bible, and distributed a letter introducing themselves. Said Charles Cousens:

> [W]e discovered that effective church planting is not a one-man job among middle-class people. This type of ministry demands top-quality work—a blend of intense forethought and vigorous legwork—from missionaries and national believers.[25]

From these beginnings, a church grew in Santa Felicia. By the end of 1980 it had thirty-five members and about sixty people attending each Sunday. Thirty-four Peruvians had accepted Christ that year. Meeting in rented quarters, the group was seeking property to build its own facility.

This young but thriving church benefitted from the combined efforts of a missionary team—the Cousens working full-time with the church and others helping part-time. The Hancocks, Boices, Gabe and Judy Agostini, and Dave Stoddard all assisted in varying degrees during 1980. Cousens was pastor until going on furlough mid-year; then Barry Hancock, Gabe Agostini, and a Peruvian man formed a pastoral team. National leaders were coming forward: four men could now preach and the church board had expanded to include four nationals along with one missionary. Peruvians taught the five Sunday school classes, reaching eighty children in all.

Cousens told of one man who walked through the church's open door one Sunday and joined the adult Bible class. This man, the foreman at a nearby brickyard, had been very unfaithful to his wife during their thirty-five years of marriage. Before the end of the class, he stood up and said, "I want to be saved." So began a change in his life. In time he became a deacon and later an elder in the Santa Felicia church.

A Maturing Church

After a difficult time in 1981 when missionaries were on furlough, the Santa Felicia church grew stronger. In 1983, attendance at Sunday services neared seventy-five. Seventy-five children attended Sunday school. The church conducted an active evangelistic program, seeing more than 100 professions of faith during the year. Believers were trained in Bible and discipleship courses. And in March 1983, the church broke ground to begin construction of its own facility in nearby Santa Raquel.

Believing that the church was ready for a Peruvian pastor, the Cousens resigned at the end of 1983 to begin a new work in La Molina Vieja, a new urbanized area. The Hancocks and Jim and Sue Kuehl continued to assist in Santa Felicia. After more than two years of construction, the church—now located in Santa Raquel—dedicated its new building in October 1985. Though strong in many respects, the Santa Raquel church was experiencing growing pains and had not yet called a pastor.

Finally in 1988 the Cousens returned to Santa Raquel and Charles became senior pastor. The following January the church took a giant step forward and chose its first full-time Peruvian pastor, assistant pastor Miguel Vasquez. Another Peruvian, Carlos

Rueda, completed the pastoral team. Missionaries Ralph and Ellen Shepard helped in the youth work and other aspects of the church's varied program.

The Christian Bible Church in Santa Raquel was now a maturing church. Membership had increased to 120, and growth led to plans for a new and larger sanctuary. Sunday school attendance had grown to 110. "The church is awakening to its need of being an aggressive evangelistic church," said Cousens.[26] It was also reaching out to people hurt by Peru's severe economic woes. Through the church about 200 people received free medical attention from a Peruvian doctor, hundreds of breakfasts were served to children on Sunday mornings, and many were helped from a fund established to aid the needy. The church continued to support its own missionary, Elizabet Torres, who worked among the destitute street children of Lima.

Church leadership was weakened during 1989 when two elders moved their families to the United States to escape Peru's economic and political problems and a third man died suddenly. Yet missionaries counted on the Lord to raise up new leaders as they taught leadership training courses to church members.

New Work in La Molina Vieja

Because the social level in La Molina Vieja was a step higher than in Santa Raquel, Charles and Barbara Cousens knew they must adapt their approach and anticipated that progress would be slow. Even so, their efforts to begin a church here in 1984 and 1985 proved frustrating indeed. A Bible study was held for a time in the home of a couple from the Santa Felicia church, but gradually people stopped coming for varied reasons—an accident, physical abuse, opposition in the home. There were problems in finding literature to distribute and a meeting place to which people could be invited. Faced with these obstacles, the Cousens taught a "Life of Christ" course to the faithful few believers in the area so that when services did begin, trained helpers would be available.

Jim and Sue Kuehl joined the Cousens in 1986, taking responsibility for the work in La Molina when the Cousens went on furlough. By 1989 the Kuehls had seen slow but steady progress. A Sunday morning Bible hour now attracted ten adults and seven children, and mid-week Bible studies were held regularly. Two new families joined the young group, bringing the number of families involved to six. Though this church was still in its infancy, missionaries trusted that it would grow and strengthen: "What the Lord has begun, He will continue."[27]

New Radio Work

To bolster TEAM's church planting work in Santa Raquel and La Molina, missionary Gabe Agostini developed a half-hour evangelistic radio program to be aired over Radio del Pacífico. Agostini was a gifted teacher, and in early 1987 the new program was already drawing a good listener response.

A Country in Crisis

Beginning in the mid-1970s, the field chairman's annual reports chronicle worsening economic and political developments. Many Peruvians already lived in desperate poverty, with a widening gulf between rich and poor. Economic crises, tensions with bordering nations, and political turmoil took an added toll. In 1976, for example, the government introduced strong and unpopular economic measures to try to combat serious economic problems. In the resulting upheaval, a state of emergency was declared and a curfew imposed, lasting many months.

During these uncertain times missionaries began to have trouble securing entry visas or visa extensions. Difficulties receded, however, and in most years which followed visas were available on a replacement basis: as one missionary left, another missionary could take over that visa. Because of cooperation in sharing visas with Evangelical Free Church missionaries, whom TEAM had agreed to sponsor in 1975, and—sadly—the small number of missionary candidates for Peru, TEAM was able to obtain the visas it needed in spite of restrictions.

The country's economic crisis deepened. Year after year, inflation soared 60-80 percent and higher. In the early 1980s came a disquieting new fact of Peruvian life: terrorism. About 1,200 acts of terrorism occurred during 1981, more than 400 of them in the Lima area where the missionaries worked. Thirteen high tension or microwave towers were blown up that year—resulting in loss of electricity as well as water, since water pumps are powered by electricity. In 1985 and 1986 the situation improved somewhat, then worsened again. Field chairman Jim Kuehl wrote in January 1990:

> We are working in a country that is facing its most difficult times in its history. The economy is in shambles. The inflation rate for 1989 was an incredible 2775%. Government *"paquetazos"* (sharp increases in prices) have put many basic food items out of reach of the poor....
>
> Terrorist activity continues at an ever increasing rate. ... At least 300 electrical towers were blown up in 1989, making blackouts and the subsequent lack of water an almost daily occurrence.
>
> The concern for personal safety and living without electricity or water have been a strain on all missionaries. The normal operations of both Radio del Pacífico and the Seminary have been affected due to a lack of electricity. Many evening meetings at the Santa Raquel church were conducted with candlelight.[28]

In these frightening times, Peruvians were responding to the gospel as never before. Charles Cousens reported that people were now being saved almost every week. The Santa Raquel church saw 100 conversions during 1989. Said area foreign secretary Gary Bowman:

> With the escalation of assassinations and bombings, there has been a corresponding increase in the spiritual awareness of many Peruvians around the country. A feeling of self-sufficiency has given way to a tremendous insecurity. People are now looking for stability and something to give them a sense of assurance and purpose.[29]

Yet the work was extremely difficult. TEAM's eleven missionaries and their families risked danger daily. They now worked among people who faced economic deprivation and the daily fear of violence, and who saw little hope for the future. Many Peruvians wanted to leave the country but could not afford to do so. Counseling and helping people in these circumstances was not easy.

Field chairman Jim Kuehl summed up the situation in January 1990. "Peruvians are still responding to the gospel," he wrote. "We as missionaries must continue to work to build God's church while it is still day, for the night will come when no man can work."[30]

BRAZIL

Although TEAM's board of directors had discussed possible work in Brazil as early as 1958, it was not until twenty-five years later that Brazil became a TEAM field—and then in unique circumstances. When Japan Evangelical Mission (JEM) merged into TEAM on January 1, 1983, TEAM gained not only a welcome boost to its

work in Japan, but also a new field in Latin America.

JEM had sent missionaries to Brazil in 1972 because there are more Japanese in Brazil than anywhere else outside Japan. Numbering about one million today, the Japanese came to Brazil early in this century to work on coffee plantations. Robert and Eleanor Spaulding and Leslie and Carolyn Grove were two JEM couples who ministered in Japan for many years before coming to Brazil. With the JEM merger, TEAM gained twelve experienced missionaries whose work in Brazil had been underway for a decade.

JEM's work centered around São Paulo, one of the largest cities in the western hemisphere with more than eleven million people. Beginning by visiting the Japanese vegetable growers who farmed around São Paulo, the missionaries eventually started a church in Atibaia. In 1981 the Lord provided a full-time Japanese missionary-pastor for this small church.

Though they had come to work among Japanese, the missionaries soon saw considerable opportunities for gospel witness among Brazilian nationals. "It was impossible not to get excited about their openness and responsiveness," said Bob Spaulding. "New churches were springing up at an incredible rate. But along with those who preached the gospel in truth were many cults, deceiving and misleading the people."[31]

Events have brought numerous religious influences to Brazil—including Roman Catholicism, Buddhism, Hinduism, Baha'i, and spiritism. Spiritism is the principal non-Christian religion, which many practice along with a nominal Catholicism. Yet Brazilians are open to the gospel. Churches have grown rapidly since evangelical mission agencies entered the country after World War I.

A Smooth Transition

The transition from JEM to TEAM in 1983 went smoothly; personnel remained the same and the missions' policies were very similar. "There has been a reevaluation of goals and a greater emphasis on church planting since the merger," reported field chairman Bob Spaulding at the end of 1983.[32]

In 1983 several churches were being established, led by missionary and national church planters. The missionaries were cooperating with an evangelical church association, *Igreja Crista Evangélica do Brasil* (ICEB). Earlier, Stephen and Lourdinha Veness had started a small church in Franco da Rocha. When they left for furlough, the ICEB church at Mandaque took responsibility for the work. During 1983 the Franco da Rocha church continued to grow and began a building program.

At Cidade Dutra, missionaries Rachel Sekiguchi, Bob Spaulding, and Les Grove led a small Japanese congregation. During 1983 this group began developing ties with a Brazilian church, the Jabaquara ICEB church, and purchased property for a new building.

Two other churches were being started by Brazilian Christians. With financial help from White Fields, Inc., a North American society which supported national church planters, TEAM had been able to place Domingos Everisto and his family at Jardim da Granja. By the end of 1983 the Jardim da Granja work was progressing well with a number of outstanding conversions, and the group had begun constructing a church building.

In August 1983 a second Brazilian couple began work in Cumbica, where a new international airport was being built to serve the São Paulo area. Together the church association, TEAM, and White Fields targeted this strategic area under the leadership of Rubens and Elizabeth Coutinho.

Training for lay leaders and a new camp rounded out the field ministries. Camp Nova Vida was a recently purchased one hundred acres of beautiful, hilly land near São Paulo. Missionaries had begun developing this land for year-round camping, aiming to reach Japanese and Brazilians for Christ and to help believers grow in their faith. During 1983 the first phase of the youth lodge was completed, along with other improvements to the physical plant.

In February 1984 Michael Pocock visited the work in Brazil. He reported:

> As in other Latin American countries I've visited this year, I was struck with the level of violence in Brazil. In this case it is personal violence and thievery rather than organized guerilla movement such as the Senderos Luminosos of Peru. We need to constantly pray for missionaries and nationals in these countries, because between truly terrible traffic conditions, crime and political violence, there are many threats to the lives of our workers.[33]

Relationships with the National Church

In 1984 TEAM Brazil ratified an agreement with ICEB, a national church association, which established a liaison committee to coordinate TEAM's ministries with those of the national church. Made up of two men from ICEB and two from TEAM, the committee's business centered primarily around the placement of missionaries and White Fields workers. The TEAM representatives on the liaison committee were also ex-officio members of the ICEB executive committee.

The following year, TEAM assigned Don and Dorothy Congo to serve in the youth ministry of Cental Church, an ICEB church in São José dos Campos.

Planting a Church in Parque América

In late 1984 the Veness family moved to the Parque América area of São Paulo to begin a church in this middle-class residential area. By November they had rented a hall and put up a sign in Portuguese which read, "Evangelical Christian Church." Using a simple PA system in their car, the family drove up and down the streets of Parque América announcing the church services. Besides regular evangelistic meetings, they held a daily vacation Bible school attended by ninety children. These children provided contacts in many homes, and door-to-door evangelism reached others. The Venesses also developed ties with an ICEB church in a neighboring area, receiving some help from the church's youth.

By early 1988, attendance on Sunday ranged from fifty to eighty, with some first-time visitors every week. The church's busy schedule included guitar classes, Bible studies, prayer meetings, choir, young people's meetings, and monthly women's evangelistic meetings. Since most of the believers were new Christians, it would take time for strong leaders to develop. Thirteen had been baptized, and another eight were attending baptismal classes.

Forming a Church Planting Strategy

Back in 1983 the missionaries had voted that their primary objective would be church planting, but it took some time to put this into practice. Long-term goals were set in 1984 and reviewed in 1986: by 1990, the missionaries aimed to establish eight new congregations and to develop Camp Nova Vida so it could accommodate sixty to eighty occupants. In the years that followed, the missionaries studied church planting strategy, seeking a clearer direction and the best approach for their situation. Except in the Japanese work and the camp, missionaries had traditionally worked each in his or her own ministry. Yet effective church planting called for so many different abilities that some began to wonder if they should try to develop a team-based strategy.

One problem in meeting the church planting goals was a shortage of missionaries devoted to this work. The field requested new candidates for this ministry, but none were forthcoming by the last years of the decade.

By the end of 1988, field chairman Don Congo could report some progress toward developing church planting teams. Ruth Kietzman was in Praia Grande, working in an extensive church development ministry with two ICEB congregations. There was the possibility that Dwain and Maxine Fowler might work with a Brazilian in a new church planting ministry. Said Congo:

> It is good to see our team approach becoming reality, both in Ruth's ministry and with the possible placement of the Fowlers. Though this opens the possibility for relationship problems, I am convinced that the team approach has advantages that far outweigh the sacrifices necessary to make it function and would stress the need to cultivate relationships on a basis of trust in each team situation.[34]

Developing Camp Nova Vida

From fairly primitive conditions, Camp Nova Vida was improved in many ways so that its program could expand. In the mid-1980s Dwain and Maxine Fowler coordinated the camps with help from Alvin Doerksen and Dave Warkentin.

From only eighteen days of camp in 1984 serving 120 campers, the numbers jumped during 1985 to sixty-four days of camp with 424 campers. Eighteen people made decisions for Christ. Remarkable growth continued, with the number of campers nearly doubling the following year and thirty-four people accepting Christ. Fowler created a system for following up those who made decisions for Christ at camp so that this fruit would not be lost.

Besides the ministry to campers was an equally rewarding ministry to the counsellors, each of whom worked for a week or more. In 1985, for example, the staff numbered close to 120.

By the end of 1989 exciting events were underway at Camp Nova Vida. Dave Warkentin was now in charge of camp programming, while Leslie Grove was overseeing major new construction. A camp director's residence had been built and a large kitchen/dining hall building was under construction. Plans for the future included additional cabin space and a swimming pool.

Teaching Ministries

TEAM provided teaching help to Pan American Christian Academy, where 300 missionary children attended kindergarten through grade twelve. Carolyn Grove and associate missionary Carma Kulish both taught music at the school.

By January 1989 Bill and Kathy Bacheller had completed Portuguese language study and were moving to Anápolis to begin teaching at the Evangelical Christian Theological Seminary of Brazil. Their ministry here would have the side benefit of further deepening TEAM's relationship with ICEB pastors and leaders.

Opportunities Ahead

As 1990 approached, TEAM in Brazil was making great strides forward at Camp Nova Vida. It had just added seminary teaching to its field ministries with the appointment of the Bachellers. And in church planting, work continued in the Japanese Cidade Dutra church and in several Brazilian churches. Missionaries were developing closer ties with ICEB, both regionally and nationally. Through White Fields, capable Brazilian leaders were starting churches among their own people.

Though long-range church planting goals had fallen short, due largely to a shortage of missionaries devoted to this task, the field was moving forward in defining a strategy and putting it to work. Doors for gospel witness in Brazil remained wide open.

MEXICO

South of the U.S. state of California is the thousand-mile-long Baja California peninsula, and it is here that TEAM chose to begin its ministry in Mexico, one of the countries currently most responsive to the gospel.

TEAM's first involvement with Baja California came in 1981

when TEAM was approached about the possibility of absorbing Missions of Baja, Inc. Carlos and Celia Freyre, its directors and only active missionaries, had worked in Baja for about fifteen years. They were seeking help for the fruitful ministry they had developed in the central part of the peninsula, which included two churches, thirteen preaching points, and an orphanage.

Further investigation found Baja California a promising area for church planting. Very little mission work was being done, yet the people were open to the gospel. Much of the Baja peninsula was barren wilderness and most of the people were poor due to political and economic isolation from mainland Mexico. Yet their future looked brighter. Large pools of underground water had recently been discovered and rich mineral deposits were being mined. Industry burgeoned and the sparse population increased dramatically as workers arrived from the mainland. The Freyre's work also showed great promise but needed additional staff and resources. Thus on January 1, 1982, Missions of Baja merged into TEAM.

Over the next year, the TEAM administrative staff developed short- and long-term plans with the Freyres for the church planting and orphanage work and began recruiting missionaries to help them.

By early 1984, a number of career and short-term workers were in Baja and others were preparing to come. Adria Anthony, formerly of TEAM's Colombia field, was discipling believers in the established churches. Frieda Johnson was assisting in the churches as well. Steve Dresselhaus was caring for administrative and financial matters. Marvin Freed managed the farm connected with the orphanage, while Ruth Workentine helped care for the children.

Plans for expanding the orphanage and providing educational and vocational training facilities were drawn up, and Freddie and Charmaine Canode went to Baja to supervise the construction.

Merger Proves Unworkable

By the fall of 1984, however, it had become clear that the merger with Missions of Baja was not the success that other arrangements like this had been for TEAM. Difficulties in developing a good working relationship with the Freyres, who were used to working alone and in their own way, reached a critical stage. Area secretary Michael Pocock told the board of directors in October 1984:

> The merger initiated three years ago has been a difficult one. Though the field is responsive and significant spiritual gains have been made by our workers there, incompatible styles of operation and disagreement over some major long-term goals have made continued work with the founder inadvisable.[35]

When issues involving TEAM's relationship with the Mexican government brought matters to a head, TEAM sought a meeting with the former board members of Missions of Baja and offered two options: that the Freyres withdraw from the work and leave TEAM to continue, or that Missions of Baja be reorganized and resume responsibility for the work. They chose the second option.

TEAM therefore withdrew from Baja at the end of 1984. Said Pocock:

> Everyone connected with these decisions is deeply saddened by this turn of events. At the same time we have not discovered any alternatives and the entire decision-making process was in strict, prayerful reliance on the promise of James 1:5, "If any man lack wisdom let him ask of God Who gives to all men liberally and upbraideth not." This being the case we trust our Lord for His grace for workers, believers and Missions of Baja as they resume the work.[36]

A Survey to the South

Although TEAM had withdrawn from Mexico, interest in this needy and receptive area remained high. The desire to make a fresh start in a different area of the Baja peninsula led to a survey trip in late 1986 by area secretary Jack MacDonald and Venezuela missionary John Conaway.

On their return home, MacDonald and Conaway recommended that TEAM re-enter Mexico, beginning its work in the lower half of Baja California Sur, the southernmost part of the peninsula. There they had found tremendous opportunities and great spiritual need, but few churches and little work by foreign missionaries.

The board of directors agreed to their recommendation at its January 1987 meeting. Mexico was once again a TEAM field.

Target Areas and Future Potential

MacDonald and Conaway identified six cities as suitable church planting targets. The first to be entered would be La Paz, the capital of Baja California Sur and its largest city with a population of 150,000.

But TEAM's vision extended well beyond these initial targeted areas. Said MacDonald:

> Entry into this part of Baja does not preclude working in the densely populated areas in the northern part of the peninsula.... Mexico has the potential to become a big field should God provide the qualified people to work there. A much more extended work onto the mainland of Mexico is part of our long-range strategy.[37]

First Steps in Ministry

The first missionaries of this new thrust arrived in Baja in January 1988. In line with the policy of sending experienced missionaries to open a new field, they were David and Joan Coots, who began service in Venezuela under ORM in 1954. Fluent in Spanish, they settled in smoothly and were soon making friends with their neighbors and establishing a cooperative relationship with the pastor and congregation of the local Baptist church.

The Coots were joined by John and Miriam Conaway, who also knew Spanish from their many years with TEAM in Venezuela. Sadly, they had to return to the United States after only a month due to John's ill health. Pat Moore, who had served in Irian Jaya and at TEAM headquarters, rounded out the first arrivals to this new field.

In any new work, the first months and even years are a time of learning the local situation and exploring how best to proceed. One matter to be settled concerned the missionaries' legal status. The Mexican government would not issue resident visas to missionaries, but missionaries could readily enter as tourists to assist a Mexican association. The association *Centro Cultural Filantrópico* was formed and registered in Mexico City with the help of a local Bible teacher and evangelist, Trino Ortiz, who served as TEAM's Mexican representative in these early years.

By the time area secretary Gary Bowman visited La Paz in September 1989, John and Becky Forcey and Dave and Debbie Tazelaar had joined the work, bringing the missionary total to seven. Bowman reported back to the board of directors that though decisions must soon be made to set the direction of this new work, the potential for expanded ministry was great. "A good foundation has been laid for future ministry," he said, "and I believe that we will see the church of Jesus Christ built in a number of those towns in that part of the world."[38]

Until 1990, TEAM missionaries worked with the Baptists in La Paz, helping them to start and develop churches while gaining valuable experience and fluency in the language. In 1990, the field began to assign missionaries to other towns.

A NEW DECADE,
A NEW CENTURY

Centennial Conference

"Workers Together—Until He Comes" was the theme chosen for TEAM's Centennial Conference, hosted by the Wheaton Evangelical Free Church in Illinois from May 8-13, 1990. This theme combined two impelling forces in TEAM's 100-year history. The motto "Workers Together," taken from II Corinthians 6:1, was chosen many years ago to emphasize that world missions is a team effort: TEAM missionaries work with God, with one another, and with homeland and national churches to evangelize the lost. "Until He Comes" recalled the firm expectation of TEAM founder Fredrik Franson—and of many others through the years—that the Lord's return is imminent. Franson literally expected him at any moment. As general director Richard Winchell said, "One had the feeling that should the trumpet suddenly sound many of us would be startled, but not Franson."[1] Winchell challenged TEAM and its supporters to be faithful to this tradition:

> Let us like our founder live every day expecting to be interrupted.
> Let us plan as though we had another five, ten or twenty years
> or more. But let us pray as though this were our last day on earth
> and reaching everyone everywhere was our sole responsibility.[2]

TEAM at One Hundred

What did TEAM look like at the age of one hundred? Like anything that is alive and growing, TEAM in 1990 cannot be adequately described in a few paragraphs. Yet some measures can help to build up a picture of the mission as a whole.

TEAM's purpose as expressed by its founders had been recently rephrased: "The purpose of TEAM is to help churches send missionaries to plant reproducing churches in other nations." In the spring of 1990, this task was being carried out in thirty countries by 1,107 missionaries.[3]

Although the organization itself was a century old, the missionary force was surprisingly young. Winchell reported that almost half of the missionary body had joined TEAM in the last ten years. They were replacing the many missionaries who went overseas after World War II and had now reached retirement age. The result was an average missionary age of about forty-five.[4]

What were these missionaries doing? Winchell gave an interesting breakdown in May 1989. Fifty-six percent of TEAM's active missionaries were working in direct evangelism and church planting. Another 10 percent ministered in Bible institutes, Bible colleges, and seminaries. Medical work accounted for 11 percent of the missionary force; while 5 percent were in radio, literature, and other media ministries aimed at evangelism and church planting. One percent were in linguistic work, and 5 percent were taken up with the essentials of administration on the thirty fields.[5]

Twenty-five Years of Growth

In his 1990 annual report, Dr. Winchell looked back a quarter century to the report I had given at TEAM's seventy-fifth anniversary in 1965. He found that the mission had grown substantially by every measure.

> Our total missionary force has grown from 840 [in 1965] to 1,107. There were 38 missionaries on the retired list then and there are 272 now, not to mention the many who have died. The number of fields has grown from 19 to 30, and the number of national churches from 735 to approximately 2,500. In the year reported upon at that conference there were 1,851 baptisms. Last year there were 7,541.[6]

The number of hospitals had increased from six to eight, with three more in the planning. Clinics had increased from 40 to 151. Together they served 403,285 outpatients and 14,041 inpatients, up from 180,708 and 13,403 respectively in 1965.

TEAM-sponsored Bible colleges and institutes now numbered thirty-three, up from ten. The number of students they served increased from 355 to 1,751.

In 1965 I had taken a leap of imagination, asking what TEAM's situation might be if the Lord did not return before the centennial in 1990. "Will there be continued expansion," I asked, "so we can look forward to having 1,500 missionaries, 2,500 churches, 250,000 members and 2,500 pastors and evangelists?" Winchell now reported that my guesses had been remarkably close to the mark. National churches did indeed number about 2,500, with their attendance reaching almost 250,000. The missionary force in 1990 was some 400 lower than my estimate, but the number of national pastors and evangelists was almost 300 higher at 2,792.

These national coworkers, though not members of TEAM, are critical to an accurate picture of the mission in 1990, for without them TEAM could not adequately do its job. In China and other older fields where TEAM is no longer able to have contact, God's work continues because faithful national Christians have carried on, sometimes through great adversity. In the thirty countries where TEAM is active, national leaders enrich the work immeasurably. They direct most of the forty-plus church fellowships to which TEAM-related churches belong, are responsible for many established churches, and help to start new churches. From these colleagues TEAM missionaries learn a great deal. In a growing number of countries, the national churches are now sending missionaries beyond their own borders.

From Here—Where?

TEAM entered its second century at a time of global upheaval. In China, the Tiananmen Square massacre had taken place the previous year. Mozambique had abolished Marxist-Leninism. The wall separating East and West had come down in Berlin, and Hungary was proclaimed a free republic. In 1990, Poland disbanded its Communist Party and Lithuania declared independence. Namibia also became independent. General Colin Powell, chairman of the U.S. Joint Chiefs of Staff, spoke prophetically when he said, in June 1990:

If you ask what can possibly compare with the unprecedented events of the last thirteen months, the answer is the yet unforeseen revolutionary events of the next eighteen months.[7]

Later that year East and West Germany reunified, the Cold War ended, and Albania gained democracy. Iraq's annexation of Kuwait led, in 1991, to war with the United States, Saudi Arabia, and other coalition forces. The USSR disintegrated. War raged in Yugoslavia as republics declared independence. The events listed here are but a sampling of all that has taken place.

At TEAM's centennial conference in 1990, Richard Winchell outlined the world changes then beginning to unfold. In them he saw new opportunities and opening doors for the gospel. He pointed out that after the global upheaval of World War II a virtual flood of new missionaries went overseas; in 1951 TEAM sent out 102. He asked:

Dare we expect that today's global upheaval may have a similar result? As then, we are now able to enter places long closed to the gospel. Will the workers come forward to take advantage of these new opportunities? Are we able to consider enlarging our areas of outreach?[8]

Winchell also pointed to the increase in mass mobility in the world, which he predicted would continue in the years ahead as many thousands of people leave their homelands to seek survival or a better life elsewhere. In Pakistan, France, the United Arab Emirates, Irian Jaya, Germany, Austria, Brazil, Taiwan, and Hong Kong, TEAM's missionaries and national colleagues face unprecedented opportunities among expatriate people.

Meeting the Challenge

Some say that any organization which has been around for a century is bound to find itself in a rut, that a malaise of some kind almost always sets in. But new thrusts, new missionaries, and long-range plans to strengthen existing ministries while launching new ones make it unlikely that TEAM will face this dilemma in the near future.

One new emphasis is on parts of the world formerly under

communist control. In May 1990, the board of directors encouraged TEAM's administration to begin aggressively recruiting workers to reach Eastern Europe. Work had already been carried on quietly across the "closed" borders of Yugoslavia and Czechoslovakia by missionaries in neighboring countries. In the climate of earlier years, this work could not be discussed openly for fear of endangering it or the people involved. Now the board could recognize this region as a legitimate TEAM field.

After much study, the board also approved TEAM's entry into the Commonwealth of Independent States (formerly the Soviet Union) in 1992. Working closely with other Christian organizations involved in that part of the world, TEAM staff traveled to the C.I.S. to ask church leaders how TEAM could best help. One need they expressed was for training in cross-cultural ministry. As 1992 was ending, TEAM was sending a team of experienced missionaries to the C.I.S.

There was also hope of a new outreach in China. Finn and Sandy Torjesen of the Java field were working toward a ministry in Shaanxi, China, building on the work Finn's grandfather had carried on there from 1921 until he was killed by a Japanese fighter plane in 1939.

New Workers

God continued to call new workers to serve overseas. During 1991, seventy-four new missionaries left for the fields, up from forty the year before. Missionary applications were lower in early 1992 than in previous years, leading Winchell to call for urgent prayer, but by the end of the year eighty-one new missionaries had begun their overseas assignments.

Long-Range Planning

In February 1992 TEAM's administrative staff met for several days of long-term planning to set the stage for ministry in the years ahead. They concluded that on the whole, the ministries TEAM is currently engaged in are sound and productive. "We must continue these services with all the strength we have given in the past—and more," said Winchell.[9] They also proposed adding to TEAM's established modes of work some "pockets of innovation" and bold new thrusts to reach a changing world. Explained Winchell:

> This suggests the possibility of new task forces who will tackle an assignment with a definite end in mind. It may be an effort that will take ten years or more to accomplish. But we shall have definite plans to get our part of the work done, with the goal of handing the work over to national believers.[10]

A special committee was set up to develop a philosophy and procedure for handing over or closing ministries when TEAM's part of the task has been completed. Committees were also working on discovering innovative tasks and determining what TEAM should look like in five, ten, or fifteen years.

TEAM was also expecting change in another area. Having served as general director since 1975, Winchell had indicated his desire to step down in 1993 at the age of sixty-five. During 1992 a succession committee met under the leadership of board chairman Dr. Terry Hulbert to prepare for the choice of TEAM's seventh general director.

Attacking the Enemy's Stronghold

In his October 1992 *Monthly TEAM Memo* to the mission family, Winchell chose as his topic Philippians 3:16: "Only let us live up to what we have already attained." When we have gained some ground, Paul says, let us keep it; don't let down the standards.

In God's power TEAM has gained strongholds for the Lord and has learned many important lessons in the past hundred years. Yet in these days of change, said Winchell, it can be difficult to know when to hold the line and when to innovate; when to change a standard and when to say, "This policy has saved us from difficulties in the past, let's keep learning from our own history."

Winchell concluded that TEAM must be open to God's leading now, must be ready to look critically at long-established precedents. Yet at the same time, he said, "caution is what separates courage from recklessness. There is nothing quite like an informed vision." When Franson sent missionaries to China, he carefully studied the country, articulated goals and strategy, and then encouraged brave steps of faith. Current needs in many areas, among them the former Soviet Union and China, seem to call for careful and yet bold new strategies. "Let us ask God to give us an eager desire to launch out with innovative means to reach the lost in unreached areas," said Winchell.

> We must take some risks and be prepared to trust the Lord for wisdom to do things in new ways under the guidance of the Holy Spirit. Join us in praying that we will be both courageous and wise. We are not called to be on the defensive. It is the enemy who is on the defensive. The church's task is to attack the enemy's stronghold. Jesus said: "...I will build my church; and the gates of hell shall not prevail against it" (Matthew 16:18).[11]

NOTES

Chapter 1 (pages 25-33)

1. Edvard P. Torjesen, "A Study of Fredrik Franson" (Ph.D. dissertation, International College, Los Angeles, CA, September 1984), p. 484, quoting Werner Schnepper, "Fredrik Franson" in *Funfzig Jahre Allianz-China-Mission*, ed. Kurt Zimmermann (Wuppertal-Barmen: 1939, p. 35).

2. *Ibid.*, p. 501.

3. As has been true of a number of other organizations, the name of the mission Franson founded in North America went through a number of changes. Given the name China Alliance Mission when the first missionaries were being called for China in late 1890, it came to be known as the Alliance Mission when, a year later, the work expanded to Japan. The first recorded mention of the Scandinavian Alliance Mission—in 1892—is in connection with the decision to open the East Africa field. When the mission was incorporated in 1897, the name was officially recorded as the Scandinavian Alliance Mission of North America. Even so, the general practice for the first thirty years was to refer to it as the Alliance Mission. The twenty-fifth anniversary history was called *Alliansmissionens Tjugufemårsminnen* (Alliance Mission's Twenty-fifth Anniversary Story). From the early 1920s the most common usage was to call the mission by its initials—S. A. M. In this book, S.A.M. is the designation mostly used until the name was officially changed in 1949 to The Evangelical Alliance Mission. TEAM, from the initials of the full name, has become generally better known and more commonly used than the official name.

4. Josephine Princell, *Alliansmissionens Tjugufemårsminnen* [Alliance Mission's Twenty-fifth Anniversary Story] (Chicago: Scandinavian Alliance Mission, 1916), p. 26. All direct quotations from Mrs. Princell's Twenty-fifth Anniversary book and her book (cited later) on Fredrik Franson's Life and Work have been translated from Swedish (or in several cases, Norwegian) by Vernon Mortenson.

5. In addition to those missionaries whose work would be under the direction of the Scandinavian Alliance Mission (now known as The Evangelical Alliance Mission—TEAM), about an equal number were sent out in this period to work under European missions which were either founded or influenced by Franson. Edvard Torjesen's dissertation "A Study of Fredrik Franson" is the source of much of this information.

6. Edvard Torjesen, *Fredrik Franson, A Model for Worldwide Evangelism* (Pasadena, California: William Carey Library, 1983), Appendix I. Torjesen lists the following "Mission Societies and Church Fellowships founded or strongly influenced by Fredrik Franson:" Norwegian Mission Covenant, Oslo, Norway, 1884; Evangelical Free Church of America, Minneapolis, Minnesota, USA, 1884; Swedish Holiness Union, Kumla, Sweden, 1887; Danish Mission Covenant, Odense, Denmark, 1888; The Mission Covenant of Finland, Helsingfors (Helsinki), Finland, 1888; The Free Church of Finland (Finnish Alliance Mission, 1895), Helsinki, Finland, 1888; German Alliance Mission, Dietzholztal, West Germany, 1889; Swiss Alliance Mis-

sion, Winterthur, Switzerland, 1889; The Evangelical Alliance Mission, Wheaton, Illinois, USA, 1890; Evangelical East Asia Mission (merger of Swedish Mongol Mission, 1897, and Swedish Mission in China, 1887), Stockholm, Sweden, 1897; Marburg Mission (Foreign mission arm of German Fellowship Deaconry Union), Marburg, West Germany, 1899; Swedish Alliance Mission (Jönköping Association for Home and Foreign Missions, 1853), Jönköping, Sweden, 1900; Norwegian Missionary Alliance, Oslo, Norway, 1901; Armenian Spiritual Brotherhood, 1906. In 1983 these missions and fellowships reported a total of one hundred countries of service (with many duplications) and a total of 1,676 missionaries.

7. New American Standard Bible, Copyright by Lockman Foundation.

Chapter 2 (pages 34-42)

1. Josephine Princell, *Fredrik Franson's Liv och Verksamhet* [Fredrik Franson's Life and Work] (Chicago: Chicago-Bladet Publishing, 1909), pp. 124-125.
2. *Ibid.*, pp. 138-139.
3. Edvard P. Torjesen, "The Missiological Ministry of Fredrik Franson" (Unpublished monograph prepared for the Third Consultation of Organizations with a Franson Heritage, Ansgar Schools, Oslo, Norway, September 2-5, 1985), p. 29.
4. *Ibid.*, p. 134.
5. *Ibid.*
6. Official minutes of the board of directors of the Scandinavian Alliance Mission.
7. Princell, *Fredrik Franson's Life and Work*, p. 148.
8. *Ibid.*, pp. 145-146.
9. *Ibid.*, pp. 154-155.
10. An intriguing question concerns Franson's decision to let this field go. Paul Sheetz states in his book *The Sovereign Hand* (Wheaton, IL: The Evangelical Alliance Mission, 1971, p. 27) that "Franson decided not to send any more [missionaries] to East Africa."

Torjesen's research shows that en route from his ministry in Turkey to the Swaziland field in South Africa, Franson stopped at a number of ports, Mombasa included. This was in March or April 1906. Hedenstrom and Palmquist were at Lamu, less than 200 miles from Mombasa at the time. Franson's visit to the East Africa missionaries, if indeed he made one, is not mentioned in Palmquist's lengthy story of the field (1915). With mail and transportation being so slow and infrequent it is understandable that he may have bypassed them. But Franson had undertaken long, arduous journeys on other fields to be with his missionaries so the question remains whether he considered himself not responsible for that field.

In other research Torjesen learned that the mission committee in Chicago had voted to adopt East Africa as a field of the mission, apparently assuming that Franson's letter introducing Eric Hedenstrom was a signal of his wholehearted approval of the plans for East Africa. It is evident that Franson took no active part in promoting this field or recruiting workers for it. It seems to have been a case of it having been the responsibility of the mission committee at home alone and one which was not followed through very well.

About fifty years after Frank Palmquist left Africa, and when his name was virtually unknown to the staff of the mission, a call came to me from the Washington Hospital in Chicago with the information that a missionary by the name of Palmquist was a patient there without much longer to live. There was just opportunity for a few brief words and prayer before he passed away. Relatives shared the information that since his return from Africa, Palmquist had continued translating the Bible into Swahili, apparently unaware that others had long since completed the task. It seems quite certain that in God's great record book there is an inscription, "Frank Palmquist, missionary and intercessor. Well done, thou good and faithful servant."

11. Edvard P. Torjesen, "A Study of Fredrik Franson" (Ph.D. dissertation, International College, Los Angeles, CA, September 1984), pp. 635, 644.

Chapter 3 (pages 43-53)
1. Josephine Princell, *Fredrik Franson's Liv och Verksamhet* [Fredrik Franson's Life and Work] (Chicago: Chicago-Bladet Publishing, 1909), p. 184.
2. *Ibid.*, p. 186.
3. Edvard P. Torjesen, "A Study of Fredrik Franson" (Ph. D. Dissertation, International College, Los Angeles, CA, September 1984), p. 601.
4. *Ibid.*, p. 605.
5. *Ibid.*, pp. 608-609.
6. *Ibid.*, p. 549.
7. Josephine Princell, *Alliansmissionens Tjugufemårsminnen* [Alliance Mission's Twenty-fifth Anniversary Story] (Chicago: Scandinavian Alliance Mission, 1916), p.71.
8. Torjesen, "A Study of Fredrik Franson," p. 543.
9. Princell, *Alliance Mission's Twenty-fifth Anniversary Story*, p. 72.
10. *Ibid.*, pp. 72-73.
11. Torjesen, "A Study of Fredrik Franson," see pp. 622-627.
12. Princell, *Alliance Mission's Twenty-fifth Anniversary Story*, see pp. 371-377.
13. Princell, *Fredrik Franson's Life and Work*, pp. 221-222.

Chapter 4 (pages 54-63)
1. Josephine Princell, *Fredrik Franson's Liv och Verksamhet* [Fredrik Franson's Life and Work] (Chicago: Chicago-Bladet Publishing, 1909), p. 229.
   Edvard P. Torjesen, "A Study of Fredrik Franson" (Ph.D. Dissertation, International College, Los Angeles, CA, September 1984), p. 632.
2. Princell, *Fredrik Franson's Life and Work*, p. 229.
3. *Ibid.*, p. 225.
4. TEAM Constitution, Article III, Section 1, p. 3.
5. Torjesen, "A Study of Fredrik Franson," pp. 533-534.
6. Josephine Princell, *Alliansmissionens Tjugufemårsminnen* [Alliance Mission's Twenty-Fifth Anniversary Story] (Chicago: Scandinavian Alliance Mission, 1916), pp. 377, 382.
7. Torjesen, "A Study of Fredrik Franson," p. 682.
8. *Ibid.*, see pp, 683-684.
9. Princell, *Alliance Mission's Twenty-Fifth Anniversary Story*, p. 144.
10. *Ibid.*, pp. 145-146.

11. Torjesen, "A Study of Fredrik Franson," pp. 726-727.

Chapter 5 (pages 64-78)

1. Josephine Princell, *Fredrik Franson's Liv och Verksamhet* [Fredrik Franson's Life and Work] (Chicago: Chicago-Bladet Publishing Co., 1909), p. 270.

2. *Ibid.*, p. 272.

3. Suggested books on Fredrik Franson:

O. C. Grauer, *A Burning and Shining Light** (Chicago: Scandinavian Alliance Mission, 1938)

Josephine Princell, *Fredrik Franson's Liv och Verksamhet** (Swedish) [Fredrik Franson's Life and Work] (Chicago: Chicago-Bladet Publishing Co., 1909)

J. F. Swanson, *Fredrik Franson: World Evangelist and Missionary Leader** (Chicago: The Evangelical Alliance Mission, 1952)

Edvard P. Torjesen, *Fredrik Franson, A Model for Worldwide Evangelism#* (Pasadena, CA: William Carey Library, 1983)

Edvard P. Torjesen, "A Study of Fredrik Franson"# (Ph.D. Dissertation, International College, Los Angeles, CA, September 1984)

(*) Out of print. Can be reviewed in TEAM library.

(#) Available for purchase at TEAM, P.O. Box 969, Wheaton, IL 60189-0969

4. Edvard P. Torjesen, "A Study of Fredrik Franson" (Ph.D. Dissertation, International College, Los Angeles, CA, September 1984), p. 711.

5. *Ibid.*, p. 713.

6. Much has been written about the great Korean revival which transformed the churches in the years 1903 to 1910 but not about Franson's part in it. After receiving a welcoming letter from Dr. R.A. Hardie, a Canadian doctor serving with the Southern Methodist Mission, Franson arrived in Wonsan, Korea in late September 1903. Dr. Hardie, who had been used by the Lord in the early revival stirrings in Wonsan, reported to his mission giving this glimpse of the Lord's timing: "I now began to realize that the Holy Spirit was working in our midst, and was at a stand as to just how I ought to proceed. But that very evening, earlier than we had expected, Brother Franson came to us. He proved to be a man of prayer and an experienced evangelist, and it was evident that the Lord had sent him to teach us how to work" (Torjesen, "A Study of Fredrik Franson," p. 719).

Another account by Dr. Hardie reveals the extent to which the Lord used Franson's ministry in Korea: "More than anything else it was Franson's visit to Korea which God used to begin the revival which spread from Wonsan to Seoul, to Pyongyang northward, and later into Manchuria" (Josephine Princell, *Fredrik Franson's Life and Work,* p. 287.)

7. Torjesen "A Study of Fredrik Franson," p. 730.

8. *Ibid.*, pp. 735-736.

9. *Ibid.*, p. 744.

10. *Ibid.*, p. 746.

11. Josephine Princell, *Alliansmissionens Tjugufemårsminnen* [Alliance Mission's Twenty-Fifth Anniversary Story] (Chicago: Scandinavian Alliance Mission, 1916), pp. 328-344.

12. Torjesen, "A Study of Fredrik Franson," pp. 744, 745, 748, 749.
13. Princell, *Fredrik Franson's Life and Work*, p. 311.
14. *Ibid.*, pp. 312-313.
15. *Ibid.*, p. 315.
16. *Ibid.*, p. 316.
17. *Ibid.*, pp. 318-320.
18. Torjesen, "A Study of Fredrik Franson," pp. 753-763.
19. Princell, *Fredrik Franson's Life and Work*, p. 322.
20. *Ibid.*, pp. 328-329.
21. Princell, *Alliance Mission's Twenty-fifth Anniversary Story*, pp. 407-408.
22. Princell, *Fredrik Franson's Life and Work,* pp. 341-342.
23. *Ibid.*, pp. 348.
24. *Ibid.*, pp. 352-353.

Chapter 6 (pages 79-86)

1. Scandinavian Alliance Mission, minutes of the board of directors, Volumes 1 and 2.
2. Letter from J. H. Hedstrom to T. J. Bach, February 20, 1923, TEAM archives. Wheaton, Illinois.
3. S.A.M. minutes of board of directors, September 19, 1923.
4. O. C. Grauer, "A Brief Biography of Pastor C. T. Dyrness" (Unpublished. Written in 1934 in Norwegian, translated into English by Camilla M. Dyrness, 1975).

Chapter 7 (pages 87-97)

1. Constitution of the Scandinavian Alliance Mission as recorded in the minutes of the board of directors, December 3, 1897.
2. S.A.M. board of directors minutes, November 10, 1908.
3. *Ibid.*, February 2, 1909.
4. *Ibid.*, December 1911.
5. The Rev. C. V. Bowman to the Rev. F. Risberg, July 1, 1914, TEAM archives, Wheaton, Illinois.
6. The Rev. F. Risberg to the Rev. C. V. Bowman, July 13, 1914, TEAM archives, Wheaton, Illinois.
7. The Rev. C. E. Peterson to Professor F. Risberg, April 20, 1915, TEAM archives, Wheaton, Illinois.
8. S.A.M. board of directors (writer not identified) to the Rev. C.E. Peterson, May 5, 1915, TEAM archives, Wheaton, Illinois.
9. Undated report (1916) prepared by the Rev. P. A. Nelson, TEAM archives, Wheaton, Illinois.
10. S.A.M. board of directors to P. A. Nelson, September 18, 1916, TEAM Archives, Wheaton, Illinois.
11. S.A.M. board of directors Minutes, February 22, 1924.
12. Minutes recorded by the Rev. Frank W. Anderson, March 15, 1924.
13. Unpublished autobiographical notes by T. J. Bach, 1960.
14. Minutes of the annual meeting of the S.A.M. held in Chicago, Illinois, April 27-28, 1924.
15. *Ibid.*
16. S.A.M. board of directors minutes, April 26, 1926.

17. Recollection by the Rev. C. T. Dyrness as related to Miss Camilla Dyrness and reported by her. There were apparently two present who were not surprised, Grauer and Bach. In his last annual report as he was retiring in 1946, as recorded in the May-June 1946 issue of *The Missionary Broadcaster,* Bach wrote, "Twenty years have passed since our beloved deceased brother, Dr. O. C. Grauer, asked so kindly if he might recommend me to the Board of Directors of the Scandinavian Alliance Mission for the position I now relinquish." It was two years later that the men of the board first considered this possibility so it is evident that Bach had not permitted his name to be put forward at an earlier date.

18. S.A.M. board of directors minutes, April 23, 1928.

19. T. J. Bach to Dr. O. C. Grauer, secretary of the board, May 1, 1928, TEAM archives, Wheaton, Illinois.

Chapter 8 (pages 98-106)

1. Josephine Princell, *Alliansmissionens Tjugufemårsminnen* [Alliance Mission's Twenty-fifth Anniversary Story] (Chicago: Scandinavian Alliance Mission, 1916), p. 151.

2. *Ibid.,* p. 153.

3. *Ibid.,* p. 155.

4. *Ibid.,* pp. 156-157.

5. S.A.M. Annual Report for 1919, *Chicago Bladet,* April 20, 1920.

6. *The Missionary Broadcaster,* January-March 1925, p. 12.

Chapter 9 (pages 107-115)

1. Ralph W. Christensen, interview, December 6, 1986.

2. For a full story of Malla Moe's life and work see the book *Malla Moe* by Paul H. Sheetz and Maria Nilsen (Moody Press, Chicago. 1956). Also available at the TEAM office library.

3. O. C. Grauer, *Fifty Wonderful Years* (Chicago: Scandinavian Alliance Mission, 1940), pp. 213-214.

4. Ralph W. Christensen, interview.

5. William Dawson, unpublished autobiographical notes, c. 1920.

6. John Christiansen, *Under the Southern Cross* (Published by the author, Chicago, IL, 1932), pp. 42, 43.

7. *Ibid.,* p. 44.

8. *Ibid.,* p. 50.

9. John F. Swanson, unpublished notes, 1963.

Chapter 10 (pages 116-125)

1. S.A.M. board of directors minutes, January 10, 1928.

2. Paul H. Sheetz, *The Sovereign Hand* (Wheaton, IL: The Evangelical Alliance Mission, 1971), p.56.

3. *The Missionary Broadcaster,* January-March 1936, p. 4.

Chapter 11 (pages 126-143)

1. William H. Pape, *China Travail* (Wheaton, IL: The Evangelical Alliance Mission, 1975), pp. 41, 42.

2. Leslie T. Lyall, *New Spring in China* (Grand Rapids, MI: Zondervan Publishing House, 1980), p. 48.

3. *The Missionary Broadcaster*, January-March 1930, p. 7.

4. *Ibid.*, p. 7.

5. Pape, *China Travail*, pp. 60, 61.

6. *Ibid.*, p. 77.

7. Reuben Gustafson, Unpublished personal diary, 1936.

8. Pape, p. 104.

Chapter 12 (pages 144-148)

1. Vernon Mortenson, personal recollection of message by T. J. Bach at meeting of student Missionary Union at the Moody Bible Institute, March 1936.

2. *The Missionary Broadcaster*, April-June 1931, p. 20.

3. *Ibid.*, July-September 1931, p. 14.

4. *Ibid.*, October-December 1933, p. 16.

5. *Ibid.*

6. *Ibid.*, July-September 1936, p. 9.

7. *Ibid.*, January-March 1937, p. 24.

8. *Ibid.*, January-March 1938, p. 17.

9. *Ibid.*

10. *Ibid.*, October-December 1939, p. 15.

11. *Ibid.*, July-September 1940, p. 11.

12. J. F. Swanson, *Three Score Years...and Then* (Chicago: The Evangelical Alliance Mission, 1950), p. 77.

Chapter 13 (pages 149-155)

1. *The Missionary Broadcaster*, January-March 1934, pp. 4, 5.

2. *Ibid.*, July-September 1934, p. 15.

3. *Ibid.*, July-September 1937, p. 13.

4. *Ibid.*, October-December 1938, p. 10.

5. *Ibid.*

6. *Ibid.*, January-March 1942, p. 16.

7. My family and I and other China missionaries had been evacuated from China in January 1945 and were in India at the time of the release from detention of some of the Congress Party leaders. One unforgettable experience came after riding in the same train as the released prisoners from Poona to Bombay and being a lone foreigner—a rather noticeable one, at that—when getting off the coach into the huge welcoming throng at the Victoria Terminal in Bombay. Fair-skinned foreigners were not popular just then with the excited mob.

Chapter 14 (pages 156-163)

1. *The Missionary Broadcaster*, October-December 1933, p. 4.

2. *Ibid.*, p. 6.

3. *Ibid.*, p. 5.

4. *Ibid.*, January-March 1934, p. 24.

5. *Ibid.*

6. *Ibid.*, January-March 1934, p. 24.

7. *Ibid.*, October-December 1936, p. 14.

8. *Ibid.*

9. *Ibid.*, July-September 1937, p. 12.

10. *Ibid.*, January-March 1937, p. 12.
11. *Ibid.*, October-December 1935, p. 23.
12. *Ibid.*, July-September 1941, pp. 19-21.
13. *Ibid.*, March-April 1944, p. 7.
14. *Ibid.*, April-June 1940, p. 21.

Chapter 15 (pages 164-172)
1. *The Missionary Broadcaster*, January-March 1934, p. 13.
2. *Ibid.*
3. *Ibid.*, April-June 1931, p. 12.
4. *Ibid.*, January-March 1934, p. 13.
5. *Ibid.*, January-March 1935, p. 14.
6. *Ibid.*, April-June 1935, p. 18.
7. Official minutes, S.A.M. Mongolia field conference, October 31 to November 2, 1935.
8. Report to S.A.M. board of directors, January 6, 1941, S. J. Gunzel.
9. *Ibid.*

Chapter 16 (pages 173-185)
1. *The Missionary Broadcaster*, April-June 1930, p. 24.
2. John Christiansen, *Under the Southern Cross* (Published by the author, Chicago, IL, 1932), p. 204.
3. *Ibid.*, p. 205.
4. *The Missionary Broadcaster*, October-December 1931, pp. 23-25.
5. *Ibid.*, October-December 1934, pp. 27, 28.
6. *Ibid.*, July-September 1936, p. 17.
7. O. C. Grauer, *Fifty Wonderful Years* (Chicago: Scandinavian Alliance Mission, 1940), p. 293.
8. *The Missionary Broadcaster*, January-March 1938, p. 6.
9. *Ibid.*, p. 9.
10. *Ibid.*, April-June 1938, p. 27.
11. *Ibid.*, October-December 1940, p. 18.
12. *Ibid.*, October-December 1943, p. 18.
13. *Ibid.*, January-March 1938, p. 7.
14. *Ibid.*, November-December 1944, p. 24, and September-October 1946, p. 28.
15. *Ibid.*, September-October 1946, p. 28.
16. *Ibid.*, July-September 1941, p. 23.

Chapter 17 (pages 186-195)
1. *The Missionary Broadcaster*, April-June 1935, p. 31.
2. *Ibid.*, November-December 1946, p. 10.
3. *Ibid.*, October-December 1939, p. 24.
4. *Ibid.*
5. *Ibid.*, October-December 1942, p. 29.

Chapter 18 (pages 196-205)
1. Arthur P. Johnston, *The Battle for World Evangelism* (Wheaton, Illinois: Tyndale House Publishers, 1978), p. 39.
2. *The Missionary Broadcaster*, January-March 1933, pp. 6, 7.

3. *Ibid.*, April-June 1937, p. 6.
4. O. C. Grauer, *Fifty Wonderful Years* (Chicago: Scandinavian Alliance Mission, 1940), p. 334.
5. *The Missionary Broadcaster*, May-June 1945, p. 8.
6. *Ibid.*, January-February 1946, p. 3.
7. *Ibid.*, April-June 1944, p. 8.
8. As related to Vernon Mortenson by David H. Johnson.

Chapter 19 (pages 206-212)
1. Report of the general director T. J. Bach, March 31, 1929, to the annual meeting of the Scandinavian Alliance Mission, pp. 6, 7.

Chapter 20 (pages 213-227)
1. S.A.M. board of directors minutes, May 29, 1946.
2. David H. Johnson, letter of May 25, 1948.
3. S.A.M. board of directors minutes, September 2, 1948.
4. *The Missionary Broadcaster*, April 1949, p. 6; June 1949, p. 2.
5. *Ibid.*, November 1950, p. 16.
6. *Ibid.*, p. 4.
7. *Ibid.*, p. 4.

Chapter 21 (pages 228-242)
1. *The Missionary Broadcaster*, September 1949, p. 5.
2. *Ibid.*, January 1955, p. 5.
3. TEAM board of directors minutes, May 13, 1958.
4. *Ibid.*, July 10, 1961.
5. *Ibid.*

Chapter 22 (pages 243-257)
1. *The Missionary Broadcaster*, November-December 1961, pp. 7, 8.
2. TEAM board executive committee minutes, June 27, 1961.
3. TEAM board of directors minutes, January 13, 1958.
4. *TEAM Topics*, mission house organ, November 1964.
5. *The Missionary Broadcaster*, November-December 1961, pp. 12, 13.
6. TEAM board of directors minutes, April 2, 1963.
7. Vernon Mortenson, *Light is Sprung Up* (Wheaton, IL: The Evangelical Alliance Mission, 1965).
8. *The Missionary Broadcaster*, July-August 1965, p. 8.
9. *Ibid.*, pp. 8, 9.
10. *Ibid.*

Chapter 23 (pages 258-276)
1. Wheaton Declaration.
2. Paul H. Sheetz, *The Sovereign Hand* (Wheaton IL: The Evangelical Alliance Mission, 1971), Introduction.
3. *Ibid.*
4. Vernon Mortenson, *This is TEAM* (Wheaton IL: The Evangelical Alliance Mission, 1965, 1987 rev.).

Topics dealt with in the in-house periodicals include the following: *TEAM Topics (Tidings),* June 1961, A Shift of Emphasis?; November 1963, The Vital Role of the Church Planting Missionary; December 1965, The Unchanging and the Changing in Missions. August 1967, What is Evangelism? August 1969, Where Does TEAM Stand? April 1972, Some Vital Questions, Five-Year Goals.

5. *Principles and Practice of TEAM* (Wheaton, IL: The Evangelical Alliance Mission, major revisions adopted 1960, 1974 and 1987).
6. TEAM board of directors minutes, April 21, 1972.

Chapter 24 (pages 277-293)
1. Richard M. Winchell, *Horizons*, January-February 1975, pp. 7, 8 (condensed).
2. George D. Martin, letter to all TEAM field chairmen, October 19, 1973.
3. Charles Willoughby, report to George Martin, December 14, 1974.
4. Earl Conrad, report to George Martin, March 4, 1976.
5. Richard M. Winchell, letter to George Martin, November 27, 1981.

Chapter 25 (pages 294-311)
1. Richard Winchell, letter to TEAM family—circulated but unpublished, September 24, 1974.
2. Lee Hotchkiss, "Servant Leadership and Management Skills Workshops," an unpublished report to the TEAM board of directors, November 5, 1987.
3. Richard Winchell, "Franson Center for Missionary Training and Personnel Development," an unpublished report to the TEAM board of directors, October 8, 1988.
4. Richard Winchell, "TEAM Training Program," an unpublished report to the TEAM board of directors, October 6, 1989.
5. *Ibid.*
6. Richard Winchell, report to TEAM annual meeting, May 17, 1989.
7. TEAM Prayer Directory, 1990.
8. Richard Winchell, report to TEAM annual meeting, May 9, 1990.
9. *Ibid.*
10. *Ibid.*
11. Jack MacDonald, David Davis, report to TEAM board of directors, "April 1 to 28, 1990, Survey of Eastern European Countries," May 7, 1990.

Chapter 26 (pages 312-326)
1. *The Missionary Broadcaster*, January 1947, p. 14.
2. *Ibid.*, March 1948, p. 4.
3. *Ibid.*
4. *Ibid.*
5. *Ibid.*, April 1948, p. 13.
6. *Ibid.*, April 1949. p. 3.
7. Vernon Mortenson, discussion paper prepared for TEAM board of directors meeting, August 17, 1949.
8. TEAM board of directors minutes, August 17, 1949.
9. *Pray for China Fellowship*, Overseas Missionary Fellowship, Seattle, Washington, January 1989, pp. 1-3.
10. Edvard Torjesen, letter to Vernon Mortenson, August 9, 1951.

Chapter 27 (pages 328-338)
1. *The Missionary Broadcaster*, February 1947, p. 13.

2. *Ibid.*, May-June 1946, p. 28.
3. *Ibid.*
4. *Ibid.*, July-August 1951, p. 6.
5. S.A.M. board of directors minutes, November 19, 1952.
6. *The Missionary Broadcaster*, April 1953, p. 3.
7. *Ibid.*, May 1953, p. 7.

Chapter 28 (pages 339-350)
1. Kenneth McVety, *The WLP Story*, pamphlet, 1985.
2. Kenneth McVety, letter to Vernon Mortenson, December 14, 1989.
3. *The Missionary Broadcaster*, October 1958, p. 5
4. S.A.M. board of directors minutes, May 26, 1946.
5. Delbert A. Kuehl, Japan field chairman, to David H. Johnson, November 1, 1964, with transcript of report by Donald E. Hoke to Japan field committee from the minutes of July 20-21, 1954. First annual report of Japan Christian College, April 1955.
6. Donald E. Hoke, annual report of Japan Christian College, April 1955, p. 1.

Chapter 29 (pages 351-370)
1. *The Missionary Broadcaster*, November-December 1959, p. 8.
2. *Ibid.*, January 1959, p. 27.
3. Donald E. Hoke, *Asahi Evening News*, May 2, 1959, p. 3.
4. Kenneth McVety, *The Japan Times*, April 20, 1959, p. 3.
5. *The Missionary Broadcaster*, July-August 1965, p. 11.
6. Ralph Cox, pamphlet, "Come help us plant one hundred churches in Japan," July 1988.
7. Stanley Barthold, Annual Report, January 1970.
8. *Ibid.*
9. *Ibid.*, January 1974.
10. Excerpts from general letters written by Verner and Dorothy Strom and Victor and Ann Springer, from TEAM files.
11. Field chairman Verner Strom's report to the TEAM 1980 Japan field conference, August 1980, p. 1.
12. Verner Strom, *TEAM Horizons*, November 1981, p. 4.
13. Brian R. Bates, *JEMS*, January-February 1983, p. 2.
14. Vernon Mortenson, *TEAM Horizons*, January-February 1983, p. 9.

Chapter 30 (pages 371-406)
1. Edvard Torjesen, field chairman's report to the Taiwan annual conference, 1959.
2. Minutes, TEAM board of directors meeting, January 15, 1960.
3. Vernon Mortenson, report to TEAM board of directors, May 8, 1963. pp. 5, 6.
4. Letter from Vernon Mortenson to C. A. Landgren, chairman of the board of Overseas Radio, Inc., August 2, 1961.
5. William S. Winchell, letter to China Radio supporting constituency, February 4, 1985.
6. *Ibid.*, December 19, 1986.
7. William H. Pape, *China Travail* (Wheaton, IL: The Evangelical Alliance Mission, 1975), pp. 128-133.

8. Edvard Torjesen, *The Missionary Broadcaster*, July 1955, p. 3.
9. *Ibid.*
10. Vernon Mortenson, *The Missionary Broadcaster*, February 1957, p. 13.
11. Morris Beck, response to ministry questionnaire, July 4, 1986.
12. Taiwan field council minutes, January 10, 1975.
13. Richard Olson, *TEAM Horizons*, November-December 1987, pp. 8, 9.
14. Youth camp committee report to Taiwan field conference, 1983.
15. *Ibid*, 1970.
16. Vernon Mortenson, report to TEAM board of directors, June 22, 1970.
17. Morris Beck, field chairman's report to 1970 field conference.
18. David Woodward, field chairman's report to 1971 field conference.
19. *Ibid.*
20. Hugo N. Johnson, field chairman's report to the 1973 field conference.
21. *Ibid.*, 1974.
22. *Ibid.*
23. Ernest Boehr, report on the Hakka ministry to the 1976 annual field conference.
24. Philip and Ann Schwab, prayer letter, Thanksgiving 1989.
25. From church work committee report to 1976 field conference.
26. Philip and Ann Schwab, prayer letter, September 30, 1982.
27. Morris Beck, field chairman's report to the 1980 field conference.
28. *Ibid.*, 1981.
29. Hugo N. Johnson, field chairman's report to the 1978 field conference.
30. Morris Beck, field chairman's reports to 1981, 1982, 1983, 1984 field conferences.
31. Ernest Boehr, field chairman's report to 1985 field conference.
32. Philip Schwab, field chairman's report to 1989 field conference.
33. Norman Niemeyer, report to the TEAM board of directors, March 19, 1985.
34. *Ibid.*, November 11, 1986.

Chapter 31 (pages 407-432)

1. Minutes of TEAM board of directors, August 8, November 19, 1952.
2. David H. Johnson, *The Missionary Broadcaster*, September 1953, p. 3.
3. Minutes of TEAM board of directors, April 6, 1953.
4. One problem complicating institutional work in Korea was the laws governing cultural, religious, and charitable activities. It was necessary that there be organized societies (juridical persons), registered with the government, for the mission, the orphan work, radio, conference grounds, college, and literature. There also were regulations relating to official meetings, minutes, and reports. Some activities required prior notice and approval.

Whether the government required it or not, there was the assumed advantage of having big names on the various boards—school presidents, politicians, big businessmen, pastors of large churches, and denominational leaders. It was clearly the purpose to have dedicated Christian men and women in these positions, but the missionaries were dependent upon the recommendation and judgment of professing Christians of their acquaintance.

George Martin, area secretary, commented to Leo Classen in his letter of October 12, 1966, "One of our problems, of course, has been that we have not had churches from which we could draw personnel. If we had planted churches first, we would have had sufficient personnel acquainted with the goals and aims of TEAM who would also be loyal to the mission and would understand what we are endeavoring to do in Korea."

A further complication was that an asset held by one ministry, such as a house used in school work, could not be transferred to another ministry, such as radio, without great difficulty. Another problem encountered in some government relationships was graft by low-level officials which resulted in loss to the mission in a number of property transactions. On no other TEAM field were relationships with the government so burdened and even hampered by red tape.

5. TEAM board of directors' minutes, October 13, 1966.
6. James Cornelson, field chairman's report, 1978, p. 5.
7. Correspondence of Tom Watson, Jr. with David H. Johnson and Vernon Mortenson, 1952 and 1953, with copies of Watson's letters to Syngman Rhee and Chief of Public Information, Republic of Korea, October 11, 1952 and December 1, 1953.
8. TEAM board of directors' minutes, July 7, 1965.

    John Rathbun, chairman of the Korea field and acting manager of HLKX in the early 1970s, related in a letter of October 17, 1990, that in 1974 "Gerardt Ham, born of German parents, and whose father was a pastor in Russia, visited Dr. You Sang Goon, Korea's Minister of Unification, and stated that from his village east of Kiev he knew of seven who had accepted Christ as a direct result of HLKX, three of them being communists."
9. *TIME*, July 2, 1990, p. 40.
10. John Rathbun, field chairman's annual report, March 1, 1976.
11. Word of Life Press, Korea, brochure, 1979.
12. Word of Life Press, Korea, *Communiqué*, October 1976.
13. James Cornelson, letter to Myra Dye, *TEAM Horizons*, April 30, 1985.
14. *Ibid.*
15. Korea Christian Conference Grounds, annual report, 1984.
16. TEAM board of directors' minutes, March 29, 1961.
17. Vernon Mortenson, report to TEAM board of directors, May 8, 1963.
18. John Rathbun, letter to Vernon Mortenson, October 17, 1990.
19. Vernon Mortenson, report to TEAM board of directors, June 22, 1970.
20. Barbara Chapman, Korea field chairman's report, 1983.

Chapter 32 (pages 433-443)

1. Norman Niemeyer, report to TEAM board of directors, March 19-20, 1984.
2. *Ibid.*, May 9, 1984.
3. "A Brief History of the Philippines Field," unpublished paper by field editor, April 1987.
4. Norman Niemeyer, report to TEAM board of directors, November 10, 1986.
5. *Ibid.*, March 20, 1989.
6. *Ibid.*
7. *TEAM Horizons*, March-April 1987, p. 4.
8. Norman Niemeyer, report to TEAM board of directors, November 6, 1989.
9. *The Basic Law of the Hong Kong Special Administrative Region of the People's Republic of China* (draft), 14 January 1989, The Standing Com-

mittee of the National People's Congress, p. 1.

10. TEAM board of directors minutes, November 12, 1985.
11. Norman Niemeyer, information included in report to TEAM board of directors, March 14, 1988.
12. Philip Schwab, Macao survey report, May 28, 1990.

Chapter 33 (pages 444-505)
1. *The Missionary Broadcaster*, January 1953, p. 4.
2. David H. Johnson, *The Missionary Broadcaster,* November 1953, p. 3.
3. Paul H. Sheetz, editor, *The Missionary Broadcaster*, January 1953, p. 2.
4. *Ibid.*
5. Charles Preston, *The Missionary Broadcaster*, November 1954, p. 5.
6. Richard and Charlotte Griffiths, annual personal report, 1962.
7. *Ibid.*, 1964.
8. *Ibid.*
9. *Ibid.*
10. *Ibid.*, 1965.
11. *Ibid.*, 1968.
12. *Ibid.*, 1970.
13. *Ibid.*, 1974.
14. *Ibid.*, 1975.
15. *Ibid.*, 1976.
16. Douglas and Julie Miller, annual personal reports, 1980-1982.
17. Griffiths, annual personal report, 1981.
18. Griffiths, annual Minyambou station report, 1982.
19. Doug and Julie Miller, annual personal report, 1971.
20. Doug Miller, *WHEREVER*, Winter 1980, p. 6.
21. *Ibid.*, p. 6, 7.
22. *Ibid.*, p. 7.
23. *Ibid.*
24. Doug and Julie Miller, annual personal report, 1981.
25. *Ibid.*, report on "Operation Bird's Head," March 1982.
26. Doug and Julie Miller, annual personal report, 1981.
27. Wolfgang Lunow, interviewed by Vernon Mortenson, June 18, 1987.
28. *Ibid.*
29. Paul F. Rhoads, report of church growth committee to the annual conference, 1986.
30. Jack F. MacDonald, journal of Irian Jaya trip, March 1982.
31. Marvin Newell, field chairman's report, 1986.
32. Ronald Hill, field chairman's report, 1984.
33. Charles Preston, field chairman's report, 1973.
34. Ronald Hill, field chairman's report, 1984.
35. Paul F. Rhoads, report of church growth committee to the annual conference, 1986.
36. Margaret Stringer, report of survey trip, December 31, 1982 to January 13, 1983.
37. *Ibid.*
38. *Ibid.*
39. *Ibid.*, February 17 to 23, 1983.

40. *Ibid.*

41. Norman Niemeyer, report to TEAM board of directors, November 10, 1986.

42. Charles Preston, field chairman's report, 1974.

43. *Ibid.,* 1975.

44. Romulo Maling, prayer letter, November 13, 1988.

45. Willem Hekman, letter to Vernon Mortenson, February 27, 1974, with attachment of letter from Department of Religion, Republic of Indonesia, February 13, 1974.

46. Norman Niemeyer, report to TEAM board of directors, June 27, 1988.

47. Jack F. MacDonald, information from report to TEAM board of directors, June 15, 1983.

48. Marvin Newell, prayer letter, November 1988.

49. *Ibid.*

50. *Ibid.,* response to strategy planning questionnaire, June 24, 1986.

51. *Ibid.*

52. Richard M. Winchell, report to TEAM board of directors, April 1985.

53. Larry Rascher, general letter to supporters, July 31, 1971.

54. Vernon Mortenson, historical notes on TEAM fields, January 1984.

55. *TEAM Horizons* issue of January-February 1983 has a brief article on the seminary: "Students of the first graduating class at the Evangelical Theological Seminary of Indonesia received their degrees on June 21, 1982. Thirty-four men and women finished the three-year program which included the requirement that each student develop a church of 30 members. In three years, these graduates and their classmates have opened 154 villages to the gospel and have baptized 2,142."

56. Craig and Brent are sons of Charles and Bernita Preston, missionaries since 1954 among the Asmat people in Irian Jaya. Candy Preston, a daughter, has worked at the Irian Jaya field headquarters in Manokwari since 1983 and has been active in the local church work. Another daughter, Tosha Godbold, and her husband are under appointment to serve in the Republic of Chad. There previously have been as many as four career missionaries from one family, but this is the first instance of four from a family—all active at the same time—and second-generation missionaries, at that.

57. Jack F. MacDonald, report on Indonesia field trip to general director Richard Winchell, March 25, 1980.

58. Finn and Sandy Torjesen are both children of missionaries who served in Taiwan—Edvard and Jenny Torjesen and Dr. Frank and Sally Dennis. After their missionary preparation and marriage Finn and Sandy expected to go to Iran, a Muslim country where TEAM had taken the first steps to open a field. The Islamic revolution which brought the Ayatollah Khomeini to power necessitated a change in TEAM's plans. Still sensing God's leading to minister to Muslims, the Torjesens next looked to Indonesia. They applied for visas knowing that they might have to wait several years and even then be refused.

They agreed in 1980, while waiting, to go to Taiwan where they had lived during their childhood. With a basic knowledge of Chinese they could be active in service. They did, however, take formal Chinese studies, knowing that proficiency in Chinese could open doors for witness. They also considered the possibility that Indonesia would not grant visas, in which case they might be asked to remain in Taiwan. In time their visas were granted and they moved on to Java in 1983.

An unusual God-given opportunity to use Chinese came in the summer of 1990, when descendants of Mr. and Mrs. Peter Torjesen, missionaries to Shaanxi Province in northwest China, were invited to attend a memorial gathering for Peter who was killed by a Japanese bombing raid in 1939. As the one in the family who spoke Chinese most easily, Finn was invited by local officials to form a team to come back to Shaanxi for short-term work among the people. Though the invitation did not specify Christian witnessing, the open door would certainly provide that opportunity.

59. Finn Torjesen, *TEAM Horizons*, March-April, 1989.
60. Romulo Maling, prayer letter, November 15, 1988.
61. Torjesen, *Ibid.*
62. Norman Niemeyer, report to TEAM board of directors, June 21, 1989.

Chapter 34 (pages 506-524)

1. Jane McNally, *The Missionary Broadcaster*, June 1952, p. 3.
2. Minutes of TEAM board of directors, January 8, 1951.
3. Letter from O. E. Meberg to David H. Johnson, March 21, 1951.
4. *Ibid.*
5. Irvine Robertson, *The Missionary Broadcaster*, January 1952, p. 3.
6. *TEAM Horizons*, January-February 1980, p. 13.
7. Einer Berthelsen, fiftieth annual report, Western India field, 1955.
8. Vernon Mortenson, report to TEAM board of directors on Middle East trip, March 4, 1966.
9. Ralph Hertzsprung, sixty-third annual report, 1968.
10. Jack MacDonald, report to general director Richard Winchell, December 31, 1975.
11. Earl Conrad, seventy-first annual report, February 14, 1977.
12. Einer Berthelsen, seventy-sixth annual report, February 23, 1982.
13. Norman Niemeyer, report to TEAM board of directors, May 4, 1983.
14. Ralph Hertzsprung, letter to Vernon Mortenson quoting Leslie Buhler, April 21, 1987.
15. Ralph Hertzsprung, sixty-third annual report, 1968.
16. Earl Conrad, eightieth annual report, February 1986.
17. Ralph Hertzsprung, eighty-second annual report, 1988.
18. Olga E. Noreen, *The Missionary Broadcaster*, May 1948, p. 12.

Chapter 35 (pages 525-554)

1. Charles Warren, annual report, 1983.
2. *Ibid.*
3. Murray Carter, *A Decade in Delhi*, Delhi Bible Fellowship, 1978, p. 2.
4. *Ibid.*
5. *Ibid.*
6. *Ibid.*, p. 3.
7. Murray Carter, letter to prayer helpers, July 25, 1968.
8. Murray Carter, *A Decade in Delhi*, p. 8.
9. Murray Carter, letter to prayer helpers, March 26, 1969.

10. *Ibid.*, July 28, 1969.
11. *Ibid.*, September 29, 1969.
12. *Ibid.*
13. *Ibid.*, June 23, 1973.
14. *Ibid.*, September 10, 1973.
15. Charles Warren, letter to supporters, October 8, 1975.
16. *Ibid.*, January 6, 1986.
17. *Ibid.*, field chairman's annual report, 1981.
18. *Ibid.*
19. Carl Flickner, field chairman's annual report, 1986.
20. Paul H. Sheetz, *The Sovereign Hand* (Wheaton, IL: The Evangelical Alliance Mission, 1971), p. 121.
21. Bishan Singh, unpublished paper on India-Sri Lanka radio work, 1976, p. 4.
22. Stanton Rubesh, *Horizons*, July-August 1976, p. 22.
23. *Ibid.*, p. 23.
24. Stanton Rubesh, prayer letter, April 1978.
25. Carol Rubesh, prayer letter, September 1980.
26. Stanton Rubesh, prayer letter, July 1982.
27. Stanton Rubesh, *TEAM Horizons*, January-February 1985, p. 11.
28. *Ibid.*
29. *The Missionary Broadcaster*, September-October 1946, p. 21.
30. Dr. Maynard Seaman, "Survey Trip of Nepal," January 11 to February 3, 1965, p. 4.
31. Dr. Maynard Seaman, letter to Charles Warren, field chairman, Tibetan Frontier Field, November 2, 1965.
32. Peter Hanks, field chairman's annual report, 1983.
33. Lynn N. Everswick, report to TEAM board of directors, March 18, 1985.
34. *Ibid.*
35. *Ibid.*
36. *Ibid.*, March 24, 1986.
37. Richard M. Winchell, report to TEAM board of directors, March 2, 1989.
38. Lynn N. Everswick, report to TEAM board of directors, June 25, 1990.

Chapter 36 (pages 555-585)

1. Agnes L. Davis, "Pakistan Pathways," an occasional publication of TEAM Pakistan field, April 1988.
2. Dr. Andrew T. Karsgaard, *The Missionary Broadcaster*, January 1948, p. 11.
3. Dr, Rob Droullard, interviewed by Bruce Rasmussen for CHP News and Views, Spring 1990.
4. *Ibid.*, Mary Droullard.
5. Paul Lundgren, Pakistan field chairman, undated letter to Vernon Mortenson, probably April 1962.
6. Vernon Mortenson, letter to Paul Lundgren, June 6, 1962.
7. *Ibid.*, June 15, 1962.
8. TEAM board of directors' minutes, March 11, 1963.
9. William C. Pietsch, field chairman's annual report, 1964.
10. Diane Evans, *TEAM Horizons*, March-April 1988.
11. Vernon Mortenson, report to TEAM board of directors, March 4, 1966.

12. G. Richard Thompson, report of evangelistic committee to annual field conference, 1966.
13. Vernon Mortenson, *I Will Build My Church* (Wheaton, IL: The Evangelical Alliance Mission, 1979), p. 14.
14. William C. Pietsch, field chairman's annual report, 1967.
15. Paul Lundgren, field chairman's annual report, 1969.
16. Vern W. Rock, evangelism report to annual conference, 1962.
17. Paul Lundgren, field chairman's annual report, 1969.
18. William Dalton, field chairman's annual report, 1975.
19. *Ibid.*, 1976.
20. David R. Davis, field chairman's annual report, 1979.
21. *Ibid.*, 1980.
22. GNS Newsletter, Good News Studios, Rawalpindi, Pakistan, 1988.
23. *Ibid.*
24. David R. Davis, field chairman's annual report, 1980.
25. *Ibid.*, 1984.
26. Jean Sodemann, *TEAM Horizons*, November-December 1986, p. 11.
27. Second generation short-term and career missionaries with TEAM from the Pakistan field, both past and present, include: David and Louise Karsgaard; David and Charles Davis; Luke and Esther Cutherell; Peter McMillan; Nate and Cindy Irwin; Mark, Marie (Lehman), and Matthew Dalton; Ruth Feldmann; Gene Stoddard; and Martha Rasmussen Hatch.
28. Vernon Mortenson, historical notes, Afghanistan, February 1984.
29. David R. Davis, field chairman's annual report, 1980.

Chapter 37 (pages 586-615)

1. Raymond H. Joyce, letter to TEAM board of directors, September 9, 1953.
2. TEAM board of directors' minutes, October 1, 1954.
3. Wilfred Thesiger, D.S.O., *The Illustrated London News*, July 3, 1954, p. 19.
4. Evangelistic committee report to annual field conference, 1978.
5. *Ibid.*
6. United Arab Emirates information paper with annual field conference minutes, 1979.
7. After the Richard Thompsons in 1968 were denied continued residence in Pakistan they spent about five years in representation work for the mission in the homeland. There followed several years in Iran where TEAM had entered into a working relationship with International Mission, Inc. The Islamic revolution which brought the Ayatollah Khomeini into power in early 1979 made further missionary work in Iran impossible.
8. UAE field information sheet, 1985.
9. Evangelistic committee reports 1975, 1977, 1981, 1984, and 1985.
10. Lynn Everswick, report to TEAM board of directors, March 15, 1988.
11. Elmer M. Tandayu, Filipino Christian Fellowship report to UAE annual field conference, 1986.
12. Lynn Everswick, reports to TEAM board of directors, November 10, 1988, and February 12, 1990.
13. Gerald Longjohn, "Church/Mission Relationships in the UAE," paper given at annual field conference, 1981.
14. Outreach Committee, "UAE Church Development," report to annual field

conference (no author's name given), 1983.

15. Larry F. Liddle, M.D., "Church Development and Church/Mission Relationships in the UAE," 1985, p. 2.
16. *Ibid.*, p. 1.
17. *Ibid.*, p. 3.
18. *Ibid.*, pp. 3,4.
19. *Ibid.*, p. 5.
20. Lynn Everswick, report to TEAM board of directors, November 11, 1986.
21. Moses Jesudass, report on Indian Christian Fellowship to annual field conference, 1986.
22. Larry F. Liddle, M.D., "Thoughts on the New Hospital Building," report to annual field conference, 1981.
23. *Ibid.*
24. *Ibid.*
25. Carl Sherbeck, field chairman's annual report, 1984.
26. Larry F. Liddle, M.D, field chairman's annual report, 1986.

Chapter 38 (pages 616-631)
1. Minutes of TEAM board of directors, January 13, 1949.
2. *The Missionary Broadcaster*, February 1948, p. 8.
3. *The Missionary Broadcaster*, May 1952, p. 4.
4. *The Missionary Broadcaster*, July-August, 1957, p. 27.

Chapter 39 (pages 632-648)
1. Chr. Christiansen, field chairman's report, 1960.
2. Vernon Mortenson, report to TEAM board of directors, March 1971.
3. *Ibid.*
4. Miss Beth A. Bromley, Unpublished Brief History of the Franson Christian High School, December 1980, p. 4.
5. Based on report to TEAM board of directors, March 1972, by Vernon Mortenson.
6. Ray Shive, letter to Norman Niemeyer, Area Foreign Secretary, May 17, 1986.
7. Paul Hayward, letter to Norman Niemeyer, May 24, 1986.
8. David Greene, "Overview of South Africa and Zimbabwe," a paper given to TEAM candidate classes, June 1983, p. 1.
9. Stewart Snook, field chairman's annual report, 1985, p. 3.
10. *Ibid.*, 1987, p. 2.

Chapter 40 (pages 649-684)
1. TEAM board of director's minutes, October 13, 1947.
2. Vernon Mortenson, historical notes, Zimbabwe, February 1984.
3. A listing of missionary children—probably not complete—who entered career or short-term missionary work with TEAM or other missions includes the following from TEAM Zimbabwe: Muriel Danielson (Elmer); Dick Dunkeld (deceased in 1972); Lynn, Dale, Joyce (Goppert), and Douglas Everswick; Paul and Tom Jackson; Gloria, Brenda, and Lorne Strom; Arthur Rilling; Jan (Catron), Nancy (Snyder), and Julie (Stephens) Hendrickson; Cheryl (White) and Rich Hoyt; and Dan Stephens.
4. Based on articles in the *The Missionary Broadcaster*, November 1954, and

June 1955.

5. Betty Mason Wolfe, *The Missionary Broadcaster*, December 1952, p. 7.
6. An interesting point of view was expressed by district commissioner Jackson when we talked with him about future plans for a hospital. The commissioner felt that missions were complicating his work by their life-saving efforts which caused the population to increase too rapidly. With this increase in the tribal areas people were moving to the crowded urban centers with the result that crime was increasing there. He felt that an educated African gave him more of a problem than the backward tribespeople. Our assurance that converted Africans would be the solution to much of the crime problem seemed not to register with him.
7. Much of the material about the ministry of the Karanda Hospital is drawn from an article by Marti (Winchell) Williams in *TEAM Horizons*, September-October 1986, pp. 6 & 7.
8. Carl Hendrickson, Evangelical Bible College report, 1976.
9. Richard Winchell, "Church Growth Challenges in South Africa and Zimbabwe," September 2, 1985, p. 5.
10. *TEAM Horizons*, November 12, 1977, p. 6, quoting *TIME*, March 28, 1977.
11. Russell Jackson letter to Vernon Mortenson, March 24, 1977.
12. *Ibid.*
13. *Ibid.*, March 8, 1977.
14. David J. Drake, *TEAM Horizons*, January-February 1981, p. 2.
15. Lorraine Waite, general prayer letter, April 30, 1987.
16. *Ibid.*
17. Dale Everswick, *TEAM Horizons*, July-August 1982, p. 4.
18. Tom Jackson, field chairman, interviewed by Vernon Mortenson, June 24, 1986.
19. Tom Jackson, field chairman's annual report, 1988.
20. Richard Winchell, report to TEAM board of directors, November 9, 10, 1988.
21. Ray Williams, letter to Lynn Everswick, July 24, 1990.
22. *Ibid.*
23. *Ibid.*
24. Lynn Everswick, report to TEAM board of directors, October 15, 1990.
25. Chris Goppert letter to Lynn and Judy Everswick, July 27, 1991.

Chapter 41 (pages 685-722)

1. Stewart F. Weber, field chairman's report to 1969 Chad field conference.
2. *Ibid.*
3. Victor E. Veary, *Pentecost on the Plains*, Sudan United Mission, Toronto, Canada, 1948.
4. Abel Ndjerareou, interviewed by Vernon Mortenson, May 27, 1987.
5. Veary, *Pentecost on the Plains*.
6. *Ibid.*
7. John Russell, *Chad Communiqué*, 1970.
8. Victor E. Veary, letter of tribute to Miss Ella Hildebrand, November 1988.
9. Vernon Mortenson, *TEAM Horizons*, 1970.
10. Vernon Mortenson, *Chad Communiqué*, Second Quarter 1970.
11. *Ibid.*

12. Jack Brotherton, *Chad Communiqué*, First Quarter 1972.
13. *Ibid.*
14. Stewart Weber, *Chad Communiqué*, Autumn 1972,
15. *Colliers Encyclopedia*, volume 5 (New York: Crowell-Colliers Publishing Company, 1955), p. 1.
16. Victor E. Veary, "Church on the Brink," privately published monograph (1984) dealing with the cultural revolution in Chad, 1973 to 1975, p. 1.
17. *Ibid.*, p. 2.
18. *Ibid.*, p. 6.
19. Richard Winchell, report to TEAM board of directors on November 1973 visit to Chad.
20. *Ibid.*
21. Jack Brotherton, *Chad Communiqué*, Spring-Summer 1975, p. 1.
22. Jack Brotherton, letter to Vernon Mortenson, August 8, 1974.
23. Vernon Mortenson, *Chad Communiqué*, Spring-Summer 1975, p. 2.
24. Nelson Bezanson, *Chad Communiqué*, Fall-Winter, 1975-76.
25. *Ibid.*
26. Committee of Six of the Evangelical Church, letter in Ngambai addressed to pastors and evangelists, translated by Victor Veary, May 1975.
27. *Ibid.*
28. Pastor Jeremie Njelarje, letter to Evangelical Church of Chad Council, October 3, 1975, translated by Victor E. Veary.
29. Charles McCordic, *Chad Communiqué*, Spring-Summer 1976.
30. Jack Brotherton, *Chad Communiqué*, 1976.
31. *Ibid.*
32. Abel Ndjerareou, interviewed by Vernon Mortenson, May 27, 1987.
33. *Chad Communiqué*, 1976.
34. *Ibid.*
35. Jack F. MacDonald, area secretary report to TEAM board of directors, November 19, 1985.
36. *Africa Report*, September-October 1990, p. 62.
37. *Chad Communiqué*, Fall-Winter 1979.
38. Carl and Sandra Hodges, *Chad Communiqué*, Summer 1980.
39. Jack F. MacDonald, area secretary report to TEAM board of directors, November 19, 1985.
40. Richard Winchell, report to TEAM board of directors, February 7, 1990.

Chapter 42 (pages 723-735)

1. *The Missionary Broadcaster*, January-February 1960, pp. 4,5.
2. Gary Bowman, chairman's report to Portugal field conference, March 1986.
3. Jack MacDonald, report to TEAM board of directors, November 16, 1982.
4. Annual field conference minutes, August 23-26, 1983.
5. Jack MacDonald, report to TEAM board of directors, November 16, 1982.
6. *Ibid.*, November 4, 1983.
7. Annual field conference reports, 1975 to 1983.
8. *The World Almanac and Book of Facts—1982* (New York: Newspaper Enterprise Association, Inc., 1982), p. 572.
9. Gary Bowman, chairman's report to Portugal field conference, March 1986.
10. Gary Bowman, report to Jack MacDonald, August 1984.

11. Gary Bowman, chairman's report to the Portugal field conference, 1986.

12. *Ibid.*, March 1986.

Chapter 43 (pages 736-778)

1. "Relighting the Lamps of Testimony in Europe," *The Missionary Broadcaster*, May-June 1965, p. 12, quoted in Robert J. Vajko, B.A., "A History and Analysis of the Church-Planting ministry of The Evangelical Alliance Mission in France from 1952 to 1974," a thesis submitted to Trinity Evangelical Divinity School, June 1975, p.1. Research copy on file in TEAM library, 400 Main Place, Carol Stream, Illinois.

2. Arthur Johnston, "Information Concerning France," March 1969.

3. Vajko thesis, p. 33.

4. Fran Johnston, "How the Church Began," *The Missionary Broadcaster*, March 1957, p. 10.

5. "Work in France Primarily With Youth," *The Missionary Broadcaster*, June 1955.

6. "Field Briefs: France," *The Missionary Broadcaster*, July 1955.

7. Vajko thesis, p. 49.

8. Arthur Johnston, field chairman's report, 1959.

9. Louise Lazaro, "Victory Day for French Church," *The Missionary Broadcaster*, May-June 1961, p. 3, quoted in Vajko thesis, p. 86.

10. Rod Johnston, field chairman's report, 1961.

11. Rod Johnston, field chairman's report, 1962.

12. Vajko thesis, p. 90.

13. Arthur Johnston, field chairman's report, 1963.

14. Arthur Johnston, field chairman's report, 1964.

15. Fran Johnston, *Please Don't Strike That Match!* (Grand Rapids: Zondervan, 1970), pp. 18-19, quoted in Vajko thesis, p. 112.

16. Rod Johnston, camp committee report, 1966.

17. Arthur Johnston, field chairman's report, 1965.

18. Vajko thesis, p. 125.

19. Arthur Johnston, field chairman's report, 1966.

20. Letter from Vernon Mortenson to Wallace Geiger, quoted in Vajko thesis, pp. 142-143.

21. Arthur Johnston, AEEI committee report, 1969.

22. Vajko, p. 150.

23. Ivan Peterson, field chairman's report, 1970.

24. Robert Vajko, theological education committee report, 1974.

25. Arthur Johnston, field chairman's report, 1974.

26. Jack MacDonald, "Report to the Board of Directors, France Annual Conference, August 18-24, 1984, Hempsted, Holland."

27. Wallace Geiger, field chairman's report, 1977.

28. "Provisional Copy of Joint AEEI-TEAM Five Year Guide Plan for Evangelism and Church Multiplication (1977-1981)."

29. Wallace Geiger, field chairman's report, 1978.

30. Wallace Geiger, field chairman's report, 1981.

31. Robert Vajko, AEEI coordinator's report, 1981.

32. Terry Regnault, camp committee report, 1979.

33. Wallace Geiger, field chairman's report, 1986.

34. Wallace Geiger, field chairman's report, 1976.
35. Wallace Geiger, AAEEI coordinator's report, 1984.
36. Jack MacDonald, "Journal of Europe Trip, August 11-September 3, 1983."
37. Jack MacDonald, "Report to the Board of Directors, France Annual Conference, August 18-24, 1984."
38. Wallace Geiger, field chairman's report, 1986.
39. Jack MacDonald, "Field Briefs," presented to TEAM board of directors March 24-25, 1986.
40. Wallace Geiger, field chairman's report, 1985.
41. Robert Vajko, "AEEI—Strengths and Weaknesses As a Union of Churches," paper presented to semi-annual conference, January 30-31, 1978.
42. Norman Kapp, "Threats to Proper Development of Church Planters," paper presented to 1982 advisory council.
43. Wallace Geiger, field chairman's report, 1985.
44. Wallace Geiger, chairman of the France field, in interview with Vernon Mortenson, June 18, 1986, Carol Stream, Illinois.

Chapter 44 (pages 779-795)
1. J. C. Gholdston, sixty-eighth annual TEAM conference, Racine, Wisconsin, 1958.
2. J. C. and Barbara Gholdston, letter to supporters, December 1955.
3. Field Survey of Spain, 1963.
4. J. C. and Barbara Gholdston, letter to supporters, April 1965.
5. Spain Orientation, draft text for the *TEAM Handbook*, February 1970.
6. Ernest Hickman, letter to supporters, February 1975.
7. Dale Vought, "An Accurate Picture of My Church," Principles and Procedures II, Winter Quarter, February 1973.
8. Dale and Anne Vought, letter to supporters, June 1974.
9. Dale Vought, Spain field chairman's report for 1979-1980.
10. *Ibid.*
11. Gary Bowman, Spain field chairman's report, 1982.
12. Gary Bowman, Spain field chairman's report, June 1984.
13. Gary Bowman, Spain field chairman's report, 1986.

Chapter 45 (pages 796-822)
1. Vernon Mortenson, "European Trip," February 15-March 3, 1963.
2. Elsbeth Baarendse, "Bids, bills, and basements: the making of a miracle," *TEAM Horizons*, November/December 1982, p. 6.
3. Richard Baarendse, Austria field chairman's report, 1974.
4. Richard Baarendse, letter to prayer supporters, February 1, 1977.
5. Stephen Stutzman, Austria field chairman's report, 1981.
6. *Ibid.*, 1987.
7. *Ibid.*, 1985.
8. *Ibid.*
9. Richard Winchell, notes on the opening of the Italy field, May 15, 1990.
10. David H. Johnson, *The Missionary Broadcaster*, November 1950, p. 16.
11. Murray Carter, Italy field chairman's report, 1983.
12. *Ibid.*

13. Jack MacDonald, "Italy Trip," report to TEAM board of directors, June 27, 1988.
14. Murray Carter, Italy field chairman's report, 1986.
15. Jack MacDonald, "Italy Trip," report to TEAM board of directors, June 27, 1988.
16. Murray Carter, Italy field chairman's report, May 1988.
17. *Ibid.*, 1989.
18. Thomas Cosmades, interview with Vernon Mortenson, January 1, 1991.
19. Estimate of believers from Richard Winchell's January 25, 1985, interview with TEAM's paid Turkish worker.
20. Karan Romaine, "Dear Daphne," *TEAM Horizons*, November/December 1982, p. 4.
21. "From a grain of sand," *WHEREVER*, Spring 1986.
22. James Romaine, "S.E. Europe (Turkey) Area Report," 1983.
23. Jack MacDonald, "Turkey Trip, August 25-31, 1987," Report to TEAM board of directors.
24. *Ibid.*
25. Thomas Cosmades, interview with Vernon Mortenson, January 1, 1991.

Chapter 46 (pages 823-837)
1. James Carmean, chairman's report to Venezuela field conference, December 27, 1989.
2. David H. Johnson, *The Missionary Broadcaster*, October 1955, p. 23.
3. James Savage, *The Missionary Broadcaster*, August 1954, p. 6.
4. *Ibid.*
5. Jack MacDonald, report on evangelism to 1962 Venezuela-Colombia field conference.
6. Charles Belch, report to 1973 Venezuela annual conference.
7. Vernon Mortenson, report to TEAM board of directors, June 8, 1965.

Chapter 47 (pages 838-855)
1. *TEAM Horizons*, May-June 1980, p. 8.
2. James A. Savage, report on seminary project to the annual field conference, January 8, 1968.
3. Gary Bowman, report to TEAM board of directors, January 11, 1990.
4. Elton Dresselhaus, chairman's report to annual field conference, 1971.
5. *Ibid.*
6. Elton Dresselhaus, *TEAM Horizons*, July-September 1975, p. 13.
7. Dan Tuggy, field chairman, response to questionnaire, July 9, 1986.
8. William Horst, chairman's report to annual field conference, 1977.
9. James Carmean, chairman's report to annual field conference, 1985.

Chapter 48 (pages 856-870)
1. Paul H. Sheetz, *The Sovereign Hand* (Wheaton, IL: The Evangelical Alliance Mission, 1971), p. 145.
2. Olav Eikland, *The Missionary Broadcaster*, August 1948, p. 12.
3. Paul Sheetz, *The Sovereign Hand*, p. 146.
4. Arthur Bakker, *The Missionary Broadcaster*, September-October 1963, p. 13.
5. *Ibid.*
6. *Ibid.*

7. Jack MacDonald, report to TEAM board of directors, March 25, 1986.

8. *Ibid.*

9. Gary Bowman, report to TEAM board of directors, January 31, 1989.

Chapter 49 (pages 871-886)

1. Earl J. Ressler, chairman's report to field conference 1980-1988.

2. Robert W. Bedard, report on Aruba radio project for 1957.

3. David H. Johnson, address at dedication of Radio Victoria PJA-6, Oranjestad, Aruba, November 2, 1958.

4. Radio Victoria dedication program, January 19, 1964.

5. Richard G. Cowser, chairman's report to the annual conference, 1966.

6. Earl J. Ressler, annual report on Bonaire ministry, 1957.

7. *Ibid.*, 1963 to 1985.

8. Richard G. Cowser, annual field chairman's report, 1982.

9. Vernon Mortenson, unpublished historical notes on TEAM fields, 1984.

10. Earl J. Ressler, annual field chairman's report, 1964.

11. *Ibid.*

12. Field chairmen's annual reports 1967-1986.

13. Earl J. Ressler, annual field chairman's report, 1963.

14. *Ibid.*, 1965.

15. Richard G. Cowser, annual field chairman's report, 1973.

Chapter 50 (pages 887-922)

1. David Crane, field chairman's report, 1967.

2. Vernon Mortenson, report of January 1-February 5, 1973, Latin America trip to TEAM board of directors, p. 9.

3. David Crane, field chairman's report for 1970, February 1, 1971.

4. David Crane, field chairman's report for 1972, January 31, 1973.

5. Guy Storm, field chairman's report for 1974.

6. Norman Niemeyer, field chairman's report for 1973, February 1, 1974.

7. Norman Niemeyer, field chairman's report for 1978.

8. Guy Storm, field chairman's report for 1975.

9. David Crane, field chairman's report for 1979, given in 1980.

10. Guy Storm, field chairman's report for 1975.

11. Norman Niemeyer, field chairman's report for 1978.

12. K. K. Bachew, "Lopinot, Trinidad," *TEAM Horizons*, March/April 1981, p. 7.

13. Norman Niemeyer, field chairman's report for 1978.

14. "112 gospel opportunities!" *TEAM Horizons*, January/ February 1982, p. 4.

15. David Crane, field chairman's report for 1979, given in 1980.

16. *Ibid.*

17. Karen Johnson, "Los Conquistadores," *TEAM Horizons*, March/April 1989, p. 3.

18. David Crane, field chairman's report for 1982, January 24, 1983.

19. Ralph Bauer, field chairman's report for 1986.

20. Dave Broucek, "Orange Juice: Benchmark of Church Growth," *TEAM Horizons*, January/February 1988, p. 15.

21. David Crane, field chairman's report for 1987, January 25-28, 1988.

22. K. K. Bachew, AEBC Chairman's Message, program guide of the AEBC/TEAM World Missions Conference, October 1988, p. 7.

23. Vernon Mortenson to David H. Johnson, October 20, 1960.
24. Jack MacDonald, report to TEAM board of directors, Peru and Colombia Trip, November 18-December 1, 1984. MacDonald also reported that in 1984 there were forty-three AM stations in Lima, with Radio del Pacifico ranking eighteenth in listenership. Of the twenty-five FM stations, Radio del Pacifico ranked fifteenth in listenership. The station was now operated by Peruvian Christians, having been turned over to a national board of directors in 1974.
25. Charles Cousens, "A Tale of Two Churches," *TEAM Horizons,* March/April 1981, p. 6.
26. Charles Cousens, Peru church planting report, January 1990.
27. *Ibid.*
28. Jim Kuehl, Peru field chairman's report, January 1990.
29. Gary Bowman, "Living in the Shadows of Violence," *TEAM Horizons,* January/February 1990, p. 11.
30. Jim Kuehl, Peru field chairman's report, January 1990.
31. Robert Spaulding, "Ministry in a Melting Pot," *TEAM Horizons,* March/April 1983, p. 6.
32. Robert Spaulding, Brazil field chairman's report, 1984.
33. Michael Pocock, "Report on Peru-Brazil Trip, February 6-19, 1984.
34. Don Congo, Brazil field chairman's report for 1988.
35. Michael Pocock, "Status of the Baja California Field," memo to the board of directors, October 12, 1984.
36. *Ibid.*
37. Jack MacDonald, quoted in "Mexico: Unlimited Potential," *TEAM Horizons,* July/August 1987, p. 11.
38. Gary Bowman, report to TEAM board of directors, March 18, 1991.

A New Decade, A New Century (pages 923-929)
1. Richard Winchell, letter to TEAM supporters, December 1989.
2. *Ibid.*
3. Richard Winchell, general director's annual report for the year ended March 31, 1990.
4. Richard Winchell, general director's spring letter, February 25, 1990.
5. Richard Winchell, letter to "Where Most Needed Fund" supporters, May 7, 1989.
6. Richard Winchell, general director's annual report for the year ended March 31, 1990.
7. Quoted by Richard Winchell in "Events of 1989, 1990 and 1991," March 18, 1991.
8. Richard Winchell, general director's annual report for the year ended March 31, 1990.
9. Richard Winchell, "Our Unchanging Task in a Changing World," general director's report to the 102nd annual meeting, May 1992.
10. *Ibid.*
11. Richard Winchell, "Monthly TEAM Memo," October 1992.

INDEX

American Council of Christian
Churches, 229-32
American Mission to the Greeks,
493-94, 500, 503
AMG, 493-94, 500, 503
*Amis de l'Alliance des Eglises
Evangéliques Indépendantes, Les.*
See Friends of the AEEI
Amis tribe, 303, 384-87
Anápolis, Brazil, 918
Anderson, Bruce, 436
Anderson, C. J., 50
Anderson, Clara, 61-62, 165
Anderson, Dale, 775
Anderson, Elof, 857-59, 861, 869
Anderson, Frank W., 92-93
Anderson, Gustav, 93
Anderson, Hilda, 61-62, 165
Anderson, Isabel, 857, 861
Anderson, Jody, 436
Anderson, Joel, 104, 144-47, photo
Anderson, Lloyd, 259
Anderson, Lynn, 865
Anderson, Mark, 776
Anderson, Mrs. Joel, 104
Anderson, Paul W., 305
Anderson, Sarah, 776
Anderson, Scott, 611
Anderson, Sherrilyn, 775
Anderson, Tim, 865
Anderson, Vernon, 843
Anderson, Wilford, 842
Anderson, Wilma Gardziella, 656-
57, photo
Ando, Pastor, 366-67, photo
André, A. E., 43
Anggi Lakes, Irian Jaya, 450, 454-
55, 469, 477-79, 483
Angola, 40
Angulo, Buenaventura, 176
Antersijn, Wilfred, 882
Anthony, Adria, 919
Anthony, Librek, 505
Anthony, Rob, 722
Anthony, Vicki, 722
Aomori, Japan, 351
Apel, Herbert, 308, 799, 821
Apel, Lorelei, 308, 799, 821

Arabian Hospital, 588
Arabian Mission of the Reformed
Church in America, 589
Arabic Literature Mission, 599
Arab World Ministries, 612
Aranjuez, Spain, 783
Arbresle, France, l', 776
Archena, Spain, 779-80
Archer, Barbara, 797
Archer, Dawn, 868
Archer, Manda, 342
Archer, Robert, 868
Archer, V. Sam, 272, 301, 306, 342
Arenas, Ismael, 855
Arevalo, Elain, 864
Argentina, 74
Armenia, 29, 71-73
Arpajon, France, 775
Aruba, 175, 186-89, 871-86. *See
also* Netherlands Antilles
ASIGEO, 178, 844, 847-51
Asmat tribe, 255, 303, 456-58, 462-
63, 481-83
*Asociacion de Iglesias Evangelicas
de Oriente,* 178, 844, 847-51
Association of Bible Churches of the
Philippines, Inc., 435-36
Association of churches. *See*
Church fellowship organizations
Association of Evangelical Bible
Churches of Trinidad and Tobago,
892-94, 897-904
Association of Evangelical
Churches, Colombia, 858-60, 864,
868-70
Association of Evangelical Churches
in Eastern Venezuela (ASIGEO),
844, 847-51
Atami, Japan, 144
Atger, Marc, 749, 751-53
Atibaia, Brazil, 913
Atkinson, Dr., 72
Attock City (Campbellpur), Paki-
stan, 566-67, 571, 573, 577
Audio-visual ministry, 265, 924
—Austria, 797-98, 804
—France, 747, 775
—Italy, 812

958

—Japan, 347
—Korea, 426
—Pakistan, 579
—Peru, 906
—Spain, 784, 789, 794
—Trinidad and Tobago, 900
—Venezuela, 827, 833
Austin, Lillian Nelson, 649
Australia, 65, 260-61, 272, 307
Australian Baptist Mission, 447, 460
Austria, 251, 302, 763, 796-806,
    808, 926
Auyu tribe, 458, 483
AVANCES, 285, 846-47
Awad, George, 598
Awju tribe, 255
Ayam, 259, 456-57, 480-82, 484
Ayoub tribe, 483
Ayres, Patricia, 550

Baarendse, Elsbeth, 797, 801-03, 806
Baarendse, Richard, 310, 797, 799-
    803, 806
Bach, Anna, 75-76, 96, 111, 116, 839
Bach, Elizabeth, 116
Bach, T. J. (Thomas John), photo
—Venezuela missionary, 74-76, 81,
    96-97, 111-14, 173, 833, 839
—general director: 96-97, 116-125,
    144, 196-205, 936; overseas vis-
    its, 120-21, 132, 150, 156-57,
    170, 175, 180-81; administrative
    style, 121-24, 204-05, 233, 247,
    270, 292
—in retirement, 94, 215-16, 243,
    253, 340
—foreign missions principles: doc-
    trinal faithfulness and syncretism,
    123-24, 196-97; on the church,
    208, 210-11; spiritual guidance,
    121-23, 247; "whatever you
    do...", 121, 124
—heritage: countries entered, 186;
    wider recognition for TEAM, 123-
    24, 232; recruitment and advance,
    207, 256; his ministry, 253
Bachaquero, Venezuela, 826

Bach Christian Hospital, 560-63,
    574, 578, 580
Bacheller, Bill, 918
Bacheller, Kathy, 918
Bachew, Ashoke, 898
Bachew, K. K., 895-96, 898-900, 904
Bachew, Stephanie, 898
Back to the Bible Broadcast, 541-42,
    666, 810, 877
Badia Tedalda, Italy, 813
Baghdad, Iraq, 587
Bah, Michael, 612
Bah, Muriel, 612
Bahadur, Tashi, 538
Bahrain, 603
Bainar, Verité, 689
Baja California, Mexico, 918-22
Bakasu, Pit, 486
Bakker, Arthur, 857-58, 862-64, 868
Bakker, Mary Louise, 857, 862-64,
    868
Baksa Duar, India, 104-05
Balman, Nolan F., 254, 273, 292,
    620
Balman, Ruth, 254
Baltistan, India, 68-69, 71
Bang, Severin and Mrs., 107, 162
Bantu Evangelical Church, 630-31
Bapiro, Stephen, 682
Baptist Mid-Missions, 701, 703, 705
Baransano, Akwila, 491
Bararkot, Pakistan, 563
Barghout, Farideh, 601, 612
Barghout, Salem, 601, 612
Barinas, Venezuela, 184, 826, 839
Barinitas, Venezuela, 179
Barnes, David, 737-38, 742
Barnes, Geraldine, 737-38, 742
Barquisimeto, Venezuela, 824
Barrie, Doreen, 696, 714
Barthold, Mary, 358, 360-63
Barthold, Stan, 358, 360-63
Barville, Edith, 188
Barville, George C., 188
Baskin, Bert, 703
Basongan, Taiwan, 385-86
Bates, Brian R., 368
Batlle, Daniel, 792

Batlle, Susan, 792
Batticaloa, Sri Lanka, 543
Bauer, Don, 805
Bauer, Lila, 891, 894, 896-97
Bauer, Marie, 805
Bauer, Ralph, 891, 894, 896-97, 900-01
Baumann, Jacques, 700
Beach, Kenneth, 756, 758, 762
Beach, Lois, 756, 762
Beach, Mary (Inky), 429, 716
Beach, Ross, 428-29, 716-18, 721
Bealoum, Joel, 699
Bebalem, Chad, 689, 701-02, 707, 714, 717-18
Bebalem Bible School, 689, 718
Bebalem Hospital, 701-02, 717-18
Beck, Janet, 389
Beck, Marleen, 864
Beck, Morris, 389, 396, 400, 402-03, 405
Beckman, Richard and Mrs., 100-01
Beckman, Ruth, 101
Beckman, Selma, 100-01
Beckman, Thyra, 100-01. *See also* Bergstrom, Thyra.
Beckon, Fronsie, 136
Beckon, Mrs. Oscar, 135-36
Beckon, Oscar, 130, 135-36, 143, 215, 312-13, 331, 388, 441, photo
Beckwith, Claire, 410
Bedard, Juanita, 874-75, 905
Bedard, Robert, 874-75, 905
Beirut, Lebanon, 588
Beja, Portugal, 723-24, 726-28, 732-33
Beladja, Chad, 688, 693, 697, 708
Belch, Charles, 831
Belgium, 64
Bell, Ralph, 334
Belledonne Camp Grounds, 768-69, 775-76
Benfica, Portugal, 729-30, 733-34
Bengal, India, 68, 70
Bennett, Betty, 625
Bennett, John E., 273, 296, 306, 562, 625
Bennett, Shirley Bradford, 273

Benoni, South Africa, 637
Benton, Lloyd, 797
Benton, Val, 797
Benton Street Baptist Church, Kitchener, 281
Berachah Hospital, 588
Berar-Khandesh Christian Conference, 230-31
Béré, Chad, 713, 716, 718
Berean Bible School, India, 286, 518, 522
Berenag, India, 527
Bergstrom, F. O. and Mrs. 104
Bergstrom, Hulda, 101
Bergstrom, Julius W., photo
—China missionary, 95, 98, 101, 132, 134, 138, 142, 314, 441
—radio ministry, 239, 319-20, 380, 417-18, 430
Bergstrom, Mrs. Solomon, 99, 101, 135
Bergstrom, Oscar, 101
Bergstrom, Solomon, 99, 101, 128-29
Bergstrom, Thyra Beckman, 100-01, 134, 320, 380, 417-18, 441
Berita Hidup, 493, 500
Bernklau, Angeline, 215, 317-18, 322-25, 373, 378, photo
Berthelsen, Einer, 154, 511, 513, 515-17
Bethany Christian School, 392-93
Bethel, Southern Africa 73, 162-63
Bethel Band of Shanghai, 131
Bethel Bible Fellowship, Shivpuri, 538
Bethlehem Church, Oslo, Norway, 85
Bezanson, Nelson I., 299-300, 307, 703, 706
Bezanson, Uda, 300
Béziers, France, 738-39, 744-45, 747, 751-52, 758, 780
Bhil tribespeople, 68-70, 105-06, 151-53, 209, 303, 508
Bhot, India, 261, 525
Bhutan, 68-70, 104
Biak, Indonesia, 459, 488-89, 497

Bible Christian Fellowship of Indonesia, 493-95, 500
Bible Christian Union, 809
Bible Club Movement, 813
Bible correspondence courses. *See* Correspondence courses
Bible House Church, 821
Bible Institute of South Africa, 636
Bible institutes. *See* Schools, institutes, and seminaries
Bible schools. *See* Schools, institutes, and seminaries
Bible translation. *See* Translation
Bindura, Zimbabwe, 194, 673-74
Binion, Eric, 644
Binion, Susan, 644
Bintuni, Irian Jaya, 479
Bird's Head, Irian Jaya, 447-55, 457, 459, 461, 464-81, 488-92, 497
Black Forest Academy, 805
Blair, Marguerite, 649-50
Blair, Orla, 649-50, 660, 683
Blanchard, Tom, 772
Blocher, Jacques, 743, 745, 748, 760
Block, Abram J., 369
Blomberg, Earl, 842
Bobby, Albert, 723
Bobby, Mary Lee, 723
Boberg, Folke, 111, 165
Bock, Henry, 453-55, 460, 477
Bock, Marjorie, 453-55, 477
Bodeen, Charles E., 198, 859, photo
Boehr, Barbara, 399-400
Boehr, Ernest, 395, 399-400
Boekhandel Evangélico, 873
Boer War, 59, 64, 73, 108
Bogdan, Elena, 310
Bogota, Colombia, 867-68, 870
Boice, Dawn, 908
Boice, John, 908
Bol, Chad, 722
Bologna, Italy, 813-14
Bombay, India, 512, 514-17
Bombay Representative Council of Churches, 230
Bonaire, Netherlands Antilles, 186, 873-74, 878-86

Bonnell, Cornelia, 377
Bookstores, 256. *See also* Printing and publishing
—Chad, 715
—Colombia, 865
—Irian Jaya, 495
—Japan, 341
—Netherlands Antilles/Aruba, 873
—Pakistan, 570-71, 574
—Portugal, 724-25, 727-29
—South Africa, 636-38
—Spain, 791
—Trinidad and Tobago, 891
—United Arab Emirates, 596-97
—Venezuela, 826, 839-40, 849-51
—Zimbabwe, 674
Bophuthatswana, 643-44
Bordreuil, Daniel, 767
Bostrom, Gustav, 179-80
Bostrom, Tillie, 179-80
Boughter, Luke, 723, 725-26, 729
Boughter, Ruth, 723, 725-26, 729
Bowdish, Albert, 262, 529, 538, 549
Bowdish, Pearl, 529, 538
Bowman, C. V., 89
Bowman, Gary
—Spain missionary, 730, 784, 788-94
—head office administrator, 306, 732-35, 843, 868, 912, 922
Bowman, Sherryl, 784, 788
Boxer Uprising, 59-63, 66-67
Bradford, Shirley, 273
Bradshaw, Iris, 873
Brake Bible Institute, Germany, 307
Brannen, Phyllis, 347
Brannen, Ted, 347
Brazil, 74-75, 299, 302, 368-70, 866, 913-18, 926
Brehm, Roy H., 103, 126, 129, 199
Brethren Assembly, 780-81
Bretigny, France, 775
Brett, Pat, 637-38
Brett, Ronald A., 284, 289, 292, 298, 306, 637-38
Breyne, Anne Marie, 770
Breyne, Michel, 770
Briercrest, Saskatchewan, 202-03

Brion, Mauro, 435
Brock, Nancy, 594, 613
Bromley, Elizabeth, 620, 640
Brook, David, 261, 307, 360
Brook, Dorothy, 360
Brostrom, A., 77
Brotherton, Jack, 688, 692, 697, 707-08, 712, 714, 718
Brotherton, Madge, 688
Broucek, David, 894, 902-03
Broucek, Gwen, 894, 902
Brougham, Doris, 372, 375-77
Brown, David L., 296, 306
Brown, Donna, 296
Brown, Dorothy, 889
Brown, Fran, 570
Brown, Isaac, 889
Brown, Raney, 814
Browning, Clara Jean, 358, 360
Browning, Neal, 358, 360
Brubaker, Jim, 797-98, 801
Brubaker, Rosemary, 797-98, 801
Bruck, Donald, 369
Brumley, Glenda, 436
Brunoy, France, 759, 775
Bruton, Lois, 673
Bruton, Warren, 673
Bucaramanga, Colombia, 867-68
Buck, Len, 636
Buck, Nina, 636
Buenas Nuevas bookstore, 849, 851
Buhler, Leslie, 518
Bulgaria, 64, 817
Bultema, Jim, 822
Bultema, Renata, 822
Bulunga, Swaziland, 51, 59
Bumhira, Edgar, 659
Buraimi Oasis, United Arab Emirates, 589-615
Burma, 67, 69-70
Burton, Betty, 571
Burton, Charles, 571
Buss, Siegfried, 349
Butts, Joe, 857-58, 860-61
Butts, Verda, 857
Byrmo, Ann-Britt, 656

C & MA. *See* Christian and Missionary Alliance
Cabagan, Philippines, 437
Cabeen, Don, 792
Cabeen, Paula, 792
Cabimas, Venezuela, 826
CADAL, 866
Calcutta, India, 39
Calgary, Alberta, 300-01
Callaway, Merrel and Mrs., 587
Calvary Bookroom, 637
Cameron, Bill, 694-95, 701
Cameron, Jean, 694
Campbell, Holly, 612
Campbell, William, 612
Campbellpur, Pakistan, 566-67, 571, 573
Camp Caravela, 726-27
Camping and conferences
—Aruba, 881
—Austria, 798, 804
—Brazil, 915-18
—France, 738, 740, 746, 749-53, 759, 763-65, 768-71
—India, 513, 517, 529, 536, 538-39
—Italy, 813-14
—Japan, 256, 334, 346-47, 369
—Java, 504-05
—Korea, 426-27
—Pakistan, 571, 574
—Portugal, 726-27
—Spain, 794-95
—Taiwan, 394-95
—Trinidad and Tobago, 888-89, 892, 897-98
—Venezuela, 833, 850
Camp Maranatha
—Italy, 813-14
—Venezuela, 850
Camp Mubarak, 571, 574
Camp Nova Vida, 915-18
Camp Praz de Lys, 750, 752, 763-65, 768
Campus Crusade for Christ, 758
Campus Fellowship, 394
Camp Washington, 881
Canada, 201-03, 265-66, 272, 281, 299-301, 306-07

—JEM merger, 368-70
—SUMNA merger, 268-69
Cana de Azucar, Venezuela, 824
Canadian International Development
    Administration, 484, 702
Candelaria, Señora, 859
Candidate school, 223-24, 283-84,
    297, 367
Canillejas Evangelical Bible
    Church, 783, 785-86, 788, 793-94
Canode, Charmaine, 898, 920
Canode, Freddie, 898, 920
Canton, China, 315, 440
Caparo Village, Trinidad, 897
Cape Evangelical Bible Institute,
    635-36
Cape Town, South Africa, 629, 635-
    36
Caracas, Venezuela, 852-53
Carache, Venezuela, 826
Caribbean Broadcasting Company,
    251, 268, 888
Carling, David, 699
Carlson, C. E., 104, 146-47, 327-29,
    332, photo
Carlson, Clara, 840-42
Carlson, Mrs. C. E., 104
Carlson, Norma, 620
Carlson, Wesley, 620, photo
Carmean, Annette, 832
Carmean, James, 824, 827, 832, 850-
    51
Carmona, Spain, 792
Carol Stream, Illinois, 258-59
Caroni, Trinidad, 889, 892, 897
Carpenter, Beulah, 703
Carter, Annette, 810
Carter, Florence, 302, 531-37, 808-
    14
Carter, Gordon, 701
Carter, Laura, 533
Carter, Murray, 302, 531-37, 808-15
Cascade, Trinidad, 889, 892
Castrocaro Terme, Italy, 809
Caterson, Joe Jr., 894, 898-900
Catron, Jan Hendrickson, 949
Catteau, Anne, 877
Catteau, Robert, 877

Cental Church, Brazil, 916
Centro Cultural Filantrópico, 922
Cercal, Portugal, 724, 732
Ceylon. *See* Sri Lanka
Chad, Republic of, 269, 303, 685-
    722, 763
Chad Christian Cooperative, 715-18
Chadereka, Evangelist, 666
Chaguanas, Trinidad, 901
Chalisgaon, India, 511-13
Chamrousse, France, 768, 775-76
Chandomba, Fanuel, 659
Chang, Esther, 377
Changhwa, Taiwan, 373
Changwu, China, 132
Chao Ho, Mongolia, 171-72, 323
Chapman, Barbara, 427, 431
Chapman, Grace, 872-73
Chapman, Wilbur, 872-73
Chapman, Zerne, 528
Chase, Dick, 422, 434
Chase, Karen, 434
Chashaya, Hamad, 682
Chefoo school for missionary chil-
    dren, 136
Chekiang province, China, 46, 49
Chen, Elder, 400
Cheng, Jonathan, 287, 377-79, 383,
    899
Cheng, Margaret, 287, 379, 899
Chengtu, China, 314-15
Chenyuan, China, 143
Chiang, Hannah, 325
Chiang, Joseph, 325, 383
Chiba, Japan, 104, 145, 329, 346
Chicago, Illinois, 64, 117, 426
Chickland, Trinidad, 902
Ch'ih Shouen, 383, 400, photo
Child Evangelism Fellowship, 882
Childs, Nan, 877
Childs, Robert, 877
Chile, 74, 905
Chilly-Mazarin, France, 757, 762
China. *See also* Mongolia
—Romanization of names, 16-17
—early TEAM work, 25-27, 39-40,
    45-50, 59-63, 65-67
—1905-1946 work, 98-103, 119,

Community movements, 464-66, 477, 480
Conaway, John, 921
Conaway, Miriam, 921
Conference ministry. *See* Camping and conferences
Congdon, Audrey, 307
Congdon, Dalmain, 307, 620
Congo, Don, 916-17
Congo, Dorothy, 916
Congreso Aliancista de América Latina, 866
Congress on the Church's World-wide Mission, 264
Conner, Craig, 814
Conner, Mary, 814
Connor, Carroll, 898, 900
Conrad, Earl, 285-86, 303, 513, 515-17, 522
Conrad, Jean, 513, 515
Conservative Baptist Foreign Mission Society, 513
Constitution of TEAM, 57-58, 87-88, 91, 198-99, 244-47, 251, 272
Convención, Colombia, 183
Cooch Behar, India, 68
Cook, Robert, photo
Cooper, Margaret, 154
Cooper, Robert, 154
Coots, David, 849-50, 921
Coots, Joan, 849-50, 921
Córdoba, Spain, 792
Coria del Rió, Spain, 789-90, 792-95
Cornelson, Barbara, 413
Cornelson, Jim, 412-13, 416, 424-25
Coro, Venezuela, 824
Coronation mine, South Africa, 628
Correspondence courses, 249, 256
—India, 240, 255, 511-12, 514-15, 517, 522-23, 528, 530, 532, 538-39, 541, 570
—Japan, 341
—Pakistan, 255, 570, 574
—South Africa, 251
—Spain, 783
—Sri Lanka, 541-42, 544
—Taiwan, 375-76, 378-79, 382, 401
—Trinidad and Tobago, 891, 897, 900

—Venezuela, 833, 851
—Zimbabwe, 674, 676
Cosmades, Lila, 816-18, 820-22
Cosmades, Thomas, 815-22
Cousens, Barbara, 907-11
Cousens, Charles, 907-12
Coutinho, Elizabeth, 915
Coutinho, Rubens, 915
Couture, James, 305
Couture, Jean, 154, 512-13
Couture, Robert, 154, 283, 512-13
Cowser, Betty, 872-73, 879-81
Cowser, Richard, 872, 877, 879-82
Cox, Eugene, 759, 770
Cox, Lois, 625
Cox, Priscilla, 759, 770
Cox, Ralph, 348, 358-59
Cox, Stella, 358-59
Crane, David, 442, 888-90, 892, 894, 896-98, 900, 903
Crane, Elaine, 442, 888-89, 892, 903
Créteil, France, 758-59, 775
Crosnes, France, 756
Cross-cultural evangelistic teams, 286-87, 379, 492, 533, 899
Cuba, Portugal, 723
Cúcuta, Colombia, 173-75, 183, 828, 856, 858, 862-63, 865, 867
Culter, Mabel, 410, 413, 588
Cumbica, Brazil, 915
Curaçao, Netherlands Antilles, 76, 175, 186-89, 871-86
Cutherell, Caleb, 570
Cutherell, Esther, 948
Cutherell, Loretta, 570
Cutherell, Luke, 948
Czechoslovakia, 310-11, 927

Dahlgren, O. A. and Mrs., 68-70, 105
Daktoho, Mr., 166
Dale, Dan, 358
Dale, Joan, 358
Dalke, Arthur, 202
Dalke, Helen, 202
Dalton, Arlene, 584
Dalton, Bill, 573, 577
Dalton, Mark, 948

Dalton, Matthew, 948
Dandeldhura, Nepal, 538, 548-50
Danielson, Mary Maluske, 190, 192-95, 646, 648-49, 660
Danielson, Muriel, 194-95
Danielson, P. L. and Mrs., 110
Danielson, Rudolph, 190, 192-94, 646, 648, 657
Daskawie, M. A. Q., 575
Davenport, Harold, 587
Davis, Agnes, 261, 289, 555-56, 559-60
Davis, Carl
—Pakistan missionary, 555-57, 559-60, 575
—home office administrator, 261, 272-73, 278, 289, 501, 576
Davis, Charles, 853, 948
Davis, David, 306, 309-11, 570, 573-74, 577, 584, 948
Davis, Mary, 570
Dawson, Emma Homme, 52, 107, 162, photo
Dawson, William, 52, 107, 162, 627, photo
Dayrit, Arseno, 436
Dayrit, Ester, 436
Day schools. *See* Schools, institutes, and seminaries
DEA, 845, 849
Dee, George, 673
Dee, Pat, 673
DeHart, Don, 570, 580
DeHart, Garnett, 570, 580
de la Cruz Bolívar, José, 184, 856
Delhi, India, 514, 530-38
Delhi Bible Fellowship, 530-38, 609
Denmark, 34
Dennis, Frank, 387-89, 945
Dennis, Sally, 387-89, 945
Deodars, India, 529, 538
Deodars Spiritual Life Center, 529, 538-39
Descheemaecker, Marc, 751, 753, 759-60, 767, 769-72
DeVries, Jeanette, 317-18
DeWhitt, Dale, 440-42
DeWhitt, Lauri, 440-42

Deyneka, Peter, 417
Deyneka, Peter Jr., 417-18
Dharangaon, India, 151, 513
Dharchula, India, 525-28, 538
Dick, Daniel, 283
Dickinson, Arthur, 401, 439, 441
Dickinson, Leona, 441
Dieterle, Gladys, 377
Digana International Village hospital, 546
Dignan, Bob, 412, 431
Dignan, Joyce, 431
Dinsley church, Trinidad, 894, 899-900
Directiva Evangelica Asociada, 845, 849
Dirks, Bonnie, 389
Dmytro, Howard, 805
Dmytro, Nancy, 805
Döbling Church, Vienna, 806
Doerksen, Alvin, 369, 917
Doerksen, Mary, 369
Doi, Pastor, 144, photo
Domei *(Nihon/Nippon Domei Kirisuto Kyokai)*
—church association, 147-48, 220, 328, 333-34, 338-39, 343-47, 350, 354-55, 365-66, 370
—sending missionaries, 367-68, 370, 398, 501-02
Donaldson, Gregg, 612
Donaldson, Kathy, 612
Doon Medical Project, 538-39
Door of Hope Children's Refuge, 377-78, 390-92
Door of Hope Mission, 268, 377-78
Dorsey, John, 532
Dos Hermanas, Spain, 789-90, 792
Dougherty, Ruth, 484, 486
Douliére, Richard, 745
Dover, Claude and Mrs., 104
Dragash, Anna, 803, 806
Dragash, Frank, 803, 806
Drake, David, 668-70
Drake, Karen Holritz, 656
Dresselhaus, Elton, 289, 827, 843, 848-49
Dresselhaus, Joyce, 289

El Salvador Church, Maracaibo,
114, 173, 178, 182, 823, 835-36,
840-41
EMEK, 700
Emerenciana, Felicia, 882
Emmanuel Hospital Association, 519
Empangeni, South Africa, 637
Endigeri, Emmanuel, 287, 899
English lessons
—China, 141
—India, 529
—Japan, 348-49, 359, 361
—Pakistan, 584
—Taiwan, 400
Englund, Anna, 134, 136-37, 382,
photo
Englund, William, 103, 127, 130,
134, 136-38, 200, 344, 382, 441,
photo
Englund, Winifred, 136
Engstrom, Mary, 40
Entering new countries, 186, 301-
02, 807-08
—Austria, 796-97
—Brazil, 299, 913
—Chad, 268-69
—C.I.S., 927
—Colombia, 113, 173-76
—Czechoslovakia, 310-11
—Eastern Europe, 310-11
—France, 736-37
—Germany, 310-11
—Hong Kong, 302, 439-42
—Irian Jaya, 445-48
—Italy, 302, 806-08
—Japan, 26
—Java, Indonesia, 499-500
—Korea, 409-10
—Macao, 442-43
—Mexico, 302, 918-21
—Mozambique, 158, 189-90, 302,
646-48
—Near East, 586-91
—Nepal, 261-62, 546-49
—Netherlands Antilles, 186-87
—Oman, 614-15
—Pakistan, 195
—Peru, 904-05

—Philippines, 302, 433-35
—Portugal, 189-92
—Romania, 310-11
—South Africa, 39-40
—Spain, 779-80
—Sri Lanka, 236, 537, 540-41
—Taiwan, 372-73
—Tibetan Frontier, 195
—Turkey, 816
—United Arab Emirates, 586-91
—Uruguay, 904-05
—Venezuela, 74-76
—Zimbabwe, 192-93
Enyatini, Swaziland, 108
Epinay-sous-Sénart, France, 760,
762, 768, 775
Epp, Theodore H., 541
Erickson, Eleanore, 625
Erickson, Harold W., 243
Erickson, Iver, 304
Erickson, James, 305
Erickson, Leonard, 300, 305
Ericson, Evelyn, 757
Erikson, Walter J., 445-53
Erikson-Tritt Bible and Theological
Seminary, 459, 489-92
Erikson-Tritt Bible Institute, 459,
489-92
Erikson-Tritt Theological College,
459, 489-92
Eriksson, Joel, 167
Erinchindorji, 324-25, photo
Esau, David, 784
Esau, Sharon, 784
Esinceni, Swaziland, 159
Espinoza, Aarón, 884
Esteban, Julio, 864
Etobicoke, Ontario, 301
Europe. See Austria, Bulgaria,
Czechoslovakia, Eastern Europe
field, France, Germany, Italy, Por-
tugal, Spain, Romania, Yugoslavia
European Bible Institute, 737-38,
742
Evangelical Alliance Christian
Churches Trust, The, 522-23
Evangelical Alliance Church, India,
518

Faenza, Italy, 811-14
Faith Academy, 434, 436
Fakhoury, 'Issa, 600
Famine relief
—Africa, 276
—Chad, 717-18
—China, 103, 129-30, 141, 208
—India, 276
—Zimbabwe, 670
Far East Broadcasting Association, 575
Far East Broadcasting Company, 319, 335, 349, 375, 380, 419, 422-23, 434, 542, 575
Far Eastern Gospel Crusade, 334
FEBC. See Far East Broadcasting Company
Federation of Independent Evangelical Churches of Spain (FIEIDE), 786, 791-93
Feenstra, Jack, 389
Feenstra, Virginia, 389
Feldmann, Ruth, 948
Fellowship of churches. See Church fellowship organizations
Fellowship of Churches, Netherlands Antilles/Aruba, 882-86
Fenglin, Taiwan, 373
Ferrant, Harry, 687
Ferreira-do-Alentejo, Portugal, 723
Fey, Virginia, 386-87
Fiak, Sahu, 487-88
Fiak, Titus, 486
Fiak, Yakub, 486-88
FIEIDE, 786, 791-93
Field conference, annual, 42, 48, 115, 233, 245-46, 264, 351
Field council, 42, 48, 115, 233, 245-46, 264, 351, 827
Filat, Jerry, 436
Filat, Marybeth, 436
Filipino Christian Fellowship, Abu Dhabi, 601-03
Fillmore, Patricia, 477-78
Films. See Audio-visual ministry
Financial support of missionaries, 34-35, 37, 55, 83, 118, 278, 287-88

Financial support of national workers and ministries
—Austria, 798, 800-01
—Chad, 688, 691-92
—China, 138, 210
—Colombia, 183, 210, 863-64, 868-70
—France, 743, 745-46, 751, 754, 756-57, 768-71
—India, 513-14, 520-23
—Irian Jaya, 493-96
—Japan, 210, 357
—Korea, 414-16
—Portugal, 727-28
—South Africa/Swaziland, 109-10, 158, 160, 210, 633-34, 636
—Spain, 784-86, 788, 793-94
—Taiwan, 373-75, 391-92, 395-97, 401-02, 405
—Trinidad and Tobago, 892, 896-98, 901-04
—United Arab Emirates, 607
—Venezuela, 176, 210, 826, 832-35, 842-44, 850-51, 854-55
—Zimbabwe, 657-58, 675-84
Finland, 34, 58, 62, 64, 69-70
Finnish Alliance Mission, 68, 70, 104-05, 931
Finnish Free Church, 105
Fisch, Edwin, 135-36, 317-18, 349-50
Fisch, Jurg, 715
Fisch, Laura, 136, 317-18, 349-50
Fish, Carol, 500
Fish, Larry, 500
Five Rivers, Trinidad, 889-90, 895-97, 899-900
Five Rivers-Khandahar Evangelical Bible Church, 890, 895-97, 899-900
Flambeaux, 703
Fleming, R. L., 548
Flickner, Brian, 431
Flickner, Carl, 538-39
Flickner, Joyce, 431
Flickner, Marie, 538
Flippin, Neil, 424
Florence Christian Academy, 619, 627

Gamede, John, 109, 158-60, 630, photo
Gandre, Alicia, 877
Gandre, Wayne, 877
García, Francisco, 176
Gardziella, Wilma, 656-57, photo
Garfield, Bertha, 410
Garfield, William, 409-10, 423-24
Garrett, Irene, 828, 857, 862, 868
Garvin, Diane, 894-95
Garvin, John, 894-95
Gateway-Harare, Zimbabwe, 683
Geffe, Bernard and Mrs., 701
Geiger, Wallace, 302, 744, 754, 757, 764, 766-67, 769-70, 772, 774, 776-77, 807
Geiger, Wanda, 744
Genden, 324
Genet, Harry, 273, 284, 289, 599
Genet, Carol, 599
George, Alfredo, 890
Georgia, Marlene, 581
Georgia, Stewart, 581, 660, 663-64
Gereja Kristan Alkitab, Indonesia (GKAI), 493-95
Gereja Persekutuan Kristan Alkitab, Indonesia (GPKAI), 493-95
Gerig, Jeanie, 434
German China Alliance Mission, 35, 59-60
German Missionary Fellowship, 308, 671
Germany
—and Fredrik Franson, 25, 28, 34, 58-59
—TEAM ministry, 307-08, 310-11, 796, 805, 816-17, 926
Gholdston, Barbara, 723-24, 780-83, 788
Gholdston, J. C., 723-24, 780-83, 788
Ghoom, India, 43, 68-70
Gieser, P. Kenneth, 305
Gifu, Japan, 356
Gillen, C. W., 54
Gillett, Clarence, 484, 487
Gillett, Twila, 484
Girgis, Safwat, 600

GKAI, 493-95
Godbold, Steve, 722
Godbold, Tosha, 722, 945
Goeku, Lydia, 367, 398, 402
Goertz, Alice, 723-24
Goertz, Herbert, 723-24
Goertzen, Henry, 891, 894
Goertzen, Marion, 891, 894
Gómez, Vicente, 859
Goppert, Chris, 683
Goppert, Joyce Everswick, 683, 949
Gorton, Dorothy, 471
Gospel for the Millions, 341, 343
Goulei tribe, 689, 692-95, 705-06, 715
GPKAI, 493-95
Grace Chapel, Pasea, 902
Grace Family Septet, 287, 379
Grauer, O. C., 85, 94, 201, 934, 936, photo
Greater Europe Mission, 742, 776, 798
Greece, 64, 803, 806, 816
Green, Inez, 377
Green, Lorraine, 719
Green, Tony, 882, 886
Greene, David, 620, 644, photo
Greenway, Dennis, 538
Greenway, Lillian, 538
Gregersen, Bruce, 810, 812, 814
Gregg, Herb, 732-33
Gregg, Linda, 732-33
Gregory, Don, 458, 463
Gregory, Joan, 458
Grewell, Margaret Hartt, 723, 727, 731
Grewell, Russell, 727, 731
Griffiths, Charlotte, 453, 457, 468-71
Griffiths, Richard, 453, 457, 465-72, 476
Grigorenko, Don, 550
Grigorenko, Margaret, 550
Grove, Carolyn, 913, 918
Grove, Leslie, 913-14, 918
Guadalajara, Spain, 783
Guasdualito, Venezuela, 826
Gudeman, Judy, 657, photo
Gudeman, Mary Ellen, 360

Gullander, Augusta Hultberg, 51
Gullander, Paul, 51
Gulzaman, Ambrose, 576
Gulzaman, Crystal, 576
Guna, India, 510-11, 538
Gundersen, Carl A., 117, 198, 202, 239-40, 244, 253-54, 264, 624, 655, 874, photo
Gundersen, Mrs. Carl A., 253, 624
Gundersen-Horness Hospital, 655-57, 663. *See also* Karanda Hospital
Gunzel, Carol, 323, 389
Gunzel, David, 323
Gunzel, James, 322-23
Gunzel, Joy, 322-23
Gunzel, Margaret Leir, 170-72, 202, 214, 265, 322-25, photo
Gunzel, Stuart J., 164-72, 202, 214, 217, 265, 272, 322-25, photo
Gustafson, Esther Nelson, 135, 240, 313
Gustafson, Fred, 69
Gustafson, Goldye, 273
Gustafson, Reuben, 130, 132, 135, 137-38, 143, 215, 312-13, 331, photo
Gutierrez, Ciro, 841
Gwalior, India, 509-11, 513, 537

Haanes, Christian, 623-24
Haanes, Esther Mosvold, 623-24
Habecker, Lydia Goeku, 367, 398, 402
Haberkamp, Monica, 722
Haberkamp, Rick, 722
Haddad, Ameal, 601
Haddad, Shafiiq, 600
Hagberg, Levi and Mrs., 113
Haggerty, Dorothy, 375-77
Haggerty, Leland, 375-77
Haglund, Jim, 809, 811-14
Haglund, Kathy, 809, 811-14
Hagquist, William, 240
Hahn, Julia, 431
Hahn, Richard, 431
Hakka people, 398-400

Hall, Ruth, 620
Halleen, E. A., 92-93
Halleen, Harold P., 304
Halvorsen, David, 744-45, 748
Halvorsen, Norma, 744-45, 748
Hammond, Rob (Butch), 802
Hammond, Shirley, 802
Hancock, Barry, 906-09
Hancock, Elieen, 906-09
Hanks, Pauline, 262, 549-50
Hanks, Peter, 262, 549-50, 552
Happy Valley Bible Fellowship, 538
Harare (Salisbury), Zimbabwe, 651-52, 674, 677-78, 680-82
Harare Theological College, 659-60, 674, 676
Harder, Alice, 867
Harder, Dan, 867
Harder, Eloise, 394
Harder, Sharon, 867
Harris, Gayle, 758
Harris, Tom, 758
Harrison, Bruce, 436
Harrison, Mitz, 436
Hart, John, 612
Hart, Joyce, 612
Hart, Ruth, 644
Hart, Wilfred, 620, 644
Harthan, David, 801, 805
Harthan, JoAnne, 801, 805
Hartt, Margaret, 723, 727
Hasan, 818
Hasan Abdal, Pakistan, 573, 577
Hastings, Carol, 154
Hatam tribe, 303, 457, 464-77, 485, 489, 492, 494
Hatch, Martha, 615, 948
Hatch, Tim, 615
Hatfield, Zimbabwe, 652, 660, 677-78
Hatori, Akira, 349
Haugerud, Andrew, 40, 51, 107, photo
Haven of Hope orphanage, 588
Haven of Rest Ministries, 426
Hawes, Marjorie Ruth, 723, 727, 729
Hawton, Merle, 570
Hayward, Paul, 643-44

Headquarters for TEAM
—Australia, 260-61
—Canada, 201-03, 269, 300-01
—U.S., 96-97, 116-17, 236-37, 258-59, 297-98
Heart Bookroom, 637
Heaven House Orphanage, 348
Heck, J. Douglas, 370
Hedenstrom, Eric, 40-41, 932
Hedenstrom, Mrs. Eric, 40-41
Hedstrom, J.H. (John Henry), 80-81, 92, photo
Hedstrom, Mrs. J. H., 83
Heinsman, William, 379
Heinz, Edna, 373, photo
Hekman, Verena, 499-500
Hekman, Willem, 493-94, 499-501, 503
Helping Hand, 348, 359
Hendrickson, Carl, 659-60
Hendrickson, Donna, 659
Henriksen, Gladys, 152
Henriksen, P. E., 48
Henriques, Bicento, 873-75, 882
Henry, Gladys, 342
Henry, Kenneth, 342
Heppner, Iona, 538
Hertzsprung, Lois, 516
Hertzsprung, Ralph, 515-17, 521, 523
Hewlett, Marvin, 389
Hewlett, Patsy, 389
Hickman, Ernest, 781-84, 787-88
Hickman, Mary, 781-82, 784, 788
Hida province, Japan, 44-45, 104
Hildebrand, Ella, 693
Hildebrand, Henry, 202
Hill, Charlene, 450, 453, 489, 496
Hill, Eunice, 581
Hill, O. D., 203
Hill, Ronald, 450, 453, 478, 482, 485, 489, 492, 496
Hill, Vicki Lynn, 479
Hillis, Don
—India missionary, 152, 216, 239-40, 511, 570
—homeland ministry, 203-04, 239-40, 244, 252, 254, 273, 278, 289, 292

Hillis, Doris, 152, 203, 216
Hill Villages Mission, 529
Hines, David, 809, 811-12
Hines, Julia, 809, 811-12
Hiroshima, Japan, 354, 359
Hitchcox, Brian, 610
Hitchcox, Ceri, 610
Hjerpe, E. G., 92-93
Hlabane mine, 628
HLKX Radio, 239, 264, 319-20, 379-80, 409-10, 416-23
Hodges, Carl, 715, 720-21
Hodges, Sandra, 720-21
Hogfeldt, Otto, 92, 198, photo
Hoke, Donald, 344-46, 355
Hoke, Martha, 344-45
Hokkaido, Japan, 65, 341
Holm, C. W., 37-38
Holmberg, George, 113-14, 176, 178-79, 182, 187-88, 833
Holmberg, Karin, 113, 187-88
Holritz, Bernard, 334, 349
Holritz, Jeanette, 349
Holritz, Karen, 656
Holt, Albert, 507, 519
Holt, Mrs. Albert, 507
Holzwarth, Dorothy, 393
Homebush, Australia, 261
Homecraft school, 660-61
Homeyer, Chris, 612
Homme, Emma, 52
Honan Church, Japan, 329
Hong Kong, 302, 324, 372, 438-43, 926
Hongo Church, Japan, 329
Honjo, Japan, 104
Honshu, Japan, 65, 347, 358-59, 369
Hopkins, Davis, 889
Hopkins, Ruth, 889
Horizons (formerly *The Missionary Broadcaster*), 265, 273, 289
Horness, Joseph, 266-67, 274, 277, 304, 624, 655, photo
Horness, Mrs. Joseph, 624
Horst, William, 827, 847
Hortaleza, Spain, 789, 794-95
Hospitals, 256, 310, 924. *See also* Medical work

Irwin, Cindy, 948
Irwin, Domingo, 174
Irwin, Nate, 948
Irwin, Phyllis, 561
Irwin, Russell, 561
Isaka, Frans, 486, 488
Islamabad, Pakistan, 570
Istanbul, Turkey, 818-22
Italy, 64, 225, 302, 806-15
Itchikawa, Ben, 369
Ito, Japan, 104, 146
Iversen, Dagny, 159, 163
Iwasaki, Kitao, 343
Iwou, Alpons, 470
Iwou, Habel, 471
Iwou, Michael, 470
Izmir, Turkey, 821
Izu, Japan, 104

Jabaquara, Brazil, 914
Jabavu, South Africa, 618
Jack, William, 283
Jackson, Lois, 683
Jackson, Mandy, 683
Jackson, Margaret, 649, 673
Jackson, Paul, 683, 949
Jackson, Russell, 649, 665-67, 673
Jackson, Tom, 675, 683, 949
Jacob, Mr., 600
Jacobson, Juliann, 176
Jakarta, 499, 502-03
Janscha, Robert, 797
Jansen, Eibrink, 448-49, 451, 453
Japan
—early TEAM work, 26, 38-40, 44-
   45, 65-66, 103-04, 144-48
—overview to 1946, 207-212
—post World War II, 215-17, 220,
   227-29, 231-32, 236, 245-46, 255,
   299, 327-70, 409-10
Japan Christian College, 345-46
Japan Christian Council, 147
Japan Evangelical Alliance Church.
   See Domei
Japan Evangelical Gospel Associa-
   tion, 369

Japan Evangelical Mission, 299, 368-
   70, 913-14
Japan Sunday School Union, 341, 350
Jardim da Granja, Brazil, 915
Jarrin, Claude, 756, 773
Jarvis, Fred, 344-45, 409
Jarvis, Mrs. Fred, 344
Java, Indonesia, 446, 491-95, 499-
   505
Jeke, Evangelist, 666
JEM, 299, 368-70, 913-14
Jenkins, Melvin, 806
Jenkins, Valerie, 806
Jensen, Anna, 141
Jensen, Arthur, 109, 156-58, 192
Jensen, C. J. and Mrs., 103
Jensen, Mrs. Arthur, 109
Jesberg, Ethel, 737, 741
Jesberg, John, 737, 741-42, 747
Jesudass, Moses, 603, 606, 608
Jesudass, Nancy, 603, 608
Jeunesse Agapé, 764, 768, 774
Jeunesse Ardente, 749-50, 753, 759,
   764-65
Jhansi, India, 511, 535, 537-38
Jhansi Bible Fellowship, 535, 537-38
Jiwan Jyoti Bible Correspondence
   Center, 538-39
Jobes, Charles, 877
Jobes, Ruth, 394, 877
Johannesburg, South Africa, 229,
   618, 622, 627, 629, 631, 635, 637,
   644
Johannesburg Bible Institute, 627,
   635
Johansen, Thorvald and Mrs., 105
Johansson, Bernard, photo
Johnson, Audrey, 889, 902-03
Johnson, B., 537
Johnson, Charles, 175, 187
Johnson, David H., photo
—earlier ministry, 198, 203, 213-14
—general director: administrative
   style, 204-05, 233-35, 270; John-
   son era, 213-43; Far East and In-
   donesia, 313-17, 322, 330-31,
   343, 352-53, 376-78, 409, 427,
   445, 447, 451-52, 458; Southern

Martins, Manuel, 732
Maruyama, Tadataka, 346
Masaichi, Matsuda, 328-29, 334, 345, 355, 366, photo
Masih, Barkat, 601
Masihi I'tahadi Jamait, 573
Mason, Betty, 655
Mass movements, 464-66, 477, 480
Matham, Wilfred, 636
Matsubarako Bible Camp, 334, 346-47
Matsuda, Pastor, 328-29, 334, 345, 355, 366, photo
Matsumoto, Pastor, 146
Mattai, 324, photo
Mavuradonha, Zimbabwe, 192, 194, 651, 653, 659, 660, 664, 674
Mavuradonha Christian school, 663-64, 674
Mavuradonha Secondary School, 663-64, 674, 680-82
Mayer, Maria, 588, 590, 593
Mbabane, Swaziland, 647
Mbaitellel, Moise, 714
Mberego, Julius, 659
Mboggdengar, Andre, 706
McAlpine, Frances, 688, 703
McAlpine, George, 688, 703
McCallister, Florence, 161-62, 636
McCallister, Irl, 161-62, 620, 630, 636-38
McClain, Margaret, 872, 881
McClain, Mildred Sawyer, 881
McClain, Robert, 872, 881
McCloy, Richard, 660
McCordic, Charles, 711-12, 718-19
McCune, Grace, 436-37
McCune, Keith, 436-37
McDonald, Betty, 902
McDonald, David, 44, 78, 105
McDonald, Monty, 902
McHutchinson, Annette, 803, 806
McHutchinson, Brent, 803, 806
McKay, Becky, 401
McKay, Ross, 401
McKenzie, Enid, 625, 636
McMillan, Peter, 948

McNally, Jane, 154, 507, 511-12, 514
McNeill, W. Arnold, 281, 299, 305
McVety, Kenneth, 340, 342-43, 355, 409
McVety, Olive, 340, 342
Meberg, Mrs. O. E., 105, 151
Meberg, O. E., 105, 151, 153-54, 506, 510
MEDAF, 702
Medical work, 256, 310, 924
—Chad, 699, 701-02, 717-18
—India, 152-53, 508, 517-19, 527-28, 538-39
—Irian Jaya, 455, 458, 462-64, 469-70, 472, 474, 477-79, 481, 483-85, 495
—Mongolia, 169, 172, 209
—Nepal, 538, 548-52
—Pakistan, 557, 560-63, 574, 579-80
—Peru, 910
—South Africa, 620, 622-27, 633
—Sri Lanka, 546
—Taiwan, 387-90
—Trinidad and Tobago, 904
—United Arab Emirates, 589-601, 604-05, 609-13, 615
—Zimbabwe, 652, 654-57, 662-63, 668-71
Médicament Pour Afrique, 702
Meleán, Eduardo, 176
Mendoza, Antonio, 855
Merauke, Irian Jaya, 496
Mergers
—Caribbean Broadcasting Company, 268, 888
—Door of Hope Mission, 268, 377-78
—Japan Evangelical Mission, 299, 368-70, 913-14
—Missions of Baja, 299, 919-20
—Orinoco River Mission, 178, 299, 847-50, 853
—Peruvian Gospel Fellowship, 281, 298, 908
—Sudan United Mission, North American Branch, 268-69, 685-93
—Tibetan Frontier Mission, 268, 526

Mérida, Venezuela, 178-79
Merrill, Kathryn, 378, 390, 393
Mersorjmem, 474
Mesme tribe, 692
Mexico, 29, 76, 299, 302, 918-22
Meyah tribe, Irian Jaya, 454, 469, 473, 477, 479-80, 485
Mhlosheni, Swaziland, 109
Miaoli, Taiwan, 399
Miaro, Irian Jaya, 483
Michaelsen, L., 37-38
Micheldorf, Austria, 805
MIJ (Masihi I'tahadi Jamait), 573
Mikkelson, Lillian, 872-73
Milfontes, Portugal, 730, 732
Millán, Santos, 864
Miller, Douglas, 459, 469, 472-76
Miller, Gerri, 505
Miller, Jeff, 505
Miller, Julie, 469, 473-74
Mimika tribe, 458
Minyambou, Irian Jaya, 457, 465, 467-69, 472
Mirza, E. B., 600
Misión Alianza Evangélica, 790
Missal, Bernita, 613
Missionary Aviation Fellowship
—Irian Jaya, 447, 452, 457-58, 460, 479, 487-88, 498
—Zimbabwe, 663, 665-67
—Chad, 700
Missionary Broadcaster, The, 164, 189, 201, 215, 265, 270. See also Horizons
Missionary children's schools. See Schools for missionary children
Missionary Gospel Fellowship, 307
Missionary Internship, 307
Missionary outreach by national churches. See Self-propagating churches
Missionary work. See Agricultural work; Audio-visual ministry; Bookstores; Camping and conferences; Church fellowship organizations; Church planting; Correspondence courses; English lessons; Evangelism; Financial support of missionaries; Financial support of national workers and ministries; Literacy work; Literature distribution; Medical work; Nationals assuming leadership; Orphanages; Principles of missionary work; Printing and publishing; Radio; Schools, institutes, and seminaries; Social concern; Self-propagating churches; Training nationals; Transferring ministries to national responsibility; Translation
Missions of Baja, Inc., 299, 919-20
Miyakejima, Japan, 104
MK schools. See Schools for missionary children
Mndebele, Abner, 630-31, 640
Mndebele, Jonas, 624
Modig, August H., 92-93
Mödling District, Vienna, 798, 801-03, 806
Moe, Malla, 40, 59, 107-10, 121, 157-59, 162, 208, 620-21, 627, photo
Moehl, Dorothy, 802
Moehl, Ed, 802
Moers, Susan, 478
Mofantsun church, 383, 396, 400
Mohara, Japan, 104
Moller, Bonnie, 394
Mongolia
—early TEAM work, 27, 41-42, 59-63, 66, 90, 110-11, 119, 164-72
—overview to 1946, 207-12
—post World War II, 214-15, 217, 228, 322-26, 373
Montaña, Curaçao, 881, 884
Montenegro, Jorge, 855
Montgomery, Marjorie, 581
Monthly TEAM Memo, 270, 303
Moodie, Janet, 413, 429
Moody Church, Chicago, 28, 308
Moon, Shim, 415
Moore, Doris, 625
Moore, Jeff and Mrs., 563
Moore, Margery, 395
Moore, Pat, 921

Moose Jaw, Saskatchewan, 203, 265, 300
Morangis, France, 752-53, 756-57, 759
Morehouse, Gerald H., 269, 272, 300, 307, 689, 694, 701-02
Morehouse, Jean, 269
Moreira, Eduardo, 191
Moriwaki, Akio, 363
Morón de la Frontera, Spain, 789, 792
Morrill, Don, 623, 625
Morrill, Geraldine, 623
Morris, J. L., 827
Morrison Academy, 392-94, 877
Mortenson, Donald, 282, 289
Mortenson, Frances, 17, 22, 135, 204, 275, 279, 320
Mortenson, Patricia, 307, 656, 660
Mortenson, Vernon, photo
—China missionary, 17, 22, 135, 138, 204, 937
—assistant general director: home administration, 204, 215-17, 219, 222-24, 234-35, 239-40; Far East and Indonesia, 316-17, 377-78, 385, 427, 447, 450-51; Southern and Western Asia, 530, 587, 590-93; Africa, 621, 653-54; Latin America, 826-27
—general director: administrative style, 270-72, 292; Mortenson era, 241-76, 304, 865-66; Far East and Indonesia, 430-31, 460-65; Southern and Western Asia, 530, 548-49, 567, 579-82; Africa, 664, 689-91, 693-95; Europe, 796; Latin America, 832-35, 888
—in retirement, 277, 279, 287-89, 304-06, 309, 320-21, 369, 665, 848
—foreign missions principles: objectives, 15-16, 29-33, 243-44, 738-39; value of good administration, 245-47, 271-72, 574-75, 734, 826-27; church planting an "in depth ministry," 247-50, 270-71, 332-33, 401, 459, 530, 574-75,

905; cluster principle, 740-41; self-governing, self-supporting, and self-propagating churches, 401, 532, 725-35, 760-61, 777, 853-55; church-mission relationships, 401, 760-61, 776-77; Bible schools and church planting, 383-84, 577, 854; resistant people groups, 568-69, 613-14; doctrinal faithfulness, 262-63, 564-65, 581-82, 640-41
Mosby, Jonathan, 305
Mosby, S. B., 176
Moskona people, 473-76
Mossbarger, Sharon, 613
Mosvold, Torrey and Mrs., 623-24
Mosvold Mission Hospital, 620, 622-27
Mother/daughter churches, 752, 756-59, 762, 773, 777, 835-36. *See also* Self-propagating churches
Moundou, Chad, 687, 715, 719-20
Mountain of Blessing Orphanage, 413-16
Mozambique (Portuguese East Africa), 158, 186, 189-91, 193-94, 302, 646-50, 682
Msengedzi, Zimbabwe, 651, 657
Mtangadura, Naboth, 682
Muir, Peter, 727
Muir, Ruth, 727
Murray, Andrew, 74
Murree, Pakistan, 571, 580
Murree Christian School, 580
Mussourie, India, 529-30, 537-38, 556
Mvurwe, Zimbabwe, 683
Mydske, Norman, 874-75, 905
Mydske, Valerie, 874-75, 905

NAE, 229
Nag, India, 530
Nagoya, Japan, 256, 354
Naidoo, John, 287
Naji, 576
Nakaichi, Ando, 366-67, photo
Nakaichi, Rutsuko, 366

186-89, 287, 207-12, 225, 236, 852, 866, 871-86
Netherlands New Guinea. *See* Irian Jaya
New Delhi, India, 514, 530
Newell, Marvin, 482, 490-92, 494-95
Newell, Peggy, 490
New Guinea. *See* Irian Jaya
Newing, James, 906
Newman, Barbara, 791
Newman, Bob, 791
New Zealand, 65
Ngambai tribe, 303, 687-89, 692, 705, 707, 714
Ngambai-Gagal tribe, 689
Ngangelizwe, Transkei, 644
Ngundu, Onesimus, 659-60
Nicholas, Edna, 892, 897, 900
Nicholson, Beckie, 570
Nicholson, Leroy, 570
Nicole, Jules Marcel, 745, 748, 760
Nielsen, Sofus, 51
Niemeyer, Norman B.
—Trinidad missionary, 290, 889-90, 892-93, 895
—head office administrator, 290, 302, 306, 405, 434-37, 439, 442, 488, 493-94, 501, 505, 544
Niemeyer, Sue, 290, 889-90, 893
Niewoehner, Marilyn, 613
Nihon Dendo Fukuin Kyodan, 369
Nihon Domei Kirisuto Kyokai. See Domei
Niigata, Japan, 356
Nijima, Japan, 104
Nikiboko, Bonaire, 878-80
Niles, Donna, 768
Niles, Steve, 768
Nilsen, Edward, 858
Ninaan, Mr., 600
Nineteenth District, Vienna, 802-03, 806
Ningsia, China, 312, 318, 323
Nippon Domei Kirisuto Kyokai. See Domei
Nizwa, Oman, 615
Njelarje, Jeremie, 689, 695, 699, 708, 710-12

Nobata, Pastor, 344
Nogent, France, 745, 748-49, 775
Nogent Bible School, 745, 748-49
Nohon, Irian Jaya, 458, 480, 483
Nordmark, Arne, 323
Noreen, Olga, 523
Norte de Santander, Colombia, 182, 856, 867
North, David, 436-37
North, Kathy, 436-37
North India field. *See* India, Tibet and Tibetan Frontier
North Salina, Bonaire, 878
Northwest Frontier Province, India, 195, 261
Norway, 25, 34, 58, 80, 85, 623
Norwegian Covenant Mission, 60, 931
Norwegian-Danish Free Churches, 87, 89, 91, 93-96. *See also* Evangelical Free Church of America
Nueva Vida Church, 795
Nuham, Petrus, 470
Numfoor, Indonesia, 459, 489, 492, 497
Nurses training, 624, 656, 670
Nyawo, Johanne, 624, 630-31, photo

Oasis Hospital, 589-601, 604-05, 609-13, 615
Ocaña, Colombia, 183, 285, 857-58, 863-64
Ocaña Bible Institute, 863-64, 868
Ochanomizu Student Chrisitan Center, 349
Odakeni, Swaziland, 159
Odingar, General, 709
Ohlson, Algoth, 82-83, 92
Okayama, Japan, 354, 359
Okinawa, Japan, 341
Ollen, Gerda, 324, photo
Olsen, Gladys, 620, 627, 629
Olsen, Marlin, 620, 627, 629
Olsen, Tom, 159, 624
Olsen, Walter, 152
Olson, Alton, 519
Olson, John, 198

Savage, H. H. and Mrs., 184
Savage, Jim, 828, 842-43
Savigny-le-Temple, France, 773-75
Sawyer, Mildred, 881
Scandinavian Alliance Mission of
    North America, The (S. A. M.),
    16, 26, 38, 57-58, 222. *See also*
    TEAM
Scharfe, Ginnie, 436
Scharfe, Mark, 436
Schlotfeldt, Larry, 843
Schneider, Kurt, 310
Schone, John, 239, 346-47
Schone, Lucia, 346-47
Schools, institutes, and seminaries,
    256, 310, 577, 924-25. *See also*
    Religious instruction in public
    schools, Schools for missionary
    children
—Austria, 804
—Brazil, 918
—Chad, 688-89, 692, 695, 700, 713,
    718-19
—China, 67, 131, 134, 142, 208, 211
—Colombia, 862-64
—France, 748-49
—Germany, 307, 805
—Hong Kong, 441
—India, 106, 149-50, 153, 209, 211,
    286, 508, 517-18, 522, 528-29,
    538-39
—Irian Jaya, 459, 461, 467-70, 476-
    78, 489-92, 495
—Japan, 211, 334, 343-46, 369
—Java, Indonesia, 502-03, 945
—Korea, 427-30
—Netherlands Antilles/Aruba, 883-
    86
—Pakistan, 564-66, 574, 577-78
—Peru, 281, 908, 912
—South Africa, 618-19, 624, 627,
    633-36
—Spain, 781-82
—Sri Lanka, 544
—Swaziland, 107, 109, 156, 211,
    619-20, 627, 633
—Taiwan, 382-84, 391-94
—Trinidad and Tobago, 893-94,

897, 902-03
—Venezuela, 113, 176-77, 200, 211,
    251, 825-26, 828-29, 833-35, 842-
    44, 849-51
—Zimbabwe, 652-54, 657, 659-64,
    674, 676, 681-82
Schools for missionary children, 851-
    52
—Austria, 804
—Brazil, 918
—Chad, 690
—China, 100, 136, 323
—Germany, 805
—Irian Jaya, 461
—Japan, 350
—Pakistan, 580-81
—Peru, 907
—Philippines, 434, 436
—Spain, 787-88, 792-93
—Taiwan, 375, 392-94
—Venezuela, 851-52
—Zimbabwe, 652
Schoonmaker, Joseph, 595
Schroeder, Marie, 612
Schroeder, Paul, 612
Schuler, Mrs. George, 377-78
Schwab, Ann, 400-02
Schwab, John, 349
Schwab, Phil, 400-02, 405, 442
Seaman, Dorothy, 262, 529, 546,
    548-50
Seaman, Maynard, 262, 519, 529,
    546, 548-50
Sebena people. *See* Moskona people
Seefeldt, Dale, 538
Seefeldt, Nellann, 529, 534
Seefeldt, Ralph, 529, 534
Seefeldt, Ruth Warren, 538
Seeland, J. Carlton, 265, 278, 282,
    289
Seely, Arthur, 334, 349
Seely, Florence, 349
Seguidores, 841
Seino, Hiroko, 367-68, 501-02
Seino, Katsuhiko, 367-68, 370, 501-
    03
Sekiguchi, Rachel, 914
Selander, Aileen, 349

25, 373, 385-86, 945, photo
Torjesen, Sandy, 504, 927, 945-46
Tornvall, Gustav, 128, 130
Toronto, Ontario, 269, 300
Torres, Elizabet, 910
Toyama Group, 352-53
Training missionaries, 223-24, 283-84, 295-98, 367-68
Training nationals, 256, 310, 577, 924-25. *See also* Correspondence courses
—Brazil, 915, 918
—Chad, 688-89, 690, 692, 695, 703, 718-19
—China, 50, 67, 137-38, 142, 211
—Colombia, 862-64, 868-69
—France, 748-49, 757-58, 768, 771-72
—Hong Kong, 441
—India, 152, 211, 286, 508, 513, 517-18, 528, 538
—Irian Jaya, 459, 466-70, 476-78, 489-92, 495
—Japan, 211, 334, 343-46, 369
—Java, Indonesia, 502-05
—Korea, 427-30
—Lebanon, 599
—Netherlands Antilles, 882-86
—Pakistan, 561, 574, 577-78
—Peru, 281, 908, 912
—Portugal, 731
—South Africa/Swaziland, 107, 109, 159, 211, 618-20, 627, 634-36, 645
—Spain, 781-82
—Taiwan, 383-84, 391
—Trinidad and Tobago, 891, 893-94, 897, 902-03
—United Arab Emirates, 601-03, 607
—Venezuela, 176-77, 200, 211, 251, 826, 828-29, 832-33, 840-44, 849-51, 853-54
—Zimbabwe, 652-54, 659-61, 674, 682
Transferring ministries to national responsibility. *See also* Financial support of national workers and

ministries, Nationals assuming leadership
—Chad, 715
—China, 142-43
—France, 758, 768-71
—India, 520-23
—Irian Jaya, 491, 495
—Japan, 342-43, 347
—Korea, 414-16
—Lebanon, 599
—Peru, 907
—South Africa, 626-27, 638
—Taiwan, 390
—Venezuela, 251, 833-35, 849-51, 855
Transkei, 644
Translation, 283, 302-03, 924
—Chad, 303, 689, 692, 714
—India, 303, 538
—Irian Jaya, 255, 303, 454-56, 466-71, 475-78, 480-82, 484-85, 495
—Japan, 341-42
—Korea, 425
—Mongolia, 324-25
—Netherlands Antilles, 188-89, 872-73
—Pakistan, 574, 578-79
—Philippines, 302, 436-37
—Taiwan, 303, 384-87
—Turkey, 303, 819-20
—Venezuela, 829, 841
Transvaal, South Africa, 40
Trans World Radio, 349, 380, 682, 817, 820
Trianni, Ivan, 810-11
Trianni, Maria, 810-11
Trincity, Trinidad, 889-90, 894, 897
Trinidad and Tobago, 251, 287, 852, 866, 887-904
Tritt, Edward, 448-53
Tromp, Coral, 453
Tromp, Leo, 875
Tromp, Roberta, 620
Troup, Louise, 624
Trujillo, Venezuela, 824
Tselapedi, Johannes, 643-44
Tsenguve, Zimbabwe, 653
Tshongwe, Southern Africa, 622

Vila Nova de Milfontes, Portugal, 724, 726-27
Vinje, Gail, 484, 487-88
Violence. *See* War and civil unrest
Visa and passport restrictions, 215
—India, 189, 302, 507, 519-20, 536-37, 539-40, 891
—Indonesia/Irian Jaya, 302, 434, 445, 461, 484, 502
—Mexico, 922
—Nepal, 546, 550
—Pakistan, 569-71
—Peru, 911
—Portugal, 236, 724, 780, 875
—Trinidad and Tobago, 290, 891, 894, 897
—Turkey, 815-16
—Venezuela, 183, 187
Vitry-sur-Seine, France, 741, 743-47, 751-54, 759, 775
Voetmann, Dave, 663
Vought, Anne, 783, 788
Vought, Dale, 730, 735, 783, 785-86, 788, 790-91
Vryheid, South Africa, 622, 628
Vust, Dorothy, 622

Waage, Minnie, 857, 862
Wahlström, Marita, 580
Waite, Lorraine, 670-71
Wakatama, Pius, 658
Wakelin, Bruce, 307
Wakelin, Nina, 307
Waldin, Margaret, 342
Waldschmidt, David, 501, 503
Waldschmidt, Pamela, 501, 503
Walker, Patty, 864
Walker, Sherman, 864
Wall, Emily, 655-56
Wall, Samuel, 655-56
Wanfang, Taiwan, 402
Wang, Stephen, 442
Wang Changlao, 99
Wangiefu, Mongolia, 111, 165
War and civil unrest, 119-20, 213, 215. *See also* Kidnapping
—Afghanistan, 584

—Canada, 202
—Chad, 715, 719-22
—China, 59-63, 66-67, 100-03, 119, 126-43, 214-15, 226, 314-19
—Colombia, 856-62
—Europe, 119, 191-92, 226
—India, 154, 226, 506, 555-57
—Indonesia/Irian Jaya, 226, 259-60, 468-69
—Japan, 119, 144-48, 215
—Korea, 226, 407-10
—Mongolia, 59-63, 66, 170-72, 214, 322-24
—Mozambique, 647
—Pakistan, 226, 555-57
—South Africa, 59, 64, 73, 108, 161-62
—Zimbabwe, 661-70, 672, 677
Ward, Charles, 904
Waridjo, Jeremias, 449, 451
Warkentin, Dave, 917
Warner, William, 654
Warren, Anita Steiner, 526, 535-37
Warren, Charles, 526, 529, 531-32, 535-37, 548-49
Waterman, Cheryl, 434
Waterman, Ray, 434
Wati, Ben, 533
Watney, Winifred, 377
Watson, Henrietta, 154
Watson, Tom Jr., 251, 264-65, 273, 334, 409-10, 416
Weber, Marion, 691
Weber, Stewart, 686, 691, 697, 715
Web movements, 755-56, 795
Webster, Beth, 776
Webster, Dick, 394
Webster, Florence, 394
Webster, Stewart, 776
Webster-Smith, Irene, 349
Weiser, Betty, 873
Weleen, E., photo
Welkom, South Africa, 619
Wentz, Fred, 394
Wentz, Julia, 394
Wernerhag, Irene, 580
Wessels, Irma Jean, 529
Western India field. *See* India

West Indies Mission, 888
West Irian. *See* Irian Jaya
Westlund, Howard, 305
Westlund, Lester, 843
Wheaton, Illinois, 258-59
Wheaton Declaration, 264
WHEREVER, 284, 289
White, Andrew, 806
White, Cheryl, 806, 949
White, Clevis, 882
White, Janice, 393, 401
White Fields, Inc., 914-15, 918
Whitfield, David, 715
Whittaker, S., 202
Wicks, Douglas, 289
Wiersbe, Warren, 305
Wilkinson, Herbert, 687
Willems, Gladys, 453-55, 477
Williams, Claudia, 821
Williams, Howard, 821
Williams, Ray, 679-80, 683
Willman, Cam, 378
Wilson, Alexander, 152
Wilson, Beatrice, 152
Wilson, J. Christy, 262, 581-82
Wilson, Walter and Mrs., 544
Wilterdink, Marian, 654
Winchell, Barry, 277, 814
Winchell, Dawn, 814
Winchell, Edna, 416
Winchell, Joan, 277
Winchell, Leigh, 277
Winchell, Marjorie, 275, 277, 279,
 618-19, 636-37
Winchell, Martha, 277, 950
Winchell, Peter, 277
Winchell, Richard M.
—South Africa missionary, 251,
 618-19, 636-37
—head office administrator, 266-67,
 273-76
—general director: administrative
 style, 292-95; Winchell era, 277-
 311; Far East and Indonesia, 321,
 435, 471, 491, 496-97; Southern
 and Western Asia, 543, 551-53;
 Africa, 665, 667-69, 678-79, 691,
 705-06, 721; Europe, 807, 814;

Latin America, 847-48, 865, 923-
 29
—foreign missions principles, 277-
 78, 295, 304, 309, 923, 927-29
Winchell, William, 321, 416, 420,
 422
Winona Lake Christian Assembly
 Grounds, 232
Wischmeier, Elaine, 729
Wischmeier, Richard, 729
Wistrand, Marie, 143, 215
Witness schools, 467-68. *See also*
 Schools, institutes and seminaries;
 Training nationals
Wittal, Ilse, 550
Wolfe, Betty, 655
Women's Bible School, Hsingping,
 142
Wonggor, Amos, 475
Woodward, Betty, 393, 402
Woodward, David, 393, 396, 402
Worden, Dick, 801
Worden, Pat, 801
Word of Life Bookstore, Harare,
 674, 676
Word of Life clubs, 882
Word of Life Press
—Japan, 334, 340-43, 347, 350, 355
—Korea, 423-26
—Spain, 783
—Zimbabwe, 658, 681
Word of Life Press Ministries, 342.
 See also Word of Life Press, Japan
Word of Life Publications
—India, 512-13, 523
—South Africa, 620, 636-38
Word of Life Radio, Zimbabwe,
 676, 682
Workentine, Ruth, 919
World Concern, 584
World Council of Churches, 221,
 263, 411, 686, 874
World Missionary Conference of
 1910, 196
World Radio Missionary Fellow-
 ship, 349, 904
World Relief, 584, 717
World Vision, 472, 584

The World of TEAM

Canada Office

International Headquarters

Mexico

Neth. Antilles & Aruba

Trinidad

Venezuela

Colombia

Peru

Brazil

Eng
Ireland
Fran
Spain
Portugal